VANISHED CIVILIZATIONS

VANISHED

FORGOTTEN PEOPLES

TEXTS BY

EDITED BY EDWARD BACON

THAMES AND HUDSON · LONDON

CIVILIZATIONS

OF THE ANCIENT WORLD

HENRI LHOTE

ROGER SUMMERS

L. P. KIRWAN

WILLIAM WATSON

CHRISTOPHER PYM

J. ERIC S. THOMPSON

DONALD STRONG

J. B. SEGAL

E. D. PHILLIPS

EDWARD BACON

T. SULIMIRSKI

GALE SIEVEKING

THOR HEYERDAHL

802 illustrations

211 in colour

539 photographs and drawings

52 maps and charts

Designed and produced by THAMES AND HUDSON

MANAGING EDITOR: Max Parrish OBE, MA

EDITORS: S.T. England BA; Ian Sutton BA

RESEARCH: Elizabeth Carmichael BA, FRAI;
R. Davidson-Houston BA, FRAI; Mark Hendy BA

INDEX: M. Beryl Bailey ALA, MSIND

ART EDITOR: Ian Mackenzie Kerr ARCA

RECONSTRUCTIONS: Gaynor Chapman ARCA

MAPS: Joan E. Bennett

ARCHITECTURAL DRAWINGS: P. P. Pratt AADIP;
Martin E. Weaver AADIP

LINE ILLUSTRATIONS: David A. Cox; Stephen Molnar;
Philip R. Ward

PHOTOGRAPHY: John R. Freeman; Josephine Powell;
Eileen Tweedy; Barney Wayne; Roger Wood

BLOCKS: Clichés Schwitter A.G., Basle and Zurich;
Klischee-Werkstätten der Industriedienst GmbH and Co.,
Wiesbaden

PRINTED in Western Germany by DuMont Presse, Cologne

PAPER: Woodfree Art and Apex Smooth Grey
Supplied by Frank Grunfeld Ltd. London

BOUND BY Van Rijmenam N.V., The Hague, Holland

CONTENTS

1 INTRODUCTION

EDWARD BACON

IT IS NOT DIFFICULT, and may be rewarding, to think of the ascent of man in terms of the story of the earth on which he lives—of a great land mass, developed, moulded and eroded by thousands of cataclysms and even more numerous minor and fluctuating influences. Rain falls, collects, sinks in and eventually develops into little streams beyond number, all of which have their various histories, separately and then together as they unite into larger streams, pools, lakes and minor and major rivers before merging into the shining sea which we call the Mediterranean civilization.

But not all rivers reach the sea; some go underground, some disappear in the sand, others end in the hollow lands and after thousands of years of evaporation turn into the desolation of salt marsh, salt-pan, dead seas. For 1800 years the citizens of Rome have looked upon the low reliefs on Trajan's column, to see barbarian horsemen represented there in scale armour. They could, had they cared, have read in their ancient books the stories of the battles on the Danube which kept these invaders in check. But nowhere do the histories of today give more than doubtful mention to this great people from the east—the Sarmatians. They are scattered and lost in the sands of time.

Over long centuries the Maya peasant, the Khmer of Cambodia, the African of Southern Rhodesia, the Tuareg of the Tassili, have looked without understanding upon the astonishing monuments and works of art tumbling in ruins around them. When the Afghan herdsmen, the farmers of the Upper Nile, of the Iranian highlands and even of Etrurian Italy stumbled over the mounds which dot their country, they had no knowledge of the treasures which lay beneath. Civilizations in many ways greater than their own were totally forgotten.

Now, in a much shorter space of time, the archaeologists and their co-workers in allied fields are re-discovering the history of these ancient peoples. Their techniques are almost infinitely diverse, as indeed are the facts which they must interpret. Their field of study is no longer confined to the few 'ancient' lands where rich discoveries have traditionally been made; it now extends across the whole world and embraces cultures in all stages of development and decay. Much thoughtfully organized, painstaking labour, much deep learning, and occasionally a flashing intuition are slowly recalling the living past to the memory of mankind.

To watch this process at work is the purpose of this book. Each of the cultures selected for study is even now yielding up its secrets, but each contains a problem, a mystery still to be solved. It is possible in these pages to follow the clues as they are discovered, to view the assembled evidence, to join in its examination and to understand the slowly emergent truth. And no-one in this exciting search can fail to add to his understanding of man and his struggle to build a durable society.

The New Light on Africa

Fifty years ago Africa, south of the Mediterranean coasts and the Nile, was a continent without a history. Now, apart from the possibility that the story of man itself has its beginning here, a host of other startling discoveries have taken the world by surprise. Three civilizations, whose very existence had hitherto been unsuspected, have in recent years come to light.

We now know that from the most remote times until the first millennium BC the Sahara was a fertile land—at one period perhaps the most densely populated region in the world. Henri Lhote, himself the discoverer of much that he describes, reconstructs what the fertile Sahara must have been like and goes some way towards explaining its greatest mystery—the desiccation of the land, the drying up of the great rivers and the total disappearance of its teeming life.

The cultures of the Sahara are known almost entirely from their art—from the multitudinous pictures painted and engraved on rocks and the walls of caves. Fortunately these pictures are of fantastic richness, those of animals stretching in time from the early elephants and hippopotami to the herds of cattle recorded so plentifully by the pastoral peoples from the East—and of humans ranging from the Europoids and the strange 'Round-headed men' to the beautiful naturalistic figures of men and women in which we can recognize the transformation of magical symbols into humanist art as we know it.

Later, round the beginning of the Christian era, on the banks of the Upper Nile south of Abu Simbel, flourished a people so little known that the only agreed name for them is 'the X-Group'. Their cemeteries were first discovered and excavated in the 1930's by Professor W. B. Emery and Mr L. P. Kirwan. Mr Kirwan now discusses the present state of our knowledge and what still remains to be solved. In their huge burial mounds the X-Group people left sophisticated treasures from Rome, Egypt, Greece, Byzantium and Meroe; yet they were savage and illiterate, filling their chieftains' tombs with human and animal sacrifices that reveal barbarism at its most primitive. Who were they and where did they come from? We have not much time left to make sure, for their remains will soon disappear for ever under the waters held back by the High Dam at Aswan.

The mysteries of Zimbabwe are likely to enjoy a longer lease of life. Although mentioned in early records, they became more generally known in what one may term the Rider Haggard era, and about the early knowledge of them eddies an atmosphere of Edwardian romance, rich, thick, mysterious and circling round the idea of gold. Roger Summers, who is Curator of the National Museums of Southern Rhodesia, is able to apply the methods and attitudes of modern science with an unusual degree of local knowledge. He deploys these in clearing away the many 'man-made' mysteries and proceeds to the true nature of this astonishing African capital.

'An Infinite Capacity for Taking Pains'

The soil of the Middle East—one might think—has been turned over too thoroughly to be able to produce surprises of quite the same order, but this is not so and the patient collection of facts and the untiring pursuit of neglected clues can still lead to conclusions equally valuable and sometimes equally disconcerting. Urartu, Mannai and the bronze-workers of Luristan are all peoples and entities which have begun to emerge in relatively recent years. Even now, scarcely any of the strangely moving works of Luristanian art have been recovered from scientifically controlled excavation; they have all passed through the hands of peasants and dealers.

The position of Afghanistan has until lately been similar. Here we are especially indebted both to the field work and to the subsequent assessment and synthesis of Dr Walter Fairservis. Now, besides being the bridgeland through which so many cultures and faiths have passed between India and the Middle East—Aryan, Hellenistic, Buddhist, Moslem—Afghanistan and Baluchistan are found to be the home of distinctive Neolithic cultures in their own right, and the discovery in 1959 of one major site—Edith Shahr—makes this an area of the very greatest significance and interest. This is pioneer work at its most exciting, when seemingly endless minutiae are adding up to the point when a new look at the history of civilization becomes possible.

If Dr Fairservis' task was like piling pebble upon pebble, Professor Segal's, in his examination of the Sabians, is like following a trail through undergrowth. Clear spaces are few, the path is lost, and its subsequent reappearance doubtful in direction. The Sabians—if they ever existed at all (that is the first mystery)—are unique in representing a sect which continued to practise a pagan religion for a thousand years, through the powerful influence of early Christianity and conquest by Islam. Their history makes a fascinating story which (like nearly all archaeological advances) has its repercussions in the world of art—the monumental mosaics which they left at Edessa and which are now being uncovered (some are published here for the first time).

Cultures in Crisis

All civilizations have their term and decay from a variety of causes, economic, political or from the monstrous growth of megalomania, as weeds collapse in morbid overgrowth from hormone weed-killers. Usually the final blow, the *coup-de-grâce*, is easy to recognize and explain, but often a civilization has been sick long before it dies, and in diagnosing this sickness the archaeologist is sometimes tempted to speak to his own society as a moralist and a prophet.

History provides three tremendous examples—the Khmers of Angkor, the Mayas and the Etruscans. Christopher Pym, who has lived for some years among the Khmers of today, describes the growth, flowering and decay of that wonderful people who produced the marvels of Angkor. Perhaps influenced by his knowledge of, and sympathy for, the Cambodian temperament, he is able to suggest, as one of several causes of collapse, that since these temples—the powerhouses, so to speak, of the Khmer civilization—had their origin in a spiritual need, their decline and loss of impetus had their origin in a spiritual change, catastrophic in effect.

Something like this solution is offered by Dr Thompson in his account of the Mayas. Their nature, their brilliant intellectual achievement, their splendid and monumental art are fully displayed by a scholar who has devoted a full life to their study and who is perhaps the world's greatest authority on them. Why did their civilization fail? The fantastic ceremonial centres, the temples, pyramids and courts were abandoned to the creeping jungle and never re-occupied. Again, a spiritual catastrophe seems a plausible answer, a failure by the priestly religion, with its incredibly complex astronomical basis, to meet the needs of the people.

The Etruscans are perhaps in a rather different category, and the mystery of their decline (reflected in their later tomb-paintings and terracottas as a sort of spiritual resignation, an abandonment of hope) is overshadowed by two other mysteries that are at first sight more intriguing—the mystery of their origins and the mystery of their language. Dr Strong reviews the present state of knowledge and the latest suggestions in both cases, but finally returns to the great intrinsic mystery of their ultimate failure—that possessing a rich artistic culture, a language and a written script, and being contemporaries of the most literate of all the early civilizations, the Greco-Roman, they should nevertheless have collapsed so completely under the dominance of Rome and left no literature, no history and no separate tradition.

Disputed Frontiers

Like every living science, archaeology is frequently at variance with traditional teaching and belief. In Japan, for instance, according to legend expressly created for the Japanese, feelings still run high on the question whether the Ainu – the white and hairy Ainu, with their strange bear-cult and customs rooted in the past – are the original inhabitants of the Japanese islands. William Watson here argues the theory that they are descended from the Jōmon, a Neolithic race who have left fascinating remains in the shape of pottery vessels and clay figurines. If that is so, we have an example of cultural continuity that must be unique.

A battle of a different kind rages over a tiny outcrop of land in the midst of the Pacific – Easter Island. Some time before AD 300 the island was colonised – from where? Thor Heyerdahl's hypothesis is a bold one, with an impressive body of evidence behind it – that the first colonists came by raft from Peru. But both the culture which grew up here, with its huge, monolithic, still immensely moving statues, and the tragic history of the 'Long-ears' and the 'Short-ears' (a political world in miniature) are absorbing and worthy of study.

Finally, back to Europe, by no means the least dark continent. Gale Sieveking's problem in his chapter on the megalith builders has been to provide a 'model' (in Professor Piggott's sense of the term) for a culture whose only remains are its funerary and religious architecture and a few objects associated with it – like trying to reconstruct mediaeval Christian society from the contents of a dozen or so cathedrals and churches. This is a field in which 'truth' is reached by the successive rejection of hypotheses until a model is designed which 'makes sense of the observed phenomena and the inferences made from them.' The 'observed phenomena' in this case are some of the most fascinating monuments created by European man ancient or modern, and the 'inferences made from them' have in the past been sufficiently extraordinary. But the migration of the megalith builders and their Mother Goddess religion can now be traced with a fair measure of accuracy: it is a story that lies near the fountainhead of our civilization.

The Sarmatians, in contrast, are truly like a great river which loses itself in the sand: a once mighty people whose name was feared by Rome and whose remains survive from the Caucasus to France and Spain, and yet who are remembered only for a few place-names, a few obscure words, a scatter of heraldic symbols. Professor Sulimirski has carried out something like a rescue operation. Sarmatian historical documentation was as dispersed as their material remains, but it can be reassembled and read as a continuous story. To do so, and to collate with it the most recent findings of archaeology, is to recover something very valuable and to shed light on the central event of early European history, the fall of the Roman Empire. It illustrates yet another facet of the archaeological method, for here the archaeologist and the historian have met and advanced together where each separately had reached an impasse.

The search for 'vanished civilizations' goes on – is indeed perhaps the most powerful motivating force behind the science of archaeology. Peaks are all the time emerging from the darkness that shrouds an unknown landscape. But the history of man, like peace, is indivisible. Such a belief must underlie every work about the past, as it underlies this.

Acknowledgements

In the work on the illustration sections the editor's first debt has been to the authors themselves, both for their advice on photographic material and for their ready assistance in the preparation of the captions, which are the responsibility of the publishers.

The task of collecting the illustrations and preparing the maps and charts would have been impossible without the generous help of many institutions and individuals. Both editor and publishers would like to express particular gratitude to: the Director General of the Service of Antiquities of the United Arab Republic, Cairo; the Director of the Musée des Antiquités Nationales, Saint-Germain-en-Laye; the Soprintendenza alle Antichità, Florence; Dr E. O. Negahban, Director of the Institute of Archaeology of the University of Teheran; Dr Linton Satterthwaite, Curator, American Section, The University Museum, Philadelphia; Mrs Katherine B. Edsall, Peabody Museum, Harvard University; Dr Raddatz of the Schleswig-Holsteinisches Landesmuseum für Vor- und Frühgeschichte, Schleswig; Dr Karin Hissink of the Frobenius-Institut an der Johann-Wolfgang-Goethe-Universität, Frankfurt; Mr Cornelius Ouwehand, Keeper of Japanese Antiquities, Rijksmuseum voor Volkenkunde, Leiden; Mme Suzanne Kahn, Keeper of the Petit Palais, Paris; Mr P. J. Hartnett of the Bord Fáilte Éireann, Dublin; Mr Azmy Rhalid of the Tourist Service of the United Arab Republic; Sir Mortimer Wheeler; the librarians of the Institute of Archaeology, London (Miss Joan du Plat Taylor and Miss G. C. Talbot), of the Society of Antiquaries of London (Mr John Hopkins), of University College, London, Dept. of Egyptology (Miss K. E. Cynthia Cox) and of the School of Oriental and African Studies, London (Mr J. D. Pearson); Dr R. D. Barnett and Mr C. A. Burland of the British Museum, London; Professor W. B. Emery, University College, London; Miss Beatrice de Cardi, Secretary, the Council for British Archaeology; Dr J. Edward Kidder, Jr, International Christian University, Tokyo; Dr Vera Leisner; and Mr Anthony Whitty.

II THE FERTILE SAHARA

Men, animals and art of a lost world

HENRI LHOTE

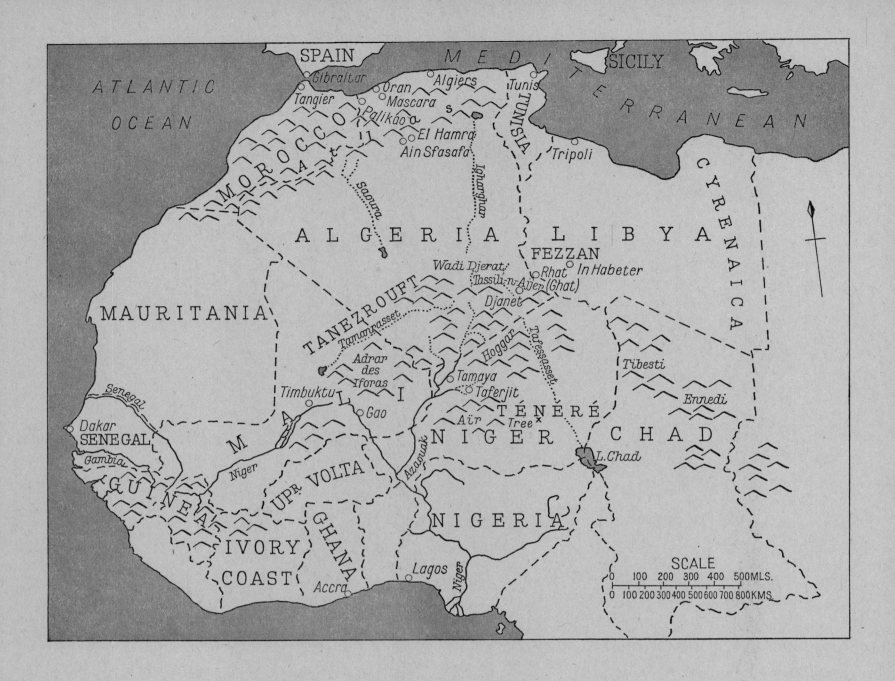

A note on chronology

It is still not possible to give any 'hard' dates for the periods of Saharan prehistory. The earliest known human artefacts, the pebble-tools, are the work of Australopithecines and are at least 500,000 years old. 'Atlanthropus', the maker of the Chelleo-Acheulian hand-axes, is roughly contemporary with Peking and Java Man, and the maker of the Aterian tools with Neanderthal Man in Europe and Asia, though it is fairly certain that this human type lasted longer in north-west Africa than in Europe. The Neolithic in the Sahara began some time between 8,000 and 6,000 BC (Carbon-14 dating is tending to lower these figures.) The start of this era is marked by the arrival of peoples who lived by hunting and gathering. They are here called 'Europoids', although we cannot yet say whether they came from the north or east. At

about the same time, or a little later, a Negroid people seems to have settled in the centre of the Sahara. They built fishing villages along the river valleys and some of them were able to devote themselves to the gathering of wild grain and, soon afterwards, to agriculture. Next came the great wave of Pastoralists, probably from the east – first with small animals (sheep and goats), then, in further waves, with enormous herds of cattle. The rock-engravings and paintings cover the whole of this period. It must have lasted for about 5,000 years. Tested samples of ash from Tassili hearths have given a date from 3,500 to 2,500 BC. First signs of the dessication of the soil appear about 2,000 BC. The invasion by the chariot people took place about 1200; horses were being ridden by 600. With the description of Herodotus (mid 5th-century BC) we reach history.

A land cursed by the gods,

a wilderness of barren rock and sand, eternally empty of all living things save a few dry grasses, insects and lizards—such was the picture of the Sahara that prevailed from Roman times almost until the present day. But over the last fifty years that picture has changed. The bones of hippopotamus, giraffe, elephant, zebra and antelope have been found mysteriously thousands of miles from their present homes; ancient trees survive tenaciously in ground where no seed will germinate; crocodiles, stunted by generations of undernourishment, eke out an existence in desert pools which they could not possibly have reached by migration. Most exciting of all, remains of men have come to light: skeletons, flint tools, food refuse, engravings of animals. Slowly the realization has grown that what are now parched valleys and arid plains once echoed to the shouts of hunters returning from the chase; herds of cattle grazed; and sparkling rivers ran through a green and fertile countryside. There is little today to tell of all this busy life, but the Neolithic peoples of the Sahara have left one enduring monument—their rock-paintings. In their hundreds and thousands these rich works of art look down from the rock-walls of Jabbaren, Aouanrhet and Sefar, once populous regions of the Tassili-n-Ajjer, now dead wastes. Only recently have they been fully revealed, and the ancient civilizations of the Sahara been given their rightful place in the story of mankind.

A few olive, pistachio and cypress trees still exist in the Tassili, one of them 25 feet in diameter and probably from three to four thousand years old. Some seeds of the *tarout* (a kind of cypress, right) have lately been found and successfully cultivated again—an almost extinct species brought back to life. (2)

The only tree in six hundred miles of desert stands almost in the centre of the desolate Ténéré (above), recalling the time when luxuriant vegetation covered the whole country. Now, the solitary landmark in a sea of sand, it appears on maps as the area's geodetic point. (1)

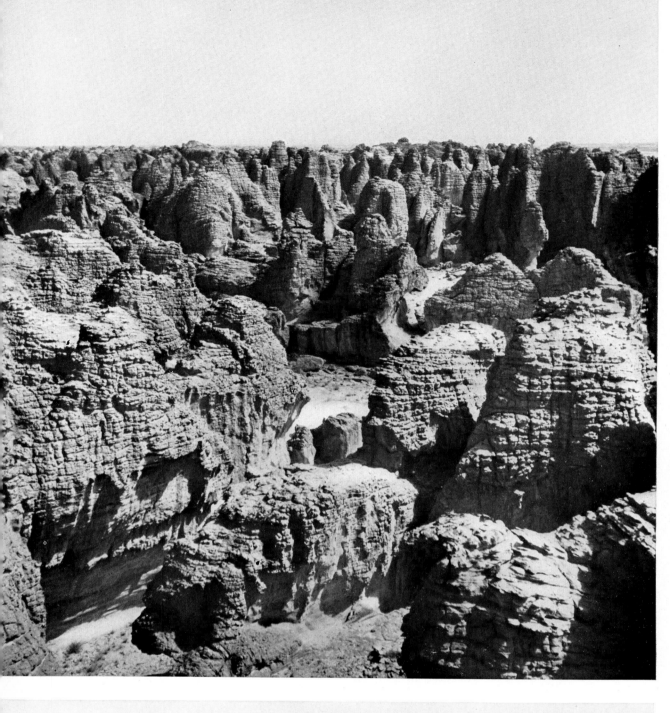

The Tassili-n-Ajjer is a sandstone massif carved into fantastic shapes by the action of wind and water (left). In the Tuareg language it means 'plateau of the rivers'. The rivers are things of the past, but weird canyons and gullies remain to show where they once ran. Sometimes they form streets and squares—a veritable 'city of the dead', the great masses of rock rising up on either side, pitted and worn by the sand like the façade of some Hindu temple, flanked by huge natural columns; or a vast stepped depression reminds the traveller of some ancient ruined amphitheatre.

The rock shelters in which most of the paintings have been found are cavities eroded at the foot of cliffs (the photograph below shows one at Aouanrhet). There are more than ten thousand of them at ground level, their walls presenting an excellent surface for painting and at the same time preserving the pictures in good condition. (3, 4)

No tomb or skeleton has been found near the painted sites. The Neolithic deposit above is further to the south at Tamaya; there is no attempt at ordered burial—skulls and bones lie in the sand in a confused heap with other refuse. (5)

Giant animals, wonderfully engraved with complete naturalism, cover the rock-walls of In Habeter, not far from the Tassili. At the top: a group of long-tailed monkeys. Centre, from the left: animal-headed hunters with a rhinoceros lying on its back; disk-symbols; a giraffe with disk-symbols; another two giraffes; a lion ready to pounce; and one more giraffe. At the bottom: two men pulling a giant giraffe's tail. (6)

A life-sized elephant is engraved on the rock-face at Wadi Djerat in the Tassili, now a dried-up watercourse, but formerly wet enough to be the home of hippopotamus. The picture belongs to the earliest phase of pre-historic Saharan art, and although not of the highest quality, is interesting in showing men and animals together. Note the young elephant underneath the big one, and men who seem to raise their arms but who carry no weapons. (7)

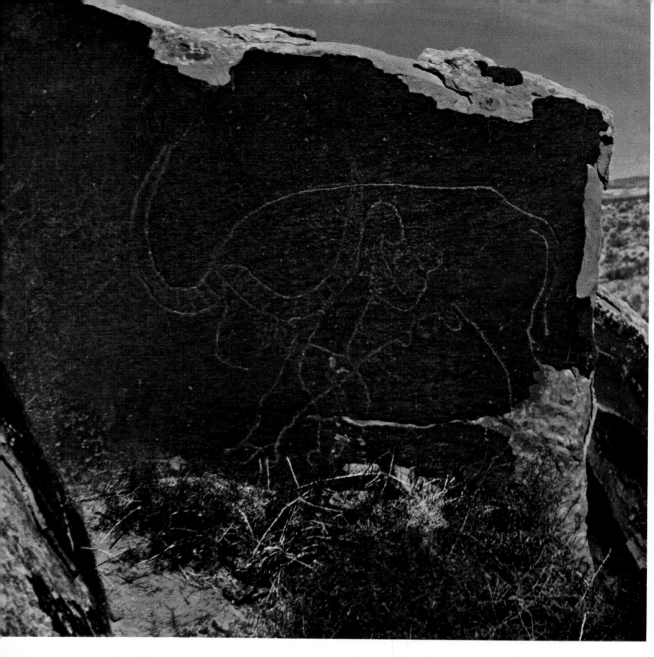

Into ancient Tassili races seem to have poured from both Europe and Africa. The 'Europoid' strain predominates in the rock engravings of the north. The man with a *Bubalus antiquus* (left) is on a rock-face in Oran Province. The Tassili itself was the home also of 'Round-headed men', who were probably negroid. Their paintings start by showing tiny doll-like men and women, but later these grow to enormous size, their heads looking like the space-helmets of 'Martians'.

The fresco at Ti-n-Tazarift (right) shows the first stage. The Round-headed men, dog-faced baboons and antelopes swarm in seeming confusion. On the same surface, but done at different times, are two other scenes —the big archer and his companion, upper left, and the strange white figure towards the right, who seems to belong with the cat-like animal opposite turning back to look at him. Below: the 'Martian' phase, the Great God of Sefar, one of the most overwhelming of the Tassili pictures. In the centre is a huge faceless figure over ten feet high. On the left women raise their arms in supplication; on the right another woman with swollen abdomen seems about to give birth. The scene is probably connected with a fertility cult. (8, 9, 10)

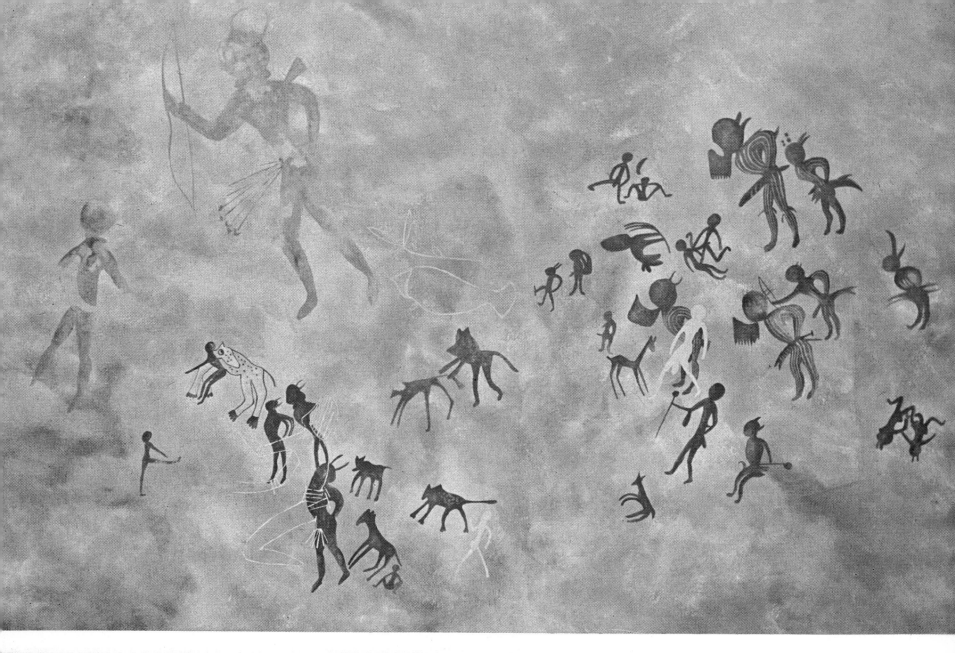

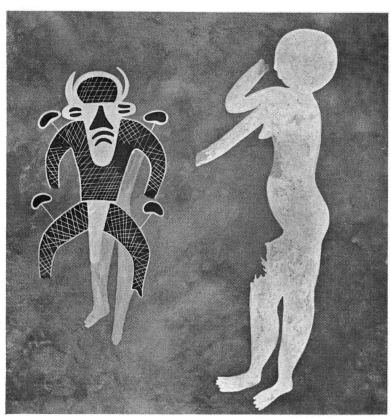

The horned mask worn by the left-hand figure is striking evidence for the presence of Negroes in the Sahara. Masks of the same type are still worn by the Sienuf of the Ivory Coast. Note also the triangular loin-cloth and stylized flowers on the shoulders and thighs. The white legs belong to another figure that has been painted over—a woman like the one that remains on the right. (11)

Away from the valleys was the untamed scrub-land with its teeming wild life: elephant, hippopotamus, antelope, wild-ass, wart-hog, giraffe and panther. To the Tassili people, however, the wild animals were evidently more than merely enemies; some were accorded a sort of devotion. The rock-walls at Wadi Djerat are filled with vivid – often over life-size – engravings of them. This hippopotamus has an endearing quality in spite of his large size—over 12 feet long. (12)

Cowering in terror a young elephant shrinks behind its mother's trunk from the attack of a panther—one of the vivid rock-engravings in the southern Atlas Mountains at Ain Sfasafa. (13)

The spiral, a magical sign, is often found connected with animals in the Tassili. At Wadi Djerat a double spiral is superimposed on an engraving of *Bubulus antiquus*. (14)

Animals long extinct join in head-on conflict. *Bubalus antiquus*, a species of wild ox with big curving horns, must once have roamed the Sahara in great numbers. The rock-engraving above is at El Hamra, on the southern side of the Atlas Mountains. The artist has managed to convey the movements of the huge beasts with vivid realism; details like the corrugations of the horns, the beard and the forelock are faithfully rendered, although the viewpoint is a simple profile and we only see two legs of each ox. (15)

Men with animal heads bring to mind the animal-headed gods of Egypt. The engraving above is at Wadi Djerat. (16)

The 'White Lady' of Aouanrhet, one of the most remarkable of all the paintings at Tassili. It shows a woman running. Fine threads fall from her arms and waist. The dots on her body and limbs probably represent scarification. Above the horns is what seems to be a cloud of grain falling from a wheat field. Is she a goddess or the priestess of some agricultural religion? (17)

The golden age of the Sahara

came with the arrival of pastoral peoples from the east. Herds of cattle now roamed the Tassili valleys and flocks of sheep grazed on the upper slopes. The hunting of wild animals continued, but life was now more settled and more civilized. Villages of thatched huts were built. Cooking-pots, heaps of kitchen-refuse, pottery and ostrich-shell ornaments all tell of wealth and sophistication. The desert was a land of plenty.

Cows and oxen are driven home— a scene full of detail and animation in a rock shelter at Jabbaren (right). The cattle belong to two breeds—one with delicate horns curved like a lyre, the other with thick horns pointing forward. In colour they range from dark violet and green to reddish brown— several are even piebald. The men too, it may be noted, are of different complexions—more evidence for the mixture of races at this time. On the right an ox has been killed and one of its legs cut off. The superb realism of these animals in movement marks perhaps the greatest achievement of the Saharan rock-painters. (18)

The first wave of settlers came not with cattle but with sheep and goats (left). The goats were of the same sort as those kept today by the Tuareg, and the sheep had short tails. The fish, which is part of a different painting, bears witness to the life that once teemed in the deep rivers and lakes of the Sahara. (19)

Bird-headed goddesses at Jabbaren▸ (right) are so like figures on Egyptian monuments of the 18th Dynasty (1200 BC) that the discoverers searched long and hopefully for a hieroglyphic inscription to explain them. But in vain. Are they the work of Egyptian soldiers on an expedition (though no known chronicle makes any mention of one), of Egyptian prisoners of war, or of Libyan prisoners returning from Egypt? It is at least certain that for centuries the Egyptians and the natives of Tassili had been in contact, usually hostile, and that each was open to the other's influence. (20)

Girls in West Africa and Senegal still wear their hair in 'sugar-loaves' like these Tassili girls of 3,000 years ago (above). The skin is rendered in red-ochre, head-dress and robes in white. Several of the details again recall Egypt, but heads and faces are Ethiopian and point to an eastern origin for the pastoralists, the closest parallels today being with the Peul of the Niger region. (21)

In its whole history, the Sahara can never have supported so large a population leading so full a life as during the pastoralist period. The fresco on the left is at Sefar. Herdsmen are driving home the cattle, two of them riding on an ox's back. The cows have full udders, showing that they were kept for their milk. Weapons consisted of bows and axes, and the dog was already part of the household. The cattle in particular are painted with skillful care for detail: note the horns, ears, hooves and tails. (22)

Big-game hunting — of rhinoceros at Jabbaren (left) and hippopotamus at Aouanrhet (below left). The rhinoceros bleeds at the nostrils and seems to have been wounded, though whether by the hunters with bows is not certain. The hippopotamus hunt is yet another striking reminder of the lakes and rivers that used to cover the Sahara. Hippopotamus bones have in fact been found not far away from this painting. The canoes are evidently of reeds, but the actual construction is left doubtful. (23, 24)

Man and woman: one of the masterpieces of the Tassili artists, an astonishing achievement which was not to be equalled until the time of the Greeks. It is painted on a rock-wall at Sefar and is life-size. The woman's head resembles the girls' in plate 21. The body is magnificently proportioned; one leg is drawn up, the other stretched out, the whole pose displaying an elegance and humanity hitherto unsuspected in Stone Age art. The other figure, probably a man, has flowers in the head-dress. (25)

The 'Marathon Race', a lively group of figures who appear to be running, painted on the wall of a niche at Aouanrhet almost at ground-level, in white, blue and red. The head-dresses are again distinctly Egyptian-looking. (26)

Ox and ram are often shown with the same attributes—crescents or disks—either above or between the horns. (27)

The face of the sun surrounded by ox heads and sacred attributes at Tisoukai recalls Ra and Apis of ancient Egypt. (28)

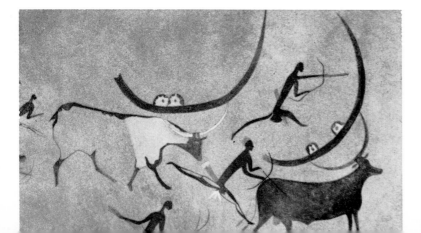

The end of prehistoric Tassili

came with invasion by new peoples from the north. They were trained warriors. For the first time the Saharan peoples had to face javelins, shields and chariots of war. The pastoralists, whose home the Tassili had been for so long, leave no more traces. They were probably driven south and became the ancestors of the Peul. The new 'chariot-people' penetrated as far as the Niger, leaving a trail of characteristic paintings behind them. They are mentioned by Herodotus in the late 5th century BC under the name of 'Garamantes'. Some of them joined Hannibal's army.

Soon after the invasion the fresco at Adjefou (above) was painted. The two chariots and the warriors in the bottom right-hand corner are the earliest in date; note the rectangular shield that one of them is carrying. Later come the row of warriors at the top and the oxen and cows (two of them with calves). The warriors have javelins and curious square objects (baskets?). There are also a goat, a dog and a tall woman in a long white dress. The odd way in which most of the figures consist of two triangles and a head that is a mere stick is typical of this style. (29)

One of the war-chariots. There are two horses; the driver holds a rein in each hand. The wheel construction is interesting. Underneath is a fainter picture of a horseman. Charioteers and riders depicted together are rare in Saharan painting. This is at Tin-Abou Teka. (30)

But more than warlike invaders were working against the Sahara. The climate was changing, the rainfall dwindling, the great rivers drying up; and by Imperial Roman times the desert had conquered.

Men, animals and art of a lost world

HENRI LHOTE

NOT SO LONG AGO, in the school atlases we used as children, the map of the Sahara bore these words only: 'vast areas of sand without water or vegetation'. The impression given was of a region swept by violent sand-storms in which whole caravans would lose their bearings and die of thirst after days of suffering. For centuries this was the picture of the Sahara and there was more legend than fact in it. Of course, the Sahara has been a desert for a long time: when Greek and Roman authors wrote their accounts of it, it was no doubt not very different from what it is today. So, naturally enough, men thought that conditions had always been the same—but this is not true. Nevertheless it was generally held that this vast area was cursed by the gods and that it had never been fit for human settlement—except for a few bands of brigands—the Tuareg—cut off from the rest of humanity because their unpardonable crimes had forced them to avoid for ever the society of civilized peoples.

Though Saharan exploration began in the middle of the last century, it only became possible on a large scale after the French occupation. What was learned then was to modify very considerably the old hazy, romantic picture. The pacification allowed the whole area to be systematically explored, whereas earlier on their thirst for knowledge had cost many British, German and French travellers their lives. The reputation for brigandage enjoyed by the various Saharan populations was not, by any means, always ill-deserved.

We know today that Africa is a very old continent where Man first became Man. South Africa, especially, has yielded up ancient hominid remains some of which represent, as it were, transitional forms between apes and men. Thanks to these discoveries we now possess an evolutionary series which, if it does not enable us to solve the problem of Man's origins, does present us with a reasonably well established picture of the different phases of this progressive evolution.

The Pebble-tool Makers

Furthermore, South Africa, the Sahara and other parts of the continent have given us the most ancient man-made implements known, the famous pebble-tools which for so long puzzled archaeologists. The makers of these artefacts were none other than the Australopithecines who were at first regarded as apes resembling men but who, in reality, possessed minds sufficiently developed and hands cunning enough to fashion tools, to create an 'industry'. These people, then must have been of a fairly high intelligence—it even looks as though they were acquainted with the use of fire.

Quite recently, with only a year's interval between them, two discoveries of capital importance were made in the Sahara. During the winter of 1959-1960 the Berliet Mission, a large-scale automobile expedition in which several scientists including myself took part, explored, with the object of tracing out a direct route between Algiers and Lake Chad, one of the most desolate regions in the whole desert—the Ténéré—where, for more than six hundred miles, from north to south, you never see a human being or come across a water-hole. The flora, with the exception of a few grasses that shoot up after the very infrequent rains, is confined to one single, solitary tree, growing almost in the centre, that has

been adopted as this desert's geodetic point and appears as such on the maps. The general aspect of the Ténéré is one of a pebbly plain stretching as far as the eye can reach. From this flat surface little peaks or eroded ridges jut up here and there, the last vestiges of a relief which was once far more varied. It is difficult to convey the strange impression you get when advancing slowly at camel's pace through these solitudes. You feel, at one and the same time, exhilarated by the splendour of their immensity and weighed down both by the absence of all life and by the profound silence that reigns. When, in great gusts, the sand-storms begin to blow and you can see but a few paces before you, the scene assumes an apocalyptic grandeur.

Nevertheless, there was a time when in the Ténéré might have been heard the cheerful shouts of men returning from a good day's hunting, when chattering women gathered around cooking-pots steaming from messes of fish and meat while men bent on fishing went gliding down a splendid stream some seven hundred and fifty miles long.

Of this stream, or rather river, hardly a trace remains. Here and there you can make out its former bed in the shape of clayey deposits containing in varying quantities both fishbones and shells, but generally speaking the sands have so thickly carpeted the whole region that you can travel for hundreds of miles without ever suspecting the fossil river's existence.

It was in the Ténéré, during the Berliet Mission that we found pebble-tools, rough pebbles from one end of which a few flakes had been struck off to form a sharp point or a cutting-edge—the impressive and earliest evidence for Man's great creative adventure which, by long and painful stages, has led up to the space-ship.

The pebbles were all together on one site at the foot of a little rocky ridge near the bed of the old Ténéré river, the Tafessasset. How long had they been there awaiting archaeologists to identify them? 500,000 years? Maybe more. It is likely that at this spot there once lived a fairly numerous community, but of the cooking-refuse these people must have discarded, and which would have enabled us to know what they used to eat, nothing has survived at all. Any remains of meals scattered about in the open must have long ago been calcined by the sun and reduced to dust by the winds.

Later journeys undertaken farther south, that is to say in the direction of Lake Chad, were to show us that the whole river

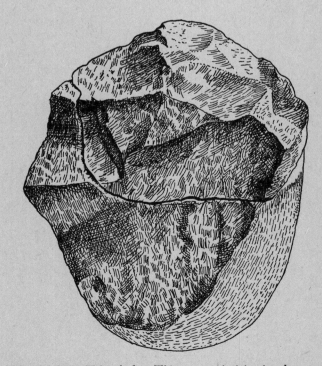

A pebble-tool from Tihemboka. This very primitive implement has been found all over Africa associated with remains of Australopithecus, who could have lived 500,000 years ago. It consists of a rough stone from which a few flakes have been struck at one end to form a cutting edge. (1)

pl 1

f 1

valley was once occupied by the makers of the pebble-tools, for we found specimens of them in several places. These first Saharan data were confirmed, in the following year, by a young palaeontologist who was studying the exceptionally rich fossil fauna of the northern Chad region. He discovered the remains of an Australopithecine whom the South African scientists consider to be the maker of the pebble-tools.

We know, then, something about the antiquity of Man in the Sahara. But the thought occurs to all of us that 500,000 years ago was not precisely yesterday. During the last half a million years all sorts of things must have happened in the Sahara.

The Hand-axe People

One of the most celebrated of the early Sahara explorers, the Frenchman, Henri Duveyrier, who spent some time at Rhat in 1861, jotted down in his note-books that Tuaregs had told him there existed in the Tihodaine *erg*, a region of sand-dunes to the south of the Tassili-n-Ajjer, and therefore near what had been the upper reaches of the Tafessasset, the remains of an enormous fossil mammal whose head was so big, said the desert men, that a woman could sit in it 'like in an armchair'. This story was verified sixty-eight years later, in 1929, by a Captain Duprez, then in command of the area, when the remains were unearthed. They proved to be those of an *Elephas antiquus*, an ancient species of elephant some thirteen feet tall. The fossil lay embedded in the banks of a former lake and buried in a mass of detritus of various kinds. Over the surrounding ground were scattered large hand-axes produced by removing big flakes from the stone. Such implements are known in archaeological terminology as 'Acheulian bifaces'. Later on, I myself was to come across a similar site in the Admer *erg*, some hundred and twenty-five miles away and on the banks of one of the Tafessasset's tributaries the clayey bed of which was still clearly visible. Although at this spot the fauna was slightly different and included fossilized remains of hippopotamus and zebra together with many fishbones, hand-axes lay all around, and it is clear that the men of Tihodaine and Admer hunted large pachyderms, fished and gathered wild fruits, roots and tubers.

Chelleo-Acheulian artefacts exist almost everywhere in the Sahara, especially in the western areas and in the Fezzan. During the course of the Berliet Mission we discovered such implements quite close to pebble-tool sites and in quantities that can be called 'industrial' since, in some places, they can be picked up in their hundreds.

Until a short while ago we knew nothing about the type of Man who fashioned these large chipped stone tools which for long—until the pebble-tools were identified as man-made—were considered as the most ancient artefacts of mankind. Once again enlightenment was to come out of Africa. In 1954 a discovery of very considerable importance was made at Palikao, a small village not far from Mascara in the Algerian province of Oran. Near this hamlet is a sand-pit which in the past was explored on several occasions by archaeologists who found remains there of animals belonging to such extinct species as *Elephas antiquus*; a primitive camel; *Hippopotamus major* etc. and, in addition to these, many Chelleo-Acheulian hand-axes.

The dig, however, had to be abandoned since artesian water from an underlying spring filled up the holes as soon as the sand was removed. But in 1954 and 1955 work was resumed on a large scale. Motor-pumps were installed to draw off the water, and, under the supervision of Professor Arambourg, a considerable amount of material was removed from the sands. It included numerous fossil bones of animals together with hand-axes similar to those of the Tihodaine and Admer *ergs*. By far the most striking find, however, was that of three well-preserved human lower jaws. For the first time human bones had been recovered in association with Chelleo-Acheulian hand-axes and a clearly defined fauna, although this type of artefact (identified for the first time at Chelles to the east of Paris and at Saint-Acheul just outside Amiens) is wide-spread not only in Europe but also in Asia and Africa.

As may be imagined, it was with a good deal of excitement that Professor Arambourg examined these venerable human relics. Their archaic appearance struck him and in fact deeply troubled him, but after careful study in his laboratory at the *Muséum d'Histoire naturelle* in Paris, he concluded that the type of Man represented by the Palikao jaws was one bearing a close resemblance to the well-known 'Sinanthropus' (*Pithecanthropus pekinensis*) of North China, a cousin of the Java Pithecanthropoids, the celebrated 'ape-men' to whom for so long a hominid status was denied.

The Palikao mandibles do, nevertheless, exhibit certain differences from those of Pekin Man, and Arambourg thought it best to class the former in a new category that he called 'Atlanthropus'. Among the associated fauna are *Elephas antiquus* (the first complete skull to be recovered); *Rhinoceros mercki*; *Hippotamus major*; *Camellus thomasi*; *Equus mauritanicus*, *Machairodus* (the 'sabre-toothed tiger'); a huge wart-hog etc. It is a fauna much like that discovered in the Somme and Thames river-terraces—except for a few species such as the camel and a horse.

So it was that a little village where French settlers had worked a sand-pit when they were building their houses provided the key to a mystery which archaeologists had been trying to solve for nearly a century. The elusive maker of the hand-axes was none other than a member of the Pithecanthropus family whose first remains (consisting of a *calotte* or brain-pan, a femur and a molar tooth) were unearthed by the Dutch army-surgeon Eugen Dubois in Java as long ago as 1891. It is true that portions of human skeletons had been found in conditions indicating that the men they represent were contemporary with the makers, if they themselves were not the actual fashioners, of the artefacts known as 'Chellean', but most of these ancient fossils were discovered isolated in alluvial deposits with no traces of fauna and no well defined industry. The Palikao finds, however, afforded additional proof that the Pithecanthropoids were no apes but real men.

The Tihodaine and Admer implements are certainly rather later in date than those of Palikao but if the former were not the work of 'Atlanthropus' then they were most likely made by a close relative of his.

These highly important discoveries concern not only Africa's past but also throw a light on Man's first fumbling efforts to free himself gradually from a condition scarcely better than that of an animal.

f 2

Chelleo-Acheulian hand-axe and cleaver from Admer, closely comparable with implements found with remains of Atlanthropus at Palikao. The hand-axe (left) is of a type known all over the prehistoric world, but the cleaver—a tool better suited to the coarser stone of the Sahara—is practically confined to Africa and hardly ever found north of the Pyrenees. (2)

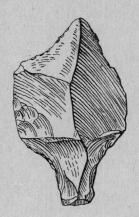

Aterian points, a type of flaked flint that marks the climax of the Middle Palaeolithic in North Africa. Its importance lies in the characteristic tang for attaching a handle or shaft; the culture extended as far south as the Niger. (3)

Lost Rivers of the Sahara

We have already mentioned the Tafessasset, a great waterway seven hundred and fifty miles long, whose sources were in the Hoggar and Tassili highlands and which emptied into Lake Chad. To map out its course was no easy task. Many camel-corps reconnaissances were needed. They were conducted with intrepidity for there was still a danger of death from thirst. This region, the *reg*, is an extensive area of flat, desert plain from which the fine sand has been blown away leaving the surface covered with small stones and gravel. The story of how men ventured into it in order to track down even the smallest topographical feature forms but one episode in the great exploration epic begun in the second half of the last century by the pioneers, the most famous of whom were the German Heinrich Barth, who worked for the Royal Geographical Society, and Duveyrier whom I have already mentioned.

pl 1

pl 3

These explorers, all men of sound scientific attainments, discovered that the Sahara was not the sand-desert of legend, but that, although there are gigantic dunes and vast sandy areas very difficult to traverse because of the lack of water, there are also huge mountain-masses scored by valleys which must once, to judge by the width of some of the canyons, have been channelled by considerable streams. Likewise the early explorers suggested that the regions so arid today must, in the past, have supported populations living in normal conditions. The pioneers, in fact, had already suspected that the engravings they had noticed on rock-faces indicated that pastoralists and cattle-breeders had once wandered in Saharan valleys.

Later expeditions were to bring to light a vast ancient hydrographic network consisting of several basins and real rivers such as the Tafessasset flowing into Lake Chad, others belonging to the Niger system or terminating in depressions, that is lakes. Among streams of the latter type are Wadi Igharghar and Wadi Saoura.

The Changing Climate

Careful examination of the Moroccan and Saharan Atlantic sea-coasts has led geologists and prehistorians to conclude that the ancient continent has hardly changed its contours for hundreds of thousands of years. Indeed, many traces of human activity in most remote Palaeolithic times—as well as in Neolithic—are still, very luckily, undisturbed. The coastal populations lived on the produce of the sea—fish, crustaceans etc. These facts are, today, accepted and suffice to dispose of fantastic theories such as that the Sahara was, until comparatively recent times, covered by the sea, or that the desert was the site of the legendary Atlantis which sank beneath the waves. Africa is, then, a very ancient continent indeed, which has not much altered in form and shape since Tertiary times.

In the meanwhile evidence of temperate climates and moist conditions has been assembled by zoologists and botanists. Thus, fish, crocodiles and batrachians have been captured in lakes that still

pl 2

survive in the Tassili highlands. Trees, such as the olive, pistachio and cypress exist on the heights of the Hoggar, Tassili-n-Ajjer and Aïr mountain masses. In this latter massif an olive-tree measuring over twenty-five feet in diameter was lately discovered by the Berliet Mission. The tree is probably from three to four thousand years old and a survivor from times when the Saharan climate was damper than it is now.

Such discoveries naturally encouraged search for traces of Man and these have proved to be very abundant. After the Australopithecines, after 'Atlanthropus', the Sahara was the home of Neanderthaloids whose presence in Europe is proved from Mid-Pleistocene times. Remains of this type of Man—characterized by heavy and prominent eyebrow ridges, protruding upper-jaw and receding chin have been found near Tangier. It is true that the remains of Tangier Man consist only of a child's lower jaw, but this is enough to assure us that Neanderthaloids lived in North Africa. It is thought that these Neanderthaloids, unlike their Australopithecine and Pithecanthropoid predecessors, were not autochthonous but came over from Europe during the last or Würmian Ice Age which caused the 'Tyrrhenian regression' of the sea.

At this period, owing to the lowering of the sea-level and the

exposure of wide expanses of land since covered by water, passage between Europe and Africa must have been easier than it is now. However, the 'Flandrian transgression' which followed, brought about a marked rise in the sea-level and the waters once again became a barrier which was to last until the time of the Neolithic peoples. As a result of the higher sea-level, several groups of Neanderthaloids which had migrated into Africa were cut off from their European cousins and so evolved as isolated communities. The African Neanderthaloid artefacts are of a peculiar sort and the Mousterian point, in Africa, acquired a tang.

f 3

In the Sahara this culture, which is known as the 'Aterian', showed considerable development and extended as far south as the Niger. Whereas in Europe the Neanderthaloids, as a distinct type, seem to have disappeared after the arrival of successive waves of *Homo sapiens* peoples—such as those of Chancelade and of Cro-Magnon—the Neanderthaloid industry persisted in the Sahara until invasions of populations with a Neolithic culture, and it is presumed that the Neanderthaloids themselves then disappeared. At any rate none of their bones have as yet been found in the desert. The climate and fauna seem to have been about the same as in preceding periods, though as no food remains have been discovered associated with Aterian artefacts we are unable to prove or to disprove this conjecture. Nevertheless, in some regions of the Sahara, especially in the territory north of the Chad and the Niger, there are ancient sand-dunes and this suggests that towards the end of the Palaeolithic conditions were getting more arid. Attempts have been made to link the various climatic phases in the Sahara with the glacial ages in Europe. The periods of great cold in our continent would correspond to periods of heavy rainfall in the desert. In other words, the four great Ice Ages of Europe, the Günz, Mindel, Riss and Würm would be contemporary with four great African Pluvials divided from each other by more or less arid intervals which would be the equivalents of the European interglacials. However, this theory is coming to be less and less held by Sahara specialists since the climatic oscillations in the desert appear to have been fewer than those in Europe. In the present state of our knowledge, it is fair to say that the Lower Palaeolithic was a time of great humidity which extended into the Middle Palaeolithic, whereas the Upper Palaeolithic was a period of aridity. All the same, what we know of Quaternary Saharan geology is not yet enough for such statements to be other than provisional.

A Green Sahara, Richly Populated

Now we come to the Neolithic which began, probably, some time between 8000 and 6000 BC though datings obtained by the carbon-14 method tend, more and more, to lower these figures. After the semi-aridity that prevailed during the Upper Palaeolithic, the Sahara came to have a heavy rainfall. Successive waves of immigrants invaded the whole area from all sides, leaving many evidences of their passage. 'Europoids' occupied the northern regions; Negroes arrived from the south and other populations, possibly copper-coloured and of Ethiopian type, poured in from

27

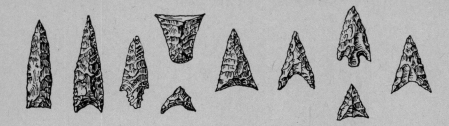

Arrow-heads of the Bovidian period, from the Ténéré. Made of green jasper, they are little gems of craftsmanship. (4)

pl 19

f 4

f 6

the east. The activities of these people were very varied, for this was the real epoch of the fertile Sahara, when the human communities were so numerous that the density of population was probably greater here than in almost any other region of the world at that time. Hunters were also food-gatherers; fishers dwelling in villages by the side of rivers and lakes lived on aquatic fauna—fish, molluscs and even hippopotamus. Later, food-gathering gave way to agriculture carried on with stone hoes in the flood-plain by the side of lakes and streams.

Finally came the pastoralists, first with sheep and goats and afterwards with cattle. We can say with confidence that at this period there was an astonishing culture in the Sahara, astonishing both for its variety and for the high quality of its stone artefacts which included polished axes and arrow-heads of the most diversified forms, pieces which are often little gems of craftsmanship.

The main paths of migration led, of course, through the great valleys on whose ancient terraces we can trace the encampment sites of the fishing folk who used bone harpoons, fish-hooks of both stone and bone and nets with egg-shaped stone weights scored with a median groove. In some places the masses of fish-bones, remains of hippopotamus, crocodiles, tortoises and fresh-water mussel shells with ash and various kinds of refuse form thick deposits covering a hundred square yards and prove how rich in fish the streams—now only dry wadis—once were. This civilization of harpoon-fishers is best represented in the southern areas of the Sahara—such as the valleys of the Azaoud and the Azaouak—and seems to have come from the region of the Upper Nile where sites of similar type are to be found. The hunters pushed on into the interior of the country following the track of

animals which, in our days, are to be seen in the savanna, the plains region lying north of the West African forest-belt—elephant, hippopotamus, different species of antelope, wild ass, wart-hog, giraffe, ostrich etc.

Love of finery was evidently wide-spread; necklaces were fashioned from ostrich egg-shells cut into little roundels, then pierced and finished off on burnishers. Pendants and bracelets were cut out of soft schist and also polished. Both quartz and amazonite were utilized to make beads. In some places stone-cutting and fashioning must have been carried on as a regular industry with workmen employed from morning to night in making the various special tools called for by the pastoral or agricultural communities. In one workshop axes would be produced, in another scrapers, in a third arrowheads.

Such workshops are especially common in the Ténéré and we can say that as far back as these Neolithic times there must have existed a definite working-class which supplied the needs of the stock-raising family groups and freed these latter from manual labour. Such specialization resulted, we may note, in the creation of very skilled craftsmen and some of the objects they made must rank among the most beautiful stone artefacts to be found anywhere in the world.

f 4

The Astonishing Art of the Rock-painters

If these remains of human industry which have been revealed up to now allow us to get a general idea about the Saharan populations from Man's earliest days, the works of art which have survived on rock-walls provide a faithful image of the Neolithic peoples and of their manner of life, which very satisfactorily completes the evidence from the deposits. The Sahara is, indeed, the great country of engravings and paintings. They exist in their thousands wherever there are rocks suitable for their execution and for their preservation, from the banks of the Nile to the Atlantic, in such numbers that we may consider this vast region as the richest area of prehistoric art in the world.

Stretching from the beginning of the Neolithic into historical times and very often superimposed one upon another, the Saharan rock pictures allow us to establish epochs and phases. Each of these constitutes a veritable chronicle, just as precious for the archaeologist as are ancient MSS. for the historian. Thus the Saharan documents differ entirely from the prehistoric pictures in south-western France and northern Spain, where human

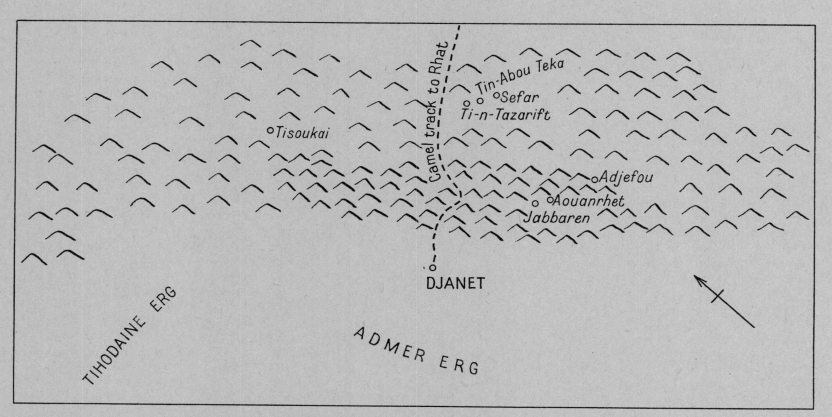

The Tassili-n-Ajjer, a sandstone massif cut into hundreds of gullies and cliffs by ancient river and rain erosion. (5)

figures are rarely shown and where there are hardly any compositions or 'scenes'. The meaning of these Franco-Cantabrian pictures is indeed so enigmatic that many theories, often fantastic enough, have been advanced to explain them. It is true we can see that some are Aurignacian in style and others Perigordian, Solutrean or Magdalenian, but their scientific interest lies mainly in the precise information they afford about the fauna of the Late Old Stone Age in western Europe. It would be vain to seek from them any indication about the migration of their authors or even the exact anthropological status of the artists. It is impossible to say what is to be attributed, for instance, to Chancelade or to Cro-Magnon Man, two physical types that existed at the same time in the area of the western European rock-paintings. We shall see that things are quite different in the Sahara where the rock art can be integrated into a world intelligible to us—because so much nearer in time to our days—and can be made to provide us with real information about the Neolithic past of the great desert.

There are three main centres which are very rich in monumental engravings of a naturalistic style—the south of the province of Oran in Algeria, the Tassili-n-Ajjer and the Fezzan in south-western Libya. These engravings are deeply incised into the rock-faces and, in most cases, the lines form a perfectly polished groove, well executed and obtained only after laborious effort. pl 6-8 Most of the pictures represent animals: elephant, rhinoceros, 12-15 hippopotamus, giraffe, horse, ass, ostrich, crocodile, as well as a large ruminant today extinct, the *Bubalus antiquus*, an animal with very long horns curving up to form the arc of a circle. All these beasts are wild, but in the south of Oran the ram is common while in the Tassili-n-Ajjer the ox occurs frequently. Both creatures are often depicted with a spheroid object between their pl 27 horns or with attributes either between or above the horns. We may have here an indication that some sort of devotion was paid to these animals. Maybe it was sought if not to domesticate them at least to tame them.

pl 8 In the south of the Oran province, elephant, *Bubalus antiquus*, ram and lion are often shown together with human beings of a Europoid appearance. These persons are raising their arms before the beasts as though to implore them or to do reverence to them.

In the Tassili, where the art-style is also naturalistic, there is no depiction of relations between animals and men and this fact alone would indicate that religious ideas were not the same in the two areas. In the Tassili are many scenes of copulation which appear very daring to our western European and 'civilized' minds. For this reason there can be no question of reproducing any of such pictures in a work addressed to the general public; still we must draw attention to them since they are surely evidence of some fertility cult such as those still practised in our days among primitive communities.

The human types in the Tassili, like those in the Oran province, have, in most cases, a Europoid aspect, though many of the pl 16 figures are furnished with animal heads—of mastiff, hare and other beasts. Maybe, one day, it will be considered that we have, on the Tassili rock-walls, early evidence for the existence of those animal cults which were so characteristic of the ancient Egyptian religion.

The fauna, as we have seen, is—with the exception of the ox and the ram about which it is well to reserve judgment—predominantly of wild species and seems to represent a complex that would be particularly interesting to communities of hunters. pl 14 Spirals, especially in the Tassili, are often associated with the animals and were possibly drawn with a view to some sort of enchantment.

The Giants of Tassili

What is very remarkable about these Tassili engravings is their extraordinary dimensions which are such as have not, up to now, been found in any other prehistoric pictures. Many of the great pachyderms, such as elephant and rhinoceros, are drawn life-size, sometimes more than life-size. Certain pictures of rhinoceros are nearly twenty-five feet long and one group of giraffes is over twenty-six feet high. It may be easily imagined how impressive these giants are, standing out from the rocky walls of the Tassili's

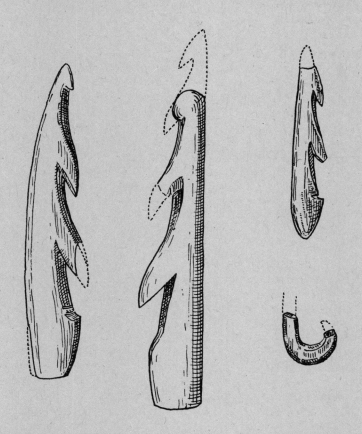

Bone harpoons and a fish-hook from the Azaouak valley and In-Guezzam. Stone weights for nets have also been found at these sites, together with masses of fish-bones and shells, proving how rich the Sahara rivers once were. (6)

great canyons. The human figures are often on the same gigantic pl 10 scale. Some men are thirteen feet tall. The numbers of the engravings are in some places remarkable. For instance, in the Wadi Djerat along a distance of less than twenty miles more than four thousand pictures can be counted; it is true that they belong to a number of different epochs.

Such a fauna as that represented indicates a rich vegetation which we may imagine not to have been very different from that of the African savanna today where the same species of animals as those shown on the rocks of the Tassili still live.

So much for the engravings. The area covered by the prehistoric Saharan paintings is immeasurably greater. These are especially abundant in the Tassili-n-Ajjer where, in recent years, some *f 5* surprising discoveries have been made. The pictures—in which more than thirty different styles, with many superimpositions, can be recognized—are, indeed, a revelation of considerable significance. At the present time more than twenty thousand separate figures, of various epochs, have been counted and the inventory is far from being completed.

Such a concentration of prehistoric art can be accounted for only by the very peculiar structure of the Tassili massif, which pl 3 is formed of sandstone that, in remote ages, was cut into and eroded by the waters so as to be in some places completely dismembered. Later on the rocks were subjected to intensive erosion by rain action, so that innumerable niches were formed, some of them pl 4 large enough to be called caves. There are more than ten thousand rock-shelters on ground level, most of them suitable as habitations, and giving on to corridors in which it is easy to move about. It can readily be imagined that such a geological formation was highly attractive to human settlers—all the more since numerous natural cisterns (which still exist) supplied water for man and beast. Moreover, not only did the sheltered cave-walls present an exellent surface for paintings, but they also preserved the pictures in good condition.

If we consider that pigment in the form of different coloured ochreous schists abounds locally, we shall realize that a people of developed artistic sense would certainly have been tempted to take advantage of all these favourable circumstances.

The Round-headed Men

f 7   The most ancient Tassili frescoes represent persons with round heads often adorned with horns or feathers. These pictures make up a very varied collection composed of many different phases which it would be tedious to enumerate here. The paintings are, in many cases, superimposed one upon another, indicating that the people who executed them lived in the Tassili for a long time.

The earliest frescoes are in monochrome, the later human figures are polychrome, while, starting with small dimensions *pl 9*   at first, they reach, at one period, gigantic size, some of them as high as seventeen feet. Despite variations in type and execution, the characteristics remain the same—stylized round heads (often reminding one of a 'Martian's' space-helmet), podgy limbs, *pl 10*   fingers and toes stuck together, bodies without any marked waist. All these characteristics remind one of Negro African statuettes. The resemblance seems all the greater when we note that our Tassili figures often display markings whose form is sometimes surprisingly like those skin-scarifications practised today by West Africans. Furthermore, among the pictures already inventoried (and not all have been copied or indeed examined) there are several representations of persons wearing a mask of a type still *pl 11*   common among the Negroes of the Ivory Coast. There can be no doubt, then, that this whole complex indicates an ancient negroid colonization which extended, as far as we can see, right up into northern Africa. This style of painting, however, is as yet known only in the Tassili and in its prolongation towards the east, the Acacous and in the Ennedi, a small range to the north-east of Lake Chad, where a very small number of frescoes similar to those of the Tassili has been noted.

We do not know, as yet, whether these negroid populations preceded or succeeded the authors of the great engravings showing Europoid faces. There is no resemblance between either the human figures or the subjects represented. On the other hand, the fauna is exactly the same in the two sets of pictures—the *Bubalus antiquus* is shown in the paintings of the round-headed men, and this suggests considerable antiquity.

pl 9   The pictures of the round-headed men do not reveal anything about their manner of life, except that their religious beliefs were certainly informed with animism and symbolism. There is no hunting scene, no incident of warfare, nothing indeed that allows us to glimpse any special form of activity. The only paintings which can be called 'scenes' are those consisting of a number of women who raise their arms, in what looks like an attitude of *pl 10*   supplication, towards a person of great height who always occupies the centre position in a shelter. Since, in one case, there is a pregnant woman lying on her back and about to give birth, we may conclude that we have here a representation of ceremonies connected with a fertility and maternity cult. The shelters with the tall central figure are always of very large dimensions and look as though they were regular temples.

Herdsmen from the East

The next period after that of the round-headed men is one marked by the appearance of invaders who practised cattle-raising on a large scale. The first wave of this pastoral people came with only sheep and goats. The goat was of the same sort as that kept today

The period of the 'round-headed men' and the 'Martians' also includes the style of the 'little devils', which shows influences from both. This example is from Jabbaren. The five figures wear horns. (7)

Cattle from a rock painting at Jabbaren. Three different breeds (or at least horn shapes) appear—downward-pointing, branched and lyre-shaped. (8)

by the Tuareg and the sheep had short tails. But, later on, pastoralists arrived who drove their cattle before them; indeed they rode on ox-back, the men going first, the women and children next *pl 22*   and the moving herd following, perhaps surrounded by dogs.

Paintings dating from the epoch of these Bovidian pastoralists exist in the Tibesti massif, in the Hoggar and, above all, in the Tassili-n-Ajjer. We may suppose that these herdsmen came from the east, especially as their heads and faces greatly resemble those of Ethiopians. The women wore their hair dressed up into crests *pl 21*   or sugar-loaves identical in form with the hair-styles fashionable among the Peul women of West Africa. (The name Fulani, more familiar to English readers, is of the same origin, but the Fulani are considered to have a greater admixture of Negro blood than the Peul.) Nevertheless, side by side with this Ethiopian type we can see negroid and even Europoid faces and this leads us to suppose that an intermingling of races must have taken place at this period. It is also possible that slavery was practised, since it is almost general among pastoral peoples who need servants to watch over flocks and herds, to lead the beasts to water and out to pasture, do the milking and carry wood and water for domestic purposes. All this may perhaps explain the presence on one and the same wall-painting of several different human types.

The cattle are of two sorts, the *Bos africanus* with long, lyre- *pl 18*   shaped horns, and the *Bos brachyceros* bearing thick, curved horns. The beasts are of lanky build and evidently accustomed to moving about a good deal. Their coats are extremely varied with markings and patches of different shapes and sizes. The horns also display all sorts of variations between the lyre form and that of shorthorns. There are even some specimens with horns bent *f 8*   downwards and this implies artificial deformation such as is practised still by the Upper Nile peoples. The cows are shown with milk-swollen udders. Such features do not suggest an early *pl 22*   stage in domestication but rather an advanced phase of cattle-breeding. As a consequence, we may assume that it did not begin in the central Sahara but somewhere else, most probably around the upper course of the Nile as is, indeed, thought by those ethnologists who have studied the pastoral cultures of Africa.

We can count in their thousands the rock-paintings left by these pastoralists in the Tassili. The pictures are of exceptionally high aesthetic quality and, taken as a whole, may be considered as reflecting the finest naturalistic school of painting in the world, so well observed and reproduced are the forms of both men and animals. As opposed to the art of the Pyrenees region where, generally speaking, only isolated figures are shown, the Tassili Bovidian painters have bequeathed to us scenes where more than a hundred persons or beasts, all quivering with life, are depicted *pl 18*   in movement. The creative artistic sense of the Bovidians was so highly developed that among the thousands of animals and human beings shown, no two are exactly alike; each has its own peculiar attitude. This may be noted especially in the case of the cattle, no one of which has quite the same coat as another; the horns are shown from different angles and, as from one picture to another, are never in the same position. We are very far removed from the stereotyped forms so common in the art of Quaternary Europe.

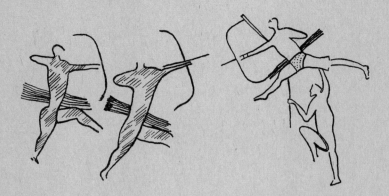

A fight between archers, Jabbaren. The men are coloured differently and perhaps belong to different races. (9)

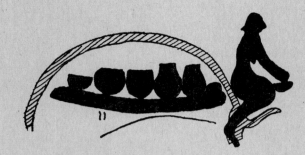

A woman cooking, with five pots behind her on a sort of bench under an arch—perhaps representing the hut: a painting at Tisoukai. (10)

A Land of Plenty

In the compositions it is always the ox that occupies the principal place. There can be no doubt that these pastoralists' whole life turned on this animal. In one scene you can see cattle, surrounded by herdsmen, coming back from pasture. In another there are calves tied with a rope. A third scene shows milking in the encampment near the huts where women are tending their children, and so forth. There was certainly some cattle-rustling between one tribe and another since we often see men, armed with bows and arrows, lined up to fight for the possession of a herd. The main weapon of the Tassili pastoralists was the bow, either straight or triple-curved.

The pastoralists were also hunters, particularly of elephant, rhinoceros, giraffe, wild ass, antelope and even hippopotamus. In one curious scene there are men in canoes chasing the latter beast. This is clear proof, were one needed, of a climate still damp and of flowing Saharan rivers. Furthermore, as though to confirm the evidence of the frescoes, hippopotamus bones have been found—not far from the Tassili—in deposits dated by the carbon-14 method to the period of the pastoralists. The old Tassilians also hunted lions; possibly they were then very common and must have ravaged the flocks and herds. The subjects are inexhaustible: here, women dress their hair; there, groups of men and women dancers circle round a tom-tom, while others shake rattles and women seated in a circle clap their hands; there are scenes of tooth-extraction, of the cutting-up of animals, of groups of men and women talking, and also erotic scenes of striking realism which are nevertheless not indecent.

The frescoes, however, afford us no clue to the pastoralists' religion. All we can say is that the oxen are often depicted with attributes above their horns and this would tend to indicate that the ox played some part in this people's faith. The sun also must have had some religious significance since representations of it figure in decorative motifs associated with ox-heads. We are reminded of the God Ra and the Bull Apis.

The Tassili pastoralists lived in oval huts made of wickerwork or the plaited stalks of dried grasses. Inside the dwellings the cooking-pots were placed on a stand. The huts themselves were in the middle of the cattle-pens, traces of which can still be seen in their hundreds; they were bounded by a stone wall too high for animals to get over. Sometimes the pen was formed by three or four rock-shelters with their exits stopped up. Again, in the case of some of the larger shelters blocks of stone were arranged in a semicircle before the entrance. The cattle spent the night in the shelters and their masters lived by their side.

In the grottoes there are often to be found remains of meals mixed with ash and rubbish, the refuse dumps formed when housewives cleaned out their huts. From the whitish, irregular layers of ash, it is clear that successive lots of litter were thrown on the same heap. It is probable that when the time came to seek new pasture a living-site would be temporarily deserted, but that the people would come back to it later on when, in obedience to the seasonal cycles that rule the life of all pastoral peoples, they sought out fresh grass.

Many pieces of broken pottery are to be seen among the refuse —where most of the bones are those of ox and goat—together with flint scrapers, arrow-heads and some stone axes. There is also a great number of bone polishers and borers, the latter used for sewing up the skins when making clothing. Beads cut out of ostrich egg-shell are scattered about here and there among the ashes—did one of the women cooking break her necklace? Inside the pens the stone grinders and pounders that lie about in such great quantities were used probably to grind wild graminaceous plants, for it does not seem that the Tassili valleys were ever suited to agriculture. All the same one painting does show women gleaning, though this picture in itself alone is not enough to prove definitely that crops were cultivated in some places. Maybe this fresco just depicts the gathering of wild grain, such as is today practised by the pastoralists of the savanna regions.

The Sahara, in the whole long course of its history, can never have supported so large a population leading so active a life as in the time of the pastoralists. The presence of the Bovidians is proved by paintings in the Tibesti, the Tassili and the Hoggar, and we may be fairly sure that they also inhabited regions where there were no rock-shelters, and where, therefore, no evidence of their existence has been preserved. Indeed, Bovidian pottery decorated with broad incisions made with comb or awl, is found over a very wide area, and has been identified in the Ténéré as well as in the sand-dune region to the north of the Tassili. It is true, also, that there are in other parts of the Sahara numerous engravings of bovines, though we cannot say whether these were or were not the work of the same people who made the Tassili paintings since they are in a different style.

Several carbon-14 analyses of charcoal from the Tassili hearths have given datings ranging from 3500 to 2500 BC and it is possible that we must set the time of the pastoralists' arrival farther back by a thousand years. However, what is certain is that cattle were common enough in the Sahara when the domesticated horse was introduced at a period fixed to round about 1200 BC. With the horse came another change in the human population.

In the pastoralists' times the flora of mountainous regions such as the Hoggar and the Tassili included conifers (e. g. Aleppo pine and cypress); arbor vitae; nettle-tree; holm-oak; lentiscus; maple; alder; lime and olive, that is to say a flora of Mediterranean type. The fauna was the same as in the preceding period, except that there was no *Bubalus antiquus*. Palynology (the study of fossilised pollen grains) tells us that from about 2000 BC there began a progressive replacement of Mediterranean vegetation by one that is, today, characteristic of the savanna.

War Chariots from the North

The arrival of the horse marks an important turning-point in Saharan history and we have plenty of evidence relating to this event, including some fine paintings whose style indicates a definite change due to the invasion of new peoples. These men and women wore bi-triangular tunics, drawn in at the waist, or bell-shaped skirts. The horses are shown harnessed to two-wheeled war-chariots. Arms and armour were javelins and round shields,

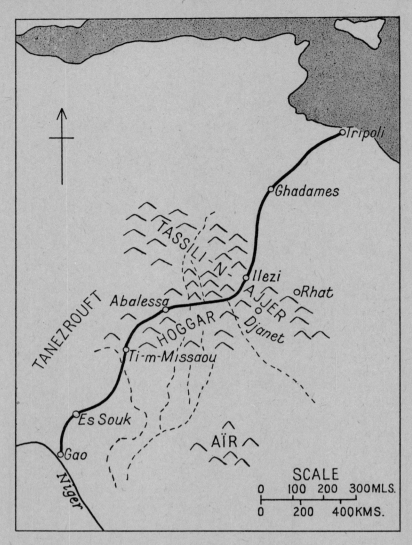

The route of the chariot-people. It is possible to trace their path across the Sahara from Tripoli to Gao, on the Niger, by following the sites where chariot paintings have been found. (11)

from Cyrenaica and adjoining territories. The distribution of this people's paintings shows clearly the line of penetration, first of all the Tassili-n-Ajjer, then the Hoggar; they made their way across the Tanezrouft and reached the Niger in the neighbourhood of Gao. The pictures of chariots to be found all along this route prove that their drivers traversed the whole Sahara. Before the 5th century BC however they learned how to ride and little by little discarded their chariots. The earliest Greek and Latin writers to mention these people call them 'Libyans' and 'Garamantes'—a lawless, warlike race. Some of these tribesmen took part in Hannibal's Spanish and Italian campaigns when they fought side by side with Gauls. Herodotus, describing the Sahara of 450 BC, mentions that whole areas were without water or vegetation and notes the existence of sand-dunes and palm-tree oases. The picture he paints does not in fact differ materially from a description of the Sahara today, except that clearly desiccation must have crept even further forward since his time. About the beginning of our era Strabo, a Latin author who was interested in North African populations, wrote that the desert men must, before setting out on a journey, take the precaution of slinging a water-skin under their mount's bellies. For men to be reduced to such an expedient it is evident that a great change must have overtaken the grassy valleys where, a thousand years before, huge herds of cattle found abundant pasture.

Why has the Desert Conquered?

To sum up: the present desert character of the Sahara appears to be a comparatively recent phenomenon whose onset dates to after 2000 BC. The process was, it seems, rapid—and that in itself is astonishing. What were the reasons for it? All the supposed explanations put forward up to now are just so many unfounded theories. Why should the Sahara which, four thousand years ago, got sufficient rain to afford water for countless flocks and herds, receive today only a few showers barely enough to keep a few camels alive?

Here we get lost in a maze of conjecture. So rapid a change of climate is almost inconceivable unless there was a great disturbance in the zones of high and low pressure. Progressive diminution of rainfall and great intensity of heat have made the Sahara what it is today. Latitude and longitude may have played their part, for we know that present-day climate is linked with the zone of high pressure round the Azores. But did not this zone of high pressure exist 4000 years ago? Is the disappearance of trees and humus due only to climate? Has not this disappearance itself played its part in modifying the climate so unfavourably? We are well aware that any change made by Man in the balance of nature may have disastrous consequences. And, in the case of the Sahara, the ancient pastoralists themselves may have been, at least partly, responsible for the spread of desert conditions, just as in our own times the Tuareg, the Mauritanian, the Arab and Tibbu pastoralists by cutting down the few remaining trees—either for fuel or to feed the higher branches to their beasts—unceasingly help on the desert's expansion.

The Tassili rock-paintings tell us that thousands and thousands of head of cattle, for several millennia, used and abused the plant life of an area which, no doubt, has always had an irregular rainfall. The factors, then, which must not be overlooked have been intense and disorderly utilisation of pasturages, the destruction of woods to permit the passage of herds, and the damage done to trees by smaller livestock, particularly goats.

Will there ever again be a fertile Sahara? Will herds of cattle again wander through the Tassili valleys and water at the banks of the Tafessasset? Despite the optimism aroused by the astonishing discoveries of modern scientists and the technical triumphs they make possible, we must doubt it.

whereas the invader's predecessors used only the bow. The martial character of the newcomers is clear from numerous scenes of combat. It is obvious that the war-chariot gave these people a great advantage over the populations already settled in the Sahara. Was it these intruders who chased away the pastoralists or did the climate alter so profoundly that they were obliged to seek new pastures elsewhere? We do not know.

In any case, the Bovidians henceforth leave no more traces on the Tassili rock-walls and everything seems to have gone on as though these pastoralists had never existed. However there now live in the savanna a curious pastoral people, the Peul, who from their physical appearance, clothing and certain of their manners and customs, look as though they might well be the descendants of our Saharan pastoralists. Moreover, the Peul are credited with having introduced the ox into western Africa and, finally, are not Negroes but are copper-coloured and of Ethiopian type.

The pictures of animals painted by the chariot-people clearly indicate a change in climate, for although giraffe and sable antelope are still included there are no representations of hippopotamus or rhinoceros. Elephants—which are shown in engravings of still later date than the pictures of the chariot-people, survived in certain grassy regions, as is confirmed by Latin authors writing of the Carthaginians' elephant cavalry, but the other pachyderms must have faded away with the drying up of many sheets of water.

The chariot-people were certainly 'whites' and apparently the ancestors of the Tuareg; they came from the north, doubtless

III CITY OF BLACK GOLD

The riddle of Zimbabwe

ROGER SUMMERS

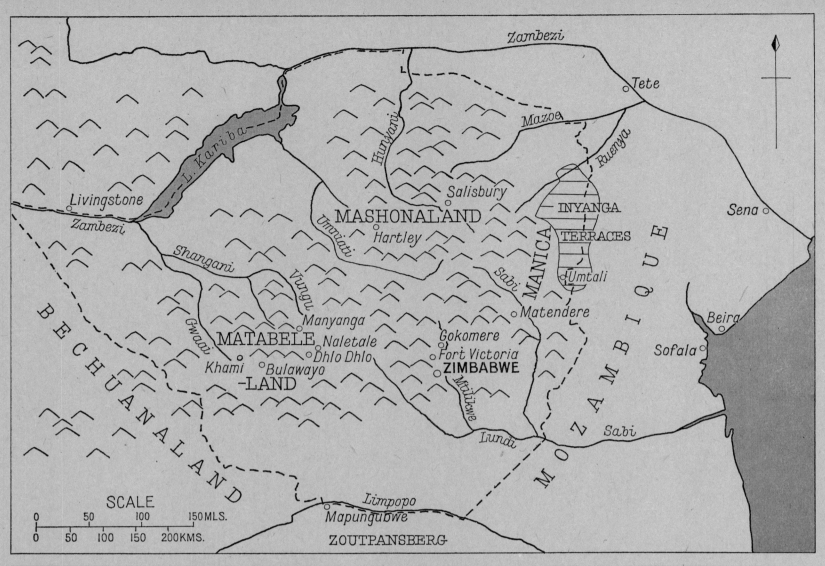

AD	ARCHAEOLOGY			TRADITION	EXTERNAL CONTACTS
	Mining	Zimbabwe	Other Sites		
300		c. 200–350 Earlier Iron Age (stamped ware) occupation			Possible Indonesian contacts via Madagascar
400					
500	Alluvial and surface collecting				
600		(Possible discontinuity in occupation)			
700					Beginning of Arab and Indian trade
800			? Earliest settlement at Mapungubwe	(No evidence of chief-tainship before 1100)	c. 700 Kilwa
900					c. 900 Sofala
1000		Pre-walling Iron Age			
1100	Underground mines in open stopes	First Acropolis walls			
1200		Mauch, Renders and No. 1 Ruins			
1300			Rozwi reach Mapungubwe; walls	? Beginning of Monomotapa dynasty	
1400		Rozwi occupy Zimbabwe First Temple walls			
1500					1505 First Portuguese 1560–1700 Portuguese settlements in S. Rhodesia
1600		Maund, Posselt and Phillips Ruins	Inyanga terracing	Mambo dynasty	
1700	Shafts	Outer wall of Temple and Conical Tower	Khami, Dhlo-Dhlo and Naletale built		
1800					
1900	Modern mechanization	1830–93 NGUNI RAIDING PERIOD Preservation, after brief but disastrous treasure-hunting		1838–93 Ndebele	Beginning of British Colonization

A chronology of Southern Rhodesian history as it is being built up from archaeological research, external records and African traditions

34

Eighty-five years ago

Adam Renders, an American hunter living in the Transvaal, came upon mysterious stone buildings in the *veld* north of the Limpopo. The natives called the place *Zimbabwe*, 'houses of stone'. A few years later a German geologist, Carl Mauch, reached the site and was held captive by the local chief for some months. What astonished the world above all was the fact that elaborate stone masonry existed in the midst of country where the inhabitants were still living in mud huts. It seemed incredible that Zimbabwe could be the work of the local people. Mauch himself thought that he had found the source of the Queen of Sheba's gold; others that it was built by Phoenicians.

The traveller of today who approaches Zimbabwe by air from the south sees first a granite hill rising precipitously 350 feet above the surrounding plain, and at its summit, amid huge natural boulders, the ruins of extensive walls—the heart of Zimbabwe, the 'Acropolis'. In the valley below lies a large oval walled enclosure, usually called the Temple, and scattered towards the hill are the tumbled walls of further buildings. (1)

As the plane swings in from the west the main buildings of the Acropolis come into view (right). In the foreground is the Western Enclosure, with the cliffs to the right. (2)

The truth about Zimbabwe
is now established with a measure of certainty: the site has been occupied since the beginning of the Rhodesian Iron Age (early 1st millennium AD); what we see there today was built by native African peoples over a period of 800 years (11th–19th centuries); and it is only one of a series of related centres all belonging to one culture and representing a phase of African history that was over before widespread European colonization began.

The Western Enclosure (left) contains some of the earliest masonry in Zimbabwe, dated to about AD 1100. We are here inside the Enclosure, looking east towards the Covered Passage. The old builders incorporated the great rocks into their own layout with magnificent effect. (3)

The living quarters have all disappeared; they were circular huts built of *daga* (daub) and thatch. All that remains are their rammed earth floors, now left sadly exposed amid the stone walls. There are many of them in the Temple and throughout the Valley Ruins. Those on the right are at No. 2 Ruins. (4)

Other 'Zimbabwes'—over 200 of them, mostly very small—lie scattered all over Southern Rhodesia. The stone-work at Khami (left) is later than Zimbabwe. Instead of forming an enclosure it consists of retaining walls supporting masses of stone and earth to make platforms or terraces. Khami was a seat of the Rozwi kings, whose main centre was Zimbabwe. (5)

Chevron, herring-bone and chequer ▶ patterns are used on the walls of a small but beautiful ruin called Naletale crowning a hill about 100 miles west of Zimbabwe. The Rozwi 'Mambo' seems to have used this place for pleasure rather than religious or political purposes. There are only a few huts surrounding the principal one, so Mambo's companions and servants must have been few in number. (8)

Surrounded by barbaric riches and hidden from eyes that must not see him, the Rozwi Mambo lived behind the high walls of his palace— for this is what the 'Temple' was. The masonry here is the most accomplished in Zimbabwe; its outer wall (above), decorated with chevron, contained 15,000 tons of stone. Inside (right) it is divided by lower walls into irregular enclosures joined by passages. Its plan resembles the chief's villages of more recent times, with the difference that it is built of stone instead of reeds. It contained the Mambo's living huts, quarters for his wives and entourage, granaries and possibly a relic hut and audience platform with upright stone stelae. (6, 7)

A strange freak of nature links the Eastern Enclosure of the Acropolis with the Temple. A man speaking in his natural voice inside the East Cave beneath its walls (below right) can be distinctly heard inside the Temple, and nowhere else in the valley or on the hill. We can only guess how this phenomenon was exploited by the medicine-men or rulers. The view below left, looking due south from a point in the Enclosure, shows the distance—over a quarter of a mile—to the Temple. (9, 10)

The Conical Tower, inside the Temple, is a mystery within a mystery. It is a truncated cone, 34 feet high and 17 feet across at the base, and is approached through a long gloomy corridor between high walls. Treasure seekers have suspected that it was hollow, but nobody has ever found a

The walls of Zimbabwe are perhaps the most spectacular achievements of man in southern Africa. Their building spreads over nearly 1000 years. The earliest walls (AD 1000–1400) consist of untrimmed stones in irregular courses and without foundations. This type is well illustrated in No. 1 Ruins (below). In the 15th century came a change, possibly coinciding with the arrival of the Rozwi—the courses run in straight lines, the walls slope back slightly and stand in levelled trenches (e.g. Enclosure 7 of the Temple, below). Nowhere at Zimbabwe was any form of mortar used, nor are there any straight lines or right angles. (12, 13)

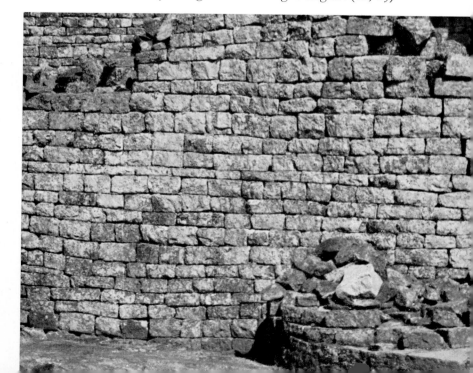

way in, and the debris of unsuccessful attempts can be seen. It is now thought to be solid, but its purpose remains unknown. As a building however, it has been called 'the finest technical and architectural achievement in these, or any other, Rhodesian ruins'. (11)

After Zimbabwe had been sacked in the 1830's it was thought to be haunted by evil spirits and never re-occupied. The Rozwi, however, did try to begin again in the Valley, but the secret of fine building was lost. Stones of all sizes are put together with little attempt at coursing. This is part of the Ridge Ruins. (14)

At Dhlo Dhlo there are again walls with chequer and herring-bone patterns, used not over the whole wall but apparently only to draw attention to the most important parts. They seem to have been built during the 17th century—a Ming bowl and a Dutch bottle of c. 1700 have been found at the lowest levels. (15)

To reach the ears of their god, Mwari, the Rozwi relied on the intercession of their dead chiefs. These chiefs are thought to have been represented symbolically by stylized bird-figures (left), odd hybrid creatures belonging to no recognizable species, with long necks and big animal-like legs. They may have served as mnemonics, like the beads of a rosary. Seven were found in the Eastern Enclosure of the Acropolis and one down in the Valley. Note the crocodile climbing up the pillar of the one on the right. (16, 17)

Strange little human figurines, reminiscent of carvings from the lower Congo, may be connected with ancestor worship. The female figure from Zimbabwe on the left is of soapstone. It was made to stand upright in a stone or mud base, but like so many objects found long ago at Zimbabwe, very little is known about it. The one on the right comes from Khami and was possibly a mounting on the end of a staff. (18, 19)

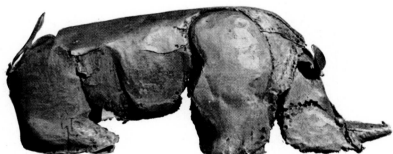

Almost none of the gold remains of the quantities that were mined over the centuries in the hills around Zimbabwe. This rhinoceros of beaten sheet gold from Mapungubwe is one of the few exceptions. (20)

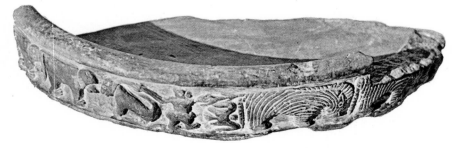

Wild animals were depicted with affectionate naturalism by these pastoral people. Above: rim of a soapstone dish from Zimbabwe showing zebras, a bird, a man with dog and baboons. Right: an ivory lion from Khami; the decoration is the same as on some divining palettes, so this too may have been used in divination. (21, 22)

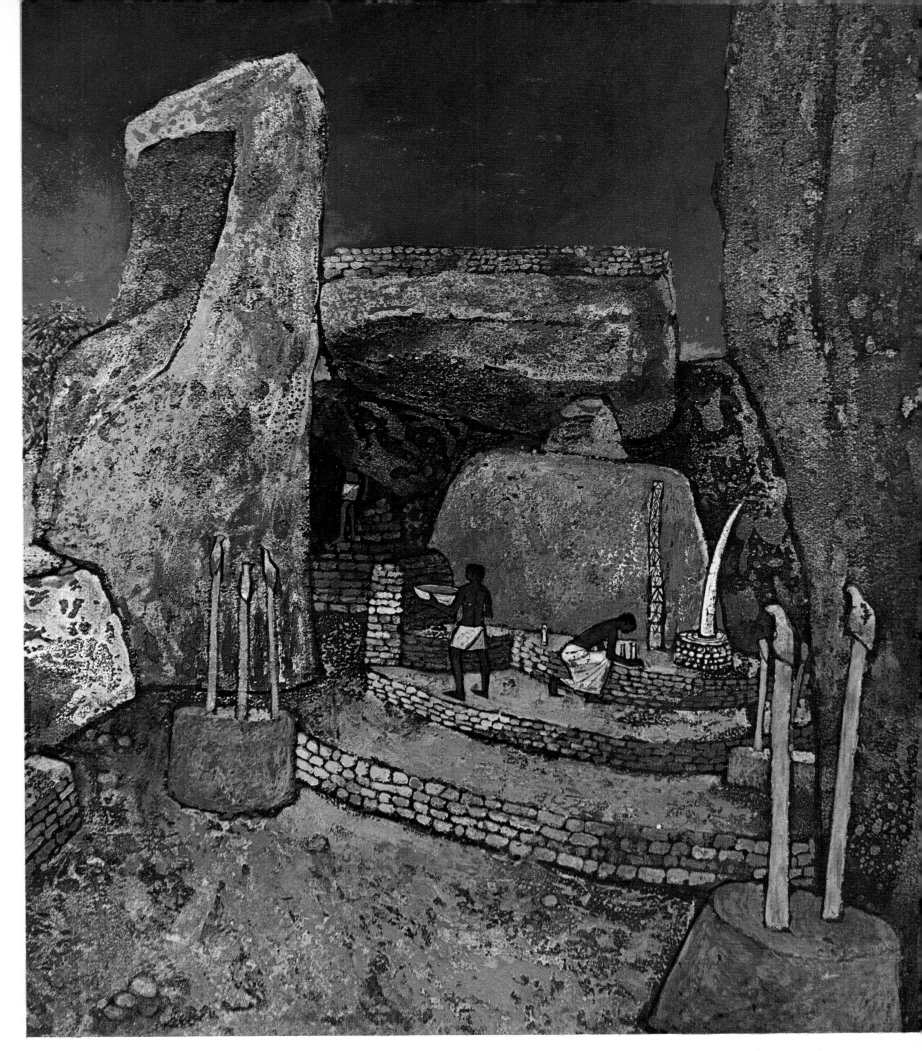

Zimbabwe was a 'church', the Eastern Enclosure its most sacred spot. It was here that the medicine men offered up prayers and possibly sacrifices to Mwari, and it was on this hill, after the centre of government had moved down to the buildings in the Valley, that the Rozwi kings were buried. In the reconstruction above we are looking to the north, into a cleft in the rock through which the sun shone at midday. Zimbabwe birds, symbols of the dead kings, stand to right and left of the stepped platform; they are set on pillars embedded in red *daga*, or mud-cement. At the back are a huge soapstone beam, an ivory tusk fixed into a rosette cylinder of soapstone, and smaller sacred objects, some covered in gold-leaf. The 'priest' in the centre wears a white skirt with fine gold wire worked into the hem. His assistant on the left, preparing for the ceremony, holds a soapstone bowl. All around the giant crags give a fantastic grandeur to the scene. (23)

Only fragments remain of the ancient pottery. The earliest examples, 2nd-3rd centuries AD (top), are decorated with channelled grooves and a row of impressions made by a bone or stick. About AD 1000 new groups appeared with a plainer type of pottery, less attractive but better in technique. (24, 25)

Made by the Rozwi themselves, a more colourful ware comes from Khami. The beaker above shows the 'band and panel' style; it is red at the top and bottom, the pattern being buff and black. All the lines are engraved on the clay after firing. Beakers like these almost certainly had a ceremonial use. (26)

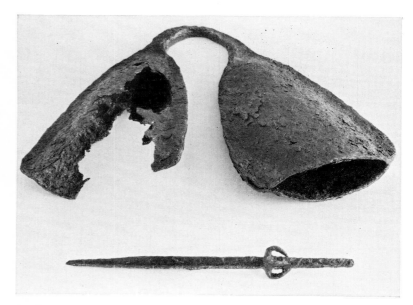

Cattle—not wild game—figure on the rim of another Zimbabwe soapstone bowl (above). This fine bull has long spreading horns, rendered as if seen from the front. The bowls may be divining bowls like the similar wooden ones used by the Venda. (27)

In the Congo forests iron gongs—either double, as above, or single—were part of the insignia of chieftainship. Their presence at Zimbabwe suggests that the Rozwi Mambos were in communication with other chiefs a thousand miles to the north-west. (28)

An intriguing collection of bronze spearheads was recently unearthed at Khami. They had been wrapped in cloth, and were found beneath a mass of corroded iron weapons. The custom of keeping 'ancestral weapons', records of past chiefs, still survives among tribes to the south, and is the most plausible explanation of the Khami hoard. (29)

The riddle of Zimbabwe

ROGER SUMMERS

FOR NEARLY a century the name Zimbabwe has had a romantic appeal, not only in Southern Africa, but to a wide public throughout the world. The word is associated in popular thought with mystery and romance, with Darkest Africa and with ceremonies whose details are better imagined than described. Added to this is the lure of the treasure believed to have been found there.

Here are the essential elements for a good mystery story, but before attempting to solve the mystery, it is as well to know what Zimbabwe is like and why it should be accounted so mysterious.

The 'stone houses' of Zimbabwe—for that is the meaning of this chiKaranga word—cover about sixty acres and are set in the middle of a square mile or so of parkland, now a National Park. The name applies strictly to a granite hill which rises precipitously three hundred and fifty feet above the surrounding park, but the name 'Acropolis', originally applied to the ruins on the hill, has now been given to the hill itself. The walls of this so-called Acropolis fill spaces between huge granite boulders and in all surround a comparatively small area divided into enclosures to which the romantically minded have given the name 'Temples'. The visitor sees first a high stone wall on the south side of Zimbabwe Hill but later, when he has climbed the hill, he realizes that the highest and most imposing walls top unclimbable granite cliffs, while there are lower and far less impressive walls on the northern slopes where the hill is easier to climb. This medley of 'Queen Anne fronts and Mary Ann backs' is common form in old Rhodesian stone buildings.

At the foot of the hill and stretching away for a quarter of a mile or so southwards lies a confused mass of buildings which cover the floor of a shallow valley and climb some way up its southern side. These buildings are dominated by a most imposing piece of stone-work, nowadays called 'The Temple', more or less elliptical in plan and nearly three hundred feet in greater dimension. The walls of the 'Temple' stand in places thirty feet above present ground level and their greatest thickness is fourteen feet. Within the 'Temple' are a number of lower, thinner walls which subdivide the enclosure into minor areas joined by passages. Dominating the interior is a remarkably fine stone structure, shaped like a truncated cone, thirty-two feet high, about fifty feet in circumference at the base and half that measurement at the present, ruined, summit.

Outside the 'Temple', the minor buildings are puny in comparison but they are of the greatest interest both by virtue of their design and on account of the finds made in them. These 'Valley Ruins' cluster together so that it is sometimes difficult to see where one stops and another starts; they have now been given various conventional names—usually those of early European travellers—but in some cases it is probable that one name covers several buildings.

The great complex of stone buildings just described is not the only one in Southern Rhodesia for, great and small, there are between two hundred and three hundred others.

Some are like Zimbabwe, with enclosure walls built on rocky outcrops. Others consist mainly of walls whose function is to retain masses of stone and earth to make artificial platforms; the best example of this type is at Khami, near Bulawayo, and the group has been named after that ruin. In the Inyanga mountains and elsewhere in the eastern districts of the country there are literally thousands of miles of stone-faced terraces, with many hundreds of associated buildings. Again, there are many roughly built places which from their position are obviously defensive in nature; in different parts of the country they are known by different names—Mashona fortifications, Venda fortified hills, Hill Refuge enclosures. Finally, there are just a few which are in quite a different class; they have regular earth-works, ditches and the remains of walls built according to European masonry traditions. For a long time these have been recognized as Portuguese forts, for there were Portuguese traders and missionaries in the north eastern corner of the country for nearly two hundred and fifty years.

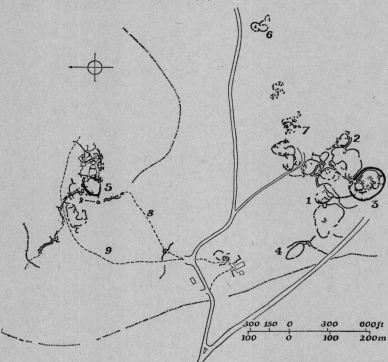

The complex of buildings at Zimbabwe, with the most important remains: 1. No 1 Ruins; 2. Mauch Ruins; 3. the Temple; 4. Ridge Ruins; 5. the Acropolis; 6. East Ruins; 7. Philips Ruins; 8. Ancient Ascent; 9. Modern Ascent. The roads are modern. (1)

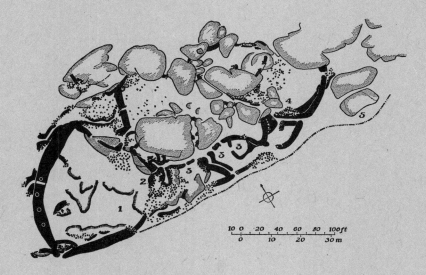

Plan of the Acropolis, showing the remains of walls between huge granite boulders: 1. Western Enclosure; 2. Covered Passage; 3. Southern Enclosures (the cliff edge is indicated by a dotted line); 4. Eastern Enclosure; 5. East Cave. The two ancient entrances were on the extreme left, one (bottom corner) between two high walls, the other (now destroyed) at the upper corner through an extremely thick wall. (2)

43

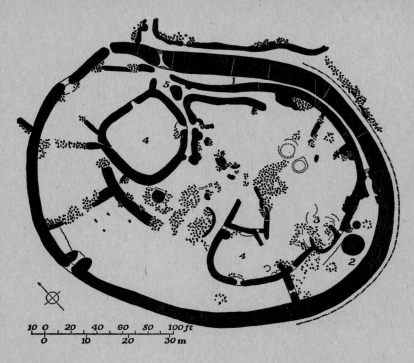

Plan of the Temple. The interior was divided into small enclosures by lower walls, now partially destroyed. 1. Parallel Passage; 2. Conical Tower; 3. Platform; 4. Enclosures with hut remains; 5. Stone platform, more or less circular—the Eastern Enclosure of the Acropolis can be seen from this spot. The dotted line indicates the extent of the chevron decoration on the top of the outer wall. (3)

Apart from the Portuguese buildings, poor relations of the colonial castles of West Africa and the 'factories' in India, all the others would appear to be of unknown origin and they pose the fundamental question....

Why were these great stone buildings reared in a land whose normal domestic architecture was the mud hut? Who were the builders and when did they build?

The Birth of the Myth

Early in the 1860's, a German missionary named Merensky was told by an African chief of buildings a hundred miles or so north of the Limpopo. The claims of mission work kept Merensky at his station in what is now the Transvaal, but he talked of the mysterious buildings to travellers, one of whom—Adam Renders—actually reached Zimbabwe about 1867. Renders was a hunter who left no record of his wanderings, but a few years later another of Merensky's visitors—the German geologist Carl Mauch—not only reached Zimbabwe, as he called it, but published three descriptions, a plan and a drawing. Mauch's visit, from September 1871 to May 1872, was not spent entirely in examining the ruins, he also explored the neighbourhood for many miles around the small 'town' where he was 'guest-prisoner' of the local Karanga chief, Mapunsure.

Despite many difficulties, Mauch examined the place in detail and has left us the only authoritative account of religious ceremonies which were conducted on Zimbabwe Hill.

It is indeed unfortunate that Mauch's only scientific description appeared after his death and the most usually quoted description comes from a semi-popular geographical magazine in which Mauch gave free rein to speculations about origins which clearly owed much to the fertile imagination of Merensky. Mauch is the modern sponsor of the 'Queen of Sheba' myth about Zimbabwe, a story which seems to have had an Arab origin in the 12th or 13th century.

Mauch apparently did not discover any gold at Zimbabwe, but it was found soon afterwards and treasure hunters visited the ruins frequently, digging little holes all over the place. One of these early visitors was Willi Posselt, a South African trader, who discovered a carved stone bird figure and bought it from the local headman for a few blankets. This figure was one of several which Posselt saw, all of them being tall beams of soft stone about five feet long and a few inches thick. The topmost

parts of the beams, eighteen inches to two feet, were carved into the form of hawk-like birds somewhat stylized to fit the material.

Posselt could not carry away the whole beam; complete beams weigh 100 pounds or more and are very awkward loads, so he hacked off the carved part and took that. On his way south he publicised his find and very shortly Cecil Rhodes bought it for his own collection. (It is still in Groote Schuur House, which Rhodes bequeathed to Cape Colony; the house is now the official residence of the Prime Minister of South Africa.)

Reports and 'Excavations'

Rhodes' purchase of the 'Zimbabwe Bird' fired his interest in the country's antiquities and, after the occupation by his Company's column in 1890, he arranged for an investigation of the Ruins. Theodore Bent, an experienced traveller and antiquary, was selected for the work and, accompanied by his wife and a surveyor—R. M. Swan—he visited, excavated and made plans at Zimbabwe and other ruins in the dry season of 1891.

Bent's results were published in *Ruined Cities of Mashonaland* which appeared in 1892 and two more editions appeared within three years; despite its superficiality, the book was of great importance in directing the attention of British readers to Rhodesian antiquities.

Bent was followed in 1892 by Sir John Willoughby, who sought to provide evidence rather than explanation, but who nevertheless did a good deal of damage.

The rumour of treasure at Zimbabwe and elsewhere led to much clandestine digging but some 'excavations' were directed by the Ancient Ruins Company Limited, an organization specifically founded in 1894 to exploit the buried treasure of Rhodesia. The folly of destroying the country's monuments for a relatively small return was brought home to Rhodes by Heinrich Schlichter, another German, who visited Rhodesia in 1899, and not only was the Company closed down but the first antiquities law was passed.

One result of the official cessation of treasure hunting was the collaboration of W. G. Neal, an erstwhile director of the Ancient Ruins Company, and Richard Hall, a Bulawayo journalist, who

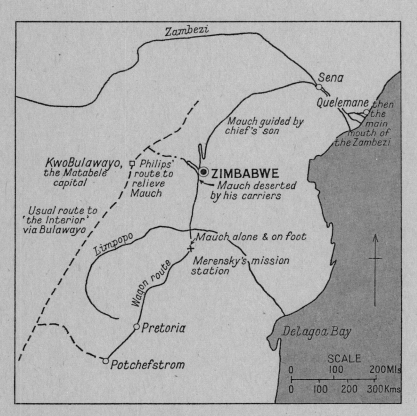

Carl Mauch's route to and from Zimbabwe in 1871–2. Mauch was the second white man to visit the ruins, and the first to leave an account of them. After being deserted by his carriers near Zimbabwe, Mauch nearly died in the veld but was rescued by local tribesmen and kept prisoner there (September 1871–May 1872). He was finally released and walked to Sena on the Zambezi. (4)

pl 16

f 4

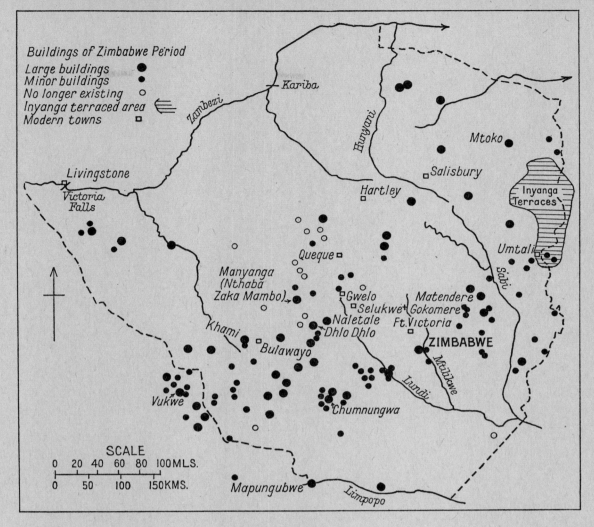

Ancient stone buildings in Southern Rhodesia and the nearby territories. There are between two and three hundred sites related to Zimbabwe scattered all over the country, dating from the 15th–18th centuries. At Inyanga, to the east, are many miles of stone-faced terraces, part of a large-scale agricultural scheme. (5)

together produced a fantastic book, *Ancient Ruins of Rhodesia*. Beside publicising the ruins still further, the book helped Hall to acquire a local reputation for archaeological expertise and very soon led to his appointment as Curator of Zimbabwe Ruins.

In the course of three years' tenure of this office, Hall probably did more harm to Zimbabwe than all his predecessors put together, for he dug out such a quantity of the deposit and trenched so deeply that modern archaeologists consider themselves extremely lucky if they find a trace of undisturbed deposit. Hall's book *Great Zimbabwe*, published in 1905, although painfully inadequate as an excavation report, does however provide us with some facts we should otherwise have lost, for all Hall's manuscript reports and plans were destroyed in the London 'blitz' in 1941.

The Myth Takes Wings

Merensky, Mauch, Bent, Swan, Schlichter and Hall were men of about the same age, nurtured in mid-nineteenth century romanticism to which was added the rather uncritical science of the last decades of that century. Moreover, the piety of their times bade them search diligently for antiquarian justification for Old Testament history.

Small wonder that all of them saw in Rhodesian 'ancient workings' the source of the gold used in Solomon's Temple; that Zimbabwe was to them an invention of the peoples of the ancient East—Phoenicians or Sabaeans; that Swan and Schlichter should have sought to apply the then fashionable 'astronomical theory' to date the ruins; that every ruin and every old mine should seem 'ancient', with dates of second millennium BC freely bandied about.

With the 'degeneracy' of the people of Mashonaland amply demonstrated every day and with the superiority of modern European, earlier Asian and ancient Egyptian civilization beyond question, who could be expected ever to imagine any but a 'civilized' ancestry for Zimbabwe?

So the first answer to Zimbabwe's riddle was that it was of high antiquity and the product of some ancient Eastern civilization.

Thirty Years of Argument

The years following the outbreak of the South African War were a period of political rethinking in Britain, and many of the older shibboleths were first questioned and then discarded. This reappraisal spread far beyond politics and antiquarianism came under fire from (Sir) Flinders Petrie while the discovery of an entirely new 'civilization' in the Aegean added to the ferment.

In such a mental context it was to be expected that the origin of Zimbabwe would sooner or later be questioned. In 1905 the British Association for the Advancement of Science nominated a young pupil of Petrie's, David Randall-MacIver, to investigate Rhodesian ruins and to report to the Association's meeting in South Africa.

MacIver's answer to the riddle was completely at variance with his predecessors': Zimbabwe was a purely African phenomenon and less than a thousand years old, some of the other ruins being much more recent. His reasons were published in *Mediaeval Rhodesia*, which appeared in 1906.

It has often been observed that provincial thought lags behind that of the metropolis and Southern African antiquarianism of 1906 was no exception. MacIver's new answer was therefore difficult to accept. Unfortunately, he also attacked Hall and local emotionalism added its opposition to the new ideas. (Incidentally, recent work has partly vindicated Hall and shown up MacIver as more than a little unfair.) Hall replied, almost incoherently, in *Prehistoric Rhodesia*.

Between them, MacIver and Hall obscured the Zimbabwe issue for over twenty years. In an endeavour to set a term to the controversy, in 1929 the British Association sent another British archaeologist into the Zimbabwe arena. This was Miss Gertrude Caton-Thompson, whose careful excavations and lucid report, *Zimbabwe Culture*, have provided models for subsequent work.

Caton-Thompson's work substantially confirmed MacIver's views both on cultural affinities and on chronology, but by an unhappy coincidence her conclusions appeared almost simultaneously with the contrary views of the German ethnologist, Leo Frobenius, and so although archaeologists were completely convinced, to everyone else Zimbabwe was still a problem unsolved.

One reason why Caton-Thompson's views were unacceptable was the apparent lack of any body of local oral tradition about the ruins. If the ruins were indeed African and recent, surely local African people should have some tradition about them.

We now know that such traditions do exist but they are esoteric, known only to a few people and extremely difficult to understand. Caton-Thompson's training did not help her in interpreting them, while Frobenius used them in a fashion which was not confirmed by archaeology. It was only when, in 1941, one of Frobenius' assistants, Heinrich Wieschhoff, combined the two methods that a thoroughly convincing synthesis became possible. Unfortunately Wieschhoff's work passed almost unnoticed, for it appeared in America in the middle of World War II.

Penetrating the Mystery: the Modern Approach

By the end of World War II there existed a myth that there was a deep and impenetrable mystery about Zimbabwe; and the sources of this myth and the climate in which it grew have now been described. But at the same time a local interest in archaeology has freed Rhodesian archaeology from its dependence on overseas experts; social and political change have enabled us to discover human resources whose existence earlier generations had denied; the practice of team-work on the widest possible front has come into being, and the problems of Zimbabwe are at last being studied by Rhodesians as Rhodesian problems.

ARCHITECTURAL ANALYSIS

Since Zimbabwe is a stone building some of its problems are architectural and are most easily solved by people trained in that discipline. Alas that only two architects should have applied themselves to it. Various individual ruins were planned in the past but it was not until 1955 that the Southern Rhodesian Monuments Commission was able to initiate a regular programme of survey. John Schofield's 1927 paper, *Zimbabwe, a critical survey of building methods employed*, is still a classic, but Schofield left Rhodesia after a brief four years and so was unable to extend his detailed studies.

In 1955, another architect, Anthony Whitty, argued that as Rhodesian stone-building techniques owe nothing to other building traditions and moreover introduce the concept of 'leaning' one wall against another, there was a reasonable chance that Zimbabwe building was a local development stimulated by a supply of easily split granite. The absence of any obvious diffusion route was not mentioned by Whitty but is an additional support for his hypothesis.

Thus far, however, architects had worked in isolation, and it was not until 1958 that Whitty, by then Surveyor of Monuments, was able to participate in the combined Monuments Commission-National Museum excavations at Zimbabwe and to analyse walling styles which could be tied, by independent archaeological methods, to distinct pottery traditions. Architectural styles were thus used to assist in defining cultural differences and a new and potent weapon was placed in the hands of field archaeologists.

ARCHAEOLOGY

An overall survey of archaeological sites had been initiated by the Southern Rhodesian Monuments Commission in 1938 but it was forgotten during the War and in 1948 the National Museum started an independent survey, soon collecting sufficient information to start drawing distribution maps. Both MacIver and Caton-Thompson had pointed out that Zimbabwe was part of a larger complex and in 1950 this was given the name *Southern Rhodesian Iron Age*, being divided into two main and several minor sub-complexes. The Commission's and the Museum's surveys were combined in 1956 and three years later comprehensive distribution maps were published.

Such work was only made possible by a 'broad front' archaeological policy whereby local workers agreed to investigate extensively throughout the country and intensively at sites other than Zimbabwe.

Although the post-war work at Zimbabwe was not undertaken until 1958, it was in effect a continuation of Caton-Thompson's dig nearly thirty years earlier. One technological advantage the archaeologists possessed: the radiocarbon method of dating. No longer was one chronologically dependent on imports, which not only introduce inaccuracies due to their (presumed) long life as 'heirlooms', but can only be used if a site has contacts with the outside world.

Like Caton-Thompson and MacIver, the modern archaeologist is deeply critical of the antiquarianism of Bent and Hall, yet a widening knowledge of Rhodesian prehistory enables modern workers to see somewhat more value in Hall's book than was at one time apparent. Despite the piling of fancy on fact, it now seems that when Hall reports facts only, he is a reliable witness. This was checked in the very place where the great Hall-MacIver controversy started—Enclosure 15 of the Zimbabwe 'Temple'—and it was found that the elderly Hall and the youthful MacIver were standing literally as well as metaphorically back-to-back and that what they saw they honestly and correctly reported. As they were not on the spot together, neither realized the exact section the other was describing and so charges of unsound excavation technique were countered by allegations of intellectual chicanery and the whole issue completely clouded. The tragedy is not that they were both right but that the bitterness of the quarrel completely misled everybody.

ECONOMIC BACKGROUND

Modern archaeologists are always interested in the economic background of prehistory and the 1958 excavators were no exception.

Fortunately, some progress in the study of the early Rhodesian gold trade had been made and a good deal of information obtained, although much of this depended on the recollections of elderly mining engineers and nothing was collected by the more usual method of controlled excavation.

Geological studies have shown that Rhodesian gold occurs as a result of the intrusion of mineral-rich solutions into veins of quartz or other fissile rocks. Consequently gold reefs tend to be more or less vertical and prolonged erosion on the surface resulted in the concentration of gold there—a phenomenon called 'surface enrichment'.

Vast quantities of gold could therefore be recovered with comparatively little effort; indeed at the outset nuggets of gold *f 6* would actually be lying about on the surface. Attempts have been made to estimate the amount mined by the 'ancients' but such calculations have so many assumptions that they are of little value.

The crude mining techniques and even cruder recovery methods will be described later; despite these, however, the total gold produced by these primitive methods must have equalled a century's production using twentieth century mechanized techniques.

Occasional finds of Indian vessels in old mines and the use of Indian units such as the *tanga* in the 19th century gold trade in Mashonaland, point to Indian participation in the gold trade and so confirm a suggestion put forward thirty years ago by Miss Caton-Thompson.

Hall considered 'ancient workings' and 'ancient ruins' as parts of the same culture but Caton-Thompson was not prepared to accept this without further evidence. This is now available and shows that they were indeed culturally separated. The gold trade commenced in the Early Rhodesian Iron Age and continued until the 19th century whereas the buildings, now in ruins, are in general manifestations of the Later Rhodesian Iron Age.

One cannot escape the interpretation that the mines and their labourers were absorbed into the political orbit of the builders of Zimbabwe but that each tended to retain their own traditional culture.

SOCIAL BACKGROUND

Work done at Inyanga, two hundred miles north east of Zimbabwe, in the early 'fifties gave some clue to the social background, for there we found evidence of peasant farming contemporary with Zimbabwe.

Cultivation was on terrace hillsides where millet, sorghums, legumes and curcubits were grown—all of exactly the same

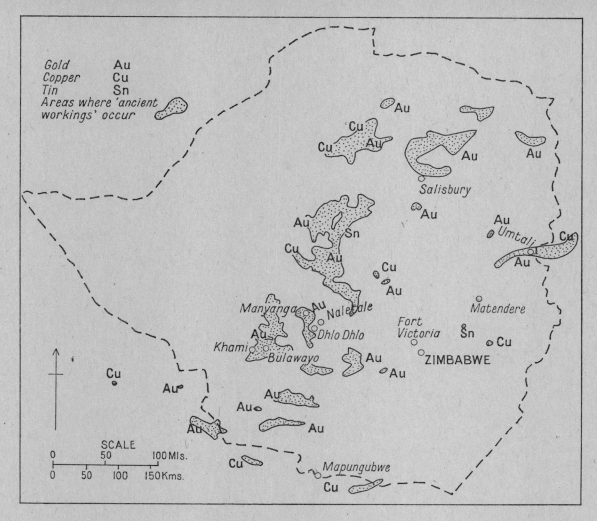

'Ancient workings' of Southern Rhodesia. The Rozwi had a flourishing metal industry. There are (or were, before modern exploitation destroyed most of them) between 4,000 and 5,000 gold workings, including alluvial, and several hundred copper workings, but only two places where tin is known to have been mined in quantity. The principal modern tin-mine, Kamativi, was not used by the early miners. (6)

species as are grown by farmers in the area today. Stock was kept in deep stone-lined pits (referred to in the older literature as 'slave-pits') and an irrigation system was installed wherever possible. Manuring was perhaps practised by using the dung from the pits either dry or washed out by irrigation water. Despite these advanced farming techniques, finds in the habitations and middens were sparse and there can be little doubt that these people had nothing to spare for such trifles as glass beads or copper bangles while their ordinary equipment of pots and iron tools was pretty meagre.

Occasional opportunities of examining the pitiful remains of mining settlements added further to our stock of general knowledge and it steadily became clear that there were extreme differences in wealth and comfort between the dwellers in Zimbabwe and other 'ruins' and the farmers and miners of the same period. The Portuguese stories of the wealth of the rulers of the country now called Rhodesia were therefore confirmed archaeologically.

ETHNOLOGY

When the Zimbabwe Museum was being opened in 1961 an African chief who lives near the Ruins got into conversation with an archaeologist and said: 'If only you white people had asked the old people about Zimbabwe when you first came to the country, we'd all know a lot more about it now.'

This sums up very neatly the failure of the ethnological approach, but the reason it was not made was that, following Mauch, all European opinion in the 1890's was solidly in favour of an exotic origin for Zimbabwe. Even in 1905 MacIver was not taken seriously in Southern Africa and it was not until the Vienna anthropological school was working out *Kulturkreise* in the 1920's that anybody thought of an ethnological approach.

Frobenius collected a good many miscellaneous stories and so have other workers but very few indeed relate directly to Zimbabwe. It is therefore necessary to use a number of scraps of information to fill in gaps in the pattern produced by other disciplines such as archaeology. Quite recently Pierre and Jacqueline Roumeguere, two French ethnologists, have collected information about Zimbabwe birds obtainable by this approach only.

Various linguistic approaches are just starting and may well add further to our knowledge of the builders.

WRITTEN RECORDS

These are very scanty and printed sources have been worked over frequently, Kathleen Kenyon's study in *Zimbabwe Culture* being the most easily available. Work is now being done on Portuguese manuscript sources and something is to be expected, but sources at present untapped are Arabic manuscripts which may be expected to throw new light on trade contacts before the 16th century, a subject about which so little is known.

Like ethnological and linguistic information, written records cannot at present provide us with a full picture and are best used to fill gaps left in other studies.

The New Story of Zimbabwe

We now possess sufficient information to enable us to outline a picture of life at Zimbabwe, and in Southern Rhodesia generally, during the past two thousand years. We have many hard facts, architectural, archaeological, ethnological; furthermore we have ample related information from which we can properly draw inferences. Finally we may, after due warning to the reader, indulge in occasional speculation in order to explain things which are at present—and may always be—incapable of rigid proof.

Before the Rhodesian Iron Age there stretched long millennia of human endeavour—in this country man may have lived and made tools for a million years and more, so it would be strange indeed if something of that heritage did not remain to the men of Zimbabwe, and even to the men of today.

On Zimbabwe Hill, on the side away from the Acropolis buildings, are some rather poor 'Bushman paintings'. Their age is unknown but culturally they belong to the Later Stone Age and provide a visible connection between Zimbabwe and the ancient past.

A more obvious connection is to be found in shell-beads, usually made from ostrich eggs, which are rare at Zimbabwe but more common in other buildings of the period. These little discs of pierced shell (very like shirt buttons with one hole) are very plentiful in Later Stone Age deposits and even today are used by Bushwomen to ornament their skirts. Their presence at Zimbabwe suggests some form of trade between surviving Bush groups and the incoming iron-users: this 'trade' was apparently a two-way affair since very early Iron Age pottery is found in the topmost layers of Later Stone Age deposits. The Bushmen were (and are) skilled hunters so they may have provided meat or skins for the Zimbabwe people, receiving not only pottery but iron arrow-heads in exchange.

Possibly the most important aspect of the Bushman connection is the physical one. Few early Iron Age burials remain, for the Rhodesian soil is too acid to preserve bone for more than a few centuries, but such as have been found show time and again that certain distinctive physical features, not only of Bush people but of even older African stock, were common in the skeletons of the people who worked in the 'ancient' gold mines. Several explanations are possible: one is that the incoming Iron Age men took Bush girls as wives, another is that the invaders conquered the Bush people and compelled them to work in the mines, yet another is that the majority of Bush people found the new Iron Age way of life more attractive than their old hunting-gathering existence. Whatever happened, there was plenty of the old physical stock remaining during Iron Age times.

Somewhere about two thousand years ago, the art of food-production began to be practised in Rhodesia. We do not yet know the mechanism of agriculture's dispersal through Africa but one suspects that Abyssinia may have been of more than passing importance in the history of this economic and social revolution. In the present state of our very limited knowledge, East Africa seems more important than West Africa in Southern Africa's development from Stone Age savagery.

Zimbabwe seems to have come into the picture early: the very oldest pottery—which Caton-Thompson called 'A' and Robinson classed as '1'—occupies a fairly thick deposit and on radiocarbon evidence its manufacture ceased about the 3rd or 4th century (AD 330 ± 150). It may have first appeared on Zimbabwe Hill in the 1st or 2nd centuries AD.

The First Miners

Just why a group of settlers goes into a new area is always an interesting problem but it is often very difficult to assign reasons for prehistoric settlement patterns. In Southern Rhodesia, however, the problem is an easy one: there was so much gold lying about for anybody to pick up that, once it was known that the yellow metal was in demand, not only did Bushman hunters become gold-diggers but many other people came down from East Africa in a veritable gold-rush. At first—like Californian forty-niners—they panned alluvial gold in the rivers and finally they started to mine for it, until in the end their mines reached right down to water level and they had extracted everything then 'payable'.

What was 'payable' to the Iron Age miner was very different from that now considered profitable and many a small fortune has been made out of the 'rubble' abandoned as unprofitable in the Iron Age.

The mine workings have now been largely cleared as a result of commercial gold mining but mining engineers have recounted what they saw and even today an archaeologist is sometimes lucky enough to see an 'ancient working' being opened up.

Usually Rhodesian reefs dip down very steeply and when the lodes are in hard rock the miners manage to follow down the reef with the minimum of wasteful cutting. Some of the stopes are so narrow that it seemed to mining engineers inconceivable that anyone should have got down them. Skeletons found in the old workings—the relics of long-past mine accidents—provide the answer: the underground workers were girls and women whose small stature enabled them to get in where men could not go. (Recently measured skeletons give heights of barely five feet for some of the mine girls.)

Some of these stopes go down to a depth of over 100 feet but the usual depth reached by the 'ancients' was 25 to 40 feet. In the dim recesses of the mines, the ore was loosened by stone wedges or by iron points held in wooden handles and driven

in by stone hammers about the size of a cricket-ball. When the reef (usually quartz) was too hard to be broken mechanically it was heated with a small fire and then quenched with water to crack it. Charcoal from this 'fire setting' has often been found in old workings.

The old miners had a horror of 'driving' into more or less horizontal reefs, and well they might, for they had no knowledge of 'timbering' so falls of roof would have been frequent. Quite recently, it was possible to examine an 'ancient working' in a gently sloping reef and grim reminders of ignorance of mine safety were soon evident when badly crushed skeletons of three women were found. Nearby on the surface was a man's grave in which another victim had been interred with as much care as possible despite the mangling of his corpse.

This last is a particularly rich mine, for the 'ancients' were only interested in visible gold yielding over 3 ozs. to the ton—values of a tenth of this amount are regarded as good today—but owing to defective techniques the mine had to be abandoned.

Shafts were sometimes sunk to reach horizontal reefs but these merely belled out at the bottom—like an English flint mine—so many shafts had to be sunk to get the ore body out. Shafts are believed to be quite late techniques, possibly learned from the Portuguese, whereas the 'open stope' method is believed to be far older and to have been learned from Arabs or Indians.

'Ancient mining' is a matter of current archaeological research and we are beginning to realize that simple as were the mining techniques, the methods of recovering metallic gold were even cruder. Ore was carried from the mine to the nearest stream

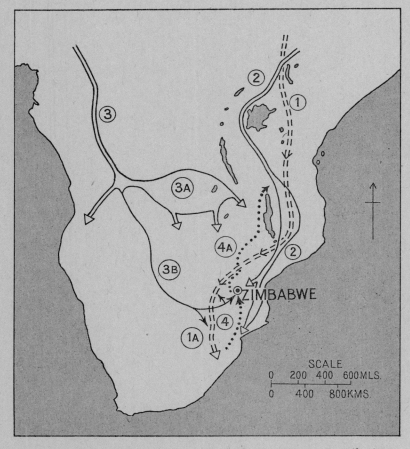

The direction and strength of the various ethnic movements contributing to Zimbabwe's history: 1. Early Iron Age groups who established mines in Rhodesia (reaching the Zimbabwe area 1st–3rd centuries AD); 1A. Continuation of 1. into South Africa; 2. Later Iron Age groups, the ancestors of the Shona-speaking peoples of Southern Rhodesia and Mozambique (reaching Zimbabwe c. 11th century AD; they built the first walls); 3, 3A. Late Iron Age groups from West Africa, giving rise to the Luba-Lunda kingdoms of southern Congo; 3B. offshoot of 3, reaching Mapungubwe c. 13th century and Zimbabwe c. 14th century AD. This is the group known as the Rozwi; 4. The Ngoni, deriving from 1A, 2 and an offshoot of 3B, invade Southern Rhodesia in the 19th century, and sack Zimbabwe and other towns about 1830; 4A. Northward route of the Ngoni. (7)

where it was crushed and the broken up quartz shaken in bowls (probably of wood), so that the 'sands' were washed away leaving metallic gold in the bottom. Very primitive sluice boxes of soapstone are known. Sixteenth century Portuguese writers comment that in the mines of 'Monomotapa' there was no knowledge of mercury amalgamation such as was then practised in the West African gold mines; they further reported that the methods of mining and recovery were so laborious that it was not worth while to employ Portuguese miners, rather should the local people be left to follow their own methods after which the Portuguese could purchase the product.

Archaeology is now confirming the pessimistic views of Portuguese mining experts of four centuries ago.

Romantic as the story of the old gold workings sounds, it has a solid basis of sober archaeological evidence, which suggests that, starting in the north-east, the miners spread slowly throughout the gold-bearing areas—roughly along the high spine of the country, the Zambezi—Limpopo/Sabi watershed—reaching the extreme south-west before the 11th century. The mining went on until well into the 19th century and was only stopped when the Matabele kings realized that gold would arouse white men's cupidity—just as it had raised the black and brown men's nearly two thousand years earlier.

f 6 There are scarcely any old gold mines near Zimbabwe, but they stretch in a quadrant to the west and north, with Zimbabwe at the centre. Copper was also mined in Southern Rhodesia but it is gold which held pride of place and an understanding of the prehistoric gold trade is of paramount importance in solving the 'Zimbabwe riddle'.

While the gold trade was being developed elsewhere in Southern Rhodesia, Zimbabwe itself may have been uninhabited. We possess but one section, dug by Robinson in 1958, which provides clear evidence of undisturbed early pottery and above it is a thick deposit of naturally accumulated 'hill earth', sand composed of quartz fragments set free from the granite through the solution of one of its other constituents and washed down by tropical rains. Thus, at the western end of Zimbabwe Hill, if nowhere else, occupation came to an end about AD 300 and was not resumed for some centuries.

Pottery is one of the archaeologist's best friends for sherds are almost indestructible and provide cultural clues when all else has disappeared. The earliest pottery at Zimbabwe is sometimes called *Gokomere Ware* from a site where it was first found.
pl 24 It is a very handsome hand-made ware, decorated in a characteristic way with impressions of square-toothed combs on a thickened rim; it often has channelled lines running round the neck and occasionally has further decoration on the shoulder; below the shoulder it is invariably plain. Bowls were also made, these being usually undecorated but nevertheless of graceful shape. The whole pottery tradition shows a sureness of touch unequalled in the wares frequently found in association with Zimbabwe walling.

Developments of Gokomere Ware are found in other parts of Southern Rhodesia and are often associated with gold mining.

Who were the miners? Archaeology always finds difficulty in answering the question 'Who?' and has to call other disciplines to her help. Mention has already been made of the Bush and older African physical characters found in the miners' bones: the same characteristics are found today among the Kalanga who originally lived in the old mining area around Bulawayo. Other explanations than direct descent are readily available so this evidence is inconclusive.

Some of the place-name elements in Southern Rhodesia, especially in the west—Matabeleland—do not seem to belong to either of the present language groups, ciShona and siNdebele, and so may be derived from the speech of earlier people. Since these elements may be Bantu one infers that the names in question were perhaps given by the miners. This is interesting and possibly significant, but it does not answer 'Who'?

One place-name, that of the whole country, may help and for this we have evidence from Portuguese writers that it was 'Mocaranga'. Turning the Portuguese phonetics into modern Bantu orthography we get *muKaranga* which means 'a Karanga

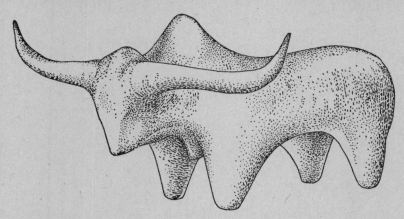

Clay model of an ox, from the Western Enclosure, Zimbabwe, c. 11th century. Cattle are also depicted on soapstone bowls of a later period. (8)

man' although a very similar word *buKaranga* means 'the Karanga country'.

Karanga and Kalanga people are today absorbed into the great Shona or Ndebele groups (the first use r's in place of the latter's l's) and traditions of their origins are vague. My own speculation (not accepted by my more cautious colleagues!) is that the Karanga had a good hand in opening up the mines.

Round about AD 1000 other groups began to appear at Zim- f 7 babwe and their cultural remains (the everlasting potsherds!) occur on sites in the surrounding districts. Culturally, they were very different from the miners—pottery was black instead of red, pl 25 distressingly plain instead of tastefully ornamented; iron implements were apparently more common (not too significant for acid soils dissolve iron as well as bones); bronze appears in quantity, usually in the form of wound wire ornaments; most important of all they definitely possessed cattle, for they made very delight- f 8 ful clay models of them. We have no evidence that the earlier people were cattle keepers but that does not entitle us to say that the later settlers introduced cattle, only that they had some high regard for their beasts, as do the present Bantu.

The First Builders

The next phase opened about the 11th or 12th century (AD 1085 ± 150) but was continuous with the preceding one, which it resembled culturally so closely that one may suggest that it was merely a 'second wave'.

Yet although there were many resemblances there was at least one tremendous difference: the 'second wave' introduced the building of great stone walls. This achievement was so remarkable that, as we have seen, it was many years before people were prepared to concede that the building was done by local tribesmen.

Whitty's hypothesis of local development of building has already been mentioned. It is still but an idea, yet it helps us in an

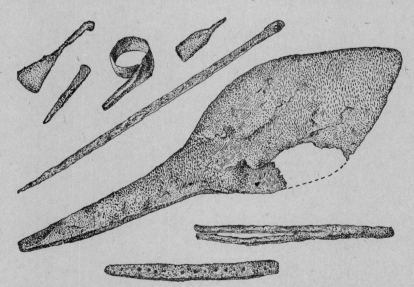

Iron tools from Zimbabwe. Top left: two razors (spatula shaped) with, between them, two tools for making wooden bowls. Centre: a long matting needle and the blade of a hoe, 12 inches long. Bottom: pincers and drawplate for making gold wire. (9)

unexpected way. Archaeologists so frequently find diffusionist hypotheses the most convenient way of explaining technological origins, that the existence of theories of local development—so useful to social anthropologists—are often overlooked. Zimbabwe stone-work has no obvious antecedents in either East or West Africa so those depending on diffusionist ideas have had to postulate seaborne diffusion to bring this stone-work into Central Africa. Whitty's ideas, based on technological considerations only, therefore provide an answer to the difficulties inherent in diffusionist theories of Zimbabwe.

f 10
pl 12
The stone walls of Phase III—dated by radiocarbon as falling between the 11th and 15th centuries—were built 'dry' without mortar, were thin in relation to their height, had almost vertical faces, were built with selected but not with trimmed stones and their bottom course ran with the ground (there were no foundations). A magnificent example is the wall of the Acropolis, which is built on the top of a 90-feet sheer cliff. An equally fine one surrounds No. 1 Ruin, lying to the north-west of the Temple but sadly gutted by Sir John Willoughby seventy years ago.

A truly magnificent building in this style is Matendere in Buhera district, about eighty miles north-east of Zimbabwe; how it compares in age with Zimbabwe is not known. There are, however, very few complete buildings in this style and one wonders if the basic defects in their design did not lead to comparatively early collapse, especially where they were not built on rock.

It must be emphasised that the walls and other buildings on the Hill are earlier than anything in the valley.

When Willoughby cleaned out No. 1 Ruin he found what he described as 'pieces of sea-green china'. Similar sherds of porcelain have been found elsewhere at Zimbabwe, especially in lower levels in the 'Temple' and have been identified as Celadon wares of the Sung or early Ming period. These imports from China were made in the 12th or 13th century and may well have found their way into the deposit a century later. Thus we have a date of 13th or 14th century for No. 1 Ruins. That this building, alone of all others in the valley, is built exclusively in the early style leads us to think that it is the earliest in the valley and hence we presume that building did not start here until between 1200 and 1400 AD.

Who were the first builders? Once more the question is a difficult one to answer and no definite solution is available. Firstly, the pottery used by the early builders is of a type and tradition which has continued in Mashonaland, and around Zimbabwe in particular, from that day to this.

pl 25
The pottery is far plainer than that found in earlier levels. Decoration is usually restricted to the shoulder and is often a mere cross-hatched band. Pottery from Zimbabwe itself shows more decoration than elsewhere although it is not common anywhere. There is a greater variety of pot forms but their shapes are less aesthetically satisfying than those of the earlier potters. Firing, too, was not so well controlled but the blemishes on the pots were covered up by an all over graphite burnish.

Secondly, the makers of this pottery type today speak Shona, a Bantu language whose dialects are mutually comprehensible all the way from Bechuanaland to the Mozambique coast and from the Limpopo to the Zambezi, an area about that of the Iberian peninsula. Recent linguistic studies suggest, too, that Shona was first spoken here about nine or ten centuries ago.

Finally, the Shona of Southern Rhodesia were, until the end of the 19th century, a stone-building people, some of whom today, in a very different social and technological environment, hold a monopoly of the craft of building in the local granite. The present custodians of Zimbabwe and other Rhodesian ruined buildings have never had any difficulty in finding stone builders able to execute repair work which is indistinguishable from the original.

While none of this proves that some early Shona group built Zimbabwe's first walls, it is more than a guess to suggest that some such group was largely responsible and that they began to come into the Zimbabwe region about the 10th or 11th century. Moreover, since pottery making by hand is a domestic craft practised by women (who also transmit language to their

f 7

children), while building in stone is a man's craft, one may also suggest that the builders came as complete family or even tribal groups.

As more and more Shona traditions are collected, the picture we have sketched from technological and linguistic considerations steadily receives confirmation and soon we should be able to fill in many more details. All that can be said now is that the early Shona seem to have established themselves as chiefs, to have exploited the already existing gold trade and to have built themselves stone walls behind which to live.

New Methods of Building Appear

During the 15th century (AD 1450± 150) there is a change, albeit a slight one, in pottery and a more considerable one in wall-building methods.

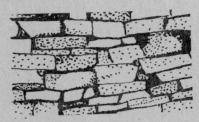

A comparison of walling methods used at Zimbabwe. Left: the earliest style, 12th century AD—untrimmed stones of varying sizes, laid in uneven courses. Right: later style, 15th century—carefully trimmed stones, accurately levelled. (10)

The new technique made use of carefully trimmed stones; set each course back a trifle so that the cumulative effect was to slope back the face of the wall (four feet batter in thirty feet height is the average); 'broke' joints wherever possible; and, most significant of all, built its base course in a carefully levelled trench. The trench levels are so well maintained and the batter so uniform that one suspects the use of some primitive level and plumb-line: however, there are no straight lines and no right angles, so apparently the use of the line and the square were unknown.

pl 13
f 10

Many of the Temple walls are in this technique but the finest example is that of the Conical Tower, while the Great Outer Wall of the Temple is in places quite as good. Stratigraphical studies made in 1958 showed that these examples are relatively late developments of the technique and they have been provisionally dated to the 18th century. The progressive improvement suggests that the later technique was a development from the earlier one rather than an importation of a new idea, although building from a levelled trench certainly looks as if it is a derivation.

pl 11
6

An eighteenth century Portuguese record speaks of the existence of a large body of Portuguese prisoners in Bantu hands (many Portuguese settlements in the interior were overrun between 1690 and 1710) and it is possible that some of the new ideas were Portuguese, although it is difficult to account for the absence of line, square and mortar—all present in Rhodesian buildings of known Portuguese origin. However, when the new ideas were first introduced in the 15th century no Portuguese had entered the Indian Ocean, so we must look elsewhere for the stimulus to improve building.

Mapungubwe is the name of a flat-topped hill in the Northern Transvaal barely a mile south of the Limpopo river which is the boundary between Rhodesia and South Africa. Rumours of buried treasure are rife in this area even today but they have a firmer foundation here than elsewhere, for in 1932 some local farmers scaled the cliffs which protect the hilltop and found a quantity of gold eroding out of a shallow grave.

pl 20

Fortunately, the authorities heard about it and the University of Pretoria acquired the excavation rights. Preliminary examination was made in 1933, while from 1934 to 1939 a regular excavation programme was carried out. Naturally comparisons with Zimbabwe were made at once, particularly as a number of low walls were uncovered and many stone walled structures were found in the neighbourhood. Connections with Zimbabwe were established as early as 1934 and later work recently supported by radiocarbon dates has confirmed the early impression.

The political influence of the Rozwi kingdom, showing the extent of Portuguese trading infiltration. At the peak of their power the Rozwi Mambo ruled over an area of 240,000 square miles, with a population of at least a million. (11)

It is now clear that Mapungubwe's history goes back even beyond the 11th century (the earliest C14 date) and that in the 14th century (AD 1328 ± 120) a change of both population and culture occurred. Fortunately, there are many skeletons from Mapungubwe and the 14th-century people are now known to be partly negroid (i.e. West African) in origin. The pottery betrays southern Congo affinities. The 'negroids' at Mapungubwe are generally known by the tribal name of Rozwi and since some of this group claim to have 'built Zimbabwe', it is possible that they introduced the new techniques in the 15th century.

f 7   The Rozwi, some of whose traditions connect them with the Congo (although there are others which suggest that they came from the South), appear to have been few in numbers, but excellent organizers and very active politically in federating small tribes into large and apparently powerful groups.

f 11   At the peak of their power, during the 18th century, the Rozwi Mambos ruled over an area stretching from the semi-desert of Bechuanaland almost to the shores of the Indian Ocean and bounded north and south by the Zambezi river and the Zoutpansberg mountains (Northern Transvaal), a huge rectangle about six hundred miles by four hundred miles. It is difficult to say how many people came under Mambo's indirect rule but they cannot have numbered less than a million and, because most of the land was fertile, the numbers may have been a lot greater.

Rozwi and Mwenye: two Skilled Peoples

In order to build one of the huge walls at Zimbabwe, much more was required than merely an ability to select blocks and lay them more or less level. Granite was split off the bare *ruwaris* by heating it and then pouring water over the hot stone, a method well known in early mining all over the world. It is both laborious and wasteful of timber. Thus the first step was to collect timber for quarrying and as time passed this would become more and more difficult. The next step was to break out the stone. Then it had to be transported on to the job, a task which could have been performed by hand but which more likely called for the use of a sledge—wheels were unknown here before 1854. Trimming of the stones was done on the job, for great quantities of granite spalls were found in the 1958 dig. Only after trimming could building commence.

A typical enclosure of Zimbabwe type. The main walls are of stone. The circular huts are built of mud (daga) on a mud foundation and roofed with thatch. (12)

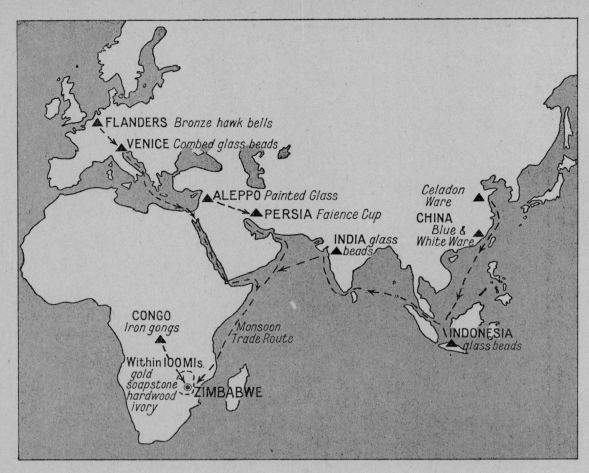

The origin of Zimbabwe imports and probable trade-routes. Most of these would have been paid for by the export of gold, but so far no article of Zimbabwe manufacture has been found outside the country. (13)

From a study of the wall itself, it appears that the Great Outer Wall was built in a clockwise direction, starting just west of the North (or main) Entrance and using the rough end of the wall as a moving ramp up which the labourers carried stone to the builders. A change in batter about half way up the wall suggests either that it was built in stages or that there were at least two teams of builders.

One visualises an architect controlling two or perhaps four teams of builders erecting the inner and outer faces simultaneously; there would be very few actual builders but there would be a veritable army of trimmers, carriers, sledge drivers, quarry-men, wood collectors and water bearers to keep the builders supplied, and the organization of this immense gang, totalling perhaps two or three hundred men and women, would call for administrative qualities of no mean order—qualities which tradition says were possessed by the Rozwi.

The Rozwi are not the only people to lay claim to have been the builders, the Lemba (also called the Mwenye) have also put forward this claim. They are as unlike the Rozwi as can be: they have no political ambitions and no communal organization, preferring to attach themselves to some other group; on the other hand, they are wonderful craftsmen—the men are superb smiths and the women's pottery is much sought after.

The combination of Rozwi organization and Mwenye craftsmanship could produce a magnificent result and the glories of the Conical Tower and Great Outer Wall may be a memorial of their co-operation. By the time the Rozwi were in the saddle at Zimbabwe the focus of importance had passed from the Hill to the Valley where the so-called Temple became Zimbabwe's most important building.

It will not have escaped the reader's notice that not only must these building projects have occupied very large numbers of people in unremunerative work but that they would all need feeding and could only operate under the most stable conditions.

pl 8
15

Undoubtedly the great buildings at Zimbabwe and the lesser ones at Khami, Dhlo Dhlo and elsewhere can only have been built in a time of prolonged peace. Portuguese chronicles speak of wars in this area throughout the 16th century and at the end of the 17th, but the 18th century seems to have been peaceful and it is to this very time that most of the large building work has been assigned on archaeological grounds.

The basis of Rozwi prosperity was however the gold trade and the greatly increased variety of imports which now included glass beads from India, Indonesia and Europe, blue-and-white porcelain from Nankin (China), metalwork from various parts of Europe and the Near East and Dutch glass bottles (which may or may not have contained the gin for which they were made!) all go to show that the Rozwi received a better price for their metal than had previously been the case. They also kept a goodly proportion to make into ornaments, usually beads of various shapes and sizes, as well as wire worked up either into bracelets or else woven into the lower part of the cloth skirts which Rozwi officials are believed to have worn.

f 13

pl 23

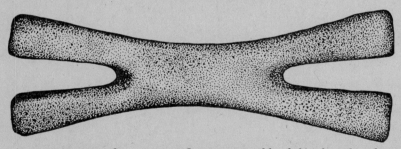

A copper ingot, used as currency. Soapstone moulds of this shape have been found at Zimbabwe and other ruins. (14)

Increased imports could of course merely imply increased exports but the impoverishment of both Arab and Portuguese East Coast towns during the 17th and 18th centuries suggests only diminution in trade, hence the argument for harder bargaining on the part of the Rozwi. No doubt ivory was another element in trade, for one tusk of every elephant killed or found dead has for centuries been the chief's perquisite, but gold seems to have been the principal export.

Unfortunately no objects of Zimbabwe or Rhodesian manufacture have been found outside the country, so we are left in doubt as to the extent of the direct export trade; even worse, we cannot apply the archaeological technique of 'cross dating'.

Before the Portuguese arrived, about 1505, this trade had been in the hands of Arabs and Kilwa, with its offshoot Sofala (a district rather than a single town), held pride of place. Although some Arabs and more Indians may occasionally have made the journey into the interior, the trade was carried on by men of

f 15

mixed blood (called by the Portuguese 'Moors', a far more euphonious name than the modern 'Afro-Asian'): tradition, customs and physical characters all point to the Mwenye as the descendants of these traders.

Even before Don Henrique started his school of navigation at Sagres, Kilwa and Sofala were known as sources of gold and were marked on maps, so gold was one of the lures which brought the Portuguese into the Indian Ocean and in due course led them to clash with the Arabs for control of this profitable trade.

Although the Portuguese succeeded for a time in controlling the gold trade from Monomotapa and Manica (northern Mashonaland and the Umtali area), possibly one-fifth of Rhodesian production, they never succeeded in laying hands on the far greater production of the western and midland mines. The rise of the Rozwi had apparently started before the Portuguese arrived, but one is not overstretching probabilities if one suggests that the dispute between the foreign proprietors of the gold trade gave the African producers their opportunity, and to see in Portuguese cupidity an ultimate reason for Zimbabwe's greatest period.

The 'Golden Age' of Zimbabwe

Although nowadays there is little enough gold to be found at Zimbabwe, very large quantities of beads (some weighing an ounce each), wire, chain, foil and even tacks have been found there. Hall, the last of a line of treasure seekers, claimed to have found £4,000 worth in three years' diggings. Doubtless Zimbabwe was once literally a 'Golden City'.

Reading between the lines of Hall's *Great Zimbabwe* and the reports of earlier excavators one cannot but conclude that much of this gold was in the top foot or two of the deposit and was probably part of a very rich 'destruction layer', the result of the sack of the town in the 1830's. Such gold ornaments would have been worn by the people living in the buildings.

Listening to the chat of 'old hands', as I have done for the past fifteen years, it has been possible to learn things which neither Hall nor anyone else dare publish, namely that a great deal of gold from Zimbabwe and from other 'ruins' was found in rifled graves. Probably there were many graves on Zimbabwe Hill—*maDzimbahwe* today means 'chiefs' graves' (although literally it is 'stone houses')—but today only one, jealously guarded, is known to exist.

This leads us to ask *What was Zimbabwe?*

Mauch describes ceremonies, commonly called 'rain-making', which took place on Zimbabwe Hill. These were in fact communal intercessions to Mwari (God) to send rain at the end of the long dry season always experienced in Southern Rhodesia. Such ceremonies are no longer held at Zimbabwe but they go on in other parts of the country where Mwari has other shrines. A cave, often with unusual acoustics, is commonly found at these shrines, so it will not surprise us to learn that there is such a one on Zimbabwe Hill close to the great rocks which an African headman once described as 'the real Zimbabwe'. pl 10

There is no place here to describe Mwari-ism in detail: it is a thoroughly respectable and reasonable religion, served by a hierarchy selected from certain families and assisted by a great number of messengers and 'children' from all walks of life. Mwari cannot be approached by ordinary folk and will listen to His people's intercessions only if they are transmitted by those (dead) who stand in His house. These intermediaries are always ancestors (hence Mwari-ism has been confused with ancestor worship) and the tribal ancestors are the departed chiefs who must be called upon by name in the ceremony. The eight 'Zimbabwe Birds', which originally stood within the Eastern Enclosure in the most sacred part of Zimbabwe Hill, pl 23 17 all have distinguishing features and are thought to have been a form of mnemonic or register of deceased chiefs for use in this ceremony. *One*, as already mentioned on page 44, is in 16 Groote Schuur House, Cape Town. *Five* are in the South African Museum in Cape Town having been taken there by Bent in 1891, there being no museum in Rhodesia in those days. *One* is in the National Museum of Southern Rhodesia, Bulawayo. This was found by Hall in 1902 in the Phillips Ruins in the valley, being the only bird not found on Zimbabwe Hill. *Part of one* is in the Queen Victoria Museum, Salisbury, Southern Rhodesia.

pl 23

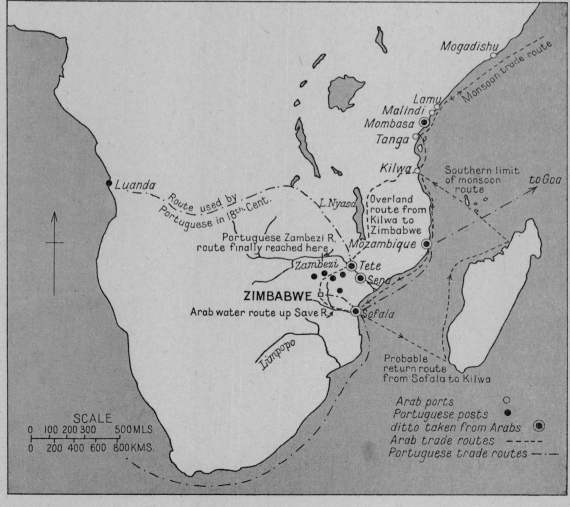

Arab and Portuguese trading in southeast Africa. Direct Arab activity was mostly confined to the coast. Sena was probably originally an Arab town at the head of Zambezi navigation; Tete lies at the point where an old African trade-route crossed the Zambezi. The Portuguese began by capturing Arab coastal towns, but then established a number of trading posts of their own in the interior. It is unlikely that any Portuguese trader ever saw Zimbabwe itself. (15)

pl 29 This was found by Hall. *Another part*, which fits the last named fragment, is in the Völkerkunde Museum, (East) Berlin, but who took it there and when is not known. Every Venda family today uses little pieces of iron which they call 'spears' as an ancestral register and a set of iron and bronze spear-heads—all different —was found at Khami Ruins, so this interpretation of 'Zimbabwe Birds' is not so far fetched as it sounds at first hearing.

In short then, Zimbabwe was a church. Probably it was the most important church in the country and indications are that it was a sacred place before anybody thought of building stone walls there.

Elsewhere I have compared it with Westminster Abbey, for both were burial places of kings and were places of public ceremonies. Just as the centre of importance shifted from the Abbey when the Parliament left the Chapter House for St. Stephen's Chapel in the Royal Palace, so did Zimbabwe's focus shift from the Hill first to No. 1 Ruin and later to the 'Temple'. Moreover, just as Government offices cluster around the Abbey and the (now vanished) Palace, so did the great officers of the Rozwi state build their houses in what is now called the 'Valley of Ruins'. It may seem a trifle far-fetched to compare the Maund Ruins to Somerset House or Renders Ruin to Scotland Yard but *mutatis mutandis* and making due allowance for scale that is not an outrageous comparison.

In fact Zimbabwe was the heart and capital of a great and rich African State. Not so well known in European literature as Mali or Ghana or Niger or Kongo because it was never in the general orbit of Atlantic trade, yet nevertheless BuKaranga, or Butwa as it was sometimes rudely called, was a place of great importance to the coastal emporia of Zanzibar and Sofala, for when BuKaranga started to exert economic pressure these same coastal towns folded up very quickly.

The End of Zimbabwe

The end of a great city is always a sad story and Zimbabwe's is no exception. In the 17th and more especially in the 18th century the place was thronged with the people of Mambo, the pl 23 Rozwi King. Ceremonies were performed on the Hill, courtiers dwelt in the Valley, Mambo himself—too sacred a figure to be seen—passed from one to the other by a hidden path, some of which still survives as the 'Ancient Ascent'. The high walls of the building we now call the 'Temple' were not built to conceal the disgusting orgies beloved of the older writers but to hide the sacred figure of the divine Great One from the vulgar gaze, for *Mumba huru*, the old name for the 'Temple'—recorded by the patient Mauch—means nothing more, or less, than 'palace'.

To people used to publicity for royalty and rulers of all sorts, this idea of Mambo's invisibility may sound strange, yet it occurs all over sub-Saharan Africa as Wieschhoff in his *Zimbabwe-Monomotapa Culture in Southeast Africa* has shown. Local traditions refer to Mambo's invisibility and to his shunning of company. Part of this may have been dictated by traditional court etiquette but it is undoubtedly also partly due to fear of witchcraft; Mambo's was too valuable a life to be risked in any way.

Mambo travelled around his domains, perhaps hidden in a palanquin, maybe in disguise since he dare not be seen, and stayed sometimes at Dhlo Dhlo, occasionally even at distant pl 15 Khami but no doubt often at lovely Naletale. Some Mambos were 5 great hunters, some like Dimbeywu were builders of great places 8 (did he, perhaps, build the Conical Tower—the 'mountain' of Rozwi legend?), others were soothsayers and one is remembered because of his mysterious disappearance (which sounds suspiciously like assassination), but all were, like Chirisamuru, proud men. For when the end came Chirisamuru sat on his chair at Manyanga—'the place of the tusks', a hundred miles and more north-west of Zimbabwe—and suffered himself to be torn to pieces by barbarians from Zululand, Ngoni driven out by the megalomaniac Zulu Shaka.

For that is how Zimbabwe and the Rozwi Federation died. It was overrun by an Ngoni horde led by Zwangendaba Kumalo of the Ndandwe tribe; everything was smashed wantonly—for little of gold seems to have been carried away—and burned. Cattle, women and young men were carried off and settled in what are today Nyasaland and Tanganyika, where there are still many old Shona and Karanga family names among people who no longer speak either of these languages.

Zwangendaba arrived in Southern Rhodesia about 1830, Zimbabwe itself was probably sacked soon afterwards, Chirisamuru was killed in 1834 and the Ngoni crossed the Zambezi on their northward march in November 1835. In a few short years the whole of the gracious Rozwi way of life was no more and such aged and honourable men as survived the holocaust ascribed the disaster as just punishment for Mambo's blasphemy against Mwari.

Zimbabwe was not immediately abandoned, although the sacked buildings were not reoccupied—they were haunted by *ngozi*, the most malignant of spirits whose bodies had been killed and not duly buried—but the remnant of the Rozwi called in Mugabe of the Duma people to help them and between them some poor buildings were erected (close to the present Museum). pl 14 For a few years ceremonies were performed, but by 1860 the Rozwi gave up hope and went away.

Today there are still tiny pockets of Rozwi living and absorbed in other tribes, their traditions are almost forgotten and are only being collected by the exercise of extraordinary patience. Even so they are most difficult to understand. In less than a century and a half Zimbabwe has become an African riddle, a foolish myth, a source of tourist income. Not really an enigma but rather a forgotten tragedy.

Yet the end of the story is not completely unhappy. Through the efforts of two British archaeologists and a handful of devoted Rhodesians, the story has become more and more widely known and Zimbabwe has become a symbol of hope to the new Rhodesia which is even now being reborn.

IV THE X-GROUP ENIGMA

A little-known people of the Nubian Nile

L. P. KIRWAN

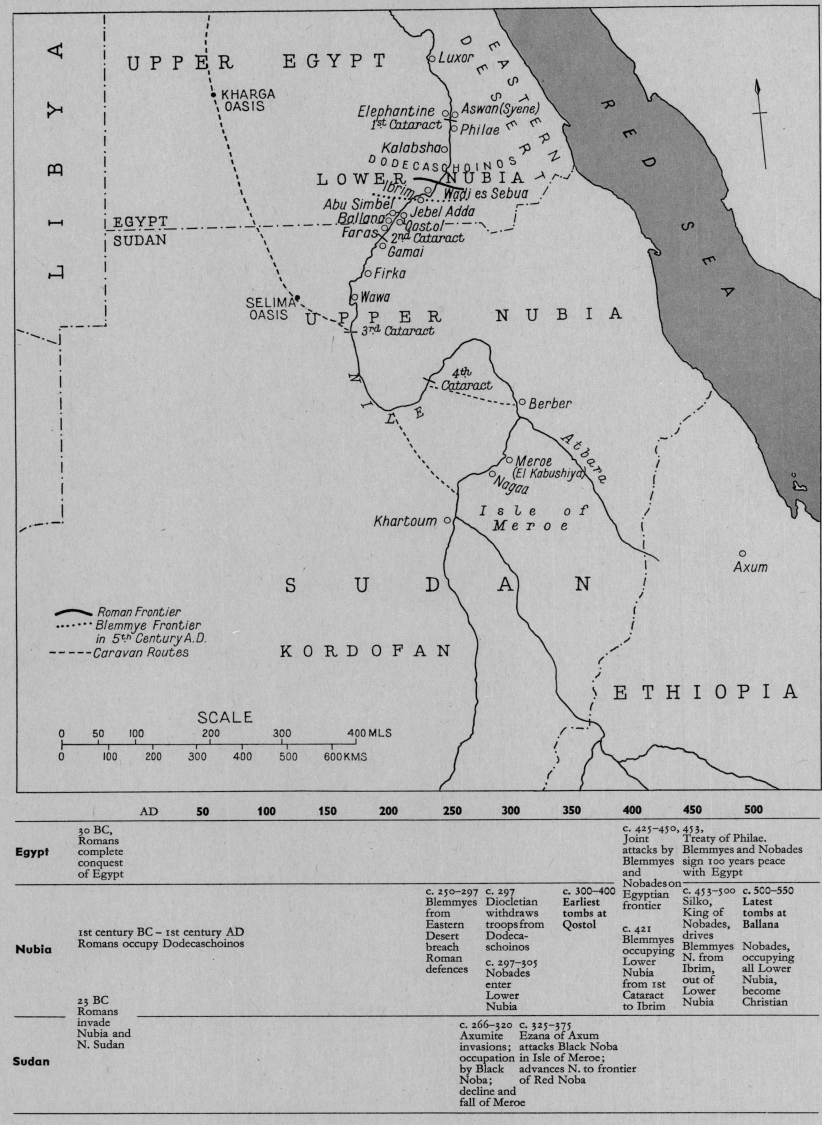

	AD	50	100	150	200	250	300	350	400	450	500
Egypt	30 BC, Romans complete conquest of Egypt								c. 425–450, Joint attacks by Blemmyes and Nobades on Egyptian frontier	453, Treaty of Philae. Blemmyes and Nobades sign 100 years peace with Egypt	
Nubia	1st century BC – 1st century AD Romans occupy Dodecaschoinos					c. 250–297 Blemmyes from Eastern Desert breach Roman defences	c. 297 Diocletian withdraws troops from Dodeca-schoinos	c. 300–400 Earliest tombs at Qostol	c. 421 Blemmyes occupying Lower Nubia from 1st Cataract to Ibrim	c. 453–500 Silko, King of Nobades, drives Blemmyes N. from Ibrim, out of Lower Nubia	c. 500–550 Latest tombs at Ballana Nobades, occupying all Lower Nubia, become Christian
							c. 297–305 Nobades enter Lower Nubia				
Sudan	23 BC Romans invade Nubia and N. Sudan						c. 266–320 Axumite invasions; occupation by Black Noba; decline and fall of Meroe	c. 325–375 Ezana of Axum attacks Black Noba in Isle of Meroe; advances N. to frontier of Red Noba			

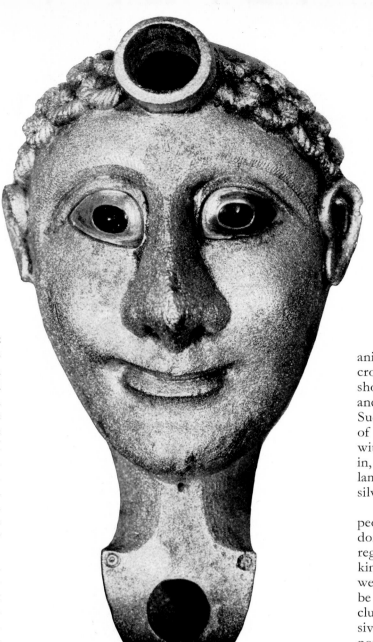

Among the most dramatic discoveries

ever made in Egypt was the 'Nubian treasure' found at Ballana and Qostol on the banks of the Nubian Nile in the early 1930s. Near the Sudanese border, south of Abu Simbel where the gigantic statues of Ramesses II gaze arrogantly out over the water, massive earth mounds were seen on either side of the river (below). Trial excavations showed that these covered tombs of a Nubian culture called the X-Group, known since 1907 but never satisfactorily identified.

Many of the tombs at Ballana and Qostol had been plundered by robbers, but enough still remained intact to throw new light on these mysterious people, who were Egypt's southern neighbours during the first few centuries of our era. Rich royal burials, accompanied by human and animal sacrifices, yielded jewellery, crowns and many other objects that showed southern influences from the ancient kingdom of Meroe in the Sudan. There were many signs too of cultural and commercial contact with late Roman and Byzantine Egypt, in, for example, the curious bronze lamp on the left, with garnet eyes in a silver setting.

Who, then, were the X-Group people? Heirs of the Meroitic Kingdom, driven north from the Khartoum region by conquering Abyssinian kings? Migrant warriors from the western desert? No final verdict can be given at present, but a decisive clue may yet be unearthed in the massive campaign of exploration that is now under way, before the High Dam is built and the waters cover the X-Group graves of Northern Nubia. (1, 2)

Slaughtered slaves and animals accompanied the king who was buried in Tomb 80 at Ballana. The skeleton (right) lay in forlorn majesty, decked with jewellery and with a magnificent crown (Pl. 17) on his seemingly negroid skull. In an adjoining room was the skeleton of a queen. The reconstruction above gives an idea of the scene when the king was buried. Slaves, some of them to be buried with their master, brought the dead king's crown and his most valued possessions. Horses and camels, richly caparisoned, were led down a ramp and pole-axed, their grooms strangled beside them. Fumes from the incense burners rose in the dry desert air. Then the tomb was sealed, the pit filled in, and a great mound was raised over the massacre. (3, 4)

An immense mound twelve metres high and seventy-seven metres in diameter covered Tomb 3 at Ballana. Gangs of labourers toiled for six weeks to remove half the mound down to ground level—and revealed an unbroken surface of smooth black soil, with no evidence of a tomb. But soon the mystery was solved: the soil proved to be mud bricks welded into a solid mass by flood water from the river. Digging down to the floor levels of the burial chambers, through layer after layer of solidified mud, the excavators were rewarded by an almost unplundered tomb. From here came the engraved silver dish of Pl. 28, emblematic of a dying paganism in the sixth century AD. (5)

Nothing could be more brutal

or at the same time more lavish than the harness of the horses buried with these warrior kings. Strangest of the finds, and most typical of the X-Group people, were some iron and silver bits of unique design (below). Curved pieces encircled the horse's lower jaw, terminating below in straight rods joined by a ring. From this ran the reins, one pull on which clamped the bit with cruel force on to the jaw in a pincer movement. With so savage a bit, a rider could halt the most fractious and unruly horse. (6)

Some secret, barbaric ritual in the African bush is suggested by this silver plaque from a wooden casket found in Tomb 17 at Qostol. A totem pole decorated with ox-horns is flanked by broad-bladed spears like those still carried by some Africans. (7)

A warrior's shield of embossed leather was found in the tumulus above Tomb 3 at Qostol. With its central boss, and the holes on either side for the wooden handle, it resembles those used by the Bega peoples of the northern Sudan today. (9)

60

Most striking of the discoveries in the X-Group tombs were the lavish and beautifully worked trappings of the sacrificed horses. The detail on the left shows a head-stall, with lion-head medallions joined by silver chain-work, still as flexible as the day it was made. Above is another medallion, a lion's head in beaten silver with garnet eyes and ivory tongue. The life-size model horse (right), in the Cairo Museum, shows a complete set of harness and trappings, with leather-work and saddlecloth reconstructed. Under a blue-dyed sheepskin is a cloth-covered wooden saddle, with silver-mounted pommel and cantle (see below), very like the modern Arab camel saddle. In the royal cemetery at Meroe remains of similar saddles, horse collars and medallions have been found. (8, 10, 11)

A popular god of Roman Egypt was the shaggy, bow-legged dwarf Bes, god of festivities and marriage. This jovial grotesque, carved in ivory, forms the handle of a knife (left) found above Tomb 3 at Qostol. (12)

Silver-mounted pommels from the Qostol tombs (right). The one on the left shows the goddess Isis with outstretched wings; on the other, two hawk-gods, wearing the double crown of Upper and Lower Egypt, face each other across an altar. Behind them are two lotus flowers. (13)

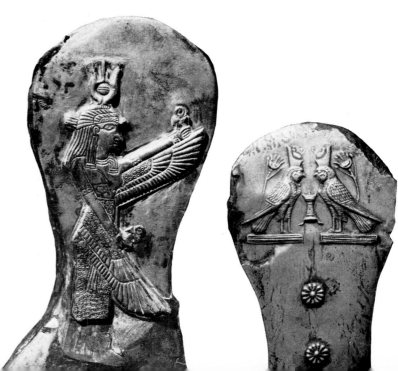

From a southern heartland

south of Nubia came the main cultural origins of the X-Group kings, from Herodotus's 'City of the Sun'. This was Meroe, in the triangle of land between the Nile and the Atbara, and from here the Meroitic kings ruled over Upper and Lower Nubia from 300 BC to about AD 300. The royal cemetery at Meroe, first excavated in 1834, had sacrificed animals, with harness and medallions similar to those at Ballana and Qostol. The X-Group jewellery, too, shows strong resemblance, and the plumed crowns, though Byzantine in their incrustation of jewels, are almost identical with the royal regalia of Meroe.

From Tomb 47 at Ballana comes the Queen's silver crown below (left), decorated with embossed busts of Isis and studded with carnelians. Round the rim are three crests composed of the disk and plumes of Isis. The best-preserved of all the Ballana crowns (centre) was on the head of the king buried in Tomb 118. This brilliant object is rich with emblems of ancient Egypt adapted by Nubian craftsmen—the 'uatchet' eye of the hawk-god Horus, and, round the rim, the *uraei*, the cobra symbols of Egyptian and Meroitic royalty, crowned with the sun-disk of Ra. The right-hand crown, which can be seen on the dead king's head in Pl. 4, gives an important clue to the identity of the X-Group people. Not only is it identical with those worn by Meroitic kings and queens in reliefs at Nagaa in Sudan, but a crown of the same type is shown in a drawing (right) from a Roman temple at Kalabsha in Lower Nubia. Here we see a horseman being crowned by a Winged Victory with a similar crown as he plunges a lance into a prostrate enemy. This (a Greek inscription shows) is Silko, King of the Nobades, commemorating his expulsion of the nomad Blemmyes (Bega) of the Eastern Desert from Lower Nubia, in the fifth century AD. The wars and alliances of these two tribes may provide the key to the X-Group enigma. (14–17)

An elegant gold necklace from Tomb 3 at Ballana, the tomb that was a mass of solidified mud. Was it perhaps dropped by robbers, fleeing as the roof started to collapse above them? (18)

The first unplundered grave at Ballana revealed a royal warrior in splendid panoply. On one wrist was this massive silver bracelet, its lion-head terminals severe, almost modern, in design. (19)

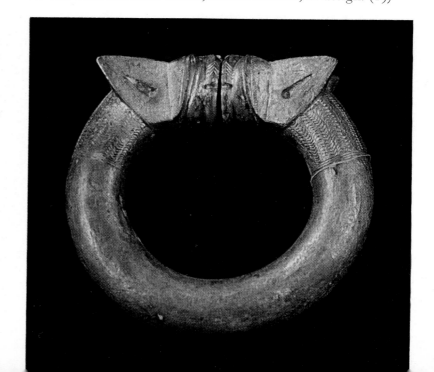

Her most precious possessions beside her, her throat deeply slashed, the young girl of Tomb 14 was the most macabre discovery at Qostol. These flamboyant earrings were hers. (20)

The Nubian Queen who wore the crown above (left) also wore these massive silver bracelets. The centrepiece is a magnificent onyx, surrounded by beryls, garnets and amethysts. (21)

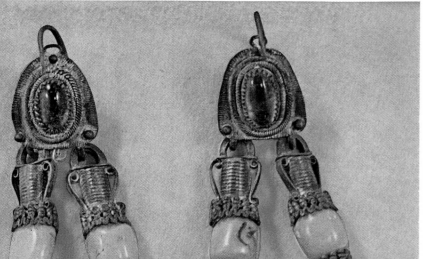

Egyptian craftsmanship
strongly influenced by the Hellenistic tradition could be seen in many of the more elaborate articles found in the Ballana tombs. Some of them, lamps and incense-burners in particular, were relatively clumsy in design (Pl. 22); others (e. g. Pl. 24) had the elegant austerity of Roman rather than Byzantine art. Mostly they are evidence not of warfare and plunder but of taste and fashion filtering down into Nubia by way of trade with the more sophisticated world of Mediterranean Egypt.

The slim and elegant shape of the tall (60 cms.) standard lamp on the right forms a stylized hunting scene, in which a hound's teeth are just closing on the tail of a fleeing hare. Such groups of running animals were popular in Coptic Egypt. Both this and the pine-cone censer come from Tomb 121 at Ballana. (24)

The Christian cross on this bronze lamp from Tomb 95 at Ballana contrasts strangely with a pagan burial. This lamp was probably imported from contemporary Christian Egypt. It is 30 cms. in height. (22)

The pine-cone was a favourite motif in Byzantine art. In this incense burner (25 cms. high) the pine-cone is hollow; the smoke and fumes came out through the perforated lid. (23)

From far and wide came the influences expressed in the native and Egyptian craftsmen's work. The tall bronze lamp on the right, with its slim fluted column standing on three dolphin-shaped legs and bearing a dolphin lamp, is topped by the bust of a bacchante. She wears the Phrygian cap imported into Egypt from Persia by way of Syria, probably when the cult of Dionysus was popular in late Roman Egypt. (25)

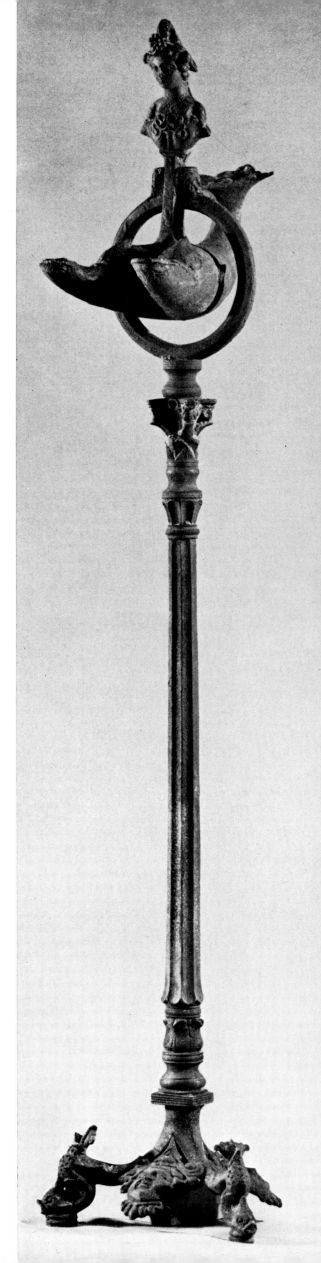

Eros holding a vine-branch, which originally supported a dolphin-shaped lamp with a Maltese cross (above), is Alexandrian work of the fifth or sixth century AD, from Tomb 114 at Ballana. Without the lamp, as here, it could easily pass for 300 years older, so persistent was the Hellenistic tradition. (26)

Only one other lamp was found at Ballana like the one above. A nude male figure holds two leaf-decked columns, each surmounted by a circular plate on which rests a detachable dolphin lamp. When it was found (in Tomb 80), there were Maltese crosses on the dolphin's tails, but these were later additions. (27)

Emblems of a dying paganism were engraved on this silver plate (left) by an artist of the Alexandrian school in early 6th-century Egypt. Hermes bears in his left hand the corn sheaf, symbol of commerce, and with his right he makes offering to the serpent of Aesculapius, protector against disease. (28)

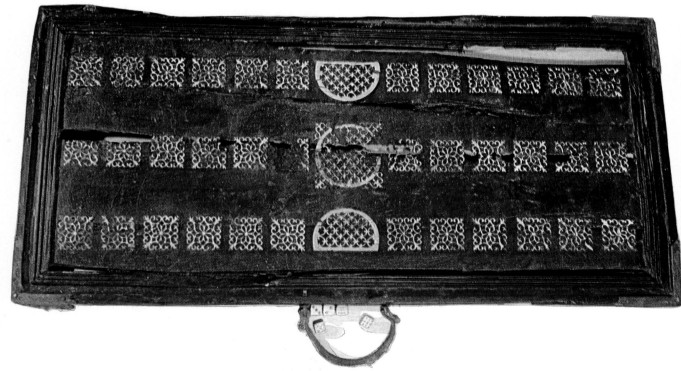

The lighter side of life among the X-Group people is represented by this elaborately inlaid board, on which a game resembling backgammon must have been played. Below it, in the mound above Tomb 3 at Qostol, lay a wooden dice-box and a bag containing fifteen ebony and ivory 'pieces' (left). The dice-box, of the kind known to the Romans as a *pyrgus*, is an ingenious device to make cheating impossible: the dice, dropped in through the top, bounced down stepped boards and out through the bottom opening. A similar dice-box is illustrated under the month of December in a Roman calendar of AD 354. (29, 30)

Broken open and rifled, this ornately decorated wooden chest was found among the debris in the tumulus over Tomb 14 at Qostol. What this chest contained we can only guess, for tomb-robbers—defeated by the complicated trick lock—had chiselled through the bronze hasps and hinges and wrenched off the lid. The front of the chest is ornamented with ivory panels on which mythological scenes are engraved, and outlined in red and green paint. Some native artist, familiar with the popular art of late Roman Egypt, has made of these scenes a curious mixture of Egyptian and classical motifs: Pan and Aphrodite appear side by side with the dwarf-god Bes, and Zeus has the Priapic qualities of the Egyptian Amun. Perseus is seen rescuing Andromeda (2nd row, 2nd from right), daughter of the King of Ethiopia (as Nubia and the Sudan were then called) from the sea-monster sent by Poseidon. (31)

Among the furnishings of Tomb 80 at Ballana was this small table, 24 cms. high, in gilded bronze. The geometrical fretwork of its hexagonal pedestal and rectangular top resembles that of the carved and fretted coffee tables found in any Arab house today. (32)

Clawing the head of a boar, this lion rears up on the sliding lid of a box. Smoke from the incense in this box wafted out through the mouths of both beasts. (33)

Strange and grotesque
bronze incense burners in the form of standing lions were among the rich and varied finds in Tomb 80 at Ballana. They have been thought Chinese in origin, but the inspiration comes more probably from Persia. Several similar vessels have been found in Egypt.

Persian influence can be seen in this snarling stylized lion (above). Head and neck are removable. The incense burned within the hollow body, emitting fumes through the mouth and nostrils. (34)

In Persia bronze censers in the shape of lions continued in use in medieval times. The lordly example on the left is of the Seljuk period (12th century AD); like the Nubian lion above, it has a detachable head and a hollow body. (35)

A little-known people of the Nubian Nile

L. P. KIRWAN

Some of the enigmas of the past are themselves ancient; that of the X-group is hardly fifty years old. Their culture was not even isolated and named until 1907, while the great mass of their remains, the 'Nubian treasure' of Ballana and Qostol, was found only in 1931 and 1932. It is possible that the present ferment of archaeolgical activity in Nubia, set in motion by the permanent inundations which the building of the High Dam will bring about, may throw more light on this mysterious people and even discover their capital. But from the fantastic treasures found in their tombs, from the barbaric funeral rites with which their chieftains were buried, it has been possible to reconstruct something of the origins of these people and to discover to some extent the part they played in the so-called Dark Age of Nubia, during the early centuries of the Christian Era.

MY OWN PART in the story starts early in the morning of November 3rd, 1931. We were on the west bank of the Nubian Nile, just south of the Great Temple of Ramesses II at Abu Simbel, beginning our third season's work on the Egyptian Government's Archaeological Survey of Nubia, our task being the exploration of all the low-lying archaeological sites between Wadi es-Sebua and the Sudan frontier before these were flooded by a new heightening of the Aswan Dam. This dam, built in 1902 and already heightened once in 1912, has been a boon to archaeologists. Before it was built and each time before it was heightened, archaeological surveys of Lower Nubia were launched by the Egyptian Government. This lonely stretch of the Nile Valley between the First Cataract of the Nile and Egypt's southern frontier therefore is archaeologically one of the most thoroughly explored regions in the world.

South from Abu Simbel

We had already spent two long winters in Nubia trudging over the desert, excavating innumerable settlements and cemeteries, and here at Abu Simbel we were at the point where we had left off the preceding year. Neither the director of the Survey, W. B. Emery, nor I, nor our Egyptian colleagues from the French-administered Antiquities Service, had any hopes of dramatic discoveries in the short stretch remaining between Abu Simbel and the frontier. Certainly, we had found much in the past two seasons. But little to add to previous knowledge, and as we moved south across the desert, leaving behind us the colossal effigies of the Pharaoh Ramesses gazing with majestic arrogance across the Nile, none of us was in an optimistic mood. Nor was the prospect in front of us exhilarating. At this point, the sandstone hills, from which the Egyptians had hewn the Abu Simbel temples, fall back from the river, leaving a great barren desert bay, shimmering in the heat even at this early hour of the morning. To the south and west, not a tree, not a bush, no matter how withered by the sun, could be seen. The only trace of green to relieve the eyes was a meagre fringe of wilting palm and acacia trees overhanging a torpid Nile.

However, as we passed the mud-brick hovels of Ballana village we noticed that this desert was not so featureless as it seemed. What at first had appeared to be massive accumulations of wind-driven sand, proved as we reached them to be sand-encumbered earth mounds between two and twelve metres high. Were these ancient barrows, blending so imperceptibly with the desert that

they had escaped the eyes of earlier archaeologists? Or were they just freaks of nature, natural accumulations? That was the problem facing us as we walked back that night to our *dahabiyah*, our houseboat and camp, on the Nile.

The following morning a party of geologists unexpectedly came ashore at Ballana. They too examined the mounds and decided that they were natural accumulations. This was expert advice but even so, hard to believe. These mounds were suspiciously regular in shape. There was a scatter of potsherds round about which could easily have come from the debris of plundered tombs. Most suspicious of all were the large green schist pebbles which covered several tumuli; surely, we thought, the work of man. In the midst of these arguments, news came from across the river, from Qostol, of the plundering of some small graves there of Byzantine date and when we crossed over we found that these lay among earth mounds exactly similar to those at Ballana on the west bank of the river.

The Tombs of Qostol

Trial excavation was obviously the only way to settle this geological-archaeological controversy. For this, we selected one of the Qostol mounds, smaller and less sand-laden than those at Ballana, and set a man to scrape round the perimeter and search for an artificial edge. I shall always remember our astonishment when we looked up a few moments later. The man had completely disappeared. We ran over and found that he had fallen into an obvious plunderer's passage tunnelled out of the alluvial soil and running eastwards towards the heart of the mound. We hauled him out, took off our shoes, and lighting candles against possible foul air, climbed in and began to crawl along the passage ourselves; painfully enough, for it was only a few feet in diameter and the atmosphere was suffocatingly hot.

We had crawled fifteen yards or more when we saw in front of us, in the flickering candle-light, a hole framed by a jagged edge of mud-brick and plaster. Squeezing through this with care, for there were hundreds of tons of earth above and the effects of an inrush of air on a structure hermetically sealed for centuries are unpredictable, we found ourselves in a burial chamber. Over the floor human bones were scattered about in all directions, a skull here, thigh bones there, but what caught our eyes were the wine-jars and cups stacked high against the walls. These we recognized as belonging to a Nubian culture called (by the late Professor Reisner of Harvard, leader of the first archaeological survey of Nubia in 1907) 'X-Group', datable to the period from the 3rd to the 6th century AD.

From this burial chamber we moved, on tip-toe, listening intently for the dropping of minute brick fragments from the sagging roof, to another very similar room. On the far side there was a sealed mud-brick door, surmounted by a cracked sandstone lintel. That the blocking of this door should still be intact suggested at once the possibility that what lay beyond might have escaped the plunderers. But this was no moment to start tampering with brick-work. Already we thought we had noticed a slight widening in the crack in the lintel. We had made our discovery. We had proved that these mounds covered tombs, rich tombs once containing treasures worth laborious and even hazardous plundering. Now evidently was the moment to leave, and we crawled back along the plunderers' passage and out into the glare of the sunlight.

The next step was to dig down from the east to see what we could find on the far side of this sealed mud-brick door. Clearing away the mound was a mammoth task of excavation. By November 30th, a large V-shaped wedge had been removed. Then a long ramp appeared, dug out of the alluvial soil, descending towards the tomb from east to west. Thereafter discoveries followed fast, discoveries among the most dramatic ever made in the Nile Valley. First two iron axe-heads, with edges so sharp that we could never have believed them ancient had they not been sealed below the mound. Then, the skeleton of a horse with a deep cleft in its skull. One iron axe fitted this exactly and the animal must have been pole-axed from the edge of the ramp as it walked down to its last resting-place. The ramp as it descended towards the level of the tomb entrance widened out into a rectangular

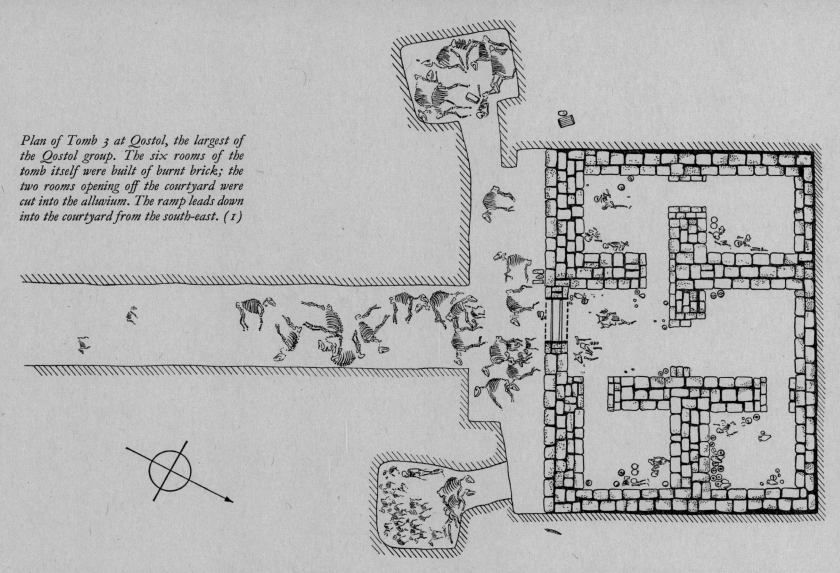

Plan of Tomb 3 at Qostol, the largest of the Qostol group. The six rooms of the tomb itself were built of burnt brick; the two rooms opening off the courtyard were cut into the alluvium. The ramp leads down into the courtyard from the south-east. (I)

court, and near the junction and in the court itself more skeletons appeared, of donkeys and camels and horses.

The horses provided the first of the many sensational discoveries we were to make at Qostol and Ballana. Several of them carried wooden saddles, covered with red or black leather, exactly similar in construction to the modern Arab camel saddle, with silver-mounted pommels and cantles. Below the saddle were fragments *pl 13* of a blue horse cloth, embroidered with an intricate pattern of birds and vines in red and green. These horses wore elaborate trappings of silver disks ranging along the flanks and across the breast bone, like the prancing cavaliers of late Roman and Coptic *pl 6* art, and in their mouths they carried silver and iron bits of unique design. These consisted of two curved end-pieces, hinged together, enclosing the lower jaw of the horse and terminating in two rods linked by a ring to which the reins were attached. One pull on the reins and the curved end pieces clamped together on the jaw in a pincer movement. Nothing could have been more brutal, nor out of all the mass of antiquities discovered did we find anything so uniquely characteristic of these owners of the Ballana-Qostol tombs.

Slaughter of the Living

Lying near the horses were the skeletons of several grooms, killed, it seems, by strangulation. This, we discovered later, was only the first phase in the holocaust which accompanied the principal burial in these tombs. Here was part of the funerary cortège, the macabre sacrifice of attendants and animals destined, like those found at Ur, to accompany the dead man on his voyage to the After World. Looking back, the scene seems now to come to life: the silver trappings glinting in the Nubian sun, the horses stumbling on the uneven surface of the ramp, then the axe-blows, the slumping animals, the anguished, stifled cries of the slaves drowned by the wailing and chanting of mourners *pl 3* and the rhythmic beat of drums.

The interior of this tomb had been thoroughly ransacked so we turned to Tomb 3, the largest of the Qostol group, and architec-

turally far the most interesting. It consisted of six rooms, with *f I* barrel-vaulted roofs, and was built of burnt brick; an extravagance in a rainless country like Nubia, and, as I remember thinking at the time, it must have commemorated some traditional link with the South, with the Savanna rainlands south of Berber, with the so-called Island of Meroe perhaps, a very ancient centre of civilization, enclosed by the Atbara and the Nile.

But much happened before we reached the interior of this great tomb. We began for one thing to find antiquities buried at random in the mound and this changed the whole aspect of the excavations. We could no longer cut out just a wedge of

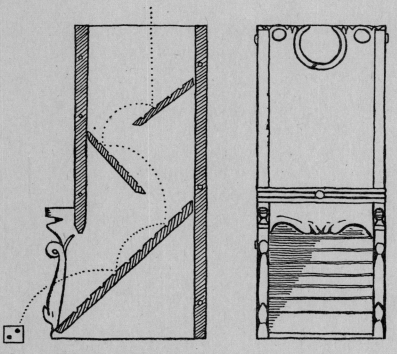

Cross-section and frontal view of the 'cheat-proof' dice-box. (2)

earth, as we had done with Tomb 2; most of the huge mound would have to be removed. An iron spear, almost rustless, an iron knife with an ivory handle in the form of the Ancient Egyptian dwarf-god Bes, and a wooden 'backgammon' board, with silver fittings and intricate ivory inlays decorating each square, were the first treasures to emerge. Below the 'backgammon' board lay a leather bag. In it were fifteen ivory and ebony pieces and a wooden dice-box, all part of the game which must have been played like backgammon. The dice-box, of a kind known to the Romans as a *Pyrgus*, was an ingenious device. You dropped the dice in through the top and they bounced down

pl 12
pl 30
pl 29
f 2

Entrance to Tomb 3 at Qostol, from inside the tomb. The wooden door was masked on the outside by mud bricks. (3)

over a ladder-like arrangement of boards and out through an opening, flanked by carved dolphin heads, as a safeguard against cheating.

We had now cleared down to ground level and to the edges of a great square pit approached by a ramp from the south-east. In the pit we could already see the red brick vaulting of the tomb roof. But knowing that the tomb itself would probably be plundered, we started first to clear the court and ramp, both filled with loose earth through which no plunderer could tunnel. The toll on the ramp was the same: slaughtered donkeys, four camels, nine horses, two sheep, and again the silver-mounted saddles, the fragments of red and green saddle cloths, the blue-dyed sheepskins, and the unique and brutal horse-bit worn by donkeys and horses alike. There was no neat arrangement of the carcasses. They were piled up above each other as if the animals had bunched together in a stampeding, snorting mass under the flail of axe-blows from the ramp-edge.

The court of this Tomb 3 at Qostol provided two surprises in the form of two small rock-cut rooms. In the south-western room we found the skeleton of a man with an iron sword and a wooden drum, barrel-shaped and hollowed out of a single block like the Sudanese drums today. On one side a lotus-flower was engraved between two 'Uatchet' eyes, the falcon's eye sacred to Horus in Egyptian mythology. The owner must have been the Royal Groom or Master of the Horse for nearby lay his six favourite chargers carrying the finest silver harness discovered, with head-stalls of heavy silver chain linked by medallions in the form of silver lion-heads with lapis lazuli eyes and ivory tongues. The silver bit was attached to the headstall by miniature couchant lions and the reins were of plaited silver chain, eighty centimetres long.

pl 8
pl 10
11

Like most of the animals sacrificed at Qostol, the horses wore engraved bronze bells round their necks, hanging from tasselled cords, and one—possibly the chieftain's favourite mount—wore a broad red leather collar ornamented with openwork silver medallions, some in the form of lions' heads with garnet eyes, others of open silver-work. One medallion framed a large scarab of green-blue faience encircled by garnets, beryls and moonstones; another a magnificent onyx cameo with a bust, probably of Constantine the Great (AD 306-337). This cameo, an elegant product of Hellenistic art, is hardly likely to have been plunder from a local Meroitic grave for it constitutes an integral part of the harness decoration. It implies therefore

f 4

a broadly contemporary contact with Egypt. Did it come by way of trade? Was it a gift perhaps commemorating an Emperor who just as he sought to promote trade (and Christianity) in ancient Abyssinia may also have had trade and diplomatic contacts with these Nubian tribes?

After these discoveries, we moved across to the second, north-western, rock-cut room, and then into the tomb itself. The rock-cut room threw more light on the life of these 'X-Group' people. It contained in addition to the skeletons of two men and two horses, the skeletons of a pack of fifty hounds, wearing collars of engraved bronze bells and leashes of plaited hair. The entrance

Onyx cameo, part of the trappings of a horse in Tomb 3 at Qostol. The elegant bust may represent Constantine the Great. (4)

to the tomb was blocked with mud-bricks, masking a rectangular doorway with sandstone jambs and lintel and a crumbling wooden door faced with circular bronze plates. The wooden door fell away in front of us and in the dim light beyond, across the bones of a sacrificed ox lying over the threshold, we could see a chaos of pottery vessels and bones and skulls, just as the plunderers had left them. In the burial chamber, nothing was left but a curious bronze lamp in the form of a human head with eyes of garnet set in silver. Several lamps of this kind have come from Coptic Egypt and they bear all the marks of a crude and ostentatious native craftsmanship. One other find in this tomb, or rather in the plunderers' passage leading to it, gave a clue to the armament of these Qostol warriors. This was part of a corrugated leather breast plate and the upper part of a leather quiver, wrenched off the corpse by the plunderers. We had already found a large circular leather shield in the mound above—we found another slashed by a sword cut in Tomb 14—and we were beginning to get some idea of the appearance of these X-Group warriors as they rode on their silver-decked horses into battle.

f 3

pl 1

pl 9

A Young Girl's Treasures

Tomb 14 was one of the most rewarding, and exciting, of these Qostol tombs and in the pit and in the mound above it we made our next discoveries. The first, in the mound, was macabre enough for any murder story: the body of a young girl, remarkably preserved by the dry soil, her beauty imaginable despite the desiccated, leathery condition of the flesh. She had been dressed in linen robes, blue, red, yellow, green, but the fragments crumbled at a touch. There was no doubt how she died. The knife slash across the throat showed clearly enough. Probably this too was a ritual sacrifice, for near the body we found this girl's most precious possessions, some in a leather satchel with iron lock and handles, some in a bundle of decaying linen. Here were all the perquisites of an oriental beauty: two wooden flasks containing eye-black, one fashioned as a mummiform figure of the ancient Egyptian hawk-headed sun-god Ra, the other as a sphinx, with eyes of ivory, seated on a pylon-shaped pedestal; silver earrings set with beryls and carnelians; four heavy silver rings, one engraved with a lotus, the other with a lion; and necklaces of silver and coral beads and silver wire. These were in the satchel. Wrapped in the linen, with several necklaces of coral, silver and carnelian, were two pairs of large silver earrings; flamboyant, barbaric but of excellent workmanship. In one a large amethyst, in

Hanging lamp shaped like a dove, from Tomb 14 at Qostol (left). Oil was poured in through a hole in the back, and the tail holds a double burner, with tweezers for trimming the wick. Right: a similar lamp from another X-Group mound tomb at Firka, northern Sudan. These were probably imports from the north, for lamps shaped like birds were common in Christian Egypt during the 4th and 5th centuries. (5, 6)

the other an oval setting of green faience, is mounted centrally on the silver pendant, while below hang drops of silver filigree
pl 20 work ending in a large coral bead.

But there was more to come from the mound than this rather gruesome discovery. Just north of the pit, beyond a group of
pl 31 perfectly preserved iron spear-heads, a large wooden chest emerged, its lid thrown on one side, its rear hasps and hinges cut through by a chisel. The lock itself was extraordinarily complicated and had defeated robbers who must have been members of the burial party. This chest, over a hundred centimetres high, was a most elaborate piece of furniture. The bronze lock clasps were surmounted by couchant lions and the lock-plate, also bronze, was engraved with a circular scroll pattern of vine tendrils, bunches of grapes and other concentric designs. On the front panel, rows of ivory and ebony bosses alternated with rows of ivory plaques engraved with mythological scenes outlined in green and red. The scenes, crudely carved, were a mixture of late Egyptian and debased classical motifs. A travesty of the Gigantomachy, a Zeus endowed with the Priapic qualities of the Egyptian God Amun, Dionysos, Aphrodite, Pan, and that favourite God of Roman Egypt, the dwarf-god of festivity and marriage, Bes, are all portrayed as best he could by some native craftsman familiar with the popular art of late Roman or early Christian Egypt. One scene shows Perseus wearing a Phrygian cap rescuing Andromeda, daughter of Cepheus, king of Ethiopia, from the sea-monster sent by Poseidon.

In the tomb itself almost nothing had been left except once again a lamp (perhaps the one the plunderers worked by) shaped
f 5 like a dove with double burners in the tail and a filling hole with a triangular hinged lid on the back. There was a chain attached for suspension, as there was to another precisely similar lamp
f 6 which I found later in another 'X-Group' tomb at Firka in the northern Sudan. Lamps in the form of birds were very common in Christian Egypt during the 4th and 5th centuries and this, like so much else found in these tombs, was probably imported from the north.

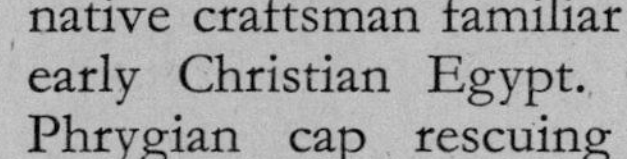

The only Meroitic inscription found in the X-Group tombs: a few characters scratched on a spear. They read, 'the good one', 'the trusty one'. (7)

Links with the Kingdom of Meroe

In archaeology it is not always the more sensational antiquities, like this remarkably preserved wooden chest, which provide the essential clues to history. Sifting some of the debris from this mound we came upon a minute bronze coin of the Emperor Valens, Emperor of the East from AD 364 to 378, a valuable clue to date. Then there was an iron spear, found near the body of the murdered girl in the mound. This had on one side of it *f 7*
a line of Meroitic inscription which reads proudly, in Dr. M. E. L. Macadam's translation, 'the good one', 'the trusty one'. Here was a link with an earlier Nubian culture. For the inscription is in the demotic alphabet invented by the Sudanese kingdom of Meroe which flourished from its capital, some 130 miles north of Khartoum, from 500 BC until c. AD 300, and during that time ruled over almost all northern Nubia.

This inscription, rudely, uncertainly engraved, was one of the many links with Meroe found in this and other tombs we explored at Qostol. The plans and architecture of the tombs showed, as W. B. Emery says in his final report on the excavations, 'a direct descent from the Meroitic pattern' and from the tombs underlying the royal pyramids near Meroe. Much of the pottery from Qostol, moreover, especially certain types of painted wine-jars, could easily have come from late Meroitic graves in this part of Nubia.

But the most striking analogies are with the royal cemetery at Meroe itself rather than with the provincial Meroitic culture of Lower Nubia. The first excavator of Meroe in 1834, an Italian doctor Joseph Ferlini, found sacrificed animals, dogs, camels, horses, on the stairway leading down to the pyramid tombs, and the remains of decorated saddles. Nearly a century later, in the days of scientific archaeology, Dr. George Reisner's Harvard-Boston expedition confirmed Ferlini's haphazard discoveries and found lion-headed silver medallions from leather horse-collars remarkably similar to those from Qostol. The Qostol jewellery too, especially the great silver and coral earrings pl 20
found with the murdered girl in Mound 14, shows similarities with the jewellery from Meroe found by these earlier explorers.

Nothing however confirmed the connection with this southern heartland of the Meroitic Kingdom more than two silver plaques from a wooden casket found in the Qostol Tomb 17. Embossed on them was the effigy of a curious composite God, a hawk- *f 10*
headed crocodile, with human hands and the hind legs of a lion, wearing the plumes and disk of the sun-god Amun-Re. This closely resembles a relief on the walls of the temple of *f 9*
Nagaa which lies south-east of the Meroitic capital. With this was another similar plaque with a design of a totem-pole surmounted by ox-horns and flanked by two up-standing spears. What pl 7
could be more African in inspiration, more reminiscent of some savage and secret ritual in the African bush? There were many other such cultural links with Meroe and the south; the stiff conventional figure of Isis, for example, on a saddle pommel pl 13
from Tomb 36, standing with outstretched wings just as one sees her in Meroitic sculpture. All this made one think that it was southwards, beyond the junction of the Nile and the Atbara, to the royal capital at Meroe, Herodotus's 'City of the Sun', that one must look for the cultural origins of these 'X-Group' chieftains.

Trade with the North

But there were links with the north too, with Christian Egypt and the Mediterranean world; commercial, political, illustrating by analogy with discoveries elsewhere the extraordinary range of trade of which Alexandria was a great international centre in Roman and early Byzantine times. Objects like the dice-box, the *Pyrgus*, conjured up visions of sophisticated leisure, of the marble colonnades and palaces of Alexandria, rather than of these desolate sands. Alexandria probably manufactured the battered silver flagon from Tomb 3 at Qostol; it is identical with one found in the famous Scottish treasure of Traprain Law, of the 5th century AD, robbed from some rich villa in Gaul by Vikings, and carried to Britain with other loot. Then, as evidence of distant trade, in Tomb 24 we found a flagon of dark blue glass, with heavily ribbed handle; an export probably through Egypt from the Rhineland where such glassware was copiously manu-factured from the 3rd century AD. Strangest of all these links with the outer world was a fragment of Tussah silk found in one Qostol tomb. How did this find its way to Nubia? Probably from India or China, by way of Ceylon, and from this entrepôt in an Ethiopian ship to the Red Sea and thence across the desert to Nubia, for in those days Persian and Ethiopian ships mono-polized the Red Sea trade route with the Far East. Finally, there was the quantity of silver found in the Qostol tombs, some of it almost pure. One of the horse-bits proved, on analysis, to contain ninety-seven per cent pure silver. Here Asia Minor was probably the source, and one certainly more likely than the exhausted Pharaonic mines of Nubia.

It has been argued that many of the imported articles in these tombs were plunder from raids on Egyptian territory rather than the results of trade. This cannot be said of the most prevalent type of amphora found at Qostol and at Ballana. This type of ribbed 'wine-jar', made of a cream-coated pink pottery, was a well-known standard container for Egyptian exports and has been found in sites as far apart as Leptis Magna in Libya, in Jerusalem, and the Crimea in deposits of the 5th and 6th centuries AD. On the shoulder they carry Greek formulae in red paint, abbreviations of invocations such as 'Christ born of Mary' or 'Christ, Michael, Gabriel', familiar from ostraca and papyri of the 5th and 6th centuries, and under the handles the names of merchants with the serial numbers of the particular consign-ment. Most of these vessels, with no coating of pitch inside and

f 8

therefore porous, carried according to the inscriptions, corn, the 'currency' of Egypt, granary of the Roman Empire. But some contained oil, and some wine; in one case, Rhodian wine, an esoteric taste in Nubia!

By the time we had excavated sixty of the Qostol tombs, we began to clarify our picture of these 'X-Group' chieftains.

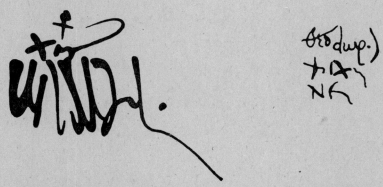

Greek inscriptions below Christian symbols (left) on imported amphorae found in the tombs. Under the handles are the names (right) of Egyptian corn or wine exporters, such as 'Theodore', 'Isaac', 'Diocles'. (8)

They were warriors riding camels and horses; the horses 'small like the largest of Egyptian asses', as the 13th century Arab geographer Abu Salih said of the Nubian horse in his day. Their religious and cultural origins were rooted south of Nubia, in the Island of Meroe, where royal dynasties dating back to the 6th or 5th century BC had developed a civilization blended of African and debased Egyptian elements, the latter an echo of the days when the Pharaohs had ruled over Nubia and Sudan as far south as the Fourth Cataract. But these 'X-Group' people were also influenced from another direction, from the north, through trade with Egypt. Turbulent neighbours though they may have been at times, this had brought them within the orbit of the Byzantine world.

This much was reasonably clear. But there was much we did not know, particularly about the principal burials, for every burial chamber at Qostol had been ransacked. Only an unplun-dered tomb could solve this problem and it was with this faint hope in mind that we moved across the river to the much larger mounds at Ballana.

A strange composite god, with hawk's head, human hands, lion's hind-quarters and crocodile's tail, and wearing the disk and plumes of the sun-god Amun-Re. The one on the left is a Meroitic relief from Nagaa in the Sudan, the other a silver plaque from Tomb 17 at Qostol—which sug-gests a close connection between the X-Group people and the kingdom of Meroe. (9, 10)

Early Christian craftsmanship from Ballana: figures of Christ and the Apostles—Syrian in style—on a silver casket found in Tomb 3. (11)

The Bewildered World of Early Christianity

pl 5 Here at first we met with unbelievable disappointment. We chose the largest mound, an immense monument twelve metres high. Day after day we laboured. Then at the end, after removing tons of earth, we came to a flat and empty surface of smooth black soil. Were we wrong? Were these Ballana mounds quite different from those of Qostol? Was this some ancient hoax designed to excite and frustrate the avarice of later generations? It seemed so. There was no crack, no crevice, nothing which suggested that below lay a tomb. In this situation, Egyptian workmen, Quftis from southern Egypt who have inherited family skills and techniques taught them mainly by Petrie, the famous British Egyptologist, in the late 19th century, are superb. Moving like human 'Geiger Counters' ceaselessly over the surface, they stopped and dug down and there found potsherds two feet below this seemingly virgin soil. The mystery was solved. Black soil proved to be mud bricks welded together by water, by some straying of the river perhaps away from its normal bed.

This tomb, No. 3, at Ballana carried us into the illogical bewildered world of Early Christianity when in Egypt Christian theology and pagan art subsisted side by side. In one room, encased in solid mud, we found a silver plate engraved, with the delicate effeminate grace so typical of the Alexandrian school,

pl 28 with all the emblems of a dying paganism. In the centre is Hermes, herald of the gods, wearing on his head the modius or corn measure characteristic of the Egyptian god Sarapis, and bearing in his left hand the corn sheaf, his emblem as the god of commerce and very appropriate to Egypt, granary of the Empire. With his right hand he makes an offering to the serpent of Aesculapius, protector against disease. The serpent is entwined round a tree from which hangs the lion's skin of Heracles (Hercules). Below are the emblems of other gods: Hephaestus, the Roman Vulcan, god of fire and metal-working, with his hammer and tongs; the shield and corselet of Ares, the Roman Mars who was also god of agriculture; and on the extreme right the griffin with the body of a lion and the wings and head of an eagle. In classical mythology, the griffin was guardian of the gold of the North. Is there some allusion here to the gold-mines of Nubia for which the country had been so famous in ancient Egyptian times?

This plate by analogy with others, some dated by hallmarks, was probably made in Alexandria early in the 6th century AD. It may have reached Nubia by way of trade like the silver plates found in Russia which were exchanged for furs, or it may, like others, have been a rich gift brought by some Byzantine embassy to placate these frontier tribes. In any event, the emphasis on commerce, industry, health and the possible allusion to Nubian gold suggests that this plate was one of the fruits of peace not war.

f 11 By contrast, the same tomb yielded a silver casket or reliquary,

embossed with figures of Christ and the Apostles, drawn with the realism, the severity, the accentuated relief characteristic of the Syrian rather than the Alexandrian school. Then there were three silver spoons, so called 'Eucharistic' spoons of which examples of the same sixth century date have been found in Cyprus and North Africa. Finally, there was a chalice-shaped silver censer, with an open-work pattern of vine leaves, one of the many censers found at Ballana.

Excavating down to the floor levels of the burial chambers was a wearisome job, probing, removing the solidified mud layer by layer so that objects could be left in their original position until we reached floor level and could see their relative distribution in the room. This tomb too had been plundered, though nothing like so thoroughly as the Qostol tombs. It contained many bronzes, among them two standard lamps in the form of a Winged Victory standing on a sphere resting on an ornate column. The outstretched arms and the wings support two rampant lions which hold a ring and through this a double-burner dolphin lamp is swung. Above it is a bust of a Bacchante. Such swinging lamps, known from Pompeii and other Campanian sites, have one practical advantage. To bring the light closer the lamp was laid horizontally so that it rested on two of the feet of the base at one end and on the lamp-ring at the other. This burial chamber also produced a very elegant gold necklace of heavy beads and pl 18 pendants, dropped perhaps by robbers escaping from a collapsing tomb.

These first discoveries at Ballana were a splendid augury and we returned in the following winter of 1932 with four hundred men and set to work on Mound 6. Below lay our first unplundered burial chamber. Behind the doorway, barred by two immense iron spears with silver hafts, lay the owner, with all the panoply of a royal warrior. On his left hand he wore a bow-guard or archer's bracer of silver. A spear and a silver-mounted sword lay by his side. On one arm he carried massive silver bracelets with lion-headed terminals, severe, almost modern, in design. pl 19 Here certainly was our first royal burial, as royal as any from the Pyramid Tombs of Meroe, for the crushed skull bore a silver crown embossed with busts of the Goddess Isis, very Meroitic in style, with a head-dress of 'Atef' plumes. Above and below and between these busts the crown was studded with carnelian jewels very much in the Byzantine manner. Indeed, this crown, with its blend of Byzantine and Meroitic elements, epitomized the two main cultural influences in this Ballana-Qostol civilization.

The Regalia of an African Queen

There were one hundred and twenty-two tombs at Ballana, five more unplundered. Tomb 47, the next to be dug, showed that here as at Qostol, the traditional Meroitic custom of ritual sacrifice had been maintained for we found on the ramp a horse with the customary bronze bells and silver trappings, and near the door of the tomb the bodies of two young slaves. Across the threshold lay the skeleton of a young woman with four bronze bowls and a bronze incense burner of a type found in Egypt in deposits of 4th to 6th century date, in the form of a pillar with open floral pattern supporting a pine cone. The perforated top serves as a hinged lid for the incense burner below. Another of a similar kind, but with the pine-cone supported by an open four-pillared shrine, was found in Tomb 121. The pine-cone was a favourite motif in Byzantine art and bronze pine-cones, cast in the round, often served as ornamental fountains. The main discoveries however came from the principal burial chamber. There we found the skeleton of a Queen wearing an elaborate silver crown inspired, like the King's crown, by the royal regalia of Meroe. As with the crown from Tomb 6, there is the same decoration of embossed busts of Isis and a studding of large carnelian jewels, the crown this time being surmounted by silver plumes and disk, emblems of the Goddess Isis.

The quantity and splendour of the jewellery buried with this African queen was amazing: twenty silver bracelets; a heavy silver torque round her neck; fourteen necklaces of silver, carnelian, quartz, jasper, olivine, obsidian, steatite, faience and glass beads; and nine pairs of earrings, many set with coral and blue faience. She wore eleven silver finger-rings, some plain, some jewelled; three silver and four coral anklets, and toe-rings with bezels in the form of silver flies, worn as amulets no doubt to ward off one of the pests of Nubia. None of this jewellery, glittering and flamboyant as it must have been against a dark Nubian skin, was so striking as a pair of heavy silver bracelets, each mounting a splendid oval onyx surrounded by beryls, garnets and amethysts. This is a type of hinged bracelet shown in some of the reliefs of the Queens at Meroe.

pl 23

pl 15

pl 21

The King in Tomb 80

None of the unplundered royal burials at Ballana was so complete or so striking as that in Tomb 80. The plan of this tomb followed the more or less familiar pattern of a burial chamber and three store rooms, all cut out of the alluvium and approached from the south-west by a descending ramp. On this lay heaped the skeletons of horses and camels. In the burial chamber, the king lay full length on what had once been a canopied wooden bier, like the wooden biers which crumbled into dust under the eyes of Meroe's first explorer, the Italian Ferlini. Here at Ballana the bier had had a bed of interlaced rope thongs, like the Sudanese *angareeb* of today, for the rope marks were clearly visible on a group of mud-encased bronze vessels lying below.

pl 4

pl 17

The dead king was a picture of forlorn majesty, an unforgettable figure, tall and strongly negroid in features. On his head he wore a massive silver crown, in design and decoration closely resembling those shown on the reliefs of the Kings and Queens in the pyramid chapels and on the temple walls at Meroe and Nagaa. The circlet is embossed with hawks, symbols of the Egyptian

gods Horus and Amun, each wearing the Double Crown of Upper and Lower Egypt carried by the Pharaohs. Rising from its upper rim are *uraei*, the cobras of Ancient Egyptian and Meroitic majesty, crowned by the sun disk of Ra.

The plumes are the most striking part of the resplendent decoration of this crown. They rise, on a short silver pillar, from a head of the Egyptian ram-god Khnum, god of the Cataracts, above all of the First Cataract where, according to Herodotus, the sources of the Nile were believed to gush forth from amidst sun-blackened granite boulders. Khnum was in particular the god of Elephantine, the 'ivory island' opposite the modern Aswan, where the ivory tusks of central Africa, the gold of Nubia, skins, incense, and slaves were traded with Egypt. Not far south of Elephantine is the island of Philae, with its great temple of Isis. This was the Mecca of all Nubians until its closure by the Byzantine Emperor Justinian in the second quarter of the 6th century AD.

This crown, with pillar and crescent supporting the plumes of Amun, flanked by *uraei* and studded with carnelian jewels, has analogies not only with Meroe to the south but with a very important drawing in northern Nubia, in a temple built by the Emperor Augustus at Kalabsha, about 120 miles north of Ballana. This shows a mounted horseman, clad in the fashion of the late Roman emperors, in a cloak and a tunic of mail, being crowned by a Winged Victory with a crown of exactly the type found in this and other Ballana tombs. His horse moreover wears elaborate trappings of disks similar to those of Qostol. With his left hand, this king or chieftain plunges a lance into the body of an enemy, prostrate in the dust. An inscription in Greek below provides the clue to this scene. In it, Silko, King of the Nobades, in bombastic language more appropriate, as the historian Bury remarked, to an Attila or a Tamerlane than to a petty chieftain of an African tribe, commemorates his triumph over the Blemmyes, a name given by classical writers to the nomad Beja of the Eastern Desert, the Ababda, the Bisharin and Hadendowa of today. This victory was the climax to a series of campaigns in which Silko drove the Blemmyes northwards from Ibrim to the First Cataract and finally out of the Nile Valley altogether. Silko's inscription, whose palaeography strongly suggests the work of an Egyptian Christian or Jewish scribe of the 5th century AD, provides an important clue to the enigma of the 'X-Group'. Firstly, it shows that the Blemmyes, for some time prior to Silko's invasion, had occupied Nubia between Ibrim and the First Cataract. More important, it shows that until that time the Nobades were confined to the Nile Valley south of Ibrim, including therefore the Ballana-Qostol district, but that thereafter they conquered all northern Nubia.

pl 14

Equipment of an African Warrior

This king in Tomb 80 carried the full equipment of an African warrior. On his left hand, covering the base of his thumb, he wore a silver bracer or bow-guard, fastened to thumb and wrist by a silver chain and leather thong. It is engraved with the horns,

f 12

The equipment of an X-Group bowman included (left) a bracer to protect hand and wrist, and an archer's loose for the finger. (12, 13)

disk and throne of Isis, and is a bracer of a kind, usually made of leather, which was used by Sudanese mercenaries from the region of the Third Cataract who served with the Egyptian army in the 2nd millennium BC. On one finger of the right hand he wore a stone 'archer's loose'. These cylindrical objects, found also in Meroitic tombs, had long puzzled archaeologists. Now their use was clear. They were used to pull back and release the bow-string after the fashion of Mongolian bow-rings. Between the king's legs lay a sword of late Roman type, about 45 centimetres long, with an iron cutting blade, hollow ground, and a wooden hilt covered with sheet silver. Some of the embossed patterns on the silver-covered scabbards of these swords have an almost European air, and it has even been suggested that they were plundered from North Italian or German soldiers stationed on the Egyptian frontier.

Necklaces of carnelian, quartz, crystal and jasper beads hung round the king's neck and he wore bracelets of silver and bead-work, but we found no trace of leather armour like that from Qostol, or of leather quivers, or leather sandals. The damp had done its work too well. Round the royal bier, against which a group of formidable silver-hafted spears had been stacked, we found several other burials; a dog, a camel, and three human skeletons, one of them of a man with arms raised as if to ward off an executioner's blow. In an adjoining room was the skeleton of a Queen, surrounded by the bodies of slaves and attendants. She too wore a silver crown, of simpler design, embossed with a frieze of standing figures of a Pharaoh holding offering vases. We found these double burials of King and Queen in two other tombs at Ballana. Could these be coincidental deaths? Or cases of *suttee*, of a ritual killing of the royal wife such as was practised in very ancient times in the Sudan? The latter is more likely and it completed the picture of the funerary cortège, of slaughtered animals, slaves, courtiers and concubines, which we had found at Qostol.

Treasures from the Mediterranean World

One unusual discovery in this same tomb, lying with a large deposit of bronze vessels, was the iron frame of a folding stool. Near by was a bronze folding table, ornamented above with goats' heads and standing on lions' paws. The loop handles are ornamented with griffins' heads. The brackets at the top of the legs originally supported a wooden board, the whole, with its movable rings sliding up and down as the table was opened or closed, being furniture of a type familiar enough from Roman sites like Pompeii.

Like other tombs at Ballana, Tomb 80 contained several bronze incense burners, two of them grotesquely decorated. One, box-like, had a sliding lid supporting a lion attacking a pig, flanked by two smaller seated lions on either side. Several incense burners of this kind have been found in Egypt, with lions attacking boars or sows, one of them in the Monastery of Epiphanius which was occupied from AD 578 to 650. The other burner was in the form of a lion with detachable head and neck, the incense escaping through the nostrils and mouth. Both burners had ring attachments for suspension. These grotesque censers have been thought to be of Chinese origin. In fact the inspiration is probably Persian and indeed a lion burner similar in type but later in date was included in the Exhibition of Iranian Art held in London in 1962.

There were two bronze lamps in this room, one of a kind never before found, in the form of a nude male figure on a pedestal, holding a leaf-covered column supporting plates carrying dolphin-shaped lamps, with Maltese Crosses above. The other lamp was quite different in style, a fluted column standing on three dolphin-shaped legs supported by human masks. The column supports a ring through which is suspended a double-burner 'Dolphin' lamp, topped by a bust of a Bacchante. These Bacchante busts were common at Ballana. They wear the Phrygian cap imported into Egypt from Persia by way of Syria and may be associated with the popularity in late Roman Egypt of the cult of Dionysos.

These lamps, native work under Hellenistic influence, were relatively clumsy in design compared with the elegant lamp found in Tomb 121 where the standard is fashioned in the form of a hound chasing a hare. This has an elegant austerity one

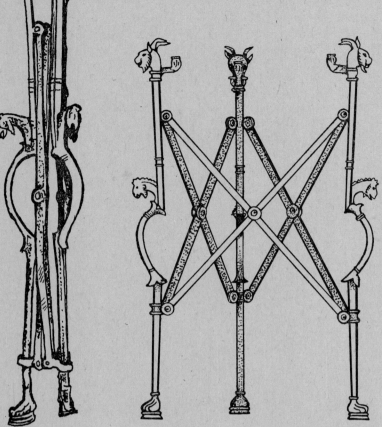

Bronze folding table from Tomb 80 at Ballana, of a type familiar from Pompeii. When it was opened out (below), the brackets supported a wooden top. (14, 15)

associates with Roman rather than Byzantine art. Such groups of running animals, however, were popular, in both bronze and ivory, in Coptic Egypt. This tomb also contained a bronze strainer with a Greek (and Christian) inscription included in its perforated base invoking the protection of God at home and on the high road.

It is impossible adequately to cover the remarkable variety of antiquities found in this tomb. In contrast to the folding tripod tables there were several miniature tables on hexagonal stands, of gilded bronze, with animals and birds set amidst the convolutions of the open-work panels in Syrian style. These resemble most closely the little wooden coffee tables, inlaid with shell and ivory, which can be seen in any Arab house today. A puzzling discovery was of a bronze samovar which since it had no spout must have been some kind of vaporizer. And then and very important for the light thrown on local industry and manufacture there was a large collection of iron tools of various kinds: hammers, chisels, saws, pincers, tongs, and metal cutters. Most of these tools were for metal-working on a fairly large scale.

How much of the metal-work found in these tombs was of local manufacture? It is a difficult question. The silver crowns, the silver mountings on saddles and on spears, the silver plaques, were certainly locally made and the same matrix was used for their distinctively Meroitic decoration in several different cases; on both crowns and saddles, for example. The majority of the bronze vessels, household utensils of the simpler kind, were probably also made in Nubia. But the more elaborate articles, lamps, censers, paterae—though there may have been Egyptian craftsmen working in Nubia—were probably imported, for in form or decoration they can often be closely paralleled, and sometimes exactly duplicated, from excavations elsewhere. An elaborately engraved bowl from Tomb 37, for instance, with a handle in the form of a lion-cub, gripping two dolphins, has an edging of hemispherical pellets. This is a technique of decoration found frequently at Ballana and Qostol, and very fashionable on bronze and silver vessels of the 5th century throughout the Byzantine world. Then there was the great bronze brazier with 'Vandyke' rim and rectangular swinging handles from Tomb 121. This was a typical Egyptian export which has been found in the

Rhineland and even in Saxon graves in southern England. The bronze flagon with trefoil mouth and high curving handle with thumb-piece from this same tomb is another example of such far-ranging trade. A silver flagon of just this type has been found in Russia and is dated by a hall-mark on its base to the reign of the Emperor Mauricius Tiberius, AD 582-602. Perhaps the most remarkable feature of these products of Egyptian craftsmanship is the persistence of the Hellenistic tradition. Nowhere is this better illustrated than in the elegant bronze standard lamp from the unplundered Tomb 114 in which Eros holds a curving vine-branch supporting a dolphin-shaped lamp to which a Maltese cross has been added. I remember removing the lamp with its cross and showing the statue to a distinguished classical archaeologist. He thought it might belong to the 2nd century AD!

pl 26

But to return to the Ballana tombs, one more, Tomb 118, must be mentioned because from it came the best preserved of all the Ballana crowns, a brilliant affair, jewel-studded, and replete with the emblems of Ancient Egypt seen through the eyes of the Sudanese people of Meroe; the winged *uraei*, topped by the sun disk, and the 'Uatchet' eye of the hawk-headed Horus. This tomb yielded many treasures, an inlaid 'backgammon' board like the one from Tomb 3 at Qostol, another folding stool, and a multitude of bronzes including a large standard lamp, carrying a very prominent Maltese cross, the duplicate of a lamp found in Tomb 95. A pair of bronze scales and several bronze weights inlaid with Greek numerals signifying their denominations showed that the system of weights and measures used in the Byzantine world was understood and used in Nubia. Generally such weights, *exagia*, were engraved with the bust of an Emperor or an official, which would have been invaluable to date this tomb. These, however, were replaced by a cross in the Ballana examples. Scales of this kind, on the simple balance principle, were generally used for weighing coins. But coins, Roman or Byzantine, are exceedingly rare in Nubia, trade with Egypt having been by barter. Probably they were jewellers' scales, for in Tomb 3 at Ballana we found a similar pair, and nearby a gold ring. As in ancient Egypt, nothing was omitted from the tomb which would enable the dead and his attendants to carry on in the Hereafter all the many activities, the amusements, the business transactions, which were part of daily life in Nubia.

pl 16

pl 22

What were our conclusions now that we had explored the majority of the mound tombs at Ballana? They confirmed, even more than our discoveries at Qostol, the close commercial, cultural, and probably political links with neighbouring Christian Egypt. Most important, they confirmed all that we had suspected of the basic cultural inheritance from Meroe, and indeed here at Ballana we found these Nubian chieftains and their spouses buried in the traditional regalia worn by the Meroitic rulers, almost as if they had arrogated to themselves the right of succession to the ancient Meroitic dynasties. Chronologically too, the Ballana discoveries were significant. Christian emblems on imports from Egypt abounded while they were infrequent from Qostol. For this, and other reasons, one can conclude that Qostol, where some tombs were probably of 4th century date, was the earlier cemetery, while some of the tombs at Ballana, Tomb 3 for example, were probably as late as the early sixth century, to judge from the imported silver and bronzes in them.

Who Were the X-Group People?

Surveying all these spectacular discoveries, there are three great obstacles to the solution of the enigma of the 'X-Group'. One is the almost total absence of indigenous written evidence. There are the few Meroitic characters scratched on the spear from Tomb 14 at Qostol, inscribed perhaps by the last man with any knowledge of the Meroitic script so plentiful on the offering tables and funerary stelae from the Meroitic graves in Lower Nubia of the 1st, 2nd, and 3rd centuries AD. Then, in Tomb 2 at Ballana, we found a very curious love-charm, an *Agage*, invoking Isis, written in barbaric Greek impressed on a strip of gold foil which had then been rolled up and thrown into the tomb. This was probably the work of a local scribe or soothsayer and no doubt for these Nubian tribesmen Greek was the *lingua franca* with Egypt, just as Arabic is for Nubians today. But none of this helps

f 7

f 16

to identify the 'X-Group', any more than the Greek inscriptions on the imported amphorae, with the Hellenized, Christian, or Jewish names of Egyptian corn or wine exporters—Heracles, Diocles, Peter, John, Theodore, Isaac and the like.

f 8

In our search for written material, we were not helped by our failure to find the capital city of these obviously settled people which must have been near their royal cemeteries. Had it once been on the island opposite Ballana, subsequently submerged in the storage lake created by the Aswan Dam? Had it been ten miles to the south, at Faras, an important Meroitic and Christian Nubian site? Or is it still to be found below the ruins of the mediaeval hill-city of Jebel Adda, a little to the north of Qostol; a city still unexplored?

Finally there was the state of the human remains. These skulls and bones might have told us something. But here again we were

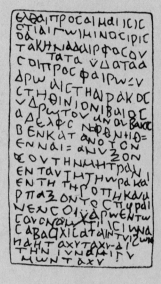

A curious love charm, found in Tomb 2 at Ballana. It was written in barbaric Greek on a piece of gold foil with a stylus, and then rolled up and tossed into the tomb. (16)

frustrated. At Qostol the subsidiary burials, of slaves, grooms and so on, were in good condition and exhibited the racial characteristics of the earlier Meroitic people of Lower Nubia. But then these people formed not the ruling caste, but the substratum of the population. At Qostol, the royal burials had been broken up by the plunderers. At Ballana, it is true, marked negroid or even negro characteristics seemed discernible, but the bones were so fragile and damp-softened that it was impossible to measure them.

How then can one solve the problem of the identity, and origin, of these Qostol-Ballana chieftains? Here archaeology needs literary aid, from papyri, from inscriptions, from the Byzantine historians; and, contrary to belief, this age which Egyptologists have called the 'Dark Age' of Nubian history, is quite well documented. But for perspective, we must first go back to Nubia in Roman times.

The Evidence of History

Lower Nubia was only partially occupied from Egypt by the Romans in or soon after the 1st century BC, their forward zone being a stretch of seventy miles south of the frontier at the First Cataract, known from its length as the Dodecaschoinos, the land of the twelve schoinoi. Here, tactically sited along the west bank of the Nile, the Romans built their characteristic mud-brick forts, not against the Sudanese and Nubian subjects of the Kingdom of Meroe to the south, but against the marauding Blemmyes or Beja nomads of the Eastern Desert. The rulers of Meroe, after their first calamitous encounters with the legionaries, became allies of Rome and maintained a profitable trade along the Nile with the Empire. The Blemmyes, on the other hand, remained implacable enemies, and so devastating were their darting raids over the desert that they gained in the second half of the 3rd century AD several footholds in Roman territory; a factor which, combined with the great poverty of Nubia and the general economic and strategic weakness of the Empire at that time, led the Emperor Diocletian to withdraw his troops to more economical defensive positions at the First Cataract about AD 297. In their place, he introduced the Nobades, of whom we have already heard in the

77

pl 14 Silko inscription. They had come, according to Procopius the Byzantine historian (writing about AD 543), from the neighbourhood of the Kharga Oasis where they had been plundering the Roman settlements and they were subsidized by the Empire—subsidies which continued to his day—as *foederati*, treaty allies, to keep out the Blemmyes, just as the Romans subsidized tribes on the frontier in Northern Britain to keep out the Picts and Scots.

The history of the Lower Nubian Nile Valley after this Roman withdrawal largely consists of the wars and alliances of these two tribes, the Nobades and the Blemmyes, and of their relations with contemporary Egypt. Indeed, the whole key to the X-Group problem lies in the relative geographical distribution within Nubia of these people in relation to the distribution of the X-Group mounds and graves, including the tombs at Ballana and Qostol, of the 4th, 5th and 6th centuries AD. Our first evidence comes from an Egyptian historian, Olympiodorus. Visiting Lower Nubia in AD 421, he found, not the Nobades, but the Blemmyes occupying former Roman territory, with their capital at Kalabsha, their southern frontier at Ibrim. Here then we have confirmation of the Silko inscription, set up in Kalabsha temple, the Blemmyan capital. This in turn confirms what must be inferred from Olympiodorus, namely that the Nobades must have occupied Lower Nubia south of Ibrim, the very region of the Ballana-Qostol tombs. But before these campaigns of Silko, the Nobades and Blemmyes, far from being enemies, were allies in joint raids on Egypt. This can be learnt from the Leyden papyrus which contains an appeal from Bishop Appion of Philae and Syene between AD 425 and 450 for protection for his churches on the frontier against both tribes whose raids about this time, as we know from Coptic sources, often drove deep into Upper Egypt.

In the end, these Nubian forays were too much for Egypt. The tribes were heavily defeated, first by the General Maximinus, then by Florus, prefect of Alexandria, and about AD 453 a treaty was signed at Philae, as a contemporary witness, Priscus, records. This allowed both tribes not only to visit the shrine of Isis there annually but even—and it shows the fear they inspired in Christian Egypt—to carry her statue south by river to their own country. The treaty imposed a peace of one hundred years and it is significant that after this date there are no further references in literature to attacks by the Nobades on Egypt. Indeed, they may have resumed their former alliance with the Empire, for a passage in the *Acta Sanctorum*, referring to events under Justin I (AD 518-527), includes Nobades among Byzantine mercenaries sent to aid the Christian king of Axum (Ethiopia) against the pagan Homeritae of Southern Arabia.

The Conquering Nobades
At the time of the Treaty of Philae, therefore, both tribes were still living on the Nile, the Blemmyes north, the Nobades south of Ibrim presumably, as they had been when Olympiodorus visited Nubia. Then the situation changed. In the second half of the 5th century—and one must assume that the alliance between the tribes preceded rather than followed Silko's invasion of Blemmye territory—the Blemmyes were expelled and the Nobades occupied the valley as far as the First Cataract. Several 6th century sources confirm Silko's claims to this conquest; first Procopius who adds that the Nobades were still receiving subsidies from Egypt in his day; then a historian of the Church, John of Ephesus, who, describing the arrival of the first missionaries in Nubia, declares that on leaving Egypt they entered the kingdom of the Nobades (Syriac *Nabados*); and, finally, a recently discovered Greek inscription of AD 577 found at Ikhmindi, north of Ibrim. This mentions a Christian king of the Nobades, Tokiltoeton, who then ruled that part of Nubia.

This geographical distribution of these two peoples during the period covered by the Ballana-Qostol tombs is of prime importance. Indeed in it lies the solution to the identity of the X-Group and of the royal burials we discovered. The crucial point on the map is Ibrim. The nomad Blemmyes from the Eastern Desert during their evidently temporary occupation in the 5th century were confined to Lower Nubia north of Ibrim. But the royal cemeteries at Ballana and Qostol (certainly in use at that time) lie to the south

of Ibrim, south of the Blemmye frontier, and in the homeland of the Nobades from which their king Silko launched his northward advance. Another significant point is the general distribution of the X-Group cemeteries. These are mostly south of Ibrim. Of these cemeteries, the great mound burials, with horse and animal sacrifices, are all south of Ibrim, not only the royal tombs at Ballana and Qostol but others which have been identified even further south, at Gamai and Firka near the Second Cataract and at Wawa near the Third Cataract, the southernmost place where X-Group remains have been recorded and where incidentally the largest tomb is built of red brick like the Qostol tomb No. 3. True, there are lesser X-Group cemeteries at Ibrim and northwards. But this is to be expected, for ultimately the X-Group Nobades, under Silko, as we have seen, occupied the whole of the Nubian Nile Valley.

Red Noba and Black Noba
This equation of the X-Group rulers with the Nobades is easier to resolve than the problem of the origin of the Nobades. Procopius, writing two centuries after the event, maintains that they came from Kharga Oasis whereas the whole weight of the archaeological evidence from the Ballana-Qostol tombs supports a southern origin. However, as against Procopius, there is other, and contemporary, literary evidence, which seems to favour a southern origin for the Nobades, in an Ethiopic inscription found at Axum, ancient capital of Ethiopia. This, the work of Axum's first Christian king, Ezana (AD 325-375), describes his invasion of the Island of Meroe, then dominated by negro tribes called Black Noba. These Noba, who had apparently occupied Meroe long enough to have absorbed much of the Meroitic culture, appear to have ruled the Sudan as far north as approximately the Third Cataract. Beyond, according to Ezana, lay the kingdom of the 'Red' Noba, a term often used to indicate amalgamation with a fairer-skinned, more advanced population. The position of the frontier between these two presumably related tribal groups is important because it appears to coincide with the southernmost limit of the X-Group culture. Are these Red Noba, then, occupying Upper Nubia in the 4th century, the people whom the Greek writers called Nobades; the Copts of Egypt, Nouba? When Ezana arrived, the Meroitic dynasty, as the result of earlier Axumite invasions, had already fallen. His enemies were the Noba, not the Meroites. Is it not possible that some of these Noba (the ancestors perhaps of the modern Nuba of Southern Kordofan) had already moved north from the Island of Meroe towards Qostol, there—beyond the reach of Axum—to establish a new Kingdom in the old northern Meroitic province, carrying with them the ancient Meroitic royal traditions?

This, built up from the dry bones of archaeology and history together, is one answer to the problem of the identity of the X-Group culture. But the Nobades are not the only candidates, as we have seen. There are the Blemmyes, the nomadic Beja from the Eastern Desert, improbable as this appears. The Italian archaeologist, the late Professor Monneret de Villard, even suggested the possibility of invaders from North-West Africa, by way of Kharga, to fit in with Procopius' ideas. And in time there may be yet other theories for archaeology is a dynamic study and fresh excavations could conceivably throw up some new and revolutionary clue. Indeed, even as this is written, archaeologists from the United Arab Republic are excavating some of the minor tombs and graves at Ballana which we, overwhelmed by the sheer magnitude and richness of our discovery, had to leave untouched. Then there are the other known X-Group settlements and cemeteries to be examined, some during UNESCO's current campaign to save Nubia's ancient heritage from the High Dam floods. There is the fortress city of Jebel Adda which could be the capital of the X-Group people. There is the great cemetery of mound tombs at Wawa, near the turbulent, rock-strewn waters of the Third Cataract; important because it is the southernmost of the known X-Group sites. These and other towns and burial places of Byzantine date must be explored in Nubia before the final verdict on the enigma of the X-Group can be given.

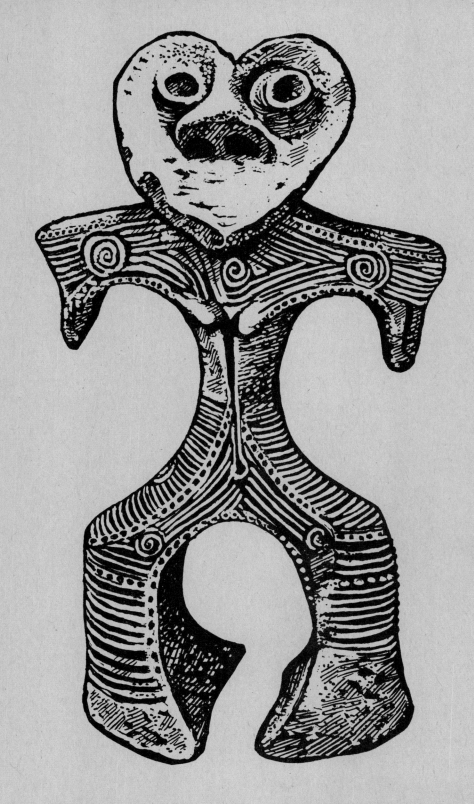

V WHO WERE THE ANCIENT AINU?

Neolithic Japan and the white race of today

WILLIAM WATSON

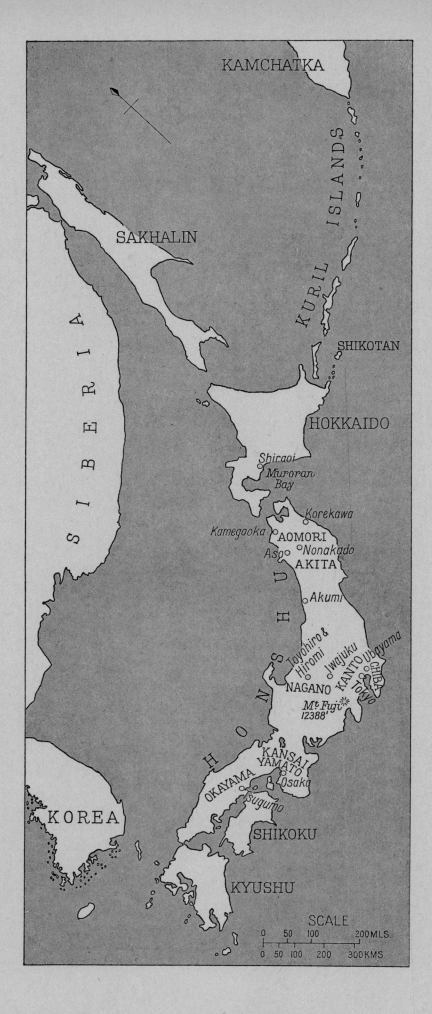

BC		
2000		Early
1000	JŌMON CULTURE	Middle
		Late
c. 200 BC	From the early 3rd century BC, gradual advance from the south of the YAYOI culture, using bronze and iron, reaching central Japan by early 2nd century BC. The Jōmon culture is progressively forced towards the north and west	
AD		
c. 300	PROTODYNASTIC period. The Ebisu (Ainu) occupy the northern part of Honshu and northern islands	
c. 500		
	8th century: Ainu mentioned in Japanese annals	
1000	Ainu treated as a subject people by their Japanese masters. They dwindle in numbers and retreat further north	
c.1880	Ainu living in the Kuril Islands	
1884	By order of the Japanese government, all Kuril Ainu are concentrated in Shikotan, but a few are left on Hokkaido	

In the chronological chart (right) the dates are only approximate, especially before 300 BC. The date of the earliest Jōmon is not known, and claims for a very early date have been made. The limit of 2000 BC indicated here is inferred from the general chronology of Neolithic cultures elsewhere in Asia.

'When our august ancestors descended from heaven in a boat

they found upon this island several barbarous races, the fiercest of whom were the Ainu.' So wrote a Japanese chronicler in the year 712. The Ainu still live in northern Japan – a white race, totally different from their Japanese rulers. But the old description scarcely fits them today; they are a gentle, charming people, dwindling in numbers (at present about 14,000), politically powerless and living on their folk-arts, their traditional dances and curious customs – a survival from the past, a tourist attraction. Who are the Ainu? How long have they lived where they do? Are they the descendants of the Neolithic people who have left such plentiful remains throughout the Japanese islands? These questions are gradually being solved by modern archaeological research.

On special occasions – a dance (above) or the conclusion of a piece of business before witnesses (right) – they don festival costume and revive the ceremonies of their ancestors. An Ainu's dress is one of his most precious possessions. Sixty years ago, when life was harder, it might take a whole year to make one. The patterns are very striking; some are for men, others for women, the distinction being strictly maintained. (1, 2)

Four thousand years ago

the Neolithic inhabitants of Japan, the Jōmon, lived in small villages like the one reconstructed on the right. Their lives were primitive although for food they had abundant fruit, animal-meat such as deer and wild boar, fish—for which they made effective bone hooks and harpoons and used elaborate canoes—and huge quantities of shellfish (the heaps of discarded shells are often our main evidence for a Jōmon village). Settlements were near a source of fresh water and usually within easy distance of the coast. To build their huts they dug a hollow about two feet deep and inserted poles along the edges, sometimes with added support inside. The poles were then slanted inwards and tied together by a ridge-pole; straw or rushes provided the covering, and they were even occasionally paved with stones. The Jōmon people could make cloth and nets, and were accomplished potters—the word 'Jōmon' means 'corded ware'. And they kept dogs. (3)

Like Neolithic peoples everywhere the Jōmon made axe and adze blades of stone for woodcutting and digging. Though agriculture was still rudimentary, the grinding and polishing of stone implements had reached a high technical finish. (4)

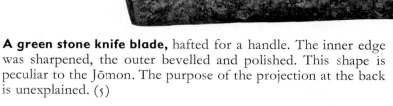

A green stone knife blade, hafted for a handle. The inner edge was sharpened, the outer bevelled and polished. This shape is peculiar to the Jōmon. The purpose of the projection at the back is unexplained. (5)

Arrow-heads of stone and obsidian have been found in great numbers. The earliest types (left, above) have an indented back; later variants (right) show the development of a tang for hafting. (6)

The hearth of a Jōmon house, partially dug out to show how it was made: stone slabs surround it on three sides and in the middle is a large pot without a bottom. (7)

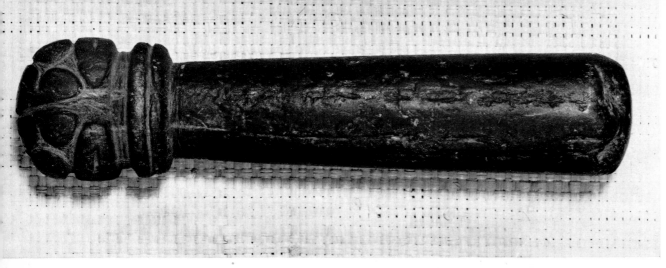

Tools that were never used have been recovered from Jōmon settlements and are thought to have been symbols of authority or to have had a ritual purpose. The 'sceptre' (left) probably began as a small pestle for grinding wild grain, the 'stone hat' (right) as a net-weight, but their careful shaping goes far beyond practical requirements. (8, 9)

What the Jōmon believed about the gods and human destiny is not known with certainty, but by analogy with related cultures we may guess that they had a shamanistic religion and practised magic. Perhaps they worshipped a Mother Goddess. On the right are figurines found in Jōmon burials. Left: Middle Jōmon; narrow eyes and claws suggest a cat rather than a human being; it is over ten inches high. Centre: Latest Jōmon; a mask-like face, slightly tilted back, and thick solid legs; was it meant to be looked at from above? Right: also Latest Jōmon; a complicated silhouette, large head and head-dress and stylized face—the eyes, ears, nose and mouth merely disks of clay. (10, 11, 12)

The 'magatama' or 'bent jewel' – a type famous in imperial times—originated in the Jōmon period. These comma-shaped stones (jade was the favourite material) were attached to the dress by a thread through the hole at one end and perhaps worn as talismans. The form changed little in succeeding centuries; some of the examples shown here may in fact be later. But the variety of ornaments, ear-rings, amulets and pendants prove that love of adornment was strong among the Jōmon people and that they were rich enough to indulge it. (14)

Heart-shaped face tilted back, wide round eyes but no mouth, and limbs formed by cutting out segments of the clay, widely separated legs meeting in a wasp-waist: a strange Late Jōmon figurine nearly a foot high. The patterning of the body is identical with some pottery decoration. (13)

Sun-worship is suggested by several sites in northern Honshu; two concentric stone circles were laid out with a 'sun-dial' arrangement (central standing and radial stones) between the two. The one shown above is at Nonakado. (15)

In this grave, underneath the shell-mound at Tsugumo, a man and a child were buried—the man in the familiar flexed position, the child inside the large jar at his head. Jar-burial seems to have been confined to infants. (16)

Without the potter's wheel and without the kiln the Jōmon craftsmen succeeded in producing a range of ceramic ware that is remarkable for variety and power, though not for technical quality. Shape and ornament changed from period to period, providing a useful method of dating.

'Corded ware' began with simple conical vessels, pointed at the bottom and crudely ornamented with cord-impressions. These soon developed into the type shown above left: the beaded diagonal patterning is made by pressing a cord wound round a stick on to the surface of the soft unfired clay. At a slightly later stage (above right) the rim is moulded and incised decoration is used for the upper part. The cord-marks are now arranged in a herringbone pattern on the body of the pot. (17, 18)

The Japanese tea-pot—at least its form—is four thousand years old. Spouted vessels appear in the Late Jōmon period. This one would have had a removable bamboo or fibre handle. (23)

Arrow-heads and blades of obsidian. Japan is rich in this black volcanic glass which in the smoothness of fracture is superior even to flint and can be brought to a razor-sharp edge. (24)

With maturity comes freedom and extravagance. The three Middle period pots (left and above) show the extreme of elaboration—curved shapes, lavish appliqué decoration and rims so fulsomely ornate that the pots must have been almost impossible to use. In the Late period (right) a return is made to the earlier simplicity: straight sides and incised patterns instead of appliqué. (19, 20, 21, 22)

Pottery techniques were used in this clay mask, where eye and mouth outlines are cord-marked. It is nearly six inches across and presumably had a religious function like the clay figurines. (25)

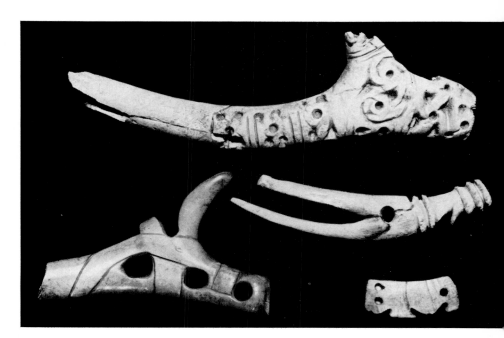

Boar's tusks and deer's antlers provided horn and ivory to be decorated by carving. The purpose of these strange objects is not known, but possibly they were ornaments of bow or spear. (26)

Were the Jōmon the ancient Ainu?

This is the great question of Japanese prehistory. The resemblances between them are striking but not conclusive. So it is useful at this stage to look at what the Ainu were like in the last century, when they were racially purer and with a culture still vigorously alive. We are lucky in having numerous illustrations of the Ainu way of life made by interested Japanese artists, most notably Tomioka Tessai around 1890. At that time Ainu religion (and to a large extent social life) centred on the bear-cult. Like other primitive peoples they believed that a special affinity existed between themselves and the animal kingdom. The bears were hunted as they were rousing themselves from their winter sleep; the object—a difficult and dangerous one—was to capture a cub alive. This would then be carefully tended ('The bear cubs are treated better than the children,' wrote a 19th century missionary)

until it was full-grown. Then it was sacrificed at a great festival. At the bottom of the picture (right, fold-out) we see the event. First an Ainu would go to the bear, sit down before it and tell it that they were sending it to join its forefathers, ask its pardon, and beg it not to be angry. The bear is then taken from its wooden cage (bottom right), and dragged with ropes, its human foster-mother following weeping behind it, to a place where two tree-trunks have been lashed together. Its neck is pushed between them and the poor beast choked to death by men jumping on the upper log. The body is then laid on a mat (top right), precious weapons are hung up behind and offerings placed before it. The men on the right are busy making *inao*. While this is happening the rest of the company join in an exuberant dance (top left). The day ends with a lavish feast, eating the bear's body and consuming huge quantities of intoxicating *sake*. (27)

After the killing the body was laid out in state. Ancient (Japanese) swords lie on either side and *inao* (sacred sticks) have been set up in the ground. Cakes in a lacquered bowl and two *sake*-salvers and cups contain the offerings. Two Ainu are exchanging salutations (a slow and lengthy procedure) and are about to partake of the *sake* in front of them. The clothes are of Japanese origin. (28)

Outside the village they built a wooden hut, a 'bear-chapel'. There the bear's head and part of the skin were fixed to a screen. Weapons and precious articles were again put out on display; *inao* were set up inside and out. In this painting (by Shunri of Chishima) five men, a woman and a child are seen at the feast. The men have their foreheads shaved; the one on the right is drinking and using his moustache-lifter. Note the criss-cross tattoo-marks on the woman's wrists, neck and lower part of cheek, a popular Ainu beauty-treatment. (29)

An Ainu village, with its busy life and varied occupations, is shown in another of Tomioka Tessai's paintings (below). The women are weaving (top left) and looking after the children, while some of the men go fishing with nets (top right). At the bottom we see how a new hut was built. First the wood is cut and roughly shaped with axes. Then they make the roof by lashing logs together and securing them by a ridge-beam. Poles are driven directly into the ground and the complete roof is lifted bodily on to them (in the picture this takes sixteen men). Finally the whole framework is thatched with reeds. As a man grew richer he would enlarge his house, the old one forming a porch or annexe to the new—hence the often irregular shapes. Note also the storehouse, on stilts as a protection against rats, the bear-cage with a cub inside, the fish hanging to dry and the group of sacred *inao* in front of the big finished hut. The interior view (left centre) shows the Ainu's sparse furniture and belongings—a bow and quiver, spear, swords and hangers and vessels for *sake*. The family sit on mats. The fireplace is in the middle, with a cauldron hanging over it on a chain. (32, 33)

The smoking habit is not an ancient Ainu custom: they learnt it from the Japanese. But their carved walnut tobacco-boxes and pipe-holders are often very old and highly prized, sometimes even being buried with their owners. The man shown here, seated on his mat and preparing to smoke, has beside him his bowl of *sake* with cup, saucer and moustache-lifter. (30)

'Instead of armour they have coats of small planks fastened together, which is ridiculous to look upon.' The Jesuit who wrote this in 1622 mistook the native Ainu bark-costume for armour. It was the ordinary working-dress. In this picture by Toyosuke of Nagasaki, the Ainu (a particularly hairy specimen) holds his pipe and bow and carries a quiver slung from the forehead. (31)

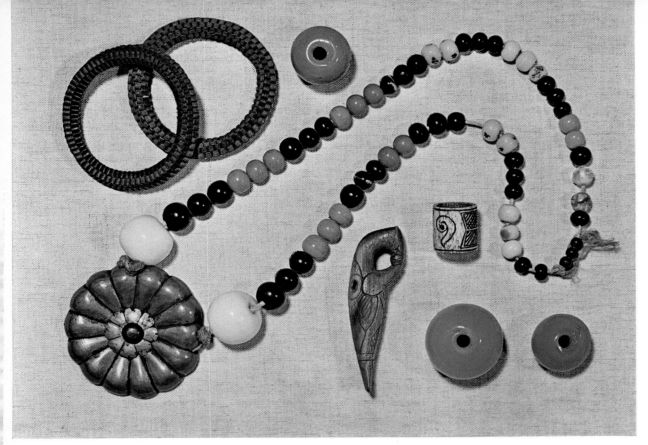

The Ainu of today
present a puzzling mixture of cultures. Sometimes they seem to be continuing Jōmon traditions; the huts they live in, the designs on their wooden utensils and woven fabrics show resemblances that can hardly be accidental. In other ways they are clearly influenced by the Japanese, and in others again they are purely themselves.

From Japan comes the bead necklace and possibly other items in this assortment of Ainu jewellery. The disk is of metal, the graceful pendant of ivory. (34)

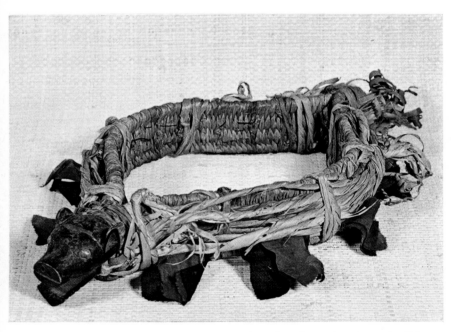

A ceremonial head-dress, made of reeds and coloured ribbons, with a miniature wooden bear's head at the front. These can be seen being worn in plates 1 and 2. (35)

Wooden sandals, which were Japanese in origin, also had a ceremonial use. Today the Ainu normally wear mocassins. In old illustrations they are nearly always barefoot. (36)

Carved wooden dishes, with delicate curvilinear ornament, are amongst the most attractive and typical works of Ainu craftsmanship. The ornament is reminiscent of that found in some classes of Jōmon pottery. (37)

Richly embroidered and decorated with appliqué work, an Ainu's ceremonial costume is an heirloom and a work of art. Both these examples are women's dresses. The left-hand one is made of black cotton fabric with fine beige stripes and appliqué of coarser material in red and white. (38, 39)

A lacquer tea-set from Japan standing on an Ainu mat and with an Ainu moustache-lifter laid across the cup. (40)

A hat for everyday made of grass sewn together with coloured thread. (42)

A quiverful of arrows was carried by the Ainu huntsman either over one shoulder or slung from the forehead, as in plate 31. (43)

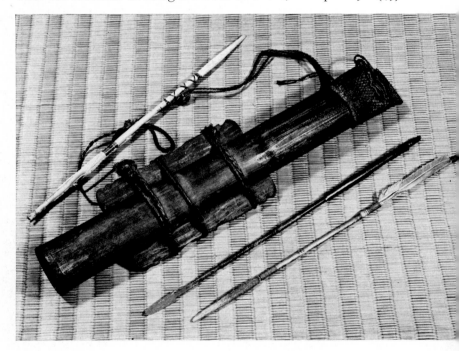

Strange sacred sticks, the *inao*, are set up in groups at the eastern end of every Ainu house (see plates 32, 33). They are willow-wands, whittled down and left with the shavings hanging. Here the skull of a wolf has been placed in a cleft stick between two *inao* as an offering to the gods. (41)

How moustache-lifters function is shown in plate 29. It is considered bad manners and even impious to allow one's moustache to go into the wine one is drinking. They were also used for offering drops of wine to the gods, by sprinkling from one end. Of these examples the upper is for ceremonial, the lower for everyday use. (44)

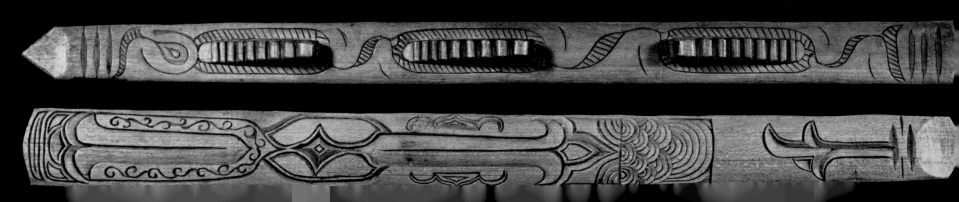

Neolithic Japan and the white race of today

WILLIAM WATSON

THE AINU, the hirsute and fair-skinned aborigines of Japan, enjoy a double celebrity. They are classed by anthropologists as a distinct and remotely isolated branch of the white race which farther west comprises the inhabitants of Europe and much of western Asia. Moreover, the living representatives of the Ainu people have a very good claim to be the descendants of the first inhabitants of the Japanese islands, who found themselves forced to retreat before the Japanese invaders. Their rôle as opponents of the newcomers is involved with the earliest history of the Japanese state and has been the subject of a debate which sharply divided Japanese historians in recent times. The crux of the problem is the connexion between the Ainu, as they have been described in the last century and are known today, with the Jōmon people whose relics form the earliest cultural stage in the archaeological record of Japan. But the modern Ainu are not conscious of any past glory. Their history as underdogs has reduced them to a humble status beside their conquerors. If any sense of cultural purpose persists among them to-day it is to preserve what remains of their traditional craft and customs for the profitable

pl 1
2

One of the earliest photographs of Ainu shows a group of them entertaining officers and men on the deck of a Japanese warship.

The Ainu today display a greater degree of racial unity than the very mixed population of Japanese. They are of medium height and averagely heavy build, with clear skin, and the men have abundant hair. Their skulls are longer than those of the universally round-headed Japanese, and by this token are classed as mesocephalic or sub-dolichocephalic Caucasoids, with the square face and high forehead characteristic of this race. Contact with the Mongoloid peoples of east Asia has left its mark in the Ainu's prominent cheek-bones; the slanting eyes which are another dominant trait of Mongol race are less common among the islanders.

pl 1
2

Ainu and Jōmon in Neolithic Japan

The historical problem which centres on the Ainu is the question of their descent both culturally and racially from the population represented by remains of Neolithic type which are found over the whole of Japan. These remains, it is generally thought, represent the pre-Japanese settlement of the territory, which as an archaeological division is termed the Jōmon (or 'corded pattern') culture, after the string-marked and mat-marked patterns which are the commonest form of decoration used on the pottery.

pl 17
18

To an observer unfamiliar with the detours of archaeological argument the identity might seem self-evident, for there is an obvious generic likeness between the ornament of Jōmon pottery and the ornament still used on carved wood and textiles by modern Ainu. But explanations of this resemblance other than that of direct descent can be entertained. Japanese theorists, ever reluctant to admit that an Ainu population once dominated over the whole of their islands, have on occasion resorted to curious reasoning. The view of traditional history, indeed the facts recorded in the official annals of the Japanese court compiled in the early 8th century AD, the *Kojiki* and the *Nihon Shoki*, is that barbarians occupied the north-eastern part of the main

pl 22
37
38
39
f 1
2
3
4

Jōmon and Ainu designs, showing their similarities and possible continuity. 1. Ainu wooden platter; 2. underside of a late-Jōmon pottery bowl; 3. decoration on an Ainu knife-sheath; 4. upper part of a late-Jōmon pot. (1–4)

entertainment of the tourists and anthropologists who still seek them out.

In 1920 the Ainu population amounted to some 17,000 of whom 1500 inhabited Hokkaido and the remainder the southern half of the island of Sakhalin and the island of Shikotan, the southernmost of the island chain of the Kuriles extending far to the north of the main islands of the Japanese archipelago. In recent times small scattered groups of Ainu were still to be found on the farther islands of the Kuriles, but in 1884 these were concentrated on Shikotan by the Japanese government. Thus finally was consummated the policy of despotic control directed at the national minority during some two thousand years. Intermarriage with the Japanese in recent years and probably from the start has reduced the size of the Ainu community, and today only about 14,000 remain distinct. They inhabit a few small and primitive villages on the coast of Hokkaido along Muroran bay, and a smaller number of villages in the inland hills. They live by expert fishing, a little simple agriculture and by selling skins and seaweed to the Japanese. Their music and dancing are highly regarded.

pl 1

island of Honshu, fought with the Japanese and were gradually pushed northwards. The annals nowhere mention the possibility of the presence in central Japan of any occupants earlier than the Japanese themselves. The latter believed that they were descended from the Sun Goddess Amaterasu, who created their land expressly for them.

But even in the 8th century there is a record of notice paid to the great heaps of shells so frequently found near what are now recognized to have been Jōmon habitation sites. In the *Hitachi Fudo-ki* the shell-heaps are correctly termed food-refuse and described as the traces of a race of giants whose footsteps measured more than thirty paces. Under the year corresponding to AD 839 there is mention of a find of stone arrow-heads on the beach at Akumi after a thunderstorm. This place is on the west coast where no barbarians of the so-called Ebisu race (or, as is contended, the ancient Ainu) were supposed ever to have been. The find was taken as an omen of imminent attack by unspecified enemies and countermeasures were prepared. It is interesting to note that two historians writing in the early 18th century (when it was

f 9

pl 6

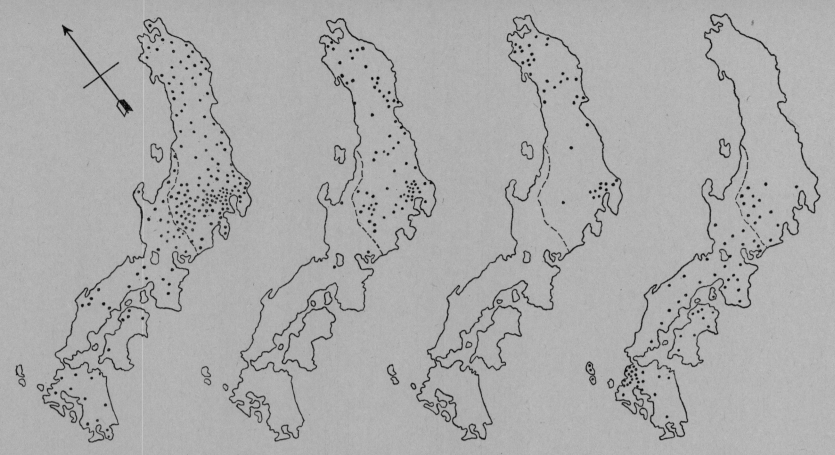

Japan in the 3rd century AD. The dotted line on each map represents the divisions between Japanese and Ebisu (Ainu) at that date. Left to right: Map 1—Distribution of Neolithic sites (each dot = 50 sites). Map 2—Distribution of late Jōmon figurines (dot = 5 sites). Map 3—Distribu- *tion of the late-Jōmon spouted vessels (dot = 5 sites). The concentrations suggest a gradual retreat to the north-west of the Jōmon population. Map 4—Distribution of aneolithic (Yayoi) sites (dot = 10 sites), suggesting the spread of the earliest phase of the incoming Japanese civilization. (5–8)*

known that finds of stone arrow-heads were particularly common in the north-west of Honshu) still avoided the conclusion that the Ebisu barbarians were ever more widely spread from the north-west than the tradition allowed. One writer suggested that the stone points had been left by a foray of Tungusic barbarians from the mainland, which is possible if improbable, and the other that the arrow-heads had been shot at geese far away in the ancient Ebisu territory, had remained fixed in the birds and so got carried to the west coast.

The scientific study of the Neolithic remains of Japan was begun by the Germans F. and H. Siebold and the American E. S. Morse. The first two believed that the Jōmon culture was the work of the ancient Ainu. Morse disagreed but still maintained that the Jōmon race, occupying the whole of Japan, was distinct from the Japanese. Opposing views were adopted by Japanese scholars. Tsuboi agreed with Morse's rejection of the Ainu theory, but with a curious corollary, for he proposed to identify the Jōmon people with the Koropokkuru of Ainu legend, a race of men measuring only a few inches in height as the story goes, who lived under the leaves of a coltsfoot plant. Kogane defended the identity of the Jōmon with the Ainu, and thus a polemic was launched which in altered terms continues among Japanese scholars up to the present time.

In more recent years, both in Japan and in the West, the view that the bearers of Jōmon culture were the ancestors of the modern Ainu has gained ground, but has still not been proved to everyone's satisfaction. The human bones excavated from Jōmon graves have been brought into the debate on both sides. Both differences and similarities between the Jōmon and modern Ainu skeletons are observable, and different selected evidence has been used by supporters and antagonists of the 'Ainu theory'. It is certain that the physical character of the ancient race, as revealed by the study of bones, is not identical with that of the modern Ainu. But if the latter are, as they admittedly must be, a local tiny remnant of the early population, mixed in the course of their more recent history with other differing but related peoples from remoter islands, then the skeletal divergences need not be an obstacle to belief in the descent from

pl 16

Jōmon to modern Ainu. The majority of ethnologists now accept this view. Thus, though Jōmon man may not be identical with the modern Ainu by the standards of the living representatives, there is no insuperable argument against equating him with the ancient Ainu, rather than with the ancestors of the modern Japanese.

In Japan the 'Ainu theory' now prevails. In the 1920's however another theory was propounded which has proved less widely acceptable and is singularly at variance with the traditional trend of Japanese thought. This is that the Jōmon people were simply the ancestors of the modern Japanese. On this view the arrival of the Japanese in the islands is put back to the Neolithic period and the Ainu are excluded, by a fresh argument, from any rôle in the major cultural history of the land. But the evidence of archaeology speaks strikingly against this view, for it reveals a sharp division between the Jōmon culture and the following bronze-using and iron-using cultures which developed continuously into the recorded beginnings of the historical Japanese state. Whatever was the degree of racial mixing between the ancient Ainu and the Japanese, and some mixing must have been inevitable, the archaeological picture shows the Jōmon culture, and hence the Ainu race, as a coherent group which remained outside the Japanese cultural and racial sphere.

At the Dawn of Japanese History

The cleavage between the Jōmon culture and what follows it is marked as much by the geographical distribution as by the nature of sites and artifacts. The cultural succession is as follows:

1. Jōmon Neolithic:
From an unknown antiquity, probably in the second millennium BC, extending in Kyushu down to about 300 BC; in the Kansai (the region around Kyoto, in Honshu) to about 200 BC; progressively later towards the north and west.

2. Yayoi culture, using bronze and iron:
Succeeding the Jōmon progressively and lasting until about AD 300.

3. Protodynastic period (Period of the Great Tombs):
The gradual consolidation of the Japanese state, which formed probably from the start in Yamato (the plain north of the modern Osaka, in Honshu), though according to some with beginnings in Kyushu, as related in the Japanese annals. This period is regarded as beginning about AD 300 and lasting until the beginning of the Asuka period in AD 538.

Systematic archaeological research in Japan, dating from the beginning of the present century, has produced a vast number of sites and a quantity of material comparable to that recovered by similar research in European countries. Unfortunately, despite the great volume of published material and the numerous popular expositions based upon it, Japanese writers have shown themselves reluctant to summarise the results of archaeological work in the form of distribution maps covering the whole country. The maps prepared however by J. Schnell in 1928, based on Japanese site lists, supply a strong argument for the mutual exclusiveness of the Jōmon and Yayoi cultures and for the recognition of the former as the culture of the Ebisu, the ancient Ainu, who retreated before Japanese pressure.

In the maps the dotted line crossing Honshu from north to south marks the approximate division of Japanese and Ainu at the end of the 3rd century AD. Each dot in Map 1 represents 50 Neolithic sites and the greater concentration of them in the north-west of central Honshu seems to indicate a longer survival of the Jōmon culture in this region than elsewhere, thus suggesting the gradual retreat of the Jōmon population from the south-west as the Japanese penetrated into this part of the country. Map 2 shows the distribution of Jōmon pottery figurines. These are specially numerous in the latest stage of the culture, which on the evidence of the geographical distribution thus appears farther confined north-westwards. The evidence of the spouted clay vessels, also a late-Jōmon feature, is shown in Map 3, and reflects a farther move of the Jōmon boundary to the north-west in the final stage of Jōmon culture. Conversely the distribution of sites shown on Map 4, that of aeneolithic sites (which would now mostly be termed Yayoi) marks the spread of the earliest phase of Japanese civilization.

Although more recent research has elaborated the classification of Jōmon potteries by defining local characteristics more closely, the broad succession of types established a generation ago still holds good. The spouted pots are still placed in the latest phase of the culture. The general movement or contraction of population demonstrated by the geographical distribution of the main pottery types, which supports the scant historical data, is not seriously questioned by archaeologists.

The Jōmon Culture

In European archaeology the term 'Neolithic' is applied mostly to communities which wholly or to a considerable degree are food-producers as opposed to mere food-gatherers. In the most favoured centres of Neolithic culture both east and west the rise of farming, both crop-growing and stock-raising, coincides with the adoption of other characteristic techniques: superior stone-working in the manufacture of weapons and tools, the discovery of the potter's art and of weaving. But on the fringes of the Neolithic culture of the good valley lands there is generally found a zone in which some or all of the new arts other than farming itself are known, while food is obtained by hunting and gathering in the old way. By these tokens the Jōmon culture, in the earlier part of its history at least, was such a case of retarded Neolithic culture. It is generally contended that the Jōmon people knew nothing of agriculture or animal husbandry, and it is clear that even if these were practised eventually (possibly under Japanese influence) their rôle was negligible compared to the place taken in the economy by hunting and fishing. Parallels can be drawn with the partial Neolithic cultures of Europe and north China. The great reliance the Jōmon people placed on easily gathered shell-fish as a source of food in addition to the yield of the hunting and fishing is a trait linking them with their earlier cultural compeers in the west, particularly in the northern European coastal regions. Only the most primitive

Neolithic economies resorted to this humblest of foods as a staple diet.

It was long thought that the remains of Jōmon culture represented the earliest sign of human life on the Japanese islands. Only in recent years has it been suggested, with reasonable evidence, that man was present there even before the knowledge of Neolithic arts had penetrated to Japan from the mainland of Asia. The problem for archaeologists interested in this question was to demonstrate that a stone-using culture, of Palaeolithic or Mesolithic type, lacking pottery, ante-dated the earliest Jōmon sites. Finds of stone tools divorced from pottery and other evidence of Jōmon settlement could not alone prove this contention. The difficulty of the case can be appreciated by considering the geological conditions prevailing over the greater part of central Japan.

In the Kantō, the region of the central eastern portion of the main island, forming the hinterland of Tokyo, the chief superficial deposit is a loam composed of layers of volcanic ash mixed with clay, a circumstance witnessing to the ancient violent activity of Mount Fuji and other volcanoes. The loam varies in thickness from a few inches to a few yards and is covered by a thin layer of humus, the modern soil, which seldom attains a depth of more than a foot or two. All Jōmon remains that have been found buried and undisturbed have been in the humus, or at most in the topmost part of the loam. But on at least one site, Iwajuku near Tokyo, stone tools of pre-Neolithic type were recovered from positions deep in the loam, so that a pre-Jōmon date is arguable for them. The earlier toolbearing level at Iwajuku was some six feet below the ground surface and contained two pieces of shale with trimmed edges, somewhat resembling the hand-axes of the European Palaeolithic. A higher level, still well below the humus, yielded blade-like implements of shale, the succession of tool types thus conforming broadly to that observed in Palaeolithic cultures elsewhere in Europe and Asia.

Such evidence from an isolated site is treated however with

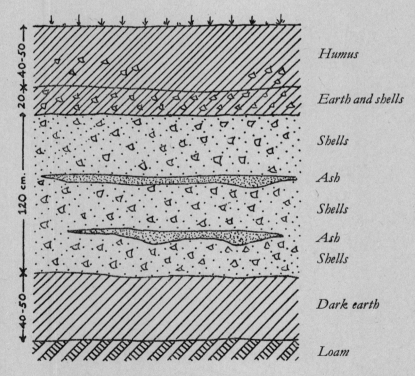

Section through the Kasori shell-mound, where the ash-layers suggest a break in occupation. All Jōmon remains have been found in the topmost levels of soil sections; stone tools from deep in the loam suggest pre-Jōmon dates, resembling the European Palaeolithic. (9)

caution, some critics maintaining that the alleged tools are natural products. Other finds of alleged Palaeolithic tools, lacking the support of stratigraphical evidence of date, have been criticised as being either stones not shaped by man at all, or as belated and degenerate stone-working. The position of the Iwajuku implements, if they are to be accepted as such, shows them to belong to a very early date, certainly in the Pleistocene period, possibly

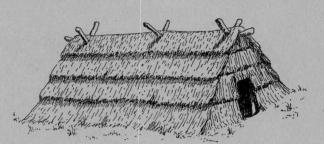

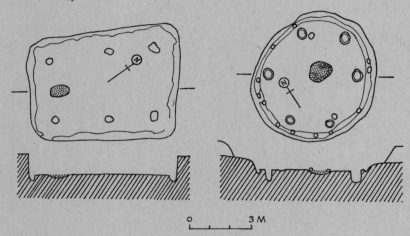

The two types of Jōmon pit-dwellings, rectangular and round, with (right) their ground-plans and sections. A typical house would be 12 to 15 feet wide, with a floor-level dug out to a depth of about 2 feet. (10–13)

even as early as the time when the Japanese islands were still attached to the continent. The absence or sparseness of traces of human habitation in the long age which separated the Iwajuku tools from the earliest Jōmon remains is perhaps to be explained (as far as concerns the Kantō, where research has been concentrated) simply as a result of the unfavourable living conditions of a volcanic region. But when the earliest Jōmon settlements were made the climatic and volcanic conditions of the country were not much different from those of the present time.

Shell-heaps: the First Jōmon Settlements

f 9 The most characteristic surviving token of Jōmon habitation is a mound, now partly or wholly buried, consisting of food debris, of which shells form by far the largest component. Shell-fish were eaten in such quantities that their remains accumulated rapidly. The shell-heaps vary in extent from a few square yards in the earliest period to areas of two acres or more at the largest settlements of the middle and late periods. The shells were tipped in fairly orderly fashion near the houses or on the fringe of a village, or thrown down on lower ground. The size of the mounds is broadly a measure of the size of a settlement, though it would naturally vary with the varying length of occupation of the site. As far as may be judged from the signs of rebuilding or extending the houses the settlements were not inhabited for very considerable spaces of time. Compared to the size of population to be expected in such primitive conditions of life the large number of sites recorded, running into several thousands, itself suggests frequent changes of habitation. The movement took place probably as much by water as by land, so that the thick woods and accidented granitic terrain need not have offered a serious obstacle to the migrations.

The kinds of shell-fish gathered for food, distinguished as fresh-water and salt-water species, and species favouring warmer or cooler water, supply interesting evidence of human movement and of climatic conditions. Investigation on these lines conducted in the region of east Honshu around Tokyo bay have shown that in the early Jōmon period the shore line was some distance (in some places over thirty miles) from its present position. Early sites marked by mounds containing salt-water shells conform to a shore line which is now far inland. Sites of the late Jōmon period, still associated with salt-water shells, are in general nearer to the shore of today. At the same time the presence of warm-water shells of species no longer found in the vicinity of Tokyo bay, suggests a cooling of the climate during the last three millennia. During the Jōmon period the sea gradually retreated, the narrow coastal plain widened somewhat, and sites of middle and late Jōmon date advanced nearer to the present coast.

pl 3 Nearly all the known Jōmon sites are located where water is still found, or where it can be inferred to have existed in ancient time, whether inlets from the sea, lakes, rivers or streams. The farther the sites are located from the ancient shore or lake bank the greater is the proportion of fresh-water shells contained in the midden mounds. The habitations were mostly on flat-topped knolls, hill spurs or ridges, the shell-mounds extending from the edge of these eminences. In the acid conditions of the Japanese soil the shells were the most durable contents of the mounds, but

An excavated pit-dwelling. The hearth is placed nearly in the middle, and in the north-west corner (left in the drawing) was a stone platform with a slender upright stone—a sort of family altar or shrine. (14)

bones of birds, fish and other animals, sometimes human bones, and potsherds and even wooden objects have also been excavated from them.

The Jōmon Pit-dwellings

The sizes of Jōmon villages are difficult to determine accurately, for there is often evidence of later houses being built over older ones, or of old house sites being used for shells and other refuse. But 23 houses traced at Ubayama in Chiba and over 100 at Toyo-hira in Nagano Ken seem for the most part to have been occupied contemporaneously. Instances are known of caves and rock-shelters used as habitations, but the Jōmon people lived mostly in huts, built either on ground level or more frequently with floors sunk below the surrounding ground. These so-called pit-dwellings are similar to those made in the Neolithic period in north China. The sunken floor must have had its inconveniences, particularly in so damp a country as Japan, and no satisfactory explanation of it has been offered other than that of heightening the head room of the hut without enlarging and complicating the timber structure of walls and roof.

f 10
11
12
13
14

The typical plans are circular and rectangular, measuring four or five yards across and sunk to a depth of one or two feet. The traces of post-holes aligned along the edge of the pit and on the sunken floor give clues to the structure. The wall posts were closer and slenderer than those nearer the centre of the hut, which were fewer, thicker and more widely spaced. This arrangement indicates a steep-raking roof, and to judge from later tradition (both Ainu and Japanese) the Jōmon roofs are likely to have been conical in the case of circular plans and pyramidal with rectangular plans, the eaves reaching to within a few feet of the ground or even touching it.

Archaeologists' reconstructions of the houses usually allow the possibility of openings like dormer-windows in two opposed slopes of the roof, forming brief gables at the apex like those of the traditional farmers' houses of Japan. Nothing survives upon excavation to show the nature of the material used in covering the roof, which must therefore have been of branches or rushes, anticipating the superb rice-straw thatch of the later buildings.

pl 7
f 12
13
14

Some house floors of the earliest Jōmon period, which are mostly rectangular, reveal no trace of hearths within, and a hearth is then generally found a few paces from the hut; but in the middle and late periods, when round and near-round houses were favoured, the hearths are indoors, first near a wall, later in the middle of the floor. The gable openings would give the smoke an escape. The hearth is often sunk into the ground and surrounded by a setting of largish boulders.

Some of the latest Jōmon houses abandon the pit plan, being built on ground level with floors paved with stone. Sometimes excavation has demonstrated that a house was enlarged by an annex. The number of people who lived in a typical hut may perhaps be judged from an excavation which revealed the bodies of five persons of different age and sex lying inside a hut measuring four by five metres, though since there was nothing to show how they met their deaths one cannot be certain that they were the living occupants. The suggestion that they were all killed by the fall of the roof seems improbable in view of the comparatively light materials that must have been used in the building.

The 'Corded Pattern': Jōmon Pottery

pl 17
18
19

In Japan as elsewhere in north Asia and Europe the corded decoration was applied to pottery by impressing on the soft, unfired clay a small stick or roller on which plaited (less frequently simply twisted) cord had been closely wound. The impressions of the beaded surface of the cord lie in adjacent lines, so that within the area of the pattern no smooth surface appears. A practical motive for the adoption of this method of decoration in the beginning may have been the need to press the clay to increase its density and to ensure that no air pockets were left in it to burst when the pottery was fired. Another suggestion was that the ornament arose from the practice of forming vessels on the inside of plaited straw baskets, which were burnt away on firing; but the recognition that the marks on the pottery surface are impressions of cord and not basket-work has disproved this view. The clay of Jōmon pottery seems to have received little other treatment aimed at refining it. The cording was exploited as a means of satisfying the eye.

Japanese archaeologists are accustomed to dividing the Jōmon culture into five successive stages. The first is characterized by vases of approximately conical shape, pointed at the bottom or standing on a disproportionately small round foot. In some pieces the mouth trumpets out slightly towards the lip, or is given a shallow convex moulding, with a wavy lip rising to three or four points. There is no sign of the use of any turning device in their manufacture, much less of a fast potter's wheel. Neither from this earliest or from any later stage of the culture have traces of pottery kilns been found, and it is presumed that the pots were fired on the ground after being covered with the twigs and branches that provided the fuel. The firing temperature can seldom have been over 500 or 600 degrees Centigrade. This low firing, combined with the impurities in the clay (the amount of vegetable matter remaining in the clay is the chief reason for the dark brown or black colour of the pottery) produced a porous, crumbly ware which stands at the bottom of the scale of ceramic quality. It is the expressiveness of the ornament and the inventive shaping which give Jōmon pottery its distinction among the primitive

pl 17
18

potteries of mankind. Nowhere is the contrast between the refinement of ornament and the primitiveness of the potter's methods more striking.

In the earliest stages the ornament is applied from simply twisted rather than properly corded string. Equally common is the use of a small wooden roller carved with incisions somewhat resembling the string marks. Sometimes an irregular pattern of crinkly lines was made with the edge of a shell. All the technical elements of Jōmon ceramic art were present at the beginning of the tradition. The special exploitation of devices such as applied ribbons of clay, moulded and wavy formation of the vessel lip and the incision of bands of parallel lines with a comb-like instrument, varied in degree at different times and in different regions. Linear ornament lies either erratically or in distinct bands composed usually of echelons of herring-bone.

pl 20

The middle stage of the development is characterized by the predominance of true corded pattern. Now the foot of the vessel is larger and well formed, the profiles still mainly conical, with convex or concave sides and larger trumpeting mouths. There is a greater tendency to place linear designs of triangles and waves against a plain ground. Occasionally some traces of red painting of haematite appear. The most original invention of the Jōmon potter appears in the middle stage of the development. The greatest delight is now taken in waved and moulded rims so elaborate that any practical purpose of the vessels on which they stand seems to be jeopardized. The wavy lip, rising to two or three ever higher points, is usually defined by a heavy grooved moulding, and this line is repeated by a similar moulding a few inches below, so that the resulting heavy collar dominates the profile. Between the two lines of moulding are generally placed patterns of bands formed by cording or applying strips of clay, in serpentine or alternating triangular or semicircular shapes, while zones of cording cover the rest of the vessel sides. Sometimes on the sides also the cording is reserved into panels of oval, undulating or hour-glass units against a plain ground.

pl 19
20
21

Regional differences become more perceptible. Pots found in the Kansai are often decorated with vertical bands of cording over which are impressed curved marks made with the end of a piece of bamboo. In Kyushu is found a family of vessels devoid of cording, on which some incised grooves around the lip provide the only ornament. While it is possible that the most elaborate of the Jōmon vases were made to honour the dead at burial, there is no clear line to be drawn regarding either ornament or shapes between the vessels placed in graves and those made for ordinary use.

The fourth chronological division of the Jōmon wares introduces a new technique in rendering the ornament. The whole pot is covered with cord impressions and a pattern is drawn by incised line over it, the unwanted patches of cording then being wiped smooth. This convenient method encouraged the elaboration of curvilinear designs whose oddly unpredictable movement is intimately characteristic of Jōmon art. At this stage appear the spouted vessels, squat in shape, with narrow mouths surmounted by large rings intended for tying on a lid, presumably made of wood since no examples survive. The spouted vessels surprisingly prefigure the shape of tea-pots in use in Japan two thousand years later.

pl 23

The latest stage in the Jōmon ceramic history is represented by the fulsomely ornate vessels found in the north-east of Honshu, especially at the rich excavated site of Kamegaoka. It is probable that the Jōmon people were to some extent in contact with the invading Yayoi population which was pushing them towards the north-west. Certain pedestal bowls, shallow basins and vases on a small splayed foot, though potted and decorated in the Ainu manner, reflect a Yayoi influence in their shapes. But the Yayoi pottery, wheel-turned, hard-fired and very restrained in ornament is at the opposite pole artistically and technically from the exuberant Jōmon creations.

When they were confined to the north-east the Jōmon potters gradually lost the most vital part of their decorative sense, the vigour of their work declined and they were increasingly satisfied with a relatively insignificant profusion of the traditional elements of pattern, applied to vessels whose more timid shapes

99

only echo the splendid old extravagance. Soon the Jōmon ancestors of the Ainu were to lose the art of pottery altogether, as they came to be overshadowed culturally and economically by their Japanese masters. Their delight was to the last in their abstract ornament, in which human, animal or vegetable forms played no part. This bias survived in the ornament used by their descendants on carved wood and textiles.

Weapons and Tools of Hunters and Gatherers

The tools and weapons of Jōmon man were very similar to those used by prehistoric communities living in comparable climatic and geographic environments in other and distant parts of the world. The equipment of the Peterborough Neolithic culture of England, whose pots represent the farthest western outpost of the tradition of corded ware, was essentially little different from that of Neolithic Japan. The Jōmon people enjoyed an advantage in material for tool-making through the numerous deposits of obsidian, a natural black glass, which Japan owes to its volcanic constitution. This substance occurs in Hokkaido, in central and east Honshu and in Kyushu. In the smoothness of fracture it is superior even to flint, and the arrow-heads and blades manufactured from it are among the finest examples of their kind. Chert, nephrite and shale were commonly used, but with them such refined fashioning was scarcely possible.

The chief Jōmon weapon was the bow, as shown by the numerous stone and obsidian arrow-heads occurring on the sites. They display a greater variety of shapes than is found in any other primitive culture. The earliest are triangular, without a tang, the back edge convex or deeply indented. Arrow-heads with a tang for mounting are found from the second of the five chronological stages onwards, but form the majority only in the fourth stage, especially in the north of the main island to which the culture was now increasingly confined. The largest specimens measure up to two and a half inches in length, while a minority are so small, measuring a bare half inch, that they have been suspected of having been made for a ritual rather than a practical purpose. Some longer pieces, shaped like a willow leaf, served as knives, and in a few instances a piece preserves traces of the resin used in attaching them to wooden handles, in the manner observed in recent times among stone-using tribesmen. The stone knives attain a length of some six inches towards the middle of the Jōmon period.

Another stone tool which is prominent in other cultures at a corresponding economic stage, the scraper used in preparing skins and bark, is less in evidence with the Jōmon, though a few rarer spoon-shaped pieces having a stumpy projection for mounting, may have served this purpose. The working of stone by removing small flakes (often in close parallel bands which suggest the employment of a 'pressure flaking' technique) is of a refinement equalling that achieved by more advanced Neolithic and bronze-using cultures in the West; while the virtuosity displayed in later Jōmon times in the fashioning of ornamental or ritual obsidian plaques with irregular and fantastic outlines surpasses the skill of any flintwork practised in early times elsewhere.

The polished stone axes of Jōmon conform to shapes associated on the mainland with the Neolithic cultures of south China and the islands of south-east Asia. They are oblong or slightly trapezoid in outline, with a flattened rectangular section, or are oval in section and pointed towards the hafting end. The flatter kind predominates in the early period, when often only the cutting edge was polished, the remainder being 'pecked' to a uniform surface. These tools were probably mounted indifferently as axes or digging implements.

Harpoons and fish-hooks were carved from antler and bone. The former vary from small single-barbed points to larger ones with rows of six or seven barbs on either side. This type is known in other parts of northern Asia and in Europe. Another variety, peculiar to Japan and east Asia, has a socket instead of a tang for mounting and is nearly always furnished with a single extra-large spur at the base. The fish-hooks are mostly of antler and range in size from one to four inches.

Such equipment is normal to primitive food-gathering peoples whose knowledge of agriculture, when it is present at all,

is confined to such small scale cropping that its results are hardly perceptible in the archaeological record. So far there is no sure evidence that the Jōmon people were acquainted with agriculture or domestic animals other than the dog. Rice growing and animal husbandry were introduced by their Yayoi successors together with bronze metallurgy and tools and weapons allied to Chinese types. The mastery of food-production gave these earliest Japanese invaders irresistible superiority and allowed for the rapid expansion of their population. It is surprising that people depending for their food entirely on hunting and gathering could live in groups as large as the remains of the Jōmon settlements suggest. Deer and wild pig were their chief prey. The bow, perhaps armed with poisoned arrows (the Ainu of recent times ground the root of an aconite for this purpose) and probably traps and pitfalls made them masters of the boar and even the bear.

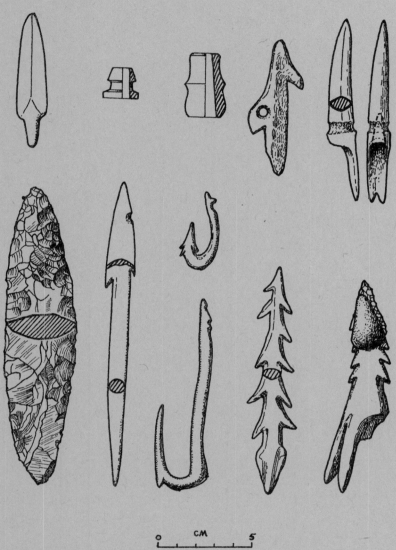

Jōmon flint and bone implements. Top: spear-point, valves for blowing up bladders, and arrow-heads. Bottom: flaked stone blade, bone fishhooks and harpoon-heads. (15)

The extent of their fishing may be judged from the frequent finds of hooks and harpoons, and finds of stones shaped to be used as net-weights show that they fished with net as well as line in the shallow waters of the creeks near which they settled. Their largest fish-hook would suffice to catch the tunny. But at all stages of the Jōmon culture the remains of shell-fish and nuts show that these never ceased to be basic items of food.

The Simple Jōmon Burials

There are no external signs at Jōmon graves of ceremonial burial in the form of grave-mounds or elaborate underground structures, such as are used in certain Neolithic burials in the West. The body was placed without a coffin in a fairly shallow pit, which was then filled with the upcast earth thrown directly on to the corpse, or, more rarely, sealed with pebbles and clay.

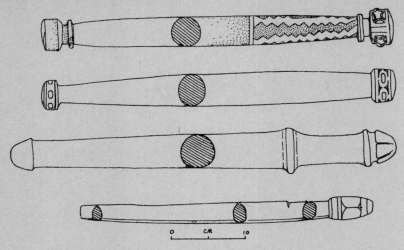

Mysterious objects that have been christened 'stone sceptres' or 'stone staves' are sometimes found in Jōmon graves. They seem to illustrate the transformation of a useful into a magical object, beginning possibly as a pestle for pulverising seeds or grain and ending as a ritual object or symbol of authority. Some are two feet or more in length. (16)

The graves are mostly in the vicinity of the habitations, often in the area covered by the shell-mound. This at first sight suggests that the dead were disposed of in the village midden, but a more probable explanation of the position of the graves is that the gradual extension of the shell-mound came in time to cover old and forgotten graves.

Before the latest phase of the culture there is no sign of organized cemeteries. In the late Jōmon period, as on an extensive cemetery site in Okayama Ken, some scores of graves might be spaced out in a comparatively orderly arrangement, although any surface mark that would make this possible is no longer visible. Around the group of graves a few boulders still remained to indicate the perimeter. In nearly every case the body was pl 16 buried with the legs slightly or completely flexed, often with a heavy stone placed directly upon it, a custom perhaps revealing a fear of the return of the dead. Apart from the crouched position the body was placed indifferently on the back, side or prone. Instances are sited in which the head of the corpse was protected by a large pot from the fall of the earth. The grave goods, even in the late period, are very simple, at most a pot set beside the body.

No special array of the corpse is noticeable, beyond occasional stone bracelets and ear-rings. Burials of adult and child or of several adults together are recorded, and there are indications that bones of an earlier burial, disturbed when a new grave was dug, were carefully replaced. In one case the long bones were arranged in a square surrounding the skull. A few burials in jars have been found scattered throughout the Jōmon area, pl 16 but these were all the graves of children, and jar-burial seems not to have been a regular rite. The lack of any obvious social distinction in the furnishing of the simple Jōmon graves is proof of the comparatively primitive level of the tribal organization.

The Arts of the Jōmon People

Some of the shaped stones served other than practical ends, and can only have had ritual or ceremonial purposes. The long sceptre-like stones with a waist defined by prominent ridges and pl 8 the curious form called a 'stone hat' by Japanese archaeologists, 9 may have originated from net-weights but their careful shaping f 16 goes beyond real requirements. The hat-shaped stones may have been symbols of authority, and this is more certain in the case of the stone staffs, some of which reach two feet or more in length. The staffs are carved with decorative terminal knobs, sometimes in designs reminiscent of the pottery ornament. A few specimens are shaped at one end into the form of a handle marked off from the rest by a rib and are designated 'stone swords', while others are clearly intended as phalloi, fertility symbols appropriated as emblems of chieftainship.

The varieties of stone used in the manufacture of these ornamental and ritual objects include greenstone, serpentine, and

for smaller objects and more rarely, a light green nephritic jade. The source of this last is not known. Jade can no longer be found in Japan itself, and possible sources on the mainland—the region of Lake Baikal and Khotan in Central Asia—are very distant. Inside Japan the trade in obsidian is well attested, and the slightest contact with the mainland, even by devious routes, may have sufficed to obtain jade in return for the no less mysterious obsidian, or for the huntsman's booty of fur and feather.

The Jōmon stone-carvers used jade almost exclusively to make simple round or oval beads, or the strange comma-shaped pendant called *magatama*, or 'bent jewel', a talisman known pl 14 also from east Asia. The *magatama* are pierced at the rounded end f 17 of the 'comma' and seem to have been attached to the dress or the person, as ornaments or charms. During the Yayoi period they were made in even greater numbers and of larger size, and their use survived even into the Protodynastic period. No explanation

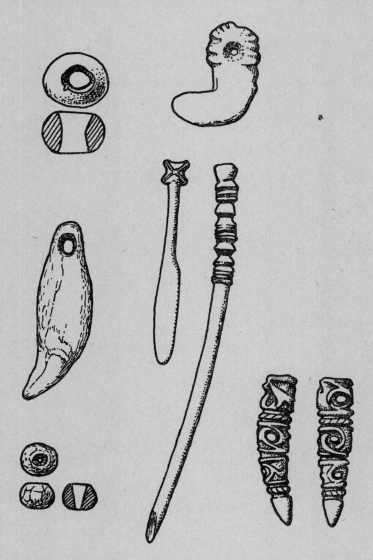

Jōmon ornaments—'bent jewels' (magatama) of bone, pendants, beads and carved pieces of antler. (17)

of the origin of the shape or of their meaning can be offered, though clearly something more than mere decoration is intended. The jade was perforated by boring from both sides, so that the longitudinal section of the perforation has an hour-glass outline, two funnel-shaped pits having met near the middle of the thickness. The same method was used for other varieties of stone. On a larger scale and in softer materials, both stone and bone, pl 26 there are examples of another method, in which a tube provided f 26 by bamboo or the bone of a small animal was used with a sand abrasive. The hole produced in this way had parallel sides and the drilling proceeded from one face.

At a site excavated in Aomori Ken at the village of Korekawa f 18 the dampness of the subsoil had ensured the survival of many 19 wooden objects such as have disappeared at other sites where the 20 soil conditions are more normal. The ancient village at Korekawa 21 belonged to the end of the Jōmon period, when the Jōmon

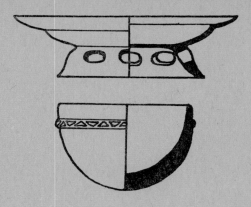

people were probably in contact with Yayoi civilization along a frontier running through the middle region of Honshu.

An important part of the Yayoi culture is its manifest indebtedness to the mainland. Its bronze weapons are derived from Chinese types. It is possible therefore to see in one striking feature of the Jōmon remains of Korekawa, the use of lacquer, an influence which reached Neolithic Japan from the Chinese mainland through the mediation of the Yayoi people. The juice of the lacquer tree provided a covering for wood both durable and very beautiful when it was coloured and polished, and it is plausible that a knowledge of it was one of the first fruits of contact with the contemporary higher civilization of the mainland. The lacquered objects found at Korekawa appear to be local Jōmon products, and this fact involves an unsolved problem. It is hardly likely that the lacquer sap was conveyed to Japan in the liquid form as it was extracted from the tree; yet there is no evidence that the lacquer tree grew wild in Japan and was available for tapping before the time of its deliberate introduction at a much later time.

The wooden objects from Korekawa include cups and bowls lacquered red, bangles and ear-rings, and instruments no longer identifiable which were wrapped in strips of bark and decorated in lacquer paint with linear designs in red on a black ground. Lacquer was used to coat baskets and other plaited objects, in some cases the top coat of red lacquer lying on a foundation of asphalt. The lacquer was stained red with haematite and mercuric oxide. A bow bound with bark and lacquered was constructed of a number of separate pieces of wood, in the tradition of the Asiatic compound bow and similar in essentials to the Japanese bow of later times. A red-lacquered wooden sword must have served as a token of office, in the manner surmised for the 'stone swords'.

f 20

f 21

A 'Medicine-man' Religion

From all the examples cited above of the industry and burial customs of the Jōmon people, little if anything can be deduced about their social practices and their superstitions. Broadly the Jōmon culture joins a vast cultural region stretching from north China to Alaska, in which traditions of tool and weapon forms and hunting methods are closely related. It is therefore tempting to argue by analogy with modern or recent primitive communities of east Asia whose material equipment preserves some ancient features resembling Jōmon types. This would lead to the speculation that the Jōmon population were observers of a shamanistic or 'medicine-man' religion combined with magical practices. The beliefs and religious customs of the modern Ainu, which are mentioned below, would make a no less plausible historical analogy.

The furnishing of Jōmon graves is evidence of the belief in some sort of spiritual existence of individuals, though there is no reason to suppose that such belief was very articulate or explicit. That some deity in human form was thought to exist is proved by small human figurines placed in the graves from the earliest Jōmon times. At first they are simple plaques defining head, trunk and arms, of indeterminate sex. But the later graves contain more distinct figures, fully formed, with strange, large-eyed faces of conventional design, wearing an elaborate head-dress and covered with impressed designs of the kind used on pottery. The decoration of the figures represents close-fitting garments, richly patterned, and the breasts are those of females. At the

pl 10
11
12
13
f 22
23
24
25

Wooden objects of the Jōmon culture from sites in northern Honshu. Far left: wooden bowl, showing exterior and section. Left: wooden spatula. More than ten of these were found together. They are sometimes called swords or daggers but their function is still not known. Their hilts have carved decoration and there are two tangs, perhaps intended for the attachment of a handle. Opposite: wooden sword (top) and bow. The sword, which must have been purely ceremonial, is red-lacquered and carved on the spherical pommel, the hand-guard and the knob at the end. The bow was also originally lacquered. (18–21)

Hiromi site near Toyohira village in Nagano Ken a female image of this kind had been carefully set erect in the middle of a circle of small stones.

These figures are thought to represent a Mother Goddess. The beliefs surrounding such a deity may have gone together with a social organization of the matriarchal kind, in which tribal and personal relations are traced through the female line even if the ruling power is exercised by men. Belief in a Mother Goddess need not have been incompatible with beliefs associated with shamanism, which is much concerned with spirit journeys into the world of ghosts. A Mother Goddess, as a personification of the principle of fertility, in the west is a creation of farming peoples. It is strange that the Jōmon people, still in the pre-agricultural stage, should have entertained this cult.

Another hint of tribal custom may be seen in the practice of removing one or more of the front teeth. A statistical study of human remains has shown that in the majority of cases this operation was performed on adolescents, from which it is inferred that it was part of an initiation ceremony, like those of some modern tribes, whereby full membership of the adult group was conferred on the young.

The Ainu of Today

The traditional life of the Ainu in recent times, when it was unaffected or little affected by the customs of their Japanese neighbours, presents a picture wholly compatible with the view presented above, that the modern Ainu are the cultural descendants of the ancient Jōmon people. Their material culture advanced

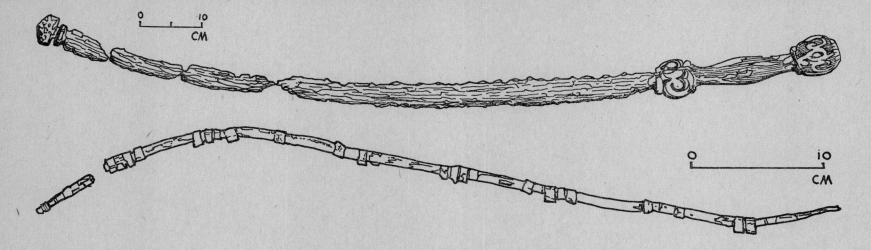

little during the two millennia which separated them from their Neolithic predecessors. They built similar houses, hunted with similar weapons and still lacked the knowledge of metal-working. Their loss of the potter's art was an inevitable result of the ready supply of superior wares from the Japanese, whose high-firing kilns they could not imitate. The accounts given by anthropologists and missionaries from the beginning of the present century describe a people content to follow the old paths, indifferent to the higher standards of economic and cultural life of their alien neighbours.

Houses with sunken floors were built by the Ainu of the Kuriles up to the time of their forced migration in 1884. In Japan they are no longer built, but Ainu architecture retains some significant differences as compared with Japanese practice, and their simple construction has hardly advanced beyond that of the Jōmon huts. With these they share a feature which distinguishes them fundamentally from Japanese buildings. An Ainu house is erected on posts set directly in the ground, while the dwelling of the Japanese peasant, however humble, is set on a rectangular frame placed on the ground surface and supported from beneath by piles driven into the ground.

The large gable openings of a Japanese house so reduce the size of the slopes on the gable ends that the roof appears to have only two sloping sides, whereas an Ainu house, with smaller gable openings, still presents the aspect of a pyramidal roof. Such differences, though slight, mark a divergence of tradition and are not merely the effect of different levels of skill. The walls of Ainu huts are often of rushes, and the roof thatch is rougher than that of Japanese dwellings—the Japanese village carpenter long ago outstripped the skill of the Ainu. In Ainu houses the longer axis is regularly orientated east and west, the eastern end being the most respected part. The door is generally on the south side and is protected by a porch.

The Ainu is very religious and every house has its sacred places: the hearth, the window in the east wall through which nothing must be thrown and through which no one may look from the outside, and the north-east corner of the main room, in which sacred objects are placed. The most mysterious of such objects are short wooden staffs, carved with simple geometric decoration, on which a number of broad shavings have been cut without being detached, so that they curl along its length. The majority of these so-called *inao* make no attempt to suggest any significant shape, though a few appear to imitate men or animals. The *inao*, or 'messengers', appear to be a means of approaching the gods, though their rôle is not explicitly stated by the Ainu themselves. They are essential to every presentation of offerings to the gods. Spiritual beings are conceived to be in a hierarchy descending from the Supreme God, who may never be addressed directly, to such chief deities as the Protectress of the Hearth, and lesser spirits such as Aioina, who was sent to create and teach the Ainu. Each living creature and lifeless object has its own supernatural essence.

Combined with these beliefs is an elaborate bear-cult, such as is found widespread among peoples inhabiting east and north-east Asia. The bear is regarded by the Ainu as a kind of *inao*, a means of conciliating the divine powers. The ceremonial bear is raised from a cub, sometimes being suckled by a woman. When it is fully grown it is paraded at a festival in a wooden cave and finally killed by crushing between the halves of a divided tree-trunk, whereupon it is eaten by all present with great ceremony. The bear is praised and receives an apology: were its soul not released from its body how could it go as messenger to the God of the Mountains to assure him of the Ainu's devotion to him and to ensure his protection for them? Women take part in the bear feast, but otherwise have little to do in religious rite.

Agriculture has even in recent times made little appeal to the Ainu. Before common modern tools were adopted the ground was tilled with a digging stick armed with a tine of antler. The hunt was the chief pastime, bear and deer the chief game. The bear was hunted towards the end of winter, being roused from its winter sleep. It was caught in pits or traps, or chased and made to impale itself on a spear implanted at an angle in the ground.

pl 28
32
33
41

pl 27
28
29

pl 1
32
33

Figurines of the Jōmon period: (a) the oldest known figurine, small and flat; (b) elongated, bell-shaped figurine, able to stand alone; (c) late-Jōmon figurine, with long eye-brows and jaw-ridge, and pregnancy indicated by enlarged abdomen; (d) figurine of the latest period—wide-faced, broad-necked and heavily costumed; she has piled-up clay on the head (hair?), huge oval eyes like snow-goggles, a necklace and cord impressed costume rolled at the knees. (22–25)

pl 31
43

The bow was still the chief weapon, and a variety of traps depending on the action of a ready flexed bow could be set to kill the smaller game. The skill of Ainu fishermen was famed in Japan. They used hinged hooks and multiple hooks made of iron bartered from the Japanese. Large sea-fish were speared from
f 27 boats made of planks sewn together and river-fish were caught in traps.

pl 37
38
39

The carved wooden utensils of the Ainu, and his embroidered and painted garments of skins and woven elm fibre, now figure among the fine craft of primitive peoples in our museums. The abstract designs used in their decoration, when they are not infected by motifs borrowed from Japanese art, are wholly in the spirit of the art of Jōmon, though some of the ancient force and variety is lost. Among the most highly prized and attractive

pl 29
44

of the Ainu carvings are libation sticks decorated with geometric designs. In libations made to the gods the stick is dipped in the offered drink and used to scatter a few drops to the divine powers. The celebrant then drinks the offering, holding aside his beard with the libation stick. These 'moustache lifters' are necessary to every feast and sacrifice.

The parallel which can be drawn between the material equipment, the art and customs of the Ainu and the prehistoric Jōmon people does not in itself provide conclusive proof that the former are the lineal descendants of the latter. But when the historical circumstances are taken into account it is hardly possible to escape the conclusion that they are closely related culturally and racially. It may be argued that what remains of Ainu culture today (leaving aside the acquired Japanese elements) has been influenced by post-Jōmon immigrants from eastern Asia possessed of a material culture generally resembling that of the Jōmon people. But such invasions, if they took place, can only have been negligible in size and confined to the northern part of Japan. There is no evidence, archaeological, anthropological or linguistic, which suggests that significant numbers of outsiders reached Japan to enter the Ainu sphere in the Yayoi or Early Dynastic periods. Thereafter, when any such arrivals, achieved or attempted, might be expected to have attracted Japanese notice, history has nothing of the kind to relate. After the arrival of the Japanese themselves in the islands only one invasion was attempted—by the Mongols in the 13th century —and this was easily repelled.

Archaeological research has nowhere else revealed so clear a picture of the defeat and supplanting of a primitive people and culture by invaders who were destined to build one of the world's great civilizations, while the remnant of the aborigines lives on beside them, oblivious of their past independence, content with their simple traditions, but very conscious of racial and social differences separating them from their clever neighbours.

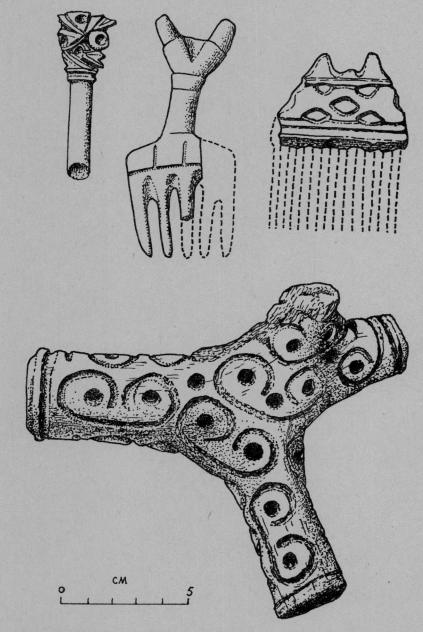

CM
0   5

Examples of Jōmon bone-carving. Top: ornamental pin and two (partially reconstructed) combs. Bottom: carved deer-antler, decorated on one side, smooth on the other. Various guesses have been made about what it is—a head-ornament, a waist-decoration, or an ornamented spindle-whorl. (26)

Ainu fishermen, from a Japanese 19th century painting. They use a harpoon with double point (of iron bought from the Japanese) to capture a seal. The canoe, of planks sewn together, shows similarities with boats used by the Jōmon. (27)

VI THE COLLAPSE OF THE KHMERS

The god-kings of lost Angkor

CHRISTOPHER PYM

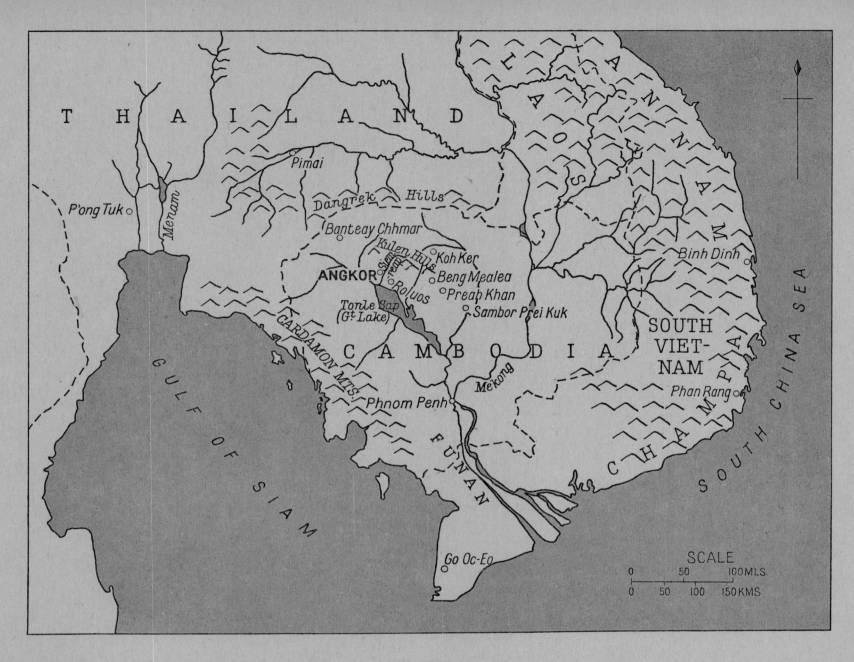

AD	KHMER KINGS	KHMER BUILDINGS	KHMER HISTORY
	802–850 Jayavarman II		Devaraja ceremony and cult begin
	850–877 Jayavarman III		Roluos becomes capital
	877–889 Indravarman I	Preah Ko (879), Bakong (881)	Reservoir (E. Baray) built at Angkor
	889–c. 900 Yasovarman	Lolei (893), Phnom Bakheng (c. 900)	Angkor becomes capital
900	900–c. 922 Harshavarman I	Baksei Chamkrong, Prasat Kravan (921)	
	c. 928–941/2 Jayavarman IV	Prasat Thom at Koh Ker	Koh Ker becomes capital: reservoir built
	944–968 Rajendravarman II	East Mebon (952), Pre Rup (961)	War with Champa
	968–1001 Jayavarman V	Banteay Srei (968)	
		Ta Keo?	
1000	c. 1002–1050 Suryavarman I	Phimeanakas?	Expansion of Khmer empire
	1050–1065/6 Udayadityavarman II	Baphuon (c. 1060), West Mebon	W. Baray built at Angkor?
	1065/6–c. 1080 Harshavarman III		
	c. 1080–1107 Jayavarman VI	Pimai?	
1100	1107–1113 Dharanindravarman I		
	1113–c. 1150 Suryavarman II	ANGKOR WAT, Beng Mealea?	c. 1125 Birth of Jayavarman VII
		Preah Khan of Kompong Svay? Banteay Samre?	Expansion of empire
	c. 1150–? Dharanindravarman II		1177 Chams sack Angkor
			Defeat of Chams. N. Baray built at Angkor
1200	1181–c. 1218 Jayavarman VII	Ta Prohm (1186), Preah Khan of Angkor (1191)	Reservoirs built at Banteay Chhmar (?)
		ANGKOR THOM, Banteay Kdei	and Preah Khan of Kompong Svay (?)
		Neak Pean, Banteay Chhmar, Bayon	Expansion of empire
1300			Arrival of Theravada Buddhism
1400			Thai invasions
			1431/2 Angkor sacked by Thais and abandoned

The Khmer civilization: chronology of the classic period at Angkor

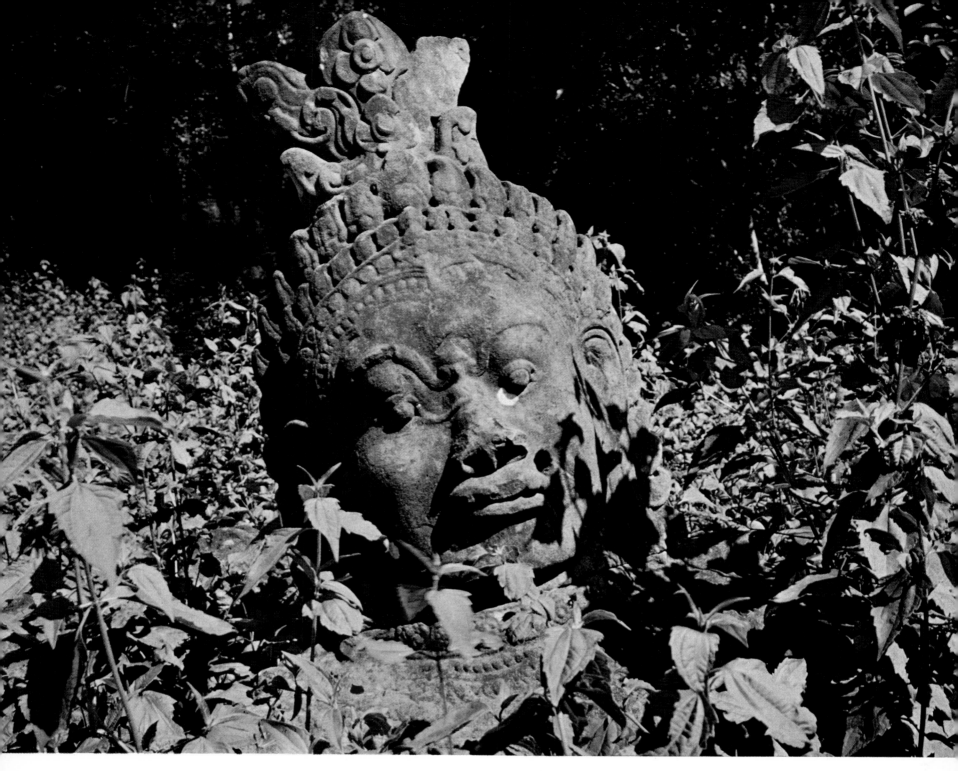

'Grander than anything left to us by Greece or Rome'

is how the French naturalist Henri Mouhot described the ruins of Angkor Wat when he rediscovered them in the Cambodian forest in 1858. As a temple he considered it 'a rival to that of Solomon, and erected by some ancient Michelangelo'.

Angkor Wat ('city temple') is simply the name of one building in what has now been revealed as a complex of buildings six miles by five, hidden for centuries in the jungle, now uncovered and in large part reconstructed by French archaeologists. We know now that this complex was the capital at intervals of the Khmers of Cambodia, when they dominated the Indo-China peninsula from the ninth to the fifteenth centuries AD. Thanks to hundreds of stone inscriptions we know much about the Khmer kings, and the gods whom they believed themselves to incarnate.

We know, too, that the wealth and prosperity of the Khmers depended above all on water, for Cambodia, far from being a tropical paradise of fertility, has great need of water during the six-month dry season to irrigate the ricefields. Specially constructed reservoirs, canals and irrigation channels covered the land in an intricate network of water, so that the ricefields could be flooded and two or even three crops a year could be harvested. And for every reservoir there was a temple, the spiritual abode of the god-king on whose favour the fertility of the land depended. Hundreds of these temples have been located throughout Cambodia, of which Angkor Wat is the best known and best preserved.

Obviously the building and maintenance of so many hundreds of reservoirs, canals and temples required not only an immense labour force but a strong, centralized administration. The key to both was the cult of the god-king, the most characteristic feature of Khmer civilization. From about AD 800 to 1200, temples and shrines were built in hundreds, a forest of sculptured stone. Well-irrigated ricefields supported a hard-working population of possibly half a million or more, bound to the service of the god-king by religious sanctions and the promise of immortal bliss to come. Then, in the next two centuries, this great machine seems to have faltered, and slowly came to a halt. Canals became choked, the jungle closed in, twining tentacles of the silk-cotton tree smothered the sculptured gods and dancing-girls. In 1431, invading Thais sacked Angkor and forced the Khmers to retreat to central Cambodia. What caused this fatal decline, this complete eclipse of a people whose artistic and engineering powers were so remarkable, is a mystery and, in the absence of written records, may remain so, though many theories have been offered.

Half-drowned in a sea of vegetation, enormous heads like this one from the east doorway of Angkor Thom were lifted from where they had fallen, and restored to their places in the causeway of giants (see pl. 38). An immense programme of restoration and preservation is still under way. (1)

The Khmers were obsessed with water — and still are. The life-giving powers of water are often referred to in ancient inscriptions, and rice, staple diet of the Khmers then as now, needs the alluvial flood-waters of the Mekong for its cultivation. In central Cambodia during the rainy season (above), forest and water merge and become almost one; houses, unchanging for centuries, stand above the floods on piles. At Angkor, however, one small river, the Siemreap, was the main source of water, and two great reservoirs or *barays* were built, with numerous pools and canals. Today water-wheels are used (right) to fill conduits leading to agricultural land, and much work is being done to restore at least the West Baray to use. The East Baray, which once held a thousand million gallons of water, is empty. Did the irrigation system fail from some cause—human or natural—and kill the Khmer empire by slow starvation? (2, 3)

Angkor Wat from the air stands out against the solid green of the forest, in a clearing made by modern hands, but does not impress, as it does from the ground, by its sheer size. The moat (foreground), some two hundred yards wide, encloses a rectangle each side of which measures about a mile. Ruins of a temple to the Hindu trinity —Brahma, Vishnu and Siva—have been found on the small hill visible in the background. (4)

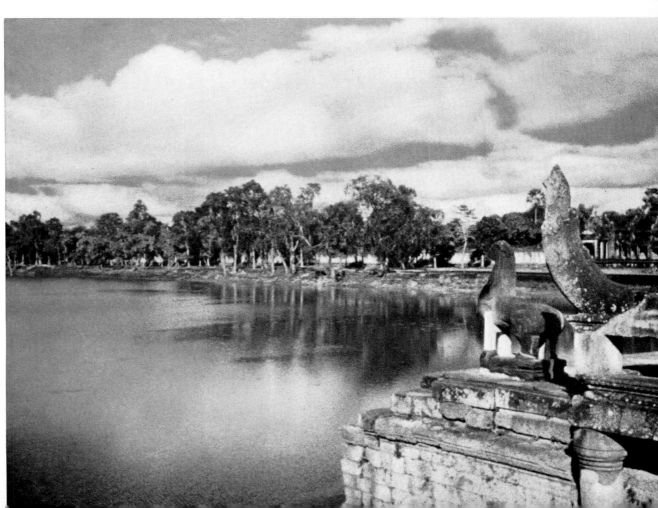

The Royal Bath, Sras Srang (right), was built about the beginning of the thirteenth century by Jayavarman VII. It was used as a bathing place, but was also a reservoir to feed the irrigation system. On the balustrade is the head of a *naga*, or serpent, representing the beneficent spirit of the waters—a frequent motif in Khmer art. (5)

Hundreds if not thousands of temples were swallowed by the encroaching jungle between the Khmer collapse in 1431 and the rediscovery of Angkor a hundred years ago. Most of them, damaged by time, the monsoon rains, and clutching, choking tropical vegetation, have had to be restored by French architects. But Angkor Wat itself, Asia's largest and most impressive work of architecture, was never altogether abandoned by its worshippers. Today (right) it stands out majestically against the sky as one approaches it down the 350-metres-long causeway from the western entrance. Heads of the *naga*, the cobra-god of Khmer mythology, rear up at intervals along the balustrade.

Angkor Wat is the culminating moment of Khmer classic architecture: the temple-mountain which symbolizes—or rather, which *is*—five-peaked Mount Meru, centre of the universe and dwelling—place of the Hindu gods. And with them dwelt the temple's builder, the god-king Suryavarman II. (6)

The god-king smiles down from the north gateway of Angkor Thom (above). Four giant faces, looking towards the four points of the compass, surmount each of the five entrances to Angkor Thom, the 'Great City'. They are *boddhisattvas* (future incarnations of the Buddha), perhaps to be identified with Jayavarman VII (1181–c. 1218), who rebuilt the city after it was sacked by the Chams in 1177. (7)

The king who established Khmer power, Indravarman, built the brick and sandstone towers of Preah Ko (below) in AD 879, to honour his ancestors. This is at Roluos, eleven miles south-east of Angkor, to which the capital was moved for a time. Here he also constructed an artificial lake for irrigation. (8)

For harmony and proportion, Baksei Chamkrong (below) is one of the gems of Khmer architecture. Built by Harshavarman I (900–c. 923), grandson of Indravarman, it shows how plateau upon plateau leads up to the temple-mountain's peak. The tower, built of brick, stands on a recessed laterite base 42 ft. high. (9)

More than two hundred monumental faces of the god-king decorate the fifty or more towers of the Bayon, crowning achievement of Jayavarman VII, the last great builder-king of Angkor. Along the walls of its galleries are long friezes extolling Jayavarman's victories and portraying the life of the people. (10)

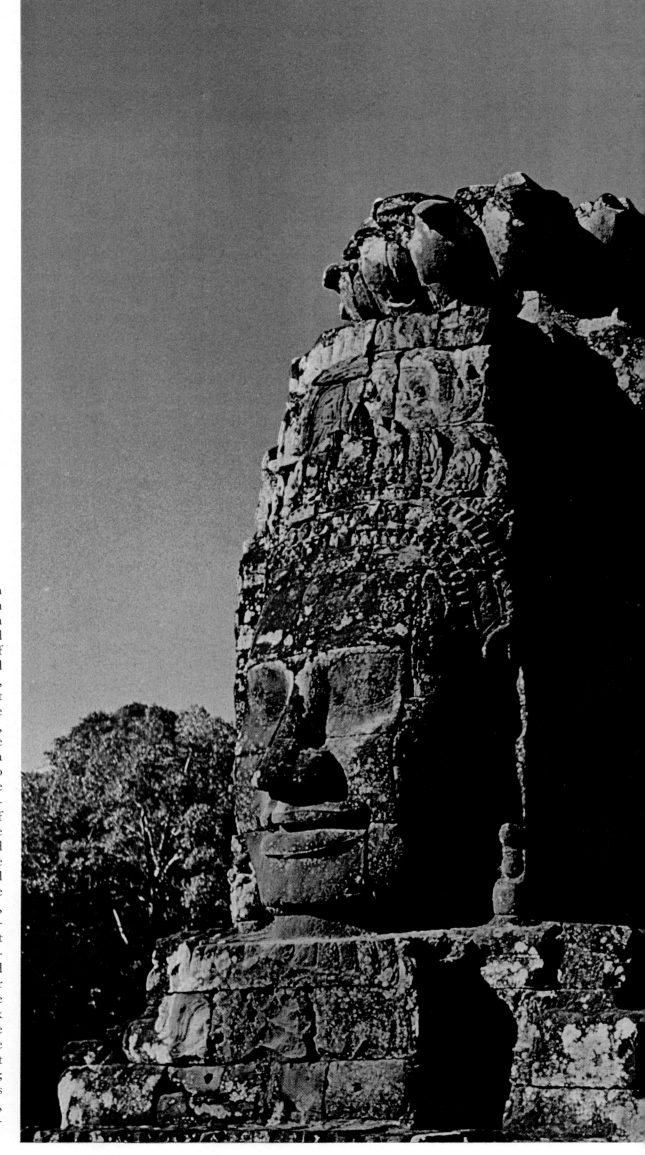

The Bayon stands for all time as a
monument to the power of one man
and the labour of his subjects. It is a
warren of courtyards, galleries and
terraces, an inextricable mingling of
architecture and sculpture, crowned
by a strange, repetitive forest of faces,
each one between five and eight feet
high. From every one of its massive
towers the Buddha-smile of its builder,
Jayavarman VII, looks out to the
four quarters of the world. It was a
world that he himself did much to
expand, for his long reign saw the
invading Chams repulsed, the kingdom extended from the Isthmus of
Kra to the north of Laos and from the
China Sea to the Gulf of Siam, and
Khmer culture spread throughout the
Indo-China peninsula. Temples and
reservoirs, roads and hospitals were
constructed thoughout the kingdom,
in the most intensive building programme in Khmer history. Summit
and symbol of this whole vast enterprise is the Bayon, the many-towered
temple at the exact centre of Angkor
Thom. The *boddhisattva* faces on the
towers (compare pl. 7) are a hallmark
of Jayavarman VII. Since he, unlike
his predecessors, was a Buddhist, he
identified himself, the god-king, not
with Siva but with the Lord Buddha;
his physical presence in the temple was
emphasized by the many *boddhisattvas*,
and by a large statue of Buddha himself. (11)

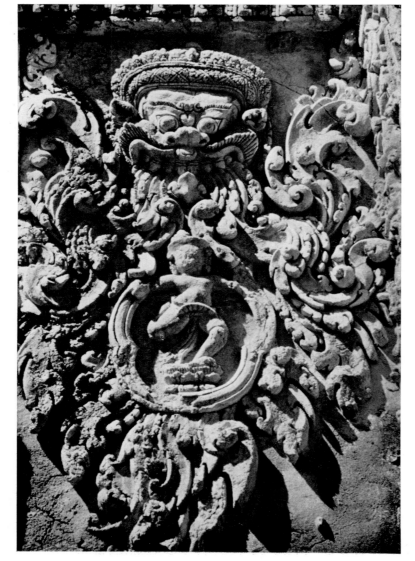

A baroque richness

of decoration covers the Khmer temples. Bas-reliefs and sculptures in incredible profusion testify to the multitude of skilled craftsmen employed in adorning these buildings, to the glorification of the god-king or his priests. These pictures show details of three temples dating to the 9th, 10th and 11th centuries.

Harmonious curves of foliage are enlivened by charming little figures in the stucco panels of Preah Ko (left, below), built in AD 879. Nearly a century later (976) a high Brahman official, one of the royal family, built the temple of Banteay Srei, 'citadel of women'. Some of the intricate ornament of this jewel of a temple is shown, top left; the *naga's* five heads rear up to decorate a corner. Animal, human and divine figures, too, were carved on the pediments of Banteay Srei (opposite). The upper picture is a scene from the Ramayana: Siva sits on the summit of Mount Kailasa, while the giant Ravana struggles to overturn it. (Comparison of its diminishing terraces with those in Pl. 9 shows how the Khmers regarded temple and mountain as one and the same thing.) On the Baphuon, c. 1060, other mythological scenes, in relief, were arranged in small sandstone panels (above) over the entrance pavilions, like paintings on the wall. Considering how every inch of space was covered—encrusted, one might almost say—with decoration, and on so many hundreds of temples, it is tempting to think that sheer exhaustion must in the end have overcome the makers of all this richness. (12–16)

Countless scenes of battle

are shown in the bas-reliefs of Angkor Wat and the Bayon, but the Khmers were not necessarily an aggressive people. The main threats to their security came from the Chams in the east, the Thais in the north-west, and the Annamites in the north-east. The Chams, a maritime people from the east coast of the Indo-China peninsula, had made frequent forays against Angkor in the classic period of Khmer civilization, but always by land. In 1177, however, the Cham fleet sailed up the Mekong into the Great Lake, took the Khmers by surprise, and sacked Angkor. Soon afterwards, however, Jayavarman VII came to the throne of Angkor, drove the Chams out, and placed a nominee of his own on the Cham throne. It is probably this victory which is commemorated in a great frieze in the Bayon, 35 metres long and 3 metres high.

Guided by a Chinese pilot, the Cham ships are rowed up the river to the attack. This reconstruction is based on the Bayon frieze. The gaudy figureheads are representations of Garuda, a mythical creature half-man, half-bird, the sacred mount of the god Vishnu who was worshipped by Chams and Khmers alike. Armed landing parties stand ready amidships while the oarsmen, behind the flimsy protection of wicker bulwarks, row them silently to the unsuspecting city. (17)

Helmets shaped like magnolias sit incongruously above the brutal faces of the Cham warriors—apparently the only way Chams can be distinguished from Khmers in the Bayon frieze. This is a detail from the left-hand edge of the picture below. (18)

With spears raised threateningly for the assault, the Cham warships race into battle. In the foreground ('below' means 'nearer' in the convention of these reliefs) men knocked overboard swim among the oar-blades and the fish. (19)

As the battle rages, peasant life continues on the bank, and in midstream a snapping crocodile adds to the carnage. Above it, one ship secures to another with grappling irons. Vivid detail makes this frieze a valuable document. (20)

Warfare by land as well as on water punctuated the history of Angkor, and two kings in particular were victorious in war. Suryavarman II (1113–c. 1150) allied himself with the Chams against the Annamites, then turned against the Chams and defeated them too. This was the high-water mark of Khmer history, marked by the supreme temple of Angkor Wat, where beautifully carved panels hundreds of yards long, extol the glory of the god-king and the valour of his armies. One such panel shows an impressive march-past of Khmer troops and their allies; from it is taken the picture below—a detail from a panel showing the martial bearing of the royal cavalry. Also from Angkor Wat is the menacing charioteer with spear and shield.

Jayavarman VII, too, commemorated his deeds in a vivid and detailed series of 'film strip' bas-reliefs. These are in the outer gallery of the Bayon. On foot and on elephant back (opposite), the armies move to the attack. In a graphic mêlée, Chams and Khmers battle hand-to-hand, the air thick with flying arrows. (Note the contrast between the squat, brutal fighters of the Bayon and the stylish elegance of the earlier bas-reliefs.) In the end, it may be that all this effort and loss of war defeated its own object, by so draining Khmer manpower as to leave them depleted and exhausted, easy prey for their enemies. (21–24)

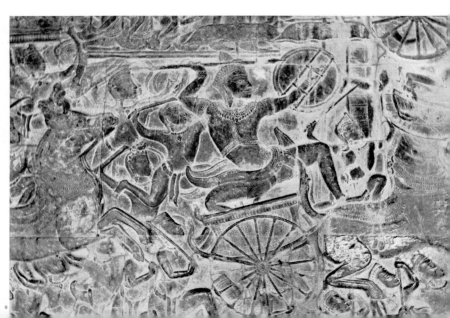

118

When the king rode forth from his palace he was escorted by a rich procession, part of which is shown in this artist's reconstruction. Chou Ta-Kouan, a Chinese visitor to Angkor in 1296, has left a description of such a procession: 'Soldiers appear at the head of his escort, followed by standards, banners and music. Next come three to five hundred palace girls, flowers in their hair and wearing patterned cloth. They carry candles, lighted even in broad daylight. Another group of palace girls follows as a separate troop, bearing the royal gold and silver utensils, and a whole series of ornaments and insignia which I do not understand. Next there comes a group of palace girls who form the private guard of the king. They carry lances and shields. They are followed by goat- and horse-drawn carriages, decorated in gold. Ministers and princes follow, riding on elephants and surrounded by innumerable red parasols.

'Next come more than a hundred golden parasols, elephants, palanquins and carriages containing the wives and concubines of the king. At this point in the procession the king appears, standing on an elephant and holding the precious sword in his hand. The tusks of his elephant are sheathed in gold, and other elephants mill around him while the soldiers protect him. He is escorted by more than twenty white parasols, decorated with gold, and with gold handles.' In this reconstruction of the scene, the procession is emerging from the south gate of Angkor Thom, past the causeway of giants (see Pl. 38). At the time when Chou Ta-Kouan was writing—nearly a century after the death of Jayavarman VII—the peak of Angkor's greatness was over, but the pomp and ceremony still remained. Two Theravada Buddhist monks watch the procession, recognizable by their yellow robes, draped so as to leave the right shoulder bare. (25)

Fold out ▶

When the king rode forth from his palace he was escorted by a rich procession, part of which is shown in this artist's reconstruction. Chou Ta-Kouan, a Chinese visitor to Angkor in 1296, has left a description of such a procession: 'Soldiers appear at the head of his escort, followed by standards, banners and music. Next come three to five hundred palace girls, flowers in their hair and wearing patterned cloth. They carry candles, lighted even in broad daylight. Another group of palace girls follows as a separate troop, bearing the royal gold and silver utensils, and a whole series of ornaments and insignia which I do not understand. Next there comes a group of palace girls who form the private guard of the king. They carry lances and shields. They are followed by goat- and horse-drawn carriages, decorated in gold. Ministers and princes follow, riding on elephants and surrounded by innumerable red parasols.

'Next come more than a hundred golden parasols, elephants, palanquins and carriages containing the wives and concubines of the king. At this point in the procession the king appears, standing on an elephant and holding the precious sword in his hand. The tusks of his elephant are sheathed in gold, and other elephants mill around him while the soldiers protect him. He is escorted by more than twenty white parasols, decorated with gold, and with gold handles.' In this reconstruction of the scene, the procession is emerging from the south gate of Angkor Thom, past the causeway of giants (see Pl. 38). At the time when Chou Ta-Kouan was writing—nearly a century after the death of Jayavarman VII—the peak of Angkor's greatness was over, but the pomp and ceremony still remained. Two Theravada Buddhist monks watch the procession, recognizable by their yellow robes, draped so as to leave the right shoulder bare. (25)

Fold out ▶

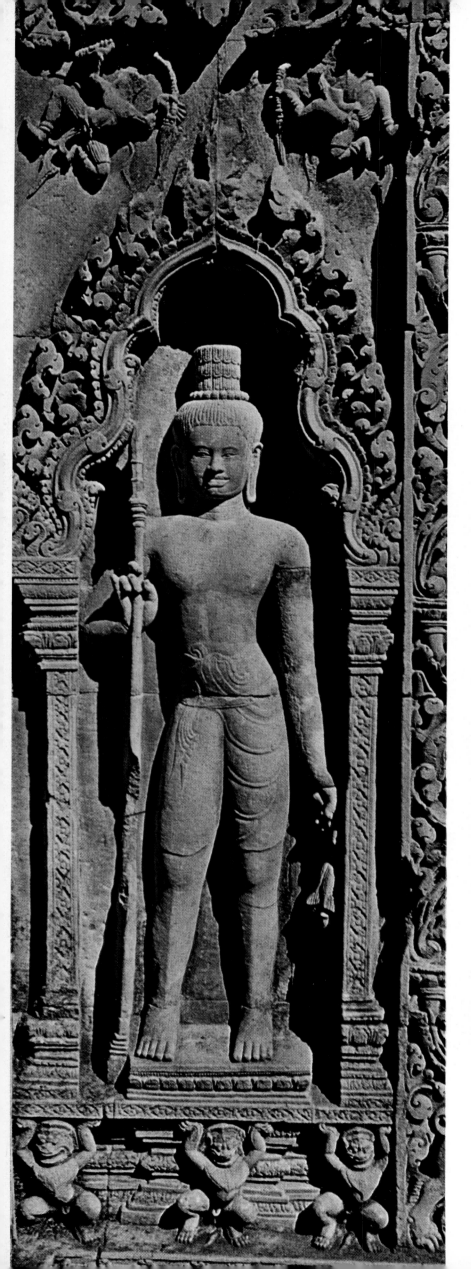

Gods and goddesses,

demons and dancing-girls, throng the walls of the Khmer temples in rich profusion. Worship of Siva and Vishnu, the Hindu gods, was adopted from India by the pre-Angkor kingdoms, and Buddhism rose to importance at Angkor in the twelfth century, in the Mahayana (Greater Vehicle) form. In both of these religions the earthly power of the king was identified with the heavenly power of the god; the linga, phallic symbol of Siva, and the statue of Buddha were considered successively as embodying the physical presence of king as well as god.

The full-blown charms of the apsarases, the celestial dancing-girls, entertainers of the gods, are a frequent theme in Khmer temples. The two above are from Angkor Wat, and the frieze on the right is from the labyrinthine temple-monastery of Preah Khan, built by Jayavarman VII in memory of his father. On the left is a dvarapala, guardian god of the temple, from the little pink sandstone temple of Banteay Srei. (32, 33, 36)

Intimate scenes of everyday life in Angkor 750 years ago still adorn the walls of the Bayon and of other buildings inside Angkor Thom. Along the west side of the great square of Angkor Thom, leading to the entrance of the royal palace, is a frieze of life-sized elephants 300 yards long. The elephant above is bearing a nobleman to the hunt. (26)

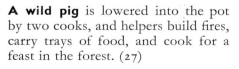

A wild pig is lowered into the pot by two cooks, and helpers build fires, carry trays of food, and cook for a feast in the forest. (27)

The gambling fever is portrayed vividly and with considerable humour in this group of cock-fighters and their supporters. Both this and the last picture are from the outer gallery of the Bayon. (28)

The cult of the devaraja, the all-powerful god-king, was the cornerstone of Khmer society. He was the lord of life and the source of all blessings, and the temple was both his abode as a god and his shrine as a king.

With waving fans and parasols a host of servants and worshippers pay homage to Suryavarman II in a relief (right) on the walls of Angkor Wat. He was devoted to Vishnu, the beneficent god; it was to Vishnu—and thus to himself as Vishnu—that he raised the temple that immortalized his name. (29)

The contemplative smile of the Buddha (below, right), on what is probably a portrait of Jayavarman VII, reveals the compassionate character of this great king. An inscription says that he cared for the ills of his subjects more than for his own. The so-called Leper King, from Angkor Thom, the only completely nude statue known to Khmer art, has the same enigmatic smile (below); who is represented, no one knows, but it may be the god Yama, judge of the dead. (30, 31)

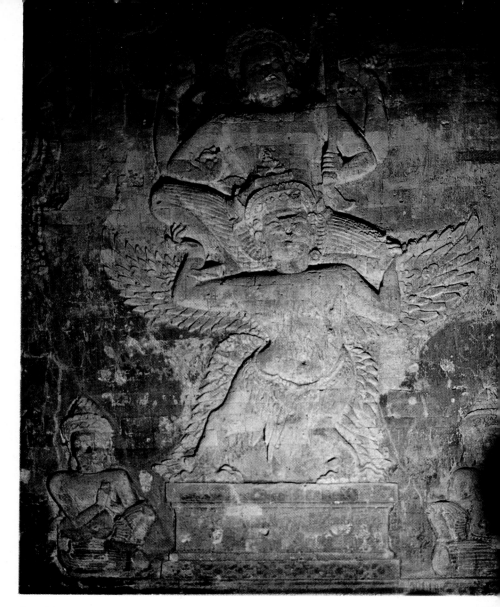

Seated on the coils of the naga, the Buddha smiles the secret, inward smile of contemplation. Behind him the naga's five heads rear up protectively. This statue was found in the Bayon, whose builder, Jayavarman VII, unlike most of his predecessors, was a devout Buddhist. (34)

Half-human, half-bird, the Garuda, in Hindu mythology, was the mount of Vishnu and the enemy of the naga. In the temple of Prasat Kravan (AD 921) this fabulous creature, sculptured in brick, carries the god on his shoulders. Later Khmer sculpture is almost all in sandstone, and brick is gradually abandoned. (35)

The god-king provides for his people in this symbolic bas-relief from Angkor Wat. This Hindu myth, a favourite theme in Khmer art, shows gods and demons churning ambrosia from the sea of milk by pulling back and forth on the serpent Vasuki, which is wrapped round a mountain pivoted on the shell of Vishnu in his tortoise form. Only the centre and ends of the frieze are shown: there are altogether 88 gods on one side and 92 demons on the other. Below is another version—the causeway of giants at Angkor Thom. Gods have a calm, gentle look; demons have round, staring eyes and terrifying expressions. (37, 38)

The blessed and the damned on the day of judgment are portrayed in reliefs of tremendous verve and imagination on the walls of Angkor Wat. Below is one small section from these reliefs, which occupy a panel about a hundred yards long. In the upper register the righteous are borne off in palanquins to Heaven, the apsarases and eternal bliss. Underneath, the sinners, roped by their noses like animals, are beaten and dragged down to Hell. Other reliefs show long files of the dead appearing before Yama, lord of the underworld. Subsequent sections show, with lurid detail, different Hells for the punishment of specific sins. (39)

Siva, the Auspicious One, god of destruction and of creation, was worshipped in the form of a linga, a stone phallus that was considered as the actual bodily presence of the god. Jayavarman VII, Buddhist though he was, could still erect this symbol in his temple of Preah Khan (above). (40)

The saffron robes of Buddhist monks pattern the grey stones of Angkor's temples today—even temples built to the honour of Siva and Vishnu. These are Theravada Buddhists, members of a reformed sect whose presence was noted by the Chinese traveller Chou Ta-Kouan in 1296. Everything the devaraja stood for they opposed; everything they upheld and believed in spelt death to the power of the god-king. Poverty and humility and the promise of suffering, against obedience and worship and the guarantee of prosperity—which would win? Theravada was certainly not the sole cause of Angkor's downfall, but today the god-kings live only in the stone of Angkor, and the yellow-robed, shaven-headed monks pray in their temples. (41)

Still enduring is the Cambodian peasant, his spiritual roots reaching deeper than the Buddhism and the god-king cults of his betters, to the ancient animism of his Khmer forbears. To propitiate the spirits of the waters on which they depend, the mountains, the forests, the forces of nature, they still erect shrines on bamboo poles, like this one which stands lonely sentinel on the shores of Tonle Sap, the Great Lake. (42)

The god-kings of
lost Angkor

CHRISTOPHER PYM

IN A GREEN FOREST clearing at Angkor in Cambodia there stands a small ruined temple, a pyramid built of reddish brick on a base of laterite. Up one of its sides run precipitous steps, leading to a tower rising in majesty at the apex. The entrance to the tower opens east; figures carved on the walls and lying inside recall the Hindu and Buddhist sculptures of India; an inscription at the entrance states that a statue of Siva was dedicated there in AD 947. The pyramid is recessed like a mountain range, with four plateaux diminishing in size towards the apex: the second is a fifth less than the first, the next is reduced by a quarter, the last by a third.

The brief story which this ruined temple tells is clear—the Khmers built pyramidal temples facing east, their recessed sides recalling the slopes of mountains; the Khmers were influenced by Indian religions, they had a strict sense of proportion in their architecture, and they were living at Angkor a thousand years ago. This one small temple has simplicity and beauty, it is a dignified building of exquisite proportions. About a thousand such temples, many of them much bigger and more complex, were engulfed by the Cambodian forest when the ancient Khmer empire collapsed in the fifteenth century. The romance of Angkor lies in the story of a civilization which flowered brilliantly for six centuries and then suddenly disappeared into the forest. Its mystery lies in—why? Why did such an accomplished and vigorous people suddenly stop building their beautiful temples? Why did the great Khmer empire collapse?

f 16

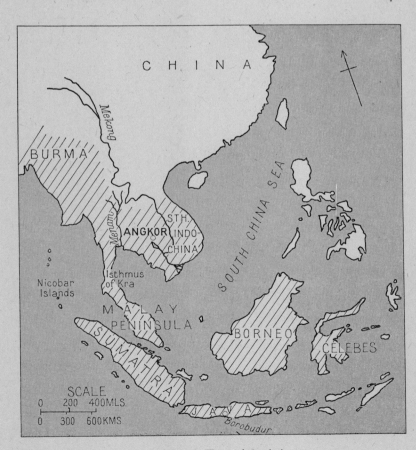

The hinduized kingdoms of South-East Asia (1)

Although plenty is now known about the Khmer civilization, the mystery and romance of its amazing ruins still attract the most fanciful theories. Angkor is a lost city of the imagination, and it still holds today the same mysterious atmosphere with which it greeted travellers in the nineteenth century. Great roots of trees clutch and enfold its sculptured walls. Monkeys play in the ruins, wild orchids grow there, lichens cover the friezes, a dank smell pervades the ruined temples, and bats make their home in the towers. Except where archaeologists have waged a successful war against the forest, there is a feeling of disaster, desertion and death. Yet Angkor is not depressing, it is an exhilarating place. The magnificent temples, some of them gigantic in size, the astonishing areas of stone covered in baroque carving, the evidences of material skill and complex spiritual imagination make the Khmer civilization one of the most remarkable of the ancient world.

The Empire of the Khmers

The Khmer empire covered the area of modern Cambodia and extended much further at the times of its greatest expansion. During the reign of Jayavarman VII the empire included much of present-day Thailand and most of Laos, probably excluding the mountainous areas in the north. Its sphere of influence certainly included all of present-day South Viet-Nam and may also have extended into the Malay peninsula south of the Isthmus of Kra. Chinese sources, and references in Burmese inscriptions, suggest that Khmer influence was also exerted over parts of Burma, but this is problematic. Angkor was linked by roads to other parts of the Khmer empire; one went north to Pimai in Thailand, and another probably went due east all the way to the Indo-China coastline. Special resthouses were established along these roads where travellers could shelter at night. There were also hospitals for the sick both at Angkor and along the roads.

The history of Cambodia starts about the beginning of the Christian era—in other words the prehistory of Cambodia continued until a comparatively late date. Various tribes, known collectively as the Mon-Khmer group, were living at this time in a large area stretching from Burma through Cambodia to the South China Sea and also including the Nicobar islands. The Khmers of Angkor are thought to be descended from one of the tribes in this group. At the beginning of the Christian era Hindu settlers from India began to trade in South-East Asia and intermarry with local tribes, and it was from this mixing of peoples that the Khmer civilization was born. It was only one of several cultures which flowered as a result of this 'hinduization' of South-East Asia. (The word 'indianized' is sometimes preferred on the grounds that 'hinduized' is too narrow in meaning and implies that the expansion from India was exclusively religious. In fact, the Indian settlers brought much else besides their religion.) Hinduized civilizations also developed in Champa (on the eastern seaboard of Indo-China), Burma, Thailand, Malaya, Celebes, Java and Sumatra.

f 1

The first hinduized kingdom of importance in Cambodia, similar in origin to the later Khmer empire at Angkor, was established near the delta of the River Mekong. Chinese writers called it Funan, and the excavations at Oc-Eo are presumed to be of a Funanese city. Funan flourished from about the first to the sixth centuries and was a strong power in South-East Asia, especially in commerce. Its decline coincided with the rise of various inland powers known for convenience as the pre-Angkor kingdoms. Sculpture and architecture from pre-Angkor sites, for example from Sambor Prei Kuk in central Cambodia, are the direct forerunners of the buildings and statues at Angkor. The inspiration of pre-Angkor art is Indian, and Hindu deities, for example Vishnu, are frequently depicted. Controversy surrounds the pre-Angkor period because Chinese writers mention a kingdom called Chen-La which is often presumed to have succeeded Funan. In fact the name 'Chen-La' is given to Cambodia by the Chinese as late as the thirteenth century, and the existence of a coherent kingdom called Chen-La in the seventh and eighth centuries is not proven. There were perhaps ten or more pre-Angkor kingdoms, lasting from the sixth until the beginning of the ninth century. It was from one of these that the first important ruler of Angkor emerged.

The temple of Preah Vihear, 1900 feet up in the Dangrek hills, was dedicated to Siva and probably founded by Yasovarman I at the end of the ninth century. In this reconstruction a small pool can be seen to the left of the long avenue. A reservoir six times as big as this pool was situated at the foot of the steps (not shown). Recently, Preah Vihear was the subject of dispute between Thailand and Cambodia, on whose borders it lies; the International Court of Justice decided in favour of Cambodia. (2)

This was Jayavarman II, whose reign in the Angkor area can be said to begin in 802. Inscriptions indicate that there was some connection with the hinduized kingdom of Java which Jayavarman II severed, and it was this that marked the beginning of the Angkor period in Khmer history, the classic period during which most of the great temples were built. Within this period, which lasted until the fifteenth century, the most important years were from 802 until 1218 (the latter date, given for the death of Jayavarman VII, being not at all certain). The chief historical events during these years were the removal of the Khmer capital from Angkor to Koh Ker during the early part of the tenth century and its return soon afterwards, the construction at Angkor of two enormous reservoirs for irrigation purposes, the building of at least four successive cities at Angkor, the sacking of Angkor by the Cham fleet in 1177, and the accession of Jayavarman VII in 1181. Jayavarman VII was the last king of any importance. Among his predecessors, besides Jayavarman II, two were especially important: Yasovarman I, 889–c. 900, who built a city at Angkor, pl 29 and Suryavarman II, 1113–1150(?), who built the temple of Angkor Wat.

The religion of the Khmers was Hinduism in which the worship of the Indian deity Siva and the *linga* (phallus) was pre-eminent. Buddhism entered Cambodia during the pre-Angkor period and was tolerated at Angkor as a minor sect until the twelfth century when it too became important. Jayavarman VII was a Buddhist, but after his death there was an iconoclastic reaction. His was Mahayana Buddhism (Greater Vehicle); Theravada Buddhism (Teaching of the Elders) did not make headway at Angkor until the thirteenth century.

A Brilliant Cultural Flowering

pl 6 The most important Khmer temples at Angkor are: Phnom
10 Bakheng, a temple on a hill at the centre of an ancient city built by Yasovarman I; Angkor Wat, built outside the city precincts by Suryavarman II; the Bayon, constructed by Jayavarman VII at the centre of his city (Angkor Thom). Angkor Wat is a temple and Angkor Thom is a city. The most important Khmer temples outside Angkor are: Banteay Chhmar, built by Jayavarman VII north-west of Angkor; Beng Mealea and Preah Khan of Kompong Svay, sites east of Angkor and built on by several kings; Prasat Thom at Koh Ker, built during the temporary removal of the Khmer capital to that region; and Pimai, a site built on by several kings north of the Dangrek hills in present-day Thailand.

The methods used by the Khmers to build these temples are not known exactly, but it seems likely that they constructed bamboo scaffolding and hauled up building materials by a simple system of pulleys and ropes. Blocks of stone were dressed before being put
f 18 into place so that every block fitted its bedfellow neatly. The sandstone from which Angkor Wat is built probably came from a quarry at Phnom Kulen, about forty kilometres from Angkor. The method of transport is not known, but water is an obvious suggestion since a river rises on Phnom Kulen and flows to Angkor.

The Khmer civilization centred at Angkor was a brilliant flowering of human endeavour. Scholars were regarded in high esteem, and colloquia were held at which learned men disputed with one another. Manuscripts of Indian epic poems were treasured and the poems themselves were recited in public. The king administered law and order, but sometimes appointed legal officials and assessors to help him. Also he exacted an oath of allegiance from leaders among the people and relied on the support of certain priestly families to maintain his position. The most influential priest had to consecrate the new king—a ceremony which seems to have declined in importance after the reigns of the early kings. Sandstone bas-reliefs at Angkor Wat and other temples indicate that pl 22 the Khmers had an army in which elephants carried the officers into battle, and a fleet which fought river-battles and sometimes ventured out to sea.

The history of Angkor is known from inscriptions, excavations, the accounts of Chinese travellers and from the nature of the temples themselves. No ancient manuscripts of the Khmer empire have survived. No book exists—no diary, no letter, no invoice, no

The Phum Da inscription (above) is dated 1054 and was discovered 160 kms. south-east of Angkor, at a village (phum) called Da. It relates the foundation of a linga by a holy man and is composed partly in Sanskrit and partly in Khmer. The Sanskrit part begins on the other side with an invocation to Siva, and the Khmer section (beginning at line 3 above) mentions both a pool and a ricefield as belonging to this foundation. Those who protect these things are offered prosperity. (3)

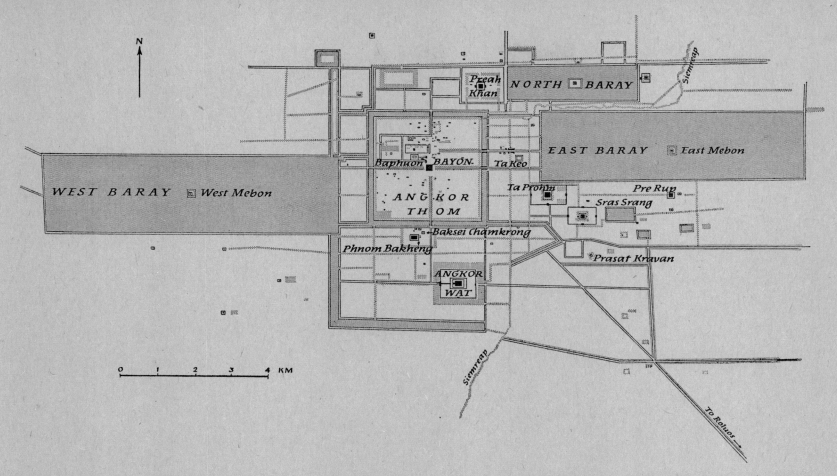

Angkor and its artificial waterways. Besides the two great 'barays', each holding a thousand million gallons, there were a large number of smaller pools and canals. One small river, the Siemreap, provided the main source of water for filling them. (4)

catalogue, no pamphlet. Khmer writings of a personal or an ephemeral nature were inscribed on palm leaves or skins which time and the tropical climate have destroyed for ever. There is little chance that future excavations will reveal ancient manuscripts preserved dramatically like the Dead Sea scrolls.

Khmer, the vernacular of the Khmer empire of Angkor, is still the language of Cambodia today. Its ancient form is known from the stone inscriptions, more than 950 of which have been rubbed and translated by French epigraphists. Khmer writing itself was derived from certain Indian systems during the pre-Angkor period. Just as the Cyrillic alphabet can be used for writing more than one Slavonic language, so written Khmer was the vehicle for more than one language at Angkor. In the inscriptions, Sanskrit passages are of interest because information is given about the Khmer kings and the gods whom they considered themselves to incarnate. Khmer passages are also important for the sidelights which they provide on life in the ancient kingdom.

An eleventh-century inscription relates the market price of slaves. A good slave could cost as much as a three-ounce silver bowl, a plate weighing two pounds one ounce, a two-pound pot, three tablets of wax and a certain quantity of stuff, whereas a much inferior slave could be bought for twenty measures of rice. A tenth-century inscription relates the case of a corrupt Khmer official who removed the boundaries of a ricefield and poached the crop. The punishment for this was a fine of ten ounces of gold for the official, a hundred and two strokes with the birch for his brother who ordered the poached field to be harvested, and a small fine for the principal workman who supervised the harvest. Other inscriptions give information on the mortgaging of property, the method of measuring ricefields, and the procedure for purchasing land.

The Water that Brought Life

The ancient Khmers were obsessed with water. The powers of water are frequently referred to in the inscriptions, and two *barays* (reservoirs) were constructed at Angkor to hold more than a thousand million gallons of water each. The Angkor region was, however, less well supplied with natural waterways than some

The natural waterways of Cambodia. The shading shows the main rice-growing areas today, served by natural or artificial irrigation. (5)

other parts of Indo-China. For example, Phnom Penh, the present-day capital of Cambodia, is situated at a point where four branches of the River Mekong meet and where there is extensive flooding when the river is in spate. At Angkor one small river, the Siemreap, provided the main source of water for filling the reservoirs. Besides building these two large reservoirs, which were situated east and west of their city, Angkor Thom, the Khmers also constructed numerous pools and artificial canals. It is misleading to paint in the mind's eye a picture of Angkor's rulers strolling for pleasure beside their lakes and pools. The Khmer kings never built, and never intended to build, a Versailles or a Peterhof. Their obsession with water was devout, not aesthetic. Neither was Angkor a spa,

131

nor did the Khmer obsession with water bear any resemblance to that which is inspired by the waters of Lourdes in modern times. The Khmers were obsessed with water because without it there could be no life.

All peoples in every age have of course depended on water for life. The Khmers needed an abnormal quantity, to irrigate their ricefields. Specially constructed irrigation systems enabled them to harvest a rice-crop more than once a year, more than twice a year, even perhaps four times a year. Cambodia's rainy season lasts about six months from May to October, and without the conservation of water after this rainy season the Khmer kings could not have grown enough rice to feed their population. There are three small hills in the immediate environs of Angkor, but they are not suitable for catchment purposes.

The rectangular shape of the *barays* at Angkor is in contrast to the haphazard shapes of water-tanks which fed agricultural lands at the ancient site of Anuradhapura in Ceylon. What can be called the geometry of Angkor is of great importance, for both Khmer temple and *baray* have a strict geometrical scheme of magic significance. Obviously one bears some special relationship to the other, for a temple was never constructed without a pool, nor a pool dug without a temple. This point is of crucial importance when one comes to consider why the Khmer empire collapsed. One of the theories put forward is that the Khmers built too many temples and exhausted themselves economically. But if pools were dug at the same time as temples and their main purpose was to irrigate the land, then the real problem is to discover which was more important to the Khmers: pool or temple.

The Struggle for Fertile Soil

The Khmer words for laterite mean 'dry rice', because laterite resembles the overcooked crust of rice which adheres to the sides of a Khmer cooking pot and which would spread to the whole pot if cooking continued for too long. The colour of laterite also resembles that of scorched rice and varies from reddish brown to black. Cambodia's tropical climate produces enough rain to nurture a dry tropical forest. This kind of rainfall makes for ideal oxidizing conditions under the surface soil. Laterite is an iron oxide derived from rocks weathering under these conditions. Oxidization of rock occurs where the surface soil is not deep (e.g. at Angkor), and the hard, infertile oxide grows upwards with insidiously increasing speed. Finally a stage is reached when water can no longer penetrate the thick laterite core, and this is when the remaining surface soil is eroded most quickly. The process, called laterization, caused the Khmers to enter upon a war of man against nature. In order to maintain fertile ricefields man had to prevent nature from reducing and eroding the surface soil.

A ricefield is bounded by miniature earthworks which act as dykes capturing rain when it falls and containing it in the field area. A muddy seedbed is thus created into which young rice seedlings can be planted. Mud provides the natural chemicals without which the crop cannot grow. When a ricefield is irrigated by rainfall year after year, there is a danger of laterization. The surface soil is gradually reduced until insufficient is left to form the seedbed. The ancient Khmer kings solved this problem by capturing the muddy waters of the Siemreap river in the East and West *barays*. These reservoirs were linked to the ricefields by canals and small catchment pools. Twice a year or more the ricefields were flooded systematically from the *barays*, the surface soil was continually replenished by deposits from the Siemreap river, the loss by laterization was made good and the ricefields of Angkor remained fertile.

The ancient Khmer road from Angkor Thom to the east passes today through a barren region from whose scattered ricefields the villagers of modern Cambodia can hardly make a living. The irrigation systems of Angkor must have stopped working in the fourteenth or fifteenth centuries, after which the Khmer kings found their economy impaired by the reduction of annual rice-harvests and the gradual laterisation of once fertile land. They must have led their subjects into the forest, cutting down trees to make clearings for new ricefields and followed wherever they went by the spectre of laterization.

In recent times waterwheels have been constructed along the Siemreap river for carrying the muddy water to otherwise infertile land. The modern Khmer government is wisely re-establishing parts of the ancient irrigation system, especially in connection with the West *baray*. More than one annual rice-harvest will soon be the general rule and doubtless the modern Khmers will proclaim that the kingdom of Angkor is rising again. But what disrupted the irrigation systems of old Angkor?

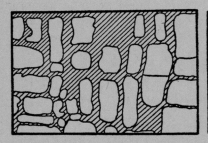

These two diagrams (from aerial photographs) show what is meant by 'intensive cultivation'. Left, in post-Angkor Cambodia, relatively large ricefields have rounded corners for ease in ploughing; the shaded ground is wasted. Right, a mosaic of smaller fields in north Indo-China—a pattern of straight lines and right angles, where every inch of space is used. (6)

The Challenge of Natural Catastrophe

An invading army could have destroyed the dykes, in which case Angkor would have been flooded by water from the reservoirs. It is reasonable to suppose that this might have happened when the Thais invaded Cambodia in the fifteenth century, but excavations have not yet offered any evidence of flooding from this cause. There is, however, other evidence which suggests that a natural flood might have taken place. The Siemreap river has changed its course since the heyday of the Khmer empire. Today an ancient Khmer bridge spans a dry watercourse outside the east wall of Angkor Thom, and the Siemreap river has carved itself a new course near by. It is not possible to say when the river changed its course, whether before the abandonment of Angkor or after. Doubtless the ancient bridge was used in the fourteenth century, but it is not in use today. A flood may well have caused the Siemreap river to change its course.

The Great Lake (Tonle Sap) is an obvious source of floodwater. The River Mekong acts on the Great Lake rather as the White Nile acts upon the Blue Nile. In summer the Mekong pushes the floodwaters along a tributary into the Great Lake which then floods the surrounding country. At high water, parts of the Cambodian forest are flooded, and in the fifteenth century floodwater could have been carried much nearer Angkor than is apparent from the Great Lake's boundaries today. In other words the north-western shores of the Great Lake have gradually encroached on the area formerly covered by the floods at high water. Perhaps the Great Lake flooded Angkor in the fifteenth century.

By good fortune a legend exists that Angkor Thom was flooded, if not at this time, at least in this way. Nineteenth-century travellers in Cambodia and Thailand were often told stories of a great flood in Cambodia's past. These stories probably originated in a history of Buddhism compiled by a Buddhist monk who lived at the beginning of the sixteenth century. According to the legend he recorded, the son of the king at Angkor Thom had a pet fly and the son of the royal chaplain a pet spider. It so happened that the spider ate the prince's fly and the king's son was much upset. The event was reported to the king who seized the son of his chaplain and drowned him in the Great Lake. The naga-king, that is to say the snake god who is frequently depicted in sculpture at Angkor, then caused a great flood which destroyed Angkor Thom. If the legend reported here is based on fact, then this flood from the Great Lake may well have disrupted the Khmer capital and its complex irrigation works.

It is fairly certain that the Khmers tried to prevent excessive flooding. There were two ways in which this could be done—by controlling the flow of water through canals, and by building dykes. The two big reservoirs at Angkor were themselves created by the erection of dykes within which the water was conserved.

The level of the water in these reservoirs was above the rice-bearing plain so that water could be channelled by gravity to wherever it was needed. To perform this operation successfully the Khmers must have had sluice-gates, but the exact nature of such gates is not known. They may have been made of wood or heaped-up earth, or possibly of laterite blocks since unexplained blocks of laterite have been discovered at suggestive points in the banks of a reservoir at Angkor and at another one in Koh Ker. However expertly these sluice-gates were arranged, they could not have controlled a massive inrush of water from the Great Lake. Protective dykes have been discovered south of Angkor at points where the flooding from the Great Lake may have been a threat, but even these would not have been able to withstand a really big flood. A flood, therefore, cannot be completely ruled out as a possible cause of the Khmer empire's collapse, but since the evidence is so inconclusive it does not seem very likely.

Recent excavations carried out at Angkor Thom have shown that the site was definitely burnt, so fire may have been a cause of the collapse. Wood was the material for building houses in the ancient Khmer empire as it still is in Cambodia now. Wherever ancient Khmer temples stand in ruins today, wooden dwelling-places must be imagined as clustering them about in the past. Doubtless these wooden agglomerations were frequently burnt down by mischance as well as by foreign invaders. The excavations from which this information is drawn also revealed the existence of four successive royal palaces, the proposed chronology for these palaces being:

Palace I   about 1000/1010 to about 1050
Palace II   about 1050 to 1177
Palace III   1177 to about 1350
Palace IV   1350 to about 1430 (or a little before)

The one clear date in this chronology, 1177, is determined from a Chinese source which says that in this year the Cham navy took Angkor by surprise and sacked it. It is also probable that Angkor Thom was burnt by the Thais in the middle of the fourteenth century. But it is doubtful whether fire could have been the whole story, for wood was plentiful in Cambodia, and the Khmers would have had no difficulty in rebuilding their houses every time they were burnt down.

There remains only one more possible natural cause—an earthquake. There is no evidence that an earthquake or volcanic eruption ever took place in Cambodia and the ruins themselves do not suggest that they ever suffered from tremors of the earth's surface. The nearest volcanic region to Angkor is the South China Sea which in 1923 threw up a section of the ocean bed—known now appropriately as *L'Ile des Cendres*.

Natural change, and natural catastrophe, were always a threat to the Khmers of Angkor. Extensive works were necessary to provide water and keep laterization at bay. Fire undoubtedly assailed them, flood was possible. What human and spiritual factors added to the challenge?

What Did the Temples Mean to the Khmers?

pl 4
6

It is difficult for a present-day mind to understand the meaning of a Khmer temple such as Angkor Wat, not because nothing is known about its purpose—it was a Vishnuite temple—but because twentieth-century ways of thinking block the only approach to its meaning. The spire of a Gothic cathedral is said to represent the soaring aspirations of its builders towards God. In John Milton's *Paradise Lost* the meaning is clear when Satan is compared, for example, with a comet. In both these examples the object (cathedral spire) or person (Satan) is like another object (aspirations/comet). A conscious leap is made in the present-day mind to compare one with the other, then a conscious leap back to the starting position. This way of thinking, so typical of the twentieth century, cripples the ability to understand ancient Khmer buildings.

It is, therefore, necessary to make an effort of the imagination to discover how a Khmer mind worked. Inscriptions indicate that the Khmers regarded their temples as Mount Meru, a mythical mountain from Hindu mythology thought of as the centre of the universe. The Khmers did not regard Phnom Bakheng, for example, as *representing* Mount Meru. For them it really *was* Mount Meru. Similarly the king who occupied this temple in the sense

This bronze palanquin hook, found at Angkor, was used to suspend a hammock from a carved wooden pole. Khmer ladies of rank sat in these hammocks and were carried through the city. The naga *motif is visible (bottom right) with the beak of* garuda *protruding above it.* (7)

that he was the founder of it and after death would be buried there was regarded as being a Hindu god. The king did not represent a god or pretend to be a god. For the Khmers he was a god. Such ideas are not uncommon among ancient peoples, but they are none the less important in a consideration of Angkor.

A further illustration can be given of how the Khmer mind might be supposed to work. For the purposes of argument the Khmer sits cross-legged under a tree with the fingers of his left hand interlocked with those of his right hand. It is a stormy day and an elephant happens to be passing by. The thoughts of this man are synchronized with the movement of his head as he looks upwards and then down. The three objects seen by him are his own interlocking hands, the elephant's trunk, and a cloud in the sky. From a present-day point of view the shape of this man's hands is like the shape of an elephant's trunk which could in turn be like the shape of a cloud in the sky. But to the Khmer mind the hands *are* the elephant's trunk which *is* the cloud in the sky. These things are not similar because of their shape, but they are actually the same thing. This illustration shows how difficult the Khmer mind is to understand and how different it is from our own. And yet the application is simple and has already been stated—a Khmer temple could be regarded as the centre of the universe known as Mount Meru. For the Khmers it actually was the centre of the universe and the man who founded such a centre was their god. Generally speaking every new king wished to establish that he too was a god capable of sitting at the centre of the universe. He would achieve this by building a new temple. There are many such temples at Angkor and their resemblance to mountains has already been noted.

pl 9
15

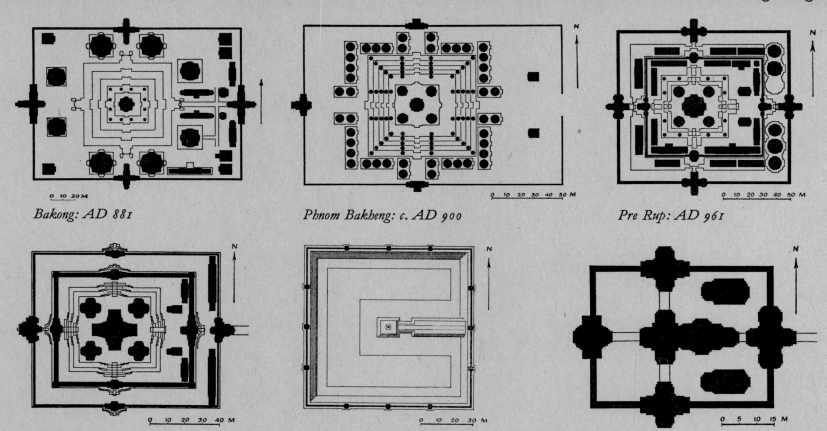

Bakong: *AD 881*   Phnom Bakheng: *c. AD 900*   Pre Rup: *AD 961*

Ta Keo: *c. AD 1000*   W. Mebon: *2nd half of 11th C.*   Chau Say Tevoda: *end of 11th C.–1st half of 12th C.*

THE DEVELOPMENT OF KHMER ARCHITECTURE

Bakong, the most important temple-mountain in the first century of the Angkor period, is composed of towers surrounding a recessed pyramid. Phnom Bakheng is comparable but with five towers at the centre. Pre Rup shows towers and uncontinuous vaulted halls. Ta Keo has an innovation —the vaulted halls are continuous and have become galleries. The West Mebon shows the same principle—a continuous vault surrounding (in this case) a single tower—in a different setting. Chau Say Tevoda, a minor temple of the Angkor Wat style, shows how towers and galleries have become integrated. The central tower is also integrated carefully into the scheme. The plan of Angkor Wat, bigger than any of the plans shown here, has the same harmony as Chau Say Tevoda. In addition, its galleries

pl 4   *besides being integrated with towers are also integrated into the recesses of*
6   *the pyramid. Compare Ta Keo, where the galleries and pyramid recesses are separate. In the Bayon, galleries and towers are still integrated, but the design is complex, confused and cramped. The central mass carved with many heads stands above the colonnaded galleries which house the bas-reliefs. (8–14)*

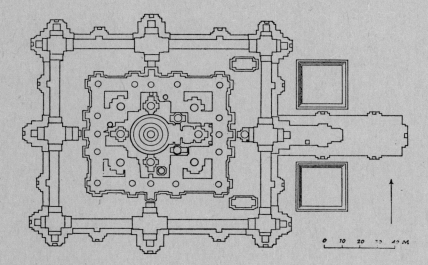

Bayon: *end of 12th C. or early 13th C.*

The Churning of the Sea of Milk

Besides taking over the idea of Mount Meru from Hindu mythology the Khmers also adopted a Vishnuite legend called the Churning of the Sea of Milk. This legend is known in India from sculpture and painting and literature, but its use in Indian works of art is as nothing compared to its constantly repeated use by the ancient Khmers. The builders of Angkor seem to have been particularly fond of it and represented it over and over again in sculpture. Nor was its use confined to Angkor, since many examples have been found all over Cambodia. A casual visitor to Angkor will at once ask the question: 'Who are these teams of sandstone giants pulling at tug-of-war with a snake's body for a rope?' This is how the Khmer's interpretation of the Churning legend appears to the onlooker, for example outside the five gates

pl 37   of Angkor Thom or on the east gallery reliefs of Angkor Wat. It
38   is necessary to consider the thought behind.

In the Churning legend Vishnu is supposed to appear in the form of a tortoise to recover things of value, ambrosia for example, which have been lost. He sites himself at the bottom of the sea of milk, and offers his shell as the base on which a mountain may be pivoted. The gods and demons twist a great serpent round the mountain, and proceed to churn ambrosia. The churn operates like a toy top, but whereas a boy spins his top, then detaches the

piece of string, the string in the Churning legend, represented by a snake, is pulled backwards and forwards by two teams and remains coiled round the pivot. Just as boiling water spurts upwards in a coffee percolator, so ambrosia is thought to rise from the sea of milk as a result of the churning process. The legend is more easily understood if one equates ambrosia and the other desirable objects with health, wealth and happiness.

The Khmers repeatedly used the Churning legend in their sculpture and since the object of the legend was to obtain health, wealth and happiness, the interpretation of the Churning sculpture is fairly obvious. The most striking of all Churning sculptures are those outside the gates of Angkor Thom, where the gods and demons straddle the moat surrounding the city. Obviously the moat is intended to represent the Sea of Milk or, as a Khmer would think of it, the moat *was* the Sea of Milk, and the gates of Angkor Thom are mountains from which ambrosia will be produced. But where one would expect to see this depicted in the sculpture an enigmatic face stares out from the gateway. These faces are   pl 7 indentified as faces of Jayavarman VII in the form of a future Buddha. There are many different future Buddhas, but this one, probably Lokesvara, is connected with providence. Now the interpretation of these sculptures is complete. The gods and demons churn the sea and produce not ambrosia but the providential Khmer monarch himself. To the Khmer mind the face of their king was a guarantee of health, wealth and happiness. Every time they passed underneath one of these gates they took part in a magic operation which guaranteed them future happiness.

The life of a Khmer citizen was not pleasant. His main occupations were rice-cultivation, building and fighting. Although there was an unknown number of slaves at Angkor to help him, his duties in service of his king must have been arduous. Inscriptions record long lists of persons and whole communities which were bound to the various Khmer temples by charter and had to serve these temple charters by working, either in the ricefields, or in the temples themselves or as soldiers. Besides building and maintaining the temples they also had to construct the irrigation systems which were part of the temple enclaves. The reward for all this arduous labour was health, wealth and happiness. Each time a Khmer citizen passed through a gate of Angkor Thom from the ricefields, the quarries or the wars, he saw the face of his king smiling from the gateway and promising ambrosia—health, wealth, happiness guaranteed by the magical Churning of the Sea of Milk.

This then may be the heart of the matter. The best guarantee of prosperity was the good running of the irrigation works. As the population grew larger, more land had to be cultivated, and therefore more irrigation works constructed—to the Khmer peasants' mind perhaps more water to be churned, more temples for the churning. At least in the Khmer mind there existed a belief that temple and pool were linked together in a magic relationship. The construction of temples and irrigation works went hand in hand and demanded an enormous labour force which in turn had to be fed. It was a vicious circle which accords with the Khmers' feverish construction of so many temples.

The Many-Towered Bayon

pl 10   The most important temple of Angkor Thom during the reign of Jayavarman VII was undoubtedly the Bayon, and its strange
f 4   appearance requires some explanation. The Bayon stands at the
14   centre of the city and is the terminus of two axial roads leading from four of the gates. While it shares the general characteristics of Khmer temples, it also resembles a gateway of Angkor Thom mul-
pl 11   tiplied some fifty times. There are many smiling faces sculptured on its towers, some of which look inwards and are hidden from view. Each tower is composed of four faces pointing to the four cardinal points of the compass. Why were so many towers grouped together and why were the smiling faces sculptured upon them?

It is an interesting visual experiment to hold a hand up to the eyes so that it masks the plinth on which the Bayon's four-faced towers are sited. The temple becomes reminiscent of a piece of textile machinery or even of a series of pitheads above a coal seam. In the first impression, that of a machine, the four-faced towers are seen as bobbins of differing heights set out on a lathe. Half-close the eyes in front of the Bayon and it is almost possible to imagine that its towers are, in fact, spinning. Each spins on its own axis and independently of adjacent towers. The central tower, more complex than the others, also spins. The second visual impression, that of the coal pitheads, suggests that some important operation is taking place beneath. When these two visual impressions are combined, the Bayon might be said to be a series of rotating towers which are imagined to stretch downwards and perform some operation below. It could be that each tower of the Bayon was considered by the Khmers to be churning the waters beneath and transforming them into ambrosia.

But why were so many towers grouped together? Four-faced towers, like those of the Bayon, are found at other places in the Khmer empire besides Angkor. These particular towers are a hallmark of Jayavarman VII, and would be recognized as such by the Khmer populace. Since the Bayon was the centre of the kingdom, it is possible that each four-faced tower represented an outlying province or temple. There can be no certainty about this, but it is the kind of idea which a Khmer mind might have conceived.

Every year the Khmer king ordered the entire population to parade in front of the royal palace at Angkor which stood close to the Bayon. The purpose of this parade was a census, though unfortunately the total number of persons who paraded is not known.

The towers of the Bayon must have dominated the parade-ground and may have represented in spiritual form a message for the human beings there assembled. It could have been the same message that greeted the Khmer citizen returning through a gate of Angkor Thom—a guarantee of health, wealth and happiness through the providential nature of the king. Since the entire Khmer population visited Angkor once a year, the Bayon might be compared to Lenin's mausoleum in Moscow in front of which large numbers of the Soviet population parade once a year. Just as Lenin's embalmed body attempts to guarantee the permanence of his empire, so the Bayon may have been a guarantee to the Khmers of present and future prosperity. As long as a Khmer citizen could prove that he had served his temple-charter faithfully, then he would be assured of health, wealth and happiness.

If this interpretation of Khmer temples, the Bayon in particular, is correct, then it begins to look as if the Khmers really built their temples for economic reasons. This is an exaggeration and clearly a building such as Angkor Wat was not built merely as an extension to an irrigation system. However, an economic theory of this kind does throw light on the mystery of Angkor—why did the Khmer empire collapse? After considering some more possible reasons for the disintegration, it should be practicable to select the most likely ones.

The Report of Chou Ta-Kouan

The importance of inscriptions as a source for knowledge about the Khmers has already been mentioned, and the result of a stratified excavation carried out at Angkor has also been quoted. One important source which has not yet been named is the account of Angkor by a Chinese official called Chou Ta-Kouan who visited Cambodia in AD 1296–1297. He does not give any assessment of the Angkor kingdom as a power in South-East Asia. His main aim seems to have been to inform other Chinese travellers how to behave at Angkor and what kind of a reception they might expect from the Khmers. There are no authorities for this diplomatic mission apart from Chou Ta-Kouan himself and his notes on the country are those of a commercial counsellor rather than the political reporting of an ambassador. But his account is of exceptional interest because it describes life at Angkor when the Khmer Empire had just started to decline.

He wrote about the rice-harvests at Angkor, the arrival of a new religion among the Khmers, and about invasions by a foreign army, the Thais. He says that there were three or four annual rice-harvests at Angkor, and although he does not elaborate on this crucial statement it must mean that the irrigation systems of Angkor were in excellent working order at the end of the thirteenth century. In his section on religion he says that certain religious persons called *tch'ou-kou* shaved their heads, wore yellow robes,   pl 25 and left their right shoulders uncovered. The word *tch'ou-kou* has been identified as a Thai word used when referring to monks of Theravada Buddhism. During the classic period of the Khmer civilization from the ninth to the thirteenth centuries Theravada Buddhism was not practised at Angkor, and therefore the reference to it by Chou Ta-Kouan means that it arrived at Angkor probably not long before Chou Ta-Kouan himself. It was in other words a new religion. Chou Ta-Kouan says about the Thais that they had recently fought a debilitating war against the Khmers and that the Khmer countryside had been devastated. He also reports the presence of Thais at Angkor itself, indicating that some kind of peaceful infiltration was taking place too.

Attack by Land and Water

It has been suggested that the Khmer civilization wrecked itself by indulging in wild imperialistic wars and trying to subjugate the whole of South-East Asia. It is true that the bas-reliefs of Angkor   pl 17–ot Wat, the Bayon and Banteay Chhmar depict countless scenes of   24 battle on sea and land. But an examination of the facts does not reveal that the Khmers set out to conquer all South-East Asia. Angkor was situated well away from the Indo-China coast and off the main trade routes. The first Khmer capital was established there as a result of gradual secession from Javanese overlordship and not because of a violent conflict with Java or any other country. In the first two centuries of Khmer rule at Angkor the frontiers were reasonably secure and were consolidated by the Khmer kings without the need for constant warfare.

f 15   However, the Khmers did have to face three main enemies—the Chams in the east, the Thais in the north-west and the Annamites in the north-east. During the classic period of Khmer civilization the Chams were the chief threat. Their kingdom Champa, which was also a hinduized kingdom like Angkor but not so brilliant, lay in what is now South Viet-Nam. Its two capitals, present-day

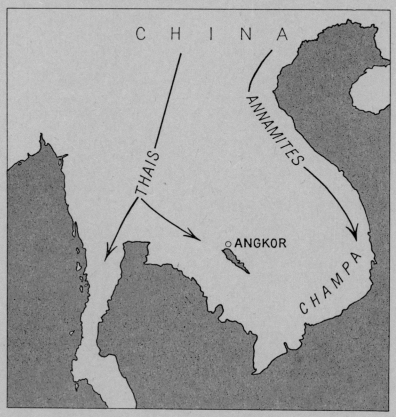

The southward advance of Thais and Annamites during the 13th century, under pressure from the Chinese to the north. (15)

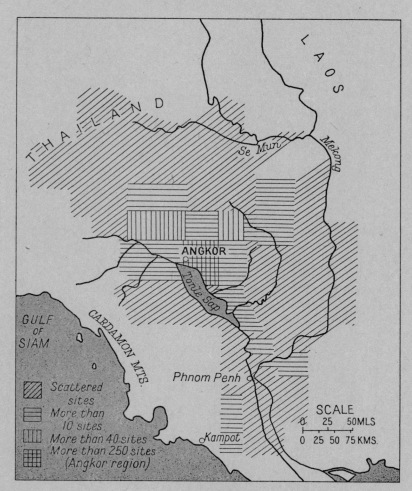

A plot of the density of ancient Khmer sites, in terms of number of sites per unit area of 800 square miles. (16)

136

Binh-Dinh and Phan-Rang, were ports on the main maritime trade route to China and on one occasion the Cham navy had to shadow the Chinese fleet which was on a punitive expedition to Java. There was a need for Champa to be constantly on her guard so the Chams used to raid Khmer territory. In AD 1177 they brought their fleet up the River Mekong, across the Great Lake *pl 17* and up the Siemreap river. They were guided by a Chinese pilot and managed to take Angkor by surprise. Although Angkor was *pl 20* sacked by the Chams on this occasion, the Khmers subsequently conquered Champa and the Chams declined in strength.

The Khmers never succeeded in beating off the Thais. In the thirteenth century the Thai people came gradually southwards from the borders of China and clashed with the Khmers, whose outposts extended far into the River Menam valley. There is disagreement about the number of times that the Thais occupied Angkor or whether any of these occupations could be said to have delivered a knockout blow; Chou Ta-Kouan reported a Thai invasion in the thirteenth century and the years 1431/32 are given as dates for the final sack of Angkor by the Thais.

The Annamites did not invade Cambodia until after the abandonment of Angkor, and although the Khmers led punitive expeditions against Annam during the Angkor period the real clash between the two peoples did not take place until later.

Obviously it was not the Chams or the Annamites who caused Angkor to crash. It could have been the Thai invasion in the mid-fourteenth century which burnt Angkor Thom and systematically blocked the waterways with debris from gutted buildings—leading to a dislocation of the irrigation systems and an economic breakdown. This reason for the end of the Khmer empire might seem to be conclusive except that by the mid-fourteenth century the Khmers were already on the decline, for it is known that no buildings of any importance were built after the opening years of the thirteenth century. If the Khmers had not already declined for some other reason, they might have been able to withstand the Thai attacks.

Massive Building and Megalomania

A favoured reason proposed for this decline is that the Khmer kings, especially Jayavarman VII, exhausted their subjects by making them build too many temples, in short that the Khmer kings suffered from megalomania, the insanity of self-exaltation and the passion for big things. Were the ancient Khmer kings megalomaniacs in this sense? Men who claim to be God are guilty of self-exaltation, but we have seen that the Khmer kings did not have to claim to be gods: they *were* gods to their subjects. Was it just a passion for big things or were there more logical reasons?

According to the economic theory there is some definite connection between the irrigation systems and the temples which they served. The size of the temples depended on the irrigation systems and were large or important according to the extent of land to be cultivated and the number of mouths to be fed. It is, however, difficult to agree that Angkor Wat was so related. This is a very monster of a building, and the thing above all else which strikes every visitor is its size. Angkor Wat was never intended to be a church, so comparison with enormous cathedrals in Europe is beside the point. This was one man's temple but even if it were admitted to be the work of a megalomaniac, it cannot be said to have caused the gradual collapse of the Khmer empire some two centuries later.

The intended culprit is the last great king—Jayavarman VII. He undertook the construction of more temples than any previous king, and did not complete the building of them in his own lifetime. Half-finished buildings, partly carved statues and incomplete inscriptions indicate that work suddenly stopped. There was moreover a violent reaction from the people some time after Jayavarman VII's death. He had himself favoured Mahayana Buddhism and allowed a number of Buddhist statues to be carved. Many of *pl 31* these were defaced by iconoclasts and torn from their niches. Perhaps this religious outburst, probably the only one of its kind at Angkor, was a reaction against megalomania. But Jayavarman VII's best-known temple, the Bayon, does not strike the visitor as the work of a megalomaniac. Rather his building programme as a whole betrays some kind of mania. In fact, Khmer history

The development of the male head in ancient Khmer sculpture. (1) Bak-heng style: straight eyebrows, prominent eyes, and a 'hard' line. (2) Banteay Srei style: a softer expression, eyebrows curved, eyes less bulging, fuller lips. (3) Angkor Wat style: less effeminate, lips longer but still full, eyebrows wavy. (4) Bayon style: softly arched eyebrows, eyes half-closed, lips full, soft and faintly smiling. (17)

shows Jayavarman VII to have been a level-headed monarch who reached the throne in late middle age after having witnessed two or three palace revolutions. And according to the economic theory Jayavarman VII's building programme was prompted by a desire to expand the irrigation systems at Angkor and put the Khmer empire's economy on a sound basis. This idea is supported by the fact that Jayavarman VII built a third reservoir at Angkor, the North Baray—not as large as the other two but an important addition to the water resources of the capital. He had also an extensive building programme outside Angkor which probably included the building of a big reservoir at Banteay Chhmar as well as many other minor works. It can be argued therefore that his programme was sensible and logical, and that it could have been fulfilled had an equally strong king emerged to succeed him.

The Decline of the God-Kings

But Jayavarman VII was Angkor's last great king, and to find a possible reason for this we must recall Chou Ta-Kouan's report of men wearing yellow robes. It seems that a new religion, Theravada Buddhism, had arrived at Angkor. It is not possible to understand the significance of this event without taking a backward look at the religions practised by the Khmers at Angkor since AD

802 when they became established in the region. Worship of the Hindu trinity, of Siva and Vishnu, and to some extent Brahma, was inherited from the pre-Angkor kingdoms and Funan. One or two temples, Phnom Krom for example, had three towers, each containing a statue of Siva, Brahma or Vishnu. Siva was usually worshipped in the form of a stone *linga* (phallus) and many such objects have been found on Khmer sites. Inscriptions were sometimes carved on them. The *linga* was considered as the physical presence of the *devaraja* (god-king) and had to be installed on a suitable mountain at the beginning of each reign. These mountains, regarded by the Khmers as Mount Meru the centre of the universe, were the actual temples. For example, when the Khmers moved the capital to Koh Ker, a new temple was built to house an enormous *linga* which embodied the *devaraja* of the new king. pl 40

Mahayana Buddhism also existed at Angkor alongside the worship of Hindu deities and the cult of the *devaraja*. One king established at the same time three hermitages in honour of Siva, Vishnu and Buddha. In one Khmer temple, the Bayon, the physical presence of the *devaraja* was not embodied in a *linga* but in a statue of Buddha—because the king at the time, Jayavarman VII, was a pl 31 Mahayana Buddhist. The Khmers must not be thought inconsistent if they grafted one sect of Hinduism on to another and mixed in Mahayana Buddhism, since the same kind of thing was happening in India. The enduring religious factor at Angkor was the cult of the *devaraja*, the all-powerful god-king, and as long as new sects or religions satisfied the demands of a *devaraja* all was well. Theravada Buddhism, the new religion, did not satisfy the demands of the *devaraja*.

The arrival of Theravada Buddhism at Angkor was in the nature of a spiritual catastrophe for the ancient Khmer empire. Theravada Buddhism is a reformed sect of Buddhism whose adherents do not fundamentally believe that Buddha should be worshipped as a god, and as the Khmers traditionally worshipped their kings as gods, this revolutionary belief had a loosening effect on their loyalties. The Khmer kings demanded obedience and guaranteed prosperity, but Theravada demanded humility and promised suffering. The Khmer kings were gods who clothed themselves in gold and lived in sumptuous palaces, whereas the Theravada Buddhist monks preached that kings should give up their possessions and clothe their bodies in rags. This was what the royal prince Buddha had done, they said. The *devaraja* had power of life and death over his subjects, but Theravada prohibited killing both of animals and human beings. One faith was harshly obsessed with material prosperity while the other mildly resigned itself to poverty. The Khmer kings were proud of their achievements in this life while the Buddhists of Theravada looked forward to a more prosperous incarnation in the next. Finally, the *devarajas* were gods, and Theravada's Buddha was a man. The Khmers, while they retained a superstition in the divinity of their king, looked for solace and found it in their new religion. They were no longer interested in health, wealth and happiness but only in finding a faith which would relieve them from their utter exhaustion.

The theory that the Khmer empire collapsed because of Theravada Buddhism is attractive but against it must be set the economic theory. The question must be asked whether as a result of irrigation systems falling into disrepair and a shortage of food the Khmers turned to a religion which preached hunger was a virtue, or whether as a result of adopting a new religion they let the cult of the *devaraja* and the temples of their *devarajas* fall into abeyance. This question also embodies a difficulty which has already been noted: which was more important to the ancient Khmers, pool or temple?

The Khmers did not differentiate in their own minds between the magic of religion, helped by the worship of statues and temples, and the magic of nature, helped by sowing rice seedlings in properly fertilized ricefields. To them there was only one magic operation to which a Western mind would say that nature and religion both contributed. Just as it was necessary to dig a reservoir to provide irrigation water during the dry season, so it was necessary for this water to play a part in the Churning legend, for example, a magic process which would change it into ambrosia. Those who built the temples also brought in the harvest, and it would have been unthinkable for the Khmers to perform one operation but not the other. The temples and the ricefields were interdependent parts of the same whole.

The Total Challenge

In the reign of Jayavarman VII, when the need to rebuild the empire after the Cham invasion of AD 1177 was pressing, irrigation systems with temples were built at Angkor and in the provinces. This programme of building came to a halt when Jayavarman died and was not resumed because the people reacted against it while a new religion, Theravada Buddhism, weakened their resolve. About a century later (1350) and possibly at an earlier date too, the Thais invaded Cambodia and dislocated the irrigation works at Angkor. The Khmer economy broke down, never recovered, and suffered further setbacks each time the Thais invaded the country. Apart from the fact that the Khmers could no longer produce as many harvests as they required, laterization probably took place on the land which gradually lost its fertility and could no longer be cultivated. At the same time Theravada Buddhism had become the people's religion and sapped their will to resist the onslaughts of man and nature. It was a challenge to which the people were unable to respond: in AD 1432 Angkor was abandoned and the Khmer empire rapidly disintegrated.

After Five Hundred Years

From this moment on the story of Angkor is like a tale of mystery and imagination. The forest ate up the temples so fast that a later Khmer king rediscovered the ancient capital while on a hunting expedition. He tried to have the capital restored but failed to maintain his court there. The forest advanced again into the temples and the whole of Angkor Thom was swallowed up. Trees sprouted from towers, tropical creepers garlanded the statues, and sprawling roots forced themselves into the foundations.

Rumours of a mythical lost city in Cambodia occasionally escaped to the outside world. In AD 1609 a European writer, basing himself on the reports of travellers, wrote a short account of Angkor in which he speculated whether it might not be the fantastic Atlantis. In the late seventeenth century a missionary wrote that pilgrims came regularly to Angkor Wat from far afield. It seems, therefore, that Angkor Wat was never abandoned in the same way as Angkor Thom. In spite of this the mystery which had settled on the Khmers in the fifteenth century persisted. Even when a

fair number of Portuguese, Spanish and French travellers had passed through Cambodia and even visited Angkor Wat, the disappearance of its builders and the bizarre appearance of Angkor Thom stimulated imaginations.

The account by the French naturalist, Henri Mouhot, rediscovered Angkor for the Western world. He wrote of Angkor Wat as being grander than anything left by Greece or Rome and as a temple which must have been erected by some ancient Michelangelo. Mouhot's drawing of Angkor Wat as it was in the mid-nineteenth century shows that it had withstood the tropical forest's invasion reasonably well. Mouhot contrasted Angkor Wat in his diary with the other monuments upon which 'the scourge of war, aided by time, the great destroyer, who respects nothing, and perhaps also by earthquakes, has fallen heavily'. So the great debate began on why the empire of Angkor collapsed.

The forest still holds part of the ruins in its grasp. The job of rebuilding temples and fighting tropical vegetation has proved difficult. There is a legend among the present-day Cambodians, who are descended from the ancient Khmers, that Angkor is destined to be rebuilt by foreigners. French architects and archaeologists have fulfilled this alleged prophecy by rebuilding stone by stone some of the ruined temples. The method of restoration is to pull the ruins down, number every stone, add new stones where necessary, and rebuild as correctly as possible.

The present-day Cambodians themselves also play an important part in the understanding of Angkor. Physically they resemble their ancestors who are portrayed in sculpture, but until recently they had forgotten their ancient parentage and could not believe that their forefathers built Angkor. It must be the work of giants or the gods, they said. But now the Cambodians are more conscious of their great past and have adopted Angkor Wat, on their national flag for example, as a symbol of resurgence. They are still Theravada Buddhists and have inherited this religion direct from the persons noted at Angkor by Chou Ta-Kouan. Saffron-robed Buddhist monks walk through the ruins of Angkor Wat today, the colour of their robes contrasting strongly with the greys and greens of the sandstone. They regard Angkor Wat as a sacred shrine, a place of pilgrimage, and to the uneducated among them— not a large percentage—the origin of this temple, for the worship of the Hindu god Vishnu, is not understood. In practice most ancient Khmer ruins have become places of worship for Cambodian Buddhists regardless of their original purpose.

Khmer masons at work dressing blocks of sandstone, from a bas-relief in the Bayon. Two teams, of four men each, grind stone blocks together using scaffolding and a crude system of leverage. The stones were ground to a perfect fit and held in place during this operation with sockets and pegs.

The two kneeling workmen in each team seem to be holding rules but are probably using them to push the block of stone backwards and forwards when it has been hoisted; the man perched on the frame tends the hoisting mechanism. (18)

VII THE GODS THAT FAILED

The glory and decay of Maya culture

J. ERIC S. THOMPSON

BC	1500 onwards	Formative period, pre-classic. Developing cultures. Tikal and many other sites occupied. Courts and mounds built.
AD	100	Proto-classic period. The threshold of Maya culture. Stone temples with corbelled vaulting. Olmec and Monte Albán cultures flourishing to the west of Maya territory.
	300	Beginning of the Classic period. Flowering of Maya culture. Dated monuments plentiful (earliest known, AD 292). Ceremonial centres multiply. 7th century—great age of *Palenque;* 8th century, of *Copán* and *Quiriguá*.
	800	Ceremonial centres begin to be abandoned. 800, latest dated monument at Copán. *Bonampak* frescoes. 869, last stele at Tikal. 928, San Lorenzo, in remote southern Campeche, erects latest dated stele of Classic period.
	900	Beginning of first Mexican period. *Chichén Itzá* occupied by Toltecs from Tula. First appearance of metal c. 1000. Rise of militarism.
	1200	Chichén Itzá captured and sacked. Second Mexican period. Rise of *Mayapán* as the capital of most of Yucatán. Marked cultural degeneration. Secular influences dominant.
	1460	Revolt of the Maya. Mayapán sacked. Yucatán divided into sixteen petty states. Collapse of Maya civilization.
	1519	Cortés lands in Mexico. 1524-45 Conquest of Maya territory by the Spaniards. 1699, Tayasal in Lake Petén, last Maya stronghold, captured by the Spaniards.

A chronology showing the main periods of Maya growth and decay.

Unlike any other civilization the world has ever seen,
that of the Mayas arose in the midst of dense tropical forest, in country where enormous labour is needed even to clear an open space.
Cities, villages, roads, the very fields in which they grew their
crops, all had to be won step by step from the jungle. The average
rainfall is ten feet a year, with a dry season of only a few months,
during which most of the building must have been done. Yet it
was under these conditions that hundreds of courts, pyramids and
temples were raised in what are now Yucatán and Guatemala.
The meteor-like glory of the Maya culture blazed between AD
300 and 900. Architecture and sculpture appeared in profusion
and of a high quality, and astronomical observation and a conception of time were developed far in advance of anything in the Old
World. Then, in a much shorter time, the great ceremonial centres of the south were abandoned one by one and in a few years

the jungle had reclaimed its own. What was the reason for this
sudden and complete collapse? Did the Mayas migrate to easier
surroundings, or did they simply shake off the rule of discredited
gods and an oppressive priesthood and revert to a peasant economy?

Totally deserted and in ruins, the very existence of the Maya cities
was forgotten for centuries after the Spanish Conquest. Only in
the 1840's were the glories of Copán revealed, through the engravings of Frederick Catherwood—products, perhaps, of the
Romantic Age, yet amazingly accurate in their details. Here, in
what was the Great Court of Copán, a broken stele lies half submerged, while in the background rises the dark mass of a pyramid-
temple. The stele dates from about AD 730. (1)

Ceremonial games were a feature of Maya ritual and every centre had its ball-court. One in the Great Court at Copán (right) consisted of two sloping ramps (of which one only is shown) with the playing-floor between them. On each side were temples, where offerings were made before the games started. (2)

In the Great Court of Copán stood fourteen monumental stelae, masterpieces of Maya sculpture over a period of 200 years. Stele B (above) can be precisely dated to AD 731. (4)

The hieroglyphic staircase, of green-tinged trachyte, rises 86 feet above the level of the Great Court. The riser of each step is carved with glyphs—on the whole stairway are no less than 2,500. Five giant human figures are seated at intervals. (5)

The great temple-city of Copán lies on the extreme south-eastern edge of the Maya area and is outstanding for the splendour of its buildings and the number of its dated monuments. In the reconstruction above a new stele is being dedicated. Priests, wearing their magnificent head-dresses, backed by quetzal feathers and decorated with emblems (including fish nibbling water-lilies) are about to place vessels containing offerings in a small pit under the stone. They have just come from a rain-making ceremony in which they walked barefoot over a bed of glowing coals. Behind them is a dummy two-headed dragon—one of the four sky-monsters—made of bark cloth and feathers and worked by two men inside. In the background, dominating the scene, is the 'Review-ing Stand', with Temple 11 above it. (3)

Terror, suffering and death were never far from the idea of the supernatural developed by the priesthood. Dragons and snarling jaguars were the constant symbols; the demon from the Reviewing Stand at Copán (below) is a larger than life human figure with grotesque features. In his hand he holds a rattle or torch; serpents writhe from his mouth and another is knotted round his waist. In contrast the maize-god, closer to the daily life of the people, is depicted in sensitive portraits of idealised youth (on the left is one from Copán), and here and there peep through evidences of a light-hearted and vivacious humanity. (6, 7)

Two-headed dragons appear all over Maya sculpture. On Altar G at Copán the jaws, fangs and eyes are still clear, though most of the other features have become stylized out of recognition, (the photograph was taken before the Great Court was cleared of undergrowth). Dragons are personifications of the sky, entrance to the celestial abode of the gods. (8)

A surprizing irony mingles with the grotesque in some of Copán's luxuriant art. The jaguar (below), in spite of his snarling expression, has one paw elegantly on hip and little pompoms and flares at the end of his tail. (9)

Mask of a god. The '3'-shape on each side of the face is an attribute of the planet Venus, feared as the bringer of famine. (10)

In the folds of the double-headed serpent (right) little human forms can be seen clambering and peering. The serpent, part of the Inner Doorway of Temple 22 at Copán, rests on a crouching Atlas-like figure, who in turn stands on a Death's-head. (11)

The long roll-call of Maya sites does not represent cities in our sense of the word. They were ritual centres, where the people gathered for festivals but where nobody lived. Priests and nobility resided on the outskirts, the people in scattered settlements, constantly on the move, as the soil became exhausted.

The Palace of Sayil (left) had a hundred rooms, ranged on three storeys. Its façade was divided in the centre by a huge staircase (in ruins, right in the photograph) leading to the upper floors. (12)

The temples of Palenque are small in scale but unusually delicate and graceful. The temple of the Sun (right, foreground) has an elaborately carved roof and 'comb', once brightly painted. Behind it is the restored tower of the Palace, rising to four storeys with an interior staircase—another rarity. (13)

The principle of the arch was never discovered by the Maya engineers. Their nearest approach to it is the corbelled arch, where each stone is laid slightly overlapping the one below, until the space between can be bridged by a single slab. The construction is easy to see in the gateway at Labná (below). The decoration on each side is based on the thatched houses of the peasants. (14)

Tulum, on the wild Caribbean coast, is exceptional in being fortified; most Maya centres had no defences. The wall was nearly 800 yards long and 10 to 15 feet high. It was pierced by five narrow gateways—the ruins of one are visible in the foreground. (15)

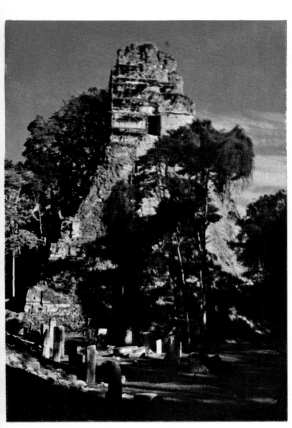

Overwhelming height was the aim of the Maya priest-architects, and nowhere does this impression remain so vividly as at Tikal. Temple 1 is 229 feet high. With its long steep flight of steps and grim altar at the top, it must have been a potent instrument of terror in the hands of the rulers. (16)

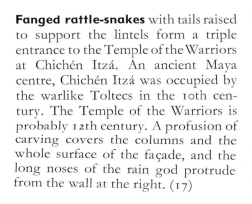

Fanged rattle-snakes with tails raised to support the lintels form a triple entrance to the Temple of the Warriors at Chichén Itzá. An ancient Maya centre, Chichén Itzá was occupied by the warlike Toltecs in the 10th century. The Temple of the Warriors is probably 12th century. A profusion of carving covers the columns and the whole surface of the façade, and the long noses of the rain god protrude from the wall at the right. (17)

The sheer quantity of Maya sculpture
is astonishing, especially when it is remembered that we know
only a fraction of what once existed. The vast army of workers
that must have been needed—quarrymen, builders, dressers of
stone, stucco-artists, sculptors and painters—was perhaps one of
the reasons why the top-heavy Maya economy collapsed.

A massive boulder, eleven feet wide, seven feet high, forms the
so-called 'Zoömorph P' of Quiriguá. On the front is a priest or
god wearing a huge head-dress similar to those on the stelae
(compare opposite page). The whole of the rest of the surface
writhes in the grotesque coils of monstrous creatures. (18)

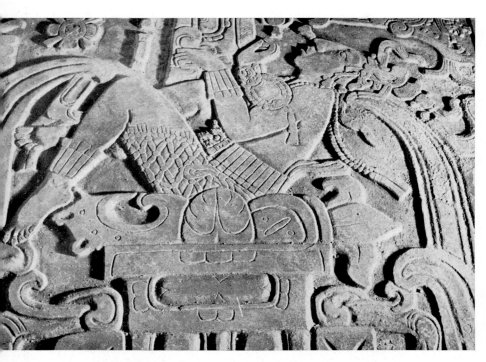

The most dramatic discovery of recent Maya research was the
tomb inside the Temple of the Inscriptions at Palenque, for it was
previously thought that the Mayan 'pyramids' had no burial purpose. The grave-slab (above) has as its central figure a man reclining, or falling, on a large mask of the god of death. Behind him
a tree-like stem sprouts upward. (20)

A mouth with bared teeth, two eyes and long S-shaped nose—
the face of the god Chac on the Labná façade (21)

Assured maturity of style and technique is evident in late Maya
carving. The stele above (the back of Stele I at Quiriguá, 13 ½
feet high) is remarkable in two ways: it shows a *seated* figure,
which is rare, and it is completely covered in the swirling plumes
of the quetzal-bird. It is dated AD 800. (19)

A ball-court marker from near Chinkultic, Chiapas. Note the glyphs round the border which give the date: the numbers, beginning at the top, are 9, 7, 17, 12, 14; the other glyphs denote the time intervals, *tuns*, *katuns*, etc. The final date is AD 591. (22)

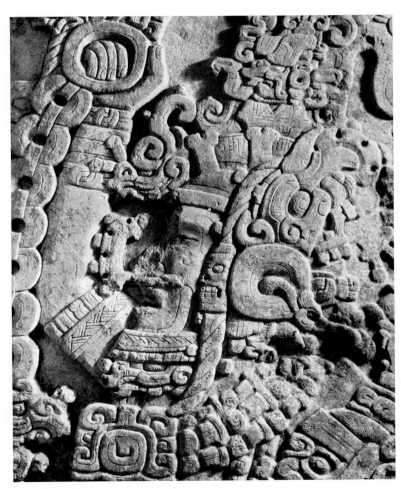

Lost in a smothering pattern of curvilinear shapes, the details of Maya sculpture are often hard for the modern eye to pick out. This detail from an early stele found at Tikal shows the profile of a priest wearing an elaborate head-dress; in his raised right hand he grasps a chain. (23)

Quiriguá, thirty miles over the mountains from Copán, is equally renowned for its sculpture. Stele D (right), dedicated in AD 766, is a masterpiece of virtuosity, from its high feather head-dress surmounted by the Death's head to the heavy ornaments round feet and ankles. (24)

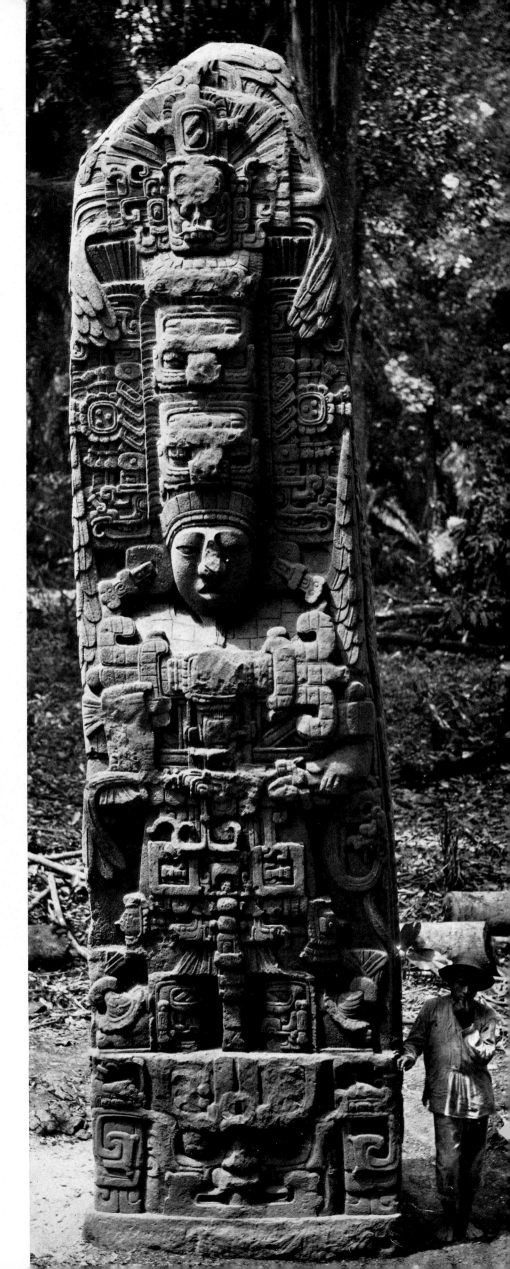

The peasant-subjects of the Maya lords
have left few traces of their lives, yet it was they who tilled the
soil, quarried the stone, laid out the courts and built the pyramid
temples, yielding huge tribute in produce and labour to the élite
who ruled.

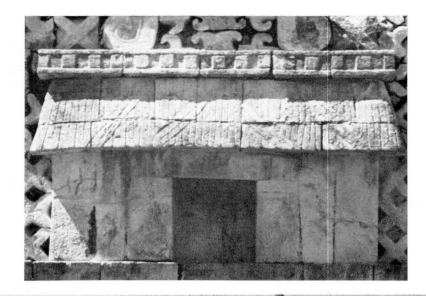

A house with palm-leaf roof appears on the sculptured façade of
the 'Nunnery' at Uxmal. If this is compared with the Labná gate
(pl. 14) and the painted examples below, it is evident that design
was standardized. (25)

Life in a coastal village: a late fresco from the Temple of the
Warriors, Chichén Itzá. On the water, teeming with sea creatures, warriors set out in canoes. Behind them are houses, trees,
merchants with packs on their backs and (right) a shrine with a
feathered serpent rising from it. (26)

The descendants of the Maya still live much as their peasant
ancestors did, and their language has remained basically the same.
It is even possible to see a facial resemblance between this modern
peasant and a relief of perhaps a thousand years ago. (27)

150

The priests,
interpreters of the will of the gods, formed the ruling class. There was no Maya nation, only a collection of small city-states each, it seems, governed from one of the ceremonial centres by a high-priest. The priestly hierarchy was, however, a close-knit one; conferences were held so that the latest advances in astronomy (on which the well-being of society depended) could be shared. In 682, for instance, a new method of computing moons was worked out at Copán and was rapidly taken up by the other centres.

Chiefs, or 'batabob', ruled the smaller centres. The famous fresco at Bonampak, which was apparently in the sphere of influence of Yaxchilán, shows such a chief being dressed for a ceremony. He wears a jaguar-skin and embroidered bell. — The fibre head-dress, with fish and other emblems, backed by green quetzal plumes has just been fixed in position. An attendant on the left fastens a bracelet; another on the right daubs his skin with red ochre. This illustration is from a copy of the fresco by Antonio Tejeda. It was by such lavish displays, by dazzling rituals and festivals that the priests were able to dominate the minds of the people and impose their will upon them. (33)

The stately progress of an important merchant, holding a fan, his badge of office, is the subject of a vase-painting from Ratinlinxul, shown below as an extended picture. The first retainer perhaps carries merchandise, the other three hold what may be staves (which with fans were the merchant insignia) but may be paddles for a canoe voyage. Note the very naturalistic dog stretching himself. (34)

The struggle for food went on endlessly—a struggle against climate, tropical animals and insects, exhausted soil and over exuberant vegetation. In this reconstruction the girl on the right carries a load of maize, the staple food; they ate it in one form or another with every meal, year in and year out. Her companion holds a papaya, a fruit rather like a melon, and carries a bundle of faggots. The headstrap is interesting—the Maya had no wheeled vehicles and no draught animals; everything had to be carried. Note the necklaces too; the man's of shells, the girl's of beetle's wings. Near the huts cooking, grinding maize for corn-cakes and weaving on the back-strap loom are going on. The man on the left plaits straw. Behind him a hunter returns with a deer while in the background rise the gleaming steps and pillars of a ceremonial centre, a remote wonder, the source of power, of knowledge, of the secrets of life and death. (28)

The dress of the people was simple—a breech-clout and often some form of head-dress. The climate made anything else unnecessary. This painted jar from the tomb of a chief at Kaminaljuyu, Guatemala, is hollow and in two separate pieces. (29)

A small family shrine in a forest clearing in Quintana Roo. These tiny late buildings are probably signs of a change from priestly worship on a community basis to the use of private 'chapels' by noble families, marking the rise of secular authority in the final two or three centuries before the Spanish Conquest. (30)

In modern Uxmal, close to the stupendous relics of the past, stands this plain thatched house, a reminder of the continuity of peasant traditions. (31)

The endless passage of time,

the prediction of eclipses, the calculation of planetary cycles, the reckoning of days, months and years—these were the constant pre-occupations of the Maya priests. Every activity had its set time, every day its special ritual and its patron deity. The calendar governed every detail of the people's lives and absorbed a crippling proportion of their energies. Yet it is here, paradoxically, that the greatest triumph of the Maya civilization is to be found. They were the first people to conceive of time on the vast scale to which modern science has now accustomed us. One stele at

Quiriguá calculates the day and month position (redrawn left) for a date *four hundred million years* in the past! Merely to contemplate this length of time would have been quite impossible for a European before the 19th century. The Maya priest-astronomers alone seem to have had the imagination (and courage) to accept a universe in which time had no beginning.

The Dresden Codex is the finest of the three surviving Maya books. It contains divinatory almanacs and astronomical data. The page reproduced here gives dates when the planet Venus would be at heliacal rising after inferior conjunction—days of bad luck. The middle picture shows the feathered serpent god Kukulcan, manifestation of the planet Venus, pointing the darts of death at the frog (beneath), symbol of rain. (32)

◀ Fold out

Trumpets, drums, turtle-shells and gourd-rattles accompany the procession on the painted walls of Bonampak. The masked figures are impersonators of gods—one wears a crocodile head, another has the claws of a crab. In the middle, not masked but wearing a white head-dress, sits the young Maize-god. (35)

'They perforate their tongues in a slanting direction from side to side, passing pieces of straw through the holes, with horrible suffering,' wrote one of the early Franciscans. The relief below shows a worshipper, probably a woman, kneeling before a priest or god and passing a cord set with thorns (not a straw) through the tongue. The blood falls onto paper in a basket. Right: it is offered to a god emerging from the jaws of a serpent. Both reliefs are from Yaxchilán and date from about AD 750. (36, 37)

The Sun, disguised in a deer-skin,—
he is bottom left and has human legs
—finds his wife, the Moon, after she
had eloped with the king vulture, top
right. A mythological vase from
Yaloch, Guatemala. At least one incident from this cycle of stories is still told
by the Maya peasants of today. (38)

The Classic Age of Maya civilization (AD 300-900) saw a luxuriant flowering of all the arts. Painted pottery developed from
simple outlines in red on an orange ground to brilliant polychrome, while modelling in clay and engraving on jade and
obsidian achieved a pitch of virtuosity which Europe and Asia
might have envied.

**Green jade—more precious than
gold**—was ancient Central America's
most treasured possession, the symbol
of life itself. It was mined in the
Mayan highlands of Guatemala. The
pendant (right) was found at Teotihuacán near Mexico City, but is
clearly Mayan work. It shows a seated
chief, with smaller figure on the left.
(39)

The Chamá Vase (left) suggests the
range of colours available on Maya
pottery. The subject is possibly a
deputation of merchants (symbol of
the fan) being received by a chief with
spear. To put the right hand on the
left shoulder—as the attendant on
the right is doing—was a symbol of
peaceful intentions. (40)

A delicate tripod-vessel (right) from
Tikal. It is pottery covered with
painted stucco. The handle is a man's
head and four faces grin from the
sides. The tomb in which this was
found bears the date AD 457 (43)

A fish (far right) portrayed in a few
simple, very assured strokes, on a
plate from Tikal. The fish, emblem of
the fish-god Xoc, who dwelt in the
sky, had a ceremonial significance. (44)

Flakes of obsidian, black, brittle, volcanic glass, with sophisticated engraving, have been excavated from sub-stele caches at Tikal. The mineral was plentiful in the highland Maya country. (41)

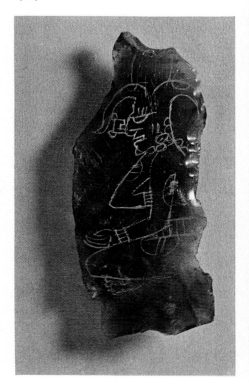

The nightmare of Maya religion— a hideous, almost toothless god, sitting on crossed thigh-bones, gloats over a human head. The figure, of hollow pottery, was recently recovered from Tikal. The eyes have a curious three-petalled form. The date is between AD 400 and 500. (42)

When the Toltec warriors from Tula occupied Chichén Itzá in the 10th century they built almost a replica of their native city. Architecture, symbolism, even the details of costume and ornament, show amazing parallels across 800 miles of jungle and plateau. Compare the two versions of Quetzalcoatl (above) and marching jaguars (below). Tula is on the left, Chichén Itzá on the right. The connexion is evident, though the later examples are slightly more naturalistic, possibly, because of contact with native craftsmen. But it may have been a semi-deserted city that the Toltecs seized. The disaster that overtook Maya civilization had already happened, and the centres to the south had been abandoned for a hundred years. (45–48)

Violence marked the end, it seems, of some of the great temple-cities. Stelae are broken, the figures of the gods defaced. The dais at Piedras Negras (below), seat of a ruler, was deliberately smashed, possibly as an act of vengeance by the peasantry in revolt. It must have been soon after AD 810, when the last dated stele was erected there. The dais itself (re-assembled from the pieces) dates from 785; its back is a dragon's head with human faces looking through the eyes. (49)

The glory and decay of Maya culture

J. ERIC S. THOMPSON

In the case of many of the peoples discussed in this book, the mystery, the puzzle, the enigma will, we suppose, yield to greater knowledge. With the Maya the enigma is intrinsic: that a people so fantastically accomplished in astronomy and time calculation and so advanced in sculpture should nevertheless have been so impractical in everyday affairs and inventions. And why did so successful, so urbane and so peaceful a society, which endured for so many years, suddenly collapse and eventually die?

THE MAYA civilization, like a meteor, came from the seeming unknown, blazed with increasing glory, grew dimmer and then became extinct, but during its greatest luminosity (approximately AD 300-900) its incandescence seared the pages of New World history.

The Maya occupied a roughly quadrangular area, about 550 miles long and about 350 miles wide at the base, embracing the Peninsula of Yucatán and the area south of it almost to the shores of the Pacific. This comprises the whole of Guatemala, all British Honduras, the western fringes of the Republic of Honduras and of El Salvador, and the Mexican states of Yucatán, Campeche, Tabasco, Quintana Roo Territory and much of Chiapas. These bounds probably never suffered much alteration, although the Maya may have once extended into what is now the Mexican state of Veracruz.

The descendants of the ancient Maya still live in this area, but they have no remembrance of the past glories of their race. They retain some of the old beliefs and customs and many still make offerings before the sculptured monuments or in the ruined temples abandoned over 1,000 years ago although with little idea why they do so. Physically, they are short, stocky, dark-skinned and with straight black hair, and some of them, particularly the Yucatec Maya who live in the north of the peninsula, are one of the most round-headed peoples in the world. In ancient times they accentuated this feature by artificial deformation of the head. In other respects they are not easily distinguished from many other American Indians.

pl 27

About two million of them still speak one or other of the fifteen principal languages or dialects of the Maya group, all of which are related to one another as are Spanish, Portuguese, French and the other Romance languages. With the exception of one small group, all the present-day Maya have been much affected by Spanish culture and are Roman Catholics although retaining much of their old paganism.

The Two Maya Lands—Mountain and Jungle

The southern part of the Maya area is mountainous, a land of deep valleys and plateaux, lakes and volcanoes, with many important Indian towns 5,000 to 7,000 feet above sea level. Although the area lies well within the tropics, the climate is pleasantly temperate and this is reflected in the flora. By contrast, the Peninsula of Yucatán and the great drainage of the Usumacinta and Sarstoon rivers is a low limestone plain with very heavy rainfall (over 10 feet per annum at the base of the peninsula). Dense tropical forest covers this hot, humid land, which today breeds much malaria, dysentery, hookworm and other tropical plagues, so that large parts are now without any permanent population.

Chicleros, gatherers of chicle, the sap of a tree which grows freely in the forest and which is the raw material of chewing gum, make temporary encampments in the forest during the rainy season when the sap flows; in very recent years oil prospectors have driven roads through the unexplored forest and built airstrips, but if they do not find oil the forest will quickly reconquer what they have cleared.

Throughout this area, particularly in the lowlands, are the ruins of Maya buildings, for the most part belonging to the great flowering of Maya culture, the Classic period, from AD 300 to AD 900. They are grouped in what are often called cities, but that is a misnomer, for they were not urban centres, but the religious and administrative capitals of districts; the usual term is ceremonial centre.

It is difficult to say how many such sites there were, partly because important ones still lie undiscovered beneath the rain forest (two large sites were found in 1961), and partly because it is hard to draw the line between small residential groups with perhaps a single pyramidal structure and undoubted ceremonial centres. By counting only those sites of sufficient consequence to possess hieroglyphic inscriptions (and many important sites lack them or have them hidden beneath debris) a total of over one hundred and thirty ceremonial centres is reached for the Maya lowlands. In contrast, only one site in the Guatemala highlands has hieroglyphic texts, all of which probably belong to the period before Maya culture developed its characteristics. No two ceremonial centres are exactly alike, but the resemblances outweigh local variations in assemblage, architecture and sculptural representation. As they are the chief surviving manifestations of Maya civilization, a brief sketch of their chief features will serve as an introduction to the subject.

Copán, City of the Gods

Copán, in the Republic of Honduras, just beyond the Guatemalan frontier, is one such large ceremonial centre. It is outstanding for the excellence of its sculpture and the large number of its hieroglyphic monuments, but its buildings have suffered, partly as a result of earthquakes and partly because the builders of Copán laid the courses of their walls in mud and weak lime in contrast to the lime mortar used at most lowland sites. It stands on the bank of the Copán river in a very fertile valley compassed about with mountains. Notwithstanding its position on the eastern edge of the Maya area, it is completely without visible defences, although conceivably wooden palisades or cactus hedges may once have existed.

At the north end lies the great court, a feature of nearly all Maya sites. This is an irregular quadrangle 260 yards long by 185 yards at the widest point. It is an artificial construction, the surface, once plastered but now largely gone, having been raised some nine feet above natural ground level. Low platform mounds enclose it on three sides. That on the west was crowned with two long stone buildings; others may have supported thatched huts. There is a wide opening or entrance on the east side. On the south stand the mass of pyramids and courts called the acropolis. The court is free of buildings except for a smallish pyramid, an insignificant platform and twin buildings at the southeast corner which formed the court in which the Maya played a ball game, their national sport, but it holds no less than thirty-one sculptured stone monuments. Some are the imposing shafts, called stelae, with figures in relief on the front and hieroglyphic texts on the sides; others, designated altars, are square blocks with simpler designs and shorter texts or are shaped as grotesque double-headed dragons.

f 1
pl 1

pl 2

pl 4

pl 8

At the south end of the court, behind the beautiful Stele N, broad stairs rise steeply 80 feet to the top of the pyramid supporting Temple 11. This building, two storeys high, is now badly ruined, but its roof must have stood nearly 150 feet above the Copán river. It is the northern flank of a towering man-made pile supporting three courts, much smaller but far above the level of the great court. Each in turn is surrounded by platforms or pyramids on which stand temples or the many-roomed buildings called for convenience palaces, although they certainly never functioned as such. These massive clusterings of courts, pyramids

Copán as it was in its heyday in the 9th century AD. The principal features are: 1, 2. the Great Court with its many stelae; 3. the Hieroglyphic Stairway; 4. the Ball Court; 5. the stairway with the jaguars; 6. Temple 11; 7. the Reviewing Stand; 8. Stele B. In the background is the River Copán. There were no defences, although Copán is on the borders of Maya territory. (1)

and platforms which rise above the surrounding structures like downtown skyscrapers in an American city occur throughout the Maya area. They are often termed acropolises. In the case of Copán the river, changing its course, has swept part of the acropolis away, exposing to view a cross-section, 100 feet high, of artificial fill, floors and drains, an extraordinary witness to past activities, for it has been calculated that this acropolis, entirely man-made, still contains more than two million tons of material brought there basketful by basketful.

f 2   The chief Maya centres almost seem to have vied with one another as to which could erect the most imposing buildings. For instance, Cobá, a large site in the distant north-east of the Yucatán peninsula, built a large and extremely impressive ceremonial centre in the isthmus between two lakes. Seemingly that was not enough; work was started on another acropolis about a mile away. A huge rectangular platform about 360 feet wide by 410 feet long and 56 feet high was erected. This contained about six and a half million cubic feet of rock and rubble, weighing nearly half a million short tons. However, the courts, flights of stairs and pyramids this great platform should have supported were never built, probably because the Classic period, during which Cobá flourished, came to an end before the work was undertaken, and the hierarchy was liquidated, leaving this monument to unfulfilled ambition.

At all sites steep flights of stairs led to the summits of pyramids or wide steps rose gently from one court to another. At sites in the basin of the Pasion, a tributary of the Usumacinta river, steps display human figures reclining full length, one above the other, and with legs crossed. Except that they are prisoners with arms bound together at the wrists, they present an amusing, but quite fortuitous, parallel to a series of seventeenth-century figures on a monument in St. Mary's church, Swinbrook, Oxfordshire. The similarity is a useful warning to students to have care in proposing cultural connections with the Old World on the strength of parallels in art.

pl 5   Copán, however, has the finest of all hieroglyphic stairways. This, ascending from the south-east corner of the great court,

comprises sixty-three steps, each carved with hieroglyphs and forming the longest text in the whole Maya area. Five giant human figures richly clad and with elaborate head-dresses are seated at intervals on the steps, adding to the grandeur of this flight of stairs, surpassed by no other in Middle America.

The Fantastic World of Maya Mythology

Perhaps because of its rulers' preference for sculpture in the beautiful local stone, a pistachio-green trachyte, to work in less durable stucco, Copán gives a better idea of what an important Maya centre looked like than many of its neighbours whose stucco embellishments have largely crumbled to pieces. Two flights of steps in Copán's acropolis are of particular interest. The first is the so-called Reviewing Stand, a flight of five steps, fifty-five feet wide, the topmost carrying a hieroglyphic text which gives the date of its dedication (AD 771). At each end there kneels on the top step a larger than life human figure with grotesque and quite un-Maya features. Each holds in outstretched hand a gourd rattle or torch and has a serpent knotted around his waist and another emerging from the corner of his mouth. It has been suggested that these steps which lead nowhere served as seats for persons of rank during some important ceremony. Above are three stone replicas of conch shells, each four feet long.

pl 3

pl 7

The second flight of steps is in an adjacent court of the acropolis and is notable for the rampant jaguars which flank it. At first sight their snarling expressions and their great bodies, once painted red and with shallow circles perhaps inlaid with obsidian or tar to represent the spots on the jaguar's skin, give them a most fierce appearance. Indeed, the jaguar in the art of several peoples of Middle America is presented as a fearsome, awe-inspiring creature, but closer examination of these sculptures makes one realize that the Maya artist is poking fun at him. Each has one paw on hip, the other pointing to the stairs, a sort of Mickey Mouse in duplicate ushering people into Disneyland. The illusion is enhanced by the dainty loin cloth each jaguar wears and the extravagant pompoms and flares at the end of his tail which introduce an element of ridicule. Surely the artist is saying that

pl 9

this supposedly dread king of the American jungle is in truth more frightened of us than we of him.

Onto this same court faces a temple which in its decoration shows a pleasant intermingling of solemn portraiture of divine majesty and gay treatment of minor supernatural beings. This is Temple 22, the lower façade of which is carved to represent a view *en face* of the head of a celestial dragon. Its gaping mouth forms the doorway into the temple, very much like those mediaeval paintings of the entrance to hell as the open mouth of a draconic monster; the top step immediately before the doorway is carved to represent the six incisor teeth of the lower jaw with a large curved fang at each end. The teeth, fangs and molars of the upper jaw are above the door with, higher up, the eyes, snout and ear ornaments of the dragon. A similar treatment of lower façades of temples to convert them into dragon features is typical of architecture in the Chenes area of distant Campeche. Dragons are personifications of the sky, so by passing through their mouths into the room beyond, one enters the celestial abode of the gods.

pl 6

In contrast to the fearsome and ill-contrived features of the dragon are the busts of the maize god set in the upper façade. The Maya had a passionate attachment to the soil and felt themselves in very intimate relationship with its chief produce. The maize god, therefore, was far more than a poetic personification of man's daily bread, and the special tenderness in which he was held found its outlet in these sensitive portraits of idealized youth.

pl 17
21

At the corners of the façade are masks of the long-nosed rain gods which occur in such profusion from one end of the Maya area to the other. In contrast to the grave portraits of those more important deities is the design which surrounds the entrance to the inner chamber of this Copán temple. This takes the form of

pl 11

a two-headed dragon, on whose body elf-like beings romp and rollick. It is a reminder that Maya artists, usually subjected to the solemn restraints and conventions of age-old religious concepts, were light-hearted and vivacious when released from such obligations.

The Roll of Maya Sites

Decoratively, Copán's temples were superb, but architecturally they were inferior to those of many other Maya cities. They were heavy, sombre buildings with far too high a proportion of structure to floor space. In the case of Temple 22, just discussed, the ground plan shows that far more space was covered with masonry than with floor. In contrast, there is an airy quality about the buildings of Palenque and other cities in the Usumacinta drainage. This was achieved by thinner walls boldly combined with wider corbelled vaulting, a matter of considerable architectural skill, for the wider the corbelled vault, the greater the lateral thrust to be countered. In the corbelled or false arch used by the Maya each course overlaps the one below until the space between the converging soffits can be bridged by a line of capstones. This same false arch was used in ancient times in parts of the Old World. Palenque and its neighbours overcame those difficulties by what to all intents and purposes was building in concrete, for the stone facings of structures were welded together into monolithic masses with concrete fill. Thereby the lateral strain was more widely distributed. This use of concrete was a great advance on the use of stone set in a weak mixture of mud and lime which Copán favoured. Later, this building in concrete was carried a stage further, and the exterior stone work became a thin coating for the concrete, a style known as veneer masonry. In buildings of that style the veneer of thin tile-like stones often peeled off for they were not bonded into the core, but the building, essentially a concrete monolith, stood. Veneer masonry is typical of the western part of Yucatán and adjacent Campeche, notably at such well-known sites as Uxmal, Labná, and Kabah.

pl 13

pl 14
f 5

pl 14

Quiriguá, an important ceremonial centre in the Motagua Valley, lies twenty five to thirty miles north of Copán and is separated from it by high mountains. Although the two cities lie in the same drainage and their builders were almost certainly of the same Chol-Chorti speaking branch of the lowland Maya, they are markedly different in various ways. Quiriguá has no dominating acropolis or even high pyramid, but what it lacks in showy architecture it more than makes up for in the grandeur of its stelae and altars. Stele E, a slender shaft with a height, including the butt, of 35 feet and an estimated weight of 65 tons, is easily the tallest stele in the Maya area, and more than twice the height of the tallest at Copán. The front and back are carved with the figures of priest-rulers impersonating gods, who stand upon intricate mask panels and have extraordinarily elaborate head-

pl 18
24

The group of ceremonial centres round Cobá; the main temples were on the isthmus between the two lakes. Cobá was the hub of an important road system. Road 1, connecting it with Yaxuná, is the finest of all Maya roads. Sixty-two miles long and straight for most of its length, it was made of stone foundations with a surface of cement. Some of the roads go straight across arms of the lake, though slight detours would have made this unnecessary. (2)

dresses. The sides of the monument are carved with hieroglyphs, among which are those giving the date of its erection. This was AD 771, the same date as that recorded on the Reviewing Stand at Copán.

Somewhat smaller, but more graceful, is the shaft to which the prosaic title of Stele F is now attached. In its arrangement of human figures on front and back and hieroglyphic texts on the sides, it resembles Stele E. Indeed, it was erected only ten years earlier. An outstanding feature of this stela is the treatment of the featherwork of the intricate head-dresses, particularly in their sweeping extensions to the sides, above the hieroglyphic texts. Maya sculptors took particular pleasure in handling the flowing *pl 19* pattern of these tail feathers of the quetzal bird which were highly prized, not only for their rarity and beauty, but because the shimmering irridescence of their greens and blues symbolized the rains divinely sent to save the maize crops. Sometimes the feathers are shown ruffled by a breeze, one plume sweeping back in a counter curve.

pl 18   Quiriguá stands apart from other Maya cities in the huge boulders it carved with the most complex designs of large two-headed celestial dragons. Other cities produced "altars" of this same general type, but none of the magnificence of those at Quiriguá, nor with such intricately carved hieroglyphs.

Thus one can call the roll of Maya sites, noting features in which each excelled. Palenque, apart from its airy, light buildings is renowned for its beautiful work in both stucco and stone, its aqueducts and its unique tower. However, it is best known for the remarkable tomb of one of its priest-rulers discovered in

1952 by Professor Alberto Ruz, the Mexican archaeologist, *f 3* beneath the massive pyramid and temple of The Inscriptions. A tunnel with two narrow flights of stairs separated by a landing led from beneath a concealed stone trapdoor in the floor of the temple to a large room, corbel-vaulted like the staircase, 70 feet below. In the centre of this room, beneath a large and elaborately sculptured stone slab, was the lidded sarcophagus. In this were *pl 20* the bones of the chief almost buried under a jade mosaic mask which once had covered the face and nearly 800 beads and ornaments of jade, the wealth of a Maya Midas, for such a haul of jade, the most cherished possession of the Maya, has not been found elsewhere in the Maya area. The decoration of the vaulted chamber is of outstanding quality. This chief was buried about AD 690, and the stairway leading to the tomb was filled in, probably immediately after burial, leaving only a sort of stone pipeline which ran down the side of the tunnel, presumably for the use of the spirit of the dead chief.

Palenque is unique among large Maya cities in recording its many hieroglyphic texts, not on stelae, but on the outsides and insides of buildings and the platforms on which they stand. Calakmul, in southern Campeche, has more stelae than any other city. Eighty carved stelae and twenty three plain have been reported from that seldom visited and remote site, and there is little doubt that excavation would add to this total. That is what has happened at Tikal, the largest and most imposing of Maya sites, where an expedition of University Museum, University of Pennsylvania, has now (1962) been working for several years. Work there has *pl 23* increased the number of carved stelae by 50%.

Tikal, in the centre of the Petén, can claim the highest Maya pyramids and temples. The estimated height of the tallest, allow- *pl 16* ing for some collapse of the top of the roof crest is no less than 230 feet, a truly awe-inspiring height when one bears in mind that all is man-made. Indeed, the figure may be even greater, for the court from which this measurement was calculated is itself raised above natural ground level.

Thus one can continue enumerating local features. Sayil, in *pl 12* distant Yucatán, erected a huge three-storey building with about 100 rooms somewhat evocative of modern architecture; Yaxchilán *pl 36* on the shores of the Usumacinta river, devoted much effort to the *37* carving of stone lintels with scenes and glyphic texts; and Bonam- *33* pak, a dependency of Yaxchilán, has bequeathed us magnificent *35* murals which covered the walls of a three-roomed temple. Despite such local variations these ceremonial centres functioned in the same way.

The People: a Life Ruled by the Calendar

A ceremonial centre was the religious and administrative capital of a district. Apparently, it had no permanent population, for the people lived in small settlements scattered over the surrounding country, coming to it for important religious feasts, courts of justice, markets and in connection with the civic administration *f 11* of the district. A somewhat similar arrangement obtains among some present-day Maya of Chiapas and the highlands of Guatemala. The people live in hamlets, in some cases at considerable distance from the town, to which they flock on Sundays, important saints' days, and secular holidays to attend church and market

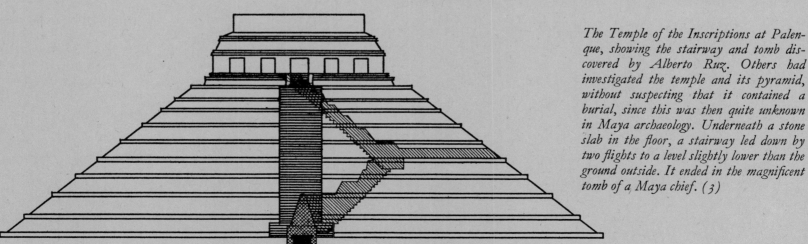

The Temple of the Inscriptions at Palenque, showing the stairway and tomb discovered by Alberto Ruz. Others had investigated the temple and its pyramid, without suspecting that it contained a burial, since this was then quite unknown in Maya archaeology. Underneath a stone slab in the floor, a stairway led down by two flights to a level slightly lower than the ground outside. It ended in the magnificent tomb of a Maya chief. (3)

The complex Maya calendar, represented here in simplified form as a system of interlocking cog-wheels. There were two ways of writing any date. On the left is the sacred calendar, consisting of 13 day numbers (the inner wheel) and twenty day-names (outer wheel). This allows a total of 260 days per sacred year (13×20). On the right is the secular calendar, consisting of 18 months of 20 days each, plus an unlucky period of 5 days, giving 365 days (18×20+5). Within each calendar every date will recur every 260 and 365 days respectively, but every date can be given a double reference (i.e. its position in both calendars) and this combination will recur only every 52 years, the Calendar Round (the Maya name is lost). Note the Maya system of numbering: a dot for 1, a bar for 5; so, for instance, two bars and a dot = 11. (4)

and perform their civic duties. At other times the town stands empty except for a small group of non-Indians and those Indians on tour of duty. Here we have a living survival of the ceremonial centre of over 1,000 years ago.

From early Spanish accounts it is known that before a big festival the participants—priests and novices—retired to the men's houses for periods of 80, 100, or even 160 days of fasting and continence. We can reasonably suppose that this retirement took place in the ceremonial centre, for the Aztec equivalent of the men's house was located there. These centres, then, were often deserted save for attendants, priests on duty, and perhaps the youths and their teachers in the religious schools; sometimes they held groups of priests and novices in retreat before some great ceremony; and on occasions of religious or civic importance they were thronged.

pl 3

Maya ceremonial centres of the Classic period were without defences. Often they were set beside rivers or lakes; some are today on the edges of swamps which may have been lakes fifteen hundred years ago; in Yucatán, where there is no surface water, they are usually near the large natural wells, called *cenotes*, caused by the collapse of the limestone crust over underground deposits of water. Generally, they do not seem to have been sited in response to natural advantage of location such as have governed in the past the growth of many of our cities.

f 11

The presence of stelae, altars, lintels, jambs, panels and stairways with their hieroglyphic texts, scarcely one without a date, distinguish Maya ceremonial centres from those of neighbouring peoples. Perhaps it could be said of the Maya that all the elements of their ceremonial centres were, directly or indirectly, manifestations of their extraordinary philosophy of time in which the calendar was a means of co-ordinating various cycles of divine influence. These ideas so deeply affected Maya culture and history that a brief comment is in order; unfortunately, a full explanation within the limits of this chapter is impossible.

f 4

The core of the elaborate Maya calendar was a divinatory almanac of 260 days, formed of concurrent cycles of 20 names and the numbers 1 to 13, both names and numbers being divine beings whose day of joint rule affected all mankind according to their natures. The whole life of the community revolved around this succession of good, bad, and indifferent days; priests were kept busy deciding what combination of day name and number was most suitable for every undertaking—sowing, taking honey from hives, hunting, curing illness, marrying, or making war. This simple divinatory almanac which still guides the lives of isolated Maya groups in the Guatemalan highlands was not the only mechanistic control of fate in ancient times.

All time periods, Maya equivalents of our week, month, year, decade, and century, were deified. Theoretically, time was an endless and exact repetition of events, for the return of any particular time period meant the iteration of its associated divine influences. As observation showed this not to be so, the Maya sought larger and larger cycles of time to explain disturbances to the ordered pattern of events which their philosophy of time postulated. With extraordinary skill they calculated over enormous distances, using a vigesimal system of counting, that is by twenties. One reckoning leads just short of 1,250,000 years, another over 2,000,000 years, into the past. Stelae at Quiriguá record much earlier dates, one carrying a date over 400 million years in the past. These are not mere statements of distances, but are calculated day and month positions, much as we might reckon that Easter day in the year 300 million BC fell on, say, April 5th. It seems a logical deduction that the Maya with their probings into the past and their measuring of greater and greater re-entering cycles of time had developed the idea that time had no beginning. Set against the belief current in western Europe until a century ago that the world was hardly six thousand years old, this was an astonishing intellectual advance.

pl 32

The Maya believed that celestial influences also affected their lives and frustrated their efforts to bring order out of the universe. Of those the most powerful emanated from the planet Venus and solar eclipses. Venus, as morning star, was feared as bringing death, famine, and destruction to man; eclipses of the sun were

pl 32

pl 10

even more direful for they might bring the end of the world. There were uncertainties about the timing and influences of both which had to be resolved, and in that the Maya priest-astronomers were brilliantly successful. With patience, cooperation and intelligent deduction they succeeded in measuring the synodical revolution of Venus so accurately that their error was only one day in a little over 6,000 years. This, an underestimate by a little less than 24 seconds of the average synodical revolution, was no mean achievement, for the interval from one heliacal rising to another varies from 580 to 588 days and bad weather must have nullified many observations.

In preparing eclipse tables the Maya were handicapped by not knowing that the earth revolves about the sun. Yet, without understanding the theory of the nodes, they discovered that an eclipse could occur only when a new moon fell within about 18 days of the eclipse half year. Their limited knowledge of the world prevented them from knowing which particular eclipse would be visible in the Maya area, but their table of dates on which eclipses could be expected was completely reliable. It would have been comforting to them to have known that eclipses which so far as they were concerned failed to materialize were in fact visible in Sweden or Siberia or Easter Island, places far outside their ken.

Astonishing Successes, Extraordinary Failures

The construction of this eclipse table and that of the synodical revolutions of Venus, the great probings scores of millions of years into the past, the arithmetical calculations which involved the invention of a symbol analogous to that of zero, and the whole concept of the eternity of time because it is cyclic were extraordi-

The corbelled, or 'false' arch, was the only type of arch understood by the Maya. At the bottom are the two varieties of true arch for comparison —the round arch, of wedge-shaped voussoirs, the stress being concentrated on a keystone, and the pointed arch, where the stress is carried diagonally to the ground. In the corbelled arch, which is much weaker, no such principles of statics are employed. Each layer of stone is simply laid slightly overlapping the one beneath, until the gap can be bridged by a single slab, or a single pair of stones leaning against each other. In one example a wooden beam, a sort of tie-beam, helps to keep the two sides together, while in another small blocks are used to give height and larger ones to carry the masonry across the opening. (5)

nary intellectual achievements without parallel among peoples on a similar cultural level throughout the history of the world. Unique, too, was the subordination of life to this pattern of divine influences which stretched forth into the universe but also affected the meanest peasant's family in a remote forest clearing. To this concept was geared the whole life of the ceremonial centre, its great pyramids and temples, its courts, and those endless texts recording the passage of time.

Yet, with such advances in purely intellectual and aesthetic fields, which we, from our very different viewpoint, might term impractical, there were extraordinary failures to advance in the practical. Imposing roads were built for religious processions, but no wheeled cart ever moved along them. Neighbours of the Maya were making pottery toys of dogs on wheels probably during this Classic period, certainly not long after its close when Maya roads were still in use, yet the idea of wheeled transport was never grasped. It is true that the Maya had no horses, but man-hauled carts would certainly have been extremely useful. On occasions, through collapse of buildings or even careless building of corbelled vaults, arches which incorporated the principle of the true arch were formed. The advantages of the true arch over the corbelled vault are so obvious that one is amazed no Maya architect ever saw these pointers to the true arch. Was it conservatism or some mental block?

f 5

Again, the Maya never learned to weigh. They had containers of standard size, roughly corresponding to our bushel, but which were carried on the back. In western Mexico certain peoples used carrying poles which, of course, worked on the balance system, and balances were known in ancient Peru. A seesaw-like game was played in nearby Veracruz and was probably known to the Maya. Yet, with all these signposts the balance never came into use, although it would have been very useful for weighing cacao beans, the currency of all Central America.

Astonishing advances in fields which to us seem unpractical, set against their failures to achieve success in such practical matters as are noted above, suggest that the interest of the hierarchy was largely confined to probing the influences that govern man's fate, how to understand their complex pattern and how to propitiate them, perhaps, ultimately, how to manipulate them. Such a civilization is perhaps comparable to some species of over-specialized Jurassic monster which died because it would not adapt itself to changing conditions.

The Ancestors of the Maya

Before considering the extinction of our cultural Brontosaurus, let us glance briefly at its infancy. Students agree that the New World was populated by immigrants crossing in small groups the Bering Strait which separates Alaska from the eastern tip of Siberia, and that such migrations continued on and off for thousands of years. At one time there was a land bridge between the two continents, but that disappeared about 8,000 to 9,000 BC. Later migrants must have come by boat—on a clear day one can see both shores from the centre of the strait. The advance and retreat of the ice-cap affected the human inflow, but slowly the new arrivals moved southward. They were of diverse racial and linguistic stocks and the earliest arrivals probably brought little culture with them.

Their trail can be picked up occasionally in Mexico—at Iztapan, for example, where a flint point lodged between two ribs of a mammoth and other flint and obsidian tools were mixed with the bones. These first Americans were wandering hunters. It was not until man started to cultivate plants and, as a consequence, adopted a sedentary life that he could make rapid progress.

Recent work by MacNeish in caves in north-eastern and central Mexico has brought to light the transition from food gathering to agriculture. The most important food plants of the Indian of Central America were maize, beans and squash; the 'Irish' potato, so important to the Indians of the Andes, was unknown to him, and manioc, the staple of the South American lowlands, was of minor importance. The whole economy of the Maya and their neighbours was based on the cultivation of maize, but there is still disagreement among botanists as to where maize was first domesticated, and what were its ancestral forms. At one time

Eccentric flints, strange pieces of highly-finished flint-work, are often found in caches beneath stelae or temples. They may be purely geometrical, as in the left-hand example, or delicately naturalistic: the one on the right shows a chief in profile with an elaborate head-dress. But their purpose remains a mystery. (6)

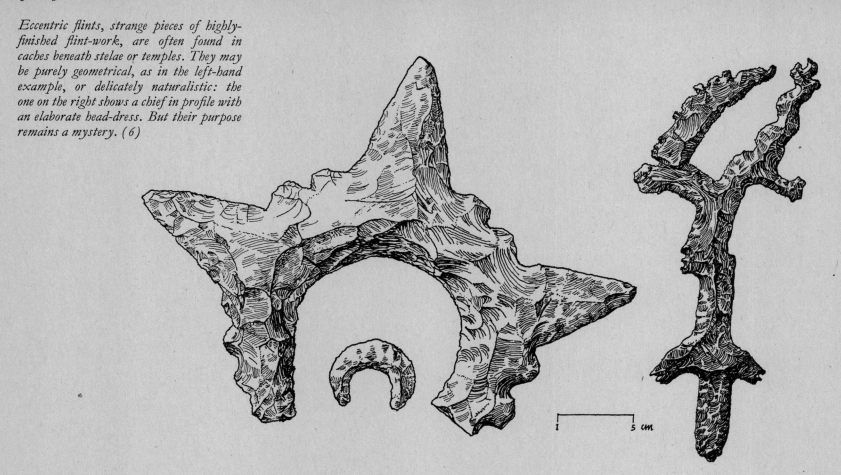

Peru was favoured as the centre of domestication, but in recent years opinion has swung to Middle America, where maize seems to have been cultivated by about 3,500 BC.

Those early centuries of farming are still almost blank pages in the book of history; they doubtless witnessed an increase of population, which brought in its train specialization and then social divisions.

By 1000 BC communities throughout Middle America had progressed to the stage that they made excellent pottery, traded with distant peoples, and had at least an emergent hierarchy or nobility, as the erection of large platforms for temples demonstrates. These early cultures, usually called Formative, do not seem to have differed greatly in essentials. Products of peasant crafts, such as pottery making, varied from one district to another, as did language, but the fundamental religious ideas seem to have been uniform. The rain gods, for instance, may have had one set of names in one area, another set in another, but everywhere, one may suppose, they were associated with serpents.

Then came the first stage of real differentiation. One might think of the evolution of these Formative cultures in terms of an assembly line for motor cars. All models start with the same chassis, and quite a few other parts are standardized, but this one gets a floor gear shift, that one has it on the shaft of the driving wheel; one has a saloon body, another becomes a roadster; some are sprayed one colour, others in two colours, so that when the models finally move under their own power fundamentally all are of the same stock, but an overlay of acquired characteristics distinguishes them from their former mates. In the case of Maya culture these are an easily recognized art style, an architecture more advanced than any other in Middle America and which made extensive use of corbelled vaulting, a hieroglyphic writing far ahead of that of any other people in the New World, and a complex calendar bound up with a unique philosophy of time and a surprising command of astronomy.

There is some evidence that Maya sculpture was evolving both in the highlands of Guatemala and the lowlands late in the Formative period. Yet, the highland Maya, despite their great advantages in climate and natural resources (they controlled the sources of jade, the most valued possession in ancient Middle America, and they had plentiful supplies of obsidian, volcanic glass, from which razor-sharp blades were easily made), never shared in the great advances of their lowland cousins.

pl 39
41

Great civilizations have arisen in the tropics, but in open or semi-open country, and some fully developed cultures moved into tropical rain forest, e.g. Cambodia and Java, but the extraordinary thing is that Maya civilization (perhaps that of their neighbours the Olmec, too) matured, not in the highland where 'every prospect pleases', but in the lowland rain forest, where the Maya had to fight the thick vegetation year in and year out, and where farm land had constantly to be cleared with fire and stone tools (it was abandoned after two years because of weed growth and falling output). Toynbee tells us that civilizations, like individuals, respond to challenge, but if the obstacles are too difficult to overcome an incipient civilization will falter and fail. The challenge of the tropical rain forest was so formidable that one is surprised the Maya did face it. Perhaps meeting it built strong character in the individual and the group, without which no culture can long survive.

The Drive to Work

The building of the ceremonial centres required much man power, good organization and a dominant minority which could impose its will on the peasant population, source of the labour. It was not merely a matter of collecting huge quantities of stone and earth; apart from the dressing of stone, it was necessary, for instance, to cut large quantities of wood for burning in the lime kilns, which produced the enormous quantities of lime used in all construction.

It has been estimated from present-day performance that the average Maya needed about half the days in a year to look after his fields, leaving quite a lot of free time for community work. pl 28

One may suppose that the peasants responded to constant demands for labour without resentment, although surely with plenty of grumbling, for in a way it was a co-operative venture. The hierarchy, they realized, alone knew how to propitiate the gods of the soil without whose help the maize crop would fail; if the gods needed a higher pyramid or an extended court or even demanded a new ball-game court for the benefit of those mortals in their confidence the required labour was a sacrifice or—to put it more bluntly—a bribe to insure that the rains would come when they were needed.

There was a constant fear that the world would come to an end (the Maya believed it had already been destroyed four times and that they lived in the fifth creation), and in that connection solar eclipses were much feared. The Maya hierarchy, by announcing ahead of time when an eclipse might be expected and what steps they were taking to win the goodwill of the gods and avert the end of the world, obviously were driving home to any sullen or doubting peasant their essential services as intermediaries between gods and men, and the need to embellish the ceremonial centre as the seat of those services. Aztec chief rulers, such as Montezuma, donned the costumes of gods and were accorded semi-divine honours; one may reasonably suppose that Maya high priests were held in the same way to be divine.

A Unity of Religion and Trade

Of the political organization of the Maya during the Classic period almost nothing is known, but the distribution of certain hieroglyphs rather suggests that the lowlands were occupied by a number of 'city-states', with semi-independent or independent status. Some of the larger ceremonial centres certainly had their satellites; Bonampak, for example, in sculpture, architecture, and its hieroglyphic texts shows every sign of having been under the cultural, if not the political, domination of Yaxchilán. There is also evidence of a similar type that at least five fairly important Maya sites in the lower Pasión drainage were joined in a similar way, but with the difference that whereas Yaxchilán was of far greater importance than Bonampak, in the case of the Pasión sites (Seibal, La Amelia, Dos Pilas, Aguateca, and Tamarandito) none towers above the others in importance.

There is also evidence of a rapid spread of new ideas and new hieroglyphs throughout the southern lowlands, and from that one might deduce some sort of federation of city states, perhaps more cultural and religious than political. It is pleasant but definitely premature to picture the Maya lowlands of the Classic period as a faint reflection of renaissance Italy with New World popes and Lorenzos competing for outstanding Maya artists. Certainly the whole area was knit together by numerous trade routes, by land and water, for the exchange of the products of the highlands, such as obsidian, jade, and quetzal feathers, for the specialities of the lowlands—chocolate, cotton textiles, flint knives, jaguar pelts, etc.

On the other hand, the prevalence in parts of Campeche and western Yucatán of certain schismatic views on the structure of the Maya calendar probably produced or were the products of political divergence because of the importance and sanctity of the whole structure of time in Maya thinking. To the Maya this schism was probably almost as important as was to Europe the great controversy between Western and Eastern Christianity over the *filioque* clause.

Among the Maya of the southern lowlands religion seems to have been a unifying factor, for the same deities are portrayed on stelae and on buildings and recorded in the hieroglyphic inscriptions throughout the area. Also, what can be gathered about Maya ceremonies and religious practices during the Classic period supports this view of religious unity. For example, the drawing of blood to offer to the gods by passing a cord set with thorns through the tongue is depicted on stone lintels from Yaxchilán, on a stela at the Petén site of Naranjo, on a mural at Bonampak, and in a hieroglyphic book, probably from Campeche, of much later date. Moreover, eye-witness accounts by Spanish writers establish that the rite was prevalent over almost all the Maya area in the sixteenth century. Again, there was a unity in mythology and folklore. At least one incident from the cycle of stories of the sun god's life still recounted by the Maya was painted or carved on Maya pottery vases over a millenium ago. pl 36 pl 38

Belief in the essential unity of the Maya lowlands during the Classic period finds support in the absence of defences and the location in open country of the ceremonial centres, in contrast to reliance on fortifications and easily defended positions at a later period. Certainly warfare was not unknown, but this appears to have been largely a matter of raiding neighbouring territories to obtain the necessary quota of prisoners for sacrifice.

The Mystery of the Great Collapse

So the Maya ships of state sailed the seas of the Classic period in mainly calm weather. Then the winds of change arose and they were scattered, dismasted and wrecked. One by one the great ceremonial centres of the southern lowlands were deserted. In some the end came so quickly that buildings were left half-finished. Because of the Maya habit of erecting dated monuments to commemorate the end of each *katun* (20 year period) or the half or quarter *katun*, it is possible to follow the sequence of their collapse. Copán erected its last monument in AD 800, the year Charlemagne was crowned emperor, and Quiriguá and Piedras Negras follow suit ten years later. Other cities lasted longer, but the *katun* that ended in AD 889 is commemorated by only four centres. There seems to have been a remote area on the Petén-Campeche border which held out a few more years, but for all practical purposes the Classic period was at an end by AD 900.

Several explanations have been advanced for the desertion of the sites. It was once thought that the whole area was abandoned either because the fertility of the soil was exhausted or because forest lands, cleared so often to feed a growing population, were invaded by grass, with which the Maya, having no plough or metal-bladed hoes, could not cope. It was also suggested that the

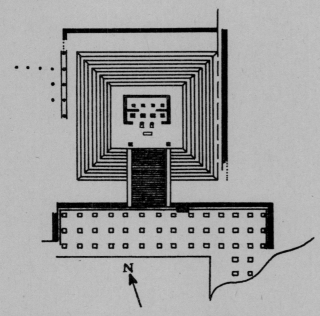

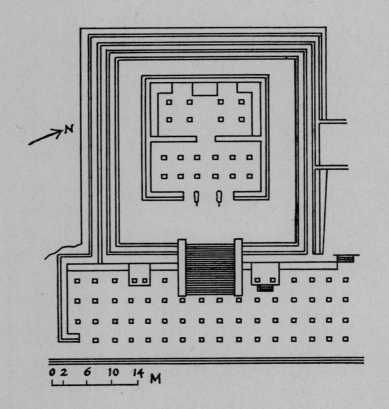

Almost exactly the same ground-plan is used for the great temple at Tula (left) and the Temple of the Warriors at Chichén Itzá (right), one of the many pieces of evidence to show that the same people, the Toltecs, planned both. Each consists of a small temple, divided into two rooms, on top of a pyramid, with a steep flight of steps. In the front are rows of columns. (7, 8)

population might have been swept off by yellow fever. Loss of soil fertility is a poor argument because Quiriguá, one of the earliest sites to be abandoned, lies amid inexhaustibly rich lands, on which the flood waters of the River Motagua deposit new soil at frequent intervals. The turf theory arose from a failure to realize that present-day savanna lands in the Petén are not former forest lands, but have always been savanna, the sandy soil being unsuited to rain forest. Finally, it is now almost certain that yellow fever, like several other diseases, was brought to the New World after Columbus' first voyage.

There is growing evidence that the whole area was not abandoned following mass migrations into Yucatán, as was once thought. Whatever happened to the hierarchy, the peasants appear to have remained in their homes. The most logical explanation is that the old co-operation of peasant and hierarch broke down, and that the peasants revolted and drove out or massacred the small ruling class of priest-nobles and their immediate followers, possibly because the hierarchy was attempting religious innovations at the expense of the old gods of the soil.

pl 49   In some sites there was deliberate destruction of monuments. Such was the fate of a magnificent dais at Piedras Negras. It had been the seat of the ruler, and one may suppose that it suffered at the hands of a mob because it symbolized his authority; alien invaders would more probably have preserved it to glorify their candidate for its occupancy.

Nevertheless, it is clear that the great ceremonial centres were not entirely abandoned; the peasants in the surrounding country, under their new leaders, the petty chiefs and witch doctors, an echelon below the old nobility, still made some use of them. As rooms started to collapse, doorways were carelessly blocked to shut them off. Burials were made in the debris of fallen corbelled vaults, and sacrifices made. Broken fragments of stelae were dragged around and set up, for worship one must conclude, but no one remained who could read the hieroglyphs or cared one way or the other if, by chance, he did understand them, for in more than one case the broken fragment was re-set upside down.

This abandonment of the ceremonial centres was general throughout the Maya lowlands, and extended to the highlands, but there the picture is not so clear because in some cases re-occupation, but seemingly by a different group, appears to have followed after a short break. The great sweep of the southern lowlands never recovered, but remained an area of small settlements and petty chiefs. In Yucatán and in the highlands of Guatemala influences from Central Mexico, discernible in some sites of the southern lowlands just before their abandonment, made themselves felt with increasing vigour. These Mexican influences are
f 11   very apparent at the great site of Chichén Itzá in northern Yucatán.

The Toltecs: Knights of the Jaguar and the Eagle

In the tenth century, not long after the abandonment of the cere-
f 9   monial centres marking the end of the Classic period, Chichén Itzá was occupied by a people who introduced the culture of the great Toltec capital of Tula, which lies about 50 miles northeast of Mexico City. They brought with them the worship of Quetzalcoatl, 'quetzal-bird snake', the deified ruler of Tula, who was represented as a serpent with feathers on his body, and other Mexican gods. They also imposed the Mexican concept of the necessity of war to insure a constant supply of prisoners for sacrifice, particularly to nourish and clothe with flesh the sun on his emergence each dawn from the house of the dead beneath the earth. To carry out this task, military orders of knighthood had been formed. Of these the most important were the jaguars and eagles, the members wearing the guise of jaguar or eagle. The new rulers of Chichén Itzá decorated buildings, presumably those in which these special rites were held, with friezes carved with jaguars and eagles offering human hearts to manifestations of the
pl 47   rising sun. These are practically duplicates of those carved at
48   Tula, 800 miles away. Indeed, the resemblances between the two
f 7, 8   cities are remarkable: the same ground plans, the same designs on columns, benches and daises carved with similar lines of warriors,
pl 45   the same representations of Quetzalcoatl everywhere, and the
46   same carvings of exotic gods. Yet the new rulers of Chichén Itzá

A gold disk from the sacred well at Chichén Itzá shows Maya warriors on the right retreating before the conquering Toltecs. All wear big feather head-dresses. The leading Toltec uses a spear-thrower in his right hand and grasps spare spears in his left. Above and below are stylized dragons. (9)

did not build a complete replica of Tula, for they utilized the Maya corbelled vault, unknown at Tula, and embellished their temples with representations of the Maya rain gods, as though seeking to   pl 17 reconcile thereby the conquered Maya.

This first period of Mexican influence, lasting from about AD 950 to AD 1200, witnessed a marked decline in all the arts, except working in metal, a craft introduced after the Classic period. Sculpture becomes dull and repetitious; files of warriors and monotonous feathered serpents lack the beauty or the life of sculpture of the Classic period. In painting, the murals at Chichén   pl 26 Itzá lack the genius so palpable in the murals of the earlier period. The same is true of pottery. The splendid polychrome pottery with scenes of ceremonial life or pleasant geometric designs and   pl 34 the finely carved or moulded vessels of the Classic period are suc-   40 ceeded in this first Mexican period by pottery which is monochrome or carries only the simplest designs in two colours. The technically interesting plumbate pottery, the nearest Middle America ever came to glazed pottery, was the product of a non-Maya group. Architecture was showy, but the buildings of the Mexican period lacked the stability of those of the Classic period. Hieroglyphic texts almost but not quite completely went out of use. In short, Maya culture had passed its crest, and was clearly going downhill.

Chichén Itzá was captured and sacked about AD 1200, and Mayapán, in western Yucatán, came to the fore as the capital of all Yucatán. Unlike the early centres, Mayapán was a real city. A stout wall five miles long, with ramparts and defended entrances, enclosed nearly 4,000 mounds, most of which were the foundations of residential huts. There is good evidence that the theocracy of the Classic period, sadly weakened during the Mexican period at Chichén Itzá, had given place to a militaristic government, whose outlook was secular. The residences of the nobility, several of which were excavated in the 1950's, were often made of better stone than were the temples, exemplifying the shift in values. Moreover, the family oratory, with much emphasis on ancestor   pl 30 worship, had grown in importance at the expense of community worship at the public temples.

Art and architecture had further declined. Sculpture of the Mayapán period is so crude and graceless that it is hard to believe that it was made by the same people who produced the magnificent work of the Classic period. Buildings are shoddy with much f 10 use of stucco to cover poor workmanship—whited sepulchres in every sense of the expression. The pottery of Mayapán is inferior even to that of the earlier Mexican period at Chichén Itzá. The only innovation was a sort of assembly line, anticipating Henry Ford by some 800 years, for turning out pottery incense burners which carried representations of the gods. Arms, legs, hands, feet, details of head-dresses and even faces made in moulds, were kept handy for sticking on the pottery 'chassis' to produce portraits of the gods. With the addition, after firing, of much colour, a showy effect was produced, but the spiritual values behind them were about equal to those of the Christmas decorations in Regent Street.

The Inspiration Fails

Mayapán smells to high heaven of cultural degeneration. It had become a militaristic dictatorship ruling the rest of Yucatán and exacting tribute by force of arms. In 1460 the Maya revolted, sacked Mayapán—full archaeological evidence for this was uncovered—and put an end to the incipient empire.

In the warfare between rival petty chiefs which marked the 80 years between the fall of Mayapán and the Spanish conquest, Maya culture degenerated even further. The old ceremonial centres were completely abandoned, and a rule of petty chiefs was established. The Spanish conquest gave the *coup de grâce* to Maya culture, but the civilization had sunk so low that its recovery would have seemed unlikely had there been no Spanish intervention.

Thus, this civilization which came to flower in Middle America 1500 years ago achieved its greatness under the leadership of a theocracy. The drive of that small group to comprehend and thus dominate the cycles of divine influences which, in their belief, set the rigid pattern of their lives, gave Maya civilization its strange form. It led them to a knowledge in the fields of astronomy, arithmetic, and the age of the earth without parallel among peoples on a similar cultural level, and it fostered the growth of a unique art and the most advanced architecture of the New World as handmaidens to this quest.

When, at the close of the ninth century, the theocracy of the Classic period fell, the inspiration of Maya culture was no more. With a swing to militarism and secular rule came cultural degeneration which continued with gathering momentum until the arrival of the Spaniards in the sixteenth century put the last

A late pottery figure from Mayapán, the only true city of the Maya. It was the capital of the last Maya state and fell in 1460, but its art was already in decline. Limbs and details of ornament were mass-produced in moulds and stuck on to a core. (10)

graceless offspring of Maya civilization out of their misery.

Had the discovery of America been postponed another century, the Maya in all probability would have been conquered by the Aztec and their allies whose rapidly expanding "empire" had in fact reached the frontier of the Maya in western Chiapas (there was an Aztec garrison at Zinacantlan, outpost of the Tzotzil branch of the Maya). Had the Aztec overrun the Maya it would have created an interesting parallel to Roman conquest of decadent Greece. One may wonder whether the Aztec would have shown for the Maya way of life a respect comparable to that of the Romans for ancient Athens.

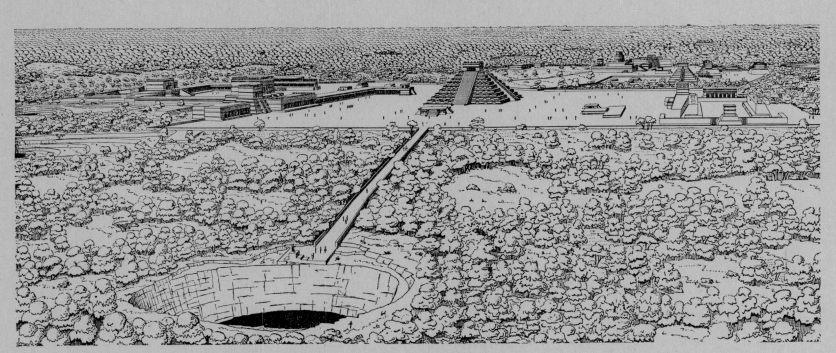

The ceremonial centre of Chichén Itzá, as it was rebuilt by the Toltecs in the 10th century AD. In the foreground is the sacred well, the cenote, into which rich offerings and sometimes human victims were thrown. The great court is dominated by the Temple of Kukulcan, connected to the cenote by the ceremonial road. On the left is a complex of buildings consisting of the Temple of the Warriors, with the 'Thousand Columns' extended in front and to the side. On the right is the Ball-court, and further back the Caracol, perhaps an observatory. (11)

VIII   THE ETRUSCAN PROBLEM

An historic people who left no history

DONALD STRONG

The main phases and events of Etruscan history are shown in this chronological table, with contemporary Greek activity on the right.

The very magnificence and profusion of Etruscan remains

make their mystery the more tantalizing. Their cities, industries, trade and cultural contacts have been traced. We could reproduce an Etruscan house and its contents, and the costumes of the people who lived in it, down to the smallest detail. And yet they remain baffling. For to some of the most intriguing questions that we ask of a great civilization the Etruscan returns no answer. There is no history, no literature, no proclamation or legal decree, no prayer to the gods. The thousands of brief inscriptions contain only conventional formulae, and the few texts of any length (the longest is 1500 words) continue to defeat all attempts at understanding.

That is one side of the Etruscan mystery: the other is the riddle of their origin. Herodotus says they came from Lydia in Asia Minor, yet their language is not Lydian, nor is it Indo-European, nor Semitic. They arose unheralded in the midst of a land barely civilized, flourished and grew powerful, creating an art rivalling that of Greece, which inspired it, and a way of life that can still cast its spell on us. Then came Rome. The Etruscan cities, sophisticated, pleasure-loving and disunited, were conquered one by one. 'The ashes on the hearths of the Etruscans were scattered to the winds,' wrote Propertius. In a process of ruthless Romanization their political life was destroyed, their customs suppressed, their art looted, the key to their genius lost. So it has remained. From the painted walls of their tombs, from countless bronzes, terracottas and stone sculptures, the sad wide eyes of Etruscan men and women gaze out at the world, a faint smile on their silent lips, as if guarding their secret for ever.

A married couple reclining at a banquet—one of a number of terracotta sarcophagi showing the dead in this pose. It was made about 500 BC and comes from Caere. (1)

The houses of the living served as models for the urns that contained the ashes of the dead. This Villanovan cremation urn from Vetulonia is particularly interesting because it shows roof construction and decoration. (2)

Before the Etruscans

the land of Etruria was the home of an Iron Age people known as the Villanovans (from Villanova near Bologna), who seem to have come from across the Alps. They were skilful metal workers and potters and they passed much of their knowledge on to the Etruscans. They cremated their dead, burying the ashes in characteristic urns.

Art grew under the influence of Greece; even Villanovan works are clearly inspired by the Greek geometric style. This *askos* with its bull's head and armed rider, is from Bologna. (3)

A single handle to a Villanovan urn may mean that it was made to hold a cremation. If a two-handled urn was used, one of them was always ritually broken. The typical shape is biconical, with incised geometric ornament. The one on the left, from one of the largest Villanovan cemeteries of Tarquinia, has a real warrior's helmet as a lid, with a high crest and three spikes back and front. Below: a reconstructed cremation burial at Bologna, showing how it was enclosed in six stone slabs. (4, 5)

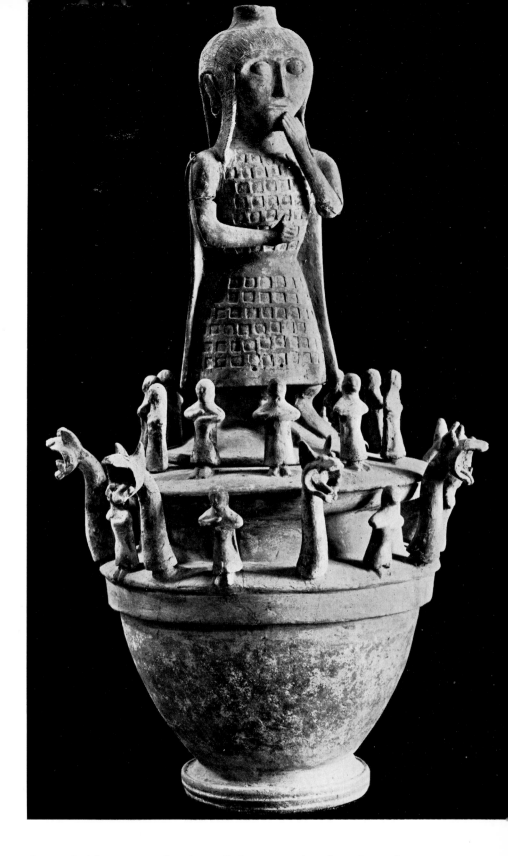

The rite of cremation continued much longer than elsewhere in Chiusi, the most important Etruscan city of the north. Peculiar to this region, where there was a specially large Villanovan settlement, are the 'canopic' urns. That shown above, c. 600 BC, has a body, lid (in the form of a human head) and 'seat' (with back), all of terracotta but imitating the details of metalwork. The urn on the right makes ornate use of oriental motifs. The two rims have griffin-heads and female statuettes, and the lid is surmounted by a large female figure in an attitude of prayer. (6, 7)

Life in the Po Valley under Etruscan occupation is vividly portrayed in a bronze situla with repoussé reliefs found near Bologna. In the zone shown below a funeral procession wends its way to the tomb. The women, bearing offerings, wear hoods and mantles with a net-work pattern. The men here have wide-brimmed hats in the Greek style, but more usually they went bareheaded. (8)

Etruscan culture crystallizes

around 700 BC, whether by a natural development from the Villanovan or by foreign invasion is still a matter for argument—the central issue, in fact, of 'the Etruscan problem.' Many of the innovations point to the east, including corbelled vaults (Mycenae), and certain kinds of grave (Asia Minor). What chiefly distinguishes the new culture from the old is the eagerness with which it absorbs ideas from abroad. There is a rush of exotic imports—vases from Corinth, Egyptian faience, Urartian pottery-stands, Assyrian goldwork, Phoenician silver. This is the so-called 'orientalizing' period of Etruscan history, when the foundations of its greatness were laid.

Trade with Egypt is suggested by the 'Bocchoris' vase (above) a faience vessel decorated with the cartouche of Pharaoh Bakenrenef who was killed in 728 BC. It shows the pharaoh between divinities, and prisoners and monkeys among palms. (10)

From Phoenicia comes this silver cauldron (below) imported into Etruria in the 7th century BC. The zones in low relief with engraved outlines show scenes of peace and war. The snakes' heads fixed to the rim were probably added in Etruria. (11)

Strong influence from the Eastern Mediterranean appears in this terracotta statuette of a woman from Caere. She wears a cloak fastened at the shoulder by a metal *fibula* and large massy ear-rings. The statuette dates from the 7th century BC. (9)

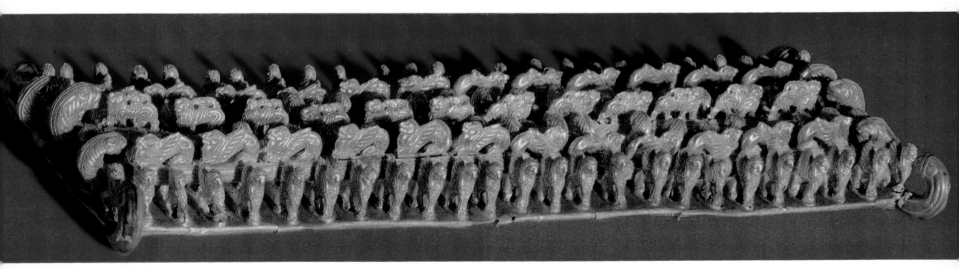

Etruscan luxury became a byword in the austere world of the early Romans. Even now the sight of their jewellery is breathtaking. There are necklaces, brooches, rings, bracelets and ornaments of every description. In 1836 the tomb of a prince and princess was opened at Caere. One of the richest pieces was a golden clasp (top) in two sections—an oval plate with five lions, connected by two hinged joints to a smaller oval plate covered with minute golden ducklings. The fibula below is another example of the same repoussé and granulation technique, this time forming lions' heads, griffins and sphinxes. (12, 13)

175

One of the most curious features of Etruscan religion was hepatoscopy, or divination by examining the liver of sacrificial animals. On a model liver from Piacenza the different parts of the liver corresponded to different sectors of the sky. This is a custom of Eastern origin—it was practised in Babylon.

'Calchas', a bearded winged figure, pores over an animal liver which he holds in his hand. This engraving on the back of a mirror from Vulci dates from the 4th century BC. Calchas is the name of a Greek priest mentioned in the Iliad. (14)

The haruspex, one skilled in interpreting the will of the gods, was an important person in Etruscan, and later in Roman, society. In the bronze (right) he wears the characteristic pointed beret and mantle, which has a short inscription. Besides hepatoscopy, the haruspex was also expected to interpret lightning and the flight of birds. (15)

One of the longest surviving texts in the Etruscan language is on a scroll held by a reclining stone figure on a sarcophagus (a certain Laris Pulena of Tarquinia). The Etruscan alphabet was almost the same as the Greek, but normally written from right to left. The scroll shown here contains sixty words; part of it describes the genealogy and career of the dead man, and the names of some Etruscan gods can be recognised, but the text as a whole cannot be understood. (16)

The Etruscan dead were given houses as costly and beautifully decorated as those of the living. The necropolis was a true 'city of death', often covering several square miles. The Tomb of the Bulls at Tarquinia (above) dates from the mid-6th century. One wall shows a scene from the Siege of Troy. Achilles, wearing a helmet, waits in ambush behind a fountain for Troilus who approaches riding on a huge horse. The amazing Tomb of the Reliefs at Caere (right) goes even further in reproducing an actual house-interior. There are imitation pillars and capitals, beams, joists and roof-planks, while all around are stucco reliefs of domestic utensils depicted in astonishing detail: on the nearest pillar a knife, pick, rope and an animal like a cat; on the further one pincers, cooking pots, a chicken and a pig. (17, 18)

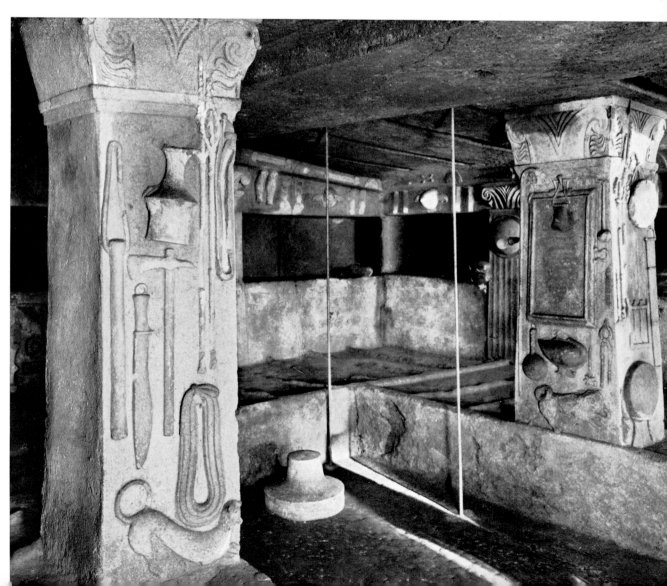

It is at Tarquinia,

one of the greatest of the Etruscan city-states, that this dazzling world comes most vividly to life. Here was a hill-city, made rich by trade, the home of an aristocracy of taste and boundless energy. On the walls of their tombs the men of Tarquinia painted everything that was most precious in their lives—feasts, festivals, music, dancing, stories from the epic poets, the pleasures of the table and the hunt, of wine and of love. At the peak of Etruscan culture (5th century BC) these paintings glow with a radiant enjoyment of physical things that makes them unique in ancient art. At Tarquinia some sixty painted tombs have been found and more are still coming to light. They are hollowed into the rock, the surfaces smoothed and covered in a layer of plaster and limewash.

The banquet in the Tomb of the Leopards. Man and wife recline together, the women fair, the men brown-skinned. Naked boys serve the wine. 'The curves of their limbs show pleasure in life,' wrote D. H. Lawrence, 'a pleasure that goes deeper still in the limbs of the dancers, in the big, long hands thrown out and dancing to the very ends of the fingers, a dance that surges from within, like a current in the sea.' Below left: dancers from the Tomb of the Triclinium, drapery flying, the girl's head thrown back in ecstasy; yet all this energy is strictly composed, the figures being separated from each other by little trees, across which their hands barely touch. Below centre: a player on the double-flute —most typical of Etruscan musical instruments—in the Tomb of the Leopards. Below right: a woman from the Tomb of the Lionesses; she dances solemnly, her costly robes flowing gracefully around her. (19, 20, 21, 22)

An excursion by the sea is depicted on a wall of the Tomb of Hunting and Fishing (above). One boy with a net leans from the prow of a dolphin-headed boat. Another on a rock aims his sling at a water-bird. In the air flocks of gaily coloured birds flutter, filling the tomb with movement. (23)

Funeral games were a part of Etruscan, as of Greek, ritual. Below left: a racing chariot from the Tomb of the Olympic Games at Tarquinia, discovered only in 1958. Below right: a wrestling contest from a tomb at Chiusi. There were once twenty painted tombs at Chiusi, but only three survive. (24, 25)

Towards the end of the 3rd century the scene begins to darken. The after-life ceases to be regarded as a pro-longation of earthly pleasures and becomes a place of judgement. Dread-ful gods menace the dead.

Grasping the hammer that symbo-lizes the blow of death, the daemon Charun advances threateningly in the Tomb of Orcus at Tarquinia. This sinister figure from the underworld shows the increasing terror of Etrus-can religion. His nose is hooked, ears pointed; snakes writhe from his head and shoulders. (26)

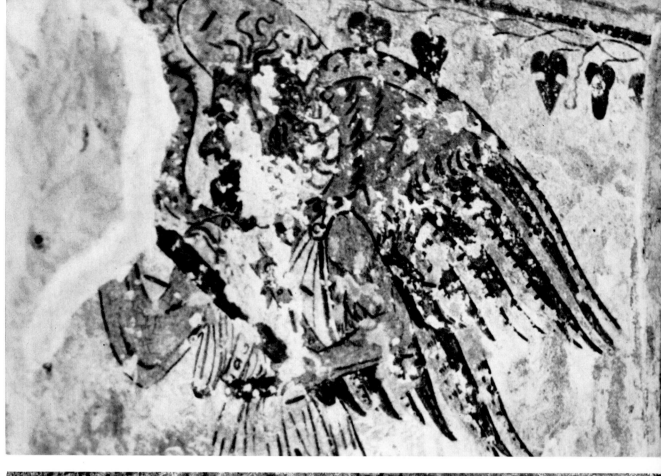

Sad-eyed, their exuberant gaiety van-ished, the Etruscans of the 3rd century sit at a melancholy banquet. The wife no longer leans happily against her husband, but sits upright. Like the man in the Tomb of the Leopards (pl. 19), he is handing her the egg, symbol of life, but now the future is without hope or joy. This painting is in the Tomb of the Shields, Tarquinia. (27)

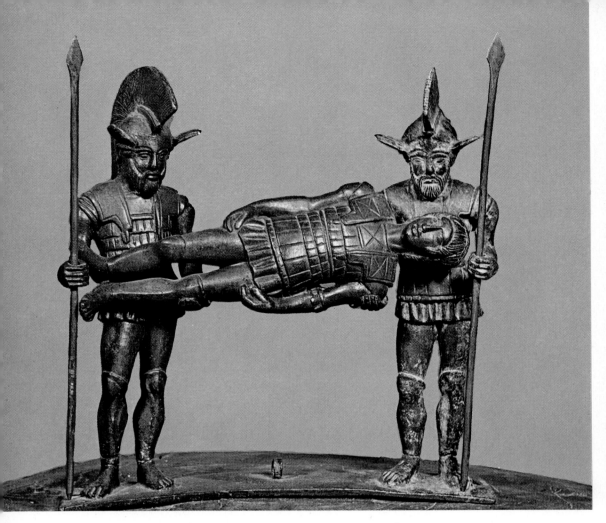

Etruscan bronze-work, whether by Etruscans or by Greek craftsmen settled in Etruria, was prized all over the Mediterranean. On the lid of a cauldron from Capua (above right) a satyr carries off a maenad, while four Amazons gallop round them shooting arrows. Above left: the handle of a *cista* from Praeneste; two warriors in armour carry the body of a third. (28, 29)

The Chimaera, perhaps the most famous of ancient bronzes, and one that caused a sensation when it was found at Arezzo in 1553. Benvenuto Cellini was given the job of restoring it (he mended the serpent-tail). The mythical beast, with its lion's body and goat's head growing out of its back, digs its claws into the ground in frenzy, ready to leap at Bellerophon, the hero who slew it. (30)

A masterpiece of bronzework is the Ficorini *cista*, typically Praenestine but made in Rome. The legs consist of groups in relief; the feet are claws resting on frogs; while the body is engraved with scenes from the story of the Argonauts—a youth practising boxing, Silenus imitating him, a lion-headed fountain, another youth drinking and a third holding an amphora already full. The detail above shows the Argo herself. (31, 32)

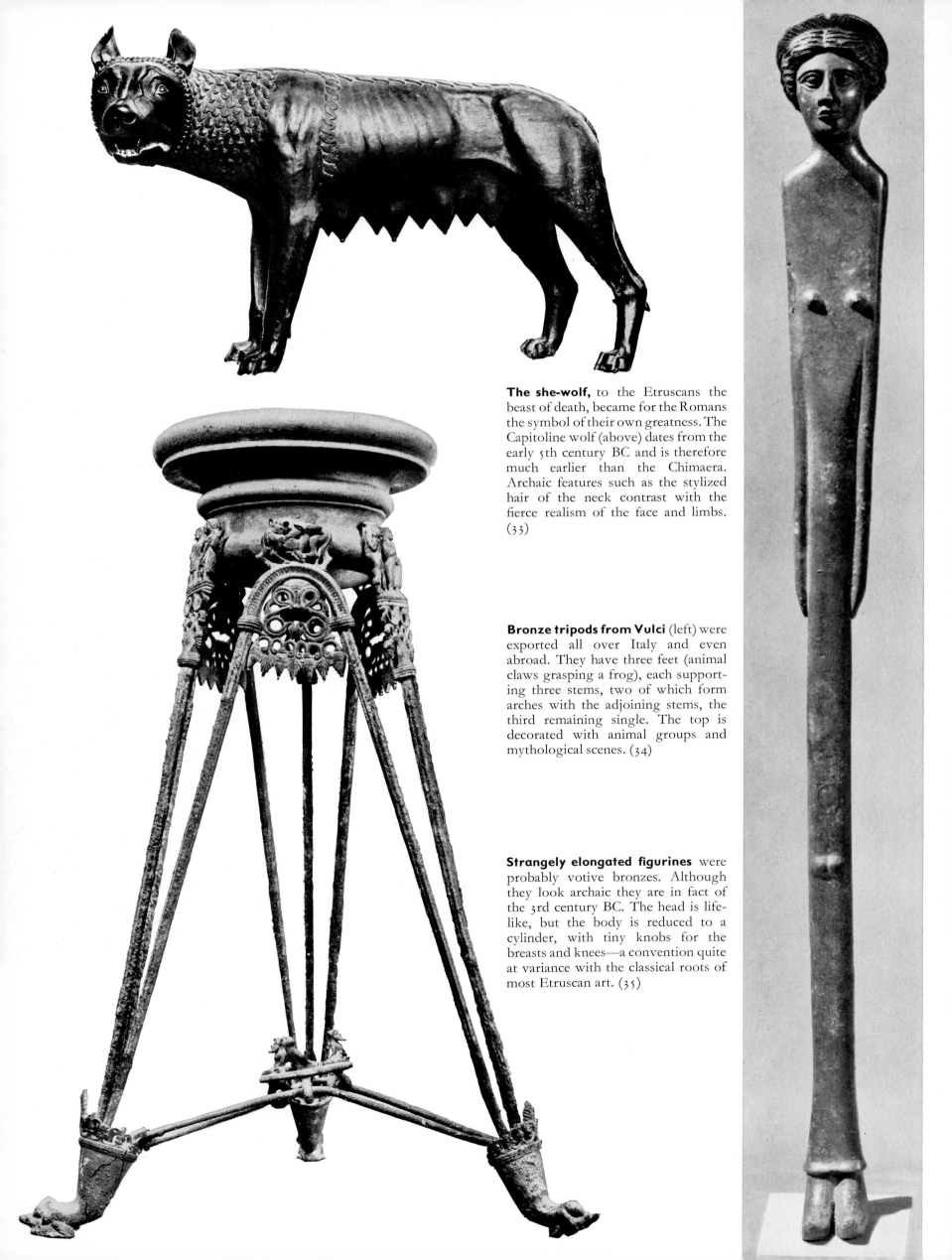

The she-wolf, to the Etruscans the beast of death, became for the Romans the symbol of their own greatness. The Capitoline wolf (above) dates from the early 5th century BC and is therefore much earlier than the Chimaera. Archaic features such as the stylized hair of the neck contrast with the fierce realism of the face and limbs. (33)

Bronze tripods from Vulci (left) were exported all over Italy and even abroad. They have three feet (animal claws grasping a frog), each supporting three stems, two of which form arches with the adjoining stems, the third remaining single. The top is decorated with animal groups and mythological scenes. (34)

Strangely elongated figurines were probably votive bronzes. Although they look archaic they are in fact of the 3rd century BC. The head is life-like, but the body is reduced to a cylinder, with tiny knobs for the breasts and knees—a convention quite at variance with the classical roots of most Etruscan art. (35)

A satyr defends himself against a snake—a small bronze that may have formed the support for a vase. A fragment of the snake remains in his left hand; in his right he grasps a dagger. The sculptor has devoted great attention to the expression of the face. (36)

The Roman art of portraiture is foreshadowed in the bronze head known as 'Brutus'. It was probably made by an Etruscan craftsman for a Roman patron in the 2nd or 1st centuries BC. As realistic as later Roman busts, the face has a deep melancholy that links it with the last phase of Etruscan painting. (38)

As supports for candelabra the Etruscan bronze-smiths often made figures of enchanting vitality showing all their love of the human form in motion. This girl, dancing to the castanets, is a sister to those who dance at the funeral feasts in the painted tombs. (37)

It is a surprising fact that of the painted pottery from Etruscan tombs, much more is of Greek than of local manufacture. And besides these imports from Greece, which must have been enormous, Greek potters settled in Etruria and began schools of their own. Throughout its development, therefore, Etruscan pottery shows a very close dependence on Greek models, though it is not difficult to tell one from another. The earliest native Etruscan

pottery is 'bucchero', a black, highly-polished ware deriving from a Villanovan type. Vessels are coarse but often attractive in shape, with incised ornament (below). Later bucchero ('bucchero pesante') shows a decline in face of competition from Greek workshops. The example from Chiusi (below right) has a bull's head at the top, and then a row of lion's heads and a zone showing a bull held by the horn and leg by an athlete. (39, 40)

The earliest Greek style to be imitated is the geometric. This vase from Bisenzio (below) is painted in black and red on a white slip; the main decorative motifs are purely geometric, but there is a frieze of schematized dancing figures forming the lowest zone. It was made about 700 BC. (41)

About 550 BC a Greek potter from Ionia (Asia Minor) emigrated to Caere. There was still an unceasing demand for Greek pots. The new workshop prospered, and the black-figured 'Caeretan hydriae' are its characteristic products. On the vase below Odysseus and his companions put out the eye of Polyphemus. (42)

The finest Etruscan vases in red-figured technique are the Faliscan made during the 4th century BC in or near Falerii (Cività Castellana). The style is distinctively different from the Greek models on which they are based, and it is often possible to see that the artists did not understand their Greek subjects or treat them very seriously. This calyx-crater by the Nazzano painter depicts the sack of Troy. At the bottom old king Priam lies on the ground, a warrior standing threateningly over him. To the left Aphrodite (with shield) is defending Helen from the wrath of Menelaus. At the top Neoptolemus kills the boy Astyanax. (43)

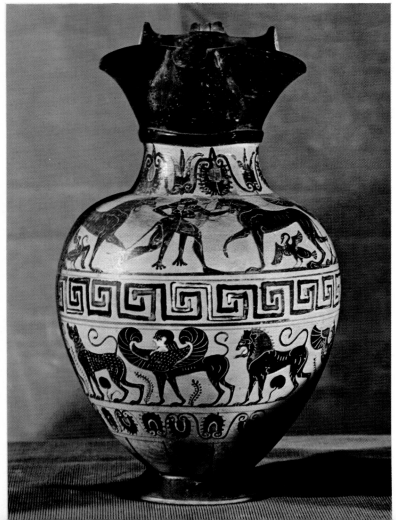

'Pontic vases' are another class of black-figured vase ware which may have been produced by a Greek immigrant from Ionia. His workshop was probably at Vulci in the 6th century BC. The vase (left) is at Florence; on the shoulder is Hercules fighting two lions, at the bottom a frieze of mythological animals. (44)

Etruscan women kept scent or ointment in elegant little jugs like this, duck-shaped and decorated in red-figured technique. The flying goddess is a 'Lasa', a type of female Eros who belongs entirely to Etruscan mythology. (45)

187

The accident of survival

accounts for the relative rarity of large-scale Etruscan stone-carving and terracotta-work. Etruscan tombs have been preserved, the temples not. And it was in the temples that the most grandiose works were to be found. Besides housing the statues of the gods, they were decorated with elaborate terracotta plaques and pedimental compositions, while the roofs had rows of 'acroteria' and 'antefixes'.

The Centaur of Vulci: a male body with the hind-quarters of a horse. The arms (missing from shoulder to wrist) were straight down at his side. When complete he would have been over three feet tall. The style is very close to the Greek 7th century tradition known as 'Dedalic'; several Etruscan carvings in this style made around 600 BC are fine works suggesting that they were made by Greek emigrants to Etruria. The Centaur once guarded the entrance to a tomb. (47)

Funeral games and the journey of the dead into the underworld in a chariot led by a daemon are shown on this tombstone from Bologna, dating from about 400 BC. (46)

Suffering and resignation show in the lined faces of this elderly Etruscan couple from a terracotta urn of the 1st century BC. The old optimism in the face of death has gone and in its place is a stoicism that bears the imprint of Rome. (48)

188

Proud winged horses, yoked to the service of the gods—one of the few large pieces of terracotta to have survived, and a masterpiece of Etruscan art. They once formed part of the façade of a temple at Tarquinia and, apart from the wing and the tail, seem to have been modelled in one piece. (49)

The lady Seianti Thanunia of Chiusi raises her veil to look into the mirror. Her effigy in terracotta, painted to display her rich clothes and jewellery, dates from the mid-2nd century. (50)

The gods of the Greeks were worshipped in Etruria, often with different attributes and different ritual, side by side with other deities whose strange names were unknown on Olympus—Tinia, of infinite power, Fufluns, Turan, Tesan, Sethlans. Apollo was one of the Greek pantheon to be taken over almost unchanged. The head of Apollo (below) from the pediment of a temple at Lo Scasato, Cività Castellana, is close in style to the work of one of Lysippus' pupils. It dates from the 4th–3rd centuries BC when Greek influence in Etruria was at its height. (52)

A peasant of Etruria, as he was in life during the late 2nd or 1st century AD. The Etruscan love of direct vigorous portraiture comes out well in this votive terracotta head. (53)

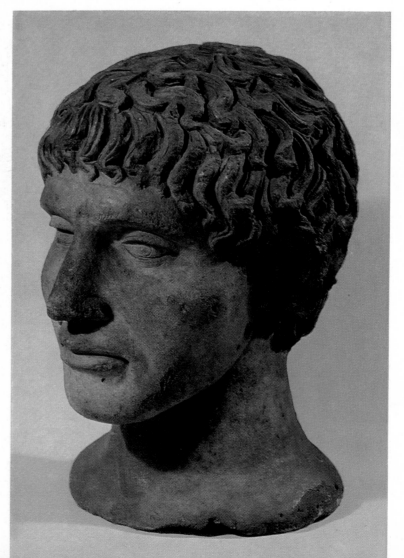

The Apollo of Veii is unmistakably Etruscan, a supreme masterpiece of terracotta sculpture that illustrates clearly the difference between Etruscan works of art and their Greek models. It is much earlier than the Apollo of Cività Castellana, dating from about 500 BC. Part of a group representing the struggle between Apollo and Hercules, it once decorated the ridge of a temple-roof at Veii. This group is associated with the name of the artist Vulca of Veii who worked on the Temple of Jupiter on the Capitol in Rome. (51)

An historic people who left no history

DONALD STRONG

THE PEOPLE we call Etruscans inhabited central Italy in the time of the Greeks and Romans; they belong, therefore, to history but they have left us no history themselves. None of the most vivid aspects of written history—the names and deeds of famous men, accounts of wars and revolutions—are known direct from Etruscan sources. From Greek and Roman writers we get a picture of the cruel and licentious Etruscan that does him far less than justice and is born of misunderstanding and political rivalry. The disease of Etruscomania—the romantic enthusiasm for all things Etruscan—which has had its victims from the Emperor Claudius to D. H. Lawrence, has done him scarcely less harm. Etruscan archaeology is still young and many of the key sites were carelessly, sometimes ruthlessly, excavated in its very early days. Nor can archaeology alone succeed in answering many of the questions which are bound to be asked about a people who were contemporaries of the fully historical Greeks and Romans.

The Etruscans, indeed, ever since the Renaissance, have been enveloped in an aura of mystery. Their cities are still largely unexplored and are often scenes of that romantic and picturesque desolation which inspires the nostalgia of vanished glories while their tomb-paintings, at Tarquinia and elsewhere, seem to re-create the life of the people with an almost overpowering immediacy. Add to all this a language about which we know very little, conflicting accounts, ancient and modern, of their origins, and the Etruscans remain as satisfyingly enigmatic as any people who have inhabited the face of the earth.

The Etruscans, who called themselves Rasna and were known to the Greeks as Tyrrhenians, inhabited part of central Italy on the western side of the Apennine range, a territory bounded on the north by the river Arno, on the east and south by the river Tiber, and on the west by the Tyrrhenian sea. It is a land of variety and picturesque landscape, endowed with rich natural resources. In the north a broad range of hilly country extends eastwards from the sea to the fertile valleys and mountains below the high Apennines; in the south the coastal tract of the Maremma rises up to a zone of fertile volcanic uplands cut by deep ravines and surrounding extinct craters like Lago di Bolsena and Lago di Vico. Olives, grape-vines, cereals and fruit grow in abundance. Besides, Etruria contained almost all the mineral resources of the Italian peninsula and several of the Etruscan cities, Populonia for example, owed their prosperity to this mineral wealth; but those of the south depended mainly on intensive and highly successful cultivation of the fruitful soil and they included the most important and rapidly developing of all.

Before the Etruscans

In this area, richly endowed by nature, archaeology has traced the development, sometime during the 8th century BC, of a material culture distinct from the rest of the Italian peninsula. A rapid accession of wealth accompanied by new and lavish burial customs is found in several centres which later became famous in history as Etruscan cities. In the 7th century foreign ideas and foreign products imported from all over the Mediterranean reflect a vast rise in the standard of living. There are inscriptions in

pl 9
10
11

One of the earliest inscriptions in the Etruscan language, dated about 650 BC. It is on a stele found at Vetulonia, of an Etruscan warrior named Avele Feluske who is armed with a double-axe. (1)

the Etruscan language as early as about 650 BC, perhaps earlier, and by about 600 BC, we can speak of a fully-developed Etruscan people. This 'orientalising' period of the 7th century BC, so called because of the predominance of imports from the eastern Mediterranean area, was obviously the decisive step in the development of the people we know as Etruscans.   f 1

It seems, however, that an equally decisive step was taken much earlier in central Italy when iron-using peoples settled on most of the sites that were later to become Etruscan cities. We should perhaps admit that many of these same centres had indeed been occupied continuously since late Bronze Age times, but the iron-users, who are called Villanovans, a name they take from the site of Villanova near Bologna, however much they may have assimilated of the Apennine Bronze Age culture must be reckoned an intrusive people closely connected with the urn-field cultures across the eastern Alps. These people buried their dead in cylindrical funerary shafts set close together, the ashes being interred in a characteristic ossuary, the biconical urn. pl 2 Helmet-urns and hut-urns, the germ perhaps of the later Etruscan 4 idea that the tomb should copy the house of the living, are also 5 found in several places. The typical contents of a rich Villanovan grave, such as have been found at Tarquinia, include finely-made bronze armour, bronze articles of dress, and metal vessels with f 2 incised ornament.

These Villanovans cannot, on any interpretation of the archaeological evidence, be dissociated from the Etruscans of history; one of the main centres of Villanovan development was the coastal region of southern Etruria—the area of Tarquinia and Caere (Cerveteri)—where they were already exploiting the local

Bronze container from a Villanovan grave at Tarquinia, 7th century BC. The vessel, on four wheels, is in the form of a bird's body ending in a long neck with stag's head. The lid has a similar neck and head. (2)

sources of mineral ore. Indeed, it can be argued that in many places the Villanovan 'shades off' into Etruscan with the influx of material wealth and foreign imports, bringing with them, inevitably, new ideas and customs. Everything depends, obviously, on a correct assessment of what took place and it will be well to begin by looking at a few of the subsequently important Etruscan places to assess the character of the change, the process and timing of which is never exactly the same in two places.

The Birth of the New Culture

f 11 We may take first Tarquinia which was to become one of the most renowned of Etruscan cities. It lay, some five miles from the sea, on a long, narrow plateau attached to a mountain chain, a classic South Etruscan site. The area of the town, known today as Piano di Città, was probably occupied from early Villanovan times and was surrounded by extensive cemeteries, the earliest being the Selciatello, the largest the Monterozzi. In the oldest

pl 4 tombs, the ashes of the dead were placed in the characteristic
5 biconical urns, of clay and later of metal, often covered with
2 bronze helmets; here as elsewhere some hut-urns have been found which are copied, no doubt, from the contemporary dwellings of the people.

About 700 the earliest inhumation graves seem to occur and one of the larger among them is the so-called Bocchoris Tomb, which takes its name from the vase of Egyptian faience with a

pl 10 cartouche of the king Bakenrenef who reigned in Egypt between 734 and 728. Other 'oriental' imports in this tomb include faience figures and fragments of faience vases, pottery stands of Urartian type, an Assyrian gold plaque, some locally made jewellery and imitations of Greek vases. A second inhumation of about the same date, the so-called 'Tomba del Guerriero', was made in a simple sarcophagus; the contents were mainly of Villanovan type but with imitations of Greek pottery and one object of precious metal. In the course of the 7th century inhumation generally took the place of cremation but the large chamber-tomb did not come in until the 6th century.

Caere, our second Etruscan city, lies about four and a half miles from the sea with its principal port at Pyrgi, some eight miles away; its wealth, from an early period, seems to have derived from the minerals of the La Tolfa-Allumiere region. Here the Villanovan Iron Age was transformed about the middle of the 7th century with a fabulously rich 'orientalising' phase. The famous Regolini-Galassi tomb is a long tunnel with side tunnels cut in the native tufa and roofed over with a false vault on the same principle as the Mycenaean tholos tombs; it contained

three principal burials with grave-goods of regal splendour including eastern cauldrons, gold and silver vessels of 'Phoenician' pl 11 make, ivory carvings in oriental and 'orientalising' styles, Corinthian vases and much magnificent gold jewellery. Both the pl 12 monumental form of the tomb and the wealth of its contents introduce a vast contrast with the preceding Villanovan phase.

In the north, Vetulonia and Chiusi may serve to illustrate contrasting developments in Etruscan cities. At Vetulonia the oldest Villanovan tombs are rather poorer than elsewhere; the later cremations are found grouped in rough stone circles and about 700 BC, it seems, a formal circle of upright slabs was arranged around groups of mainly inhumation tombs containing rich 'orientalising' grave goods of bronze, jewellery etc. Monumental tombs appear at the end of the 7th century. In Chiusi, the most important Etruscan city of the north in historical times, there was a large Villanovan settlement and the rite of cremation lasted much longer than elsewhere. There are two characteristic local forms of burial; in one, the so-called burial 'a ziro', the ash-urn is placed in another, larger vessel, and in the other, the vessel is shaped in imitation of the human body and has a lid in pl 6 the form of a head, the so-called 'canopic' jar. Prosperity seems to 7 have come to Chiusi at the end of the 7th century with chamber tombs and imports from abroad as well as from the coastal Etruscan cities.

Who Were the Etruscans?

In the course of these developments during the 8th and 7th centuries BC, the historical Etruscans had appeared. The 'far-famed Tyrrhenians' are mentioned in Hesiod's *Theogony* dating from about 700 BC and it is arguable that as early as 750, when the Greeks were beginning to colonize the southern parts of Italy, the centre of the peninsula was already controlled by the Etruscans, who were strong enough to discourage the Greeks from attempting to settle further north and induce them to accept instead the rich market for their pottery, oil, perfume etc. in return for raw materials. The crux of the Etruscan problem, as it is so often called, is to decide whether the rise in the standard of living and the transformation from Villanovan to Etruscan is explained simply by trade or whether the new elements which have no obvious connexion with the earlier culture derive from foreigners settling in the country. Moreover, even if the archaeological evidence does not seem to demand a foreign invasion to explain the transformation of Etruria in the 8th and 7th centuries, many people believe that it is the only possible explanation of the deep-seated differences which exist between the historical Etruscans and the peoples inhabiting the rest of Italy, for the Etruscans lived lives, worshipped gods and spoke a language very different from that of their neighbours.

This problem of the formation of the Etruscan people is coloured by two conflicting ancient accounts of their origins which have formed the basis for all future discussion. Herodotus, the 5th century Greek historian, gives what is, apparently, the traditional foundation myth of the Etruscan people, that sometime after the Trojan Wars a body of Lydians under the leadership of Tyrrhenus left their own country and at length settled in the land of the Ombrikoi 'where they built themselves cities and where they live to this very day'. This account deserves no more and no less credence than the story of Rome's foundation from Homeric Troy—perhaps a little more, in that Herodotus did not get it from Etruscan but from Lydian sources—but it was certainly believed by the Etruscans themselves and the ancients in general. Among Roman writers 'Lydian' or 'Maeonian' are the commonest adjectives for Etruscans; the Tiber is 'the Lydian river'. It was left to the learned and pedantic Dionysius of Halicarnassus, writing at the time of the Emperor Augustus, to state a reasoned case against the story; basing his argument upon a comparison of language, religion and customs, Dionysius set out to prove that the Etruscans were 'autochthonous' i.e. indigenous to Italy.

It seems certain that no solution of the Etruscan problem is possible in terms of a simple choice between the alternatives of Herodotus and Dionysius of Halicarnassus; nor can any modern theory, or ingenious modification of the ancient ones, such as that which would bring in a new people as invaders from the

north, be accepted as a total explanation of the Etruscans. At the present we can only ask questions. Does the orientalising phase in Etruria demand a foreign immigrating element to explain it? Are the regularly planned monumental tombs of this period a decisive argument for this because the construction of corbelled domes and vaults related to Minoan-Mycenaean methods of construction is not indigenous to Italy and quite unknown in the pure Villanovan phase? Do the tumulus-graves of Populonia and Vetulonia with their parallels in the coastal regions of Asia Minor confirm the Herodotean story?

f 10

Supporters of an eastern immigration into Etruria are now generally prepared to accept small groups of highly-organized colonists arriving, perhaps, at various periods in the 8th century; they can hardly claim more. Others believe that the period around 700 is too late to bring in the Etruscans and would argue for a much earlier immigration, some time during the Dark Ages of Mediterranean history (say between 1100 and 750). The Etruscans might then be the unpronounceable Twrws.w (Turusha?) who appear in 13th century Egyptian records among the sea-raiding peoples. There is hardly any archaeological evidence to support this theory although it has been suggested that some of the chamber tombs at Populonia with architectural analogies in Asia Minor as well as some of the imported objects found in the same place could be as early as 10th or 9th century BC.

An Alien Speech and Religion

What sustains this enquiry into the origins of the Etruscans is, as we have seen, the difference in language, religion and other aspects of life between them and their neighbours. We shall return to their language and religious beliefs later but here we must consider briefly what evidence, if any, they contribute to the solution of the problem. Dionysius of Halicarnassus observed that the language was quite unlike the other ancient languages of Italy which, like Latin, are of the Indo-European

Iron fasces from Vetulonia, 7th century BC. The bundle of rods and the axe—symbols of authority—were later adopted by Roman magistrates. This example, the earliest known, is made of small hollow iron rods and a double-bladed axe (compare the axe in fig. 1); it disintegrated when moved but was put together again in the Archaeological Museum in Florence, where it now is. (4)

Inscribed funerary stele, 6th century BC, found on the island of Lemnos in the Aegean. The language, of which there are other examples, seems to be related to Etruscan. The link may be merely semantic, or it may be evidence for Etruscan migrations. (3)

Religion is obviously an even more precarious argument than language in determining the 'origins' of a people but scholars have argued strongly for the 'oriental' alternative on the grounds that there are obvious oriental characteristics in the Etruscan religious beliefs and practices. The practices of hepatoscopy, the examination of the liver of sacrificial victims to discover the will of the gods, seem to have originated in Babylonia, but we cannot be sure that these practices about which we know, in the main, from late writers were original to the Etruscan religion or were derived from later contacts with oriental ideas by the processes of religious syncretism. A people as receptive to foreign ideas as the Etruscans, who certainly assimilated much of the religious mythology of the Greeks, might also have borrowed directly or indirectly from Chaldaean sources.

pl 14
15
f 12
13

Most recently, the genetic evidence of the distribution of bloodgroups in modern Tuscany and ancient Etruria compared with other parts of the Mediterranean world has been called upon to help solve the 'Etruscan problem'; if there is any possibility of progress in this field it will clearly depend upon much more extensive statistics than are as yet available. For the present we must allow that there are many questions still left unanswered about the process of the formation of the Etruscan people; it may be hoped that they will be answered when archaeology and field-work in Etruria have provided more evidence about the development of her cities and countryside from Villanovan, and even Bronze Age times, down to 600 BC. But finally it should be said that there are many who prefer to shelve the 'problem' altogether. Instead they look for unifying elements which make a homogenous culture from a mixture of tribal groups with different race and language; the Etruscan religious beliefs are one such element and the written language is another. To them Etruria means not a race but a culture, a language, a religion; it is not necessary to ask 'Who were the Etruscans?'.

group. Linguists generally believe that Etruscan though it may have assimilated some Indo-European elements is basically a non-Indo-European tongue. The 'orientalists' have claimed some connexion between Etruscan and the 6th-century inscriptions in a pre-Greek dialect surviving on the island of Lemnos in the North Aegean and have argued that this fact supports an Etruscan immigration from Asia Minor. What precisely this connexion means is another matter; both Etruscan and Lemnian could be survivals of pre-Indo-European Mediterranean languages pushed into restricted areas by the Indo-European advance. Furthermore, Etruscan seems to have no obvious affinities with Lydian or any other languages of ancient Anatolia.

f 3

The Rise of Etruscan Power

Turning from the problems of her early development, we may now look at Etruria during the 6th century BC, the period of her greatest power and influence. The developments of the 7th century had seen the creation of a number of independent city-states ruling surrounding territories of varying size. In their earliest contacts with the Greeks the Etruscans seem to have won the reputation of being piratical seafarers; their maritime interests developed rapidly from 700 onwards and in the 6th century Etruscan sea-power, in alliance with the Carthaginians, could more than hold its own against the Greek colonists of the southern part of the peninsula. From a very early period the Greeks found in Etruria an important outlet for trade and a source of valuable materials. Their relations with several Etruscan cities were very good and many Greeks settled in Etruria to carry on trade. A Greek trading post was later established at Spina on the Adriatic and there was always a large Greek element in the population of Caere whose port, Pyrgi, had a Greek name; Caere also had a treasury in the sanctuary of Apollo at Delphi. The Etruscans, at the height of their prosperity, also traded widely beyond the Alps and with the Carthaginians with whom they were often in alliance to protect common commercial interests; this alliance led inevitably to clashes with the Greeks.

In the course of the 6th century the Etruscans were able to extend their sphere of influence over a very large part of Italy and one ancient writer goes so far as to say that 'almost the whole of Italy had been under Etruscan rule'. How this Etruscan territorial expansion was achieved we do not know; our authorities suggest the existence of a league of twelve principal cities but we know very little about the nature of the league or its composition. It is generally agreed that Caere, Veii, Tarquinia, Vulci, Volsinii, Clusium (Chiusi) and Vetulonia should be numbered among the twelve principal cities in the period of Etruscan power; other important cities, Arretium (Arezzo), Perusia (Perugia), Volterra, Populonia and Rusellae, were powers to be reckoned with at certain periods. We know that these cities met together to celebrate an annual festival of religious character but it is highly doubtful whether they ever combined their resources into a federation which could serve as the basis of Etruscan power; political and economic alliances between individual cites and groups of cities either for joint military action or colonization seem more likely to have been the mainspring of her brief and successful imperialism. But it is unlikely that the naval and military organization of the Etruscans was ever geared to maintaining successfully a territorial empire against aggressive enemies.

An Etruscan helmet, captured at the Battle of Cumae by Hieron of Syracuse, who dedicated it as a votive offering at Olympia in 474 BC. The inscription reads: 'Hieron, the son of Deinomenes, and the Syracusans; Tyrrhenian booty from Cumae to Zeus.' (5)

194

The Etruscan expansion outside Etruria proper took two main directions, southwards over Latium to Campania and, a good deal later (end of 6th century), north-eastwards over the Apennines into the valley of the Po. The high-water mark of Etruscan power came when she became mistress of Capua and Rome; the Etruscan domination of Rome, which was for some time the centre of an Etruscan monarchy, is recorded in legend and confirmed by archaeology. In Campania, Capua was the centre of Etruscan rule and at Pompeii inscriptions and architectural remains have been found that prove a period of Etruscan occupation. The expansion into the Po valley took place at the end of the 6th and early 5th century BC; as a result, several important centres of Etruscan influence sprang up, among them Felsina (Bologna), Mantua and Spina, a trading station established at the mouth of the Po. The Etruscan dominion in north Italy lasted hardly more than a century, but in the 5th century when the Etruscan hold over the southern colonies was being weakened, the northern cities seem to have enjoyed their greatest prosperity, until, about 400, they were overrun by the invading Gauls.

During the 5th century BC Etruscan power was generally on the wane. Early in the century Rome seems to have thrown off the Etruscan yoke by expelling the last of the Tarquins and so breaking down Etruria's land communications with Campania. The expansion of the Greeks and of Carthage provoked a serious economic crisis in Etruria; in 474 BC her sea-power suffered a *f 5* severe blow in the Battle of Cumae when her ships in alliance with the Carthaginians were defeated by the Greeks led by Hieron of Syracuse. The Etruscans seem to have been expelled from Capua some time between 445 and 425 and by the end of the century their domination of the Po valley was collapsing under attacks from the Gauls. At the same time, Rome was undermining Etruscan power in central Italy; when Veii fell in 396, the Etruscans, already heavily engaged in the north, were unable to muster effective resistance. The last Roman triumph over Etruscans is recorded in 281 BC and very shortly afterwards Rome planted her first military colony, Cosa, a permanent symbol of her authority over Etruscan territory.

The collapse of her Empire seems to have broken the spirit of Etruria. While later Greek and Roman impressions of Etruscan life give us a picture of decadent loose-living that is probably without justification, many have noted how the lively spirit and joyous good humour of painted tombs at Tarquinia in the 6th and early 5th centuries gave place in the 4th and 3rd centuries to an atmosphere of despair that seems to reflect Etruria's fall from *pl 27* greatness.

Cities and City-life

The kind of city-state that the Etruscans introduced to central Italy was very close to the Greek pattern, each city being the hub of its surrounding territory. The earliest form of Etruscan government seems to have been a monarchy, the external symbols of which—the golden crown, the sceptre, the throne etc.— survived in the regalia of the Roman magistracies. Later, the *f 4* monarchy seems to have been replaced by oligarchically elected magistrates; although we know the names of some of the magistrates—the *zilath*, who is found in many Etruscan cities and the *maru* are two of them—we can say nothing of their functions nor of the political history of individual cities. Wealth was no doubt concentrated in the hands of the aristocracy especially in those cities of southern Etruria who owed their prosperity to agriculture. In the industrial cities such as Populonia where the iron of Elba was smelted we must suppose a class of wealthy businessmen concerned with its manufacture and export. In addition there must have been a large free working population, colonies of resident aliens, especially Greeks, and a heavy slave population.

The basis of Etruscan life was the economic prosperity of the country. Apart from the production of iron and copper, several of the cities manufactured bronze objects which, from their consistently high quality, were in constant demand abroad; *pl 34* Vulci produced its tripods, candelabra and weapons, Perugia *f 17* tripods and wrought iron all of which were exported widely. *18* But the Etruscans were primarily an agricultural people; Etruscan

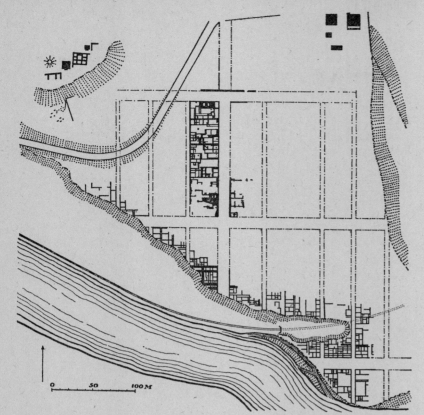

An Etruscan town now in process of excavation: Marzabotto, only 15 miles from the great city of Felsina (Bologna). The site is being eaten away by the River Reno and has also been disturbed by a modern road and railway, but enough remains to make it the best example so far discovered of Etruscan town-planning. On a height in the north-western corner was the 'Acropolis' (apparently not a defensive position) with temples and altars. The rest of the town was laid out on a chequer-board pattern, with long rectangular 'insulae', a scheme later taken over by the Romans. (6)

corn is frequently referred to and wines and olives from Etruria were renowned then as they are today. The administration of individual cities was able to tackle considerable works of land reclamation and drainage; the Maremma, the coastal region of southern Etruria, a malarial swamp till a few years ago, seems to have been well-drained and fruitful under Etruscan rule and the drainage of the Po valley is specifically referred to by ancient writers as an Etruscan achievement. Some remarkable evidence of Etruscan land-drainage has survived in the country round Veii and elsewhere in southern Etruria.

The sites on which the Etruscans chose to live were easily defensible and in their earlier period were without artificial defences except ditches and banks at the weaker points. The size of the cities may be judged by the fact that the later walls of Perugia have a perimeter of 7.3 km. and Veii and Tarquinia of about 8 km. These walls, of solid ashlar masonry, are generally not earlier than about 400 BC, the walls of Veii seem to have been built not long before the destruction of the city. The monumental arched gates and architectural façades are even later and designed under the influence of Hellenistic architectural ideas. Of the internal layout of the cities very little is known since none of the important cities has been extensively excavated. Most of them must have grown up in a haphazard manner from Villanovan beginnings. What little is known of the arrangement of the houses and streets does nothing to confirm the conception of a city laid out in accordance with the rigid rules of Etruscan religious ritual. Vetulonia has no obviously regular plan; only the later city foundations outside Etruria proper illustrate some of the methods of axial planning that are usually associated with the name of the Etruscans. Marzabotto, a small Etruscan town near Bologna has a principal street crossed by subsidiary streets in a strictly formal plan. These streets were well-paved and furnished with stepping stones; the principal one is extremely wide, as much as 15 m. in one place. At Marzabotto as elsewhere, there is ample evidence of an efficient system of street drainage.

The houses were of brick, stone or timber; very commonly the

f 6

foundations would be of stone and the superstructure of timber or mud brick. The basic form of Etruscan house was rectangular, consisting, perhaps, of a single room partitioned in various ways. We may also discover something of the design of the more elaborately planned dwellings of the wealthy because the Etruscan conception of the tomb as the house of the dead has left us a number of large family vaults, such as the Tomb of the Volumnii at Perugia, which probably preserve something of the characteristic layout of the wealthier private house. A typical plan has a large central chamber with three rooms opening off the far end and approached on the opposite side by a corridor with two flanking rooms. The central chamber would correspond with the *atrium* of a Roman private house and indeed one method of roofing the later *atrium* with an inward tilt in all directions, the so-called *atrium tuscanicum*, is specifically attributed to Etruria by the Roman architect, Vitruvius. No evidence has been found for this form in Etruria but the central opening with the roof sloping down from it may be seen on a house-urn from Chiusi; it serves to give both ventilation and light. Some of the internal arrangements are also known from tombs, especially those at Caere where details of ceiling construction, doors, windows, and even furniture are carved in stone; best known

f 7
8

f 9

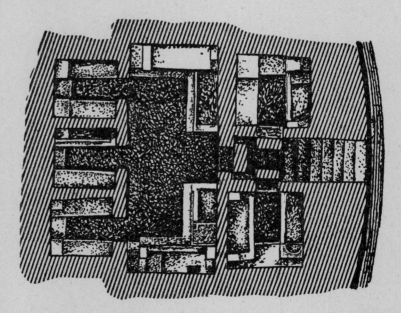

Plan and section of the 'Tomb of the Greek Vases' in Tumulus II at Caere (5th century BC), showing how Etruscan tombs imitated the layout of private houses. Tumulus II contains four separate tombs, each with its own entrance, burrowing into the circular mound from different directions. They were cut into the solid rock (diagonal shading) and the earth heaped up over them. This one consists of a descending entrance passage, flanked by two small rooms; a main chamber, corresponding to the atrium of the house, with funerary couches around three walls; and three small cubicles opening off the fourth. The dead lay on real wooden beds placed on top of the stone ones. (7, 8)

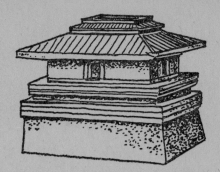

Funerary urn from Chiusi in the shape of a house on a high podium. The central space (atrium) was open to the sky, with the rooms of the house opening off from it—a plan copied by the Romans. (9)

pl 18 of all these interiors is the so-called Tomb of the Reliefs at Caere with its coffered ceiling and representations of everyday objects modelled with remarkable realism in stucco.

A Buried World: Tombs and Tomb-paintings

From Etruscan tombs we draw much more than our knowledge of Etruscan domestic architecture for they are almost our only source for reconstructing the life of the people, designed as they are to be the centre of an enhanced life after death. These tombs generally line the roads that led out of the Etruscan cities or were grouped into necropoleis in the surrounding country. The roads which provided direct communication between neighbouring cities are often considerable works of engineering; deep road cuttings were made for the roads out of Veii, stone and timber bridges carried them over mountain streams, and tunnels were excavated through stubborn rock. At Caere (Cerveteri) some of the road cuttings are honeycombed with tomb-chambers. The forms of Etruscan sepulchres varied from place to place according to the building materials available and to local differences of taste. In regions where the hills are of soft volcanic tufa, as they are for example round Caere, chamber tombs are f 7 cut into the solid rock and surmounted by an earthen tumulus. 8 In other places, for example Populonia, the tombs are built up from ground level and vaulted over, with a tumulus of earth to cover them. In the country around Viterbo, at Norchia and Castel

d'Asso, the tombs are cut into the face of the rock and designed with elaborate architectural façades imitating houses or religious buildings.

The most precious legacy for our knowledge of Etruscan life pl 17 and customs is the painted interiors of chamber-tombs at 27 Tarquinia and elsewhere. At Tarquinia some 60 tombs with f 11 paintings have been found, of which about 20 may now be seen; 20 have come to light at Chiusi but only three survive. The Tarquinian series ranges in date from the mid-6th century to the Hellenistic period; the prevailing technique is that of fresco on a layer of plaster or of clay and limewash.

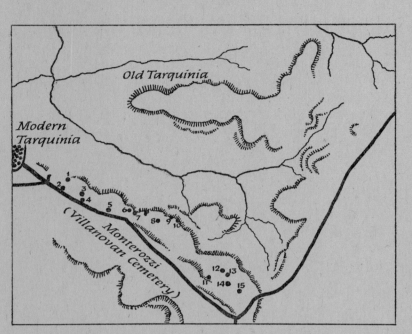

Tarquinia, ancient and modern, showing the position of the most famous painted tombs: 1. Tomb of the Lionesses; 2. Tomb of Hunting and Fishing; 3. Tomb of the Triclinium; 4. Tomb of the Leopards; 5. Tomb of the Typhon; 6. Tomb of the Shields; 7. Tomb of the Cardinal; 8. Tomb of Orcus; 9. Tomb of the Painted Vases; 10. Tomb of the Old Man; 11. Tomb of the Chariot; 12. Tomb of the Baron; 13. Tomb of the Bulls; 14. Tomb of the Olympic Games; 15. Tomb of the Augurs. The Etruscan town stood on the opposite side of the valley from the necropolis, the normal practice. Even older burial places lie in the vicinity, the largest being the Villanovan cemetery of Monterozzi. (11)

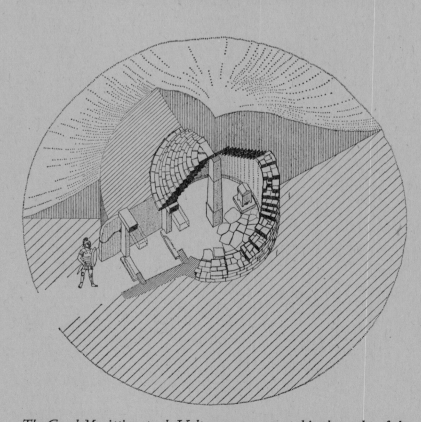

The Casal Marittima tomb, Volterra, now re-erected in the garden of the Archaeological Museum at Florence. The vault is of the corbel type, with layers of stones overlapping each other. The central pillar reaches up to the centre of the vaulting but does not actually support anything. After it was built the whole tomb was covered with a mound of earth. (10)

A few of the subjects are taken from Greek mythology. In the Tomb of the Bulls, one of the earliest of the Tarquinian series, pl 17 Achilles is lying in wait for the Trojan prince Troilus as he comes to water his horses. But the majority of paintings, from the late 6th century onwards, illustrate scenes of Etruscan life and customs. The back wall of the Tomb of the Augurs shows two mourners at the door of the tomb; on one side wall a brutal and bloody contest between a man and a dog, which reminds us of the Etruscan connexion with the gladiatorial games of Rome, is part of the funeral games in honour of the dead. On the back wall of the Tomb of the Leopards a lively banquet scene shows us the pl 19 lordly Etruscans freely indulging in the delights of wine and love 22 to an accompaniment of music and dancing which they so much enjoyed. Husband and wife dine together, a custom which shocked the Greeks and reflected the important position held by Etruscan women in both private and public life.

The paintings of the Tomb of Hunting and Fishing show us pl 23 other pleasures the Etruscans enjoyed during life; so, too, do the paintings of a tomb recently discovered in the Monterozzi Cemetery at Tarquinia. Boxing contests, races of two-horse chariots, discus-throwing, jumping and foot-races are depicted and the tomb was christened the Tomb of the Olympic Games. pl 24 The nobles of Etruria were famous for their horses and chariot teams; one peculiarly Etruscan game was the so-called Trojan Game, later adopted by the Romans, which seems to have been a horse-race over a maze-shaped course.

Although the scenes of mourning remind us of the essential purpose of the paintings, the early paintings usually strike a joyful note of the pleasures of life and hopes for the future. In the later tombs the mood changes. The fearsome demons, Charun and Tuchulcha, in the Tomb of Orcus, the burial place of an aristocratic Tarquinian family, are among the sinister underworld beings that we meet with increasing frequency in the later paintings. Cruelty and despair, even terror about the future life dominate many of the painted scenes.

pl 26

'Disciplina Etrusca': the Worship of the Gods

This development of Etruscan views about the after-life is one of the few aspects of Etruscan religion for which we have the evidence of the Etruscans themselves; for the rest of their religious beliefs we depend very largely upon non-Etruscan sources drawing upon an Etruscan religious literature that is now lost. The community of widely held religious beliefs kept the Etruscan federation together and the religious league lasted long into the Roman Empire. An annual meeting took place at the shrine of Voltumna, an unidentified place in the territory of Volsinii; its chief business was the election of a high-priest who was to hold office for one year but it also provided the opportunity for exchange of ideas and discussion of matters of common interest. We cannot doubt the truth of the remark of Livy, the Roman historian, who tells us that the Etruscans were 'a race, above all others, devoted to religious beliefs and ceremonies, all the more so because it excelled in the art of their observance'.

The gods of Etruria were many and various. Some were purely Etruscan as we may judge from the names that have come down to us; others were Greek or thoroughly conflated with Greek gods. The chief deity was Tinia, of infinite power, associated with Uni (Juno) and Menrva (Minerva) in a triad which was also worshipped on the Capitol of Rome. Among the lesser divinities some, like Nethuns (Neptune) have Greek names; others like the goddess Turan, Etruscan. Pantheistic religions always extend hospitality to foreign gods but the identification of so many local Etruscan deities with Greek gods is a surprising phenomenon. It is due, perhaps, as much to the influence of Greek art, which first gave the Etruscan divinities visual form, as to the direct influence of Greek religion. Many of the gods who take on Greek physiognomy and were given Greek names probably retained their own characteristics while many others were never assimilated to the forms of Greek anthropomorphism. Tinia, though in form he is sometimes indistinguishable from the Greek Zeus, has quite different powers; conversely, the Greek myths of the gods which play so big a rôle in Etruscan art are often only half-understood by the artists who depict them.

pl 51
52

The fundamental differences between Etruscan and Greek religion are most obvious in the ritual that accompanied the worship of the gods, the so-called *Disciplina Etrusca* about which we know a good deal from Roman sources. Our knowledge of the Etruscan ritual books comes from quotations and references in Roman works dating from the 1st century BC and later; the books themselves may not have been codified much earlier than this but, traditionally, they constitute a body of knowledge revealed to the Etruscan people by Tages, grandson of Tinia, greatest of all the Gods. We learn that the principal sections were rules concerning hepatoscopy or divination by means of the liver of sacrificial victims, the rules of divination from lightning and, lastly, the rules governing other aspects of behaviour and daily life and the methods of discovering the intentions of the gods concerning them.

pl 14

These practices were carried out in Etruria by the so-called *Haruspices* who could recognize and interpret the will of the gods, and long after the decline of Etruscan nationality the Etruscan *Haruspex* in the retinue of Roman generals and emperors continued to wield influence in the course of Roman history and institutions. The Romans held it essential, for example, to be skilled in the rules of the Etruscan discipline when planning a city. From direct Etruscan sources comes an interesting document of the practices of hepatoscopy in Etruria; the bronze model of a liver found in 1878 near Piacenza is marked out in sections—40 in all—corresponding to the Etruscan divisions of

pl 15

f 12
13

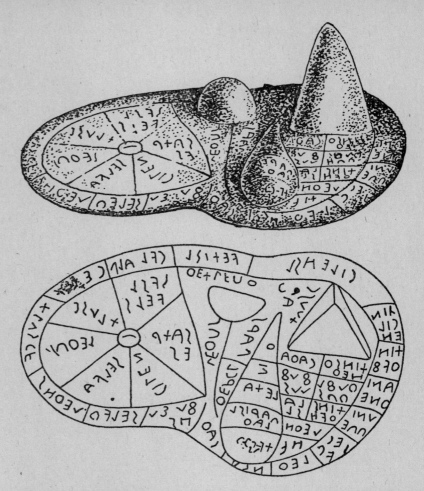

Bronze image of a liver from Piacenza, probably used as a model for instruction in divination. Its upper surface is divided into forty sections, each with the name of a god or goddess inscribed on it, corresponding to a division of the sky. (12, 13)

the sky, each of which is inscribed with the name of an Etruscan god. It is usually thought of as a kind of text-book for *Haruspices*.

Dominating the domestic architecture of Etruscan cities were the sanctuaries and temples of the gods. An Etruscan sanctuary included an altar and a temple building to contain the cult-statue of the god. The Etruscan temple, unlike the Greek, was not transformed from wooden origins into a monumental stone

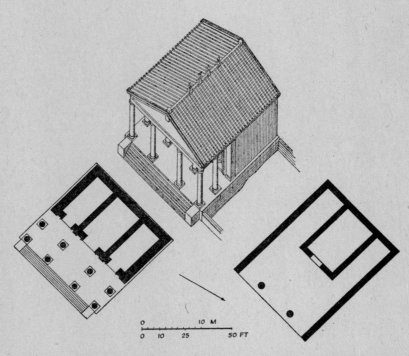

Two types of Etruscan temples: Veii (left) with three parallel chambers and Fiesole (right) with a single chamber and flanking corridors. The reconstruction of the Veii temple is only conjectural. Etruscan temples, unlike Greek, were made of wood with facings of terracotta slabs. (14, 15)

construction; the walls might be stone and mudbrick but most of the superstructure continued to be of wood protected by facings of terracotta slabs. Vitruvius, who has much to say in his academic way about 'Tuscan architecture' assigns to Etruria *f 14* the origin of the temple with a cella divided into three parallel chambers or with a single chamber and flanking corridors. The basic Etruscan temple plan seems to have consisted of a broad cella fronted by a row of timber columns of wide span. In the *f 15* temples at Fiesole and the Portonaccio site at Veii we seem to have examples of the second of Vitruvius' two arrangements with a narrower cella and flanking corridors.

The architectural details developed very little. Columns were unfluted with capitals derived from early forms of Greek Doric; another common form of capital in Etruria is related to the Aeolic form which many believe to be the ancester of Ionic. In Hellenistic times the Greek forms of Doric, Ionic and Corinthian seem to have been introduced into Etruscan architecture. The terracotta facings of the timbers—frieze slabs, raised gutters, acroteria and antefixes—which are among the most characteristic products *pl 49* of Etruscan craftsmanship were richly modelled and gaily decorated in paint. Many of the free-standing acroterial figures and pedimental compositions are included among the unquestioned masterpieces of Etruscan art; the acroterial figures from the *pl 51* Portonaccio temple at Veii and the 5th century pedimental figures recently discovered at Pyrgi, the port of Caere, are some of the finest pieces. The Veii figures of about 500 BC have been associated with Vulca, the sculptor of Veii who, we are told, was brought in by the Romans to make the cult-statue of the Capitoline Jupiter; artists of his school were responsible for other parts of the decoration.

The Mystery of the Etruscan Language

It has already been remarked that Etruscan literature seems to have been almost entirely religious in character; we have references besides to historical, medical and dramatic literature none of which is probably any great loss to us. In fact, the longest Etruscan text that has come down to us is a linen roll which by some curious chance was used to wrap a mummy in Alexandria and is now in the Museum at Zagreb. It contains about 1500 words among which may be recognized the names of many Etruscan gods, and it seems to have been a ritual calendar; a similar ritualistic roll is shown in the hands of a certain Laris *pl 16* Pulena on the lid of a 2nd century sarcophagus from Tarquinia. Laris Pulena seems to have been the author of books on divination and held high office in Tarquinia; of the 60 words inscribed on his roll, 22 also occur on the mummy-wrapping in Zagreb.

Although we can recognize the meaning of many words, we cannot translate the texts of the Zagreb wrapping, the Pulena roll and the few other long Etruscan inscriptions, and it is a matter of great surprise to non-specialists in the field of Etruscology that this state of affairs prevails today. The truth is that up to the present our knowledge of the grammar and vocabulary of Etruscan remains comparatively slight. The main difficulty has been the lack of lengthy texts; with few exceptions among the many thousands found over large parts of Italy, the inscriptions are short, funerary in character and largely repetitive. They can be read easily since the Etruscan alphabet now presents no *f 16* problems; it consisted originally of 26 letters derived from the Greek and was usually written from right to left. Later this alphabet was modified to suit the special needs of Etruscan. The earliest writing seems to belong to about the middle of the 7th century BC, perhaps as early as 700 BC.

The short funerary inscriptions, for many of which there exist Latin bilinguals, can very often be translated, but the knowledge of Etruscan syntax that is obtained from them is too slight to give much help with longer texts. Only a long bilingual text could provide a rapid solution to the problem; all attempts to relate Etruscan with other known languages have been unsuccessful and we are left with the laborious process of internal comparison of the various texts, a process by which the meanings of words and the formation of grammatical endings are won with the utmost difficulty. Here we can do no more than summarize very briefly what is at present known about the Etruscan language.

Some 30 or 40 words are known to us from Latin and Greek literary sources and they include, for example, the names of the months. By what is known as the combinatory method, the study and comparison, that is to say, of the formulae used in votive and funerary inscriptions, we have acquired a knowledge of several words expressing family relationships and a number of highly probable meanings for various verbs. We know the Etruscan names for many of their gods and also, from the inscriptions accompanying the scenes engraved on bronze mirrors, *pl 14* their versions of many Greek names. From the famous dice found at Tuscania now in the Bibliothèque Nationale, Paris, we get the names for the numbers 1-6, but, tantalisingly, we cannot be sure which is which. Some grammatical endings of nouns and verbs seem quite certain—the form of the genitive singular, for example, and the past and present tenses of some verbs.

The total achievement is the ability to translate short funerary and dedicatory inscriptions with a fair degree of accuracy. A typical one, of some length, may serve as an example; it is to be found on the walls of the Golini Tomb at Orvieto and reads:

vel lecates arnðial ruva larðialisa(m?) clan velusum nefs marniu spurana eprðnec tenve meχlum rasneas clevsinsl ʒilaχnve pulum rumitrine ði ma(l?)ce clel lur

It may be freely translated:
Vel Lecates, Arnth's brother, son of Larth and descendant of Vel. He held the offices of Maro Urbanus and Eprthe and was Zilath of the Etruscan people in Clusium.

In conclusion, it may be repeated that, so far, no convincing connection has been found between Etruscan and any other language; though it shares certain roots with neighbouring Indo-European languages in Italy it is generally excluded from the Indo-European group. Dionysius of Halicarnassus seems to have been right when he said that the Etruscans spoke a language unlike that of any other known people.

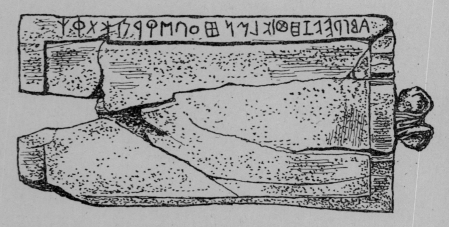

Ivory writing-tablet from Marsigliana d'Albegna, c. 650 BC. The inner surface was coated with wax, of which traces remain. On the rim is the Etruscan alphabet of twenty-six letters (written from right to left), evidently the scribe's model. (16)

A Rich Legacy in Art

The products of Etruscan craftsmanship maintained a consistent quality which made them highly-prized far beyond the bounds of Etruria; Etruscan mastery of bronze techniques is shown in *f 17* chariots, helmets, candelabra and vases decorated either with *pl 36* engraving or extremely skilful embossing. Engraved bronze *37* mirrors are an attractive and typically Etruscan group of products *14* ranging in date from the 6th to the 3rd century BC; the subjects are generally taken from Greek mythology though some few are Etruscan. This art of engraving on metal came to quite astonishing fruition in the series of cylindrical or rectangular containers most of which seem to have been made at Praeneste, the out- *pl 31* standing example being the so-called Ficorini *cista*. *32*

Small votive bronze figures have survived from all periods and pl 35 they include several peculiarly Etruscan forms, among them a number of curious elongated figures. Of the many large-scale bronzes which are known to have adorned Etruscan cities very few have survived. Perhaps this is not surprising when we remember that 2000 statues were taken in the booty of Volsinii by the Romans in 264 BC and that throughout the Empire Etruscan 'objets d'art' were still highly prized by the connoisseurs.

A very large output of stone carving and modelling was mainly religious and funerary in character. Sarcophagi, funerary urns and other kinds of funerary sculpture were worked in local materials in many Etruscan centres. We have the stone
pl 1 sarcophagi of Tarquinia, the terracotta sarcophagi of Caere, the *cippi* of Chiusi, illustrating funerary banquets and other funeral
pl 6 scenes, the Canopic urns and funerary figures of Chiusi and,
7 in the Hellenistic period, the series of richly-sculptured funerary
50 urns made of alabaster at Volterra, of limestone and terracotta at Chiusi and of limestone at Perugia. Terracotta workers throughout Etruscan times were occupied first and foremost with the decoration of religious buildings. Their work ranged from the simplest kind of low-relief plaque with repetitive scenes to the most grandiose pedimental composition involving difficult problems of modelling technique. They also made sarcophagi and small funerary urns for their private patrons.

The characteristic domestic pottery of Etruria is the ware known as bucchero, which develops from the typical Villanovan fabric generally known as *impasto*. This *impasto* is often made from coarse unpurified clay and is sometimes poorly fired; its successor is a bright black highly-polished ware produced by an extremely skilled process of firing; a red bucchero also exists but
pl 39 is less common. The early bucchero shapes are often very attractive; ornament is generally incised on them and follows an
pl 40 'orientalising' repertory. In the 6th century the 'heavy' bucchero ornamented with reliefs of various kinds is much less attractive. The decline of bucchero is explained by the fact that the workshops were losing ground to imported Greek wares and painted Etruscan imitations.

Etruscan painted pottery from the very first copies Greek
pl 41 shapes and designs. Geometric wares of Greek derivation occur from about 700 BC onwards; copies of imported Protocorinthian and Corinthian vessels were made in the 7th and 6th centuries. Then about the middle of the 6th century a workshop in Caere began to produce black-figured pottery, the so-called
pl 42 Caeretan *hydriae*, in Ionian Greek style; these came, no doubt, from the workshop of an Ionian Greek who had emigrated to Etruria about 550 BC. The so-called 'Pontic vases', of which
pl 44 one of the best-known is an amphora in Munich with a Judgement of Paris scene, were made in some other Etruscan city, perhaps Vulci, a little later. Local production of a red-figured
pl 45 pottery in imitation of Greek began about 450 BC; it seems to have been made in several centres, among them Chiusi, Orvieto and Volterra.

The style in the 4th century is often very lively and refreshingly different from the mass of South Italian red-figure. The most
pl 43 ambitious red-figured vases made in central Italy are the so-called Faliscan vases—which are known to us mainly from finds made in tombs at Civita Castellana and were probably made there. These vases, closely related in style to Attic work of the period may well be the result of an immigration of Attic vase-painters into central Italy. Another important if short-lived branch of ceramics in Etruria is the relief-vases made in imitation of Hellenistic gold and silver vessels; they are sometimes gilded and silvered to complete the imitation and they were most probably produced in the area of Bolsena.

Among the finest products of Etruscan craftsmanship are the gold jewellery and other work in precious materials which attracted the talents of the best craftsmen in Etruria, especially in the archaic period. The wealthy lords and ladies of Etruria
pl 12 were buried in rich dress adorned with jewellery; other costly
13 grave-goods, cups of gold and silver, ornaments of ivory and amber were set beside them. The gold ornaments often have details outlined or drawn in with tiny granules of gold soldered on to the surface, a technique in which the Etruscans achieved
pl 12 a high degree of mastery. The gold dress-pin from the Regolini

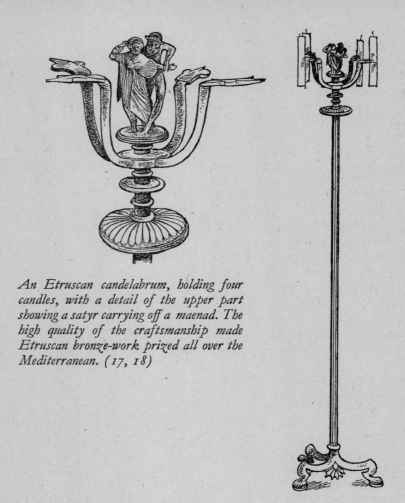

An Etruscan candelabrum, holding four candles, with a detail of the upper part showing a satyr carrying off a maenad. The high quality of the craftsmanship made Etruscan bronze-work prized all over the Mediterranean. (17, 18)

Galassi tomb at Caere, the gold cup of Greek shape from the Barnardini Tomb at Praeneste and the ivory cup from the Barberini Tomb, also at Praeneste, are outstanding works of this period in precious materials. After the 7th and 6th centuries there are very few objects of comparable quality although the tomb paintings continue to depict very considerable private riches.

The Debt to Greece

Every branch of Etruscan craftsmanship was dominated by the influence of the Greeks. Greek craftsmen had been resident in Etruria from an early period; it was the Corinthian Demaratus, according to one historical tradition, who first introduced artists into Etruria. As early as the middle of the 7th century BC, the Aristonothos who made the mixing-bowl found at Caere was a Greek. Immigrant Greeks must have made the so-called Caeretan hydriae and Greek inscriptions have been found on Etruscan painted vases and on the walls of tombs. In Campania the Greeks and Etruscans were for long neighbours and to the direct Greek influences we must add the vast quantity of imported Greek objects which served as models for Etruscan imitation. Yet despite this dominating Greek influence, it is hardly ever difficult to identify Etruscan from Greek work, not by reason of its inferiority but because it has clear independent characteristics.

pl 42

It is only recently that unqualified praise has been given to Etruscan works of art. The fact is that every artistic achievement in Etruria can be recognized as more or less derivative from foreign sources. No continuous creative process seems to dictate its development; as M. Pallottino observes 'there is no continuity of artistic development but sudden forward leaps, long pauses, rapid and inspired adaptation of the very latest novelty from Greece...'. Etruscan artistic history is dictated by its reaction to contact with, firstly, the civilizations of the eastern Mediterranean and then with Greek art from its geometric to its Hellenistic phase. Throughout, the Etruscans maintained a high level of craftsmanship and every now and then their artists achieved something of the highest quality which lifted Etruscan art out of its derivative and provincial status.

The early influence of Greek geometric art was superseded by the 'orientalising' phase which is so well represented by the contents of such graves as the Regolini Galassi Tomb at Caere. This 'orientalising' did not act as in Greece, as a step in the process of creating a characteristically Etruscan representational art; instead, it gave way to new and clearly defined foreign influences and from 600 BC onwards Greek art was the source of inspiration for Etruscan artists. The Centaur from Vulci in the Villa Giulia Museum, Rome, is a work of this time; it is closely inspired by the so-called Dedalic style of sculpture in archaic Greece, yet it has none of the marks of inferior provincial work. Together with the well-known alabaster statuette from the Isis Tomb at Vulci, now in the British Museum, it can claim to represent an important and independent branch of the Dedalic tradition.

pl 51   The Apollo of Veii was made at the end of the 6th century and it is probably the best known of all Etruscan terracotta sculptures. It is associated with the name of the only Etruscan artist that has come down to us, Vulca of Veii. Undeniably the Apollo owes elements of style to the Ionian school of Greece but when this is said we are left with a masterpiece of Etruscan art, constructed in a technique which the Greeks never mastered in the same way. The Apollo has rightly become one of the key-pieces for assessing the basically different qualities of Etruscan and Greek art; here we seem to have something in obvious contrast with Greek formulae, evidence of a strongly expressionistic art that is peculiarly Etruscan.

    In the realm of painting, the Greek sources of inspiration are no less obvious. Some of the earliest examples like the plaques from the Campana Tomb at Veii are closely inspired by Greek vase-painting which, no doubt, provided models for the artists. The same source may well have served the artist who painted the scenes in the Tomb of the Bulls, the earliest of the Tarquinian series, but he has created a style which is essentially his own.

pl 20   In the paintings of the Tomb of the Triclinium the work has become so thoroughly Etruscan in character that its Greek sources recede entirely into the background. The artist has created something which is independent of its sources of inspiration. The same is true of the two magnificent animal bronzes, the famous Capitoline Wolf, a work of the late archaic period, and the Chimaera from Arezzo, made in the 4th century BC, which are both to be reckoned as independent creations of brilliant sculptors and are justly admired as two of the finest bronzes that have come down to us from antiquity.

    In the 5th century BC Etruscan art did not develop in the same way as art in Greece. The archaic conventions lingered on and very few terracottas and bronzes are directly inspired by the art of the later 5th century in Greece; exceptions are the terracotta figures from a temple at Orvieto which seem to reflect the Pheidian tradition in Attic art. But it was not until the late 4th century that Greek art again evoked a widespread and creative response in Italy. By this time Etruria was already giving way to Rome as mistress of central Italy and it seems that we should now speak of Etrusco-Italic rather than pure Etruscan art. Several non-Etruscan centres were now producing important work. The Latin city of Praeneste, home of the finely engraved *cistas* in Etruscan style had always been closely connected with Etruscan art, but it is significant that the finest of all the *cistas*, the

so-called Ficorini *cista*, was made in Rome, which was now becoming the most important city of central Italy and attracting artists from many places.   pl 31 32

    Yet much of the central Italian art of the Hellenistic period still belongs to the pure Etruscan tradition; such are the masterly terracotta figures inspired by the Praxitelian and Scopaic traditions of Greek sculpture, like the outstanding Apollo from Città pl 52 Castellana. One important aspect of later sculpture in central Italy, that of portraiture, seems to be both a response to the realism of later Greek sculpture and a positive expression of Italic taste. It is exemplified in the finest bronze heads and the humblest pl 38 funerary portraits on stone and terracotta sarcophagi and funerary urns. The famous statue of the *Arringatore* in Florence was found near Lake Trasimene; it bears an Etruscan inscription but the man, with his Roman dress, seems to belong already to the series of portraits of Roman patricians in the last century BC.

The Rôle in History

The picture of a gay and pleasure-loving people that we get from many Etruscan tomb-paintings has an immense attraction for those who admire an apparently uninhibited and unambitious existence devoted to enjoyment. It is even used to explain the failure of the Etruscans: 'You cannot dance gaily to the double flute', says D. H. Lawrence, 'and at the same time conquer nations and rake in large sums of money.' But this picture of the Etruscans is surely quite false. They emerge in truth as highly successful managers of their natural resources, efficient businessmen, able to command a very high standard of technical production but lacking the qualities and perhaps the desire to maintain a position of power. Perhaps much is explained by the domination of a ritualistic religion that determined all the activities of everyday life and seems to have degenerated in later years into a morbid and fatalistic preoccupation with the future. To the Etruscan it seemed that religion, not circumstances, guided the course of history and, indeed, after the rapid flowering of Etruscan life in the 7th century and a period of imperialistic expansion in the 6th century, the rest of Etruscan history is a record of decline.

    Yet the Etruscans played an immensely important rôle in the history of Italy and indeed of our western civilization. The areas of the Italian peninsula that came directly under Etruscan control were considerable, but they were small in proportion to those affected by her influence; the life of the Ligurians, Umbrians, Picenes and Latins all contained a strong Etruscan element. It was the Etruscan who introduced the idea of the city-state in central Italy and transformed a village into a city civilization. We owe to the Etruscans the diffusion of writing by means of the alphabet they had themselves borrowed from the Greeks. The special debt of Rome to Etruria lies deep-rooted in all her achievements; her direct borrowings include elements of military organization, the ceremonial and regalia of her public life, many aspects of her art and religion. The civilization of Rome was founded on Etrusco-Italic beginnings and famous Romans like Maecenas, who counted among his ancestors the nobility of Etruria, could take pride when they saw Rome's Etruscan past reflected in every part of her private and public life.

IX THE SABIAN MYSTERIES

The planet cult of ancient Harran

J. B. SEGAL

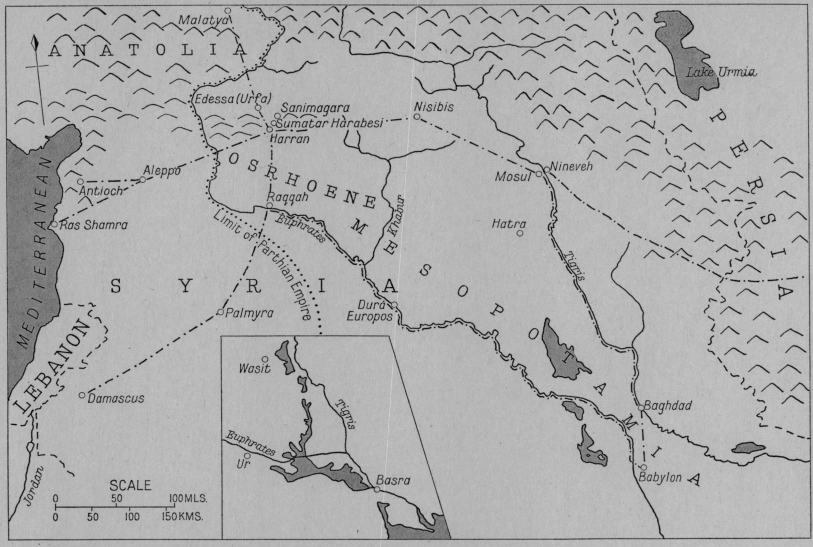

Syria and Mesopotamia, showing trade routes passing through Harran

BC

c. 1850?	Abraham lives at Harran
c. 1850	Temple of Sin at Harran mentioned in letter from Mari
c. 1365	Sin and Shamash of Harran mentioned in treaty of Mitanni
c. 850	Shalmaneser III restores temple of Sin at Harran
c. 750	Sin of Harran mentioned in treaty of Arpad
675	Esarhaddon visits Harran on his way to Egypt
c. 650	Asshurbanipal instals his brother as High Priest at Harran
610	Harran sacked by Umman-Manda
553/2	Temple of Sin at Harran restored by Nabonidus
53	Crassus defeated by Parthians near Harran

AD

c. 100	Sect of Elkesaites active
165	Reliefs and inscriptions set up to Marilaha at Sumatar
2nd Cent.	Coin to Sin-Marilaha at Hatra
c. 205	Abgar the Great adopts Christianity at Edessa
217	Emperor Caracalla assassinated on return from Harran
227/8	'Orpheus' Mosaic made at Edessa
235/6	'Phoenix' Mosaic made at Edessa
277/8	'Funerary Couch' Mosaic made at Edessa
363	Emperor Julian visits Harran
5th Cent.	Abbess Aetheria visits Edessa on pilgrimage
549	King Chosroes refuses to take ransom from Harran

AD

c. 600	Koran mentions Sabians
639	Harran pagans surrender to Moslems
c. 745	Caliph Marwan II makes Harran his capital
814/5	Governor of Harran allows pagans to perform rites in public
830/2	Caliph Ma'mun meets pagans at Harran
836	Thabit ibn Qurrah born at Harran
c. 854	Al-Battani born in neighbourhood of Harran
c. 880	Ahmed ibn al-Tayyib describes pagans of Harran
c. 925	Ibrahim ibn Hilal born
943	Mas'udi visits Harran
1032	'Round' Sabian temple destroyed at Harran
1184	Ibn Jubayr visits Harran
1260	Last Sabian temple at Harran destroyed by Mongols
c. 1310	Al-Dimashqi writes on pagans of Harran
16th Cent.	First European contact with Mandaeans in S. Iraq

Note on chronology. The Sabians are such an elusive people, with so many tantalizing gaps in their history, that a full chronology is not possible. The list above tabulates their fleeting appearances in history and in contemporary writings.

At the crossroads of two trade routes

in north-western Mesopotamia stands the ancient city of Harran. Here a caravan route from India and China to the Mediterranean crosses the highway from Anatolia to the cities of Syria and Palestine. Here too lived Abraham and Sarah, before they 'went forth to go into the land of Canaan', and it was at Harran that Jacob, after fleeing from Esau, tended the flocks of Laban. But it was as a cult centre that Harran was specially renowned—a centre of the worship of the moon-god Sin, 'greatest of the gods and goddesses'. This cult, with the worship of the sun and the planets, persisted after the rise of Christianity and even into the Islamic period. Its followers were known as Sabians. But who these Sabians were, where they came from and where they finally went—whether indeed they were entitled to the name of Sabians—is a mystery.

The last king of Babylon, Nabonidus, restored the temple of Sin in 552 BC. A stele commemorating this (above) shows the king holding a sceptre and worshipping the signs of the moon, the sun, and Venus. After the fall of Babylon the moon-god was still worshipped at Harran. A stele (left) bearing the crescent emblem of the moon-god Sin was found about four miles from Harran on the road to Edessa. This may correspond to the location of a temple of Sin that was visited by the Emperor Caracalla just before his death in AD 217. (1, 2)

The first kingdom to adopt Christianity as the state religion was Edessa (modern Urfa), some 50 kilometres north of Harran. Side by side with the new religion, however, the pagan rites persisted. The first Christian king of Edessa was probably Abgar the Great; on the steep-sided Citadel Mount, in the southern part of the town, stand two 60-foot Corinthian columns (below), one of which once bore a statue of Abgar's Queen, Shalmath. The statue has disappeared, but an inscription still bears witness to the high status of women in Edessa. (3)

The everyday life of the people of Edessa in the 3rd century is shown in the funerary mosaics that have been discovered in rock tombs in and around the city. The 'Tripod' Mosaic (top right) shows a family, probably of modest means, dressed in Parthian style. The central figure holds a leaf, probably aromatic, in his hand and is applying it to a censer on a tripod foot. The woman at the left has what is perhaps a flower—this may have been a cult-symbol of the Sabians. The family in this mosaic must have been pagans, for there is no Christian formula in the Syriac inscription. That the Sabians believed in a future life is suggested by the words at the foot of the mosaic, 'May he have a goodly latter end.' (4)

'Shining and succulent', as they are described by the pilgrim abbess 'Aetheria of Aquitania', who saw them in the 5th or 6th century AD, the sacred carp in the fishponds of Edessa are evidence of the worship of Atargatis, or Venus. To this day they are never eaten; traditionally inviolate, they even leap out of the water to snatch pieces of bread. (5)

Women are prominent in the monuments of pagan Edessa, where they evidently enjoyed respect under the law and an honoured position in the family. The only stone effigies found at Edessa are of women; the one pictured above shows the high, draped head-dress, reminiscent of those worn by European women in mediaeval times. (6)

Wealth and sophistication are shown by some of the mosaics of Edessa. In the 'Family Portrait' Mosaic (above) Moqimu poses with his wife on his left, his three sons, his daughter and, behind him, his grand-daughter Shalmath. His wife and daughter wear tall head-dresses with bands of contrasting colours, grander than the one in Pl. 4. The girl in the background, too young for the head-dress, decorates her hair with three curved combs.

In the 'Funerary Couch' Mosaic (right) the central figure reclines on a couch, a stoup of wine in his left hand. His wife, in elegant robes and a high head-dress, sits on his left, and their children, younger than those in the 'Family Portrait' Mosaic, are disposed around them. This mosaic was made in AD 277–8, the 'Family Portrait' is undated but may be earlier. (7, 8)

Through the Harran Gate of Edessa (below), its citizens related, the emissary of King Abgar returned bearing the letter from Jesus and a portrait of Jesus on a kerchief. The adoption of Christianity at Edessa was in fact two centuries after the Crucifixion. The Sabian rites of moon-worship continued, however, at Edessa and in the nearby hills, until well into the Islamic period. Remains of the Byzantine wall can be seen on the right. (10)

The pagans of Edessa believed in a future life. Rock-cut tombs in the hills outside the city testify to this, with sculptured reliefs in a style that is familiar from the better-known sculptures of Palmyra, nearly three hundred miles to the south. The winged figure above is a detail from one of these tombs. The reclining figure below, set in a semi-circular niche, recalls the personage in the mosaic of Pl. 8. With their belief in a day of judgement the Sabians were listed in the Koran as members of a tolerated religion. The writing here, as in the mosaics, is Syriac. (9, 11)

In a remote watering-place
called Sumatar Harabesi in the Tektek hills, east of Edessa,
are ruined buildings, reliefs and inscriptions which shed some
light on the Sabians in the 2nd century AD. In their long frock
coats, with their hair dressed in ringlets—as Harun al-Rashid's
son was to see them 600 years later—they practised their secret
rites to Sin, the moon-god, and to Marilaha, 'the Lord God'
possibly one and the same supreme deity.

Every planet had a temple of special shape and colour in the
Sabian ritual. Some of the Sumatar shrines also appear to have
been cylindrical, some rectangular. The one shown above is
circular on a square base; the outer perimeter of the circular wall
just touches the outer edge of each side of the square base—a
feat of some architectural skill. (12)

A headless stone statue near one of the ruined shrines of
Sumatar (above) wears a long frock coat, beneath which trouser
legs appear. On the central mount is a standing figure (below,
left) wearing a shorter version of the coat. Close by it is a bust
in a niche (below). The dedicatory inscriptions are in Syriac:
one invokes 'Sin the deity', with a date corresponding to AD 165.
(13–15)

The moon temple, Deir al-Kadi, may have been at Sanimagara,
where these ruins, with their florid decorations, now stand. At
such sites perhaps were celebrated—mainly in honour of Shamal,
lord of the *jinn*—the central rites of Harran, the 'mysteries'. (16)

Re-birth is the theme of the 'Phoenix' Mosaic (above), from the floor of a cave tomb at Edessa. The phoenix (its name is inscribed in Syriac at the top of the picture) stands on a wreathed pillar, symbolic of the soul; before it is a conventional stone tomb. The theme is thus clearly stated, with symbols of death, the soul, and rebirth. This mosaic (dated AD 235–6), and the one opposite, were only found in the last few years, and are here reproduced in colour for the first time. (17)

Orpheus with his lute is the theme of a mosaic from the floor of another Sabian cave at Edessa (right), dated AD 227–8. Here Orpheus, seated on a mound, plays to a docile group of birds and animals. It is strange to find this myth pictured so far from Greece, but the theme was a popular one in Rome's eastern provinces, and throughout their early history the Edessans loved dancing, song and poetry. The Emperor Alexander Severus is said to have worshipped Orpheus; he passed by Edessa in AD 231. (18)

Harran today still retains vestiges of its variegated past. A village of about a hundred beehive-shaped huts (above) occupies the south-eastern part of the old city, overlooked by the ruins of the Great Mosque and the Citadel, where stood the last Sabian temple in Harran. In the first millennium of our era the Sabians resisted the overtures of both Christianity and Islam, but in the face of persecution clung steadfast to the basic tenets and ritual of their strange planetary religion. In the 12th or 13th century the last remaining centre of their worship was destroyed by the Mongols, and the Sabians disappeared from Harran. (19)

The Sabians survive, it has been maintained, to this day in a small sect, mainly metal-workers and boat-builders, in the lower reaches of the Tigris and Euphrates. These people, known as Mandaeans or Subba, were wrongly identified by travellers as followers of John the Baptist, though baptism in running water is the most important of their sacraments. A priest of this sect is shown (left) performing the rite of baptism, which includes complete immersion and giving of water to drink from the flowing stream.

There are similarities with the little that is known of Sabian ritual and beliefs—for instance in the induction of priests and in the mystery rites —and the Mandaean language is akin to Syriac. But there are also radical differences: the Mandaeans, like the Sabians, hold that human fate and actions are subject to the influence of the planets, but, unlike the Sabians, they believe that this influence is entirely evil. Their own traditions place their origin in Palestine, with a period of exile at Harran, but here history lies on the borderland of legend. (20)

The planet cult of ancient Harran

J. B. SEGAL

THE SABIANS present an enigma as elusive as it is tantalizing. They are mentioned obscurely in the Koran. Thereafter we know that they were a religious community who performed strange rituals during the first centuries of Islam. Yet early historians—some of them men of integrity, but all of them opponents of Sabian beliefs and practices—were at a loss to identify them. The name of Sabian had, they darkly allege, been assumed by impostors. Later writers regard the name Sabian as a general title to designate the heathen and all that was hateful in heathendom.

Much of the information on the Sabians was assembled over a hundred years ago in a monumental work by a Russian scholar, Daniel Chwolson. Since Chwolson's book, little original material has appeared—some texts, some archaeological finds and sociological studies. Recent research, however, enables us to set out the problem afresh; whether it provides the answer to the enigma must be left for the reader to decide.

Ancient Harran and the Sin Temple

Harran in North-west Mesopotamia is familiar to the Western world from the Bible. Abram and Sarai 'went forth. . . . from Ur of the Chaldees. . . . and they came unto Haran, and dwelt there' (Gen. 11). It was to Harran that Abraham sent his servant to bring a bride for Isaac (Gen. 24), and it was to Harran that Jacob fled from Esau to dwell with the family of his mother (Gen. 29). At the time of the patriarchs Harran was already famous. It stood at the intersection of two major highways; one connected the mountainous regions of Anatolia with the populous cities of Syria and Palestine, another joined Asia Minor and the Mediterranean seaboard with the distant wealth of India and China. Harran was a great emporium. Ezekiel mentions it among the merchants of the East 'in choice wares. . . . in chests of rich apparel, bound with cords, and made of cedar' (Ezek. 27: 23 f).

But it was as a cult centre that Harran was specially renowned and particularly for the cult of Sin, the moon-god. Sin of Harran is invoked in treaties over a wide area between the 19th and 9th centuries BC. His emblems, the crescent and disc, have been found in North Syria as well as at Harran itself.

Many of the inhabitants of Harran had 'Sin' or 'Si' incorporated into their names. The Harranian temple of the moon-god and his family was known in Sumerian as E-hul-hul, the Temple of Rejoicing. It was restored by the Assyrian Shalmaneser III in the 9th century BC, and two centuries later it was restored again by Asshurbanipal, who installed his younger brother as its High Priest. Esarhaddon on his way to Egypt paid his vows at this temple. It was roofed with cedar of Lebanon, its friezes were inlaid with lapis lazuli, and its doors were of silver.

A striking episode in the history of Harran—and a matter of significance to the present discussion—is the sojourn there of Nabonidus, the last king of Babylon, recorded on stelae discovered at Harran and in its vicinity. Nabonidus, probably of Aramaean descent, had been directed in a dream to rebuild the temple of Sin, which had been destroyed by the Medes in 610. His mother, who died at the remarkable age of 104, was priestess there. But the people of Babylon refused to assist in the holy task; and for ten years the king abandoned his capital, until the temple was restored at Harran, to the glory of Sin, 'king of

the gods' and 'greatest of the gods and goddesses'. On the stelae of Harran, king Nabonidus is depicted holding a sceptre bearing a divine symbol; he worships the emblems of the moon (a whole circle with a crescent below), the sun (a disk with an internal pattern of four points with spreading rays) and Ishtar/Venus (a seven-pointed star in a circle). pl 1

The stream of worshippers at the temples of Harran did not cease with the fall of the Babylonian kingdom. It was on his return from a visit to the temple of the moon at Harran that the Emperor Caracalla was assassinated in AD 217. The young Emperor Julian, who led a pagan reaction against Christendom, made Harran his headquarters for several days in 363; and it was from Harran that he set out to carve an empire in Persia. His defeat and death flung Harran into consternation and mourning. Nevertheless, Harran's pagans continued to resist the encroachments of the rising religion of Christianity. In the 5th or 6th century Harran was visited by a pilgrim abbess from Spain, and she records in her Latin diary: 'Except for a few clerics and holy monks, I found not a single Christian; all were pagans.' pl 2

When the King of Persia invaded this region in the 6th century he spared Harran as a bastion of the 'old faith'. And in 638-9 it was the pagans of Harran who took the initiative in the surrender of their city to the Moslem army.

The Beginning of the Problem

It is against this background that we have the first historical record of the Sabians—two centuries later, in the year 830 or thereabouts. The Caliph Abdallah al-Ma'mun passed by Harran to launch an attack on the territory of Byzantium. Our chronicler relates:

'People met him to wish him well. Among them were a group of Harranians. Their attire at that time was a frock-coat, and their hair was long and in locks, like the locks of Qurrah, grandfather of Sinan ibn Thabit.' Al-Ma'mun wondered at their attire, and he said to them: 'To which tolerated community do you belong?' They replied, 'We are Harranians.' He asked, 'Are you Christians?' They replied, 'No'. He asked, 'Then are you Jews?' They replied, 'No'. He asked, 'Then are you Zoroastrians?' They replied, 'No'. He asked, 'Then have you a (revealed) book or a prophet?' Then they became confused in their speech. He said to them, 'In that case you are pagans who worship idols; you are the men of the (talking) head of the days of (Harun) al-Rashid my father. Your blood (may be shed) with impunity; you are not a tolerated community.' They replied, 'But we pay the poll-tax.' He said to them, 'We accept the poll-tax only from non-Moslems who follow the religions which Allah (may he be exalted and magnified!) mentioned in his book and who have a (revealed) book. For this reason the Moslems made peace with them. But you belong neither to one group nor the other. Therefore you shall choose now one of two courses—adopt either the religion of Islam or one of the religions which Allah (may he be exalted!) mentioned in his book. If you do not, I shall slay you utterly. I grant you respite until I return from my present journey. If then you have entered into Islam or into one of the religions which Allah (may he be exalted and glorified and magnified!) mentioned in his book, (it will be well). But if you have not, I have given orders that you shall be slain and wholly extirpated! . . . .'

So they changed their attire, and shaved off their locks and abandoned their frock-coats. Many of them became Christians and put on the girdles (prescribed for Christians), and a group of them accepted Islam. But a section of them remained as they were. These began to be perplexed and troubled, until a sheikh of Harran, a jurist, acceded to their enquiry. He said to them, 'I have a scheme whereby you will escape and be saved from slaughter.' They brought him a great sum of money from their treasury which they had renewed from the days of al-Rashid for this purpose. . . . (The jurist) said to them, 'When al-Ma'mun returns from his journey, say to him, 'We are Sabians', for this is the name of a religion whose name Allah (may he be magnified!) has mentioned in the Koran. Adopt it, and through it you will escape.'

Al-Ma'mun did not return to Harran. He died at Budendun in AD 833. 'But', continues our chronicler, 'from that time (the Harranians) adopted this name, because there had been no people called Sabians at Harran and its regions (previously). When the report of al-Ma'mun's death reached them, most of the Harranians who had become Christians apostatized and returned to the religion of Harran. They let their locks grow as they had done before al-Ma'mun passed by Harran, on the grounds that they were Sabian. But the Moslems prevented them from wearing frock-coats, since this was part of the dress of those who were in authority. The Harranians who had accepted Islam were not able to apostatize for fear of being slain. They continued to dissemble within Islam. They used to marry Harranian women; they made their male children Moslem, their female children Harranian.'

The chronicler of this incident lived probably no more than sixty or eighty years after the events he describes, and he had first-hand acquaintance with the people of Harran. Yet we must hesitate to accept his account at its face-value. He was a Christian, and there was a long history of bitter strife between the pagans of Harran and the Christians. He has implicit reproach for the Moslems. The Moslem jurist who rescued the Harranians from their predicament did so, he claims, for a reward. Moreover, he insinuates, Moslems permit even heathens to shelter under the title of 'people of a (revealed) book' and to claim thereby the toleration of Islam.

It is incredible that pagans should have been allowed to continue their practices at Harran undisturbed—unless, for some reason, they were formally tolerated by Islam. Harran was not an obscure village remote from Moslem authority. It was an ancient city of great renown. It had played a prominent part in Moslem history before the time of al-Ma'mun. It was at Harran that Marwan II, last of the Umayyad Caliphs, had established his residence. Harun al-Rashid, al-Ma'mun's father, had visited the region of Edessa and Harran in about 792. He cannot have been ignorant of the religious background at Harran. Further, Syriac Christian chronicles—probably written at Edessa, but in any case no friends to the pagans of Harran—tell us that, about 20 years before al-Ma'mun's visit, the governor of Harran, Ibrahim, 'ordered the pagans of Harran to carry out these mysteries openly; and they were paying the tax'.

Can we believe that the Moslems were suddenly, shortly after al-Ma'mun's visit, hoodwinked into granting toleration to the Harranian pagans—merely because they had adopted the name 'Sabians'? Was this the first time they had applied the term to themselves? And what did it denote?

In the eyes of Moslems the earliest references to Sabians occur in the Koran. One passage declares:
'Surely those who believe, and those who Judaize, and Christians, and Sabians, whoever believeth in God, and the last day, and do that which is right, they shall have their reward with their Lord; (there shall come) no fear upon them, neither shall they be grieved.'

Clearly the Prophet Muhammad regarded Sabians as belonging to the general category of monotheists—Moslems, Jews and Christians—who believe in God and the day of judgment. Another reference in the Koran is less informative:
'God directeth whom he pleaseth. (As to) the true believers, and those who Judaize, and the Sabians, and the Christians, and the Magians, and the idolaters; verily God shall judge between them on the day of resurrection; for God is witness of all things.'
From this we can deduce no more than that the Sabians were probably a recognized religious community.

There were, however, unknown to the Moslems, possible allusions in Christian writings to a sect of Sabians some four centuries before the coming of Islam. It is alleged that the prophet-founder of this sect, Elkesai, from the city of 'Serai' in Parthia, had been handed a book for men called Sobiai by an angel. Elkesai proclaimed forgiveness of sins for those who believed in this book and who received baptism, fully clothed, in a river or fountain in the name of the Great and Most High God and his son the Great King. The doctrines of the sect were a confused mixture of Jewish, Christian and pagan—the acknowledgment of a single God, the rejection of earlier prophets, the veneration of water as the source of life, belief in the male and female principle of Christ and the Holy Spirit and belief in reincarnation—Jesus was

reincarnated in Elkesai. Epiphanius connects the sect with the baptizing sects beside the Jordan at the beginning of the Christian era; by some scholars they have been identified with the Mandaeans, or Subba, who claim to have migrated from that region (and whom we shall discuss later). It is improbable that they are the Sabians of the Koran, since their membership can never have been great and they lived remote from the milieu in which Muhammad moved. But we should also take into account the allegation that their leader derived from 'Serai' in Parthia. Parthia comprises also the area of Harran and Edessa; and the name Serai (from the Chinese term for silk) may allude to the silk trade which brought much prosperity to the inhabitants of those cities at the period to which Elkesai is ascribed.

We must touch briefly on the derivation of the name Sabians. They are not, of course, the Sabaeans of Arabia, nor are they to be connected with the Queen of Sheba whose visit to King Solomon is recorded in the Bible. The name was probably not Arabic but Syriac, the language spoken at Harran and Edessa, the language apparently of the Elkesaites and also of the Mandaeans, or Subba. The theory has been propounded that the name Sabians denotes the Baptizers, a term which might aptly describe both Elkesaites and Mandaeans. But would the Harranians have adopted for themselves the name of Baptizers, since baptism had a minor role in their religion—a religion to which they remained faithful for centuries? We may doubt this. It is possible, on the other hand, to interpret the term Sabian as 'Conventicler' or 'Congregationalist'. Finally, the name may be connected with Soba, a geographical term applied, at this period, to the city of Nisibis. Nisibis was a centre of Syriac culture. To Muhammad, then, the Sabians might be speakers of Syriac from the area of North Mesopotamia. They believed in a single God, and in the Day of Judgment; they are likely to have had affinities with Jews and Christians. They were, we may presume, people of a superior cultural level.

Let us now look at the environs of Harran in the first three centuries of the Christian era—the period, that is, at which Elkesai and the mysterious Sobiai were apparently active.

Abgar the Great, the first Christian King of Edessa: portrait on a coin of the late 2nd century AD. (1)

A Disordered Pantheon—Sin, Marilaha and Be'el Shamin

Forty kilometres north of Harran stands the city of Urhay, now the Turkish Urfa. Under its Seleucid name of Edessa it won fame in Christendom as the first kingdom to adopt Christianity as its state religion—probably under Abgar the Great in the early 3rd century. According to the legend, its king corresponded with Jesus himself, and Syriac chronicles tell how the apostle Addai addressed the people of the city, probably on the Citadel mount now crowned by two Corinthian columns. The story is, of course, apocryphal, but it was widely believed, and pilgrims came to Edessa from distant parts of the Christian world. But the native religion of the people of Edessa was the cult of the seven planets —the Moon, the Sun, Jupiter, Venus, Mercury, Saturn and Mars. One of the city gates was called after the temple of the Sun, Beth-Shemesh. The symbol of the crescent moon appeared on the coins of the pre-Christian kings of Edessa. Names of planets were incorporated in the names of its citizens. Bardaisan, the philosopher of Edessa and contemporary of Abgar the Great, wrote,

A coin from Harran of the time of the Emperor Caracalla, showing the crescent symbol of the moon. Caracalla was assassinated returning from a visit to the temple of Sin. (2)

we are told, a treatise on the conjunction of the planets. The planet cult at Edessa survived for several centuries after the introduction of Christianity, and even after the coming of Islam.

Light has been shed on this planet cult by recent work at Sumatar Harabesi in the Tektek mountains, a remote and deserted watering-place for the herds and flocks of the region, and about 50 kilometres south-east of Urfa (Edessa) and 30 kilometres north-east of Harran.

At Sumatar, a group of seven or eight ruined stone buildings, probably tombs, stands in a half-circle at irregular intervals around a central mount. They are of various shapes—one is round, another square, a third round on a square base. Due north of the central mount, and at some distance, are more imposing ruins, perhaps administrative buildings, including what is today called the 'castle'. Beside one is the headless stone statue of a man, dressed in a long outer garment reaching below the knees—we are reminded of the frock-coats of the pagans whom al-Ma'mun encountered at Harran; below this garment appear trouser-legs. On the northern flank of the central mount—clearly a sacred site— is a relief which illustrates another garment of this period. The coat is somewhat shorter, and no trouser-legs are visible. Beside it is another relief, this time the bust of a male personage, and without a head-dress; his hair is secured by headbands, a bow and a half-loop on either side of his head. We are reminded of the Harranians of al-Ma'mun, who wondered at their long locks.

Beside these reliefs are two short Syriac inscriptions dedicated to 'the deity'. A third inscription declares that the relief which it accompanies was dedicated to Sin.

A fourth inscription is largely indecipherable. But it appears to mention again Sin, the moon-god, and the dedication of a treasure; perhaps the treasure was in his care. Here we may recall the payment from the treasure of the Harranians to the Moslem jurist following their encounter with al-Ma' mun.

The summit of the central mount is a bare rock. A number of Syriac inscriptions are incised deep in the surface. One states: 'May Absamya son of Adona the *nuhadra* be remembered. May he be remembered before Marilaha. . . .'

Two other inscriptions are dedicatory and are given pride of place, one on the western, the other on the eastern side of the summit. The first reads:
'On the New Moon of Shebat (February) in the year 476 (AD 165) I Tiridates son of Adona ruler of the Arabs built this altar and set a pillar to Marilaha for the life of my lord the king and his sons and for the life of Adona my father. . . .'

The second records an event in the same month:
'In Shebat in the year 476. . . . we set this pillar on this blessed mount and erected the stool for him whom my ruler nourishes (or, whose shepherd is my ruler). He shall be *Budar* after Tiridates the ruler. And he shall give the stool to him whom he nourishes (or, whose shepherd he is). His recompense shall be from Marilaha. And if he withholds the stool, then the pillar will be ruined. He is the god who knows us (?).'

The last words are uncertain. It is possible, but not probable, that they should be rendered, 'He is the god Sin'.

The year in which these inscriptions were recorded, AD 165, was a turning-point in the history of Osrhoene, the province in which Edessa and Harran are situated. Roman armies occupied Edessa and expelled its pro-Parthian monarch Wael. 'The king' of the Sumatar inscription is probably the king of Edessa, the

pl 12

pl 13

pl 14

pl 15

principal city of the province. There was a direct political bond between Sumatar and Edessa at this time.

There was also, it seems, a religious bond between the two places. The chief deity of Sumatar was evidently referred to as Marilaha, 'the Lord God'. His cult emblems were a sacred pillar and a stool. The motif of the sacred horned or crescent pillar is a not uncommon lunar symbol in this region. We have the motif on reliefs in a rock-cut vault at Sumatar; we find it on the ancient stelae of Harran; and, for example, on the coins of Harran in the reign of Septimius Severus. But the more complex theme of a sacred pillar and a stool is depicted on two coins of Wael, the king of Edessa whom we have mentioned. Another Edessan coin of the reign of Elagabalus, some fifty years later, carries the same motif in miniature. The Wael coins, however, bear also a legend,

f 3

The sacred pillar and stool on a coin of Edessa. These were the symbols of the god Marilaha. (3)

unfortunately unclear, in the script of the Sumatar inscription. It may be deciphered as the name Marilaha.

Who was this deity Marilaha? In Nabataean, Mara ('lord') is one of the epithets of the god Be'el Shamin, 'master of the heavens'. At Palmyra, too, in the first centuries of the Christian era Mara, 'lord', is a title of Be'el Shamin, here the central member of a triad of deities; he is called variously 'lord of all', 'lord of the universe', 'great god'.

In the 2nd-3rd centuries AD a small Aramaean kingdom was established at Hatra, about 80 kilometres south of Mosul. Inscriptions from Hatra—in a script akin to the scripts of Syriac and of both the Nabataeans and Palmyrenes—indicate that there, also, the god that was invoked most frequently was Be'el Shamin; he is called 'great god', 'king'. And we find on coins from Hatra, the legend 'Sin Marilaha'. Was Sin here elevated to a supreme role, or was he identified with a central deity, Be'el Shamin?

f 4

Coin of Hatra, a small Aramaean kingdom south of Mosul. The inscription on the obverse (left), in a script akin to Syriac, invokes the god Sin Marilaha. (4)

It is not profitable to speculate on the identity of this central godhead. Cults appeared, merged and disappeared, and we cannot seek to resolve the disorder into a tidy pantheon in which each deity is allotted his particular sphere with peculiar attributes and peculiar duties. It is sufficient to observe that the general atmosphere over a large area of North Mesopotamia and Syria during the first centuries of the Christian era favoured the conception of a central deity attended by lesser deities. At some places—notably Beth Hur—Be'el Shamin was worshipped as 'chief of the gods' as late as the 5th century; at Harran the practice continued considerably longer.

Edessa and its Mosaics

Before, however, we turn to consider Harran, we must study more closely certain religious practices of pagan Edessa. Evidence of the ancient worship of Tar'atha or Atargatis, that is, Venus, the goddess of fertility, is to be found in the pools of teeming fish which have survived to the present time. The pilgrim abbess who visited the city in the 5th or 6th century described them as 'shining and succulent'; and so they are today. To this day these fish are never eaten. Another sign of the Tar'atha cult is perhaps to be found in the leaf carried in the right hand of the central figure of the 'Family Portrait' Mosaic of Edessa; the mosaic, found in 1952,

pl 5

pl 7

Relief from Palmyra (the Hypogeum of Atenatan, AD 229). The reclining male figure, and the female figures grouped in the background, strikingly resemble the 'Funerary Couch' Mosaic at Edessa. (5)

is undated, but certainly belongs to the 2nd or 3rd century AD. The same motif is to be seen in the 'Tripod' Mosaic, found in 1956 and also undated; here the leaf is applied to a censer. A leaf is shown also in sculptures from Hatra.

The pagans of Edessa believed in a future life. The elegiac inscription at the foot of the 'Tripod' Mosaic ends with the words, 'May he have a goodly latter-end'. Resurrection is the theme of the 'Phoenix' Mosaic, found in 1956 and dated AD 235-6. It depicts the tomb in the form of the conventional arcosolium of the Edessa rock-caves; above the tomb stands a wreathed pillar—we recall the sacred pillar of Sumatar—and the whole is surmounted by the Phoenix, the symbol of rebirth.

Reliefs in three cave tombs at Edessa show a funerary theme familiar from the sculptures of Palmyra. The dead man reclines, one elbow resting on a cushion. This is also the theme of the 'Funerary Couch' Mosaic, also found in 1956 and dated AD 277-8. Here the dead man holds a stoup of wine in his left hand. Around him are his wife and children; one holds a napkin, another a spice-box (?). Other accessories in the funeral of an Edessan pagan are portrayed in the 'Tripod' Mosaic. The central object, mounted on a tripod, is for burning incense. A woman proffers what may be identified as a flower; a man holds a cap—possibly a cap of state.

David with his harp, from a wall painting at Dura Europos. This may represent another variation of the Orpheus myth. (6)

The theme of another Edessa mosaic, the 'Orpheus' Mosaic, found in 1956 and dated AD 227-8, is one which will recur in our analysis of the religion of Harran. The bard is depicted sitting, his lyre in his hand; around him are a lion, a goat and birds in attitudes of becoming docility. We should not be surprised to encounter Orpheus at Edessa, for throughout its history its citizens loved dancing, song and poetry. Moreover, in the 3rd century, the Orpheus theme had acquired a considerable follow-

ing in Rome's eastern provinces. A variation of the Orpheus motif may be found in the presentation of David in the Synagogue at Dura Europos. More significant, the biography of the Roman Emperor Alexander Severus, a Syrian by origin, informs us that the busts of Abraham, Jesus, the philosopher Apollonius of Tyana, and Orpheus stood together in his private chapel. Alexander Severus was acclaimed Emperor in 222, five years before this mosaic was made at Edessa; he passed through the region of Edessa in 231 on his way to the East.

The broad synthesis of cults and beliefs of which Alexander Severus was a proponent is amply reflected in the liberal philosophy of the school of Bardaisan the Edessan, to whom we have already referred. Born pagan, he adopted Christianity and wrote against heretics; later, however, he encountered the violent opposition of churchmen for what they regarded as his gnostic views. A century after his death St Ephraim attacked Bardaisan without mincing words:

'Let us pray for Bardaisan, who departed (this life) in heathenism —a legion of demons in his heart, and our Lord on his lips.'

Further evidence of gnostic beliefs at Edessa is provided by the remarkable, if obscure, stone epitaph found there some fifty years ago:

'Pleasant is the resting-place of Shalman son of Kawkab (Star). They have answered thee and called thee, and thou hast answered them whom thou hast touched. Thou hast seen the height and the depth, the distant and the near, the hidden and the evident. And they—they know well the usefulness of thy reckonings. . . .'

Now, we have seen that the pagans of North Mesopotamia were devotees of the planets during the first centuries of the Christian era. There was among them also an evident trend towards the conception of a single godhead—whether he stood alone above all other deities, or whether he was merely *primus inter pares*. At Edessa, as we have already observed from the monuments, the pagans believed in a future life. All the inhabitants of this area were speakers of Syriac. If, then, the interpretation of Sabians as the people of Soba—hence, speakers of Syriac—is accepted, there is justification for regarding the Sabians of the Koran as the pagan Semites of North Mesopotamia.

The identification may be applied with particular force to the inhabitants of Harran. They were for the most part Semites— more exactly, Aramaeans—and worshippers of the planets. Further, the inscriptions of Nabonidus elevate Sin above all other gods. He is 'king of the gods of heaven and earth' and 'greatest of the gods and goddesses'. That this universalistic conception is no accident is proved by the inscription of Nabonidus at Ur; there Sin is described as 'lord of the gods of heaven and earth, king of the gods, god of the gods'. There is another reason for maintaining the view that the pagans of Harran were exponents of universalistic beliefs. The Koran uses the term *ḥanīf* of a person who professed monotheism before the appearance of Judaism and Christianity—before, that is, Moses and Jesus; in the opinion of Muhammad the true *ḥanīf* was Abraham. Now, Harran at the time of Muhammad had long been the centre of the Syriac *ḥanpe* (*ḥanpa* or *ḥanīf*)—and Harran was the home of Abraham. *Ḥanīf* is, in some measure, a synonym of Sabian; the latter is a member of this religious community, the former professed the beliefs of the community.

We shall discover later in this study that the Harranians possessed a sacred book—called, significantly, the book of the *ḥanpe* or Haniphites—and that they recognized certain prophets. True, the book was concerned solely, it appears, with ritual and not with ethics or law, and the prophets were legendary rather than human. But the Harranians satisfied the conditions required by Islam for recognition as a tolerated community. Why, then, it may be asked, did they falter and grow confused when the Caliph al-Ma'mun asked for their credentials? Several reasons may be advanced. Twenty years before the Caliph's visit, the rites of the Harranians had received the formal approval of the Governor of Harran. The sudden disapproval of al-Ma'mun must have found them off their guard and bewildered. Moreover, the Harranian pagans spoke Syriac and may well have been ignorant of the speech of the Caliph. This supposition is supported by their recourse to a Moslem jurist. But the most likely explanation for the confusion of the Harranians in their encounter with al-Ma'mun is their unwillingness to expose their book, with its description of the holy mysteries, to the eyes of an outsider.

The Sabians through Moslem Eyes

From the 10th century onwards antiquarians, mainly Moslem, interested themselves in the beliefs and customs of the Sabians. Not all of them accepted the equation of Sabians with the pagans of Harran—we shall return to this problem later. The world of paganism had shrunk; vast regions to which Christianity had not reached had been converted to monotheism through Islam. Moslem writers swept into the ragbag which they labelled Sabian all the miscellaneous fragments they could find—from ancient Greece and ancient Egypt to contemporary India and China. It was not easy for the Sabians to counter these insinuations. Like every religious minority in the Islamic empire they were engaged in a constant struggle to maintain their very existence as a community. The creed of the Sabians was not one that could acquire general acceptance, and they seem to have made no effort to win converts. Their cult revolved largely around their mysteries; even their language, Syriac, was a 'secret' language to most of their Moslem neighbours. The descriptions of the Sabian religion by Sabians have not been preserved. The accounts that have survived show us the Sabians through the eyes of their detractors, Moslem, Christian or Jewish, who were inclined to accentuate those details of Sabian practice calculated to arouse the hostility and repugnance of their readers. They contain allegations that are clearly preposterous but this will not surprise us. After all, allegations that ritual murder is practised by the Jews, a minority more accessible than were the Sabians, have been a recurrent theme in Asia and Europe even in the 20th century.

A brief account of Sabian beliefs is given by a 9th-century writer, Ahmed ibn al-Tayyib. The Sabians, he maintains, held that a supreme power, single and eternal, was the primal cause of the Universe. He is beyond the worship of men; and he has delegated the administration of the Universe to the planets who proclaim his supremacy. Furthermore, he has sent prophets—the most famous of whom are Arani (others omit this name), Agathodaemon (whom other writers equate with Seth and Orpheus—represented, it will be recalled, in a mosaic at Edessa) and Hermes (whom other writers equate with Idris or Enoch) to guide mankind. Sabian views on the nature of the deity, on natural phenomena, on the soul and dreams followed the views propounded by Aristotle. A contemporary of Ahmed ibn al-Tayyib tells us that the planets are deities, some male and others female, some benevolent, others malevolent, with passions and lusts like human beings.

Ahmed states firmly that the Sabians were united in their doctrines and free from sectarian feuds. But another writer of the same century tells—with greater probability—of two dissident groups. One group, the Rufusiyyah, wore no jewellery and held solemn sacrifice of swine; members of the other group never went out of their homes and shaved their heads closely.

These alleged Sabian sects are unlikely to be the pagans of Harran. The mosaics of Edessa depict jewellery prominently on the women's costume, the pig was a forbidden animal, the Harranians wear their hair long. A later source, Mas'udi, an acute observer who himself visited Harran in the 10th century, uses the term Sabian for pagans over an ever-broadening area. He writes, it is true, of the Sabians of Harran and those Sabians whom he describes as *Kimariyyun*. The former, he declares, are Greek and follow eclectic forms of philosophy; the latter are clearly the Mandaeans or Subba (whom we shall describe later), since they live near Basra and Wasit. Mas'udi, it must be admitted, contradicts himself. In one passage he maintains that the founder of both groups of Sabians was Budhasaf (Buddha), believed —as we are told elsewhere—to have come from India. In another he writes of four categories of Sabians, the Chaldaeans who are the Mandaeans, the Chinese who follow Budhasaf, the Greeks and Romans, and the Egyptians who survive at Harran ! Later writers advance theories that are even more improbable. The more distant our 'authorities' in time and space from the Sabians—however we identify them—the more reckless is their definition of Sabian doctrines.

Nevertheless, we can arrive at a plausible outline of these doctrines. Sabians directed their prayers, as we have already seen, to the spiritual beings which (they held) act as intermediaries between men and the Supreme deity; these beings inhabit and guide the planets, which stand to them in the relation of the body to the spirit. The activity of these spiritual beings produces movement in space, and this creates material things—plants and animals and men. But matter is bad by nature, and human beings have prejudices and passions; only through the influence of the spiritual beings are they endowed with love and amity, knowledge and healing. The Sabians therefore rejected the Moslem—al-Shahrastani calls it Haniphite—teaching that a human prophet can mediate between man and the supreme deity. They did not believe in resurrection in the conventional sense; every 36,425 years, they maintained, a new order of men, animals and plants is created afresh.

The Daily Ritual

The ordinary Sabian could not conduct his life by general principles of elevated philosophy such as these. The mass of Harranians followed a complex scheme of ritual, worshipping idols in the temples as representations of the remote and often invisible planets. There were temples, however, not only to the seven planets, but also to the Primal Cause, the First Intellect, World Order, Necessity and the Soul. All these temples were round. The temples to the planets were each, our sources declare, of a special shape—we are reminded of the buildings at Sumatar Harabesi—and each reflected the ideas of those times about the colour and metal peculiar to each planet and the day of the week which it was supposed to govern. The arrangement and order of the temples and the height of the idols conformed to the distance of each planet from the earth. The temple of Saturn was hexagonal and black, his statue was of lead, his day Saturday; the temple of Jupiter was triangular and green, his statue of tin, his day Thursday; the temple of Mars was oblong (or square?), his colour red, his statue of iron, his day Tuesday; the temple of the sun was square, his statue was of gold, his day Sunday; the temple of Venus was probably a triangle inside a rectangle and it was blue, her statue was of copper, and her day Friday; the temple of Mercury was probably a triangle in an oblong, it had no allotted colour, Mercury's statue was of clay and his day Wednesday; the temple of the Moon was probably octagonal, her statue—the moon was now regarded as female—of silver, and her day Monday.

We do not know where these temples were located inside Harran—except for a temple of the Moon which will be mentioned later. Outside Harran were two villages called Tar'uz, the gate of Venus, and Salamsin, the idol of Sin, which were celebrated in the 9th and 10th centuries for the devoutness of their Sabian inhabitants. The latter name recalls the present-day village of Sanimagara, east of Sumatar in the Tektek mountains, where may still be seen an altar and a large complex of ruined buildings. Here may have been the site of the temple of the Moon which was called Kadi. Legend, obviously apocryphal, related that the idol of the waters (Arabic *ṣanam al-ma'*) had fled to India, but upon entreaty had consented to return only 'thus' (Syriac *kadi*), 'so far'. This temple was the scene of important celebrations, both monthly and annual. Other Sabian ceremonies were held annually at a temple of Sin named *Sini* (or Sibti?).

In prayer the Harranians looked towards the North (less probably, with other writers, the South). They prayed each day at sunrise, noon and sunset; there were also supererogatory prayers. They washed before prayer.

The regulations concerning special prayers were stringent. Worshippers were instructed:

'If you wish to address a prayer to a planet and to make some request, first fill all your being with the fear of God the Most High, cleanse your heart of evil thoughts and your garments of uncleanness, and make your soul sincere and pure. Consider to which of the seven planets you should make your request and to which it conforms in character. Then put on your garments and address your prayer to that star when it has arrived at the place in the sphere which I shall indicate. If you do this, your request will be granted and you will receive the boon you desire.'

Each of the planets had influence over a special category of persons—Saturn over persons of authority, Jupiter over wise men and philosophers, Mars over men of violence, the Sun over persons of distinction, Venus over women, children and artists, Mercury over men of learning and science, the moon over cultivators and vagrants. Each planet, too, had its own temperament; Saturn and Mars, in particular, were malevolent. The right time for prayer was fixed by observation of the station of the planet in the sky. The suppliant, dressed in the colour and style appropriate to the planet—in praying to Jupiter, it should be noted, the suppliant wore the 'volume of the Haniphites' around his neck—offered incense according to prescribed formulae. The incense of Saturn contained opium and the skull of a black cat, and that of Mars contained human blood; the incense to the sun and moon is called respectively the 'greater' and the 'lesser incense of the Haniphites'. We have an account of the prayers to each planet, the name of its special angel, its magic appellation, and its chosen victim for sacrifice—Saturn demanded a black he-goat, Jupiter a white lamb, Mars a striped cat, the Sun a crested cock, Venus a white pigeon, Mercury a white cock, the moon a small calf.

The Harranian calendar was lunisolar; as elsewhere in the ancient Near East a series of twelve lunations was adjusted to the tropic year by the intercalation of an additional month every two or three years. Only two month-names peculiar to Harran have survived. One, the 'Date-month', is the name of the spring month which opened the year; the other, the 'month of the Chief of praise', corresponds to our January, and probably followed the election of the chief of the community.

The spring month was ushered in by a thirty-day fast which ended on the eighth day of that month. The full moon of the spring month was celebrated by a mystery. So, too, the full moon of the month nearest the autumn equinox was marked by solemn offerings of food and wine and sacrifices to the dead. At the full moon nearest the summer solstice women bewailed Tammuz, the young vegetation-deity whose bones, according to the myth, had been ground by the millstones. This pattern of changing seasons was reflected in the collection of the poll-tax for the Harranian treasury (to which we have already alluded) in the summer, autumn and winter months.

Certain festivals, all of them marked by lavish sacrifices, were celebrated at shrines outside Harran. One, on 28th Nisan (April), was the occasion of the sacrifice of a bull to Hermes and offerings to the 'Lord of Hours'. On 3rd Elul (September)

Harranians bathed in secret in warm water, with tamarisk, wax, pine-cones, oil and sugar. The ceremony was completed before sunrise; they then made sacrifice and drank seven beakers of wine. On the 26th day of this month was held the festival of the Conception (or, the Mountain?). Those who made vows attached a burning torch to a chicken; if the chicken was burnt before the torch, the vow, they believed, was accepted by the 'Lord of Luck'. At the beginning of Former Kanun (December) the women celebrated a festival to Venus and the water-nymphs, also outside Harran. The image of the goddess, 'hidden, far and near', was set up on a marble plinth in a tent, and the officiants brought fruit, flowers, herbs and animal victims.

Side by side with the lunisolar religious calendar which opened in the spring, the Harranians evidently observed a civil year beginning in Latter Kanun (January). On the last day of the previous month the chief priest, standing on a pulpit at the head of nine steps, struck each person with a branch of tamarisk —a familiar fertility rite. He then prayed for the long life, increase, power and eminence of the community; and he invoked the destruction of the buildings at Harran where once had stood the shrines of Venus—the Great Mosque, the Church of the Byzantines and the Women's Market.

The 'Mysteries' of Pagan Harran

The central rites of pagan Harran, however, were the mysteries. They were celebrated principally to Shamal, lord of the *jinn*, perhaps the deity of the North to which Harranians turned in prayer and which they believed was the source of wisdom and might. It is possible that on the 27th day of every month, worshippers went out to the Kadi shrine to sacrifice to the moon, and on the following day they burned animals to Mars in a pavilion of baked bricks constructed in the form of a cone. Certainly mysteries took place on the 27th day of Haziran (June), Tammuz (July), Elul and Latter Kanun. Some mysteries had special features. In the Latter Kanun it was called the 'birthday of the Lord', who was, we are told, the Moon. The occasion was marked by the burning of pine-branches called Dadi—the name and ritual recall the *ded* ceremonies of Osiris worship in ancient Egypt, which had parallels in other regions of the ancient Near East. In Haziran the mystery was directed to the 'god who causes arrows to fly'. The priest shot into the air arrows bound to a burning torch cut from Harranian timber. He then crawled to retrieve the arrows; if the torch still burned the omen was good.

Extracts from the formulae at five Harranian mysteries have been preserved. Unhappily they are garbled; the translator from Syriac knew little Arabic—perhaps, too, he was reluctant to divulge the secret words. The words of two mysteries, the second and the fifth, are fairly complete, but only in the opening and closing phrases. At the second mystery—addressed to the devil and the idols—the priest exclaimed, 'Have I not given you what you handed to me?' The boy novice answered, 'For the dogs, the ravens and the ants!' 'What must we do,' asked the priest, 'concerning the dogs, the ravens and the ants?' 'O priest!' replied the boy, 'they are our brothers. The Lord is victorious and to him we celebrate the mysteries.' The mystery ended with the formula, 'Like the lambs in the flock, and the calves in the herd, and the youth among the men ... who approach and enter the house of the Bughdariyyun, the house of the victorious one —we celebrate his mystery.' The fifth mystery opened with the exclamation of the priest, 'O son of the Bughdariyyun, hearken!' The novices replied, 'We are content.' 'Be silent' called the priest, and the others answered, 'We hear.' The priest then declared 'Ho! I say what I know, and naught do I omit.' The mystery ended with a formula like that at the end of all the mysteries, 'Those who depart to the house of the Bughdariyyun. Our Lord is victorious, and to him we celebrate his mystery.'

The ceremony apparently lasted seven days. During that time the priest proclaimed 22 words with trilling and cantillation. The novices were not to be seen by any woman. They ate and drank. Before proclaiming the words they smeared their eyes with the drink, they received bread and salt and partook of consecrated bread and chicken. The drink was stored in a corner. The novices said to the priest, 'Our master, let the strange thing be declared.'

The high, draped head-dress of the women of Harran is shown in this bust of a certain Shalmath (left). An English missionary recorded a similar female head-dress (right) when he visited Harran a century ago. (7, 8)

He replied, 'Let the bowls be filled with mystery; let what remains be collected (?).'

We cannot, of course, expect to reconstruct these mysteries; no Sabian, one author tells us, would reveal these secrets even if he had abandoned his religion. But light is thrown on them by the Sumatar inscriptions which I have quoted. It is reasonable to equate Budar of Sumatar with the Bughdariyyun of Harran —whatever the name means. The office of Budar seems to have been transmitted from one dignitary to another. In Shebat 165 Tiridates, the ruler (of the Arabs?), had chosen his successor at Sumatar; perhaps 'nourish' in the Sumatar text implies a ritual of feeding, as with the novices at Harran. The symbol of the Budar was evidently a stool, and indeed the chiefs of the Harranians in the 7th century were said to occupy a stool. It was evidently handed down from Budar to Budar; if the chain of transmission was broken, the pillar which rested on the stool would fall. The Sumatar text shows that we may perhaps identify Shamal of Harran with Marilaha of Sumatar.

Much has been written on human sacrifice among the Harranians. On 8th Ab (August), at the pressing of new wine in honour of the gods, they are said to have sacrificed a newly-born male child, and to have employed the flesh with the addition of flour, saffron, spikenard, cloves and oil, as the food at the mysteries. (One writer, however, declares that this sacrifice was performed whenever the earth was five degrees in the ascendant or the reverse.) The allegation must be rejected, at any rate for the Moslem period. Al-Dimashqi in the 14th century goes so far as to declare that human sacrifice appeared in Sabian rites directed to every planet—except, significantly enough, to Saturn to whom a bull was offered. To Jupiter, he maintains, was sacrificed an infant born of a bought (in Arabic Jupiter is the 'buyer') woman, the infant's mother to the sun, to Mars a redhaired man, to Venus a whitehaired woman, to Mercury a cultured youth, to the moon a fair man. This cannot be taken seriously. Al-Dimashqi's taste for the horrific is shown by his story that the idol of Mars held a bloody head in one hand; from an earlier writer we learn that it was a burning torch, not a human head!

There are three accounts of a severed human head which uttered oracles in the Harranian temples, one account in each of the 8th, 9th and 10th centuries. But in one important detail the accounts vary. One maintains that the head was dedicated to Mercury, another to Mars, while the third states that the ceremony took place in the temple of the Moon. Al-Biruni declares that the Sabians sacrificed children to Saturn. Elsewhere he writes that the Sabians were notorious for human sacrifice, but 'at present they are not allowed to carry it out in public'. We may wonder whether it was ever performed during the Christian era. With one dubious exception, no Christian chronicler indicts the Harranian pagans with this offence. An explanation for the naïve reports of Moslem writers may be found in the Syriac history of Bar Hebraeus, which was compiled from earlier sources. Ibrahim, governor of Harran in the 9th century, permitted the Harranians to celebrate their mysteries in public. They led in procession, our chronicler relates with distaste, a bull decorated with garlands of flowers and bells, and accompanied by singers and musicians; it was then solemnly sacrificed. This bull is evidently the sacrificial victim to Saturn of al-Dimashqi. We read of it elsewhere. It was wholly black—an unusual colour in Harranian sacrifices. It was fed with grass plucked by virgins at sunrise. Drawn by a chain of gold, with incense burning before it and amid prayers, it was taken to the place of sacrifice. Its head was smeared with salt and wine, it was decapitated and its organs were examined for omens. We may find here the origin of the stories of the human victim placed in a bath of sesame oil and fed with figs for the period of one year; then, rumour had it, the severed head would advise the Sabians for one year— others held one week—on their scientific and economic affairs. The stories derive from a popular Harranian proverb—'he is in oil', that is, he is in distress. Not unrelated is the phrase 'preparation of the head', a well-known term among alchemists.

That there was hocus pocus in the ritual of Harran is implied by descriptions of the ordeals to which young male neophytes were subjected. We read of four vaults below a temple where stood idols in the shape of the heavenly bodies. The eyes of the lads were bandaged. As they sat wearing slippers made of the skin of sacrificial victims and crowned with garlands of willow, they heard frightening noises from copper instruments, and lights flashed in the darkness. Their eyes were uncovered, and they swooned. The historian Mas'udi will have none of this. The fearful words and sounds did not, he reveals, proceed from the idols, but from temple priests plying bellows behind the walls. These are the mysteries described by a Sabian poet:

'. . . The strange things; a temple set upon vaults. In it they honour the stars, and in it are their idols and vows to the absent ones . . .'

Manners and Fashions

We know something of social customs at Harran. They did not perform circumcision. They took care to avoid persons afflicted with leprosy or other contagious diseases. After pollution of any sort they washed with natron. They considered procreation as the sole purpose of marriage. Nevertheless, they did not practise polygamy. The marriage ceremony was performed before witnesses; marriage between close relations was forbidden. Divorce was granted only after clear evidence had been shown of shameful behaviour, and a divorced woman could not be re-married to her previous husband.

At pagan Harran women enjoyed equality under the law. The high status of women is evident from the monuments of early Edessa. Some tomb inscriptions commemorate women. Shalmath, queen of Edessa, was honoured by a statue on one of the Corinthian columns still standing on the Citadel mount at Urfa; the statue has gone, the Syriac inscription remains to this day. The only two effigies in stone found at Urfa are of women. Women appear prominently in the mosaics of Edessa. Their necklaces and gold brooches and, most of all, their placid features, indicate the dignity of their position. We can trace the change of fashion in female headwear. In the 'Family Portrait' Mosaic (as in another mosaic now destroyed) a young girl wears three combs in her hair. But her aunt and grandmother wear high hats with two bands of cloth (?); and so, too, does a lady in the 'Funerary Couch' Mosaic. In the less wealthy family of the 'Tripod' Mosaic the woman's hat is lower. A different hat is found in the sculptured bust of a certain Shalmath; this type of hat resembles the headgear worn by Kurdish women of Urfa at the present day.

The Harranians ate meat only if the animals had been slaughtered in accordance with ritual regulations, by severing the jugular vein and the gullet. The method resembled that of Islam, and there was much argument by Moslem theologians as to whether it was permissible to eat meat prepared by Sabians. More species of animals were forbidden to the Harranians than to Moslems. Not only were dogs and pigs prohibited, but also camels; Sabians believed that ill luck would follow if they passed under the nose-rein of a camel. They would not eat fish, pigeons and chickens. It is related of the famous Sabian secretary Ibrahim ibn Hilal that he declined to eat these foods when he was entertained at the house of the Vizier. 'Do not let the food grow cold', urged the Vizier. 'Eat some of these beans with us.' 'O Vizier', replied the Sabian, 'I shall not disobey God in my food.' For garlic and broad beans, too, were forbidden to Sabians; some refused to eat also kidney beans, cauliflower, cabbage and lentils. The rules are said to have derived from medical considerations.

The Harranians seem to have had high regard for wine. The pressing of new wine was an annual occasion for religious festivity. Wine appeared among the offerings to the dead at the festival of the autumn full moon, and the 'Funerary Couch' Mosaic depicts the dead man holding a bowl of wine. Wine was poured over animal victims at the time of sacrifice. Nevertheless, abstemiousness in intoxicating drink was held by the Sabians to be a virtue. Indeed, the Sabian Ibrahim ibn Hilal indited verses in honour of wine—but he owed his first advancement to his sobriety. He was at a drinking party with the Vizier and his friends when a messenger arrived for the Caliph demanding the immediate despatch of a letter to a provincial governor. Ibrahim alone had a cool enough head to compose a suitable document – to the admiration of his companions.

Amulets were widely used in Harranian ritual. The left wing

of chickens, stripped of the flesh, was worn by boys and pregnant women. Rings engraved with the shapes of animals were highly esteemed. One of our authors asked why. '(The Harranians) maintain', he writes, 'that they came across them in the tombs of their dead long ago, and that they would win the blessing of God through them.' This may refer to rings worn by the dead, but perhaps it refers rather to pictures of animals in the tombs. Some animals are depicted in the 'Orpheus' Mosaic. In another Edessa mosaic which I have entitled the 'Animal' Mosaic the central section has been largely destroyed, but in the borders animals are represented with lively art. We may imagine the Harranians engraving pictures upon their rings to acquire the *baraka* transmitted from the dead.

The Sabians suffered certain disabilities in their relations with their Moslem neighbours. Some Moslem theologians forbade Moslems to intermarry with Sabians and to share their meals; others permitted it. The separateness of the Sabians was accentuated by their regulations on prayer and festivals and their restrictions on food. In consequence, loyalty to the Sabian community made exacting demands on its members. Nevertheless, those Sabians who achieved distinction in the world of science and letters maintained their links with their fellow-sectarians.

Culture and Science; the Sabian Achievement

It was particularly in the fields of astronomy, medicine and the exact sciences that Sabians won renown. The Syriac-speaking communities, both Christian and pagan, received and transmitted the learning of Greece and Babylonia to the Islamic world and thence to Europe. But the proper observance of Sabian ritual in all its minutiae required an exact acquaintance with natural phenomena that was not required for the practice of Christianity. The association of certain metals with individual planets that was current among the Sabians has its counterpart in the Greek treatises. Knowledge of the relative distance of the planets from the earth was derived by the Sabians from Greece; and from this they allotted each day of the week to a planet, in the order of Saturn, the Sun, the Moon, Mars, Mercury, Jupiter and Venus. The Sabians, then, made their own distinctive contribution to contemporary science, and the extent of their contribution may be recognized in any general analysis of Islamic civilization.

The first Sabian to achieve an outstanding reputation was Thabit ibn Qurrah, born, probably at Harran, in about 836—that is, six years after the visit of al-Ma'mun to Harran. On returning from his studies at Baghdad, Thabit came into conflict with the Sabian authorities at Harran. We are told that he was forbidden access to their temples. Subsequently he recanted, but afterwards his relations with the community again became so strained that he withdrew altogether from Harran. He was later appointed an astronomer to the Caliph at Baghdad, and there he spent most of his life. He was, we are told, on such intimate terms with the Caliph al-Mu'tadid that he alone had the right to sit in the royal presence; even the Vizier stood. Thabit was a prolific translator and writer, and his treatises—which range from metaphysics, history, music and astrology to medicine, mathematics and astronomy—had great influence on contemporary thought. He established a Sabian community at Baghdad and directed its affairs. Thabit's treatise on the doctrines and rites of the Sabians has apparently not survived.

Thabit died in 901. He had established a family tradition of culture which extended over two centuries. His son Sinan, in particular, was physician to the Caliph and founded several hospitals. Sinan's attainments were not confined to medicine; he was also astronomer, philosopher and historian, and he was celebrated as a man of great humanity and tolerance. He adopted Islam, much against his will, but his children remained Sabians. They, too, achieved fame in the same fields of learning.

Another famous Sabian family was descended from a Harranian physician who had settled at nearby Raqqah. His two sons were well-known doctors at Baghdad. His grandson was the celebrated Ibrahim ibn Hilal, to whom we have already alluded, Court secretary in the 10th century and a man of many parts—poet, prose-writer, historian, mathematician and astronomer. He was a devout and loyal Sabian, and he won toleration for Sabian

pl 3
6

pl 7

pl 8
4
f 7
8

pl 8

communities throughout the Empire. Indeed, he refused the post of Vizier rather than desert his faith, and he would not leave Baghdad for fear that his community might suffer in his absence. He typified the Sabian virtues of self-restraint, service, modesty and tolerance; he knew the Koran well and would fast during Ramadan. His son and grandson were well-known writers. The latter also attained high rank as Secretary, but he seems to have become a Moslem.

The Sabian Muhammad ibn Jabir al-Battani, who died in 929, was one of the greatest astronomers and mathematicians of all time. He lived at Raqqah. His astronomical tables and his works on the precession of the equinoxes, on the orbits of the planets and on eclipses were highly esteemed in Europe as well as in the East—as, indeed, they are to the present day.

This efflorescence of Sabian culture and science at Baghdad and other centres of the Moslem Empire—there were other Sabian astronomers, mathematicians, physicians and writers who cannot be mentioned here—had unfortunate consequences for Harran. Its most distinguished sons left it. It declined rapidly. An aura of mystery, it is true, clung to the place. Men told of fossilised skeletons in the nearby mountains. At Byzantium a pleasant story is related of a lady healed of childlessness by a stone believed—falsely—to come from Jacob's well at Harran. From Persia we hear of a Christian deacon educated at Harran, who had learnt there to do service to the devil. He recanted, refused to sacrifice two chickens to his master, and was—his pupils believed—flung to his death. The renown of the alchemists of Harran was known at Court. A certain monk of Harran received rapid promotion to a Bishopric and even to the Patriarchate on the Caliph's personal intervention. But his undertaking to justify this promotion by transmuting base metals into gold was not honoured, and he did not survive long.

Harran's condition worsened. It was a victim of the internecine feuds of petty warlords between the 10th and 12th centuries. In the 11th century the Sabian temple, which had replaced the temple destroyed to make place for a mosque at the beginning of the Moslem occupation, was itself destroyed; but some of the fine buildings erected on the site of Sabian shrines were still to be seen by the Spanish traveller Ibn Jubayr at the end of the 12th century.

'(It) has markets that are admirably disposed and wonderfully arranged. They are all roofed with wood, and men within them are never out of the long shade. You pass through them as you would pass through a house with large corridors . . . The venerated cathedral mosque, which is old but has been restored, is of surpassing beauty . . . We have never seen a mosque with wider arches . . . In the beauty of construction of this mosque and in the fine arrangements of the adjoining markets, we observed a splendid spectacle; and the harmony of design is such as is rarely found in cities. . . .

Harran . . . is a considerable town, with strong and formidable walls . . . It has a strong fortress on its eastern side; . . . the walls of the fortress itself are strongly fortified.'

A century later we have a brief description of the gates and the wide streets of Harran. In one tower were deposited copper *jinn* which were regarded as a talisman against snakes; the Sabian Thabit ibn Qurrah had written a treatise on statuettes as a prophylactic against snakes. The citadel of Harran still stood on the site of a round Sabian temple. But a few years afterwards this last remnant of Sabian worship was razed by the Mongols. The Sabians had disappeared from Harran.

Today Harran retains vestiges of its variegated past—thanks to the labours of archaeologists, notably D. Storm Rice. The imposing ruins of the Great Mosque dominate the countryside, and fine carvings in the walls of the Citadel belong to the Islamic period. Stone lions of 'Hittite' workmanship recall the earliest history of the city. So, too, the well still today called the 'well of Jacob's woman' outside Harran may be identified with the well from which Jacob drew water for the flock of Laban (Gen. 29:10). Between these two widely separated periods of Harranian history the sparse relics of the Sabians serve as a link. The ruins of the Citadel, where stood the last Sabian temple, survive. In the Great Mosque a chapel has been excavated that may once have been a

f 9
10

In the ruins of the Citadel of Harran fine carvings of the Islamic period can still be seen, such as this relief of two dogs on leashes. (9)

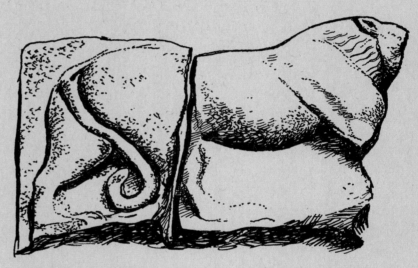

Carved stone lion of Hittite workmanship from the ruins of the Harran citadel. This and similar reliefs are reminders of the earliest period in the city's history. (10)

Sabian shrine. The legend of the local Moslem saint, Hayyat al-Harrani who is said to have had connection with India, reminds us of the Sabian associations with India. Even the peculiar shape of the beehive hovels of the modern village of Harran recalls the cult house of baked bricks shaped like a cone to which the Sabians went out to sacrifice to the planet Mars.

pl 19

Mandaeans—the Sabians of Today?

The Sabians survive, it has been maintained, to the present day, not at Harran but, for the most part, in the marshes at the lower reaches of the Tigris and Euphrates. Here live the Subba, or Mandaeans (perhaps the Syriac term for 'Gnostics'). Their earlier title was Nazarene, and travellers have wrongly called them the 'Christians of St John'. The members of this strange sect—mainly boat-builders and craftsmen in silver and gold—number today no more than a few thousand. Like other isolated minorities in this region of overriding nationalism, they are a rapidly declining community.

The Mandaeans believe that the upper world is represented by the Great King of Light, the Great Life. Inferior to him are countless spiritual beings, some beneficent, others demoniac. The earth was created out of black waters; the Zodiac and the seven planets are the work of evil spirits. The 'Knowledge of Life' and the light-giving powers seek to direct men and women to good actions; the planets and the spirit of physical life incite them to error through Judaism, Christianity, Islam and other 'false religions'. The teacher of the Mandaeans was John the Baptist, himself baptized, while yet a boy, by the 'Knowledge of Life'. Those who lead a good life pass after death to a world of light, others undergo torture, but even the most evil will be purified in a great baptism at the end of the world.

Baptism in flowing water—which the Mandaeans call *yardna*, perhaps connected with the name Jordan—is the most important and characteristic sacrament of the Mandaeans, and from this they derive their name Subba. Simple baptism is performed before all religious ceremonies and daily before sunrise; a state of ritual uncleanness must be removed by triple immersion. Priests carry pl 20 out more complex rites of baptism. A second form of sacrament is the sacred meal of fish, pomegranate, coconuts, and other fruits and nuts. Most religious occasions are marked also by the drinking of consecrated water and the eating of consecrated bread and of *sa* (dough in the shape of a phallus). The burning of incense and the sacrifice of sheep and pigeons are other familiar accompaniments of religious ceremonial, although Mandaeans are reluctant to slay animals. The Mandaeans construct their cult hut (*mandi*) of reeds and mud beside running water. An oblong flat-roofed hut (*andiruna*) is used for weddings and the consecration of priests.

The rites of baptism and the sacred meal are performed at decisive turning-points in the life of the observant Mandaean —at birth, marriage and death. The last is the most momentous, since Mandaean belief in the after-life leads to the punctilious observance of minutiae of ritual at the death bed and funeral. Formal ceremonial is conducted by priests, bearing their insignia of turban and fillet, myrtle wreath, staff, gold signet ring and, on certain occasions, an iron ring carrying the picture of certain animals (as among the Sabians)—lion, scorpion, bee and snake. As among the Sabians, the induction of a new priest lasts seven days; on each day he is instructed in three secret words. At Sabian mysteries 22 words were solemnly uttered.

Mandaeans, like the Sabians, hold that each day and hour of the week is under the influence of a planet. They will not willingly commence an important enterprise unless the omens are favourable. Their year consists of twelve months of thirty days each, followed by five inauspicious days of epact. At the New Year they keep vigil at home for 36 hours, for it is believed that the spirits of light depart from the world to congratulate the Supreme Being at this commemoration of Creation. The New Year is marked by the rebuilding of the cult hut, by the preparation of food, and by baptism. Among formulae uttered by communicants is the phrase, similar to that of the Harranian mysteries, 'Ask and find, speak and listen'. But the Harranians worshipped the planets; the Mandaean invocations include a formal denial of the power of the sun and the moon.

As among the Sabians, Mandaean women may own and inherit property. Divorce is not recognized; the married woman is not expected to remarry—but may in fact do so. A man may have as many wives as he desires. Any plant that produces seed may be eaten by Mandaeans, and vegetables may be eaten freely, provided they are first washed. Animals must be killed by methods of ritual slaughter, but birds of prey, fish-eating birds, fish without scales, camels, horses, pigs, dogs, rabbits, horses and cats are forbidden food.

Are the Mandaeans lineal descendants of the pagans of Harran? Or are they the true Sabians, whose name the Harranians had usurped? According to their own tradition, the Mandaeans originated in Palestine, and went into exile first to Harran, then to Mesopotamia. But Mandaean history lies on the borderland of legend, and although some Mandaean stories go back to the beginnings of Islam or even earlier, their compilation was much later. True, the Mandaean language is akin to the Syriac of Harran. We have seen, too, isolated points of resemblance between Mandaean and Sabian ceremonial—in the formulae of mysteries, the ceremonies at the induction of priests, the use of rings engraved with the pictures of animals. Yet the resemblance may be accidental. The cult of Harran was based upon worship of the planets; in the early Mandaean books the planets are regarded as malevolent. Mandaean religion contains much that is Iranian in origin; there is little trace of Iranian influence at Harran. Mandaeans use a solar calendar; the calendar of Harran was lunisolar. Most important, baptism is the central sacrament among the Mandaeans; it had a minor part at Harran—and it could never have been of importance there, since Harran suffered always from a shortage of water.

We can only speculate on the origin of the Mandaeans and the identity of the Sabians. *Allah a'lam*, the mediaeval historian would say, 'Allah knows best.'

X THE PEOPLES OF THE HIGHLAND

The vanished cultures of Luristan, Mannai and Urartu

E. D. PHILLIPS

U. S. S. R.

CASPIAN SEA

BLACK SEA

Bosporus

Caucasus Mountains

Derbent

TRANSCAUCASIA

ARMENIA

L.Sevan

Karmir Blur (Teshebani)

Mt Ararat

Aras

HITTITE EMPIRE

Halys

Gordium

PHRYGIA

ERZINCAN (Altintepe)

URARTU

L.Van

Van (Tushpa)

AZERBAIJAN

Uaush (Sahend)

Marlik

Amlash

Elburz Mts.

TURKEY

ANATOLIA

Malatya

KURDISTAN

L.Urmia

Kalar Dasht

LYDIA

CAPPADOCIA

LATE HITTITE KINGDOMS

MITANNI

Tell Halaf

HURRIANS

Khabur

Khorsabad

Upper Zab

MANNAI

Hasanlu

Teheran

MESOPOTAMIA

Lower Zab

Ziwiye

IRAN

ASSYRIA

Tigris

Hamadan (Ecbatana)

Siyalk

MEDIA

SYRIA

PHOENICIA

Kermanshah

ZAGROS Mountains

LURISTAN

MEDITERRANEAN SEA

Baghdad

KASSITES

ELAM

PALESTINE

Jordan

Dead Sea

ARAMAEANS

Babylon

AKKAD

SUMER

Euphrates

Ur

PERSIAN GULF

EGYPT

Nile

SCALE
0   100   200   300 MLS.
0   100   200   300   400 KMS.

CASPIAN SEA

L.Urmia

MANNAI

Teheran

Zagros

LURISTAN

IRAN

Harsin

Kermanshah

Tepe Giyan

Nihavand

Siyalk

Kirind

PISH-I-KUH

Alishtar

Khurramabad

Baghdad

Saidmarreh

Kashgan

Surkh-i-Dum

PUSHTI-KUH

Mountains

Euphrates

Tigris

Karkheh

Susa

Babylon

SUMER

KHUZISTAN

0   50   100   150 MLS.
0   100   200 KMS.

Luristan: the dotted line shows where the bronzes were found

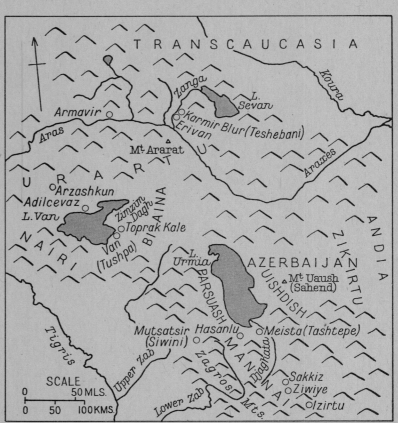

TRANSCAUCASIA

Kouru

Zanga

L.Sevan

Armavir

Karmir Blur (Teshebani)

Aras

Erivan

Araxes

Mt Ararat

URARTU

Arzashkun

Adilcevaz

Zinzin Daghu

L.Van

Toprak Kale

ZIKIRTU

NAIRI

Van (Tushpa)

BIAINA

L. Urmia

AZERBAIJAN

ANDIA

Mt Uaush (Sahend)

UISHDISH

BARSUASH

Tigris

Mutsatsir Hasanlu (Siwini)

MANNAI

Meista (Tashtepe)

Upper Zab

Zagros Mts

Sakkiz

Ziwiye

Lower Zab

Izirtu

SCALE
0   50 MLS.
0   50   100 KMS.

The kingdom of Mannai and the central part of Urartu

222

In the rugged highland

that rises steeply to the east and north of Mesopotamia, country and climate both contrast strongly with the hot, fertile plains of the Tigris and Euphrates valleys. The climate is cooler, the cultivable areas smaller; the people, fewer in numbers but hardier, were frequent raiders of the Mesopotamian lowlands from the 2nd millennium BC to the time, about the middle of the sixth century BC, when they became lost to sight in the history of the Persian Empire. Three of these mountain groups in particular are described here—the peoples of Luristan, Mannai and Urartu. Of the last two we know a little from Assyrian records, but Luristan is known only as the home of the makers of strange decorative bronzework, found by tribesmen in ancient graves which have never been scientifically excavated. All three of these cultures have points in common with other contemporary cultures of the Middle East, but each has also its own unique characteristics. Of the Luristanians nothing certain is known, but they may be of the same stock as the Kassites and Hurrians from Armenia and the Caucasus, and they were certainly involved with those other invaders from the steppes, the Cimmerians and Scythians. Like these, they used the horse in war; elaborately worked bits and cheekpieces are frequent finds in their graves.

A variety of styles influenced the art of these highlanders, several sometimes combining in one piece, as in this Mannaean gold plaque from Ziwiye. The human-headed winged bull is pure Assyrian, the lion-griffin (top left) Assyrian too, but with Iranian influence. The Tree of Life (right-hand edge) is a Mesopotamian symbol, and the prancing ibex is partly Scythian. (1)

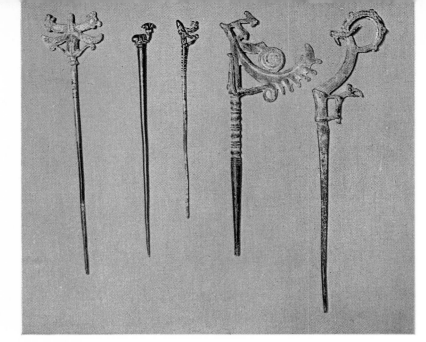

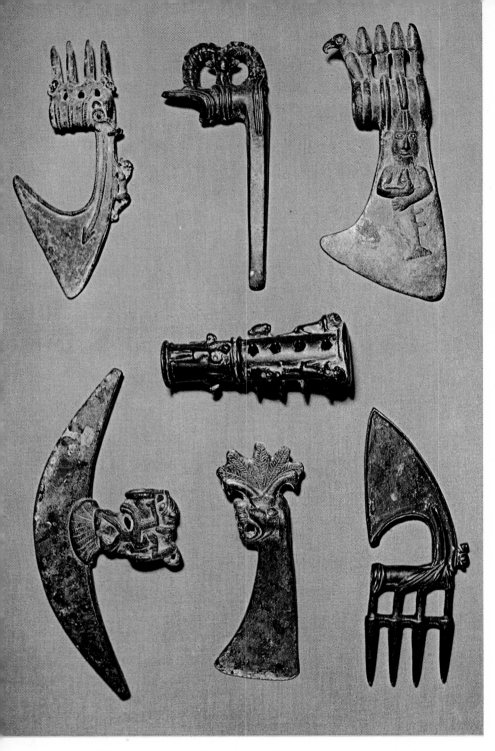

The ornamental bronzes of Luristan are unique in their strange mingling of human and animal motifs. Complete figures appear on the faces or backs of axe-blades (above), or on the socket or the strange finger-like decoration at the back of the socket. Sometimes blades are modelled in such a way as to appear to be coming out of an animal's mouth. In some, the cutting edges are set at an angle, even at right angles, to the haft; these would have been quite unpractical as weapons or tools and must have had some ceremonial use. (2)

The decoration of horses' bits is one of the most elaborate and typical forms of Luristanian bronzework. Linked bits with fairly simply figured vertical side-bars (above) resemble others often found outside Luristan. More peculiar are those with a rigid mouth-bar and intricately worked cheekplates. The latter may be simple animal figures (left); or animals with wings or human heads (opposite); or they may be compositions, in a square or oblong frame. At the foot of the opposite page is one which uses the sweeping curve of rams' horns to form an attractive design. Another example (this page) shows a hero or a god mastering two heraldic beasts, which may be a native artist's variation on the Babylonian theme of the hero Gilgamish. (3–7)

◀ **Even on pins** the same strange motifs are found (left), with animal heads, simple at first, soon elaborated out of all recognition. (8)

The 'Gilgamish' hero appears again in bronze finials (below), sometimes with a second face at the navel and extra heads springing, in the Scythian manner, from the beasts' hindquarters. Or the hero may dwindle and vanish altogether. Bearded gods decorate these finials, too, and charming little fertility goddesses clasping their breasts (right). (9–12)

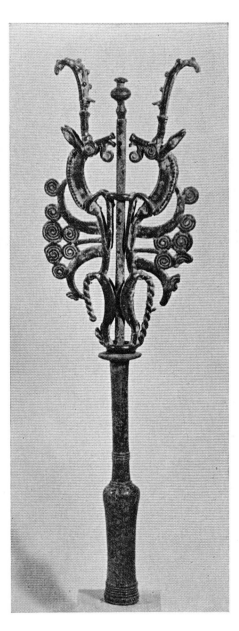

Bronze vessels with long beaked spouts, some with lively animal handles, have been found in Luristanian graves. That these are widespread Iranian types is shown by comparison with the 9th-century BC pottery vessel below, from Siyalk. (13, 14)

A most impressive piece of Luristan metalwork is this bronze ewer, uncharacteristic in the simplicity of its line. A succession of rib mouldings round the body adds strength and dignity. It may have been a cult vessel. (15)

The round face of the sun-god Mithra figures on many large disk-headed pins, probably of a votive nature, that are often found in Luristan graves. In the example above, fantastic animals gallop after each other round the central face, and among them a strange creature, apparently human but with a tail, squats on his haunches. (16)

The central boss of a shield also bears the face which may represent Mithra. On either side can be seen a rampant lion, representing the animal attribute of the god, and underneath is a bull, his sacrificial victim. (17)

226

Tantalizing glimpses
of the religious life of Luristan are
given by the figures on plaques and
quiver-plates, but interpretation is
highly conjectural. The three bronze
quiver-plates below can be roughly
dated (l. to r.) to 12th–11th century
BC, 8th–7th century, and c. 1000 BC.

In the ruined temple of Surkh-i-Dum many straight-sided
plaques were found, like the three above, which may have been
belt or quiver plaques. For the most part they show none of the
obsession with horses that is so prominent among the bronzes
from Luristan graves; instead, in light repoussé, they show
religious scenes which, if they could be interpreted with certainty,
would tell us much about the Luristanians and their interaction
with the peoples around them. The Tree of Life on the left is a
Mesopotamian symbol. In the centre Mithra and his lions are
again among the figures. The right-hand plate has been interpreted as a hierarchy of Indic deities. In the topmost of the three
registers containing human figures are Varuna with his sacred ox,
and Mithra, the twin rulers of the universe; below these, Indra
the storm-god with the Maruts, his attendants, in the form of

lions; below these again the Nasatya twins render medical service
to an aged being whom they are perhaps rejuvenating. In other
plates, Magian priests appear, with their sacred wands of tamarisk,
and, as we shall see (pl. 23), the Zoroastrian gods Ahura Mazda
and Ahriman. Whatever the true interpretation of these strange
figures may be, they seem to belong to the Aryan religion introduced by the Iranian Medes and Persians, if not to the earlier
religion of the Kassite nobility with the influences absorbed from
their long domination over the Babylonians. Perhaps these two
kindred stocks, and their religions, overlapped for a time in Luristan. However that may be, the absence of the horse motifs in
the Surkh-i-Dum bronzes indicates that their makers were settled
cultivators, though of the same race as the nomad horse-breeders
farther north. (18–20)

227

A small bronze deity from Pusht-i-Kuh, in south-west Luristan, dated to c. 1000 BC, is a silent witness to troubled times. Across his skirt a much later (c. 600 BC) neo-Babylonian cuneiform inscription tells how this statuette (a local god) was plundered from its temple and later restored. The style of the figure is entirely native, particularly in the face. (21)

Imports from Mesopotamia are sometimes found among the Luristanian bronzes. This bronze bowl, much earlier in date than the bits and other Luristan bronzes, is inscribed with the name of King Shargalisharri of Akkad (2233–2208 BC), and may have been a present to a native chieftain. (22)

Undoubted evidence of old Iranian religion is seen in this silver plaque from Luristan. In the centre is Zurvan, the hermaphrodite god of infinite time (note the female face below the bearded male face). From either shoulder emerge the twins Ahura Mazda, Lord of Wisdom, and Ahriman, spirit of darkness and evil. Zurvan was also the embodiment of the three ages of man, and here we see rows of figures representing adolescence (seated, left), maturity (standing, left), and old age, presenting the sacred *barsom* as symbol of authority to the newborn twins. The opposition of Ahura Mazda and Ahriman, and this myth of their birth, are certainly characteristic of Zoroastrianism, but this plaque suggests that they are older too. (23)

Between the hammer and the anvil,
a buffer state attacked alternately by Assyria and Urartu, Mannai had a troubled history. The Mannaeans inhabited the fertile plains and valleys south of Lake Urmia, and throughout our period the Assyrians and Urartians fought over them. Sargon II of Assyria has left a full account of his campaign of 714 BC which he fought to assert his power in Mannai, when, as he says, the cities he destroyed were 'countless as the stars of heaven'. By the time of Sargon's grandson Esarhaddon, the Mannaeans were a danger to Assyria once more, and the nomad Scythians from the northern steppes also made their first appearance in the Assyrian chronicles —some on the side of Mannai, and others, under their chief Bartatua, as allies of Assyria. When the Medes swept in from the east in 616 BC, Mannai was allied to Assyria once more, and

the Assyrians and Mannaeans went down to extinction together.

With no certainly native inscriptions of their own, the Mannaeans live only in Assyrian records of conquest, and in the magnificent finds of Ziwiye and Hasanlu.

A rich treasure of gold was found, packed in a bronze coffin, at Ziwiye in Kurdistan, on the southern edge of the Mannai country. One theory is that this treasure, which shows a wide variety of styles, belonged to the Scythian chief Bartatua, and was buried with him. The gold plaque above shows two Assyrian winged lions, their heads curiously merged into one, under a Tree of Life. (24)

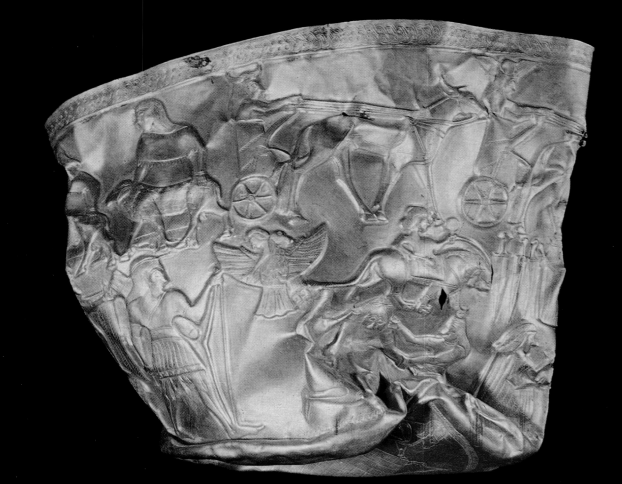

The golden bowl of Hasanlu, a solid gold vessel of great value, was found in eerie circumstances in the burnt ruins of a fortress that must have been sacked by the Urartians. Together with the skeletons of three men, it was found crushed under the debris of a collapsed upper floor; whether the men were looting, or rescuing a precious object, one can only guess. On the upper register (above) a procession of deities in light chariots is led by what seems to be a weather god, drawn by a bull from whose mouth comes a stream of water. This recalls the weather gods of Syria, Asia Minor and Mesopotamia after 2000 BC. In the lower register a hero with mailed boxing gloves fights a fearsome monster whose fish tail ends in three snarling dogs' heads. On the reverse (left) are a god with horned head-dress in the Mesopotamian style, and a goddess riding an eagle. Everything indicates that this is a piece of local art, made under Hurrian influence a considerable time before the fall of Hasanlu. (25, 26)

Fold out ▶

A rich royal burial has recently been uncovered at Marlik, just south of the Caspian Sea and a little way east of the Mannaean country. The Marlik finds, which date from the early first millennium BC, belong to a culture which shows affinities with Mannai. The gold vase (left) has two registers of graceful, long-legged unicorns prancing round in opposite directions. The unicorns may be modelled not on horses but on the wild ass or onager of Iran, since their tails are not like horses' tails and their ears are too large for horses'. The tuft-like ornaments on back and legs may represent wings, which would suit heavenly creatures. The same tufts and the same form of tail appear on fully winged horses (or onagers) in some Luristanian cheekpieces. The rosettes in the background have some religious significance, to judge by others found in mythological scenes on the plaques from Surkh-i-Dum. The high relief of this vase is developed further in the gold vase below (left), where the heads of the winged bulls, worked in one with the body of the vase, stand out a full two centimetres from the surface. This vase in turn recalls a bowl (below) from Kalar Dasht near the Caspian Sea, on which three lions, similarly vigorous in style, are not worked in relief but made separately and riveted on. All three objects on this page are roughly contemporary with the Hasanlu and Ziwiye finds, and the lively, stylized animal figures may well have influenced the bronzesmiths of Luristan. (31–33)

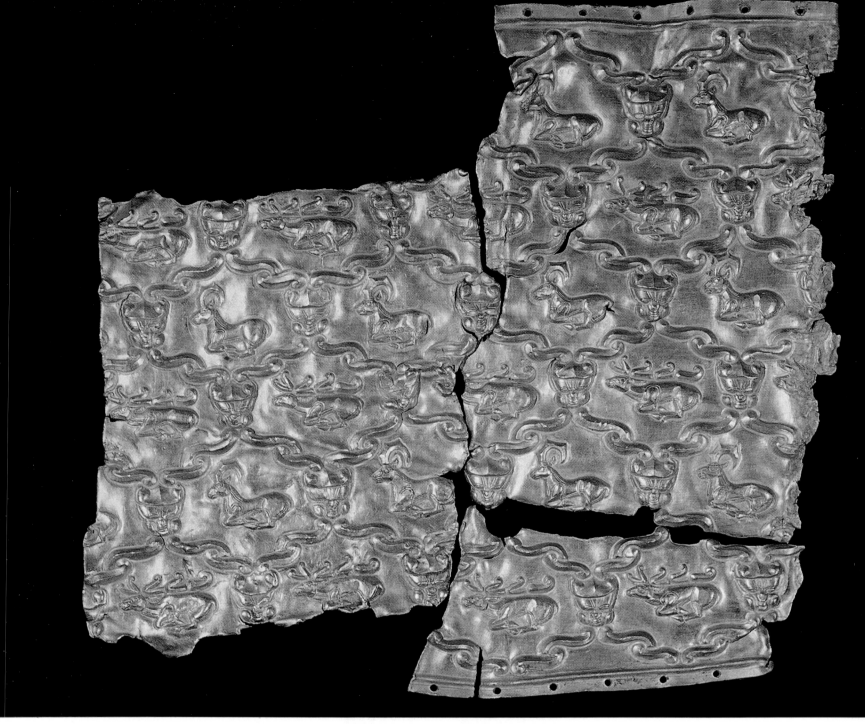

Crouching Scythian stags alternate with Iranian ibexes in the same position, on this gold plaque from Ziwiye (above). The repetitive design is enclosed in conventionalized branches spreading from lions' heads of Iranian type. The piece might have been designed as an exercise in the mingling of two styles. (29)

One of the finest pieces of craftsmanship among the Ziwiye treasure, this magnificent gold bracelet dates to the 7th century BC. One of the lion-head terminals is detachable, to make the bracelet easier to put on and take off. The teeth and tongues were separately made. (30)

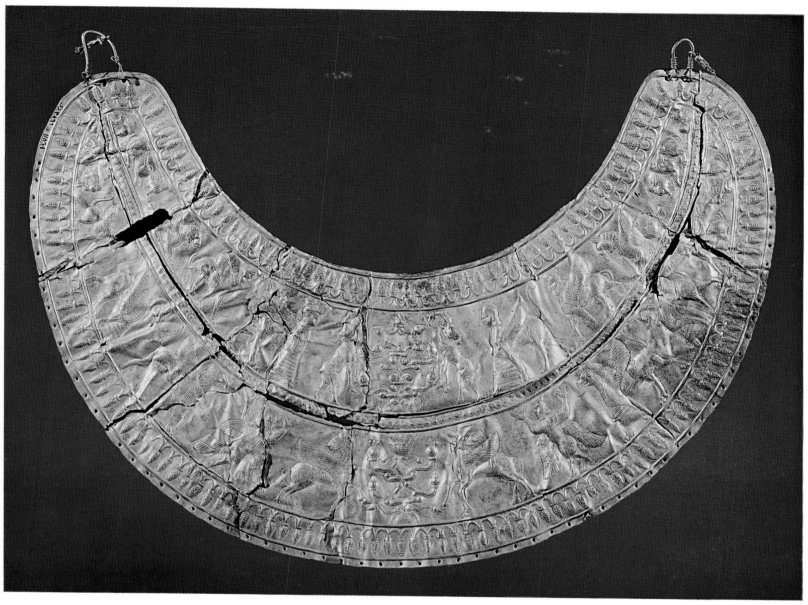

An elaborate gold pectoral from the Ziwiye treasure (above) shows Egyptian and Assyrian mythological figures, Scythian animals and a Mesopotamian Tree of Life all combined in one object. (27)

A ram's head in gold, astonishingly life-like in spite of its sophisticated stylization, forms a drinking-cup or a rhyton—an Iranian theme enriched by Mannaean craftsmanship. It was found at Ghaflantou near Ziwiye. (28)

One of the great powers

of the Near East in the early 1st millennium BC was the Kingdom of Urartu, centred round the shores of Lake Van. The Urartians, remnants of the wider Hurrian world of the second millennium, first appear as a unified state in the middle of the 9th century BC, when Shalmaneser III made great efforts to crush it. From both Urartian and Assyrian records much of the stormy history of Urartu can be pieced together, though there is some difficulty in distinguishing between new conquests and the defeat of rebellions in already conquered territory. The Urartians were road-builders and engineers of great skill; to hold down their subject peoples they built military roads and constructed massive fortresses at strategic spots. At the period of its greatest extent, the power of Urartu was felt from the Caspian to the shores of the Mediterranean; in the east they were in conflict with the Medes, and in the north they may have encountered the first Scythians to come down into Transcaucasia. By the 7th century BC, in the time of Esarhaddon of Assyria, the Scythian flood began in earnest. The great Urartian fortress of Karmir Blur was destroyed by these invaders from the steppes, a blow from which Urartu never fully recovered. The kingdom lingered on, in a reduced state, and actually outlasted Assyria, until finally, about 585 BC, it fell to the Medes who had already annihilated Assyria.

Enough examples of Urartian art have now been recovered from the well-known Armenian sites and, among other objects, from such places as Ziwiye and Scythian sites north of the Caucasus, to show not only the influences that shaped it but also the influence that it exerted in its turn. In bronzework this may be traceable as far off as Greece and Etruria.

Siwini, city of the sun-god, otherwise called Mutsatsir, contained a temple devoted to Haldi, the national god of Urartu. This reconstruction shows how the temple probably appeared when, newly built, it was adorned with statues and objects of gold and silver, ivory and bronze, in preparation for the crowning of the king, Urzana, a vassal of Urartu. In the background is the temple, with bronze shields hanging between the pillars and a tall, lance-shaped finial, symbol of the god Haldi, rising above the gable. By the temple steps the king watches from his chariot as the temple furnishings are brought in. Huge bronze cauldrons, piles of votive lances in bronze or gold, massive eagle-headed winged griffins, tall diademed statues in painted stone like the one shown here of the former king Argishti I—all these and many more would have been brought to beautify the temple for the king's coronation. This we know from a bas-relief at Khorsabad, which records in detail the plundering of this temple by Sargon of Assyria. (34)

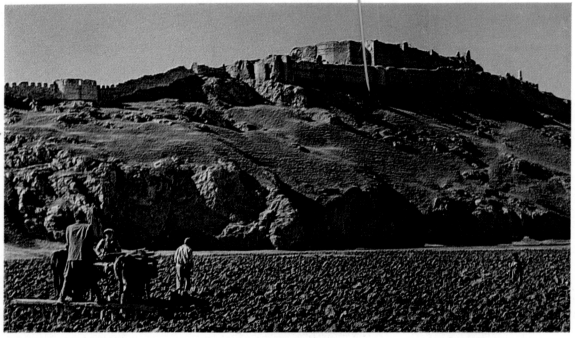

The royal citadels at Van Kale (left) and Toprak Kale were tremendous examples of Urartian military engineering. In the hills above Lake Van, Sarduri I, king of Urartu (832–825 BC), built a battlemented fortress both as a base for the control of his subject provinces and as a defence against the Assyrians. On the northern side (opposite) the rock face is precipitous and easily defensible. Later, this site was abandoned by Rusa I for the heights of Toprak Kale (opposite, right), five kilometres farther from the lake. A rock-cut chamber, and vast storage jars of as much as 130 gallons' capacity, indicate that Toprak Kale was designed to withstand a long siege. (35–37)

In remote mountain valleys

south-west of the Caspian Sea, bordering on Mannai and Urartu but to a large extent cut off from contact with other cultures, potters and bronzesmiths of the early 1st millennium BC were producing work that shows some affinities with neighbouring lands. The Marlik culture we have already met (pls. 31, 32); Amlash, in the same region, is another such culture, dating to about the 9th-8th centuries BC, and coming to light only in the last few years when some of its products, found by peasants, reached the antiquities market of Teheran.

A bronze mace-head (above) from Amlash is decorated with three merging human faces. The jutting noses, which doubtless added to its lethal qualities, echo the facial characteristics seen on some Urartian pieces (see opposite). (38)

From the royal burial at Marlik comes the silver cup above, with its linear and relief design showing a warrior grappling with two leopards, and also two fine pieces of pottery. The charming seated bear may have been some kind of jug; the mouth is extended to form a short spout. The animal figures in pottery from Marlik are very like those from Amlash. The triple vase, an elegant, sophisticated form, is in fine grey slip, now cream-coloured with age. (39-41)

236

The bony, arched nose of the Urartian aristocracy—so different from the typical Assyrian face—is clearly seen in the 7th-century BC gold medallion and silver pectoral above, which were found at Toprak Kale. Both of these show the same scene, a seated goddess approached by a female worshipper. In the pectoral, the worshipper is bringing a sacrificial animal. (42, 43)

Assyrian influence is stronger in the helmet and shield of bronze belonging to Argishti I of Urartu, which were found at Karmir Blur. The figures ritually tending the Tree of Life are typically Assyrian, but the strange curving snakes are Urartian. The stalking lions, too, on the shield are leaving the Assyrian tradition behind; they are longer-legged and less ferocious, and quite un-Assyrian in their tip-toe stance and curving tails. (44, 45)

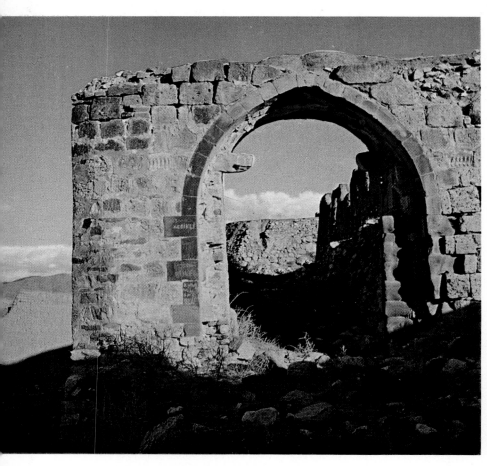

On the hill of Van Kale are also the ruins of a mediaeval fort. This sturdy archway, which was part of it, shows masonry taken from the Urartian citadel. (46)

To withstand a siege of long duration Karmir Blur was provided with storage facilities for its defenders and the citizens who gathered within its walls. Soviet archaeologists have found two great storerooms (one of which is shown below), containing 152 huge storage jars, which would have held 350,000 gallons of wine or oil, or 4,400 bushels of corn. (47)

An outpost of the Urartian empire was the fortress of Teshebani, now Karmir Blur near Erivan in Soviet Armenia. Here Russian archaeologists have carried out excavations which have provided a clear picture of this centre of imperial government, and of its destruction by the Scythian hordes about 625 BC. The reconstruction above, based on these finds, shows the scene as it must have been when the Scythians broke through a side gate into the citadel. Blazing arrows shot over the walls set fire to wooden-roofed buildings, and horses and cattle, herded on to the roofs for safety, crashed through to the floors with the burning rafters. Here, lying on top of the charred timber and amid the debris of collapsed walls, their bodies were found two and a half millennia later, some still partly preserved in the ashes. Trilobar Scythian arrowheads sticking in the walls of the lower town add a vivid touch to the grim picture this excavation presents. (48)

The military architecture of the Urartians is strikingly illustrated by this bronze model of a fortress, found at Toprak Kale. Information can be gained from it about their treatment of doors, windows and battlements, such as seldom if ever emerges from actual excavations. These models were quite common; one is shown being carried in a procession bearing tribute for a king of Assyria. (49)

This bronze ritual cauldron, inscribed with Urartian cuneiform, was found at Altintepe, 200 miles from Van towards the Black Sea. It is ornamented with bull's-head protomes as handles. (50)

Similar protomes are found as far afield as Italy. Of the two examples above, the lower is a bull's head from Toprak Kale, the upper, a griffin head on a cauldron from Praeneste, Etruria. (51, 52)

Human heads were also shown in the form of protomes, and the aristocratic Urartian nose appears in a number of these attachments from widely separated sites in Anatolia and the Mediterranean region. Of the four strikingly similar examples on the left, the uppermost is from Toprak Kale, the right-hand one from Gordium in Phrygia, the lowest one from Praeneste and the other from Olympia in Greece. Some of this spread may be due to the influence of skilled Urartian metal-workers, some to direct exports for which access to the Mediterranean must have been possible. (53)

The vanished cultures of Luristan, Mannai and Urartu

E. D. PHILLIPS

Of the three peoples discussed below, the Urartians, the Mannaeans and the makers of the Luristan bronzes (whoever they were), the two first do appear in written history, namely the records of Assyrian conquest, but the last survive only as the makers of a great number of objects, discovered by Lur tribesmen and sold to dealers of antiquities during this century. It was of course only in the last century that the Assyrian cuneiform yielded its secrets; and our knowledge of all three is therefore modern and as yet fragmentary. All three are in fact lost peoples, whose vague features are just beginning to emerge through the mists of antiquity. Archaeology can indeed provide facts from which reputable hypotheses can be built up; but in all three cases archaeology has been bedevilled in a number of ways. There has been no scientific excavation of a Luristan bronze site; Mannaean sites are just beginning to come under the spade, the Ziwiye treasure having been discovered clandestinely; and Urartian sites, from their geography, lie on the frontiers of Turkey, Iran and Russia and tend to fall in areas of military security, with all that that signifies in the world of today.

THE REGION now called Luristan and those once known to the Assyrians as Mannai and Urartu all belong to the great stretch of rugged highland that rises steeply to the east and north of Mesopotamia. Here parallel ranges of mountains run north-westward from the eastern shore of the Persian Gulf to form the western edge of the Iranian plateau, and continue afterwards in a westerly direction through Armenia into Anatolia. All parts of the highland have much in common to contrast them with the hot and fertile plains of Mesopotamia, where in ancient times irrigation from the great rivers supported a dense population and great cities. The climate is much cooler, indeed extremely cold in winter, there is more rainfall, and the cultivable areas are mostly small and light in soil, and except in certain favoured places much less rewarding to any irrigation that may be possible. The population is therefore much sparser and much more mobile, and has in most periods of history been ready enough to make raids into Mesopotamia.

On the Fringes of the Mesopotamian Empires

The peoples of Luristan, Mannai and Urartu in such a geographical situation all owed something to the great civilizations of Sumer, Babylonia and Assyria, but each had its own culture, which was not merely a provincial or barbarous version of the Mesopotamian. We shall be concerned with their histories from the later part of the 2nd millennium BC onward for some centuries, until they merge with the history of the Persian Empire. Though the best known remains in all three regions belong to these centuries, the highland cultures of this period are the result of widespread migrations and conflicts which had involved the whole of Western Asia in the 2nd millennium. These earlier disturbances claim our attention first.

During the 2nd millennium the long process began by which Indo-European peoples from the northern steppes beyond the Caucasus established themselves about Western Asia, Iran and northern India. Their earliest pressure perhaps drove some of the native peoples of the mountains to migrate or infiltrate and sometimes to come as invaders into Mesopotamia and northern Syria, even in the 3rd millennium. The Indo-Europeans then drove their way through these peoples, drawing many of them in their train as subjects or allies, and appeared themselves early in the 2nd millennium as invaders and conquerors in the Near East. For the first half of the millennium the highlanders under Indo-European leadership dominated the older peoples of the plains, most of whom were Semites. The most powerful of these Indo-Europeans were the Hittites who ruled Anatolia, and later extended their dominion over northern Syria, but their connection with our three cultures is not direct, unless more Hittite influence was felt in Urartu than has so far appeared. Two other peoples are directly relevant, namely the Kassites from the Zagros mountains in the region of Luristan, and the Hurrians, who spread from regions further north, particularly from Armenia.

Both were themselves native peoples of the highland, and spoke languages which were not Indo-European, but belonged to a group sometimes loosely called Caucasian, once widespread but later surviving only in the Caucasus. They were led by Indo-European aristocracies small in numbers but great in energy and achievement. They were the first to use the horse in war to draw the light chariot with spoked wheels. Indo-European names of gods at least appear among the Kassites, and of gods and rulers much more obviously among the Hurrians, in whom this element was clearly stronger. In both cases the names reveal the Indic branch of the Indo-European family, of which the main body moved through Iran to conquer northern India.

The Kassites were already dangerous enemies of Babylon by the 17th century in the time of Hammurabi's successors, and at the end of the 16th they had established their own dynasty there. This lasted until 1171 BC, longer than any other domination of the mountaineers, and never lost touch with its original home in Luristan. During their rule the Kassites formed a military caste keenly interested in horses and somewhat separate from the ordinary population. In their time Babylon was the least of the major powers, and little achievement is recorded of them, but in any case their memory was not cherished by the Babylonians.

The Hurrians on the other hand were at their height as active as any other power. Their states in northern Mesopotamia and Syria under the chief of them, the kingdom of Mitanni, endured until the 14th century. The Mitannian kings, ruling from their capital at Wassuganni on the Khabur, fought for a time on equal terms with the Egyptians who were pressing northward through Syria under the Eighteenth Dynasty, and for a time they held Assyria in subjection. On their northern frontier they were at first equally successful against the third partly Indo-European power, the Hittites. But in the 14th century their realm was destroyed from opposite sides by the Hittites and the resurgent Assyrians. They never again formed a state of their own in the lowlands.

Thereafter until the early years of the 12th century the Near East was dominated by four great powers who achieved a certain equilibrium, the Egyptian and Hittite empires in the west and the Assyrian and Kassite Babylonian kingdoms in the east. This international order was finally broken by a new wave of migration from the north, set in motion by further Indo-European peoples but involving others, which left Assyria and Babylonia intact, but overthrew the Hittites in their homeland, and ended the Egyptian empire in Asia. In Central Anatolia the Indo-European Phrygians from Thrace became the dominant people, but on the southern edge and in northern Syria small states persisted which still used the Hittite language for some purposes, as their kings' names show, and which counted some remnants of the Hurrians among their subjects. They and the Phrygians further north were the western neighbours of Urartu. They were eventually destroyed by the expanding power of Assyria.

The growth of the Assyrian power was in one aspect a strong reaction against the earlier dominance of the highland peoples. Assyrian records tell of highland campaigns with a particular pride and give much detail. They are in fact the main source of historical information on the peoples of Mannai and Urartu

EAST ANATOLIA ARMENIA URARTU   NORTH-WEST IRAN MANNAI

BC	EAST ANATOLIA ARMENIA URARTU	NORTH-WEST IRAN MANNAI	BC
1600			1600
1500			1500
1400			1400
1300			1300
	Urartu mentioned (as Uruatri) by SHALMANESER I		
1200	END OF THE BRONZE AGE IN THE NEAR EAST		1200
1100			1100
1000			1000
		Citadel of Hasanlu built? Iranian tribes moving south *Metal work of Amlash and Kalar Dasht?*	
900	Arame begins to form kingdom of Urartu. SHALMANESER III attacks; captures Arzashkun. Urartians adopt cuneiform script	SHALMANESER III attacking Medes and Parsuash; takes Zirta	900
	SARDURI I 832–825? Capital moved to Tushpa (Van Kale)		
800	ISPUINI 824–805? Urartian empire extended		800
	MENUAS 815–790?		
	ARGISHTI I 789–766? **Urartian power at its greatest**	MENUAS captures Hasanlu? and Meista	
	SARDURI II 765–733?	Urartian domination in Mannai. SARGON's 8th campaign in Mannai (714)	
700	RUSA I 732–714 Capital moved to Toprak Kale		700
	ARGISHTI II 713–679? Attacks by Cimmerians and Assyrians		
	RUSA II 678–654? Scythians in Urartu	Scythians temporarily in Mannai. *Treasure of Ziwiye? c. 670*	
	SARDURI III 654–625? Destruction of Teishebani?	Median empire	
	ERIMENAS 624–606? Armenians beginning to enter Urartu	Persian empire	
600	RUSA III 605?–585 Armenia part of Persian empire		600

during our period, though they have little to say of Luristan. Urartian inscriptions are much more difficult to interpret and are much fewer, but they do reveal that the Urartians were a Hurrian people. The Urartians were mostly no doubt descended from Hurrians who had never left Armenia, but they must have recognized their kinship with the Hurrian elements further south and have received support from these when they attempted to dominate the remnants of the Hittite states and northern Syria.

The Urartians are still the best known, as they are the most important, of our three peoples. But now the pace of discovery is quickening in Iran, which until this generation had been little explored for remains of our period, except in the area of ancient Elam in the extreme south-west. The native peoples of its western highlands are beginning to be revealed in their own homes. We are learning more of their interaction with yet other Indo-European invaders, the creative Medes and Persians and the destructive Cimmerians and Scythians, whose movements decided the history of the 1st millennium, in the highlands at first, and later throughout Western Asia. This is the background to the archaeological discoveries made in the region, which will now be described.

Herdsmen and Bronze-workers of Luristan

Among the several distinct regions of the Iranian plateau Luristan in the southern Zagros Mountains has become famous during the last thirty years for the peculiar bronze-work which will be our primary interest here. Though they have affinities with other metal-work, the Luristan bronzes in their full development seem to be peculiar to this one region. The first problem for archaeologists and historians of art is to date them and to decide who

made them; the second, to explain why they should be confined to Luristan and its immediate neighbourhood, except for a few stray specimens which might be exports. There are also the questions of the foreign influences that they show and of the influence which their style in turn exercised on the art of nomad peoples often far from Iran. Lastly there is another class of bronzes from Luristan executed in a different manner and apparently having a purely religious significance.

Most of the Luristan bronzes were found in graves belonging to large cemeteries in the upland plains and in the valleys among the Zagros to the south of the well-known route that runs from Baghdad through Kirind and Kermanshah to Hamadan, the ancient Ecbatana, and northern Iran. The first were discovered accidentally in 1928 by a Lur tribesman working in his field. When they proved to be valuable antiquities, the Lurs, living in difficult country and famous for robbery and violence, easily kept the supply entirely in their own hands. They discovered more and more graves by prodding the ground with rods about three feet long at likely places near springs and ancient settlements, until they struck the covering slabs of stone below. Naturally they rifled the graves without any scientific supervision, and perfectly destroyed most of the evidence apart from the bronzes themselves.

In such circumstances no map can be attempted to show the distribution of sites. The area from which the typical bronzes came lies to the south of Kermanshah, Harsin and Nihavand, on the plains of Khava, Dilfan and Alishtar, further west in the plains of Hulailan and Turkhan, and generally in the basin of the river Saidmarreh as it flows through the gorges of the region called Pish-i-Kuh into Khuzistan. Similar bronzes, but of more archaic

f 1
2

	WEST AND SOUTH-WEST IRAN LURISTAN	ASSYRIA BABYLONIA	
BC	Kassites under Indic rule begin to be dangerous to Babylon	HAMMURABI 1728–1686	BC
1600		Hurrians dominant in Assyria; begin to form states in N. Mesopotamia under Indo-European rulers of the Indic branch	1600
1500		Kassite conquest of Babylon, c. 1530 Kassite dynasty in Babylonia	1500
1400		Mitannian kingdom (Wassuganni) dominates N. Mesopotamia	1400
1300		ASSUR-UBALLIT I (1356–1330?)	1300
1200		SHALMANESER I of Assyria 1265–1235 revives Assyrian power, destroys Mitanni	1200
1100	E N D O F T H E B R O N Z E	A G E I N T H E N E A R E A S T Kassite dynasty overthrown, 1171	1100
1000	Iranian tribes begin to move through Iran. *Earliest Luristan bronzes?*		1000
900			900
800	SHALMANESER III fighting Medes near Hamadan, 836 Median power steadily growing	SHALMANESER III, 858–824	800
700	Cimmerians with Medes in the Zagros. *Late Luristan bronzes?* CYAXARES, reigning in Media, drives Scythians back north	TIGLATH-PILESER III 745–727 SARGON II 721–705 SENNACHERIB 704–681 ESARHADDON 680–669 ASSURBANIPAL 668–626 Fall of Nineveh 612 End of Assyrian Empire 606	700
600	CYRUS, King of Persia, defeats Medes, 550	New Babylonian Empire until Persian conquest in 539	600

character, come from Pairavand, north-west of Nihavand. Far down the Saidmarreh near its junction with the Kashgan in the plain of Kuh-i-Dasht, the ruins of a temple, this time properly excavated, on the hill of Surkh-i-Dum yielded bronzes of a different type and of great interest.

The graves were shallow and of various shapes, some square, some rectangular, some more rounded, some of a long oval form. They were usually less than one metre wide and seldom more than two long. They were walled with vertical slabs of stone or with smaller stones, and roofed with two or more large slabs according to size and shape. In the shorter graves the skeletons were in crouching position, in the longer laid out at full length. Exceptionally, very large graves contained several skeletons, even twenty or more, laid cross-wise in a row, and according to some reports, the skeletons of horses. Sometimes skeletons were in great jars laid horizontally, a form of burial known also from Transcaucasia. These varieties of burial seem to have been determined by local circumstances and cannot be arranged in a chronological sequence. None were so elaborate as to deserve the title of royal tombs.

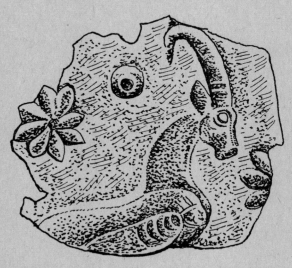

Fragment of a Luristan bronze (left), showing head and part of the body of an ibex. Comparison with the Scythian-style gold ibex from Ziwiye *(right) suggests that Luristanian bronze work may have had some influence on the Scythian animal style. (1, 2)*

243

The contents of the tombs were all of the most portable
kind. The pottery was little different from that of neighbouring
parts of Iran during the same period: yellowish-grey vases and
pots, particularly pots with long spouts painted in black with
geometric or animal designs. Of the bronzes a high proportion
were ornamental trappings for horses or chariots, often representing horses and other hoofed animals, wild or tame. These
would be the remains of a people of herdsmen and horsebreeders
who had few settlements and little agriculture. They could have
lived very much as the modern Lurs, who live as herdsmen in
tents of black goatskin, practising a little cultivation but regularly moving with their animals and gear between winter and
summer pastures at different altitudes. Transhumance, as this
mode of life is called, has always been common in Iran and in
eastern Caucasia, and differs only in degree from the full nomadism
of the wide steppes.

The Bronzes

Though the swords, daggers and vessels differ little from those
found in neighbouring regions, the ornamental bronzes are
unique, and the animal decoration of axe-heads and whetstone-
handles at least distinctive. To assume that stylization of animal
and human figures increased with time is natural but risky.

Horses' bits are of two fundamental kinds. Those with mouth-
pieces in two links, and cheek-pieces which are simple vertical
bars with ring-attachments, are like those used by other horsemen
or charioteers outside Luristan. Peculiar to Luristan are those
which consist of a heavy mouth-bar in one piece and of cheek-
pieces most elaborately worked. Some of the cheek-pieces are
in the natural forms of horses, bulls, sheep, deer or other animals;
others represent these with wings or human heads, or more
fantastic animals with a head at either end of their backs. More
elaborate still are compositions of figures, sometimes in a square
or oblong frame, in which a hero like the Babylonian Gilgamish grasps and masters two beasts symmetrically disposed on
either side of him, or again stands glaring on the back of a horse,
or rides with bent bow in a chariot drawn by fantastic long-legged
lions. Rein-guides for chariots are also known, which show
some of these motifs in square or round frames, the latter often
made by the curving horns of a ram.

But the strangest ornaments are the tubular figures or finials.
The tubular figures often represent a bearded god or a goddess of
fertility holding her breasts. The finials, like some of the pin-
heads, once more represent a hero mastering beasts, but the
development is much more fantastic. The hero and beasts
sometimes appear to be fused into one, or the hero may grow a
second face at the navel and a third at the groin, or he may
dwindle into a pole, or vanish into a space, across which the beasts
confront one another heraldically. Pendants in animal form are
usually more realistic. There are also curious amulets in the
shape of human hands, as in Transcaucasia.

The whetstone-handles are in the form of heads of lions,
rams, deer or ibex, sometimes with long necks. The axe-heads
seem to develop from ancient Mesopotamian types. Some have
remarkably long tubular haft-holes or sockets, and some have
blades set crosswise as in adzes, again a Mesopotamian feature.
The backs of the sockets are decorated with digitations, rows
of finger-like spikes which in later specimens are fashioned into
animals' heads. Sometimes complete animal figures appear on
the backs of the sockets or on the borders of the blades. Sometimes the blades are modelled at the root so that they appear
to be spat out of an animal's mouth. Some are semi-circular
with two large holes at the sides, some are crescent-shaped, and
some droop on their upper borders and have cutting edges that
retreat, so as to be quite unpractical if they were used as weapons
or tools. More difficult to classify are pleasantly naturalistic
figures such as that of a naked goddess holding her breasts and
supporting an ibex on her head, various vessels which are decorated with hunting scenes very much in the Assyrian manner, or a
little figure of a man holding two puppies on leads fastened
round his waist. Mesopotamian influence is shown in a bronze
dagger which is exactly like a Sumerian gold dagger discovered
at Ur. Now and then there are such imports as a bronze bowl
of much earlier date inscribed in the name of King Shargalisharri
of Akkad (2233–2208 BC) and weapons inscribed with Babylonian kings' names, perhaps presents to native chiefs who had
served as mercenaries. Direct traces of Assyrian contact are rare.

Among the pins from the graves are some with large disk-
shaped heads adorned with repoussé work and not pierced
through like the typical bronzes. These, and certain round or
straight-sided plaques suitable to be plates on belts or quivers,
were found much more abundantly among the ruins of the temple
at Surkh-i Dum. The faces, figures and scenes shown seem to
belong to the Aryan religion introduced by the Iranian Medes
and Persians, if not to the earlier, perhaps Indic, form practised
by the Kassite nobility. It is possible that these two kindred
stocks and their cultures overlapped for a time in Luristan.

The figures on one quiver-plate have been interpreted as
a hierarchy of the Indic deities Mithra and Varuna, Indra the
storm-god, the Maruts his followers and the Nasatya twins,
who are certainly known among the Mitanni. In other plates the
Magian priests appear with their sacred _barsoms_, wands made
of bound twigs of tamarisk, and the round face of the solar god
Mithra is figured with his animal attribute the lion, and his
sacrificial victim the bull. A silver plaque, no doubt of later date,
even shows the birth of the Zoroastrian high god Ahura Mazda
and of his twin the devil Ahriman from the primeval hermaphrodite deity Zurvan, the embodiment of endless time.

Who Were the Makers?

It is tempting to believe, with some scholars, that the original style
and themes of ornament on the horse-trappings and finials is
that of the Kassites, late in the 2nd millennium, when they
returned to their mountains. They could have picked up from
their long stay in Mesopotamia the conceptions of the beast-
mastering heroes Gilgamish and Eabani, and of the great goddess
Ishtar and the Tree of Life. Their leading families may have
concentrated themselves in the area where the bronzes are found.
The disks and plaques of Surkh-i-Dum should on the whole be
later than this, because of their Iranian character, for the Iranian
branch of the Aryans is not now supposed to have entered Iran
before the 10th century. If, as is now increasingly believed, the
Aryans of both branches arrived by way of Caucasia, the affinities
of the swords and daggers and of the pendants and amulets
with Transcaucasian types would be a natural result.

These affinities suggest that the earliest Medes and Persians,
and after them those Cimmerians who, as we shall see, went
south-eastward into Iran, were the makers of some of the bronzes
or at any rate customers of local smiths who met their demand.
The Scythian style of the northern steppes likewise owes something to Luristan in such things as animal-shaped whetstone-
handles and animal representations in which the extremities

_Bronze bit of a type peculiar to Luristan, consisting of a single ridged bar
and two cheekpieces. These represent a horned god holding two human-
faced bulls—perhaps a native variant of the legend of Gilgamish._ (3)

Luristanian situla, or drinking vessel, in bronze repoussé, of about 800 BC. The scene, a hunter pursuing an eagle, shows strong Assyrian influence. (4, 5)

turn into the heads of animals or birds. These features could have been picked up by the Scythians during their stay in Western Asia and carried back north of the Caucasus. Something of the style of the typical bronzes reappears oddly as far west as Etruria and as far east as Tibet and the Ordos desert of north China, by what routes of transmission it is fascinating to speculate. The distinctive art of Luristan comes to an end under the Achaemenian Empire of Persia.

A Buffer State: Mannai and its Troubled History

The territory called Mannai in Assyrian records, Mana in Urartian, and Minni in the Old Testament lay in Persian Azerbaijan south of Lake Urmia, and was separated by the northern Zagros from Assyria to the west and Urartu to the north-west. The Mannaeans, apparently natives of the highland, possessed a little-known culture of their own, based on the resources of their fertile plains and valleys. The boundaries of Mannai are not certainly defined, but its core was the plain south of Lake Urmia between the Zagros and the river Djaghata. Its history is inseparable from that of north-west Iran, through which the Medes and kindred tribes were moving at the time that concerns us. No certainly native document or inscription has been found among the remains of Mannai, so that this culture, like that of Luristan, cannot speak for itself.

The territory of Mannai was attractive to conquerors. Throughout our period the rival powers of Urartu and Assyria contended for it as a source of tribute if not as an actual province. The political history of the Mannaeans, as revealed by written sources, consists of the various phases of this struggle, complicated by the ever increasing power of the Medes and towards the end also by the episode of Scythian domination.

Under Shalmaneser III the Assyrians, operating in 858 BC against Urartu and against Parsuash, west of Lake Urmia, entered Mannai, took Zirta, a royal city, and drove out its king Ualki. Such warfare continued until the middle of the eighth century, when the Assyrians fell into a period of weakness, of which the Urartian kings took full advantage. Menuas took and garrisoned the capital Meista, on the site now called Tash Tepe, and left an inscribed stele to commemorate his conquest. Argishti I held Mannai against the Assyrians in continual cam-

paigns and took captive its king Aza. Sarduri II deported many of its people to the shores of Lake Van, but was checked in the south by the revived power of Assyria under Tiglath-Pileser III.

We next hear that Iranzu of Mannai, who favoured Assyria, was overthrown by his neighbours Bagdatta of Uishdish, Metatti of Zikirtu and Tibusina of Andia, all of whose lands lay east of Lake Urmia and who were in league with Rusa I of Urartu. The first two of these at least have Iranian names, and Andia, which extended to the Caspian coast, must have been traversed by the incoming Iranian tribes. Iranzu's son Aza was killed by the same party, and replaced by another son, Ullusunu, who was at first subservient to Rusa.

Sargon II of Assyria was determined to assert Assyrian power in Mannai. He has left a full account of his eighth campaign dated 714 BC, which was fought in Mannai and Urartu with this aim. His narrative is a main source for the political and economic state of these countries at the time. He struck eastward through Zamua on the western edge of Media and approached Mannai from the south, in order to subdue it and to strike terror into the peoples of Parsuash on the west of the lake and of Andia and Zikirtu to the east. Ullusunu, who was now favourable to Assyria, met him near Messi (Meista) and went down on all fours in submission, and a great banquet was held of Mannaeans and Assyrians jointly. Sargon then marched round the eastern side of the lake, defeating the men of Uishdish, Zikirtu and Andia, who had deserted Ullusunu for Rusa, and finally met Rusa himself with his allies in a defile of Mt Uaush (Sahend) near the eastern shore. Sargon took the great Urartian border-fortress of Ushkaia, seizing huge stores of food, and then advanced into Urartu. He gives suspiciously large totals of cities destroyed which he even says were 'countless as the stars of heaven'. It is clear that here, as elsewhere in western Iran, there were many fortified towns of moderate size and more villages.

Shortly after this, Rusa was defeated in his northern territory by the Cimmerians, and committed suicide. Mannai appears to have remained under Assyrian control, except for the region round Meista which fell back into Urartian hands. By the time of Sargon's grandson Esarhaddon the situation in Mannai had become dangerous for the Assyrians. He had to defeat 'the intractable barbarians of Mannai', and their ally, the Scythian Ishpakai. This is the first definite mention of the Scythians in Assyrian records. Mannai is a natural place of arrival for them after their advance along the Caspian coast by Derbent and Transcaucasia. About the same time the Mannaean Ahsheri, a determined foe of Assyria, appears allied with some of the Cimmerians under the dangerous Median chief Kashtarit. Though the Cimmerians soon left Mannai, some became allies of Rusa II against Assyria. Esarhaddon was driven to negotiate with another band of Scythians for help. These had occupied Mannai under their chief Bartatua, and remained there for the rest of Assyrian history, often raiding far and wide, until they were finally defeated and driven back across the Caucasus by the Medes.

The next king of Assyria, Assurbanipal, sent his marshal against Ahsheri of Mannai, now allied with the Scythians. The Assyrians took Izirtu and drove out Ahsheri, who was killed in a rising and succeeded by his more compliant son Ualli. Some towns were handed back to Assyria. Between Assurbanipal's death and the destruction of Assyria by the Medes the Mannaeans are mentioned as Assyrian allies against Babylon. This is their last appearance before Mannai falls to the Medes. During this time the Scythian horde must have continued to move about the countryside as difficult neighbours for the settled cultivators.

Into this imperfect framework of history we have to fit the results of the little excavation that has been carried out in Mannai and its neighbourhood. So far the two most notable sites are Hasanlu, west of Tash Tepe in the Solduz valley, and Ziwiye near the town of Sakkiz.

Hasanlu: the Golden Bowl

The mound of Hasanlu contains layers representing occupation from neolithic to modern times. For our period the most significant area is the citadel, dated from 1000 to 800 BC, which rises from the larger area of the outer town, first settled as a town about 2000 BC. The builders of the citadel were a people new to the site, who made foundations of stone for walls and large buildings, had iron weapons, and used fine grey polished pottery, of a type known widely in Iran. The citadel had been surrounded by a great wall of sun-dried brick nine feet thick, rising from a stone base eight feet high to a probable height of thirty feet. The wall was strengthened with large towers and intermediate bastions, and had the main gate to the west, flanked by bastions. Like the outer town, the citadel contained blackened earth and other signs of burning.

In the area so far excavated the main building was a large palace or temple which faced eastward on a front of eighty feet on to a paved street and courtyard. It had two storeys, as the amount of collapsed brickwork showed. On the ground floor it consisted of an east room, linked by a narrow entrance to a west room, and a roofed courtyard reaching to the west wall of the citadel. The débris on the floor of these rooms, and of small storerooms attached, included weapons, pottery, glazed tiles, ritual vessels, a bronze stand and two remarkable finds, a cup and a bowl.

The cup was of silver, about eight inches high, and decorated with two registers of electrum figures: above, a scene of victory with chariots, prisoners and soldiers, below, a lion and a horse heraldically opposed and flanked by archers. Quite different in style was the bowl of solid gold, eight inches high. It was found in a small storeroom attached on the south side to the east room, and had evidently fallen from the upper storey, along with the bodies of the man who was trying to carry it out and of his two armed companions. The three skeletons were found crushed by the collapsed wall and roof which had also flattened the bowl. The decoration of the bowl is in two registers. pl 25 The upper one represents a procession of deities in chariots drawn by various animals, met by a priest with a curious hair-cut, who is followed by men leading sacrificial animals. The bull drawing the leading chariot pours water from his mouth, which streams down into a scene on the lower register. The lower pl 26 register is not unified, but contains an assortment of divine and heroic figures; the most remarkable is a hero wearing a kilt and knuckle-dusters who fights a male monster. The monster emerges from a mountain and has a curious curving tail ending in three dogs' heads, on which the water from the divine bull descends.

It is likely that the art of so rare and elaborate a ritual vessel has ancient connections with a wider world than Mannai, and that the vessel is more ancient than most of the objects with which it was found. In the upper register the bull drawing the leading god is like the animal companion of weather-gods in

Asia Minor, Syria and Mesopotamia after 2000 BC, and here it sends down a shower. The rays spreading from the head and shoulders of the second god are like those that spread from the sun-god Shamash in Akkadian art of the 23rd century BC. The crescent-shaped horns of the third god's head-dress are likewise Mesopotamian. In the lower register a female figure rides an eagle, as the Sumerian hero Etana did in myth. The goddess riding a lion and holding a mirror has the attributes and posture of the north Syrian goddess Kubaba. The demon attacked by two heroes has a prototype in a Hurrian relief from Tell Halaf in north Mesopotamia. The battle between the hero and the monster may be connected with a Hurrian myth in which the weather god Teshup overcomes a giant man of diorite, begotten by an older god, Kumarbi, to destroy him.

The style shows no late Assyrian influence, but is linear, like other styles from Iran to Palestine in the 11th and 10th centuries. The light chariots are also typical of the late 2nd millennium. The hair-styles and dress, male and female, have affinities in Iran. Everything suggests that this is an ancient Iranian style under Hurrian influence. The enemy who destroyed Hasanlu is almost certain to have been Urartian or Assyrian. The excavators are inclined to believe that it was one of the towns conquered by Menuas when Urartu was at its most powerful. This would be consistent with everything found, and particularly with the lack of Assyrian influence.

The local and purely native art of Mannai may be illustrated by a bronze dish from north-west Iran which has crudely vigorous reliefs of a feasting scene with a herd of cattle and a pair of fighting horses, and of a lion hunt. There is a certain likeness between the Hasanlu bowl and another gold bowl from Kalar Dasht, nearer the Caspian, south of the Elburz range and considerably farther east. This has riveted to it three figures of walking lions done in a similar vigorous style and marked with the swastika on the haunch, like the lion on the Hasanlu bowl. At Amlash, south-west of the Caspian, two gold goblets were found, adorned with figures of animals and monsters. One is engraved above with a winged lion attacking a goat, and below with stags separated by a palmette. The other has a hunting scene in the upper register and a procession of cocks in the lower. The borders between the scenes recall those on the Hasanlu bowl, and the style of the figures might be ancestral to that of some on the Luristan bronzes.

pl 33

The Treasure of Ziwiye

Equally famous with the Hasanlu bowl is the rich treasure discovered at Ziwiye in Kurdistan, on the southern edge of ancient Mannai, on the spur of a mountain, a position commanding the routes east and west between the Djaghata and Lake Urmia, and south and north between Transcaucasia and Hamadan. The fortress there had thick walls of sun-dried brick. Among the remains of arms and furniture found within it was a collection of gold objects, placed with some others in a bronze coffin. The coffin is decorated in Assyrian style with a frieze of men led in procession, who may be captured Medes. The treasure included the following objects: an elaborate gold pectoral ornament, a magnificent gold bracelet adorned with lions' heads, a dagger-sheath of gold, a gold torque adorned with animal heads in strong relief, fragments of gold plaques for covering chests or caskets, hollow gold heads of lions and bird-headed monsters, a forehead-band of gold with enamelled roses, a gold vase with palmettes, a gold girdle and earrings, ivory plaques from furniture and ivory panels from a casket, and some silver ornaments for harness and for a chariot.

pl 30

pl 24

Peculiarly interesting is the variety of styles not merely distributed among several objects but sometimes combined in one. The pectoral has figures of at least three styles and possibly more in its two symmetrical registers. In the upper register the central Tree of Life is a Mesopotamian symbol. The ibexes rearing up on either side are of a type well known in prehistoric Iran; the human-headed winged sphinx is originally Egyptian and wears a north Syrian kind of apron on its forelegs; the winged bull with the head of a bearded man is pure Assyrian. The lion-griffin crouching behind him is Assyrian with Iranian influence, and the little figures of a lion cub and a hare at the end are in Scythian

pl 27

f 7

8

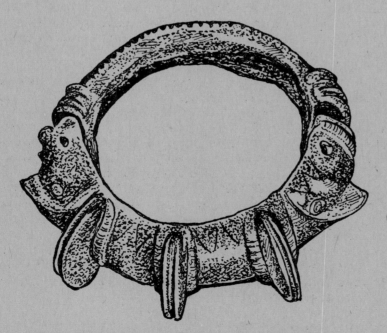

Bronze 'knuckleduster' from Luristan, reminiscent of the Roman 'cestus'. It was held in the closed fist, with the disks projecting between the fingers. Another type of 'cestus' is worn by the hero in pl. 25. (6)

Right: detail from the right-hand end of the Ziwiye pectoral (pl. 27). Compare this lion cub with the Scythian lion (left) from the Kuban. (7, 8)

style. In the lower register the Tree of Life again occupies the centre. The winged bull approaching with averted head is Assyrian, like the winged man who follows. The eagle-griffin is Assyrian, but wears the north Syrian apron; the ram is Iranian, but wears the same apron. The winged sphinx is Egypto-Syrian, and the quadruped and the hare at the outer edge have a Scythian appearance. The same types of monster appear on some of the

pl 1 plaques. A repetitive design in gold plate encloses Scythian stags with drawn-up legs, alternating with Iranian ibexes in the

pl 29 same posture, in frames of conventionalized branches spreading outward from lions' heads of Iranian type.

Dating of the objects has varied from the 9th to the 7th century BC, and they need not all be of the same date; dating of the burial is now late in the 7th century. According to one suggestion the treasure was collected and partly made for the Scythian chief Bartatua, the Protothyes of Herodotus, at the time when he ruled Mannai and was courted by Esarhaddon, and was buried a generation later after the Scythian power had fallen. More prosaically it has been called the collection of an Assyrian governor. At any rate it mirrors the extreme variety of influences flooding into this region at a time of violent change.

A Great Power: the Kingdom of Urartu

We come finally to the kingdom of Urartu, one of the great powers of the Near East in the early centuries of the 1st millennium. Naturally its remains are much more abundant, elaborate and widespread than those of Luristan and Mannai, and Assyrian and native sources for its history much fuller. As a remnant of the wider Hurrian world of the 2nd millennium it has its peculiar interest, but it is no less famous for its resistance to Assyria and for its sufferings at the hands of the northern invaders who passed through its territory.

The general region of Armenia appears commonly in earlier Assyrian records under the name Nairi, though even in the 2nd millennium there is mention of Uruatri, an earlier form of the familiar Urartu, which appears in the Old Testament as Ararat. This territory had been known to the Hittites, but was never part of their empire, nor was it overrun by the Phrygian invaders when they first destroyed the Hittite power in Anatolia. So far as is known, it was still inhabited by the same Hurrian population during our period. No native name is known for the entire region. The core of Urartu consisted of the territory called Biaina on the shores of Lake Van, separated by mountains from Assyria and Iran, but more exposed to the north, where there are large plains between the ranges.

The beginning of the state of Urartu, which brought the small principalities of Nairi under its rule, is recorded in the middle of the 9th century by Shalmaneser III of Assyria, who spent much effort in attempts to crush it. The founder is called by the Assyrians Arame. He is the historical original of the great king Aram, still remembered even in Christian Armenian tradition, who was said to have defeated the Medes and the Assyrians and founded an empire. Shalmaneser on accession took from Arame his city of Sugunia in the south near the upper Zab, and advanced to Lake Van. Two years later he attacked the capital Arzashkun, perhaps to be identified with Mollakent near Liz, north of the

lake. Arame fled to the mountains, Arzashkun and other cities were plundered, and the Assyrians claimed to have subdued the entire country. The plundering army and its booty and prisoners are represented on the famous bronze gates of Balawat.

No further Assyrian operations are mentioned for more than twenty-five years from 857 BC. During this time the Urartians adopted Assyrian cuneiform and at first also the Assyrian tongue for the royal inscriptions. Later they used the same script to write their own language, and there are some bilingual inscriptions.

Arame's successor was Sarduri I (832-825) who transferred the capital to the historic site of Tushpa, the modern Van. This was the origin of the town of Van, still sometimes called Tosp or Vantosp in Armenian sources. Tushpa also gave the lake its Greek name of Thospitis. Van lies by the lake at the foot of the height Van Kale, which was rightly thought to be a more defensible site for the royal citadel than Arzashkun. But even this was later abandoned by Rusa I for the heights of Toprak Kale, five kilometres further from the lake. Territories lying southward toward Assyria were added and control established over the kingdom of Malatya, under Ispuini (824-805) who reigned for a time (815-805) jointly with his son Menuas. Under Menuas as sole king (804-790) a beginning was made with northern conquests, as well as with interference in Mannai. This was continued under Argishti I (789-766) and Sarduri II (765-733) until the Urartian empire included wide regions north of Mount Ararat, extending into the land of the Qulha, the Colchians of Greek writers, into the country round Lake Sevan and into the upper basin of the Aras. On the west the boundary remains uncertain, though for a time under Argishti II (713-679) it lay in Erzincan, where the important site of Altintepe has yielded Urartian metalwork. The Urartian annals, though much less full than the Assyrian, describe in the same manner continual campaigns, frequent massacres and devastations, and the deportations of large numbers of captives with their cattle and other possessions to the central region of Biaina.

There is the same difficulty as with the Assyrian annals in distinguishing new conquests from the crushing of rebellion in conquered territory, or from mere raiding. Most of the country concerned is extremely mountainous, so that these operations demanded great skill and perseverance, and such feats of engineering as the making of military roads, in which the Urartians were as well practised as the Hittites, who first did so, or as their own contemporaries the Assyrians. In the north their harrying and cattle-lifting campaigns may have made enemies of the first Scythians who reached Transcaucasia. In their eastern campaigns they are likely to have pressed upon the Medes in regions further north than the Assyrians did in the same period.

The number of small districts claimed as provinces in the Urartian annals is surprisingly large. Urartu proper apparently had eight provinces between Lake Urmia and Lake Van. Seven more bordered on Assyria and were Urartian in culture and sympathies. The conquered territories were much more numerous; they have been estimated at one hundred and two, most of them in the north, though some were on the upper Tigris. Urartian influence extended even further than the lands between Transcaucasia and Assyria; it reached the Caspian in the north-east, and was felt at the time of greatest expansion under Menuas, Argishti I and Sarduri II through Syria as far as the Mediterranean, and by trade and diplomacy in Anatolia. Under these kings it may have seemed that the old dominion of the Hurrians would be restored even south of the highlands, among peoples who contained many Hurrian descendants.

The details of administration are very slightly indicated by native and Assyrian sources, supplemented a little by the evidence of archaeology. The empire seems at first to have been of the same pattern as the Hittite or the early Assyrian, having a combination of royal and feudal elements. The true provinces, metropolitan and other, came to be governed by prefects, with subprefects and other officers under them, who commanded troops of their own. The prefects would thus have exercised both civil and military powers. They were no doubt members of the nobility, but they governed as royal officers appointed by the king. There is reason to believe that there were other nobles who were not royal officers, but had their own estates and were no doubt required to provide troops. These would be feudal grandees by hereditary right. There were also the numerous members of the royal family, who cannot all have held administrative office. The developed system of prefects was no doubt modelled on the later Assyrian system.

Cities and Rock-built Citadels

Outside Urartu proper, conquered territories were often governed at first by their own kings as subject rulers paying tribute to the Urartian King of Kings, and then, when these proved unsuitable, by royal governors in the Assyrian manner. Tribute was also paid by some dependent kings who were not so much vassals as allies, particularly against Assyria. There was a set policy of building Urartian towns in the conquered provinces, partly emptied as they were by deportations. These towns, and the many fortresses at strategic points, were occupied by soldiers and officials with their families, but whether there was regular colonization with Urartian settlers is not certain. The fortresses or fortified citadels were built in positions of natural strength, such as a spur of a hill with precipitous cliffs, and some have traces of towns outside the walls. The typical fortification consisted of massive blocks of basalt or more rarely of limestone, laid without mortar in courses from half to one metre deep to a thickness of three or four metres, surmounted by courses of brick to a total height of some twelve metres. The walls were buttressed for their entire height and, as appears from bronze models, battlemented too. In the Van region alone more than forty such sites have been discovered, and they would have been more numerous in exposed provinces.

pl 49

Sargon's account of cities taken and laid waste on his eighth campaign does much to clothe these remains with life. The fortress of Ushkaia, for instance, on the border of Mannai and Urartu, barred his way into the province of Zaranda. It stood on the flank of Mount Mallu 'the cypress mountain' with walls eight cubits thick, watching over the land of Subi, where Rusa bred countless horses for his cavalry. The city of Ulhu at the foot of Mount Kishpal had a great canal 'flowing like the Euphrates', from which channels drew off water to irrigate an orchard. There were fruit trees and vines, high plane trees 'which cast wide shadows', sown lands and pastures, and stamping grounds for horses and cattle. By the river was a palace roofed with cypress beams. The city of Mutsatsir, ruled by the vassal king Urzana, and known to the Urartians as Siwini, the city of the sun-god, contained a temple of Haldi, the national god of Urartu, as well as the king's palace. Sargon despoiled it of enormous wealth in precious metals, objects of gold and silver, vessels and ceremonial shields and weapons, inlaid furniture, rich garments and textiles, ivories and statues of gods and kings. The plundering is shown in a bas-relief from Sargon's palace at Khorsabad.

pl 34

The successive royal citadels on Van Kale and Toprak Kale and the towns below them were perhaps the greatest examples of Urartian building and engineering. At Van Kale Sarduri I built a great wall and keep, with at least the lower courses made of stone slabs weighing several tons each, to control access to the

248

Reconstruction of a relief from Adilcevaz on Lake Van, perhaps showing the Urartian god Haldi. The spearhead finials, symbol of this god, can also be seen on the temple in pl. 34 (9)

north-west corner of the rock, where it was not precipitous. The slabs must have been brought by raft across the lake. Menuas built the great canal that still runs from an abundant mountain spring through the valley of Hayothdzor for at least fifty kilometres, to irrigate the gardens of the town of Van before entering the lake. Its dykes, and the stone aqueduct that carries the water over the river Khoshab, still remain, but the ancient town of Tushpa is covered by the modern Van. Menuas and Argishti between them hollowed out three great chambers of uncertain use, complete with tunnels and stairways for access, in the south face of Van Kale, which still bears their cuneiform inscriptions. The canal, now called Shamiram-su, and the works and inscriptions on the citadel were credited later in Armenian legend to the masterful Queen Semiramis of Assyria. She invaded Armenia for love of its king, Ara the Beautiful, who had rejected her advances, and after he died in the fighting, spent much time there in building, landscape gardening and debauchery, to console herself.

pl 36

pl 35

Rusa I moved the citadel to Toprak Kale, further east on a southern spur of Zimzim Dagh. He built a new town at its foot, which for a time appears to have been called Rusahina. Since this could not be served with water by Menuas' canal, he collected the waters of a spring on the mountain to the south of the town in the artificial lake *Rusa sue*, 'Rusa's lake', now called Keshish-Göl, and led down the waters in another canal. The citadel on Toprak Kale was excavated at various times before the days of modern archaeology, and no plan was ever made of its walls and buildings. It yielded a very various collection of metal work, remains of furniture and statuary, ivories and polished red pottery, as well as older types of grey ware. The chief building known was the temple of Haldi, looking down from the west side of the rock on a foundation 13.50 metres square. Inscriptions on bronze shields from the site make it probable that the temple was finished in its final form by Rusa III, the last king. On the west side of

pl 37

the citadel were also a wall and a repository of human and animal bones. Some distance to the east were remains of magazines containing vast jars of 500 and 600 litres capacity, and a rock-hewn chamber. The centre of the citadel was apparently an open space, but various buildings occupied the slopes, some of them surely outside the walls.

The Burning of Teshebani
The only scientific excavation of any Urartian city was carried out in recent years by the Russians at Karmir Blur near Erivan on the river Zanga in Soviet Armenia. This was shown by an inscription on a bronze bolt among the finds to have been the site of Teshebani, the centre of government for Urartian Transcaucasia, where a viceroy or governor held court, and where large stores of tribute in kind were kept, and provisions for the garrison. There appear to be two distinguishable periods of occupation, an earlier, marked by objects bearing the name of Menuas the conqueror, and a later in which Rusa II was most active. Late in the 7th century, perhaps about 625 BC, Teshebani was destroyed by the Scythians, as is shown by the remains.

f 10

f 11

The mound on its northern side overlooks the Zanga, which flows at the bottom of a steep slope. The domestic wing and storehouses of the citadel were flanked on the north by a series of towers arranged in indented fashion facing the river, while on the south an inner line of such towers bordered on a huge courtyard. The courtyard was entered by two gates, and enclosed the houses of the richer inhabitants. On the south side were the residences of officials. The whole building covered 1600 square metres and had at least 120 rooms. Its walls had bases made of huge unworked stones, surmounted by courses of sun-dried bricks containing chopped straw, and must once have been ten metres high. The roof had been flat and made of beams of poplar, oak and beech, overlaid with twigs, rushes, or reeds, and then by beaten earth. Windows had been made in the walls near the roof, and there were also remains of light-wells. The inner rooms had been plastered with clay and showed remains of mural painting. The central part was two storeys high, and in some places there was a cornice with crenellations. Small huts and houses, obviously improvised, showed how towards the end the population had crowded in from the countryside.

In various rooms there was ample provision of food and drink. In one was a deposit of 550 bushels of wheat, 9–12 ins. thick and containing the remains of insects and weevils. There were also remains of barley, millet and sesame, in prepared trenches or in vessels. In one room was a great trough cut in a block of tufa, from which stone pipes ran out of the fortress. This had been used for softening the sesame before it was dried and pounded in stone mortars, which were also found; an indication that

sesame oil was regularly made. In another room was a deep vat from which a gutter ran out, and above it a stone funnel, while near by were a long-handled shovel of iron, and a clay pot containing a filter of straw and twigs over a hole in its bottom. This was evidently an apparatus for brewing barley beer. Two great storerooms contained 152 vast jars which would have held 160,000 litres of wine. All vessels were marked in cuneiform or hieroglyphs with their capacity in *akarki* (240 litres) and *terusi* (about 24 litres). There were also remains of textiles, some thick woollen fabrics and others of plant fibres. The pottery included polished red ware, as at Toprak Kale, as well as cruder black or grey ware.

pl 47

Teshebani seems to have been in decline before it was destroyed, to judge by broken vessels and remains of wasps' nests and small rodents. The final destruction was by fire. Charred remnants of collapsed roof beams covered much of the floor space and red dust from bricks was very common. Lying on top of the roof beams were found skeletons and even soft parts, preserved in the ashes, of horses, asses and cattle, which must have been on the roofs for lack of room, and have crashed down with the blazing timbers. Some of their stomachs contained grass and other vegetable matter, whose stage of growth indicated that the disaster occurred in August. There were Scythian trilobar arrowheads lying blunted, or sticking in the wall by the postern gate at the west end of the river-wall, which shows that the Scythians must have mastered the lower town to reach the fortress. Scythian horse-trappings and other objects inside the fortress showed that there were some Scythians among the defenders. Relations with the Scythians must have been very close at the time.

pl 48

The Art of Urartu
From these sites and others enough material has now been gathered to give a fair sample of Urartian art. Of foreign influences the Assyrian is very obvious during the 8th century. The helmets and shields and quiver of bronze belonging to Argishti I and Sarduri II, which were discovered at Karmir Blur, and were evidently kept there as symbols of royal authority, are of Assyrian type. Their decorations of charioteers and horses, and of winged genii and other figures ritually tending the Tree of Life, are scarcely conceivable without Assyrian originals. But something distinctive appears in the facial type of the figures with their sharp, jutting noses. The remarkable curving snakes on the helmets, with their peculiar heads, are not Assyrian. The figures of lions and bulls in Urartian art are generally less ferocious and longer-legged. This divergence grows more marked after the 8th century.

pl 44
45

In the 7th century the finds from Toprak Kale show the influence of late Assyrian art in their animal and human figures, but the lions and bulls on the bronze shields have longer legs,

f 12

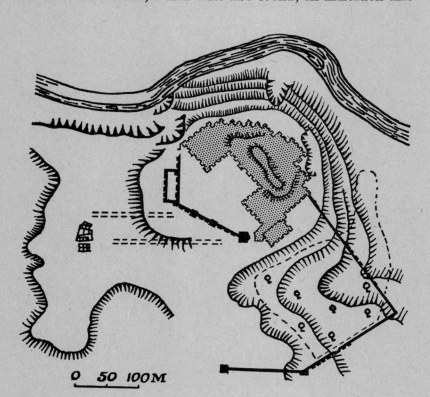

0 50 100M

Plan of the city and fortress of Karmir Blur. The tinted area shows the fortress itself, part of which is also shown in the detailed plan (right). The steep slope down to the river is commanded by a series of towers, and similar towers also face the other way towards the central courtyard. (10, 11)

0 10 20 30M

Bronze figure of a so-called eunuch, a royal attendant from Toprak Kale, 37.5 cm. high. This may have been a free-standing figure or possibly part of the ornamentation of a throne or bed. (12)

curling extremities, a different convention for showing muscle, and a curious appearance of stalking on tip-toe, all of them features that are foreign to Assyria. The bony, arched nose pl 42 distinctive of the aristocracy in Urartu is shown on a gold medal- 43 lion and on a silver pectoral ornament from Toprak Kale, both representing a seated goddess approached by a woman votary; it appears on the many metal attachments in the form of human heads and shoulders which are found on Urartian bronze caul- drons; and most notably on a relief from Adilcevaz which is taken to represent the god Haldi himself, standing on the back and f 9 head of a bull in the manner of Anatolian and Assyrian gods.

pl 50 Some features of Urartian art, such as the protomes of lions −52 and griffins, which distinguish it from Assyrian, are often thought to be derived from the late Hittite or Aramaean kingdoms. Since the Hurrians had been so powerful in these borderlands of Syria and Anatolia, it has been suggested that this is their tradition, carried northward into Urartu by craftsmen who left them to escape the Assyrian attack.

The influence of Urartian art, at least in metal work, has been pl 53 definitely traced in Phrygia and claimed much further afield in Greece at Delphi and Corinth, and even in Etruria. Some of the metal objects found in these places may even be Urartian exports. The routes by which Urartian influence or exports could have reached the west are various: Syria and the Phoenician ports,

Central Anatolia and Lydia, and the Pontic sea-route leading to the Bosporus and the Aegean, have all been suggested with good reason.

The Decline: a Forgotten People

From the point where we left the narrative at the height of Urart- ian power the rest of the kingdom's history can be briefly told. The expansion under Sarduri II was rudely and decisively checked by Tiglath-Pileser III of Assyria, who drove the Urart- ians out of Syria in 743 BC, and chased Sarduri at the peril of his life across the Euphrates. In 735 Tiglath-Pileser besieged Sarduri in the citadel of Van Kale, but failed to take it. Urartian power was destroyed in the lowlands. The attack was continued against Rusa I (732-714) by Sargon II who, as we saw, detached Mannai from Urartian allegiance, and made destructive raids through Urartu itself. In reply Rusa brought Phrygia and Tabal in South Anatolia into a loose alliance against Assyria, but his power was weakened by the invasion of the Cimmerians from beyond the Caucasus. Rusa was severely defeated by them and committed suicide. They overran much of Urartu, and after they had passed through it they threatened Assyria along its entire northern fron- tier. They were checked by the Assyrians under Esarhaddon, and moved off in two directions, some into the Zagros as far as Luristan, but the main body westward to destroy the Phrygian kingdom and to devastate Lydia and many Greek cities of Asia Minor.

Argishti II (713-679) maintained the central area, Biaina, intact, along with some of the nearest provinces. Rusa II (678-654) kept some Cimmerians as mercenaries, no doubt for use against the Assyrians, and had some fighting on his western frontier with the Phrygians before their power fell to the Cimmerians. Neither under Sennacherib, son of Sargon, nor under his son Esarhaddon, did the Assyrians make any move against Urartu. But by Esar- haddon's time an even more dangerous enemy had crossed the Caucasus, the Scythians, who had driven the Cimmerians off the South Russian steppe and now followed them into Western Asia.

The main horde of Scythians arrived by the Derbent route along the shore of the Caspian and established itself in Mannai and Media, at the same time overrunning Urartu and doing such damage as is known from Karmir Blur. The Urartian state never fully recovered from this invasion. It lingered on from Sarduri III (654-625) to Rusa III (605-585), who still left inscriptions as far north as Armavir. It thus lasted through the reigns of Assurbani- pal and his short-lived successors, to survive Assyria. It is men- tioned in this period by Babylonian sources and by the Hebrew prophet Jeremiah. The end of Urartu is generally dated about 585, when the Medes, who now faced it on its Iranian and Assyrian frontiers alike, closed in and destroyed Tushpa. Though this is not mentioned in any historical source, the fall of Urartu is pre- supposed in the Median advance to the river Halys in Cappadocia to fight Alyattes the Lydian at that time.

Simultaneous or nearly so with the Median conquest must have been the Armenian immigration, probably from Cappadocia, which brought into the old country of Urartu an Indo-European language, not Iranian, but of the Thracian group. The confused state of the country is shown by a passage in Xenophon's roman- tic biography of Cyrus the Great, which may not be true of Cyrus but may be true of the Medes. Cyrus is said to have reduced the king of the Armenians, who had rebelled against Cyaxares of Media, and then to have helped him in a war against the plunder- ing Chaldaeans of the mountains, restoring peace and regulating the use of land by the two peoples. The Chaldaeans are likely to be the Urartian worshippers of Haldi, now driven into the moun- tains by the Armenians, who had taken the best land. Under Persian rule the Urartians must still have maintained something of their identity, for Darius in his struggle for the throne had to subdue an Armenian pretender who raised his standard in Baby- lon and called himself Arakha son of Halditi. The two names contain those of the Urartian gods Ara and, once more, Haldi. In Herodotus the obscure Alarodians of this region are probably the Urartians, who continued to serve in the Persian armies. Thenceforward memory of this energetic people was lost, except in some Armenian legends, until the days of modern archaeology.

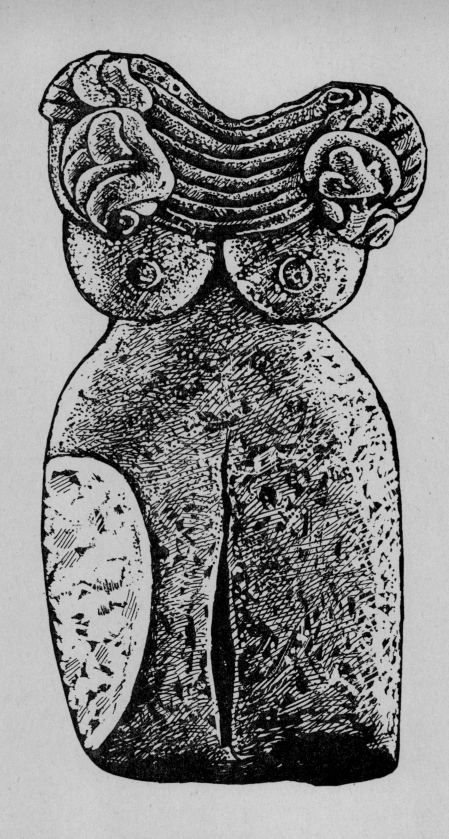

XI BRIDGE TO THE ANCIENT EAST

The new knowledge of early Afghanistan

EDWARD BACON

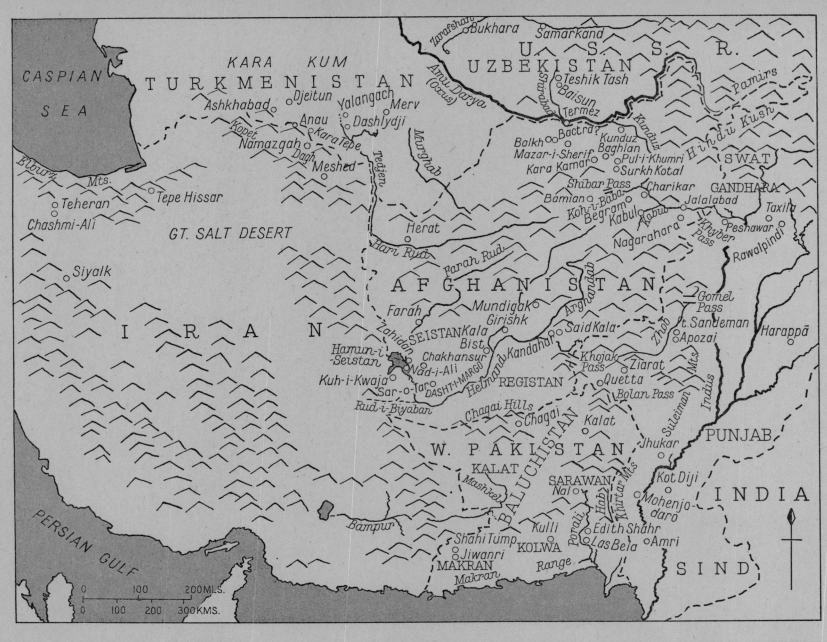

BC	WEST	AFGHANISTAN and adjacent regions	EAST
Pre-4000	Jericho (Tell-es-Sultan) First occupation of Siyalk (1)	EARLY NEOLITHIC First occupation of Djeitun, Kile Ghul Mohammad 1	
3000	Siyalk 11 Chashmi-Ali culture Siyalk 111 Proto-literate period	FULL NEOLITHIC Developed village cultures: Namazgah Tepe, Kara Tepe, Anau 1-11, Hissar 1-11 Togau ware. Kile Ghul Mohammad 111	
	Sumerian civilization	Kechi-Beg culture: Kile Ghul Mohammad 1v, Damb Sadaat 1, Early Said Kala	Kot Diji and Amri cultures
2000	Akkadian period	Quetta culture: Deh Morasi, Damb Sadaat 11, Sur Jangal 11-111	Beginning of Indus civilization
	Hammurabi	Late Quetta culture: Damb Sadaat 111, late phases at Mundigak Complex A at Edith Shahr. 'Zhob Mother Goddesses'	Climax of Mohenjo-daro and Harappā
	Kassites	LATE PREHISTORIC PERIOD: falling off of population and decline of village cultures	
1000	Beginning of Assyrian Empire Cemetery B, Siyalk	Invaders from outside: Lando ware, Complex B at Edith Shahr, Nad-i-Ali grey ware	Destruction of Mohenjo- daro and Harappā Dark Age
	Fall of Assyria Achaemenid Empire 330 Alexander	Loose Achaemenid rule in Afghanistan; Zoroaster Collapse of Achaemenid empire. Alexander in Seistan Beginning of Seleucid rule	Life and death of Buddha Alexander reaches the Indus
0	Roman and Parthian empires	c. 130 Invasion by Parthians and Scythians	
AD	Rise of Sassanian empire	Kushan conquest and rule: fire temples 123-53 King Kanishka. Buddhism introduced; Bamian founded	Kushan rule in northern India

Chronology of Afghanistan and adjacent regions, in relation to the civilizations of Mesopotamia and the Indus

252

The high valleys of Afghanistan
are the ancient bridge to India and
the Far East. Along them have passed
six thousand years of human history—
primitive hunters, nomadic herdsmen,
caravans of merchants, conquering
armies overwhelming whole civilizations and peaceful missionaries
bringing new ones to birth. It is a
land dominated by forces from outside, the route by which ideas and
cultures have spread, but whose only
permanence lay in its epic geology
and tough climate and in the farmers
and herders who wrested a living from
its watered valleys. It was the tenuous
thread that joined the ancient Indus
with Persia; Aryan invaders crossed
it on their way to subdue India, and
so later did Alexander the Great,
bringing Greece to the threshold of
the East. Here Buddhism found one
of its holiest places—in turn to be
overrun by Islam. Few regions of the
world are richer in traces of man's
past, and few have until recently been
so completely unknown. Now the
complex and disjointed story is falling
into place, giving us the key to much
that was mysterious in the history of
Inner Asia.

A tiny Mother Goddess from the
Quetta culture, c. 2000 BC, and the
immense Buddha of Bamian, 173 feet
high, hewn from the living rock
during the 3rd or 4th century AD,
symbolize the long chronicle of religion in Afghanistan, though they
represent neither its beginning nor
its end. The figurine, modelled in
clay, comes from Damb Sadaat in
Baluchistan; the heavy, multiple-
strand necklace points to influence
from the Indus valley, where the
great cities of Mohenjo-daro and
Harappā were reaching the peak of
their achievement. (1, 2)

Only where the life-giving waters run

can man make a home in this parched landscape. It is a land of barren mountain chains and bare plains with little or no rainfall, fiercely hot in summer, icy in winter, swept with the changing seasons by winds of hurricane force. Many of its rivers are dry for half the year; others flow inland and evaporate in salty swamps.

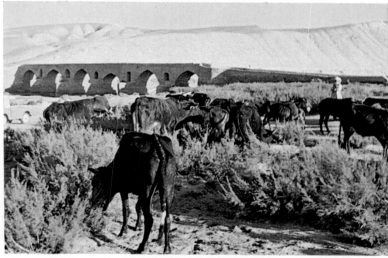

The broad steppes of the north (above, left), stretching away into the remote grasslands of Central Asia, support nomadic herdsmen, tent-dwellers, who find food for their animals only by a constant search for new pastures. Yet a stream from the hills will transform the desert into a garden. In the Konach-Mar valley (above), 10,000 feet up in the shadow of the mighty Hindu Kush, irrigation makes it possible to grow crops and establish farms. From the mountains, west into the desert, flows the Hari-Rud, bringing fertility to the city of Herat, where cattle graze today (left). Further south, on the edge of the central Iranian desert, lies Seistan, its villages (left, below) struggling under a climate of extremes and living from the waters of the Helmand. (3–6)

Still every winter large numbers of Afghans migrate to the warm plains, returning in the spring to their homes on the high plateaux. The picture on the opposite page (above) shows such a group winding its way through the Panjshir Valley in the Hindu Kush. The colourful costumes (below) stand out against the arid grey of the landscape. This family is coming home to the highlands after spending the winter in the Punjab. (7, 8)

The pattern of living has hardly changed here for thousands of years. Cultures have risen and died, but all have been conditioned by the nature of the country and the climate, and all have depended, as they do today, on the flow of the rivers and on the historic passes through which trade has continued unchecked by invasion and war.

Stone Age farming communities
are known to have existed in the north of Afghanistan from the 4th millennium BC. The people lived in mud houses; they were beginning to keep sheep and goats, grew wheat and barley, could make stone tools and clay pottery with attractive painted ornament, and seem to have had a fertility religion centring on a Mother Goddess. By 3000 BC metal had been introduced and copper implements, bangles and rings were common. Pottery decoration had reached a high level of sophistication, though the potter's wheel was still unknown. At Namazgah Tepe, just across the modern border with Russia, 150 whole pots have been excavated. Most of the designs (below) are geometrical, but a few have animal figures, including the spotted snow-leopard (top left), familiar from Siyalk and Tepe Hissar in Persia. Namazgah Tepe was a flourishing town, with a central square and houses of up to twenty rooms, manufacturing copper tools, woven fabric and stone sculpture. Model carts with wheels show that cattle- or goat-drawn vehicles were used. (9)

Villages in Seistan were more numerous in prehistoric times than today. This site had small single-roomed houses. (10)

The cemetery of the same village lay close by. Burials were in brick-lined pits, with the skeleton in a flexed position. (11)

To seal or stamp goods the villagers of about 2500 BC used these 'compartmented' seals, shown here slightly enlarged—one from Damb Sadaat, near Quetta (left), the other from Said Kala, further north. Two seals have so far been found at Damb Sadaat, both of clay and both based on a cross-shaped design. The Said Kala seal is of steatite and has a more elaborate pattern. (12, 13)

The climax of the early ware known as Kechi-Beg pottery is found in the Loralai District of north-west Baluchistan. The big pot with *bucranium* design (stylized bull's head and horns) is from Sur Jangal; next to it a sherd from Damb Sadaat—possibly a barking dog; top right, a sherd from Rana Ghundai interesting because it shows western cattle with no hump (the normal breed was the humped *Bos indicus*); bottom right, part of a line of strutting partridges, arbitrarily marked with the zigzag. (14)

Long perished basketry and fabrics can be recognized, and even the fabrics identified, by the 'basket-markings' on clay vessels; on the right are four positive casts made from fragments (where the impression is of course negative); top row, twill-plaited matting; bottom row, coiled basketry. (15)

Faiz Mohammed ware: a shallow plate (wheel-made) with an elegant design using the pipal-leaf. (16)

Prosperity and peace

make this period (c. 2500–1500 BC) one of maximum population for Baluchistan. The valleys are crowded with villages, some large enough to be called towns. Parallels with the Indus (especially with the culture known as Amri B) are astonishingly close, and inevitably they pose the question: What was the relation between Afghanistan and the great cities further east? Is it possible that the Indus civilization was conceived here, by remote contact with ancient Mesopotamia?

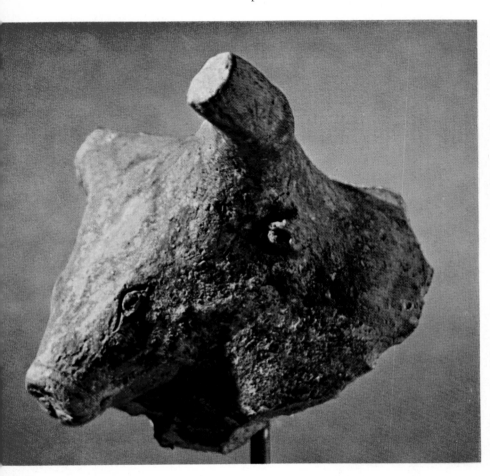

Bull-figurines and strange goggle-eyed Mother Goddesses have been found in numbers at Periano Ghundai in the Zhob valley—pointers to a fertility religion that has been called the 'Zhob Cult'. On the attractive Quetta pottery, bulls are also among the favourite motifs but here there seems to be no religious meaning. The vessel below is from Damb Sadaat. (17, 18)

The most important discovery so far made in this region is the huge site of Edith Shahr, just north of Bela. Here in 1959–60, eight miles of ancient buildings were found, the walls still standing in places to a height of five or six feet. The central—and most intriguing—structures were stone-built pyramids or ziggurats whose original height must have been about 30 feet. They were ascended by steps. At the top were small buildings with what seems to be a drain-pit. Around them were other groups of buildings—stone-based with upper parts of mud-brick—which may have been tombs. Indeed the whole complex was most likely not a town but a ceremonial centre. In the reconstruction above the artist has imagined a bull-sacrifice, with a procession ascending one of the ziggurats. Priests carry offerings of flowers and figurines of the Mother Goddess and the bull. (19)

A mysterious new culture replaced that of the original Edith Shahr some time in the 2nd millennium BC. The earlier buildings show signs of having been destroyed by fire; around them immense new avenues and circles of stone were laid out—perhaps the centre of a sun-worshipping religion. Some walls (right) continue the old technique, tiers of dry round stones. Who were the invaders? Is the destruction of Edith Shahr part of the same sequence as the catastrophe that overtook Mohenjo-daro? (20)

These marks are more than ordinary decoration. They occur on pots of the Quetta culture and could be a first simple attempt at recording by symbols. If so, we may be seeing the earliest stage of the still undeciphered Harappān script, the writing of the Indus civilization. (21)

The bull-cult of Edith Shahr has left numerous painted clay figurines, sometimes with fragments of a wheeled cart—yet another detail pointing to connections with the Indus valley. (22)

West Central Iran seems to have been the earlier home of the invaders who conquered Edith Shahr. The evidence so far is sparse but consistent. Below: 'Lando' ware, a coarse painted pottery, often with running spirals and horses' heads, is found over much of Baluchistan and is virtually certain to be connected with pottery from Siyalk. Right: a spouted vessel from Seistan; the type is also familiar from Western Iran. (23, 24)

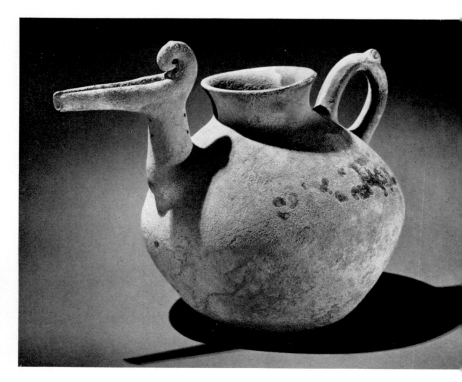

A dark age

follows the last phase of Edith Shahr. When the clouds lift it is the mid-1st millennium BC. The Achaemenid dynasty rules in Persia and exercises a loose control over Afghanistan. Now we hear for the first time of a great city already, according to tradition, ancient—Bactra, 'Mother of Cities'. It was situated in the north, between the Oxus and the mountains, but where? Earlier this century archaeologists searched for it beneath the mound of Bala Hissar (below), the fortress of Balkh. They did not find it. Bactra may still lie under any of the countless mounds that cover the plain (right)—one of the great discoveries that await the future. (25, 26)

Alexander's march through the defeated Achaemenid empire brought him to Seistan and the passes of the Hindu Kush in 329–8 BC. At Bactra he married the princess Roxana. Six years later he was dead, his immense kingdom split up among his generals. Two Greek dynasties ruled in Afghanistan for nearly 200 years before falling to the Parthians and Scythians about 130 BC. They issued coins which show how their original Greek traditions were gradually overlaid by Central Asian and Indian. Classical motifs die out, and the Greek language is replaced by Kharoshti. The kings on these examples are (top row): Menander (c. 162–148 BC), Eucratides I (c. 167–159 BC), Heliocles I (c. 159–139 BC) and (bottom row) Pantaleon (a pretender to Eucratides' throne, whose emblem was the panther) and an unidentified king, possibly Azes I, a Scythian ruler. (27)

261

The monastery of Bamian

at the foot of the great Hindu Kush mountains, stands for ever as one of the holy places of Buddhism. It was founded under the rule of the Kushans, a Central Asian tribe who had fought the Parthians in the 1st century AD. Originally a fire-worshipping people, the Kushans accepted Buddhism as the state religion. To Bamian, monks came from all over north-west India and established a monastery in its peaceful valley (below). Their cells were hollowed out of the rock, and in the southern cliff they carved two colossal statues of the standing Buddha. Masterpieces of the sculptor's art, they have made Bamian world famous (the one illustrated in pl. 2 is marked on the extreme left). From here, during the 3rd—4th century, Buddhism spread to the whole of Central Asia, for it lay on the caravan route of the silk-traders. Today some of the caves are used by the modern populace as shelters. Above: caves round the remnants of a seated Buddha also carved in the rock. Right: modern mud-brick walls transform the once great monastery into crowded dwelling-places. (28–30)

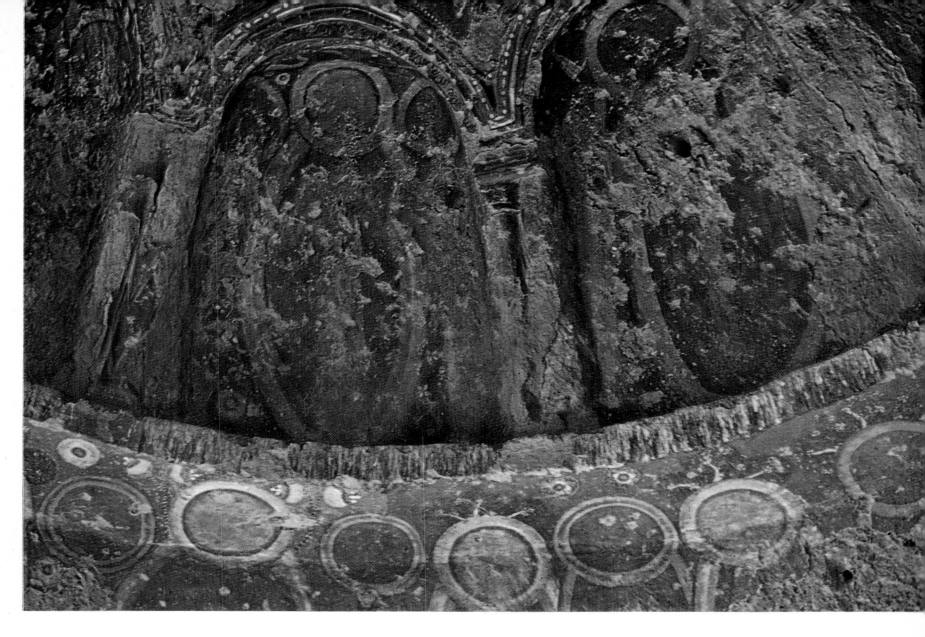

Inside the cliff is a warren of cells, sanctuaries, galleries, passages and stairways. Thousands of monks worshipped here. Some larger caves are domed or given imitation 'lantern' roofs and painted with frescoes expressing Buddhist concepts. The style is that of Gandhara—a product of united Hellenistic and Indian traditions. Above: frescoes on the domed ceiling of a circular chamber close to the smaller of the two Buddhas; it is reached by climbing stairs at the side of the statue and then walking round the top of the head. Several features of the style recall Early Christian and Byzantine art—the haloes, the position of the feet and hands and the decoration between the figures. Right: two more details from the cells—a Bodhisattva and a Corinthian column, symbol of the relationship between Central Asia and the classical world.

In the 9th century Bamian was conquered by the Moslems. The monks were massacred, the Kushan city nearby destroyed, the faces of the two Great Buddhas systematically hacked away. In 1221 the Moslem city across the valley (from which pl. 30 was taken) was itself wiped out by Genghis Khan. (31–33)

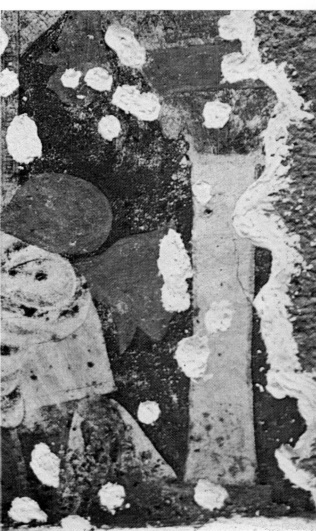

One of the most cosmopolitan cities in the world

during the 3rd and 4th centuries AD must have been Begram, the capital of the great Kushan dynasty whose kingdom stretched as far as the Ganges. All the objects on this page were excavated at this one site. Top left: a Hellenistic bronze figurine—the club and apples belong to Hercules, but the vine-decorated *modius* on the head is an attribute of the Egyptian god Serapis. Centre: a *yaksi* or river-goddess, in ivory—part of a larger composition; the voluptuous pose, the transparent drapery, the half-smile, are completely Indian. Top right: plaster medallion of a youth wearing a helmet—'Pompeiian' decoration; the same head appears on Roman coins and gems. Lower right: Syrian glass goblet painted with figures. Bottom: engraved ivory casket-lid, showing ladies at their toilet, in the same Indian style as the ivory relief. (34–38)

The new knowledge of early Afghanistan

EDWARD BACON

The enigma of Afghanistan and its neighbours is one that is in course of solution; and it can be compared with the missing books of a history which are still coming to light and for the most part await decipherment. It seems that this great region played in prehistoric times much the same part as it played in later years—that of transmitter and bridge-land. Just as Hellenism and Islam passed through it on their way to India, so it seems possible that the influences which first stimulated the Indus Valley civilization passed the same way. And was it Aryan invaders, crossing the same bridge, who so radically changed the old order and destroyed and superseded that great civilization? Many clues are there to be found and although the way of archaeology has been difficult—for political and geographical reasons alike—the situation has improved and French and American archaeologists in particular have made extensive, important and often surprising discoveries.

It is their discoveries and theories which are described in the following pages; and the descriptions and conclusions reached are based entirely on the researches of Dr Walter A. Fairservis, Jr, of the American Museum of Natural History and Director of the new Museum of the University of Washington, Seattle.

IT IS ALMOST 1200 miles from the valley of the Zarafshan River, on whose banks stands Samarkand the Golden, south to the Makran shores of the Arabian Sea. It is about 1000 miles from the Khyber Pass to Teheran, capital of modern Iran, the city which stands between the watered Elburz Mountain valleys that fringe the Caspian Sea on the north and the arid wastes of the great Salt Desert of Persia on the south and east. This vast area which lies between Mesopotamia, India, and ultimately, China, is geographically a part of the Iranian plateau. As such, it is characterized by a series of desert basins and the barren mountain chains that form the borders of the basins. Over much of the region rainfall is exceedingly sparse, less than ten inches annually, and in some years none at all.

It is a melancholy but attractive land, witnessing on every hand the inexorable forces of an epic geology. Immense talus fans spread out in their thick pebbled masses from the mouths of ravines cut into the flora-less brown slopes, bearing testimony to centuries of sudden devastating floods; the kind of floods that destroyed a part of Alexander's army during the march on the return from India. Many striking scenes meet the eye: enormous playas glaring white in trackless salt wastes, great sand dunes engulfing ridged stone hills, the rays of the moving sun, the changing colours of the exposed rock strata. It is a thirsty land, exposed to a relentless sun in summer and to bitter cold winds in winter. It is the wind which is memorable, for it forms the paradox of the region. In its steady blowing in summer man has an ally which blows away the vicious biting flies native to the few watered places, and a wholesome agent which dries and cools the sweat on his brow and whisks down the shafts of mud ventilators to refresh the air of the houses; but in the spring when the wind picks up the winter-loosened sand and carries it at velocities of 60 to 70 miles per hour across the basins of Seistan, or in winter when it hurtles in an icy blast down the Quetta Valley, it is man's true enemy.

On the east of the region, mountain ranges fan out from the central knot, the Pamirs, sometimes called the Roof of the World.

Like the fingers of a hand these mountain ranges stretch generally westward: the Suleiman, the Khirtar, Hindu Kush, Koh-i-Baba. Each has had a prominent rôle in the course of human history. The Suleiman and Khirtar ranges mark the eastern fringe of the Iranian Plateau and make a clear division between the Indo-Pakistan subcontinent and Inner Asia. The Hindu Kush and Koh-i-Baba constitute the mountain backbone of modern Afghanistan. On the south of this mountain chain is the desert country Registan, and Dasht-i-Margo, while on the north is the broad grassy plain which proclaims Central Asia as surely as salt water symbolizes the sea.

pl 7

The Waters that Bring Life

But it is not as boundaries that the mountains gain greatest importance. It is because their high slopes intercept the Atlantic winds which are the rain-bringers here. The high valleys are well-watered and many are the seats of considerable forests. It is the gathering of the waters in the high valleys and their subsequent descent to the arid lands below that means life to the region. How storied are the rivers of this region; storied in a continent of storied rivers. The Helmand, whose valley is a highway in a virtually impassable land; the Hari Rud, the moisture basin for the city of Herat, sometimes called the key to India; the Kabul River whose abrading flood cut the Khyber Pass; the fabled Central Asian rivers, Murghab and Zarafshan, and above all the Amu Darya, the Oxus, seat of empires.

f 2
pl 5

But it must be remembered that it is not really the rivers of history that mean survival to the thousands of modern villages whose field patches delineate the tillable soil of mountain valleys and desert rim. It is the small streams like Porali of Las Bela, the Kunduz of Baghlan, and the Hanna of Quetta whose perennial flow is a constant in the lives of settler and traveller alike. It is the reservoir of water hidden deep in the talus of even the barren ranges of the Great Salt Desert which, tapped by means of deep wells and the painfully wrought but efficient karez (khanat) systems of shafts and tunnels, is the most significant source of all. For when knowing men realized that water was hidden even in the desert, the terrors of a precarious existence were somewhat mollified.

It is obvious that this terrain prescribes men's actions. Farmers are limited in the amount of soil they can till. A season of exceptional rain may open normally desert areas but inevitably a return has to be made to that area which artificial or natural means of bringing water has made dependable. The staple crops are wheat, millet and barley but the wondrous ability of melons to retain sweet water in plenty makes their cultivation greatly desired. Dates, onions, pomegranates, and lovely roses are common. But it is a rare village that does not have its quota of sheep and goats to provide essentials of hide, hair, milk and meat. Transhumance—a sort of annual 'shuttle' migration—is the practice of many inhabitants. Until recently the passes leading into the Punjab and Sind were choked annually with the comings and goings of Brahui and Pathan whose caravans moved seasonally from traditional highland homes to lowland camps in time-honoured search for grass and trade.

pl 7
8

The Bridge of Peoples

The region is criss-crossed with ancient routes: the Makran coast with its old sea ports, the east-west and north-south valley roads of Baluchistan, the Helmand River road from Seistan to Kandahar, the mountain road from Herat to Kabul, the desert roads from Meshed to Merv, Balkh, Bukhara and on to China, the difficult road from the Turkestan plain over the high passes to Kabul and beyond and finally the historic passes Mula, Gaj, Bolan, Gomel, Tochi, and Khyber. These routes follow the easiest courses nature has created: they lead from spring to stream, to wells and oases, to rivers and ravines, and eventually from villages to cities. Their existence has been the reason why so many writers have labelled Turkestan, Afghanistan, Baluchistan and Seistan the 'bridge-lands'. They are the geographical links beween such centres of high human achievement as Mesopotamia and India.

pl 5

But to take the term too literally is to misunderstand these lands. One of the real surprises to the wanderer travelling in the region is the revelation of areas of natural prosperity in the midst of waste. The great plains of grass now largely replaced by cultivated cotton have made Uzbekistan one of the leading textile producers in the USSR, and surely everyone has heard of the apricots and roses of Central Asia. The luxuriant pastoral scenery around Kandahar is worthy of a Millet, and any who have travelled in the broad valleys of Charikar, Jalalabad and Bamian know how fecund the upland valleys of Afghanistan can be. Even poor Baluchistan, which has been described as 'thousands and thousands of sheep living on nothing' has a bright return for those who reach her easternmost regions. Apozai, Ziarat, the Quetta Valley, and Kolwa are celebrated for natural vegetation. Some of these places are now seats of prosperous farms, among which the fruits of Quetta are famous all over the subcontinent. Las Bela town on the extreme south-east is set in a ten mile square area of fertile fields and old trees among which graze some of the fattest cattle in Pakistan. Makran is celebrated for its dates. To this extent there are areas that belie the region's reputation as inhospitable to man.

It is necessary to be aware of these features of the geography in order to understand the peculiar importance to the story of mankind of the archaeological remains found in the region. For as long as men have existed there since the Palaeolithic, it would appear that essentially the same scenes have met their eye: barren mountain, vast desert, and luxuriant patches of vegetation. Such an environment limits human actions. It forces men to congregate wherever there is water and to build where there is tillable soil. It delineates the highways along which men had to move and dictated thereby the places where cities and fortresses were to stand. In spite of these limitations, or perhaps because of them, communication between men was made easy. It is no coincidence that some archaeological remains found in Turkestan can be almost duplicated by those unearthed in Baluchistan far to the south. The traveller could find familiar things no matter how far in the region he might travel. Strangers were and, in fact, are commonplace in this land and the gossip of the world has been known to villagers from the shores of the Caspian to the jungles of Kolwa. The region then is varied in context but similar in both its general geographical and human cultural character. It is this paradoxical quality which puzzles the archaeologist studying the past of the region, a quality which was unquestionably a motivating factor in the development there of the characteristic cultures which played an important rôle in human history.

The Millennia of the Hunters

The first human occupation that we know very much about was that of the Neanderthals of Upper Pleistocene times. Soviet archaeologists working in the Oxus River region in the 1930's had found stone working of Mousterian character. Particularly important was the region of Baisun in Uzbekistan not far to the north of ancient Termez. Here a great many caves are found in the valley of the Shirabad River. Under the direction of the eminent prehistorian A. P. Okladnikov, the lower cave of a group known collectively as Teshik-Tash has been excavated. Five culture layers were found, each separated from the others by a sterile layer. The five layers represent a longevity of occupation but a general homogeneity of culture. The stone tools encountered are the flakes, scrapers, points, and cores of the Mousterian tradition, and a bit of worked bone completes the artifact inventory. The outstanding find was made in the uppermost layer. Here, surrounded by six pairs of Siberian mountain goat horns, was the skull and skeleton of a Neanderthal child. The evidence indicated that the child had been buried in a pit not far from a hearth.

We are given an insight by this discovery of a primitive world of food-gatherers and hunters. They were living in a cool climate of mountains and valleys and preying upon the goats, deer, wild horses and such birds as the Asiatic rock partridges and the rock pigeons, fauna which mark the unchanging Central Asian character of the times. The brown bear, leopard and hyena gave an element of danger to the hunt and in fact there is evidence that after burial a hyena dug to the corpse in search of flesh.

The Neanderthals of Central Asia were cave dwellers in winter and campers in summer, a seasonal factor familiar in another form in later times. The basis of the cave economy was the mountain goat; the difficulty of hunting this elusive beast in the wilds of the mountains was surmounted only by the individual skill of each

hunter and their group co-operation in driving the game to a place where the simple weapons of the time—spears, clubs, and rolling stones could be brought into play. The successful hunter brought the carcass to his cave where a family waited about the fire. Here was the social centre whose symbol was the hearth, centre of warmth and protection. As did the Neanderthal men of Western Europe, the men of Teshik-Tash appear to have had a belief in an after-life. For the disturbed child's pit-grave close to the hearth and surrounded by the horns of the mountain goat indicates a ceremonialism in which cogniscence was paid to activity after death whether for good or for bad.

That Neanderthal man was widespread in the Indo-Iranian area appears to be indicated by the sporadic occurrence there of the Mousterian and Levalloisian type tools generally associated with him. In northern Afghanistan Louis Duprée has discovered a number of cave sites at which Middle Palaeolithic tools have been found. Chance finds of similar tools are reported for Seistan and the Mashkel basin. At the latter place cursory examination of the find spots by geologists suggests the existence of a large interior lake or inland sea on whose shores Stone Age men hunted and camped. Though outside the area, the discovery of Middle Palaeolithic flake tools in the terraces of the Indus River indicates a farther spread of Neanderthals into the sub-continent.

Carlton Coon's excavation of the rock-shelter of Kara Kamar in northern Afghanistan revealed the presence of an Upper Palaeolithic tool tradition there which may have flourished some 30,000 years ago. But except for scattered finds of bladetools here and there throughout the region, the important period between the time of the Teshik-Tash Neanderthals and the coming of food-production is still largely hidden from us. There are, however, evidences for Mesolithic hunters and fishers around the Caspian Sea, particularly in cave sites.

Farms and Houses: the Mound of Djeitun

The surveys and excavations of V. M. Masson in Turkmenistan have produced the first full evidence we have for agricultural settlements east of the Caspian Sea. Close to the present border of north-eastern Iran the Russians have investigated a number of village sites which present an almost unbroken sequence from the 4th to the 1st millennium BC. The earliest of these sites is the small mound of Djeitun. The excavations there have revealed a settlement of small one-room houses erratically grouped about one another with irregular lanes between. These houses were made of sun-dried clay blocks of adobe type. Each house has a small yard presumably to retain a few goats and sheep. There are also small storage buildings connected with the yards. A typical house was approximately square, varying from 2 to 35 square metres in size. There was a storage area partitioned off and in at least one case a storage pit set in the plastered floor; a hearth against one wall and what might have been a ceremonial niche in the opposite wall completed the house plan.

The settlements were in the midst of the cultivated fields and one can assume that each farmer had direct access from his house and yard to his own field. Impressions of wheat and barley grains have been found in the clay of the houses. Bone sickle handles and flint blades, storage vessels and bins within the houses demonstrate how important agriculture was in the life of the Djeitun farmers.

It is the stone industry of Djeitun that indicates that the farmers were in a transitional stage during which hunting still had a prominent place. The industry is essentially microlithic. There are the diminutive geometric forms of borers, trapezes, notched blades, polyhedral cores, blades and micro-scrapers familiar to the Mesolithic culture of an earlier period. Bone implements include the usual food-gatherers' repertoire of needles, pins, borers and shoulder bone scrapers. There are fine bone beads cylindrical in shape and frequently grooved. The remains of the desert gazelle (subguttorosa) and of wild goats and sheep outnumber those of domesticated animals. This is a situation familiar at other comparable sites of the Near and Middle East. It is indicative of the fact that domestication was still an uncertain process; perhaps breeding was slow. Meat had still to be drawn largely from the hunt.

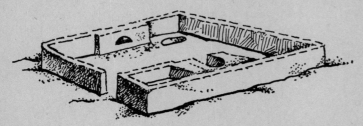

Partial reconstruction of a house at Djeitun. It consisted of a single room, the floor covered with lime-plaster. In the wall left of the entrance was the hearth, and on the right a walled-off corner for storage and another square structure with a niche. Nineteen houses of this type have been excavated at Djeitun. (1)

In spite of the flourishing hunting aspect of Djeitun there is little doubt of the relatively advanced state of settled life there. Pottery, while handmade and coarse-tempered, is rather sophisticatedly decorated in patterns of wavy lines painted with a dark colour on a cream or buff surface. Simple clay figurines of animals, small conical clay objects of unknown usage, demonstrate an easy familiarity with clay as a mouldable medium. Polished stone axes quadrangular in section, pierced stone discs and grinding and polishing stones prove the depth of the involvement of Djeitun in the Neolithic World.

The Djeitun farmers' world was not unlike that of his equivalent in Western Iran and Mesopotamia. To the north was the arid waste of the Kara Kum desert, while on the south were the Kopet-Dagh ranges from which came the streams bearing the water which made agriculture possible. The best areas for agriculture were along the piedmont zones and immediately adjoining flat lands. These extended approximately north-west and south-east. Masson would derive the Mesolithic elements of the Djeitun culture from the Mesolithic cultures of the Caspian Sea region to which they bear many similarities. Whether this is the result of their derivation from a common ancestor or a contemporary integration, or both, is not certain on the present evidence.

It is clear, however, that Djeitun in its food-production aspects ultimately links with earlier farming cultures known in the Near East. Masson has pointed to the plastered floors, terracotta cones and the storage facilities as common to both Djeitun and sites such as Jarmo and Tell-es-Sultan at Jericho. He also emphasizes the importance of the bone sickle handle as a possible link with the Natufian of Palestine.

The Djeitun culture gives one the impression of a situation in which farming was forcing a kind of enclave of settled life into the home grounds of highly skilled hunters who already knew the food value of local plants. Farming was successful in finding disciples but even its most loyal adherents were unwilling to give up entirely the hunting which had formerly been the sole basis of the economy, and which, until domestication was proved feasible, was still the best source of meat. It must be remembered in this regard that man is omnivorous and meat consumption a natural part of his diet. Until he had other sources, hunting was still important.

Djeitun is extraordinary in its revelation of a Mesolithic hunting culture integrated with a full Neolithic. On the present evidence it cannot be given a date much before the middle of the 5th millennium BC, a date which would seem to mark the progress of food-production towards the east.

Djeitun is the earliest of the series of developing farming cultures that we know for Turkmenistan and north-eastern Iran. Later cultures demonstrate, as expected, the increased control of agricultural and domestication techniques and the gradual reduction of food-gathering to a lesser rôle in the economy—though it never disappears completely. These changes are symbolized by the augmenting farming tool repertories and the perfecting of methods of technology. Brick, for example, replaced adobe; copper makes its appearance as early as the Dashlydji stage which is immediately subsequent to that of Djeitun. Copper tools and weapons of various kinds: axes, spearheads, needles, etc., appear in quantity from this stage on.

The painting of pottery and the forms of the vessels demonstrate increased sophistication in the knowledge of this medium by the potter. Simple monochrome painting is later supplemented by polychromes. Designs extend to the stylized depictions of animals and people. Clay figurines of women frequently steatopygous may be indicative of the existence of a fertility cult though this evidence, *per se*, is not conclusive. These figurines, at first simply moulded, were in the early stages incised and (or) painted, but in later stages appliqué decoration was used. Weaving of bast fibres and possibly flax and hair became commonplace, if the number of spindle whorls recovered by the excavators is any criterion.

Villages and Towns: the North

After the Djeitun culture, settlements grow more numerous and more complex. One of the earliest villages, at Yalangach, in the Tedjen River delta, consisted of groups of small, oval, single-roomed houses set in a compound wall at odd intervals. Within the wall were other utility and living houses set closely together. This type of settlement developed into real towns, not unlike those that are to be seen in the Middle East today. At Kara Tepe, midway between the Tedjen Delta and Ashkhabad, the houses were situated along narrow alley-ways leading to a square which was probably used for markets. The houses contained numerous rooms grouped round inner squares open to the sky, in some of which were located the kitchen-hearths. The rooms, various in size, were both for living and for utilitarian storage. In the living areas were hearths (in the centre) and an occasional heating oven. The latter consisted of a large bottomless vessel sunk into the floor. A fire within this vessel could heat the floor and thus the room.

By now (c. 3000 BC) copper implements, bangles, rings and the like were commonplace. Figurine decor was sophisticated; pottery painted decoration included a variety of geometric designs, together with goats, birds, and human figures. The style had become loose and the crisp horizontality of the earlier potters had generally given way to overall patterning rather rich in detail. A characteristic feature is the compartmented seal. This is diamond-shaped or triangular in form and cut with geometric designs frequently concentric in pattern. Of great interest are two-wheel model carts which are probably indicative of the existence then of cattle- or goat-drawn vehicles. Strangely, the potter's wheel was still not used in this area. Evidence of the skill which this people had acquired is provided by necklaces made out of finely cut and polished beads manufactured out of comparatively hard stones such as agate, carnelian and lapis. Examples have been excavated from Kara Tepe (level III), Namazgah (level III) and the famous site of Anau.

Burial customs give us strong clues to ancient religious beliefs. Many of the burials found by the excavators were in pits, some of which were lined with brick. These burials were usually loosely flexed and were commonly found among the houses, where presumably the deceased had once dwelt. The early inhabitants of Tepe Hissar (Hissar I) consistently buried their dead on the right side in a loosely flexed position with the face generally towards the sun. The Hissar burials occur among the houses as do those of Turkmenistan. However, the Hissar I people seem to have been more generous in supplying their dead with funerary furniture. The dead were apparently well-dressed though cloth has not survived, but an abundance of beads, diadems, bracelets and anklets were recovered from these grave pits. With these are fine painted vessels and copper objects, including daggers in the case of the men.

This treatment of the dead more than suggests that there was a prevalent belief in an after-life of sorts. Certainly the willingness to bury the deceased in the proximity of the living suggests strong family ties and a lack of fear of ghosts so prevalent in other cultures. Proper orientation, funerary furniture and a standardized burial position are also indicative of expected future activities for the deceased.

The evidence tends to show that all the sites in southern Turkmenistan and north-eastern Iran belonged to a single culture, with local variations. All over the region there is a clear evolution

pl 9

pl 12
13

from simple farming by a few families clustered in a small village, to large settlements with numbers of specialists like the metal-smith, potter and weaver, carrying on non-farming activities. But how much of this evolution was the result of local creativity and how much due to the diffusion of cultural traits from developing regions elsewhere is not so clear.

Northern Afghanistan is rich in archaeological remains but at present only a bare handful of painted sherds serves to represent what must have been an extensive settlement there. Provocative is a single sherd of obvious prehistoric ware found in the moat of the Bala Hissar at Balkh which has a painted design of a spiral. The spiral motif is found in the painted pottery of Tripolje west of the Caspian and is known in a somewhat different form in Kansu.

A Land of Extremes: Seistan

The flow of the rivers of north-western Afghanistan is generally to the north-west. The river valleys form natural routes to the east and south-east. Future exploration of them should provide us with sites linking Northern Iran to Baluchistan. The great valley of the Hari Rud which forms a natural road into the heart of Afghanistan is virtually unexplored archaeologically. Yet here is found the city of Herat, set in the midst of a fine cultivated plain on whose surface are numerous mounds that mark the site of ancient villages. Here is a proper goal for future archaeological work.

South of Herat is the city of Farah, located at the strategic point where the road from the north has passed the western extension of the Central Ranges of Afghanistan and turns eastward toward Kandahar and the Indian passes. Here too the Farah Rud creates a natural road into the Seistan basin and the Lower Helmand Valley. The Farah plain is dotted with mounds. Cursory examination of these has indicated that a prehistoric people, making a fine black on buff slip pottery, once built their villages there. They were living at a period probably somewhat later than the Hissar I culture.

pl 6

The Seistan basin is the delta of the Helmand River. It marks the lowest portion of the great Tertiary depression of Southern Afghanistan. The Helmand River leaves the mountains near Girishk. At Kala Bist, where are the ruins of the palaces of Mahmud of Ghazni, the river is augmented by the flood of the Arghandab. The Helmand Valley at this point has cut a valley in the desert basin at places 7 to 8 miles in width. The southern rim of the basin is marked by the low hills of Chagai along which runs the present Pakistan frontier. The elevation of these hills turns the river course from south to west. The long gentle slope (187 feet in 70 miles) to the west terminates in the great Hamun-i-Seistan, a shallow lake whose western rim is formed by the arid mountains of Eastern Iran. The Hamun fluctuates with the river flood. In spring it is a broad expanse made idyllic by great flights of birds who flock to the reed jungles at its rims. In the autumn it is a shallow pond whose shores are hard, brown and lifeless.

Seistan is a land of extremes. The British Seistan boundary commission of 1904–1905 recorded a winter wind of 120 miles per hour. In May, the so-called wind of 120 Days commences. This can average 40–50 miles per hour with gusts up to 70 miles per hour. The heat is intense in summer, and the cold bitter in winter. The Seistan biting fly is an excruciating plague to the traveller.

Yet the abundant water, the lovely green vegetation in such contrast to the endless brown of the desert, the good soil which provides fine crops when used correctly, make Seistan attractive and men have been willing to accept the difficulties to enjoy the benefits. In fact, large numbers of ruins have been found, most of which have since proved to be Muslem or Partho-Sassanian. But on the southern portion of the basin there is an old course of the Helmand called the Rud-i-Biyaban (Dry River). In the ancient delta of this river the British observers of the Boundary Commissions of 1875 and 1904–5 noticed black-topped hills or mesas. The black colour, on closer inspection, proved to be caused by masses of slag and pottery. This material had acted as a cover for the underlying silt during the violent Seistan windstorms. As a result, as the surrounding area had been eroded away, the protected areas remained as small black-topped hills. The observers noted a great

pl 5

f 2

Prehistoric and protohistoric settlements in the Seistan basin. In the north and west lies the Hamun-i-Seistan, a large shallow lake whose area and level fluctuate with the seasons. Into it flow the Farah Rud from the north and the Helmand, by a delta, from the south. In ancient times the Helmand, instead of bending north as it now does, continued westward and entered the Hamun-i-Seistan at its southern tip. The old course, known as the Rud-i-Biyaban (Dry River), is marked by dotted lines on the map. It is here that the prehistoric sites are concentrated. (2)

many of these hills in every direction. In Partho-Sassanid times some of them were used as the sites of a line of watch-towers. Obviously, each of these hills represents the location of a small habitation. It remained for that indefatigable archaeological explorer, Sir Aurel Stein, to prove that these habitation sites were largely prehistoric. He found abundant painted pottery of the black on buff type along with flint blades, beads, alabaster cups, and other prehistoric artifacts. All these sites showed a striking homogeneity. One gets the impression that Seistan was occupied by prehistoric farmers for a limited time only. But of course later excavations may tell a different story.

One of the best preserved villages consisted of small single-roomed houses set in fairly regular order along a series of lanes. The inhabitants appear to have had good sources of copper ore and alabaster in the vicinity, for those raw materials and artifacts made from them are in no little abundance in these sites.

pl 10

Close to this habitation was the cemetery. What graves were perceptible were completely excavated by the wind and the contents strewn about. Enough remained, however, to prove that burial had been in a brick-lined pit, that the body had been flexed and surrounded by funerary furniture which consisted, as far as can be determined, of painted pottery, alabaster cups, copper mirrors, and necklaces.

pl 11

The Seistan artifacts have a close affinity with the culture identified by Sir Aurel Stein in south-east Iran along the Bampur river, a culture which in its turn is related to the Kile Ghul Mohammad cultures of West Pakistan. In general it would appear that Seistan was not on the direct line of diffusion from northern Iran to Baluchistan.

East of Seistan, in the plain of Kandahar, flourished the Morasi culture, so-called from the type site of Deh Morasi. Here the people lived in small mud-brick houses set in the midst of cultivated fields. Sheep, goats, and cattle were domesticated, the latter of Bos Indicus or humped type. They used copper, carved and polished stone beads and compartmented seals. Their pottery is characterized by black on buff painting and by squat, small-mouth jars and stemmed vessels. Bull figurines of terracotta and stone were commonly made. The most striking object recovered is a mother goddess figurine of pedestal type. Her appliqué goggle-eyes and heavy necklace prove that she belongs to the so-called 'Zhob Mother Goddess' family, well known in northern Baluchistan. This Afghan representative has a sharp incision in her forehead and red colouring matter on her body suggesting some ritualistic role.

Another site, Said Kala, revealed an early phase of the Deh Morasi culture in its upper levels. However, below these levels the fine wheel-made pottery of the Morasi culture is replaced by a crude hand-made ware associated with flint blades, crude brick houses, and the usual plentitude of sheep and goat bones. No figurines were found at these levels.

The Mound of Mundigak

The best picture of ancient Afghanistan is provided by the excavations, only very recently published, of the high mound of Mundigak, north-west of Kandahar. This site was occupied over a long period and has been divided by the excavators into ten levels. The first inhabitants were a semi-settled people who probably practised transhumance. But soon it was occupied all the year round and its people formed increasingly strong contacts with areas to the south and west. Copper implements appear at level 6 and painted pottery gradually comes into use. The later levels show an intimate relation with Quetta ware.

During the final phases of Mundigak's history the character of the occupation changes. This change is in keeping with a similar phenomenon in the Baluchistan sites to which Mundigak is related. In spite of the badly eroded condition of the upper part of the mound the French were able to unearth features of a truly monumental building. This building was fronted on its northern side by a double row of clay half-columns set on a platform and covered by an ornamented roof to form a kind of porch colonnade. The building itself appears to have risen in terraces to a flat top. This was reached by entering a red-painted door in the middle of the columns and moving along a passage to the west of the building where a stairway led upwards.

On the side facing the colonnade were the remnants of rather complex structures consisting of various rooms and courtyards. On other sides of the main building were storerooms or cells at various levels as if in the service of the main structure. Associated with the main building were globular vessels painted handsomely with animals: ibex, birds, and pipal leaves.

The colonnaded building is eventually replaced by a similar but more massive, less well-built structure with which was associated a rather degenerate female figurine of the 'Zhob Goddess' type. The last occupations of the mound are unimportant to this part of this account except that they illustrate more troubled days for the people of Mundigak.

This truly remarkable site presents a vivid insight into the changing world of the late prehistoric farmer. A radio-carbon date of 2625 BC plus or minus 300 for the 5th level adds further proof to the suggestion made by other sites in Baluchistan that those farming cultures of the area on the easternmost reaches of the Iranian Plateau were very localized and lagged behind their western counterparts in the development of their technology. Kandahar did not have the attraction of Turkmenistan to early farmers, perhaps because of its remoteness.

The Iranian archaeologist finds much that is familiar in these Kandahar sites but he becomes aware particularly in the remains of the upper levels of a new and strange influence. Pipal leaves, humped bulls, goggle-eyed 'goddesses', and elaborate structures

set on high parts of the sites are symptomatic of other interests and influences. These can be summed up in the single word 'India'. To understand what this means one must examine the prehistoric sites of Baluchistan.

Approach to India: Baluchistan

Baluchistan is the mountainous eastern rim of the Iranian Plateau. It is also a part of the mountain barrier which sets off the Indian subcontinent from the rest of Asia. Too far to the west to come under the rain shadow of the monsoon, the region depends for its moisture on the same Atlantic winds that sporadically bring rain to the plateau. What rainfall there is is jealously stored in the talus gravels of the valley slopes or in some fortunate cases channelled into perennial streams, but the rate of evaporation is high and few indeed are the streams that reach the Indus Valley or the Arabian Sea.

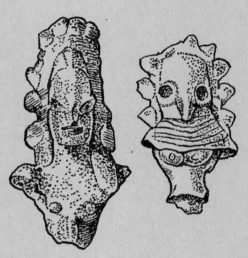

'Zhob Goddesses', strange goggle-eyed figurines, have been found at several sites, including Mundigak, Dabar Kot and Periano Ghundai. The two shown here are from Damb Sadaat. (3)

It has been customary in recent years to regard the ancient farmers whose village mounds occur in every valley as members of peasant cultures. This term 'peasant' carries a connotation that they were subject to overlords or at least cultural inferiors of the Indus Valley civilizations. The term is inappropriate, for the bulk of the Baluchistan prehistoric cultures now known were rather in the ancestral line towards the Indus civilizations than subjected contemporaries. The development of civilization outside the Near Eastern centres of civilized origins, particularly in areas as remote as India, is a phenomenon of no little importance to the history of man. We ask ourselves: was the civilization of Harappā and Mohenjo-daro the result of contacts no matter how remote with ancient Mesopotamia or was it the natural climax of ever developing cultures placed in a favourable environment, or was it indeed something of both? There is no clear answer yet, but prehistoric Baluchistan provides two valuable contributions to the problem: 1) It was the screen through which many west-east cultural traits had to find their way; 2) Its position at the very edge of the Indus Valley made its cultures a kind of mirror reflecting the developments in the valley itself.

The emphasis upon the forbidding qualities of Baluchistan in the literature have done much to give the region a relatively minor place in the story of the Indus civilization. But evidence demonstrates how very important was Baluchistan's rôle. It is a matter of some astonishment to discover how thickly settled were the valleys of prehistoric Baluchistan. The Quetta Valley for example in one period supported more than 20 villages; the Ornach of southern Kalat had 8; the plain around Duki in Loralai had at least 5, one of which was so large as to warrant the term 'town'; northern Las Bela had such a concentration of settlements as to approach urbanization. These quantities not only compare favourably with the modern situation but in some cases exceed it.

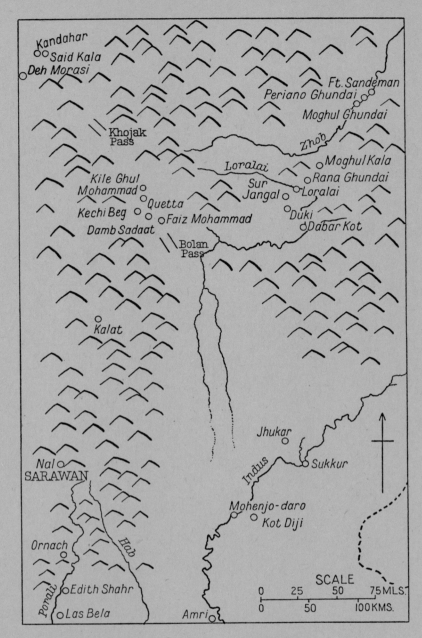

Map of the Quetta area, in relation to the Indus Valley sites. (4)

How such populations were supported in an arid land with relatively primitive means is uncertain. There are great dams or *gobarbands* which certainly had a rôle in conserving the water supply. Our evidence indicates that a variety of specialized workers were available. We can assume at least that the farming communities were beautifully adapted to the land and were prepared to anticipate her whims.

In our present knowledge of the archaeology of Baluchistan the Quetta Valley is of prime importance. This valley lies at the head of the Bolan Pass on the south and is connected by easy roads to the Zhob Valley and to Kalat-Chagai in several directions. The difficult though effectively passable Khojak Pass gives access to Kandahar. At the centre of the valley is Quetta City, favourably situated in the midst of a system of artesian wells and the drainage of the Hanna River. The city is dominated by a huge mound, whose inner core, tossed out on its slopes by British engineers in the 19th century to make an arsenal, evidences some five thousand years of human occupancy from a primitive flint knife to a Victorian coin. From this hub of archaeological continuity one travels a few miles north or south and finds on every side the familiar village mounds of ancient man.

One of these mounds, Kile Ghul Mohammad, provided vivid evidence for the longevity of man's occupation in this part of Baluchistan. Here the very earliest inhabitants did not know the use of pottery. They were apparently semi-nomadic pastoral people who lived in adobe and probably wattle and daub huts and later made them of mudbrick. They herded goats and sheep and possibly aurochs-like cattle. They had sickles (the flint blades have been found but not the bone handles they were hafted to). On the evidence it would appear that they grew wheat and barley. This period of the culture has been labelled Kile Ghul Mohammad I (KGM I).

The next stage (KGM II) is marked by the arrival of pottery. It is coarse and hand-made, frequently basket-marked. Dabs of red paint suggest some decorative intent. The excavations have revealed traces of houses with substantial brick walls.

With Kile Ghul Mohammad III we reach wheel-made pottery, decorated by simple geometric designs in black on a red slip. This pottery is symptomatic of what must have been a strong diffusion of north Iranian influences. It is possible to trace these borrowings from earlier Iranian cultures and to establish their sources—one of them is Chashmi-Ali, near Teheran, upon which a type of pottery known as Togau ware is based. This has been found in the state of Kalat, south as far as Las Bela on the Arabian Sea and west almost to the Iranian frontier. It is a black-on-red painted ware, specially distinguished for open bowls with decoration on the interior. The characteristic design is a row of goat or deer heads whose horns or antlers are depicted with considerable flourish. In subsequent periods the heads disappear leaving in their stead the curving horns which in a final stage are merely commas.

New Ideas from the North

After KGM III came an influx of new ideas and developments, mostly from northern Iran. A fairly unified cultural pattern emerges, which is found in virtually all parts of Baluchistan and which has interesting parallels with the pre-Harappān cultures of

pl 15

f 5

A comparison of pottery designs from the Chashmi-Ali culture of northern Iran, with Togau ware from Baluchistan, showing the similarities of design between west and east. (5)

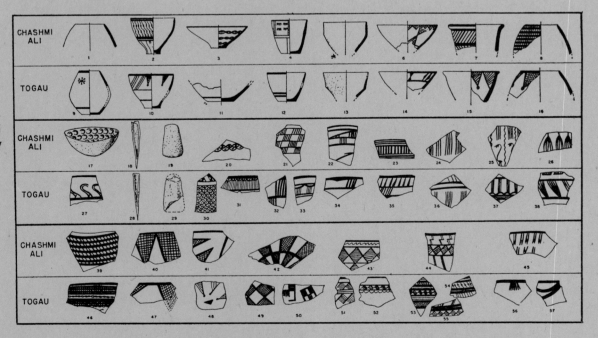

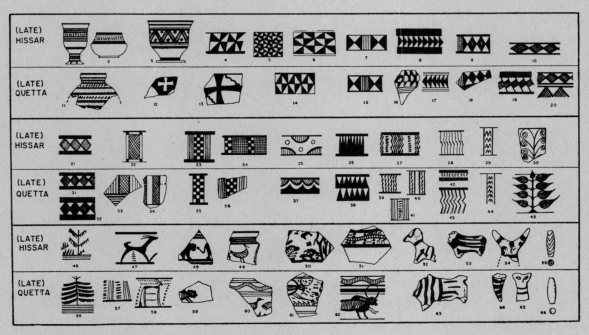

Chart to show stylistic links between the Loralai and Quetta districts of Baluchistan and the pre-Harappān Amri-A culture of the Indus valley. (6)

f 6   the Indus valley—the Amri culture in western Sind and the Kot Diji culture further to the north. The name of Kechi Beg has been given to it, from the type-site excavated near the village of that name a few miles south of Quetta. It is characterized by new pottery types, advances in building techniques and increased use of cattle, though it also includes survivals from the earlier cultures. Examination of some representative Kechi Beg sites will make this clear.

  One of the earliest is the uppermost level of Kile Ghul Mohammad itself (KGM IV). Here the old black-on-red ware is found in conjunction with a new black-on-buff ware related to the so-

f 7   called Hissar cultures of Iran.

  Polychrome pottery was achieved slightly later; it occurs at the lowest levels of the large site of Damb Sadaat, some eleven miles south of Quetta City. Here also two other important features appear for the first time: the use of boulders as foundation for

pl 21   mud-brick walls, and pottery marks—perhaps indicating the beginning of a system of communication by symbols, in other words of writing.

  The typical Kechi Beg pottery is a beautiful thin-walled deep vase with parallel sides decorated in horizontal rows of black and red painted designs. These designs are drawn with exceeding fineness and demonstrate complete mastery of the medium. Other common types are finely made open bowls and small-mouthed globular jars with a band of chocolate or black paint round the rim or the shoulder, or both.

  Progress in engineering is shown by a site in the Upper Hab River valley in Las Bela, built on the talus of the eastern slope of the valley. This site is close to the mouth of a ravine which leads out of a natural reservoir formed by the principal mountain mass and its piedmont. The inhabitants of the site were able to build a fine dry-stone dam across the ravine thus imprisoning the run-off of the barren slopes. The water was then released at will into irrigation channels and the whole of the alluvial plain in the vicinity irrigated. This is in contrast to the miserable fields of the modern villages which are virtually confined to the flood plain below the silt bluffs cut by the Hab River.

  At Nal, in the Sarawan district of Kalat State, excavation has uncovered the usual settlement of mud-brick huts, some of them with the stone foundations characteristic of the Kechi Beg culture. The inhabitants seem to have practised two kinds of burial. The first is the familiar flexed burial in a brick-lined pit in the floor of the houses; the second, fractional burial in which parts of skeletons were placed either in or among funerary vessels. These vessels, which also occur among the pit burials, are superb examples of the potter's art. The finest are canister or globular in shape painted in

A comparison by means of pottery designs and figurines between the late Hissar culture of northern Iran and the late Quetta culture of Baluchistan. (7)

polychromes of black, red, green, and blue in wonderful patterns of precisely arranged geometric, floral, or animal designs. Fish, birds, and goats are favourite design elements and are delightfully rendered. Flat copper chisels and numerous beads attest to the same after-life interests as those of the farmers of northern Iran previously mentioned.

pl 14   At the little site of Sur Jangal and at Rana Ghundai in Loralai District of north-eastern Baluchistan the Kechi Beg-Amri style of pottery painting reaches a kind of climax. The largest repertoires of design are used. These include the depiction of rows of cattle, both humped and otherwise, and of black buck or goats. Stuart Piggott some years ago pointed out the striking parallel in the drawing style of these animals of Baluchistan and those made by the potters of ancient north-eastern Iran. It is of interest that at Sur Jangal by far the largest number of animal bones identified in the excavations were of cattle. This is in contrast to the usual Iranian plateau emphasis on sheep and goats. It is indicative of a changing world.

The Prosperous Quetta Culture

Baluchistan had now reached the period of its greatest prosperity. More sites of this time have been found than of any other. It is the phase first recognized by Stuart Piggott and now known as the Quetta culture.

Damb Sadaat, whose earlier occupation belongs to the Kechi Beg culture, provides in its upper levels a good example of the later period. It was made up of multi-roomed houses divided by lanes. Brick hearths, storage jars or pottery ovens were a feature of many rooms. The brick walls were frequently laid on a foundation of flat marble or limestone slabs. Entrance to a room was made by a wooden doorway whose hinge was a stone socket set in the pounded earth floor.

Copper, bone, alabaster, agate, flint, shell, and teeth were used to make a variety of needles, knives, beads, spatulas (for weaving), and bangles, among other things. Clay was used to make elegant
pl 12   round rattles, compartmented seals, model houses, and figurines.
17   The latter include animals such as the wild ass, the bull and the
f 8   goat. Female figures with legs thrust forward and delicately
pl 1   modelled appliqué hair and necklaces demonstrate a fineness of workmanship.

The decorated pottery is of two major types: Quetta ware, which is a black-on-buff ware, includes stemmed vessels and a

Chart showing the stylistic links between the Namazgah culture of Turkmenistan (N) and the Quetta culture (Q). Top left are figurine-heads and compartmented seals. (9)

variety of goblets, flaring cups, deep vases, and open bowls. These are decorated in bold skilfully laid out geometric designs that are painted in broad brush strokes that emphasize horizontality—probably a result of using a fast wheel. The second major type is a fine ware called Faiz Mohammad. This is usually grey in fabric   pl 16 though other colours do often occur. The vessel is almost always a plate or shallow open bowl decorated with black or red-brown designs on its interior. Quetta ware is a full step away from the painstaking minute decorative qualities of the Kechi Beg potters. It is not surprising therefore to find in the development towards Quetta ware intermediate phases—an evolutionary action which was stimulated by a similar development in north-eastern   f 9 Iran and Turkmenistan.

Elsewhere in Baluchistan this same stylistic evolution took place. It was a period however of considerable local variations on the common theme. For a long time archaeologists have been puzzled by the seemingly endless variety of pottery styles in Baluchistan. Now it would appear that most of them are merely localizations in which the perceiving eye can detect relationships to other areas. In north-eastern Baluchistan, particularly in the Zhob Valley, potters continued to use red-slips as a background but their design repertory included most of the Quetta ware motifs as well as local motifs. In Central and Southern Baluchistan the so-called Kulli culture in its early phase is characteristically symbolized by a black on buff pottery which on one side utilizes the concentric design drawing techniques of the older Nal type and on the other possesses a repertory very close to that used by the Quetta culture potters.

The Zhob, Quetta, and Kulli cultures have in common not only the evolution of their pottery designs but also the more concrete diffusion of trait elements one to the other. Identical potter's marks which by now have achieved some complexity and popularity in the Quetta Valley are found as far as Fort Sandeman   pl 16 in Zhob. Faiz Mohammad pottery occurs as far south as southern Kalat. Details of figurine form and décor are widespread: model houses, alabaster cups, bead types are seemingly shared among these cultures.

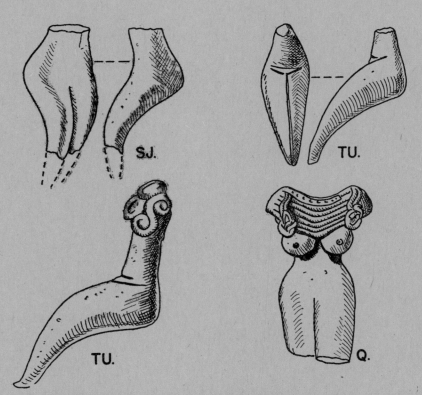

Figurines from prehistoric Turkmenistan (TU) compared with those from Sur Jangal (SJ) and Damb Sadaat (Q). (8)

The Cradle of the Indus Culture?

A significant point in this regard is that in the Indus Valley the late phase of the Amri culture, the so-called Amri B, is very closely related to these developments in Baluchistan. From what we now know of it virtually every trait identified with the Amri has its equivalent in Baluchistan. This is a remarkable parallelism of enormous significance to our understanding of the developments towards the Harappān civilization.

The uppermost levels at Damb Sadaat represent the final phases of the Quetta culture. The whole top of the mound appears to have been given over to a ceremonial complex. The principal feature of this was a huge brick platform roughly square in shape which appears to have been the foundation for a brick building. Set into the platform were stone drains and a kind of storage chamber. In the debris of the building were found painted humped bull figurines and the 'Zhob goddesses' already described. Significant of the ritual aspect of this structure was the find by Leslie Alcock, the excavator, of a stone cache in the corner of the structure in which was a disarticulated human skull. Lower on the mound a portion of a massive brick wall which presumably enclosed the higher structure was uncovered.

these means of ascent were cell-like compartments rising with the terraces. Around these structures are complexes of formal buildings with stone-paved floors divided into small rooms in some of which drain pits are located. In several cases these pits are located at the very top of the high structures. Associated with the ruins are bull figurines and the so-called 'Kulli goddess', a variant on the more familiar Zhob type. The location of many of these Complex A structures is on the highest points of bluffs overlooking the Porali Valley.

It is obvious that the Las Bela sites conform very neatly with what has been described for other parts of Baluchistan and for Mundigak. The late Kulli culture is contemporaneous with the mature Harappān civilization as it is known at Mohenjo-daro. One cannot help but compare the buildings on the 'citadel' mound at Mohenjo-daro with those of the areas we have been describing. Drains, access stairways and ramps, and location, all demonstrate similarity. In fact, if we take into consideration the evolutionary trends whose salient points we have touched upon, the parallelism of development is very clear. There is no doubt that the remoteness of the Afghan-Baluch region from northern Iranian food-production centres was sufficient to retard develop-

Edith Shahr, Complex A, about 2000 BC. The high pyramid-like structures are thought to have had a religious use; they were ascended by steps and at the top were mud-brick rooms sometimes with a drain-pit.

Around them stood groups of rectangular buildings with stone foundations and upper parts of mud-brick. Some of these seem not to have been houses but —from fragments of human bones found—may have been tombs. (10)

The situation on the highest part of the mound of such a building with its particular artifact associations recalls at once the pillared building at Mundigak. But there are numerous other parallels. At Dabar Kot in Loralai a brick drain has been found associated with a large unidentified structure containing a Zhob goddess figurine. At Periano Ghundai in Zhob these figurines were also found high on the mound. At the site of Kulli in southern Baluchistan Sir Aurel Stein found Mother Goddess figurines of a style more elaborate but still similar to those of Zhob as well as bull figurines high on the mound associated with rather sizeable buildings of unknown use.

In northern Las Bela there is a series of sites located along the gravel terraces overlooking the Porali River Valley and just north of the fertile plain of Welpat. These sites are remarkable for their preservation. The foundation of the ancient walls and in fact the bulk of the structure of the most monumental buildings was made of tiers of boulders. Much of these tiered walls still remains so that it is possible to trace the outlines of the ancient structures by merely visiting the scene. The complex of sites is called Edith Shahr and consists of two aspects: the earlier Complex A, the Kulli culture in both phases, and Complex B, a foreign culture to be dealt with later.

The Complex A structures of the later phase are best symbolized by large pyramidal-shaped structures rising in terraces to a flat top on which was located a fired or mud brick building. Access to the top was gained by ascending ramps and (or) staircases. Besides

ment of the early pastoral peoples whose settlements have been found in Kandahar, Quetta, Loralai, and Kalat.

For perhaps two thousand years the Indo-Iranian borderlands were sparsely occupied by wanderers whose sheep and goat herds sought seasonal grass and whose primitive agricultural methods never permitted a development beyond that of small plots of grain growing wherever nature herself made their agriculture possible. Sometime during the later part of the 3rd millennium BC the acceleration of technology and the growth of population in the northern Iran-Turkmenistan region caused the spread of new methods, some of which may have included the use of cattle as draft animals. Perhaps new people accompanied these ideas. In any case this new farming moved into the vale of Ferghana on the north-east and it came into southern Afghanistan and Baluchistan right to the Arabian Sea. From there on the diffusion of ideas and styles across the intervening area was accelerated. What effect did this have upon farming cultures already established in the Indus Valley? Do the Quetta potter's marks underlie the Harappān script? Did western cattle interbreed with a wild humped zebu in the Indus Valley so as to produce the humped cattle which in turn provided the energy source for the development of civilization? These and other questions we cannot now answer on the present evidence.

But our view of the Indo-Iranian borderlands indicates that cultural development was so rapid in the Indus Valley that it affected the neighbouring regions to the west. The predominantly

273

Iranian derived cultures of the Baluch-Afghan region were increasingly influenced by the east. By the time of their latest development the farmers were involved in religious activities that included non-Iranian features such as water ablutions, human sacrifice, Mother-goddess, and bull worship. They were decorating their pottery with humped bull, fish, and pipal-leaf motifs and may even have practised cremation (few burials of the later periods have been found). Seasonal movement by pastoral people persisted as it does today, bringing news of events both on the plateau and in the Indus Valley. There can be no doubt that the two areas were intimately associated. But it would appear that it was the Iranian farming world that planted the seeds for ancient Indian civilization. Later that civilization planted seeds of its own on the plateau, for the child had outgrown its parents as it should do.

Invasion or Decay? The Old Order Ends

The later phases of the village cultures in the Indo-Iranian borderlands demonstrate a maximum control of their environment by the prehistoric villages. The number of settlements identified for this period (c. 2500–1500 BC) exceed those of earlier periods and in fact most of the historical periods. We can assume therefore that populations of men and domesticated beasts were at a maximum. This means that the use of natural resources, soil, water, indigenous vegetation, clays, wild life, was also at a peak. Yet the end of this period is marked by a pronounced falling off in the number of settlements and obviously of population. In the Quetta Valley for example there is a drop from some 20 settlements to 8 or less. In Seistan we are hard put to find any sites that we can identify as representing successors to the prehistoric ones previously described. Even the Indus Valley neighbour of Baluchistan is characterized by a pronounced diminution of the number of villages, successors of the Harappān civilization there. As far west as the Lake Urmia region of north-western Iran the old farming villages virtually disappear.

It is becoming clear that this falling-off of population though rapid was possibly not a sudden process. At Mundigak, there is evidence for a deterioration in the latest phases evidenced by smaller and less well-made structures. The same thing was happening in the Quetta Valley and at no less a site than Mohenjo-daro in Sind. In Las Bela on the other hand there are signs of a conflagration in the last of the Complex A phase at Edith Shahr. Similarly a burned layer has been noted at Rana Ghundai in Loralai. One also has to consider in this context the famous contorted skeletons in the streets at Mohenjo-daro. Mohenjo-daro however was already on the decline when this attack came.

It is obvious that here we are dealing with a fundamental problem in the story of human cultures and the complex civilizations deriving from them. Older theories, for example those of the geographer Ellsworth Huntingdon, ascribed these apparent collapses of ancient cultures to climatic change. More recently, particularly among history-minded colleagues, the process has been credited, principally, to invading forces from outside. There is little doubt that new forces were appearing. At Tepe Hissar in north-eastern Iran the painted pottery prehistoric village culture was gradually replaced by an apparently more militant culture symbolized by grey ware and bronze weapons. This process started somewhat earlier than the late phases of the painted pottery culture of the Indo-Iranian area. The situation at Tepe Hissar seems to have been one of gradual replacement of one culture by another until the earlier was completely absorbed and thereby lost its identity.

However we are probably not far from the mark when we observe that it was possibly over-exploitation of the natural resources more than any other reason that brought about the decline of the prehistoric farming cultures, in the Indo-Iranian borderlands at least. The populations had become too large and the cultures too elaborate. When we uncover the ceremonial structures of these late phases we wonder how many specialists were being supported by the farming populace. The priests, the servants, the time spent in construction of the buildings were drains on the primitive economy. Conversely why the need for these ceremonial structures? Was it because the economic situation

was precarious? So much so in fact that there was real need to propitiate the gods of nature in order to avert natural calamity, an event all too possible on the arid plateau.

It is well-known that great flocks of goats and sheep have a devastating effect upon the landscape in their consumption of every blade of grass, shrub and shoot. The continual deep-ploughing made possible by draft-cattle had an adverse effect as well. We have no idea at all as to the prehistoric farmers' understanding of the need for fertilizers and (or) the process of rotating crops, though we can assume that they were not entirely ignorant of such things. In any case the increasing cognizance by archaeologists of the value of biological and physical evidence for interpreting the past gives hope that future excavators will be able to solve these problems.

An Aryan Invasion?

The second millennium BC was a restless period in history. The technical advances in metallurgy, farming, the process of domestication, the development of wheeled vehicles, etc. made in the early ancient world had spread to other regions where they both found root and stimulated new advances. Especially in the grass-lined areas of Eurasia this had the effect of creating beautifully adapted pastoral cultures. These cultures had a tribal social organization which centred around the extended family and its expression in a clanship. This kind of social subdivision was perfectly suited to the expression of strong loyalties and independent action by clans within the tribe. Horse domestication emancipated the tribes from too close regional ties but it also brought them into conflict, a conflict enhanced by growing populations and frequent droughts. The result of this situation is familiar: the tribes were forced to move to other areas and eventually the southern regions were invaded. The first of these invasions with which the Indo-Iranian borderlands were directly involved is that of the Aryans.

Northern Afghanistan and the adjacent Turkestan plain is sometimes called Aryana, especially in the older German texts. The implication is of course that these lands were the homeland of the Aryans. The time-honoured story tells how these people forced the Indian passes, especially the Khyber, and in chariot-riding hordes fell upon the settled lands of the Indus and Ganges where they had the dual effect of causing a kind of dark age and of creating the foundation of traditional Indian religion and social form.

Archaeologists are in general in agreement that the story of the Aryans is based upon fact. No one doubts that pastoral people were forced into the settled lands of Afghanistan and India. However archaeologists are hard put to recover the material evidence for pastoral people. The destruction of the settlements of settled people is often taken as the mark of the invader but it does not tell us very much about that invader. Finding positive evidence constitutes one of the great problems for modern archaeology.

On the present evidence however it seems clear that in south-eastern Iran, southern Afghanistan and Baluchistan the prehistoric settlements were either abandoned or on the wane when these new people arrived. In Sind it would appear that the Jhukar culture which succeeds the Harappān there represents hill tribes perhaps not unlike the Pathans who were either drawn by the prospect of loot or were driven from their homeland by invading tribes. At Fort Sandeman near the Gomel Pass Jhukar-like pottery has been found in apparent confirmation of this theory.

This part of the story is best understood by returning to the Edith Shahr sites in Las Bela. Complex A, belonging to the Kulli culture, has already been described. The evidence suggests that as a part of the movement of the early Iranian tribes into the more southerly reaches of the plateau towards the end of the second millennium BC there was an invasion of this Complex A or Kulli culture, bringing it to an end and establishing a new cultural form. The new people were horse users, made weapons of iron, and had a religion in which sky deities had a major rôle.

The sites of this period—Complex B sites—are characterised by stone circles, rectangular buildings and white stone-outlined avenues and rings, orientated east-west and apparently connected with a sun religion. Such structures occur high on the talus or slopes of mountain walls surrounding Welpat Tahsil. At least one mound located in the midst of the fertile fields there also

pl 18

f 11

pl 20

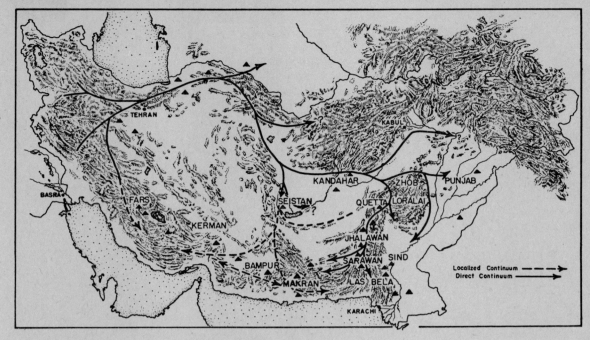

The probable routes of cultural diffusion from the Iranian Plateau to Seistan and Baluchistan during late prehistoric times. (11)

belongs to Complex B. It is somewhat square in plan but its interior is hollow, giving one the impression of a fortress-like building with earthen walls.

Alongside new importations, objects from the earlier Complex A culture are still found. In one case, a piece of a pottery fruit-stand, the artifact is evolved from the design form familiar in the earlier complex.

Where did the new people come from? The evidence now being accumulated points to the area round Siyalk in west central Iran. Here a people known as the Cemetery B people have been identified. According to Ghirshman, an outstanding authority on the subject, they were probably the first Iranian tribes to reach western Iran. They were the prime motivators of 'the large scale movements that took place on the Plateau at the very end of the second millennium'. In our context, their most interesting product was a distinctive pottery type, which has genetic relationships to ceramic material found on a great many sites in Baluchistan, ranging from Kalat to Las Bela, and called 'Lando' ware. Lando ware is rather thick, coarse in fabric, painted ware. It is characterized by carinated bowls painted with horizontal running designs, which include spirals and horses' heads.

Associated with it at a number of sites is a coarse-tempered thick ware decorated with loops, band, and other simple forms made by applying clay to the surface of the completed vessel. The appliqué lines are frequently incised or pencilled. This pottery is characteristic of the Edith Shahr Complex B sites of Las Bela.

Other evidence about the new people comes from the mound of Shahi-Tump in Makran. In one grave was found a copper shaft-hole axe and a spear head. The axe is of a type familiar in South Russia at the famous Bronze age site of Maikop. Nearby at Jiwanri a cairn field produced a pottery type not wholly unlike that found in the Siyalk Cemetery B. Again at Moghul Ghundai near Fort Sandeman in north-eastern Baluchistan a fine assortment of bronze objects came to light, including a tripod vessel, what may be regarded as horse bells, and some iron objects including leafshaped arrowheads. The bronze objects of Moghul Ghundai also bear some resemblance to those found in the Siyalk Cemetery B.

At the mound of Kile Ghul Mohammad there is an intrusive level of coarse painted pottery with supplementary appliqué decoration. This pottery is called Ghul ware. It has a wide distribution, being found as far east as Moghul Kala in the Loralai district and on the upper reaches of the Hari Rud in Central Afghanistan. This ware is not dissimilar to the Lando-Complex B coarse wares though it may represent a later variant.

At the high mound of Nad-i-Ali near Chakansur in Afghan Seistan Ghirshman located in the lowest part of his excavations there the fine grey wares familiar as the type fossil for the successors to the painted pottery farmers of north-eastern Iran. At the time of writing this seems to be the farthest south for these north-

easterners. Ghirshman sees these grey ware cultures as forerunners who fleeing from the north-east came to western Iran as a result of pressure brought by the influx of other people who later overcame them and who created Cemetery B at Siyalk. The grey wares of Seistan must then be indicative of another branch of the same people of north-east Iran. So far however none of the characteristic Siyalk Cemetery B related assemblages have been found in Seistan, though they may be there if the evidence from Baluchistan is any indication of the routes by which they reached the borders of India.

The Achaemenid Empire: Bactra, 'Mother of Cities'

The almost two thousand year span between the period of invasion and the coming of Islam is strangely almost less well-known than the previous prehistoric period just described. In part this is because archaeologists of the later periods have concentrated on the splendid art and architectural remains and have had an understandable lack of interest in the more prosaic culture history which they and more modest sites represent.

The Achaemenid Persian Empire, the earliest historical empire we know about here, included most of the Indo-Iranian borderland region. Most of this control was nominal and very loose indeed. Baluchistan was called generally Gedrosia and with the possible exception of the Makran coast and the Quetta-Gomel area was of little importance. Arachosia, which included mountainous southern Afghanistan and the Kandahar region, was the home of warlike tribes and control of the region was erratic. Seistan or Drangiana was the centre of many Iranian traditions. Zoroaster's flight to eastern Iran in the 6th century BC brought him under the protection of the Achaemenid chief Vishtaspa whose son Darius later became the greatest of the Achaemenid rulers. Drangiana at that time was a prosperous settled area watered by the Etymandrus (Helmand). Its citizens were peaceable and early were substantal allies of Cyrus, founder of the Achaemenid Empire. Zoroaster's home during his exile in Seistan was on the Kuh-i Khwaja. This is a volcanic neck that sticks, mesa-like, out of the Helmand delta. It became a sacred place, the goal of pilgrimage and the seat of fine temples after Zoroaster's time. Unfortunately the archaeological investigations so far carried out there have failed to reveal any substantial evidence for the Achaemenid period. For Parthian and Sassanian times however there are substantial monuments, as there are all over Seistan.

It is noteworthy that during Achaemenid times the territories in north-west India were reached via northern Afghanistan (Bactriana) and the mountain roads and passes which include the Kabul Valley and the Khyber (Parapamosidae). This route was at once a token of the traditional roads from the more settled and populous regions north of the Central Afghan range, and the difficulty of passing through more southerly regions as well. Tradition has it that there was a great city already ancient in those

pl 23

pl 24

days located on the plain between the Oxus river and the mountains in northern Afghanistan. This was the city called Bactra, sometimes surnamed 'Mother of Cities'.

Archaeologists have always been interested in Bactra. Today the site of the ancient city has been assigned generally to the Muslim city of Balkh which is located about twelve miles west of Mazar-i-Sherif. The open plain about the place is dotted with countless mounds, the village sites of various periods. Balkh itself is featured by an enormous mound topped by a Bala Hissar—a fortress of Timurid times. One of the first acts of the French Archaeological Mission to Afghanistan (1924–1925) was to sink sondage trenches into the great mound but these produced few traces of pre-Islamic occupation. In the season of 1946 another assault was made on the site under the direction of Daniel Schlumberger. Sixty-one sondages were sunk systematically into the main mound and surrounding submounds. These probes located Kushan remains below the Islamic. Finally a University of Pennsylvania expedition sank a test pit into a wall of the lower part of the site in 1953. This also encountered Kushan material but nothing earlier.

Balkh has frustrated its investigators and the Achaemenid and Hellenistic remains, which must be somewhere there, are still buried. As some archaeologists have suggested, Bactra may not be at Balkh at all but somewhere out in the surrounding plain which so badly needs systematic archaeological survey. The search for Bactra goes sporadically on. A token of the lure of the 'Mother of Cities' is Sir Aurel Stein's bequest of a considerable sum of money to finance a British expedition that would seek, find, and excavate Bactra. Stein himself had always wanted to visit Afghan Bactriana but was prevented by political barriers. He died in Kabul just before setting out on another of his wonderfully sensitive archaeological tours which might have located Bactra after all.

On the Edge of the Greek World

Alexander's destruction of the Achaemenid Empire and the break up of political unity among his successors after his death, the rise of the Parthians and their wars with the invader Saka-Scythians, the Roman trade, the establishment of the empire of the Kushans in the east and of the Sassanids in the west, are historical events about which anyone can read in the standard histories on the subject. The archaeological record for these important times is a sparse one in Afghanistan and barely perceptible in Baluchistan.

For Alexander himself there are traditions, mistakenly labelling this ruin or that as one of his cities, still existing among the local populace. Alexander's historians wrote of stays at Bactra and Seistan. Cities in Arachosia, Bactriana, Seistan, and Gedrosia were supposedly built by command but we have no trace of them. Yet there is always the hope that some day one of those nameless mounds that dot these areas may reveal that the conqueror's orders were indeed carried out.

Coins which one could still buy in the bazaars of Afghanistan in 1949 in abundance, form a substantial body of evidence for the Hellenistic rulers of Bactria and adjacent states which arose with the weakening of Seleucid power in the east. These coins indicate that there exist Bactrian sites in Afghanistan awaiting the spade. The coins are among the finest in the ancient world. The portraiture is sharp, and close observation rewards one with some sense, no matter how slight, of the living monarch. It is of interest that whereas the earlier coins of the Bactrians bear classical motifs and Greek inscriptions, the later ones and those of the Scythic and other successors demonstrate both Central Asian and Indian influences which gradually displace the Hellenistic. Kharoshti joins Greek on the coins and in the end replaces it. Elephants and humped bulls become common elements in the coin maker's repertoire. The coins thus represent one of the most graphic demonstrations of the diffusion of styles and their integration with already established modes known to the archaeologist.

The coins tell us things which the ancient writers do not. In effect it is possible to perceive how the Greek way of life was submerged into the Central Asiatic and the Indian. Part of this submergence was political. Both the Saka-Scyths and later the Kushans attacked the Greek kingdoms and the resulting conflict caused the withdrawal of the Greeks and their Hellenized subjects towards north-west India, where their presence helped to create

pl 25
pl 26

pl 27

276

the famous architectural and sculptural art style of Gandhara. Those were the days of the rise of Parthian control in Iran and Mesopotamia. This control effectively cut off the Hellenistic kingdoms of the east from their cultural counterparts of the Mediterranean and this of course intensified the Asianization of their world. By about the middle of the 2nd century BC the Greek political power was centred in north-west India and had completely lost its grasp on its homeland across the central Afghan ranges.

The French archaeological delegation in Afghanistan has been particularly interested in this extraordinary period which saw such changes in cultural form. The names of Foucher, Hackin, Carl, Ghirshman, and at present Schlumberger are associated with pioneer and far-sighted excavations and other researches that have produced remarkable results. If ever the rôle of archaeology in providing evidence on which to build history is doubted, here is irrefutable proof to give the quietus to the most ardent sceptic.

The Fire Temples

The French excavations have been many and extensive. However there are several highpoints which stand out. In 1952 Schlumberger investigated a site where Greek-inscribed stone blocks had been found near Pul-i-Khumri in northern Afghanistan. The site called Surkh Kotal is not far from Kunduz where on several occasions Hellenistic remains have turned up. Schlumberger was in hopes that the site would at long last be one of the Bactrian period. Instead it turned out to be a temple complex of Kushan times dating between the middle of the 2nd century AD and the early 3rd century AD. This was a time when the Kushans who ruled most of northern India as well as Afghanistan had accepted Buddishm as the state religion and had become patrons of religious institutions throughout their empire.

The Surkh Kotal is a hill almost surrounded by a ruined mudbrick wall. One ascended the hill after passing this wall before reaching another walled enclosure at the top. The visitor in ancient times entered this enclosure through one of several narrow openings located between square towers. The courtyard he first encountered was surrounded by a columned portico or gallery perhaps for worshippers awaiting their turn. The temple was in the centre of the enclosure and was entered at one end of the western side. The visitor walked up a stairway into a gallery that completely circled the sanctuary. The excavator has suggested that a rite of circumambulation was involved in the worship of the deity whose image or symbol would have been in the sanctuary.

The sanctuary consisted of a series of connecting galleries surrounding a central chamber. Entrance to the galleries and the chamber was on the east. The central chamber had at its centre a fine masonry platform, square in shape with steps reaching up to it on its western side. By each corner of the platform were pillars that supported the wooden roof of the sanctuary and along the walls of the chamber itself were pilasters that tied the whole unit into an aesthetic and functional whole.

On the south side of the outer enclosure was a smaller temple not dissimilar to the main one. By great good fortune a fine altar— the one in the larger temple had disappeared—was discovered *in situ* in the smaller temple. This altar was very striking in its day. Though made of mudbrick its sides were decorated with fine reliefs including two birds. Pilasters at each corner and a column in the centre of the eastern side supported decorative arches now lost. The top of the altar had a pit which held the sacred fire.

This impressive building located in the rather awesome setting where the last fringes of flat alluvium reach among the soaring piedmont of the Hindu Kush Mountains is clearly non-Buddhist. It belongs to the old Iranian world out of which the worship of the fire god Agni developed. It is at once a part of the old cult and of Zoroastrianism. Its location so near the major route between Central Asia and India suggests that these old cults were not isolated survivals but were a flourishing faith in northern Afghanistan. Perhaps they stood to Zoroastrianism much as Lamaism stands to Buddhism, as a kind of compromise.

A late Parthian and early Sassanian palace-temple complex has been identified on the Kuh-i-Khwaja in Seistan. Ernest Herzfeld has ascertained that there was a fire temple in this complex. Other fire temples also have been identified in Seistan. The Kuh-i-Khwaja temples contained mural paintings which made Sir Aurel Stein, the original discoverer, believe that he had found a Buddhist sanctuary, but it is now clear that the temples belong to a magistic faith completely Iranian in character and very probably not far removed from that identified at Surkh Kotal.

Buddhism: the Monastery of Bamian

pl 30

Among the archaeological splendours of Inner Asia one of the foremost is Bamian. The site is located in a side valley on the northern side of the Shiba Pass in east central Afghanistan. The place was visited in AD 632 by the Chinese monk Hsiun-Tsang when it was very much a flourishing Buddhist community and had been so from at least the 2nd century AD. Genghis Khan is said to have destroyed Bamian in the 13th century when it was the seat of Moslem power, a power which during the 9th century had finally extinguished Buddhism there. During the First Afghan War British prisoners were kept at Bamian, among them Lady Sale who described her experiences in her famous account.

Stories of blood and thunder do not accord with Bamian. The valley is fertile and lovely in appearance. Surrounded by high mountains, supplied by a cool abundant stream and isolated from the turbulent world, it is a place of peace. To it Buddhist monks travelled from north-west India and established a monastic settlement there. The places of meditation were the caves which the monks painstakingly cut from the rock especially along the southern cliff of the valley. Some of these caves were simple cells, others were complexes of cells, sanctuaries, and galleries connected by a variety of passages and stairways. The main caves were integrated to Buddhist concepts. Many of the ceilings were domed in imitation of the sky and, as were the walls, painted *al fresco*. The paintings depict the various Buddhas and Bodhisattvas whose mystic powers move the universe. After centuries of assault by natural and human forces there still survive fragments of the frescoes with which the caves were decorated. These brightly coloured fragments are precious representations of parts of the pantheon of Mahayana Buddhist divinities recognized then. Most memorable are the divinities who float in the celestial sky like will-o-the-wisps, the finite boldness of the Byzantine-like standing Buddhas which appear in pathetic remnants around the base of a ceiling dome, the rich contrasts and blinding shades of the painting where blue, orange, and green are used in wonderful array.

pl 31-
33

The carver cut coffers, niches, squinches and pillars out of the stone in imitation of free-standing structures which he must have known from Buddhist centres at Taxila and Swat. Among the most important caves at Bamian is that which has a rock-cut imitation of the so-called 'lantern' ceiling. This type of ceiling is very ancient and was a solution to the problem of roofing over a square opening, especially one which was too wide to span with a horizontal beam. The method was simply to lay beams diagonally across the four corners of the squares, repeating in the same way on top of the new square thus formed; each time reducing the size of the opening until only a small hole remained at the very top. To imitate this kind of roof-working in the unadjustable situation of a cave ceiling required great skill on the carver's part and the fact that he succeeded so well is a symptom of the advanced state of craftsmanship in those far days.

f 12

The triumphs of the sculptors' art were the gigantic statues of Buddha which have made Bamian world-famous. There are two of these colossi at the site. Both stand in niches at either end of the major cave complex on the southern cliff. The western figure stands 173 feet in height and the eastern is 120 feet high. The niches were once covered with frescoes; the niche of the larger Buddha must have been spectacular in its detail and vivid colouring. Still to be seen in the vaulted ceiling are the Bodhisattvas which like Christian angels transfer the firmament into a heaven merciful in aspect. Below on the lower rim of the vault are medallions framing richly caparisoned apsaras who toss flowers and jewels about the divine scene. Below these, though little indeed now remains, were rows of seated Buddhas, each with its specific *mudra*.

pl 2

These rows reached to the very bottom of the niche where at the ground level there were sanctuaries each painted and decora-

The imitation 'lantern' ceiling (beams laid diagonally across the corners) carved in the solid rock at Bamian. (12)

ted according to its ritual function. The larger image was dressed in flowing robes, made it is said of ropes set into the rock with wooden dowels. This is in some contrast to the robes of the smaller and earlier Buddha which were made of clay covered with plaster. Both images were painted and the smaller Buddha probably entirely covered with gold leaf. What wonder these images must have provoked during their hey-day! From afar the colour of the decoration must have drawn the attention of the visitor. As he drew nearer the images became larger until in their proximity the colossal size and splendour of decoration invoked the all-encompassing Buddha in whom the universe resides.

The Ancient Cultures Meet

Earlier it was pointed out that Afghanistan was a bridgeland. Especially were eastern and northern Afghanistan important as crossroads for routes going in all directions. The Hellenistic and Roman worlds were international. The rise of the Kushans in the east and of the Parthians in the west did not interfere with the overland trade. Rather these empires stimulated the use of the trans-Iran roads. Roman trade reached to China at least as early as the 1st century AD. Parthian traders were commonly seen in Taxila and Indians appeared in the market towns of Syria and Palestine. There was little interruption of the overland contacts with the collapse of the older empires and the achievement of power by the Guptas in India and the Sassanids in Iran. The profit to be gained by participation in this trade made all the powers whose territories were concerned encourage the overland commerce.

It is no coincidence then that the styles, fashions, and advances of much of Asia and the Mediterranean had their expression in the bridgeland countries. At Bamian one can find hundreds of examples of the other cultures and civilizations whose contributions made up the hybrid cultures of mediaeval Afghanistan. Buddhism is of course an Indian faith and the floating apsaras and Bodhisattvas on some of the painted walls, full-bodied and warm in aspect, have their parallels in the famous caves of Ajanta. But the stiff finite figures of, for example, the 120 foot Buddha, suggesting Byzantine mosaic, are Sassanian in style.

The coffer-decorated ceilings however are familiar to those who know their Roman mosaics. The robes with their toga drape, the Corinthian capitals, and in fact the creation of colossal statues to awe mankind emphasize the Graeco-Roman world which was the ultimate source of many style traits then common in Central Asia. Some of these, including the earlier naturalistic carving of the Buddha image came from the Gandhara integration of East and West. But Bamian is a Central Asian site and while we can acknowledge the foreign sources of the many iconographic and stylistic elements which make up the art of Bamian there is no question that these are integrated into an aesthetic whole which is purely Central Asian.

The impression one receives even from the ruined and sometimes pathetic remains of the splendours of Bamian. is a very great one indeed. Ajanta leaves one stunned by its utter beauty set in the companionable warmth of a teeming Indian ecology. Nara still lives and the vital aliveness of a temperate forest setting and the vulnerable quality of the ancient wood which supports the temples suggests that loving care has always been present. Bamian by comparison is isolated and infinitely lonely. All about are the indications of people, whose prayers and labours made their community vital and active. If there is such a thing as a vocal stillness Bamian is a notable repository for such a quality. It is indeed a place of meditation and was meant to endure intact forever. But perhaps it does in the visions it will always invoke of the piety of its creators.

Kapisa, Capital of the Kushans

Bamian suggests the international world of which it was a part. The discoveries at Begram give proof of it. Begram is located at the head of the Charikar Valley to the north of Kabul at the junction of the Ghorband and Panjshir Valley routes. The town was the royal capital of the Kushans before the early part of the 3rd century AD. In those days it was known as Kapisa. It was flourishing at the very height of the Roman Empire in the days when the Antonines were masters of the western world. Ghirshman found three main levels of occupation of the site, the earlier (I) dating from the 2nd century BC to the middle of the 2nd century AD. The second and intermediate level (II) apparently represents a reoccupation of the site by King Kanishka after a short abandonment. A feature of this level were the finds of jewelry which suggests Central Asian influences were strong then; a suggestion not unwarranted in view of both the Saka-Scythian invasions of a century or so before, and of course the Central Asian origin of the Kushans who were one branch of the Yueh-chi pastoral nomads. These had moved west from their east Central Asian homeland near the Han Chinese border as a result of pressure brought by the Hsiung-Nu.

The final level (III) dates to the late 4th century AD and contains evidence of strong Sassanid influences as well as a quantity of iron weapons indicative perhaps of the troubled times that saw the collapse of the Kushan empire.

pl 35-38 It was the earlier excavation of Hackin in Kanishka's royal city that produced the most remarkable finds. In two rooms of the palace were found a veritable museum of fine objects which reflected the cosmopolitan world of those ancient days. Included were lacquer boxes from Han China, traditional Buddhist sculptures of Gandhara type, Syrian glass, superb carved Indian ivories, ornamental disks with Pompeiian decoration, and a number of fine late Hellenistic and Roman bronzes. One of these was a Hercules which might as easily have been found in sites of Roman Britain. It is of interest that during the British excavation of the Quetta Miri in the 19th century in the preparation of an arsenal there a fine bronze Bacchus was found of the same type as the Begram Hercules. Unfortunately this object was lost and a photograph alone remains.

The Kabul Valley is actually a part of the same cultural area as Gandhara. The route to Peshawar is spotted with the ruins of Buddhist stupas indicating how strong that faith was in mediaeval Afghanistan. It is a strange twist of circumstance that that exact area is now the centre of the strongest Moslem adherence.

One should mention the fine stucco heads found at the ancient Buddhist city of Nagarahara or Hadda, near the modern city of Jalalabad. These heads vary from strictly Gandharan types, through Early Empire Roman portraits, to what can only be called a French Gothic style. The heads represent the peoples familiar to the monks of the Kabul Valley. We have here a portrait gallery which leads our eye over the often-emotional visages of Indians, Mediterraneans, Iranians, and barbarian Central Asians. Many of the portraits are sensitive moving studies of men devoted, warlike, pious, and blasphemous. Others are static, intended only as decorative elements of an architectural unit. But all of them are illustrative of a teeming world in which many people and cultures had significant rôles.

The southern and western areas of the Indo-Iranian borderlands seem to have been localized distant regions outside the pale of the more dynamic events of north and east. Seistan however was of some significance in late Parthian and Sassanid times. In fact the populations reached their peak there in those days. This was because of the development of a fine canal and dam system which brought water into the arid alluvial land where the Sar-o-Tar ruins stand today in crumbling desolation. Likewise, a canal system was operative in the Rud-i-Biyaban channel. This brought water into the southern delta, along whose expanse a *limes* system was maintained against raids from the warlike tribes, some of whom may have been the Saka whose bases were on the Middle Helmand for a time. The great ruined expanse of the city of Zahidan in the northern delta indicates how truly prosperous Seistan was under Sassanian rule. It is no wonder that the place is celebrated as more than just the birthplace of Rustam.

The Changing Pattern of Living

It is of great interest to note that on the present evidence the centres of important settlement in prehistoric times were in north-eastern Iran, southern Turkmenistan, southern Afghanistan and eastern Baluchistan. These were mutually influential with the chronological priority in the north-east. In historic times however, northern and eastern Afghanistan were the most important centres while at the same time the more northerly areas of Russian Central Asia grew in importance. In the Indo-Pakistan subcontinent Sind, which in prehistoric times was the cultural centre of the Indus Valley, falls far behind the north-west frontier and Punjab areas in importance after c. 1200 BC. Much of the reason for this shift is of course due to the changing world in prehistoric times. Agricultural needs dominated and travel was limited more or less to a circle of villages and diffusion was of the stimulus type. In historic times the horse made travel and efficient communication possible. The trade routes were chosen for speed of passage. Centres developed and flourished where trade was easy. Agriculture was often at best a poor second in the economy. Kapisa, Kabul, and Hadda needed the support of commerce and (or) the loot of empire to flourish. They rose to full expression where the old prehistoric settlements could not. Through Islamic times to our own era the advantage to a settlement of locations on trade routes near natural resources of metal and fuel has been greater than that given to settlements set in the midst of the fields tilled by the residents. But the latter pattern of living is most enduring, seemingly little affected by the events which cause the rise and fall of the dynamic cosmopolitan cities which lie in the midst of those events. In this sense the modern situation of the Indo-Iranian Borderland countries is a lucid demonstration of old events and evolutions which archaeology is only beginning to describe.

XII THE FORGOTTEN SARMATIANS

A once mighty folk scattered among the nations

T. SULIMIRSKI

Chronological table showing the main events of Sarmatian history, so far as they can be reconstructed. The Sarmatian tribes included here are the **Aorsi, Siraces, Iazyges, Roxolani** and **Alans.** Other peoples— **Scythians, Goths** and **Huns**—are shown where they affect the Sarmatians. Some of the chief archaeological discoveries are indicated by italics.

Date	Poland / Western Europe	Hungary	Roumania / Bulgaria	Ukraine / West of Dnieper	Don-Dnieper / Crimea	Kuban / Caucasus	East of Don
BC				Early **Scythian** culture	**Scythians** in steppes; **Greek** Bosporan kingdom in Crimea; Arrival of **Royal Sarmatians**	**Scythians** *Royal tombs in the Kuban*	**Sauromatae** being replaced by **Early Sarmatian** culture
300 BC			*Thraco-Scythian tombs in Bulgaria*	*Late Scythian tombs*		Arrival of **Sarmatians**. **Scythians** move west. **309 Siraces** in Bosporan dynastic war	*Imports from Greek cities and central Asia*
			Scythia Minor in Dobruja	Late **Scythian** culture	**Royal Sarmatians** in the steppes. Bosporan kingdom in eastern Crimea. **Scythian** kingdom founded in western Crimea	**Siraces** in the Kuban	Domination of the **Massagetae** over Eastern **Sarmatians**
200 BC				**Royal Sarmatians** in the steppe. **Bastarnae** further west	**Iazyges** on the Don-Dnieper steppes. **Roxolani** cross the Don and settle north of **Iazyges**. **Roxolani** allied with Crimean **Scythians**. **110** Bosporan kingdom seized by **Mithradates**	**Siraces** dominate Kuban area	**Huns** defeat **Massagetae**. Rise of the **Aorsi**
100 BC			*Isolated finds connected with Royal Sarmatians*	**Iazyges** cross the Dnieper. **Roxolani** cross the Dnieper and dominate Ukrainian steppes	**Aorsi** and **Alans** north of Crimea. Sarmato-Thracian dynasty rules Bosporan kingdom	*Siracian cemeteries and barrow-graves*	**125** Chinese mission to **Aorsi**. **Aorsi** at the summit of their power. *Treasure of Novocherkassk*
			78 Iazyges reach the Danube delta. First fighting with Rome		Roman suzerainty over 'Sarmatized' Bosporan kingdom	**Siraces** become tributaries of Rome	
0			**20 Roxolani** reach the Danube delta. **Iazyges** move west. *Description of Roxolani by Strabo*	**Roxolani** retreat before the Alans	Western **Alans** mixed with **Aorsi** dominate Don-Dnieper steppes. *Bosporan tombs and stelae. Tamga signs*		Rise of the **Alans**
100 AD		**Iazyges** settle in Hungarian plain	**69 Roxolani** invade Moesia. Dacian wars. **Roxolani** defeated. *Trajan's column*. Dacia becomes a Roman province	Western **Alans** cross the Dnieper and seize the steppes	Close Bosporan-Western **Alan** relations develop	**Alanic** pressure on **Siraces**	**73 Alans** attempt to invade Parthia
		Dacian wars. **Iazyges** fight on the Roman side. *Earliest Iazygian remains*			*Bosporan-Sarmatian polychrome decoration*		**123 Alans** attempt to invade Roman Asia Minor. **133 Alans** invade Media and are defeated. **Hunnic** pressure on **Alans** begins
	Detachment of **Iazyges** sent to Britain. *Beads, stelae, etc*	Sporadic wars with Rome. **176** Peace treaty between **Iazyges** and Marcus Aurelius		Western **Alans** retreat under pressure from Eastern **Alans**			
200 AD		**Iazyges** raid Moesia and Pannonia. *Grave at Szil*			Western **Alans** driven west by Eastern **Alans**	**Siraces** driven west by Eastern **Alans**	**Hunnic** supremacy over Eastern **Alans**. *Burials with deformed skulls*
	Offshoot of Antae (**Alans**) established in Poland. *Zakrzów graves*		**Antae** (**Alans**) arrive in Bessarabia and Moldavia. *Alanic graves*. **271** Arrival of **Visigoths**. Romans abandon Dacia. **Visigothic** kingdom established in Transylvania	*Siracian barrow-graves on the Dniester*. **Goths** move south from Baltic down the Dnieper. **250 Goths** capture Olbia	Eastern **Alans** in Don-Dnieper steppes. Steppes near Sea of Azov and Western Crimea seized by **Goths**. Decline of Bosporan kingdom. *Last Bosporan coins*	**Alans** in the whole Kuban area	
300 AD		Eight successive Roman expeditions against **Iazyges**. *Barrow graves at Herpály*. **321 Iazyges** attacked by **Visigoths**. **332** Civil war amongst the **Iazyges**. **358 Iazyges** defeated by Constantine	**322 Visigoths** defeated by Constantine. Arrival of **Huns**. **Ostrogoths** and remnants of **Roxolani** cross into Roman Moesia	**Ostrogothic** empire	**362 Goths** capture Bosporan kingdom. **Huns** cross the Don and advance across the steppes. Some **Alans** retreat into Crimea	**Huns** pass north of the Kuban. Some **Alans** join them. Other groups remain	**350 Huns** advance across lower Volga and Don. Some **Alans** retreat westwards, others join the **Huns**
				375 Huns move west. Collapse of **Ostrogothic** empire			
400 AD	**410** Sack of Rome by **Visigoths**. Polish kingdom of Antae (**Alans**) overrun by **Huns**. **453** Death of Attila	**Visigoths** in Hungary. **432** Invasion of Hungary by **Huns**					
	Alans in Hunnic service gain independence	**Huns** retreat. **Iazyges** regain independence. **472 Iazyges** decisively beaten by **Visigoths**	**Huns** retreat. **Antae** (**Alans**) revive and extend power	**Huns** retreat	**Huns** retreat	**Huns** retreat	
500 AD	Serboi and Choroates (**Alanic** tribes) remain and are gradually absorbed by the Slavs over whom they reign			Kingdom of **Antae** extended to Kiev	Groups of **Alans** survive in Crimea	**Alanic** kingdom in Caucasus	
				Slavicization of the **Antae**			
600 AD				Invasion of kingdom of **Antae** by Turkish **Avars**. *Martinovka hoard*		**Alanic** kingdom survives until 12th century	

'Whenever these Barbarians issued from their deserts

in quest of prey, their shaggy beards, uncombed locks and fierce countenances, which seemed to express the innate cruelty of their minds, inspired the more civilized provincials of Rome with horror and dismay'. So Gibbon, taking his tone from those same dismayed Romans. Yet in truth the Sarmatians were themselves the victims of destiny and their curious and often tragic history has still to be fully told. Scattered herdsmen and pastoralists on the broad steppes east of the Volga, they were caught up in the huge tribal movements of Central Asia (3rd century BC – 4th century AD) and driven further and further west. Their history became a long running battle for survival, first against Rome and then against the fresh waves of peoples from the east who followed in their wake and finally overwhelmed them. Traces of their passage survive from the Caucasus to Portugal, from Germany to North Africa. They appear, fleeing before the victorious emperor, on Trajan's Column in Rome (above), and in AD 175 over five thousand of them were sent as legionaries to remote camps in Britain. The relief on the right is part of a funeral stele from the camp at Chester. (1, 2)

The nomadic life

that had been natural to the Sarmatians in their homelands across the Volga was never abandoned by them. 'Wherever they come, that place they look upon as their home', wrote Ammianus Marcellinus in the 4th century AD. The description he gives of them does not differ in essentials from that of Herodotus eight hundred years earlier, so little had they changed during the interval. To form an encampment they placed their wagons ('with rounded canopies of bark') in a circle. Here the women and old people stayed. The younger men were all warriors and skilled riders. Horses were reserved for them, the wagons being drawn by oxen. From the contents of their graves their everyday life can be reconstructed with some confidence. Many of their more valued possessions would have been made far away (perhaps on the shores of the Black Sea) and kept for generations, or else acquired (by trade or war) from their neighbours. The cauldron in the foreground of this reconstruction is based on that in pl. 27, and shows the interesting high foot or pedestal on which it stood. Weapons consisted of bows (which underwent drastic modification when the Sarmatians came into contact with the more warlike Huns) and spears. In the background are the flocks and herds upon which all the nomadic peoples depended. The search for pasturage is the key to the whole history of these confused times. (3)

Where a Sarmatian chieftain died, there he was buried, often with his weapons and treasure around him. Burials with almost the same grave-goods may come to light anywhere in Europe. The beads (above left) are from the Roman fort at Chesters in Northumberland, where we know that a detachment of Sarmatians was posted. They are totally unlike any British or Roman jewellery and the only parallels are with beads from Sarmatian graves in Hungary. Left: jewellery from the Caucasus, 3rd–4th centuries AD: two gold rings, a bronze mirror with cast ornament on the back, a silver buckle and bronze brooch, and a long necklace with glass beads. Right: Sarmatian iron sword, 15 inches long, double-edged and pointed, probably made in the Black Sea area. (4–6)

The Bosporan Kingdom
a Greek foundation of great antiquity between the mouth of the Dnieper and the Sea of Azov, was the cultural centre of many scattered Sarmatian tribes. Passing through it or close to it on their migrations, they absorbed its characteristic mixture of styles and traditions — from Greece, from Iran and from Central Asia.

A golden ceremonial helmet from a grave near Bucharest may belong to the 'Royal Sarmatians', a powerful tribe who flourished in the 2nd century BC. It has certain Greco-Scythian features, but the main influence (e.g. the animal on the side) is from Iran. (7)

Precious horse-trappings were amongst the treasures of the Royal Sarmatians. This *phalera* from the shores of the Black Sea (2nd century BC) is cast in silver and gold-plated. Its animals recall the art of Iran: in the centre a hyena devours an antelope; above, two winged buffalo pursue a leopard; below, two griffins with an ox-head between them. (8)

A Bosporan warrior on a funerary relief from Tanais, near the mouth of the Don. His armour may be compared with that worn by the Sarmatians on Trajan's Column (pl. 1). Tanais was part of the Bosporan Kingdom and served as a market between Greek merchants and Sarmatians of the surrounding steppes. The inscription is Greek. (9)

'Sarmaticus' was the title taken by Roman emperors after victories over the Sarmatians. Marcus Aurelius (top left) defeated them on the Danube in AD 169. The two reverse designs (right) date from the reign of his son Commodus (issued AD 177–8) and show stylized barbarian armour as trophies. The gold coin (below left) is of Constantine II (317-40). (10-13)

284

A silver treasure-hoard, hastily buried as a new wave of invaders advanced west, has come to light at Martinovka in the Ukraine. It belonged to a ruling family of the Antae, 'Slavonicized' descendants of the Alans, overrun by the Turkish Avars about AD 600. In the top row are belt-buckles and a martingale, a piece of horse-harness for joining three straps; in the centre a bracelet, a large brooch with human head and animals in profile, and an ornamental animal plaque. At the bottom, a plaque with late 'tamga' signs, and a strap-end. (14)

How a motif can be transformed as it passes from culture to culture is well illustrated by the gold fibula (below) from Maikop in the Kuban, (1st–3rd century AD.) The god's head 'cut short at the chin' occurs first at Cemetery B at Siyalk, Iran, c. 1000 BC. It became popular with sculptors and metal-workers throughout Mesopotamia, especially the Parthian region (e.g. the 'masks' on the Palace of Hatra) and even Italy (Pompeii) and Siberia. Then the Sarmatians adopted it and turned it into something quite different—the severed head of an enemy brandished by the victor. (15)

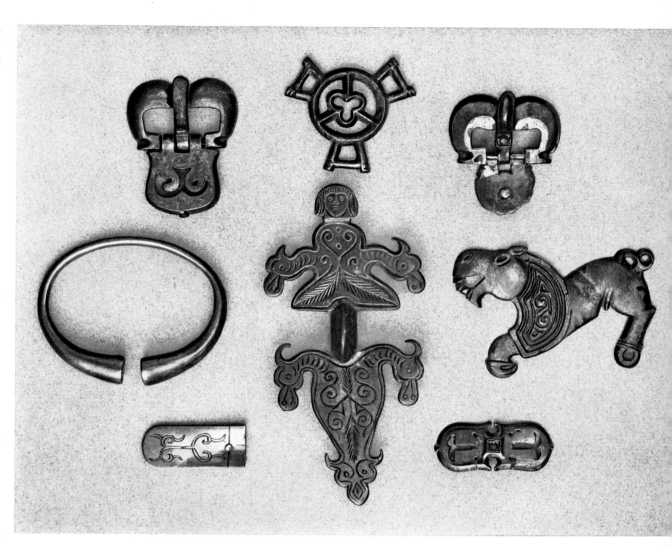

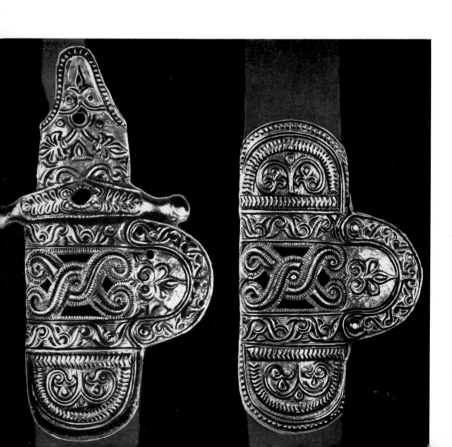

Through the centuries Sarmatian art changed as little as Sarmatian life. The engraved bowl from Poland (above) dates from the 3rd or 4th century AD, yet with its rows of animals—griffin, lion, elk—shows no great development from the *phalera* reproduced opposite (pl. 8) 500 years older. Left: two sabre-sheaths decorated with thin metal sheets, from the late Alanic kingdom in the Caucasus, 10th century AD. (16–18)

'They could afford to wear gold ornaments' says Strabo; an understatement when one is faced with the staggering riches uncovered a hundred years ago at Novocherkassk, near the mouth of the Don. It was the grave of a woman, probably a queen of the Aorsi in the 1st–2nd century AD. Top: a coronet studded with precious inlays. Below it a gold jug with stag handle, a needle-box and perfume-box covered in intricate repoussé decoration and (right) another perfume-box with a lid secured by a golden chain. Other discoveries have been almost as impressive. A late hoard from the Caucasus (left) included a glass beaker, a necklace of gold and carnelian beads and a garnet ring. Above right: a bronze gilt shield boss from Herpály, Hungary, 3rd century AD, ceremonial only, not for use in war. The type is Germanic (actual iron bosses have been found with a spike instead of a knob) but the ornament is Sarmatian. Far right: jewellery from several sites showing a mixture of Sarmatian, Greek and Gothic influences. The belt-plaques and ear-rings are the most Sarmatian. (19–23)

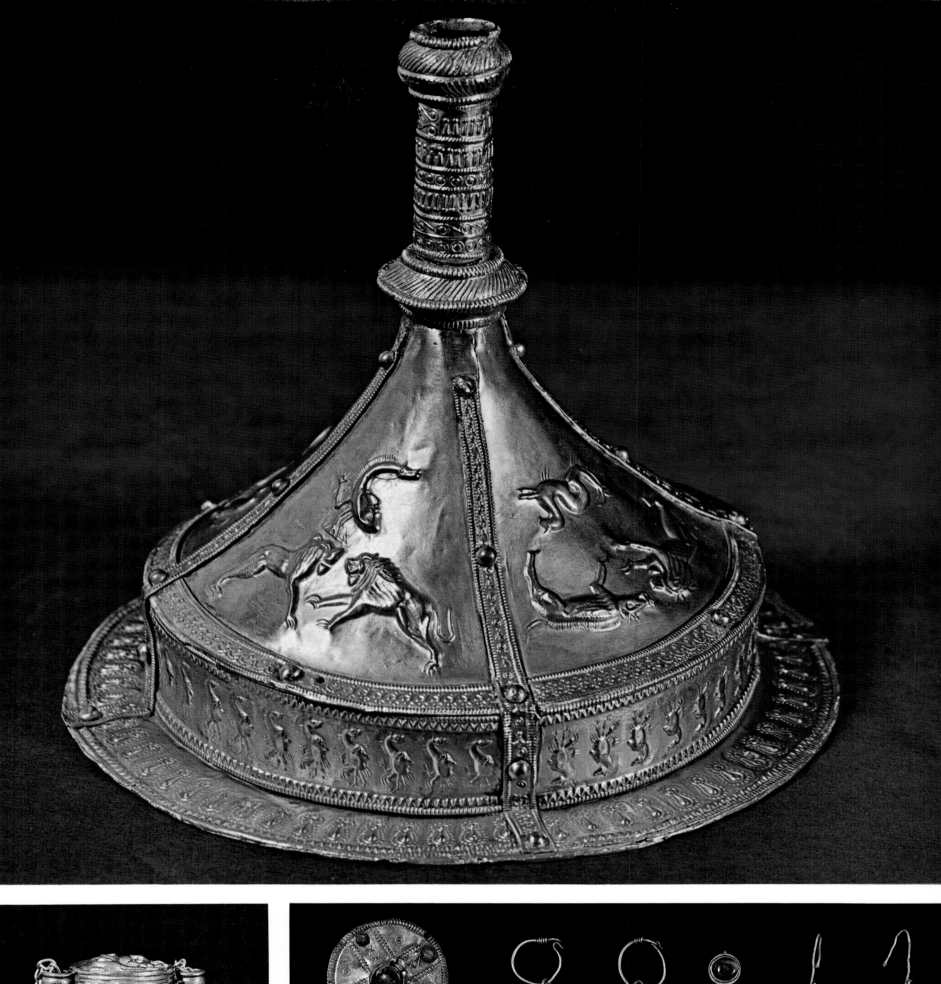

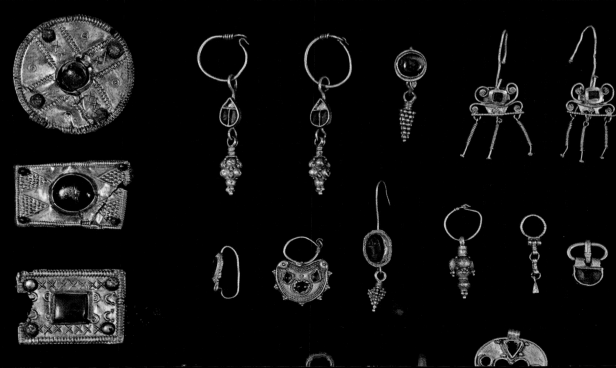

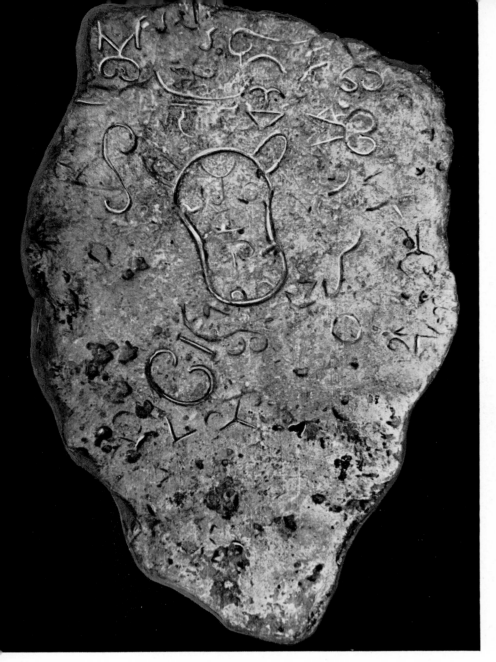

Sarmatian religion

remains a mystery, compounded of magic, sacrifice, divination and a smattering of Greek mythology. We hear of them worshipping swords fixed in the ground and muttering 'secret incantations' to see into the future. Certain places were regarded as holy and ritual centred round sacred stones, a few of which still exist. They are covered in 'tamga' signs, strange cyphers remotely based on the Greek alphabet, originating probably in the Bosporan kingdom but soon becoming a hall-mark of Sarmatian culture and undergoing remarkable transformations. The Krivoy Rog stone (left) was used for centuries, and the tamgas inscribed on it show every stage of development. In the middle is what looks like a horse's head; the rest of the surface is covered with tamgas quite at random, running over the head and over each other. There are no signs at the bottom—proving that it was originally fixed upright in the ground. (24)

Before the 5th century AD all the signs are magical or religious. They occur on a variety of objects including grave stelae and belt-buckles (the one below left is from Kerch, 1st–2nd century, and the tamga on it is based on a Greek monogram for 'Helios'). The cauldron (below), from the Don-Donets region, bears a tamga that also appears on Bosporan tombs. With the coming of Christianity the signs lose their old meanings and become property marks and family crests. On the two rings (above), surmounted by the Christian cross, they identify Vsievolod Yaroslavich, an 11th century Grand Duke of Kiev of the Ruric dynasty. (25–27)

A once mighty folk scattered among the nations

T. SULIMIRSKI

BY THE BEGINNING of the Christian era, the term *Sarmatia* appeared in ancient written records, replacing the name *Scythia* given formerly to the eastern part of Europe. It derived from the *Sarmatians*, a people which superseded the Scythians in the steppes north of the Black Sea.

The Sarmatians seem to be at present a forgotten people, but in antiquity they were a large and mighty folk, with whom the Romans often had to fight. Their rôle in reshaping the ancient European order at the turn of Antiquity and the Middle Ages, and their contribution to mediaeval art were considerable although usually ignored. Their impact on the Slavonic peoples was important and lasting, and the vocabulary of almost all Slavonic languages comprises many words of Sarmatian origin.

The Sarmatians were of Iranian stock, and were close relatives of the ancient Scythians, Medes and Parthians and also of the Persians; their language was related to that of Avesta. Herodotus, the Greek historian of the 5th century BC, mentions that 'they used the Scythian language, speaking it corruptly'. No Sarmatian written texts have come down to us, except a number of personal names usually of their rulers. But the tongue of the Ossetians, in the central part of the Caucasus, which has evolved out of the ancient Sarmatian-Alan dialects, can be considered to be modern Sarmatian.

Conditions in the steppes were never stable and the Sarmatians were never a united people. Minor friction was constant between tribes, and from time to time major wars drove a large group from their areas to seek new pastures at the expense of other neighbours, causing further disturbances. The movements call to mind a billiard table on which one ball striking another stops in putting the other in motion.

The Ancient Homeland of the Sarmatians

The name under which the Sarmatians were mentioned for the first time by the ancient authors in the 5th century BC was 'Sauromatae'. Herodotus says that their land lay 'three days journey' east of the Don, and 'three days journey' northwards from the Sea of Azov. Archaeological research has shown that they extended over the wide grassland of the Eurasiatic border east of the Don nearly up to the Ural river, and northwards along the Volga up to Saratov. They were of mixed origin, combining features of various Late Bronze Age cultures, particularly the Maeotians and the Scythians, with whom the Sauromatae were in close contact.

They had no permanent settlements. They lived on horseback and their dwellings were wagons drawn by oxen. In their dress, customs and culture they did not differ from the Scythians. They wore trousers and pointed caps. Their wives retained the 'ancient Amazon' mode of living, joining their husbands in the hunt and in war, and wearing the same dress as the men. No virgin was permitted to marry until she had killed an enemy.

However, the Sauromatae were not fated to live quietly in their country, moving around from time to time with their herds in search of fresh pastures. Events in central Asia during the 4th century BC had a great bearing on their further development.

In 331 Alexander the Great destroyed the Achaemenid Empire of Persia. During the next two years he conquered Bactria and Sogdiana, but did not succeed in subjugating the peoples further north, the Chorasmians and the Massagetae. In fact the effect of his conquests was to bring about a strong union of these two peoples, and during the 3rd century BC they became the masters of all the nomad tribes of central Asia, and even the Huns, a Turkish people who lived east of them up to the Chinese border, had to acknowledge their suzerainty.

The culture of the Massagetae was typical of the steppe peoples but was at the same time very strongly influenced by the Achae-

The main area of Sarmatian history—but detachments reached as far as eastern China, northern England and the Iberian Peninsula. (1)

menid civilization of Persia. The extension of their rule, therefore, meant the spread of Achaemenian culture and ideas; the Sauromatae were among the peoples profoundly affected by these.

Another innovation was the adoption of new warfare tactics and armour. The armour consisted of leather or material on which were sewn small copper or iron plaques; horses were protected in the same manner. The main weapons were long, heavy lances held in a hooked bar fixed to the horse's neck, and long iron swords. This cavalry fought in close array and no adversary could resist it. The new tactics resulted in a reorganization of all the armies in the east, even those of the Huns and the Chinese. Light mounted archers were replaced by armoured cavalry which became the typical Sarmatian war-formation. Even the Romans were in the end forced to equip some of their units in the same fashion.

A New Culture: the Royal Sarmatians

Massagetian-Chorasmian rule, or some sort of political dependence, had a profound effect on the old Sauromatian culture. It began to lose its 'Scythian' characteristics and to acquire an eastern, central Asiatic appearance, known as 'Early Sarmatian'. The transition seems to have started (early 4th century BC) in the region of Orsk-Chkalov in west Siberia, the area nearest to the Massagetian border. Here, to judge from the diversity of the furniture of the graves, was a society divided into social ranks and even different racial groups. Grave-goods are mostly of Iranian, central Asiatic or oriental origin, but in the western part of the area Greek imports have been found. Women were often buried with arrowheads, which some authors consider to be a survival of ancient 'Amazon' (matriarchal) tradition. An entire carcass of a sheep or horse has often been found in richly furnished graves; the animals always had the head removed.

By 338 BC the Sarmatians had crossed the Don. We know this both from Greek historical records (Pseudo-Scylax) and from archaeology. The region west of the Don had been occupied at the beginning of the 4th century by the Scythians, who had built spectacular royal tombs in the Kuban valley in the north-western Caucasus. At the end of the century the Scythians have disappeared from the Kuban and are found much further west, on the other side of the Dnieper. The implication is that they were pushed westwards by advancing Sarmatians, who were doubtless

themselves under pressure from other Sarmatian tribes further east. By 300 BC the Sarmatians controlled the whole area between the Don and the Dnieper.

These Western Sarmatians were evidently united under a strong central leadership. Written records call them 'the Royal Sarmatians'. A branch of the Scythians who had retreated into the Crimea became their vassals and Olbia, a Greek city on the mouth of the S. Bug, paid them tribute. One of their kings, Galatus, is mentioned in a peace treaty concluded about 179 BC by the King of Pontus (in Turkey, south of the Black Sea) and a queen, Amage, appears in the records some decades later.

The only finds that can be linked with the Royal Sarmatians are golden or silver gilt horse trappings (*phalerae*) dated to the 2nd century BC. They have an embossed ornament, either geometrical or in animal style reminiscent of ancient Assyrian or Ionian, but at the same time closely connected with Graeco-Indian art. *Phalerae* of this type have been found at eleven sites mainly within the presumed territory of the Royal Sarmatians. Two were found outside that area, one in Transylvania, the other on the Danube in Bulgaria. The latter may be connected with a branch of the Royal Sarmatians which under pressure from other Sarmatian tribes had to retreat further west. For by this time the might of the Royal Sarmatians was near its end. Most of the population presumably submitted to the newcomers; but at least some of their tribes set off again on the migration westwards.

pl 8

Outpost of the Greek World: the Bosporan Kingdom

The Sarmatians who entered the Pontic steppe (the region between the Don and the Danube) in the 4th century BC were the first to make direct contact with the classical world, in the shape of the Bosporan kingdom. The origins of this kingdom go back to the 6th century BC, when the Greeks founded several colonies on the northern coast of the Black Sea. In the 5th century BC the Bosporan kingdom embraced all colonies on the shores of the Sea of Azov and a wide stretch of land along the eastern coast, inhabited at first by Maeotian but later by Sarmatian, or Sarmatized tribes.

The aim of the Bosporan state was to protect Greek cities from seizure by the steppe nomads. But the Scythians and after them the Sarmatians were content to preserve the Greek cities and to use them as commercial agents. During the Sarmatian period the Greek cities, and above all the Bosporan state, kept their position as centres of production and exportation.

Its subsequent history may be briefly told. After absorbing successive waves of Sarmatian invasion, it was seized in 110 BC by Mithridates of Pontus, who involved it in his wars with Rome. A period of disorder followed, but by the mid-1st century AD a new dynasty of mixed Sarmato-Thracian origin was established. It ruled until the arrival of the Goths in the 3rd century AD. Members of this dynasty bore mainly Thracian or Sarmatian names and 'Sauromates' was one of them. Rome exercised a nominal overlordship.

The wealthy middle classes, engaged mainly in trade and industry, were chiefly of Greek origin, but a large proportion of the population was indigenous, Maeotian, Scythian and Sarmatian, only partly Hellenized. The official language was Greek and the funeral ritual of the middle class shows that it tried to keep to ancient Greek traditions. But descriptions by ancient authors of the North Pontic cities in the early Christian era, the sepulchral stelae with sculptural figures and above all paintings in grave chambers, show us Bosporans whose appearance was evidently Sarmatian. They wore trousers, soft leather shoes, long cloaks probably of wool, etc., a thoroughly Scytho-Sarmatian dress. Their armour was Sarmatian too. Bosporan nobles are depicted as cavalrymen with a conical metal helmet, a corselet of scale or ring armour, a long lance, a dagger fastened to the leg with a ring at the top, a sword with a round stone pommel, a bow and bowcase (*corytus*) and a small shield. The same armour has been found in Bosporan tombs of the period. The Sarmatians who appear on Trajan's column (the Roxolani) or on the Arch of Galerius at Salonica were clad and armed in the same manner. Infantry had usually no corselets and were armed with lances, javelins, large shields and sometimes a bow.

pl 9

f 2

pl 1
f 6

Figure of a warrior on a rhyton from the Bosporan region, showing the mixture of Greek and Sarmatian features. (2)

A tendrilled fibula, or brooch, 'with the foot turned over', was one of the most characteristic pieces of Sarmatian jewellery. They have been found at sites as far apart as the Volga, the Kuban and Poland. The one shown here is from eastern Germany. (3)

Masters of the Central Steppes: the Eastern Sarmatians

The years between 174 and 160 BC were a turning-point in the history of the Sarmatians who stayed in their original homeland east of the Volga. Hitherto they had lived under the domination of other peoples, chiefly the Massagetae. Now the Massagetae were defeated by the Huns, and the Sarmatians were able to shake themselves free. Remnants of the Massagetae were assimilated and the Sarmatians now had the Huns as their eastern neighbours. Their might is well illustrated by the arrival, in 125 BC, of a Chinese legation which tried to incite the Sarmatians against the Huns, in order to relieve Hunnic pressure on the Chinese borders.

The result of these changes was a transformation of the Sarmatian culture, which reaches a new period in its development called the Middle Sarmatian period. It was a time of unification, and obliteration of regional differences. Grave goods from all over the Sarmatian territory east of the Volga show only minor variations. Long swords become less frequent and were gradually replaced by short swords and daggers with a ring on the top of the hilt instead of a pommel. Spear-heads, or lance-heads, were an exception. By the end of the period (2nd century AD) the Eastern Sarmatians were no longer heavy armed cavalry: they were primarily armed with a new, more effective bow introduced by the Huns and designed to combat the cavalry that had previously been invincible. The new bow was strengthened by bone inlays and fired a heavy arrow with three-edged head. It was this invention that eventually gave the Huns superiority over all their adversaries.

Many of the grave goods bear witness to strong ties with Central Asiatic countries: mirrors, bone spoons, jewellery, horse harness, red-coloured pottery of Kushan type and distinctive jugs with a handle in the shape of an animal. On the other hand, graves in the lower Volga show connections with the Bosporan kingdom —*fibulae* of various types made sometimes of silver, including the *f 3* 'tendrilled type with the foot turned over', glass, carnelian and amber beads, Egyptian-type faience pendants and amulets, wheel-made pottery, etc. Small bronze plaques (sometimes golden) sewn on to garments are common to the whole Sarmatian territory. Gold apart from plaques is rare. Fragments of sheep's bones are often found in a dish or bowl, but entire carcasses are now an exception.

The best known of the Middle Sarmatians are those who migrated across the Dnieper and began pressing upon the frontiers of Rome. Two groups, however, remained nearer to their ancestral homelands and may conveniently be described first.

The Aorsi, living mainly to the east of the Volga, were the most remote. After the defeat of the Massagetae they increased in strength and became a mighty people, mentioned in Chinese annals of c. 130 BC (where they are said to have had 100,000 archers as their fighting force), and by the Greek geographer Strabo (early 1st century AD), who says that an important trade route ran through their territory and they could 'afford to wear gold ornaments'.

A branch of the Aorsi (probably fugitives from the main group) settled west of the Volga, around the lower Don, and it was here, *pl 19* at Novocherkassk, that the most splendid of all Middle Sarmatian *22* graves was excavated in 1864. It was the grave of a woman, probably a tribal chief or queen. Grave goods included at least thirteen gold objects, mostly decorated in the animal style and studded with precious stones—turquoise, amethyst and coral. There were richly ornamented diadems, bracelets, perfume-bottles, cases and jugs. One of the latter had a zoomorphic handle (a stag) of the same type as those of the clay jugs in ordinary Sarmatian graves. There were also hundreds of small plaques sewn on to garments.

In the middle of the 1st century AD the Aorsi lost their leading position among the Eastern Sarmatians and were replaced by the Alans (see p. 294).

The Siraces of the Kuban

The second group, the Siraces, lived further to the south, in the valley of the Kuban and the steppes immediately north of it. They were not a large people. Strabo says that their king Abeacus had at his disposal in c. 66–63 BC only 20,000 horsemen, whereas Spadines, King of the Aorsi, who bordered them to the north, had 200,000.

During the dynastic feuds of the Bosporan kingdom, the Siraces became involved in Mithridates' wars against Rome. They became tributaries of Rome in the 1st century AD, but were soon conquered by the Alans, and do not appear in written records after the 2nd century.

They were partly nomad wagon-dwellers, partly tent-dwellers and farmers. Large numbers of their permanent settlements, usually hill-forts, are recorded in the Kuban valley. Houses were built of beaten clay, and the inhabitants practised agriculture— wheat, barley and millet and animal husbandry. Cattle, horses, sheep and pigs were reared, and fishing was an important part of their economy.

It was a severely stratified society. At the top were kings and princes, beneath them a series of social classes, differing widely in wealth and privilege. Our knowledge of Siracian life comes chiefly from their graves, which were of two types—the 'flat' cemeteries where the majority of the people were buried, and the princely 'barrow graves', confined to the upper classes.

The largest of the 'flat' cemeteries is at Ust-Labinska. Here a variety of grave goods has come to light. The pottery is mainly a wheel-made ware—bowls, vessels with spherical body etc.—but most characteristic are jugs with handles in the form of animals, or at least the top of the handle in the shape of an animal head. Jugs of this type were common among the Sarmatians on the lower Volga and the steppes further east. They were probably adapted from Central Asiatic peoples, where jugs with zoomorphic handles were common from the 2nd century BC.

Weapons were more numerous than before. There are daggers and swords of two types—either long and narrow, or short, *pl 6* double-edged and pointed. Iron spear-or lance-heads are common. Socketed arrow-heads are replaced by three-edged tanged points.

Jewellery is also plentiful, including the characteristic 'Sarmatian' tendril-*fibulae* of the so-called 'type with foot turned over', *f 3* and the *fibulae* of *arbalest* type. Mirrors were usually decorated. In richly furnished graves there are imported goods—glass vessels, *terra sigillata* bowls, beads made of glass, paste and semi-precious *pl 5* stones, and Egyptian *scarabei* and similar figurines.

In most graves animal bones were excavated, the remains of food for the journey into the next world: mainly sheep, seldom cow or pig. Occasionally there are complete skeletons, chiefly cows, seldom horses.

Of the princely barrow-graves the best known are at Ust-Labinska (situated in the vicinity of the flat cemetery), Vozdvi-zhenskaya, Armavir and Zubovskii. They consist usually of small mounds with a grave-shaft (with niche) underneath. Sometimes a man is buried alone, sometimes a man and woman together. The grave-goods do not differ much from those of the flat cemeteries, but there is a profusion of gold objects and goods imported from distant countries. Another difference is that all the princely burials are of horsemen.

The principal weapons were heavy, long lances and long swords with a wooden hilt, oval in section, topped by a round or square pommel of some precious or semi-precious stone. Both men and horses wore corselets, but by the end of the 1st century AD the sealed corselet is replaced by ring-armour. Conical helmets have been found in several graves. Bows and arrows played a secondary rôle in the armament of these knights. Their horse-trappings differed from those of the Scythian period, but *phalerae* were still in use. The bits had simple rings.

Jewels and ornaments have been recovered in quantity—torques, fibulae of the same type as those in the flat graves, diadems and bracelets. Belt-buckles and clasps are mostly open-work, often with coloured filling. The polychromy (related to Persian goldsmiths' work) considerably modified the animal style by filling the bodies of the animals with gems and cut pieces of coloured glass, enclosing them in a coloured frame.

Very characteristic are small thin metal, usually gold, plaques sewn on cloth, hundreds of which have been excavated from Kuban barrow-graves. They differ from those of the Scythian period in being very small, their shapes geometric—rounds, triangles, crescents, rosettes, etc. All are of Oriental type.

Some of the goods mentioned are products of Bosporan workshops, but others are of local Siracian manufacture. Others again come from even further afield—Greek goods imported through the Bosporan town of Panticapaeum (Kerch), and Oriental luxuries (especially beads) reaching the Siracian country by the caravan routes described by Strabo. Iranian and Indian ideas, as well as jewellery, must also have followed the same route, considerably influencing the Siracian culture and that of other Sarmatian tribes.

Two objects from Kuban barrow-graves are of Greek origin and can be dated 6th century BC, i.e. six centuries or so before the graves in which they were found. According to an inscription on one of them they originally belonged to the temple of Apollo at Phasis. They were evidently looted during an incursion south of the Caucasus.

The Great Migrations

When the Sarmatians burst upon the frontiers of the Roman Empire in the 1st century AD they were already split up into tribes with distinct names, and it is by these names that they are usually mentioned by Roman historians. The most famous are the Iazyges, the Roxolani and the Alani. Their relations with Rome and with each other are now fairly well understood, but before examining the story in detail it is helpful to have a picture of the great migratory movements of Eastern Europe as a whole.

Sarmatian history consists of a series of waves moving from east to west, each pushing and being pushed, until they reach the barrier of Rome and break up into yet more complex eddies and cross-currents.

f 4   The first wave—the vanguard of the Sarmatians—was the Iazyges. In the 2nd century BC they lived north-west of the Sea of Azov between the Dnieper and the Don. Behind them (i.e. to the east) were the Roxolani; in front of them a non-Sarmatian people, the Bastarnae. Pressure from the Roxolani pushed the Iazyges across the Dnieper up to the Dniester (early 1st century BC) and then to the Danube delta, the frontier of Rome. The first recorded fighting between Sarmatians and Romans took place in 78 BC. By AD 20 the Iazyges had crossed the Carpathians and settled in the Hungarian Plain. Here the war with Rome went on, with various shifts in the situation (sometimes the Iazyges sided with Rome against later Sarmatians) for 400 years. Then they disappear from history, squeezed into oblivion by pressures too great to be resisted.

At their heels came the Roxolani. In their 'starting-position' (2nd century BC) they lived east of the Don. Their movements closely follow those of the Iazyges—across the Dnieper (early 1st century AD), at war with Rome (AD 62).

After these large-scale movements came a lull. The place of the Iazyges and the Roxolani in the steppes north of the Black Sea is filled by the Aorsi and the Siraces, who, as we have seen, attained a high degree of civilization and did not at once follow their compatriots to the west. The current, however, had not stopped. In the 1st century AD they were subdued by a new tribe from east of the Don—the Alans. The resulting mixture of tribes is referred to by ancient writers as either 'Alanorsi' (i.e. Alan-Aorsi) or Western Alans'. But the Alans, instead of repeating the familiar pattern and adding to the tension on the Roman border, expanded

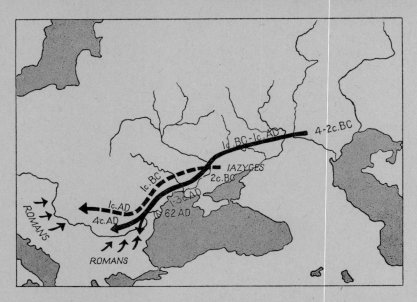

The approximate route of the Iazyges and the Roxolani, the first two waves of Sarmatian nomads to reach western Europe. (4)

south into the Caucasus, west into Bessarabia and north-west into Poland.

In the early 3rd century AD came a new threat, this time from the north—the Goths, fighting their way from the Baltic to the Black Sea. In 332 they captured the 'Sarmatized' Bosporan kingdom. Later they too joined the march against Rome.

Finally the ultimate enemy—the Huns. The greatest of the Gothic kingdoms—the Ostrogoths—broke under the Hunnic onslaught in 375, crossed the Danube and allied themselvees (temporarily) with Rome. This was virtually the end of the Sarmatians as a distinct people. Split into smaller and smaller units, dispersed in many unconnected regions, they had little chance of maintaining their national identity and were doomed to be absorbed by either their successive conquerors or the subdued peoples in the country of their retreat. There are a few partial exceptions which will be described—the Alans in the Caucasus and some small groups in the Ukraine and Bessarabia. But 'Sarmatia' had ceased to exist.

With this summary in mind we can return to the first of the Sarmatian tribes to make its impact on the West, the Iazyges.

The Invasion of the West: the Iazyges

The earliest history of the Iazyges is unknown. They may have been identical with the 'Royal Sarmatians'. But around the beginning of the Christian era they are mentioned by Strabo and then by Tacitus as living between the Dnieper and Dniester, and ruling over a Celtic people called the Bastarnae. Tacitus says about the Bastarnae that 'in consequence of frequent intermarriages between their leading families and the families of Sarmatia, they have been tainted with the manners of that country'. No archaeological remains of the Iazyges have been found in the Pontic area, in spite of the fact that they lived for at least a century in the region close to the Sea of Azov and for another century in the steppes west of the Dnieper.

In their migration westwards the Iazyges came first to the Danube delta, an outpost of the kingdom of Dacia, centred on modern Transylvania. On the other side of the river was the Roman province of Moesia. The Iazyges allied themselves with Mithridates Eupator of Pontus (in Asia Minor) in his war against Rome. We hear that in 78–76 BC a punitive expedition was undertaken by the Romans against the Iazyges north of the Danube, obviously in connection with an incursion of theirs into Roman territory. It was the first of many encounters. The Iazyges were to become familiar adversaries. Ovid, who was banished to Tomi (modern Constanța) in AD 8, has left several descriptions of them.

The way south was blocked, but the way west still lay open. Soon after AD 20 the Iazyges crossed the Carpathians and settled in the Hungarian Plain between the Theiss and the Danube. The Dacian tribes that were already there had to pay them tribute. The Roman province of Pannonia now faced them to the west, but instead of trying to invade it at once they seem to have come to an agreement with the Romans and received subsidies in return for service as auxiliaries. They were on the Roman side in the Dacian wars of Trajan (AD 85–88 and 101) but raided Roman Moesia at the same time.

The earliest remains of the Iazyges date from this period. Their graves were flat and were grouped into large cemeteries. They were poorly furnished: clay vessels, sometimes an iron knife, beads, occasionally a brooch and exceptionally a short iron sword with a ring at the top of the hilt. The influence of the subdued indigenous population is illustrated by brooches and arm-rings of La Tène type. A few early graves contain objects of Pontic origin (e.g. decorated gold plaques sewn to garments) but these soon die out, which implies a break between the Iazyges and the North Pontic lands from which they came.

The Fight on the Frozen Danube

Trajan had made Dacia into a Roman province with the aid of the Iazyges, but in AD 117 this peaceful arrangement was broken. Hadrian had to defend Dacia against the Iazyges from the west and the Roxolani from the east (see p. 294). The Iazyges continued sporadically at war with Rome for the next fifty years. In AD 169 they crossed the Danube and invaded Pannonia, only to be severely beaten by Marcus Aurelius. Dio Cassius has left us a vivid description of the battle between the Romans and the fleeing Sarmatians on the frozen Danube. The Iazyges, expecting easily to overcome the pursuing Romans once they were on the ice, turned back on them. In response the Romans formed a compact body, laid their shields flat and placed one foot upon them in order to reduce the chance of slipping, 'and thus they received the enemy's charge. Some seized the bridles, others the shields and spear-shafts of their assailants, and drew the men towards them; and thus, becoming involved in close conflict, they knocked down both men and horses, since the barbarians, by reason of their momentum, could no longer keep from slipping. The Romans also slipped, but those who fell on their back would drag their adversaries down on top of them, while those that fell forward actually seized their antagonists, who had fallen first, with their teeth. For the barbarians, being unused to a conflict of this sort, and having lighter equipment, were unable to resist, so that but few escaped out of a large force.'

pl 10 In AD 175 peace was concluded, Marcus taking the title 'Sarmaticus' and his victories being celebrated in Imperial coinage. Hard conditions were imposed on the Iazyges. They were required to dwell far away from the Danube and had to contribute 8,000 cavalry to the Roman army, 5,500 of whom were sent to Britain.

These Sarmatians in Britain were distributed through the northern frontierland in units of 500. Traces of them have so far been discovered at three sites. In the Roman fort at Chesters on Hadrian's wall, an eye-shield from a cataphract horse was found,
pl 4 probably Sarmatian, and also a number of beads typical of the Sarmatians in Hungary. There is a funeral stele showing a Sarmatian horseman at Chester, and in the ancient fort of Bremetennacum at
pl 2 Ribchester near Lancaster, inscriptions bear witness to a Sarmatian cavalry unit 500 strong.

Nothing is known about the fate of these men, but at least some of them never returned to their homeland. A settlement of veterans was established at Bremetennacum; it never became a real town, but it was still in existence in the early 5th century AD.

In Dacia the war broke out again only two years after the peace just described, and the Iazyges obtained some mitigation of the former conditions. They were allowed to sail on the Danube in their own boats and to communicate with the Roxolani who dwelt east of Dacia. They were anxious to maintain relations with these, since it was through them that they were able to provide themselves with beads and other commodities of eastern origin which were their most common grave-goods.

Conflict with Rome continued intermittently. We hear of the Iazyges losing a war in AD 236–238, raiding Dacia in 248–250 and Pannonia in 254. They were evidently a strong people whom the Romans were unable to subdue permanently. Archaeological remains from this period (c. AD 160–260) are plentiful. The Iazyges seem to have gone on living a nomadic, pastoral life. A

new feature in graves is the so-called 'herdsmen's bag'—an assemblage consisting of an iron knife, iron awl, fire-stone and flint, and sometimes a whetstone. The ruling classes continued to be buried in barrow-graves, of which a notable example has been found at Szil in the centre of Roman Pannonia. It is possibly the grave of a Sarmatian prince who fell in battle during an incursion in the 2nd century AD.

By the middle of the 3rd century the position of the Iazyges had decisively deteriorated. In 260 the Goths had entered Dacia, which the Romans could no longer defend, and in 271 had established the powerful kingdom of the Visigoths. But in spite of this danger on their eastern border the Iazyges continued their raids into Pannonia, until the Romans finally decided to finish them. Between AD 290 and 313, eight successive Roman expeditions entered and devastated their territory, after which the Emperor Galerius Maximus and his successors, Constantine and Licinius took the title 'Sarmaticus'.

Roman punitive expeditions had not broken the Sarmatians but had considerably weakened them. They were no longer in a position to resist the Visigoths who attacked them in AD 321. But the Visigoths, after beating the Iazyges, crossed their territory and invaded Pannonia. Their incursion ended in a great victory for Constantine in 322. The Gothic king was slain and the Iazyges were saved.

The renewed activity of the Iazyges at the beginning of this period (AD 260–330), to which the Romans reacted so strongly, seems to have been connected with internal changes, most probably a new wave of immigrants from the east. The contents of the graves seem to indicate three distinct layers of society—a lower class, possibly the indigenous conquered Slavs; a middle-class, perhaps the first wave of Iazyges; and a ruling upper-class, the 3rd century newcomers. Graves of the first group are without weapons; the second, consisting of careful coffin burials, contain 'herdsmen's bags', personal ornaments and a few iron swords and Roman coins; the third are barrow-graves, furnished with weapons, horses, and fine Pontic jewellery. A particularly interesting barrow-grave, dating from about AD 300, has been found at Herpály, on the eastern fringe of Iazygian territory. Here a Sarmatian warrior was buried with his horse; in the grave were characteristic Sarmatian beads and a fine shield buckle covered with pl 21 a gold-plated silver sheet decorated in the Pontic style. The shield buckle was of Teutonic type.

The final stage of the Iazyges began about AD 332. A disastrous civil war broke out amongst them, ending with the flight of one whole tribe, the Ardagarantes, partly to the Goths, partly to the Romans. The remainder were again beaten, this time by Constantius in 358, and, after an attempt at peaceful settlement, massacred.

Fighting went on through the end of the 4th century AD. In the early 5th century came the Huns. By about 432 they were masters of most the Hungarian plain, having subjugated the Goths and what was left of the Sarmatians. But after the death of Attila (453) the Sarmatians freed themselves from Hunnic rule, and there are again records of clashes between them and the Romans. In 472 they were beaten by Theodoric, king of the Visigoths, and two Sarmatian kings, Beukan and Babai, fell in battle.

This seems to be the last reference in written records to the Hungarian Sarmatians, the descendants of the Iazyges who had arrived 500 years before. They had gained the name of 'Latrunculi' (free-booters, robbers) and one historian says that they were 'a tribe most accomplished in brigandage.' Yet they were suffi- pl 10- ciently formidable for six Roman emperors to take the title 'Sar- 13 maticus' after defeating them, and special coins were several times minted to commemorate victories over them.

The Roxolani: 'Impetuous, Fierce and Irresistible'

The Roxolani, the next great tribe of Sarmatians to reach the West, crossed the Don in the mid-2nd century BC. They first ravaged the country and then settled north of the Iazyges in the steppes between the Don and the Dnieper. They must have partly subdued the 'Royal Sarmatians' and partly forced them to move west of the Dnieper.

About 110 BC they became involved in Black Sea politics, first allying themselves with the Scythians against the Bosporan-Pontic alliance and then, after being defeated by Diophantes of Pontus, aiding the Pontic army in its conquest of the Bosporan kingdom. Their defeat in the first campaign is described by Strabo. They were 50,000 men strong and had the reputation of being warlike, but were light-armed and could not stand against a well-ordered and well-armed phalanx. They used helmets and corslets of raw hide, carried wicker shields and had for weapons spears, bows and swords.

By the middle of the 1st century AD, as part of a much larger movement of the tribes, the Roxolani had moved west of the Dnieper. From here part of them seem to have settled between the Dnieper and the Danube delta (ousting the Iazyges, who were there before), but the bulk of them went further south and by AD 62 had arrived in the plains of southern Roumania. We have a description of them by Strabo of about this time (AD 17–23). He calls them 'the wagon-dwellers'. 'Their tents made of felt were fastened to the wagons in which they spent their lives. Round about the tents were the herds which afforded the milk, cheese and meat on which they lived. They followed the grazing herds, from time to time moving to other places that had grass.' He also says that they are 'warriors rather than brigands, yet they go to war only for the sake of the tributes due to them. They turn over their land to any people who wish to till it, and are satisfied if they receive in return a tribute for the land, which is a moderate one. But when tenants do not pay, they go to war with them.' Their horses, like those of the Scythians, were exceedingly quick and hard to manage, they therefore castrated them. They also hunted deer and wild boar in the marshes, and wild asses and roe deer in the steppes.

We know from their grave goods that they had iron swords, small iron arrow-heads, and quivers of birch-bark—the weapons of light-armed mounted archers. According to ancient descriptions, they lassoed their enemies in battle.

As soon as they arrived on the Danube the Roxolani invaded Roman Moesia. They were hurled back, but thousands of 'Transdanubian' (presumably Dacian) fugitives sought shelter in the Roman province and were allowed to settle there. Tacitus has left a vivid—if hostile—description of the Roxolani as they appeared to their Roman neighbours. 'Plunder, and not war, is their passion,' he writes, '—a band of freebooters, determined to ravage the country . . . Their courage has no inward principles, but depends altogether upon external circumstances . . . In an engagement with the infantry nothing can be more dastardly; in an onset of the cavalry they are impetuous, fierce and irresistible. Their weapons are long spears or sabres of enormous size, which they wield with both hands. The chiefs wear coats of mail, formed with plates of iron, or the tough hides of animals, impenetrable to the enemy, but to themselves an encumbrance so unwieldy that he who falls in the battle is never able to rise again.'

In the winter of AD 69 the Roxolani again invaded Moesia and annihilated the Legio III Gallica. But they were soon taken by surprise by another Roman army and severely punished, a heavy fall of rain and a sudden thaw having deprived them of all advantage from the speed of their horses. In AD 85–86 they attacked Moesia yet again, and in the Dacian wars of Trajan they fought on the Dacian side (the Iazyges, it will be remembered, were on the side of the Romans). When Trajan celebrated his triumph in AD 107, captive Roxolani were led with Dacians pl 1 through the streets of Rome. On Trajan's column we can see a detachment of Roxolani archers on horseback fleeing before the victorious Romans, and their armour exactly answers the description given by Tacitus.

After the Dacian wars they were given a subsidy on condition that they kept away from Roman frontiers. In AD 117 the subsidy was discontinued; another war ensued, Hadrian, Trajan's successor, had to leave Rome to quell the disturbance, and the subsidy was renewed. In AD 118 the king of the Roxolani became a Roman vassal.

Thereafter the Roxolani suffered eclipse. The Goths, as we have seen, wrested Dacia from the Romans in AD 271. During the 3rd and 4th centuries there are many records of raids by Sarmatians into Roman territory, often undertaken jointly with the

Goths, but the identity of the Sarmatian tribes taking part is left doubtful. Those depicted on the Arch of Galerius at Salonica (AD 297), for example, may be Roxolani, but may equally well be Alans.

In AD 377 those Roxolani who still remained in the Roumanian plain east of the Danube had to abandon the country under pressure from the Ostrogoths, who, in turn, were then retreating before the Huns. Some of the Roxolani sought refuge in Roman Moesia, others retreated further west, and joined the Iazyges in the Hungarian plain.

New Tribes from the East—the Western Alans

The last great migratory movement of the Sarmatian people was that of the large group known as the Alans (Alani). In its numerous ramifications, this tribe was once to be found in almost every country of Europe, from the Volga to Spain.

By the middle of the 1st century AD the Alans had won the upper hand over all the eastern Sarmatian tribes. In 68 they were reported in the vicinity of the Sea of Azov, and by the beginning of the second century they were masters of the whole territory previously held by the Aorsi and the Siraces. Some of the Aorsi moved west; others accepted Alanic rule and, merging with them, became the 'Western Alans'. The Siraces too seem to have retreated west. In the steppes of the lower Dniester, in the Ukraine and Bessarabia, are found richly furnished barrow-graves exactly similar to those built earlier by the Siraces in the Kuban. They date from the 2nd and 3rd centuries AD and seem to be the burials of Siracian princelings displaced by the Alans before the arrival of the Goths. Grave-goods include a bronze mirror, a bronze kettle with zoomorphic handles, vessels of Gallic or Pannonian origin, richly decorated horse-harness and an iron battle-axe.

The Alans' first attempts at further expansion were to the south. They invaded Parthia in AD 73 and Roman Asia Minor in 123. Both attacks were repelled. In AD 133 they invaded Media, advancing along the western coast of the Caspian and crossing the narrow passage of Derbent. The historian Josephus has left an account of the Alans in battle. 'They came in great multitudes and fell upon the Medes unexpectedly and plundered their country without opposition.' Pecorus, the king of the Medes, had fled and 'had yielded everything he had to them, and had only saved his wife and his concubines by giving them a hundred talents for their ransom.' The Alans then entered Armenia, where they were met by King Tiridates. In the battle which followed, the king was lassoed by an Alan, and failing to cut the cord with his sword was drawn to his captor and slain. The Alans subsequently 'laid waste the country and drove a great multitude of men, and a great

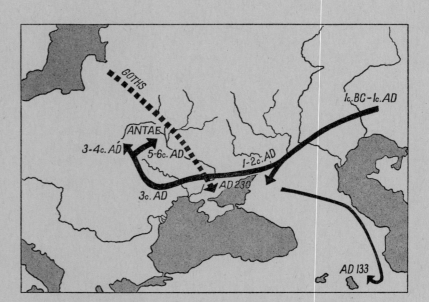

Map showing the migrations of the Western Alans. In the steppes north of the Black Sea the Alans merge with the Aorsi and it is this mixed stock that is known as the Western Alans. The invasion of Media in the 2nd century AD proved to be only a brief raid, not a true migration, but in the Crimea groups of Alans survived for centuries. (5)

quantity of other prey they had gotten, out of both kingdoms along with them and retreated back to their own country.'

The Ukrainian steppes east of the Dnieper also fell under Alanic power. But before they could reach Dacia and add to the pressures already being exerted on the Roman border they had to face a new threat from the north.

The Goths move South

There is no exact agreement about the date at which the Goths reached the Black Sea area. About AD 230 seems appropriate, and archaeological evidence supports the assumption that they came along the Dnieper from their former home on the Baltic coast.

About AD 250 they captured Olbia, the city under Roman protection at the mouth of the S. Bug. The Bosporan kingdom, still under nominal Roman superiority, was subdued; in 332 Bosporan coins ceased to be minted. The last Bosporan king was Rheskuporis IV who died in 361/2.

The eastern reach of the Goths, or the Ostrogothic Empire, has been put usually on the Don. Archaeological evidence suggests that it extended only to the Dnieper, or slightly east of that river in the steppes, and only a relatively narrow strip north of the Sea of Azov was in possession of the Goths.

The conquest of the steppes and the seizure of the almost completely Sarmatized Bosporan kingdom had an enormous effect on the culture of the Ostrogoths, leading it to acquire many Sarmatian characteristics. The fine Bosporan workshops began to supply the new customers, adapting the old Sarmato-Bosporan models of jewellery to the taste of their new masters, and adding some elements brought by the newcomers. The new 'Gothic' art which thus developed spread later over the whole of Central and Western Europe, carried and promoted by the Goths and other peoples, including the Sarmatians, retreating before the Huns.

pl 23

The most westerly branch of the Alans, at the time of the Gothic invasions, lived in the northern half of Bessarabia and the adjoining part of Moldavia on the other side of the Pruth. Here the population was mainly Slavonic, but the Alans must have constituted the dominant class since the country is referred to by contemporary writers as 'Alania' and the Pruth is called 'the Alan river' *(Alanus fluvius)*. This group of Alans may almost certainly be identified with the Antae who are recorded as living there in the 4th century AD.

There is an interesting description of the Alans by Ammianus Marcellinus in the 4th century AD which is almost identical with that given of the Sauromatae eight hundred years earlier by Herodotus. It seems that the centuries had had little effect on the mode of life and habits of the steppe nomads.

pl 3

Ammianus Marcellinus says the 'Halani' (the Alans) 'live upon flesh and abundance of milk. They have no huts but dwell in wagons with rounded canopies of bark. They drive over the boundless wastes and in places rich in grass they place their carts in a circle, to move again as soon as the fodder is used up. Wagons form their permanent dwellings, in which they live and their babies are born and reared. Wherever they come, that place they look upon as their natural home.

'They drive their cattle before them and pasture them with their flocks, but give particular attention to breeding horses. All aged and women unfit for war remain close by the wagons. The young men grow in the habit of riding from their earliest boyhood, and regard it as contemptible to go on foot.'

Almost all the Alans, he says, were tall and handsome, their hair inclining to blond; 'by the ferocity of their glance they inspire dread.' They were light and active in the use of arms. 'In their manner of life and their habits they are less savage than the Huns. They delight in danger and warfare. The man who falls in battle is judged happy, while those who grow old and die by natural death they assail with bitter reproaches as degenerate and cowardly. They take pride in killing any man whatever and as glorious spoils of the slain they tear off their heads, then strip off their skins and hang them upon their war-horses as trappings.'

As their god of war they worshipped a naked sword fixed in the ground. 'They have a remarkable way of divining the future.

Sarmatian soldiers depicted on the Arch of Galerius at Salonica (erected AD 297). Galerius, later co-emperor with Constantius, was in command on the Dacian frontier around the turn of the 3rd century. The Sarmatians in this relief are serving in the Roman army and are equipped with typically Sarmatian arms and armour, but it is impossible to say from what tribe they come. (6)

They gather very straight twigs of osier and sort them out at an appointed time with certain secret incantations and thus clearly learn what is impending.' They did not have slaves, 'they all are born of noble blood'. They chose as chiefs 'those men who are conspicuous for long experience as warriors.'

Alanic graves in Bessarabia and Moldavia contain typical furniture of Sarmatian burials—bronze rings and other personal ornaments, necklaces of glass or carnelian beads, occasionally an iron sword and once a Roman imported glass beaker. Of particular significance are some bronze mirrors (and one stone slab) engraved with 'tamga' signs, proving that the earlier home of these Sarmatians must have been the Sea of Azov close to the Bosporan kingdom.

The 'Tamga' Signs

These 'tamga' signs are especially interesting because they are the Sarmatians' closest approach to a written script. Scholars disagree about their precise meaning and function. Some are of the opinion that they had a magical purpose, others consider them to be property-signs which later, in the Middle Ages, developed in some countries into the coats-of-arms of the nobility and in others, e.g. in the Caucasus and parts of Central Asia, retained their old meaning of family or clan property-crests. There is likewise no agreement as to their origin, which has often been sought in Iran.

The recent work of E. I. Solomonik provides a list of 160 objects with 'tamga' signs found in the USSR. This reveals that over half of the 'tamgas' were found within the Bosporan kingdom, mainly at Kerch (Panticapaeum) and another 20 at Chersonesus and Olbia; thus about two-thirds of all known 'Sarmatian' signs

f 7

pl 24-
27

295

were found within Greek territory. Of the remainder about two-thirds were found in the Crimea and the Kuban valley, both regions strongly affected by Bosporan influence. Only one-eighth of the total were found within Sarmatian territory proper, and only three were traced east of the Volga.

This distribution, and the fact that they do not appear until the 1st century AD, implies that 'tamga' signs must have originated in the Bosporan kingdom and were a Greek invention. The signs at Kerch and other Greek cities were either carved or incised on grave stelae, in grave chambers, or appear as open-work on belt-buckles and clasps. The earliest of these represent monograms of three Greek deities: Apollo, Helios and Dionysos, all connected both with the cult of the sun and with belief in an after-life. Later the rigidity of the design slackened, details were omitted and the monograms simplified; finally only a few characteristic features served to recall the original patterns, but the derivation is still recognizable.

The 'tamga' signs were adopted by the Sarmatians who lived close to the Bosporan kingdom, the Siraces and the Aorsi. The few objects found outside this region are obviously of Bosporan or Kuban origin. The more or less simplified 'tamgas' found further west in late assemblages were evidently connected with the migration of those Sarmatian tribes which adopted the signs.

The signs had a religious or magic meaning. Those on grave stelae and in tombs had to guide and guard the deceased in the after-life. Those on cauldrons, mirrors and belt-buckles had to protect their owners, and after the conversion to Christianity were replaced by the cross or Christ's monogram. Their tradition in this respect was continued in the Middle Ages by the belt buckles with a representation of 'Maiestas Domini'.

But the old 'Sarmatian' signs which lost their meaning after the conversion, were not abandoned but gradually acquired the character of property signs or family crests, and finally, in mediaeval Kievan Russia and in Poland, entered into heraldry. In Poland, especially, they survived for an amazingly long time. Many coats-of-arms of the 12th–14th centuries are identical with 'tamgas'; other later examples show stylized versions in the form of crescents, arrows, horseshoes, crosses, etc.

The Antae in Bessarabia, in spite of conflict with the Goths, seem to have resisted any pressure to move further west and even to have extended their rule eastwards. In the 5th and 6th centuries we find them ruling over the whole Ukrainian forest-steppe zone west of the Dnieper, and also east of that river. They had probably taken advantage of the downfall of the Ostrogoths under Hunnic onslaught and enlarged their dominion. The centre of their power was now transferred to the region of Kiev. By this time they had become so completely 'Slavicized' that ancient writers refer to them as Slavs. But Byzantine sources of the 6th century still distinguish them from all remaining Slavs, though they emphasize that they spoke the same language.

Dramatic traces of this last period of the Antae have been discovered. At Pastyrske, near Kanev, is an earthwork which probably defended the capital of one of their kings. At the end of the 6th or the beginning of the 7th century the Antae were over-run by a new wave of eastern nomads, the Turkish Avars. Before fleeing, the ruling families managed to conceal hoards of silver which they were never able to reclaim. Among the most important is that found at Martinovka also near Kanev, west of the Dnieper, a large portion of which is at present in the British Museum. It includes human and horse figurines, brooches, bracelets, rings and belt-buckles and strap-ends bearing 'tamga' signs. Signs closely related to these are found on objects in Hungary, Yugoslavia and Bulgaria. Their geographical distribution in a single line from the north-eastern corner of the Carpathians to Croatia across Hungary suggests that they follow the route of the retreat of the Antae before the Avars.

An isolated offshoot of the Antae seems to appear in southern Poland. Here in the first two centuries AD lived a Slavonic people, bearers of the Przeworsk culture. At the beginning of the 3rd century this culture underwent considerable changes. Wheel-made pottery of the Pontic type appears suddenly, together with the characteristic Sarmatian tendrilled *fibulae* 'with the foot turned over', and 'tamga' signs on the weapons.

Who were those who caused the change? The evidence points to Antae from Bessarabia. A number of richly furnished graves, a feature hitherto unknown in the Przeworsk culture, were evidently burials of rulers of the country, presumably its conquerors. Some of the most notable are at Zakrzów (Sackrau); the grave goods include objects of North Pontic origin and Sarmatian belt-buckles, besides some Roman imports.

The kingdom of the Alanic Antae in Poland was not of long duration; in the 5th century AD they seem to have been subdued by the Huns from Hungary.

The Onslaught of the Huns

The Huns, fieriest and most ruthless of all the nomad peoples who hurled themselves upon the West ('they ate, drank, slept and held counsel on horseback' according to Ammianus Marcellinus), had already seized the ancient homelands of the Sarmatians during the 2nd and 3rd centuries AD. Those Sarmatians who still lived in the steppes of the lower Volga and the Caspian, an eastern branch of the Alans, came strongly under their influence, if not under their direct rule, and adopted many of their customs. In their graves we find long swords, long composite bows of Hunnic type and Hunnic arrow-heads, larger and heavier than the former ones. Hunnic horse-trappings and bits were also used, and Central Asiatic pottery types are the most common. At the same time, Bosporan jewellery and gold-work continued to be imported.

A new feature of this late Sarmatian period, confined almost exclusively to the Sarmatians east of the Don, was cranial deformation. The custom of binding the child's head in a special manner in order to make it grow to a special shape has been recorded in various prehistoric cultures. It became common in

Tamga signs. The upper row is a selection of typical signs from various sources—belt-buckles, grave stelae, bronze mirrors etc. They range in date from the 1st century to the 7th, the sign at the left being still fairly close to the Greek monogram standing for 'Helios'. In the lower row the signs are adapted for Polish coats-of-arms of the 11th century to the 17th, becoming progressively stylized and heraldic. (7)

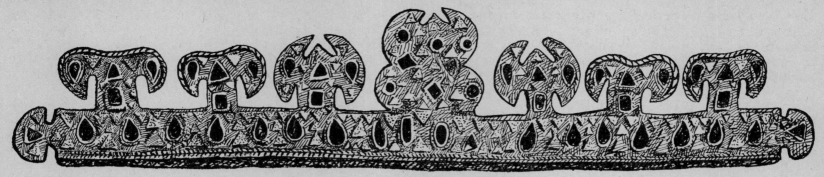

A gold diadem from the outskirts of Melitopol, 4th–5th century AD. Between 1945 and 1947 some spectacular finds were made at this site, just north of the Sea of Azov—swords, rings, bronze cauldrons, gold horse-trappings and gold encrusted dishes. This diadem came to light in 1948. It *seems to belong to a branch of the Eastern Alans, perhaps mixed with the Huns (a skull found in the same grave had typical Sarmato-Hunnic deformation). The stones are amber, garnet and carnelian; diadems of the same type have been discovered in Alanic graves in Hungary. (8)*

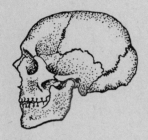 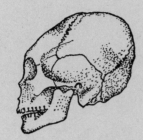

Skull deformation, as practised by the Sarmatians, with a normal skull (left) for comparison. The custom of artificially deforming the skull in childhood seems to have been introduced by the Huns. It was adopted by the Eastern Alans in the 4th century AD and survived amongst small groups for an astonishingly long time—even as late as the 17th century in the Crimea. (9)

Central Asia during the early Christian centuries especially among the Huns, and was then adopted by the Eastern Alans. About 70–80 per cent of skulls from eastern Sarmatian cemeteries of this period were artificially deformed.

About AD 355 the Huns advanced across the steppes of the lower Volga and the Don. Some of the Alans retreated westwards, some were caught up in the Hunnic tribes and dragged into Central Europe (these groups will be traced later), but a large portion retreated south and established themselves in the Crimea and the Caucasus. Westward the impetus of the Huns continued with irresistible force; in 375 they broke the Ostrogothic kingdom (the bulk of the nation entered Roman Moesia, thereby setting in train the fateful series of events that ended with the Sack of Rome by the Goths in 410); in 405 they reached Hungary; in 451 (under Attila) they crossed the Rhine; in 452 entered Italy. But in 453 Attila died. The conquered peoples immediately rose against them and in a single year thrust them back again to the Dnieper.

The Alans in the Caucasus established a strong kingdom that lasted, in some form, for 800 years. They survived the Huns, the Avars and the Turks. In the 8th century the whole country north of the Caucasus was called Alania. Their heyday was in the 12th–13th century when they withstood the Tartar-Mongol invasions. Alanic princes and princesses often intermarried with the royal house of Georgia and with aristocratic families of Byzantium.

Graves of this late period have been discovered at Zmeyskaya in the northern foothills. Most of them were furnished with weapons and many with horse-harness. The usual weapons were sabres of the so-called Khazar type, common in East Europe during the whole early mediaeval period. Their wooden sheaths were usually decorated, often covered with a thin, richly ornamented sheet. Bows were common, but only a few spear-heads have been found. Foot warriors had iron double-edged battle-axes. In female graves the abundance of amber is striking, and points to connections with the Kiev country and the Baltic coast. Cranial deformation, which had been practised up to the 8th century, was by now abandoned.

Ultimately the Sarmatians of this region merged with the indi-

pl 16
17

genous inhabitants and the names of modern Caucasian peoples begin to appear in place of 'Alani' and 'Alania'. But these later cultures clearly derived from them and one of them—the Ossetians—still preserves many features of the ancient Sarmatian traditions and language.

In the Ukraine some groups of Alans managed somehow to survive the Hunnic disaster. We find a number of Sarmatian graves of the 4th–5th centuries in the region of the lower Dnieper. Some scholars believe them to have been left by Alans mixed with Huns. Characteristic of this group are the so-called 'river-graves': flat graves with no mound, situated on the lowest river terraces and overflowed by the spring tides. In them warriors were buried, sometimes with their horses, richly provided with gold ornaments, weapons and decorated horse-harness.

f 8

Other small groups of Alans are found in various parts of Europe and Asia throughout the succeeding centuries. In the Crimea they are mentioned as late as the 17th century, when they were still practising cranial deformation. Another small community was living in Bessarabia in 1462, and Alanic mercenaries served in the Byzantine army in their wars against the Seljuk Turks. Most extraordinary of all are the 30,000 Orthodox-Christian Alans who are mentioned in 1318 by Brother Pellegrini, Bishop of Zaytun in China, as living with their families on the Chinese coast opposite Formosa. They are said to have been 'in the Great King's pay', but nothing more is known about them.

Across a Continent in Forty Years: the Alans in France and Spain

The fate of the Alans who retreated westward before the Huns is complicated and often pathetic. The story of one group can be traced in detail. This large detachment crossed the Danube in AD 377. Together with a group of Huns, they joined the Visigoths and Ostrogoths and ravaged the Roman territory in the Balkans. In 378 the Alanic cavalry played a decisive rôle in the famous battle of Hadrianople in which the Roman army was routed and Valens, the Emperor, slain.

f 10

Two years later, in 380, the Alans, jointly with the Ostrogoths and the Hunnic detachment, drove northwards, entered and settled in Pannonia. Twenty years later they joined the Vandals and crossed to Noricum, the province adjoining it in the north-west, and were opposed by the Romans under Stilicho. He granted them territories in return for pledges of service. So in 402–405 they fought in the Roman army against the Visigoths.

But in 406, jointly with the Vandals and Suaevians, they set out to invade Gaul. Under their king Respendial, they crossed the Rhine near Mainz and defeated the opposing Franks. Part of the Alans, under King Goar, then offered their services to the Romans, but the bulk of them, under Respendial, and the two allied Teutonic peoples, began a 'tour de France', ravaging and laying waste the country and cities in their way. Their route led from Mainz through Trèves, Rheims, Tournai, Arras, Amiens, then Paris, Orléans, Tours, Bordeaux and Toulouse. There was no Roman army to oppose them. In 408 the Alans, after oppres-

297

sing Gaul for two years, passed into Spain and with their allies ravaged the whole peninsula, finally settling in Lusitania, modern Portugal.

In 418 the Alans were routed by the Visigoths, who were driving out 'barbarians' on behalf of the Emperor. Addac, king of the Alans, was killed, and the remnants of the people fled to Galicia where they joined the Vandals. Gunderich, king of the Vandals, assumed the title of 'Rex Vandalorum et Alanorum', which was retained by his successors up the the very end of the Vandal kingdom in AD 533.

Thus finished the independent history of this branch of the Alans, who during the 40 years since they had left their original steppes had crossed a whole continent. Even now their wanderings were not ended. Gradually merging together, the united peoples, Vandals and Alans, left Galicia for southern Spain in 422 and in 429 crossed into Africa.

These Alans were not the only ones who reached France. The group under King Goar was at different times allied with the Visigoths and the Romans. These are probably the Alans who are recorded at Narbonne in 416 and later at Orléans. They seem not to have resisted the Huns in 451 but were subdued by the Visigoths in 452. We hear of other Alanic kings (Beogus 'Rex Alanorum' in 464; Eochar 'ferocissimus Alanorum rex' in 440) taking part in the confused struggles of the beginning of the Dark Ages.

Only a few archaeological remains attributable to the Sarmatians have so far been found west of Hungary—a grave at Siebenbrunnen in Austria, a tomb at Valméry in Normandy, a fragment of a bronze kettle near Chalon-sur-Saône, and some small gold plaques from a grave at Carthage in North Africa. Witness to their presence in France, however, is to be found in over 30 French place-names connected with 'Sarmatians' or 'Alans', among them the name of the town of Alençon.

'Serboi' and 'Choroates' in Central Europe

Large numbers of the Eastern Alans, like other eastern European peoples, joined the army of the Huns. It is futile to try by archaeology to trace their route and the places in which they settled. But some traces of them remain in the names of modern Slavonic peoples. The name 'Serb', for instance, is non-Slavonic. It occurs in Ptolemy in the 3rd century AD as the name of an East Alan people dwelling on the steppes of the lower Volga. They were presumably overrun by the Huns in the 4th century. In the Middle Ages a country called 'White Serbia' extended over Saxony and Thuringia up to the Saàle, i. e. within what was once the Hunnic Empire. We may guess that the detachment of the Hunnic army that gained power in that region consisted chiefly of East Alans, Serboi. After the death of Attila in AD 453, they might have gained independence and ruled the country on their own account.

The German population west of the Saale seem to have got rid of the Alan yoke, but the Alanic Serboi seemingly maintained their power over the Slavs east of the river. It is interesting to note that the greatest concentration of artificially deformed skulls at the turn of the 5th and 6th centuries comes precisely in this region.

The most plausible conclusion is that the Alanic Serboi ultimately merged in the subdued Slavonic population and that the name 'Serbs' is at present the only trace of their sojourn there. Some such process presumably took place in Yugoslav Serbia where probably another branch of the Alanic Serboi was engaged.

The name 'Croat' has a similar history. The form 'Choroates' has been found among the inscriptions in ancient Tanais on the mouth of the Don. In the 10th century the 'Belochrobati' (White Croats) a Slav people, occupied the upper Vistula and parts of Bohemia. They had a number of Sarmatian characteristics—the king was fed on mare's milk and they practised cranial deformation—and the names of their chiefs were non-Slavonic. Here again, we may conjecture that an East Alan tribe bearing a name similar to 'Croat' was entrusted by the Huns with the task of keeping the country north of the Carpathians under control. After the downfall of the Huns, they may have ruled the country on their own account and were ultimately Slavicized.

Scattered and Forgotten: the Fate of the Sarmatians

There is something pathetic in the fate of the Sarmatians. In the various stages of their history they were pushed over almost all the countries of western Europe. The descendants of their detachment of AD 175 probably still live somewhere in England. Sarmatian history has been interwoven with that of many peoples and nations. But in spite of that they are now a nearly forgotten people. Little remains to remind the modern world of their existence—the Ossetians, the names of a few Slavonic peoples, some European place-names, some words of Sarmatian origin in Slavonic languages, parts of the coats-of-arms of Polish nobility (abolished in 1920) and an increasing number of objects recovered by archaeology. The Sarmatians were a 'barbarian' people; but they did not distinguish themselves like the Vandals and the Huns, whose names came to be the symbol of atrocious barbarian outrages. They contributed to the development of the splendid Sarmato-Bosporan art, and to its 'Gothic' successor, which later gave birth to the many branches of mediaeval Western European art—Merovingian, Anglo-Saxon, Romanesque. But here again their rôle has been passed over in silence.

Perhaps the most important achievement of the Sarmatians was their part in the formation of the various Slavonic nations. But later expansions of eastern nomads—Avars, Bulgars, Magyars, which did not reach Western Europe, have partly obliterated the structure that they helped to create.

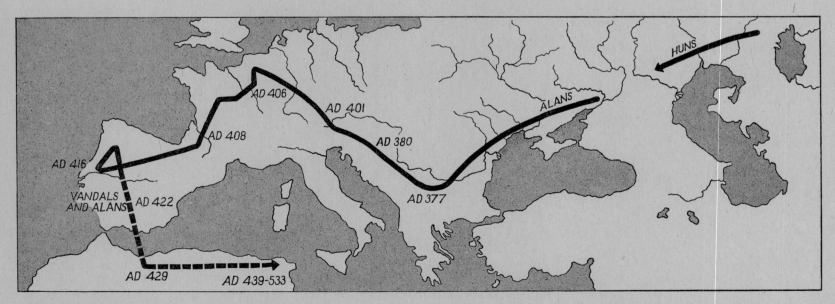

The wanderings of the group of Western Alans described in the text. A similar history was no doubt true of hundreds of other groups, who have *left no record. The Vandal kingdom in North Africa lasted until AD 533. (10)*

XIII THE MIGRATION
OF THE MEGALITHS

A new religion comes to ancient Europe

GALE SIEVEKING

	SPAIN	MALTA	SICILY & SARDINIA	SOUTHERN FRANCE	BRITTANY	IRELAND N Wales Scotland	ENGLAND	DENMARK	
3500									3500
3000	Huelva group								3000
2500	◄ Fall of Los Millares settlement Alapraia			Arles group	Carnac tombs	West Irish settlements	Severn-Cotswold gallery-graves	Bygholm hoard Tustrup	2500
2000		Hal Tarxien	Giants' Graves			Boyne Valley tombs			2000
1500									1500
1000									1000

Passage-graves
Gallery-graves

Diagram to illustrate the dates of erection of passage-graves and associated monuments in the west Mediterranean and north-west Europe

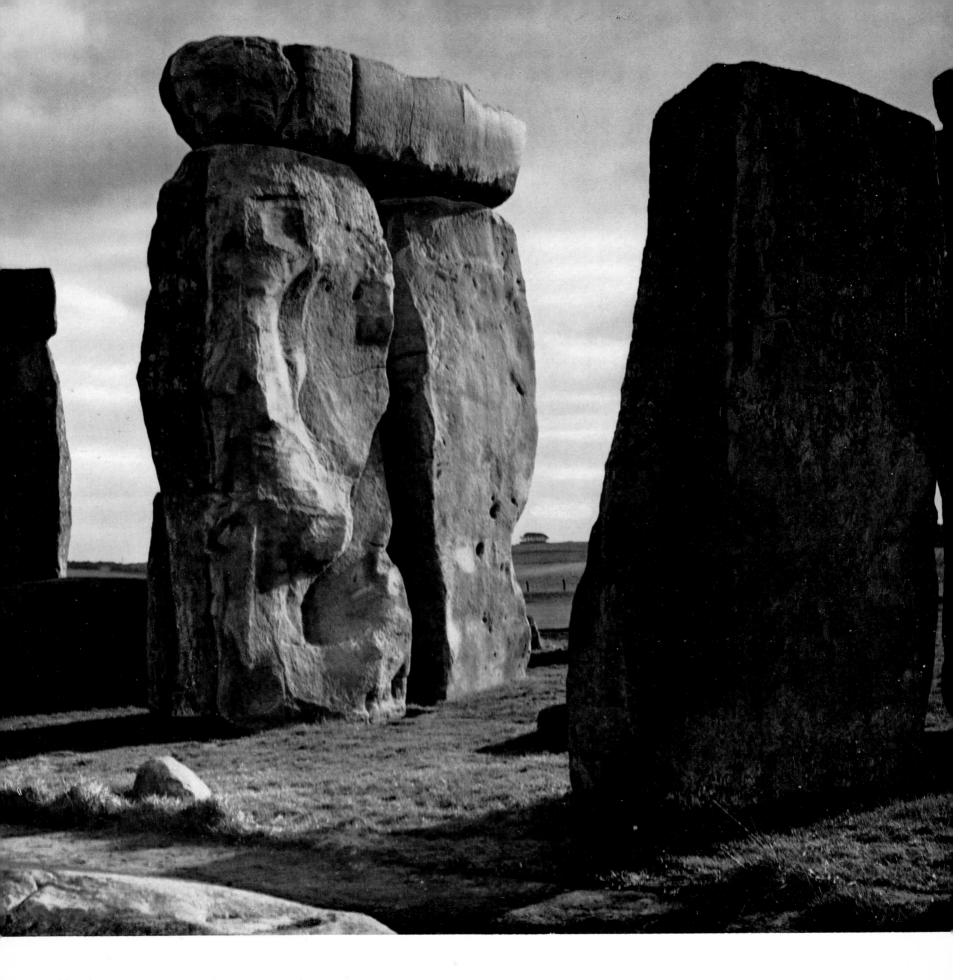

Massive stone monuments

of great age are widespread in Western Europe. The horseshoe enclosure of Stonehenge (above), the long avenues of megaliths in Brittany, and many others have long been a puzzle to the layman and a challenge to the archaeologist. What was the impulse that drove men to this tremendous labour? It must have been an overwhelming one. In the case of Stonehenge (about 1660 BC), the smallest inner circle seems to be a reconstruction of an earlier temple with lintels (Bluestonehenge) transported from the Prescelly hills in Wales, 135 miles away, and the huge blocks of sarsen came from twenty miles away, near Marlborough.

Megaliths began to appear in Spain and Western Europe around 3000 BC, as the outward forms and manifestations of a religion, or series of religions, based on ancestor worship and a cult of the Mother Goddess. The building of large collective tombs for multiple burials is a characteristic part of this religion, though the actual use of large stones (megaliths) did not necessarily have any religious significance. In various different forms these megalithic graves and the accompanying religion spread from the western Mediterranean northwards through France, Brittany and the British Isles, to northern Germany and Scandinavia. Though our knowledge of the megalith-builders is still scanty, much can be pieced together by considering the obvious relationships of the different groups of megaliths, and their architecture and decoration. (1)

The first staging-post

in the migration of the megalithic religion was in the Tagus estuary in Portugal and the south-eastern corner of Spain, the small coastal province of Almeria. Here, before 3000 BC, the Los Millares culture arrived, a fully developed megalithic culture with a Mother Goddess religion and a ritual for the propitiation of the dead. Los Millares and the other towns appear to be colonies from settlements far to the east in Greece, the Cyclades and Anatolia, where ancestor worship, communal burial and the Mother Goddess are well known. But the distinctive form the megalithic religion took is a Spanish invention. The stone and bone idols, the eye and other decorative motifs derived from these mother goddess idols, like the passage-graves themselves, are a distinctive colonial form of religious practice, and reappear later, to the north and west, as the megalith builders spread.

Portable mother-goddess figurines with round, owl-like eyes were part of the apparatus of the megalithic religion in the western Mediterranean. The carved Spanish leg-bone idol on the left was probably fully clothed. The slate plaque above, a flat native copy of the idol from Farisoa, Portugal, has incised eyes and a herring-bone design on the skirt. The native designer misunderstood the design, which now consists of just face and skirt. (2, 3)

The eye motif recurs in a vessel from one of the later Danish passage-graves (above, left) as on a fine pot (above, right) and bowl (below) from Los Millares, perhaps 500 years earlier in date. The all-seeing eye of the earth-mother, with what may be intended to represent hair, also appears on an alabaster idol from Almeria (right). This was probably also given grass material or woven clothing. (4–7)

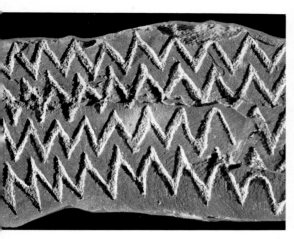

The herringbone reappears on a decorated stone from Fourknocks, Ireland (above), as well as on a stele (right) from Trets in Southern France. This stele is a valuable cultural pointer, a translation into a monumental size of the Iberian slate and schist plaques such as pl. 3 opposite. (8, 9)

The Spanish goddess cult seems to have been particularly strong in Southern France. Undecorated schist plaque goddesses like pl. 3 are found in many Hérault megaliths, and after these achieved monumental size a native cult of full-scale statue goddesses developed in the Hérault and Gard regions. This one (left) from St Sernin shows the fully clothed goddess in hieratic pose, with a six-strand necklace round her neck. (10)

Passage-grave influence is rare in England, but occasional imports crop up to confuse the picture. The Folkton drums (below), local chalk copies of Iberian idols, made in Yorkshire about 2200 BC, repeats the pair of spectacles or owl-like design of their Spanish forebears. (11)

A clear case of contact with Spain: rock-carved stags at Val Camonica in the Italian Alps recall similar animals in Spanish rock-paintings and in Los Millares pottery. If the Millaran bowl in pl. 5 is turned round (right), a very similar stag is seen. (12, 13)

303

The passage-grave developed from relatively crude beginnings. The cross-section model above shows an early example at Los Millares, in which a short passage leads to an approximately circular chamber lined with large standing slabs. The roof of the passage is of corbel construction, the slabs overlapping until they meet. (14)

A very fine tomb with a long passage at Antequera, the Cueva del Romeral (below), is a late megalithic development from the short passage-graves of Los Millares. The model shows the 70-ft. passage leading to a central chamber whose corbelled dome is closed by a single slab 18 ft. long. The whole was covered by a 30-ft. mound of earth. (15)

Rock-cut tombs and megaliths often exist side by side: the use of large stones had no religious significance. On the left are the entrances to rock-cut tombs in Sardinia, where such tombs are locally known as 'Witches' Houses'. (16)

Very large upright stones are sometimes found in the chambers or in the passages, especially in the tombs of the Millaran culture. In the great mausoleum of Menga (above), three massive columns, perhaps of ritual purpose, divide the main chamber. (17)

The true passage-graves of Los Millares, with their corbelled roofs rising to a beehive-like dome, recall the 'tholos' tombs of Greece and Mycenae. Sometimes the entrance to the short passage is through a small 'porthole' (left), which had a part in the complex ritual that accompanied and followed the numerous different burials. (18)

The corbelling method of construction is clearly seen in this photograph of New Grange, the largest and most important tomb in the Boyne valley group of megaliths near Dublin. All round the central vault, horizontal courses of stone overlap on their inner edge, each course held in position by the weight of stone above, until a single capstone can close the gap. The result, when the sheer weight of rock is considered, is a spectacular achievement. (19)

The northward spread of the megalithic religion can be traced as far as north Germany and Denmark. The engraving below (early 19th century) shows a passage-grave in the North Frisian Islands with typical passage and chamber, large free-standing stones set edge to edge along the wall and a single massive slab for the roof. The old woman contemplating the cooking pots is the artist's 'reconstruction' of the tomb as a fairy's or witch's dwelling-place—the same sort of error that gave the name 'Witches' Houses' to rock-cut tombs in Sardinia. (20)

Out of the main stream

of collective tomb-building the Maltese Islands developed their own specialized forms of the megalithic religion, receiving influences perhaps from the Iberian 'seedbed' but remaining to a large extent autonomous and different. Ancestor worship and collective burial were the main features of Maltese religion in the 2nd millennium BC, as they were in Spain and Portugal, but there the resemblance ends. In Malta the megalithic temples were not used for burial but only, like the forecourts of the Western Mediterranean passage-graves, for the ritual of propitiation of the ancestor spirits. The temples are built with soft limestone blocks of great size, uprights and lintels equally weighty like the trilithons of Stonehenge. Often, as in the temple at Hagar Qim (right), the blocks are decorated with small drilled holes. On the mushroom-shaped altars libations were poured or animals sacrificed. In the great temple of Hal Tarxien (opposite, right) the double spiral decoration is another formalized expression of the two eyes and nose of the ancestral goddess. (21, 22)

The horseshoe plan of Stonehenge

inner trilithons (below) stands out vividly when seen from the air. Dated by carbon-14 to about 1660 BC, this is probably the latest megalithic monument in England. Stonehenge has been compared to such later monuments as the Lion Gate at Mycenae, but its nearest relations seem to be the contemporary Maltese temples. Hagar Qim, for instance (below, right), shows not only pairs of similarly horseshoe-shaped chambers but also an outside retaining wall surmounted (at the back of the picture) by a continuous line of lintel stones. (23, 24)

The use of the running spiral in decoration is seen on a stone in the passage at New Grange (left). The stone basin above—also at New Grange—is another echo of Mediterranean practice: compare the Maltese version in pl. 24 above. In Irish tombs such basins held burnt and washed cremations. (25, 26)

Other forms of megalithic tomb have been found in England and Wales—the gallery-graves, which differ from the passage-graves in plan though the construction is similar. The engraving above illustrated a paper read to his 'brother antiquaries' by an amateur archaeologist in 1817, and shows a section through a gallery-grave at Stoney Littleton, Somerset. Instead of a passage leading to a burial chamber, the gallery-grave consists of a passage with transepts or small chambers leading off it—in this case three on each side. This design, which is thought to have originated with the megalith-builders of the Loire estuary, is found in tombs along the Severn valley and in the Cotswold hills. Somewhere on the banks of the Severn the immigrants from France must have made their landfall. Other gallery-graves, such as West Kennet near Avebury, were built further inland. (27)

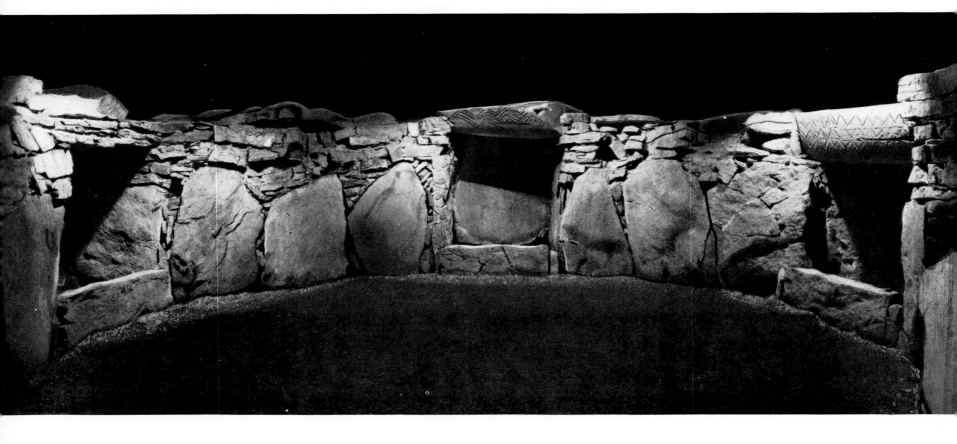

Great avenues of standing stones, called alignments, are a feature of megalithic burial sites in Brittany. The picture below shows the alignments at Kermario from the air. Several of these alignments are known, consisting of up to eight rows of stones, and running for as much as 2–3 kms. in a straight line. They are believed to be ceremonial ways or approaches, like the ditched approach to Stonehenge, but no monument has ever been discovered at their ends. (29)

Native workers were plentiful and conditions peaceful when the megalith builders settled in the Boyne valley. One of the passage-graves there, Fourknocks, is dated by carbon-14 to around 2000 BC, some 800 years after the earliest megalithic tombs in western Ireland. A specialized local type, the Boyne graves are cruciform in plan, with recesses leading off the main chamber. In contrast with the small, window-like recesses at Fourknocks (opposite), those at New Grange are almost the size of the central chamber itself. The photograph (right) shows the east recess with the stone basins (pl. 26) in situ and herringbone and eye motifs visible. Both monuments are outstanding among European megaliths, Fourknocks in its vast chamber, New Grange in its immense covering mound. (28, 30)

Across the Irish Sea the Boyne people established a colony in west Wales, where they built at least one passage-grave of cruciform type. The early 19th-century painting below shows the exposed remains of another passage-grave, at Plas Newydd, Anglesey; all but the most rugged constructional features have vanished, while traces of the mound can just be seen (31)

The migration of the passage-grave builders along the coasts of Western Europe may have been largely motivated by trade. In Denmark the megalithic people mingled with the earlier funnel-beaker folk. This reconstruction shows a settlement based on that of Barkjær in East Jutland, where traces have been found of two long houses that would have held as many as fifty families. The sea served as a defensive moat on three sides. Little or nothing is known about their ships; the canoe shown here is of a type that is known to have been in use in the Bronze Age while the larger craft is suggested by engravings in tombs. The clothes are also from Bronze Age times but are believed by archaeologists to be derived from those used in megalithic times. (32)

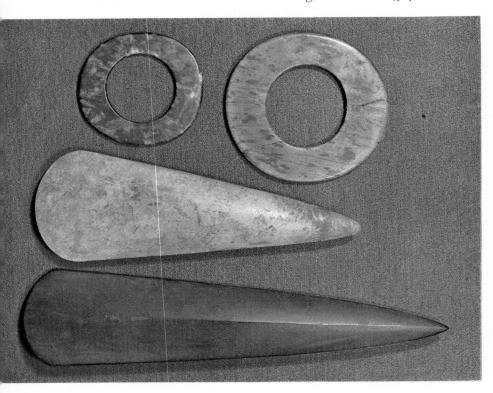

Jadeite axes and arm rings (above) from Mané-er-Hroek in Brittany probably belonged to the earliest users of the tombs, for similar axes are carved on the grave stones. The pottery below, from Ferslev in Denmark, belongs to a late stage (about 2500 BC) in the development of passage-grave pottery. Below (right) is the Bygholm hoard, also from Denmark, the earliest group of metal tools in Northern Europe associated with a funnel beaker of the type made in earliest Danish megalithic times. The spirals are copper bracelets. The copper dagger on the right has a cast rib on one side, a design which is found at Los Millares, and must have come from Spain or Portugal about 2800 BC. (33–35)

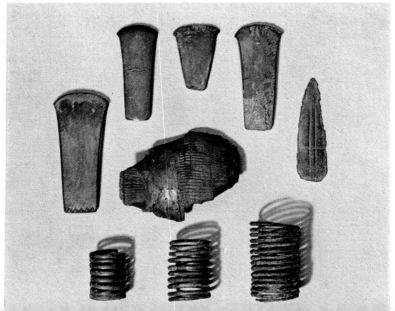

Trade links are vividly shown by two necklaces made up of very similar beads, the one on the left from Alapraia, Portugal, and the other from Odoorn in Holland. The latter shows amber from the Baltic, tin beads of English origin, and faience beads from Egypt. (36–37)

311

When they came to the north, the megalith-builders found, already living there, people of an earlier Neolithic culture, known from their pottery as the funnel-beaker culture. These buried their dead in small stone cists or boxes. On the right is a funnel-beaker grave at Keitum in the North Frisian Islands, in which a rectangular outer wall of small stones encloses individual cists. This form of grave when covered with earth misleadingly resembles the long rectangular mounds of the gallery type of megalithic grave but is thought to be derived from the design of the long houses in which these people lived. (38)

The ritual ancestor worship took special forms in the Danish Neolithic, with separate ceremonial houses associated with passage-graves. Built of timber and wattle-and-daub, they contained benches littered with rows of pottery with food and drink for the dead. A reconstruction of one of these (Ferslev, from which came the pots in pl. 34), is shown above and left. (39, 40)

In the megalithic cemetery of Tustrup, East Jutland, a similar 'temple' can be seen, the outer stones and footings restored to show the plan. The walls were built of wood posts held in place against the heavy outer slabs by a packing of smaller stones. (41)

A new religion comes to ancient Europe

GALE SIEVEKING

CHRISTIANITY IN EUROPE originated as a missionary movement from the East Mediterranean in the 1st century AD. But a study based on the principal architectural monuments in the West, if these alone survived, would have to concentrate on the development of such styles as Romanesque and Gothic, more than a thousand years after the arrival of Christianity in the West. These styles are indigenous developments in England, France, Germany and Italy and show few direct traces of their East Mediterranean inspiration.

It seems certain that the megalithic tombs and temples which appear in Western Europe around 3000 BC are the apparatus of a religion, or series of religions, like Christianity, which originally came from western Asia or Asia Minor but which after developing distinctive forms in Spain and later in Western Europe continued to exist and develop for more than a thousand years. The religion was one of ancestor worship connected with an actual cult of the dead and their resting places. Megalithic burial monuments are often the only traces of this religion and, like Gothic cathedrals or parish churches, were used for hundreds of years, for ceremonies of veneration as well as for burial, and added to or altered as fashions changed or prosperity increased.

Our knowledge of this religion is scanty and often seems contradictory. The different groups of megalith are clearly related. Architecturally they are similar in a number of ways; they are decorated with religious symbols which are related; they contain furniture, such as tables and stone receptacles, which are evidence of closely similar ritual observances; but the debris inside the tombs in different countries, the broken pottery, and the stone and metal weapons, which represent the persistent use of the megaliths, are locally made and differ with each group of monuments. The archaeologist is apparently faced with a series of related monuments in different countries built by quite different people.

In many countries the arrival of the megaliths seems to bring with it no corresponding change in tools and pottery, which continue to be made by methods previously in use. This shows that there has been no general change in the population and that the religion the monuments represent cannot have been introduced by conquest or invasion. The megaliths themselves have been assimilated to the locally pre-existent culture (and many of them could have been local developments). However, certain classes of megaliths and related monuments, known as *passage-graves*, represent small intrusive groups associated with defensive hill-top settlements close to the sea. It seems that the builders of these passage-graves arrived by sea, since the related monuments are far apart on the coasts of Spain, Brittany, Ireland and Denmark.

To trace the origins of the megalithic religion which these tombs represent and the steps by which it moved from western Asia to the Baltic one has to follow the movements of colonists, first to the west Mediterranean and later from Spain and Portugal to Atlantic Europe, over a period of more than 1000 years. The reasons why the colonies were founded is not yet known, but they must have been a result of imperial or economic expansion from what was at that time the only city-dwelling part of the Western world. There may possibly be some connection with the occur-

rence of metal ores in Iberia and Western Europe, but this is unlikely to have been the main impulse behind colonization. The megalithic cult associated with this colonial movement represents only a crystallization of their existing religious beliefs in the new environments of Spain and the West. The colonies provided the milieu for its propagation, as did the Roman Empire for Christianity: religion, like trade, followed the flag. If the passage-graves represent the direct transmission of this religion in a new colonial form evolved in Spain, the remaining megaliths represent the indirect influences of East Mediterranean and of Iberian religious ideas in the native cultures.

3000 BC: the Great Stone Tombs

In the megaliths we find traces of a cult or religion believed to be a form of ancestor worship or propitiation of the dead, and the building of large collective tombs for multiple burials is a characteristic part of this religion. The best-known types of tomb are those built of extremely large, roughly dressed or unhewn boulders and known as *megaliths* (lit. 'large stones'). The ritual with which these tombs are related may be called the *megalithic religion* as a form of shorthand, as one might call Western Christianity the *Gothic religion* after its best-known monuments.

The use of large stones is of no religious importance in itself, though monuments built in this manner do not resemble civilized architecture and so appear unusual and surprising. Tombs closely related to the megaliths are often of quite different construction, some being built of small unmortared stones, while others consist of artificial caves cut into the rock. A megalithic monument entirely built of very large upright stones is said to be of *orthostatic* construction, while artificial caves are known as *rock-cut tombs* and courses of unmortared stone are known as *dry stone walling*. This last may be used for an entire monument, as the roof may be corbelled upwards by overlapping each horizontal course pl 19 of stones on a circular base until they rest against one another in the centre to form a beehive tomb, known by the Greek word *tholos*. Dry stone walling, however, is often used in combination with orthostatic construction to fill in the gaps between the large boulders. The megalithic form of construction, then, cannot have been of primary religious importance. Apart from similarities of design which show that these tombs are closely related, it is the fact that they are *collective tombs* representing churchyards rather than individual burials which throws the most light on the religious ritual. Collective tombs imply a form of communal worship unknown before the arrival of the megaliths in Western Europe.

Most of the difficulty in understanding the megalithic religion comes from studying the funerary monuments in isolation. While the general character of ancestor worship is easy to recognize we can only find the slightest trace of the differences and peculiarities which must have differentiated it from other religions of this kind and which would enable us to understand why it became so widespread in Western Europe. To go further it is necessary to study the other cultural movements taking place at this time, and see the religion against the background of the separate cultural development of each country.

The Coming of the Mother Goddess

Megalithic monuments are widespread in Western Europe and they can best be understood by studying the movements of small passage-grave colonies in the west Mediterranean and later on the Atlantic and Baltic coasts. South-eastern Spain and Portugal form the first staging post in these migrations. Here one can recognize a number of direct East Mediterranean influences in the cultural record associated with the introduction of collective burial and the development of complex funerary monuments, including megaliths.

The earliest relevant cultures are those making a style of pottery known as impressed ware, because of the way it is decorated with simple impressed lines and patterns. Impressed ware groups generally form the earliest Neolithic culture in the coastal areas and islands in the west Mediterranean, and prototypes of this pottery have been recognized in Crete, Greece and possibly in Anatolia. The Spanish and Portuguese people related to this

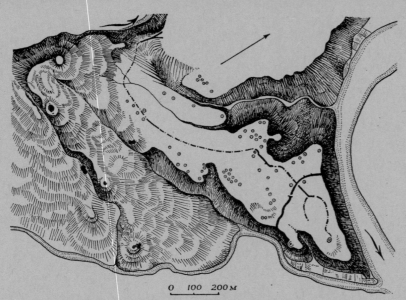

Plan of Los Millares showing the defended hill-top town of the colonists on a promontory overlooking the river, with the cemetery beyond the town wall on the lower plateau to the north. Circles mark the sites of collective tombs. The town is 14 miles inland. (1)

early migration from the East are only recognized by their pottery and by their use of trapeze-shaped flint arrowheads and certain bone implements. A more characteristic group of migrants is recognized in the key area in south-east Spain, the small coastal province of Almeria.

The graves of the Almerian Culture, which include the earliest Spanish monumental tombs of stone, fall into two classes. One class contains ritual implements and ornaments representative of earlier cultures in Iberia and now part of the native tradition —objects such as polished stone axes, bone points, shell bracelets and trapeze-shaped flint arrowheads—and the second class contains obviously exotic grave goods unrelated to those of any other Spanish cultures, but directly paralleled in the East Mediterranean. The most obvious imports are the so-called flat idols. These are violin-shaped representations of a female deity or Mother Goddess cut out of flat (undecorated) pieces of polished stone which must be related to similar idols found in the Cyclades and at Troy. Green stone beads and bifacially worked flint arrowheads were also imported.

The tombs of the Almerian culture were built of small fairly regular stone blocks. They were small and circular and apparently unroofed, or perhaps provided with a wooden roof. Most of the tombs are too small for the burial of more than one individual, but a few graves, not larger than the rest, do contain more than half a dozen disarticulated skeletons—the first traces of some form of communal burial.

The Almerian culture seems to have lasted several hundred years before it was superseded, partly submerged and partly driven westwards, by the fully developed megalithic culture of Los Millares at some date before 2800 BC. The significance of this culture (the Almerian) lies in the fact that west of Crete it is the earliest recognizable culture anywhere in the Mediterranean associated with a Mother Goddess and with a complex ritual involving expensive equipment for the dead. It represents the arrival by sea, in a coastal province of south-east Spain, of a group of people whose religion must ultimately have derived from western Asia. The later phases of this religion in the west are often associated with megalithic funerary monuments and temples.

The two known settlements of the Almerian culture are small and poorly equipped, and tell us little of the origin of its customs, so that we cannot tie down its originators to a particular time or place in the East Mediterranean. All that one can say is that it appears, as is usual with prehistoric cultures, already fully formed, and does not bear a close resemblance to any particular culture in the East.

Its successor, in the same small region of south-east Spain, the Los Millares culture, is one of a group of true colonies established in southern Iberia between 3400 and 2500 BC: the earliest recorded

examples of the Greek colonizing principle. These settlements consist of hill-top towns of East Mediterranean type, like those of Greece and Asia Minor, surrounded by stone walls, sometimes multiple, strengthened by heavy semi-circular bastions, and provided with complex winding entrances for ease of defence. *f 1* Inside the walls are square stone-built houses.

Only three or four colonies and sites related to them are known in Spain and Portugal and, even if nothing else was known about them, their heavily defended character would suggest settlements in a hostile neighbourhood. In fact both the architecture of the settlements and the objects found in them and in the tombs can be closely paralleled in the Cycladic Islands of Greece, at Troy and elsewhere in the East. The town walls at Los Millares and those of some of the Greeks are built of stones laid in herring-bone patterns, also in fashion at Troy and other early Eastern settlements. Many similar examples can be given. The semi-circular bastions on these walls are themselves a peculiar trait known so far in only one site in the East, at Chalandriani on Syros, which may therefore have a direct connection with the colonies, but the architecture as a whole is part of a very ancient tradition in western Asia and Asia Minor, transplanted as a whole to Spain and Portugal.

Many of the more portable 'imports' may be inspired by the East, but made by the colonists in Spain, and the clearest and most acceptable archaeological evidence for relationships between the two regions lies, as usual, in the imported pottery. With this commonly used material design is a matter of custom rather than of ritual importance, so that it is easy to recognize the imported wares identical with those from the sites in Crete, the Greek islands and the region of Troy when these are found in Spain and Portugal.

The most convincing imported pottery is the stroke-burnished ware found in the Tagus region of Portugal. The main colony in this region is Vila Nova de San Pedro, a hill-top fortress town *f 4* surrounded by three walls, the innermost of which is known as the citadel. The settlement was occupied for a long period and the earliest traces of occupation are found under the wall of the citadel, and presumably belong to a period before the site was fortified. The earliest settlement contains fragments of a finely made stroke-burnished pottery decorated in herring-bone patterns, a ware which is identical with that found in the Cyclades. The red colour of this pottery and the careful stroke decoration are believed to imitate metal vessels from Asia Minor.

Though in general terms their culture and religion were very similar, a number of different types of imported pottery distinguish the different colonies, and they are likely to have been connected with different mother settlements in the East Mediterranean. As the direct imports are so few the interesting thing is the wide variety of dates at which the connection between the two areas was maintained. Some imported pottery seems to have been as late as 2300 BC. Yet Los Millares was apparently destroyed in 2500 BC, and its megaliths were imported into Western France before 3000 BC.

The Inspiration for the Passage-Graves

The builders of the Los Millares settlement constructed large-scale collective tombs the design of which became the inspiration for the later passage-grave series of tombs, the builders of which arrived by sea in Brittany, Ireland and Wales, and Scandinavia. These tombs are often set in a rough cairn of stones and are seen in plan to consist of a circular chamber and a short passage, both of which can contain niches or small side-chambers. *f 2*

Stone revetment slabs or stone blocks mark the edge of the *pl 14* cairn or are built into the body of the mound. Outside the entrance to the tomb is a semi-circular forecourt lined with stone slabs set upright in the ground, edge to edge, and one or more free-standing circles of stone slabs may surround the tomb. The method of construction of the passages and funerary chambers is of the greatest interest. These are made of dry stone walling and are often extremely carefully cut. The lower part of the construction may be of squared-off slabs set edge to edge but the roofs of the circular chambers were corbelled, that is, built of horizontal courses of stones overlapping in the inner side and held in posi-

A classic tholos grave at Los Millares, showing the small forecourt and short passage. Dotted lines indicate the slabs covering the passage, the overhang of the bottom courses of the corbelled roof, and what was probably a hole for a central post or pillar. A closely similar grave contained pottery ornamented with stag and eye motifs. (2)

tion by the weight of stone above them so that they rise to a single cap-stone in the centre.

This form of construction is a very spectacular achievement. The only comparable tombs for which we have certain evidence in the Aegean are the much later Mycenaean *tholoi* such as the 'Treasury of Atreus' which dates from the 15th century BC. At Los Millares there is an earlier simpler series of (mostly unroofed) round graves with passages with which a considerable part of the more exotic grave goods can be associated. The corbelled-roof passage-graves, or *tholoi*, as they are also sometimes called after the Greek examples, are later constructions developed in Spain for the same ritual.

Interest centres on these earlier round graves with passages since they in turn must have been responsible for the design of the earliest, non-corbel vaulted, passage-graves in Western Europe. It is important to note the character of the grave goods with which they and the earliest colonies in Iberia are associated. In addition to obvious imports—such objects as the decorated ivory dagger pommel from Nora, or alabaster jars from Los Millares resembling those from Egypt and Crete—there is also a characteristic ritual assemblage and a series of specialized copper tools and weapons. Both are equally notable. The ritual assemblage includes the famous symbol pottery decorated with the oculus or eye ornaments and with stags, and also stone cylinder idols and phalange-bone idols decorated with the emblems of the female deity. There are also various cult objects, objects copied in stone for purposes of deposition with the dead such as stone sandals, stone lunulae (necklaces) and hafted stone adzes or mattocks.

The metal finds provide some clue to the economic status of the colonists. This was somewhat higher than that of the Beaker culture which succeeded them since the Los Millares culture and the Portuguese colony possessed an East Mediterranean metal technology and could cast weapons in closed two-piece moulds while the metal weapons of the Beaker culture are hammered out and not cast. Heavy cast weapons such as axes are not present in the later period. Many of the early weapons imitate those found in Anatolia, the Cyclades and Crete, and the flint daggers found in the Spanish and Portuguese graves are also copies of metal types from these regions. A small copper dagger with a cast rib down the centre at one side is found in the earliest settlement at Los Millares and in the Portuguese tombs of this period. The Bygholm Hoard in Denmark, dating from this period, also contains one of these very distinctive weapons. As we shall see this is one of the earliest examples of close contact between the two regions.

But it is the minor constructional details of the tombs which are most closely paralleled in Western Europe. These and the finds associated with them show that the Los Millares graves were used not merely as tombs but as funerary chapels. In fact they are almost the only religious constructions in the culture and the main practice must be associated with actual burials. These are collective tombs and tombs of families, though not necessarily families of great wealth for although many 'ritual' objects are known there is little that resembles the panoply of chieftainship. The graves must sometimes have contained several hundred in-

dividuals which were deposited over a considerable length of time. Apart from the Millaran grave goods a considerable quantity of deposits were made by the Beaker culture after 2000 BC.

However, apart from actual funerary deposition it is proper to suppose there were other complex rites of which we have some archaeological hints. The semi-circular forecourt in front of the entrances to these tombs must have been the scene of many of these public or private ceremonies. Special niches and offering tables are erected in the forecourt, near which are found broken pottery and broken female idols. There are also single standing stones in the forecourts or in the actual chambers of some of these tombs, and the passage towards the chambers was constricted by the use of special porthole entrances and by obstructions such as raised stone divisions in the floor or upright septal stones. Finally within the chamber itself there is evidence of further specialized rituals. Some of the side chambers are niches which do not reach to the floor, but are merely shelves in the side of the tombs. These are carefully lined or paved with stones, and were used sometimes for gifts, sometimes for the burial of children. Many of these architectural details are also found in the West European tombs.

The New Faith Takes Root

It is instructive to see what effect the arrival of the colonists had on the local cultures in southern Spain and Portugal. We find a variety of local copies of the tomb types cropping up in different parts of the country, and also the occurrence of isolated Millaran round graves or tholoi in a barbarian grave cemetery, while the gigantic monuments these people built show a combination of a high degree of sophistication of religious worship with the native architectural traditions. These native traditions are generally recognizable by the use of the megalithic form of construction, that is the substitution of very large stones for the more exact technique of dry stone walling.

An early form is recognizable in the Portuguese Dolmen Culture, which developed from the Almerian culture when this was driven west by the arrival of the colonists at Los Millares. The grave goods, trapeze-and leaf-shaped arrowheads of flint and round-sectioned polished stone axes show their relationship with the Almerian culture and the most characteristic ritual deposit, the highly decorated slate plaques, are a development of the Almerian flat idols with decoration derived from the Los Millares cylinder and phalange bone mother goddesses. One of these slate plaques recently turned up in Eire, showing the derivation of at least a part of the Irish megalith tradition.

Many of the groups of tombs of this Dolmen culture found on the borders of Portugal and south-western Spain are passage-graves, but they are almost exclusively passage-graves built of megalithic blocks, a design that clearly developed here. Very few are of dry stone walling or tholos construction. The less sophisticated techniques of the indigenous Iberian group have been employed to build tombs approximating to the Millaran plan. A typical tomb group that was found near Reguengos in east Portugal contained 134 passage-graves and two tholoi, both the

One of the mounds at Farisoa, Reguengos, south-east Portugal, showing a fine tholos tomb inserted into a mound already containing a native passage-grave constructed of very much larger stones than the later tomb. As at Los Millares (pl. 14), the wall of the tholos chamber is composed of tall, carefully fitted standing stones. (3)

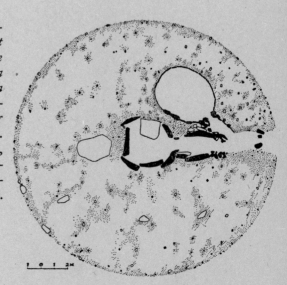

pl 17

pl 18

pl 2
3
5
6
7
13

pl 35

315

f 3 latter being secondary constructions inserted into mounds already containing passage-graves of orthostatic (i.e. large stone) construction. This shows that the designs of the native dolmens had already evolved while the Los Millaran tholoi were still being built.

The influence of the Millaran culture is not shown merely in the grave architecture, but also in the fact that these are all *collective* tombs representative of the rituals introduced by the Millaran culture. The normal accompaniment for a burial was one or two pots and a stone adze; one of the Reguengos collective *pl 3* tombs contained more than 200 burials accompanied by 355 pots and 135 decorated schist plaques representing the Mother Goddess.

This combination of architectural traditions can be seen in many parts of Northern and Western Europe where the collective tomb burial and ritual practices were introduced and married to already existing traditions of individual graves built of stone blocks or outlined by stone rows. But the tradition transmitted by sea from Spain and Portugal has in it a strong *native* Iberian element. Apart from corbelled and dry-walled constructions, some of the most characteristic productions in Ireland and Brittany are simple passage-graves of orthostatic construction with round burial chambers and simple passages, built on the ground surface in round cairns of stones, like the graves found in such large numbers in Portugal. It is therefore interesting to see how soon the primary effect of the Millaran colonists on the native architectural tradition wanes near to these colonies. The passage-graves of the Huelva group on the Spanish side of the Portuguese frontier, which are adjacent to the graves we have described from Reguengos, and which still contain a proportion of actual Millaran tomb offerings, are built to a plan which has evolved from the simple circular chamber and passage of Los Millares and now consists of a number of elongated chambers opening off the passage.

Two other alterations which take place in the primary design lie in the lengthening of the passage and the gradual movement of the tomb underground. Generally speaking, the tombs of the colonists at Los Millares are above ground, but some of the largest and finest constructions of the neighbouring province of Malaga, *pl 15* the orthostatic passage-graves of Menga, Veira and Romeral, whose design and ritual trappings suggest that they are a product of the colonists, are inserted in the side of natural hillocks, and the dry-walled corbelled Millaran passage-graves at Alcalá, on rising ground, must have been built in trenches partly or wholly below ground. This tendency also produces the so-called rock-cut tombs, among the earliest of which are those on the Tagus Estuary.

The plans of these tombs represent almost an overstatement of the Millaran tholos, with a single porthole entrance at the mouth of a comically small semi-circular forecourt and admittance to the chamber without an intermediate corridor. The grave goods of the Palmela tombs confirm their early date since they consist of cylinder idols and metal objects proper to the Portuguese Millaran culture and decorated schist plaques and trapeze-shaped arrowheads deriving from the indigenous Neolithic groups.

A second type of rock-cut tomb in the same region, that found at Alapraia, has, like the great passage-graves of Malaga, an elongated passage in front of the burial chamber, and should represent a later stage of development. The same line of development, from simple tholoi and passage-graves with a circular chamber and a passage, and rock-cut tombs with short and non-existent passages, to graves and rock-cut tombs with elongated passages, can be recognized elsewhere in megalithic architecture in southern France and Sicily and in the Atlantic in Brittany and the British Isles.

A parallel architectural development seems to have taken place in the Cyclades, Crete and Greece. Round graves without passages built on the surface of the ground are found in the Cyclades dating from c. 3000 BC. The earliest Cretan graves of this sort, about 3000 BC, had short passages, and probably corbelled roofs of mud brick, while the Mycenaean tholos of the 15th century BC is a magnificent beehive chambered tomb, like the finest examples in Spain, but built below ground and equipped with a *long* passage. It is also not a collective tomb at all but a princely burial vault.

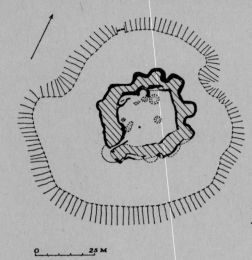

The fortified hill-top town of Vila Nova de San Pedro, south-west Portugal, showing the citadel and three encircling walls. The inner two walls are contorted into semi-circular bastions, especially on the north side, away from the entrance. These bastions are faced with well-laid dry stone walling. (4)

Except at the earliest stages, these architectural styles in Spain and the Aegean do not seem to have developed in the same cultural or religious environment, so that the coincidence of the tholos form found in Mycenae many centuries after its first appearance in Spain illustrates the closeness of trade and other connections between the two areas.

A carbon-14 sample taken from beneath the destroyed town wall at Los Millares gave a reading of around 2500 BC, and this may be the date of destruction of the Spanish settlement itself. However, in Spain and Portugal the collective tomb tradition seems to have lingered on and to have been only partly overthrown by the succeeding Beaker culture. The latest tomb offerings at the rock-cut tombs as at Los Millares itself are those of the Beaker people, who took over some of the fortified towns such as Vila Nova de San Pedro and used the tombs for their own separate ritual, based on individual rather than collective burial. There, as elsewhere in Europe, the impressive megalithic monuments retained their sacred character long after the religion that produced them had been forgotten. The Beaker culture itself appears to be an indigenous Spanish development, which spread to Western Europe shortly before and after 2000 BC. However, at this time they may not have subdued all the Millaran settlements. There is some evidence for contacts between individual tombs at Los Millares and the Cretan Empire as late as 1800 BC and in Almeria these settlements probably remained in existence until after the arrival of a new wave of hill-top town settlers in the 17th century BC.

The Megalithic Temples of Malta

Spain and Portugal are the key to the spread of collective tomb building on the Atlantic and the Baltic coasts of Europe but the west Mediterranean, at this period, seems to have been broken up into a number of autonomous regions each of which witnessed the growth of strange megalithic cults whose architecture and ritual owe a great deal to those of Spain in general terms but which often seem to be cut off from the mainstream of religious orthodoxy. This may be because they belong to a period after the one in which the Iberian religion was at its highest peak of development.

The most specialized development takes place in the Maltese Islands. Here there is a long series of megalithic temples which are not used as burying places. Their function is purely that of the tomb forecourts in the Iberian megalithic cult, that of chapels or chantries for the performance of rites for the propitiation of ancestor spirits. Funerary chapels re-occur with passage-graves in Northern Europe but not on this scale. The latest temple at Hal Tarxien, near Valletta, has a façade 30 feet high attached to a semicircular forecourt 110 feet in diameter. Collective burial was practised by the Tarxien Temple Culture as in the Los Millares Culture in Spain, but the burials are confined to natural caves and rock-cut tombs, the latest of which, the Hypogeum at Hal Saflieni, is a full-scale reproduction underground of a Tarxien Temple, a maze of halls and grottoes containing at least 7,000 burials. No evidence exists here to suggest that collective burial ritual or the megalithic temples were introduced from outside. As in Spain and nearly everywhere else in the west Mediterranean the Maltese Islands had been inhabited before 3000 BC by people using impressed pottery. A long succession of such peoples has been discovered in Malta and, though a simple form of collective burial in natural caves forms part of their religion from the earliest times, the sudden appearance of the megalithic temples in this cultural stream is difficult to explain without any other corresponding change.

It is possible to show that the development in design from the earliest to the latest of these temples is indigenous to Malta. The simpler temples are those with the so-called clover leaf plan set in an approximately round mound. They are approached by a concave façade which gives onto a short passage leading to three adjoining circular rooms, an end chamber and two side chambers. This design is succeeded by others clearly developed from it. The rooms themselves become horseshoe-shaped. Additional side chambers larger than the first are added with passages between them and the end chamber is entirely suppressed or reduced to a concavity in one wall.

pl 21

The temples are built with blocks of great size, the most truly megalithic architecture in the Mediterranean, but they are finished to a degree unknown elsewhere. Their design consists of entrances formed by orthostats and lintels, and walls formed by upright megalithic blocks and surmounted by horizontal courses of stone blocks of the same size. The use of a soft limestone enabled a fine finish to be given to the blocks which, after they were dressed to their exact shape, were often decorated all over with small drilled holes. Though the Maltese architecture is unparalleled elsewhere, there is plenty of evidence to connect the ritual purposes for which it was used with the megalithic cultures of the West, and with the Aegean religion of Crete and later of Mycenae.

pl 22
26

Ancestor worship and collective burial relate the Maltese temple culture to the western megalithic tombs, and one notices a number of common elements such as the use of the forecourts for ritual purposes. One or two Maltese fashions such as the use of the standing pillars and large stone basins are imitated in late Spanish and Western megalithic tombs, and the female deity, probably related to ancestor worship, is represented in Malta by statuettes and by relief carvings of the eye ornament on the temple stones resembling those found on the symbol pottery of Los Millares. But the decoration in the Maltese temples includes a number of direct imports from the Minoan and the later Mycenaean cultures, such as the use of the 'Growing Plant' motifs in the altars and the running spiral decoration, found respectively in the earlier and later temples. The discovery of large numbers of animal bones and the carvings of animals show that the practice of animal sacrifice had been imported from the Aegean.

Giants' Graves and Witches' Houses: Sicily and Sardinia

The Maltese temple culture dates between 2350–1500 BC when it was overcome by alien peoples rather like those of the Argaric Bronze Age who finally put an end to the Los Millares cultures in Spain. The period of existence of the other megalithic cultures in the West Mediterranean is much the same or in some cases even later. Little can be said of these monuments except that their design differs from region to region and that they are nearly always collective tombs. In the case of the rock-cut tombs of the Castelluccio culture in Sicily, there is a close resemblance to Spanish models such as Palmela. But in the Balearic islands and Sardinia strictly local models seem to have been followed in the tomb architecture.

pl 16

In Sardinia both rock-cut tombs and megaliths were in use. The megaliths are known locally as Giants' Graves and the rock-cut tombs are called Witches' Houses. These megaliths are of some importance as they are examples of a type known as a gallery-grave where the interior is a rectangular corridor of large stones set inside a long mound or cairn of stones. Gallery-graves are met with all over Europe and are one more example of the translation of the collective tomb idea into terms of the local cultural preferences. In Sardinia, as elsewhere, the gallery-grave has been provided with a semi-circular forecourt for the performance of the necessary ceremonial. This has led to the design of exceptional monuments, the 'lobster claw' cairns, which consist of a gallery with separate horn-like projections in either side of the entrance. Closely similar monuments are found in Scotland and Ireland, the so-called horned cairns or court cairns. The similarity of design between these and the Sardinian 'lobster claw' cairns is due solely to the concave stone settings used to mark out the ceremonial forecourt, and it is probable that many other monuments had *temporary* structures of this kind. The Sardinian tombs have been robbed and no settlements can be related to them so that it is difficult to connect them to the general megalithic story.

The Spread to Southern France

The southern French littoral is more closely connected with Spain and there is even one settlement at Lebous (Hérault) defended by walls with semicircular bastions, which may be an east Mediterranean colony. The megalithic tombs appear to be Spanish. One small group of passage-graves is found in the département of Hérault; this grave pattern was imported by sea into France by Spanish megalith builders from the Barcelona district. Their design is not closely related to that of the best passage-graves of Spain and Portugal—in place of the circular chamber and central passage, the tombs consist of a roughly square chamber with an asymmetrically placed passage. However, we have already seen how quickly the native designers in Spain modified the first conception of what these tombs should be, so that tomb design does not prove an accurate guide to their period of existence. Some megaliths in the Hérault contain small flat schist plaques (undecorated), like the goddess plaques made by the native Spanish megalith builders. But nearly all the burial deposits in the passage-graves are late insertions belonging to the Beaker culture, showing that the megaliths were still sufficiently revered in 2000–1800 BC to be suitable places for burial rites, but telling us nothing of the original builders.

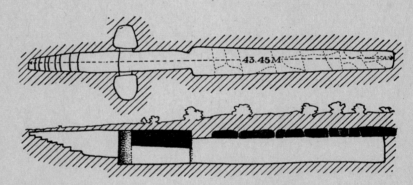

Plan and section of the Grotte-des-Fées, Arles-Fontvieille. The largest of the group, this tomb, lies apart from the others. (5)

A second group of south French tombs which seem to be closely connected with Spain are the five magnificent rock-cut graves near Arles (Bouches-du-Rhône). These were built on what were then islands in the Rhône estuary, though they are now hills many miles inland. The Arles grottoes, as they are called, are trench graves excavated in the rock and roofed with megalithic slabs, set inside round or oval mounds. The inside of the tomb consists of a narrow rectangular chamber entered from the end by a long open approach passage like those of the later Portuguese rock-cut tombs. There is no doubt that the Arles graves are quite unlike anything else in the south of France. They appear to be a parallel development to those we have discovered in Iberia.

f 5

Here again, tomb contents provide little assistance in determining the place of origin of the tombs. The fine series of burial deposits in these tombs are all late secondary individual inhumations. The traces of the earliest collective burials have been swept aside or cleared away. However, one or two pieces of plain pottery and the occasional leaf-shaped arrowhead are relics of the earliest use of these tombs. Fortunately another trench of this type, recently found at Labastide de Trets, contained these early grave goods in quantity, and was related to a nearby coastal settlement, where this south French culture could be more fully studied. Trets is also the site of one of the two really valuable cultural pointers in south French megalithic art—the stelae of Orgon and

pl 9

Trets. These are stone slabs decorated with designs derived from those found on the little flat decorated schist and slate plaques, the native Mother Goddesses found in the Spanish and Portuguese tombs. After their arrival in southern France these little portable objects were translated into large flat standing stones—but traces of their geometric decoration still remain. Sometimes this decoration looks Greek rather than Spanish: another instance of the closeness of the links between east and west.

These two sites with Spanish megalithic art are related to the Arles grottoes nearby. The lowest layers of the Trets settlement contained both the plain pottery found in the tombs and also early impressed potteries of the Mediterranean region. In the same deposit further fragments of the broken Trets stelae were excavated. The Bouches-du-Rhône tombs and megalithic art can thus be directly related to developments in Spain and, as the impressed pottery is likely to be early, this argues that there was continuous contact between the two regions, or that the tombs themselves may belong to the initial period of expansion from Los Millares. Further traces of Spanish influence can be seen in the rock carvings on the French and Italian Riviera and in the central Alpine region at Fontanalba. The stags drawn by the rock carvers are very like those in the symbol pottery bowls at Los Millares and in south-east Spanish rock and cave paintings directly related to this settlement.

In much of the rest of southern France and the Pyrenees, as in northern Spain and Portugal, there are small collections of native megalithic tombs which must be related in design at one or two removes to the original dry stone walled passage-grave. These are a very real religious and cultural manifestation to the tomb builders themselves, though architecturally they have degenerated from the original Spanish designs. They represent, in fact, the adoption of the ancestor worship collective burial religion outside the immediate hinterland dominated by the colonists. In northern and western France and the British Isles, as in central Europe, this native revised edition of the megalithic religion was to prove at least as important as the direct importations from Spain.

Moving North by Sea: Western France

Southern Spain and Portugal are the first stage in the migration of the megaliths. Western France, the British Isles and Scandinavia are further stages along the main dispersal route. In Spain and Portugal collective burial, and the megalithic and dry-walled graves where this rite was practised, can be seen to form part of a religious ritual, involving ancestor worship and reverence for a female deity or Mother Goddess, which included ideas derived from the Near East but was developed in Iberia itself, among the colonists from Greece and Anatolia. In Western Europe, Spain and Portugal can be seen as the principal centres of influence. It is no longer possible to trace influences from Greece and the Near East among the megalith builders. The immigrant traditions are those derived from Spain, though of course local inhabitants are naturally involved in building at least the larger tombs, where manual labour was employed on a large scale.

In western France several groups of passage-graves can be recognized. There are some in the Charente near Angoulême, some on the south coast of Brittany, some on the mainland and in the islands off the north Breton coast, some in the Channel Islands and some, well inland, near Caen in southern Normandy. The builders of all these tombs arrived by sea from Spain and Portugal. Most of the tombs are near the coast, though in the case of the Caen group the tomb builders seem to have travelled up river from a landing place between Cherbourg and Le Havre.

There is no reason to believe that all the French passage-graves are of the same date or come from one and the same Iberian centre. In fact there seems to be every likelihood that in the same way as the five or six Near-Eastern colonies in Spain and Portugal come from different parts of Greece and Anatolia, the sea-travelling megalith builders in the Atlantic came from different parts of Spain and Portugal at different periods. Though it is not yet possible to tie up each group with a mother settlement in Iberia, the different colonies in the Atlantic can be arranged in some sort of chronological order. Small tombs with circular chambers and

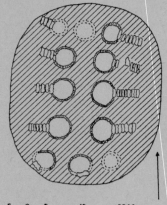

Plan of Fontenay-le-Marmion, near Caen, the best-known of megalithic sites in Normandy. The mound is of stone and contains twelve passage-graves, inserted more or less symmetrically. The passages are dry-walled and roofed with large slabs, while the chambers are also dry-walled and must originally have had corbelled roofs, traces of which remain. (6)

short symmetrical passages, such as those at Fontenay-le-Marmion near Caen, are likely to be early since they so closely resemble the early Iberian type. On this criterion a particularly early group can be recognized in Normandy and the north Breton coast. One north Breton passage-grave was dated by the carbon-14 method to approximately 3100 BC, and this suggests that some of the first passage-grave builders may have sailed direct from Spain to Ushant across the Bay of Biscay, instead of coasting along western France. A second early feature of the Atlantic passage-graves is their association with hill-top settlements fortified by walls. The passage-graves seem to fall into two classes: small monuments associated with defended settlements, and large isolated tombs of great splendour whose builders no longer needed to be defended. The Lizo camp near Carnac, the earliest Breton defended settlement, is built in the centre of the largest group of megalithic sites in Europe, including tombs of all characters, and also the stone rows or alignments, which may be an Atlantic form of the megalithic temple or purely ritual site.

Lizo camp must have been built by an immigrant settler group. Its situation overlooking an estuary is very similar to that of Los Millares in Spain, but as the French camp contained circular houses while the Millaran houses are square, there is unlikely to be a direct connection between the two. However, a similar defended camp, Peu-Richard, near Saintes in the Charente Maritime, is clearly connected with Los Millares. It contained a considerable quantity of a form of symbol pottery related to that of the Spanish town. Peu-Richard camp is one of a group of settlements surrounded by rock-cut ditches on the chalklands in the Charente. Most of these settlements are small and unimportant, but Peu-Richard is very considerable and it is defended by multiple ditches and ramparts and complex entrances whose general character recall that of Vila Nova de San Pedro and the Spanish sites.

Few megalithic tombs of early design can yet be closely related to the west French settlements, which suggests that these settlements may belong to a period after the introduction of megalithic architecture into western France. Tomb morphology suggests that many of the French passage-graves themselves belong to a later period than the initial expansion. This is true of small tombs with elongated passages, like those found together in the Barnenez South mound in north Brittany, and of large tombs with squared-off chambers like those at Kercado and Ile Longue near Carnac and La Hougue Bie in Jersey, the largest and most splendid megalithic monuments of Atlantic coastal France. Both tomb-

f 6

pl 29

f 7

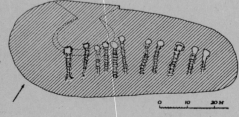

The long mound of Barnenez South, in northern Brittany. One-quarter demolished (dotted lines) by a road contractor, the mound revealed, on excavation, eleven passage-graves using different methods of construction, some megalithic, some built of dry stone walling, yet certainly contemporary with each other. (7)

pl 10

pl 12
13

types have long passages and square chambers instead of the short passages and circular chambers of the true Spanish and Portuguese tholoi. The Barnenez long mound seems to have grown sideways by accretion, one small chamber and elongated passage being placed next to another. As some of these Barnenez tombs are built of megalithic blocks, while others are entirely built of dry stone walling with carefully corbelled roofs, it seems clear that both methods were employed at the same time.

Large monuments such as Ile Longue and La Hougue Bie are built of megalithic blocks with dry wall made up between them, and in the case of Ile Longue the chamber is surmounted by a corbelled cupola and dry stone walling, though the passage is roofed with enormous stone blocks. These and comparable Irish tombs of great size, with their long passages and their combination of an extreme megalithic form of construction with a most elaborate architectural treatment bear a distinct resemblance to such tombs as Menga and Materabilla, believed to belong to the latest style in southern Spain. Ile Longue itself is set in a cairn of stones with four concentric revetting walls or stone settings surrounding the chamber, a feature which comes direct from the Los Millares tombs.

Most of the megaliths in southern Brittany contain only relics of a period later than their construction. For example, there are many Beaker culture burials with barbed and tanged arrowheads, Pressigny flint daggers and the characteristic Bell-Beaker pottery. But in some of the finer passage-graves such as Kercado, one can recognize the distinct and possibly original ritual grave furniture pl 33 including very large highly polished jadeite axes and rings, small beads of callais and certain gold objects. The large quantities in which these axes were deposited suggest that they accompanied collective burials, and there seems no doubt that we have here funeral gifts very like those identified in the Portuguese and the Irish tombs, which can be associated with the megalith builders themselves. Similar pointed-butted jadeite axes, though of a material imported from a different source, are recorded from the Portuguese megaliths, and that these are contemporary with the building of at least some of the Breton tombs is shown by their occurrence in sculptures on the tomb walls as at Gavr Innis.

Other elements of the elaborately carved decoration to be found in these Breton tombs must be related to the Spanish and Portuguese background. As in the south of France and Ireland, the ritual designs for the small cylinder idols and flat decorated stone plaques of Iberia have been translated into monumental form and can be found as decorations for large dressed megalithic blocks. The finest example of this is the interior of the Gavr Innis passage-grave, 22 of whose standing stones are entirely covered with laboriously carved monumental decoration. Plain pottery, often in the form of open bowls, also occurs in many of these graves and this is probably derived from the native impressed ware tradition in Iberia. It seems likely that the practice of cremation may have replaced simple burial in the Breton tomb ritual as it did in Ireland. This is also the best explanation for Breton collective tombs such as that of Gerbors, now filled with *individual* inhumations that are secondary. In the Conguel passage-grave an apparent cremation was separated from later deposits by stone slabs like those used in Irish tomb ritual, and this should be related to the use of special ritual grave furniture, also found in Ireland and in Brittany.

Both in western France and in the Paris basin further megalithic collective tomb groups have been recognized belonging to the locally inspired gallery-grave tradition. The Paris tombs are trench graves set in the ground or, in the Marne, rock-cut galleries and are probably not earlier than the Beaker culture in date, about 1800 BC. A few Breton graves are recognized as belonging to this tradition. It is not possible to identify the native strain which they represent. The other west French gallery-graves found in the lower Loire valley are of more importance, and the native group which they represent seems to have carried out a migration of its own by sea to the Welsh hills and the Cotswolds on either side of the Severn valley. There is some evidence that this migration from France to the British Isles may have taken place before 2800 BC; that is to say, very soon after the arrival of the passage-grave builders in western France.

A Change of Ritual: Ireland and Scotland

In the British Isles the main passage-grave groups are those found in Ireland and in the north of Scotland. Small groups of particularly early types are found in the Scilly Islands and in the Tramore region in southern Ireland, and also near Inverness at the north-east end of the great glen of Scotland. The latter, known as the Clava group, are the only British graves associated with the type of jadeite axe found in the Breton tombs. With the exception of the Scilly-Tramore group of passage-graves none of the groups of settlers use the original passage-grave plan with a circular burial chamber. All the later graves have square or polygonal chambers or have developed designs, such as the cruciform passage-graves of the Boyne valley.

f 8

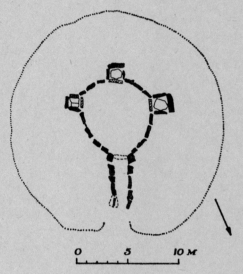

Fourknocks passage-grave, showing the 'cruciform' plan and large central chamber, the side chambers reduced to recesses. Of 'classic megalithic' orthostatic and dry-walled construction (pl. 28), the tomb was roofed with a corbelled vault, the largest megalithic vault in Europe. It may have been partly timbered; the large central 'posthole' and small number of roofing stones found by the excavators certainly suggest this. (8)

The other early Irish passage-graves are those in the cemeteries of Carrowmore and the earlier graves at Carrowkeel, on the west coast of Ireland, near Sligo. The megalith builders must have coasted or sailed well round into the Atlantic to make a landfall on this coast. Both are hill-top sites with cemeteries of passage-graves rather than single isolated burial monuments. Carrowkeel cemetery is related to a village of houses placed in an extremely strong defensive position. In marked contrast to this, the later Irish monuments, the Boyne valley group of megaliths near Dublin and their relations in Anglesey, are large-scale constructions several miles apart and are not related to defended settlements. Evidently when these tombs were built native labour was cheap and sudden onslaughts were no longer expected from the surrounding countryside. The Boyne valley tombs are embellished by numbers of large stones carved all over with spirals, eye- pl 25 ornaments and other Iberian motifs derived from portable objects but translated, as in France, onto the monumental scale. The carvings are similar but not directly related to those found at the French sites, and though none has survived it is likely that paintings or hangings in the same designs were used to decorate these tombs. The design on the standing stone at the entrance to the burial chamber of Fourknocks passage-grave bears a close resemblance to some form of hanging cloth.

New Grange is the largest and most important tomb in the f 9 Boyne cemetery. The mound is about 200 feet in diameter and covers an area of approximately an acre. Its present height is 44 feet. A circle of standing stones seems to have surrounded the tomb, and around the edge of the mound runs a kerb of large flags set edge to edge, about half of which are ornamented. The kerb stone in front of the entrance is richly carved with spirals and lozenges and the burial chamber contains a number of other decorated stones. Opening off the central corbelled vault are a pl 19 single terminal chamber and there are two chambers on either side. The plan of the Boyne tombs (and that of the later tombs at Carrowkeel) is that known as cruciform—chambers and passage together make up the shape of the cross. The side chambers may pl 28 be complete rooms or small recesses in the main room, but they are usually adequately marked off from other parts of the tomb, as if they were chapels belonging to separate families or to

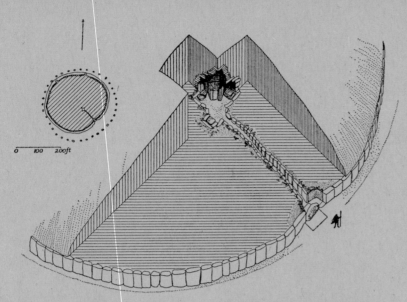

View through the mound at New Grange, showing the stone basins (pl. 30), and the corbelled roof (pl. 19). The plan (left) shows the vast area of the mound. (9)

different forms of ritual. It is in these recesses that much of the megalithic art is found, but the entrances of both tomb and chamber are also specially emphasized with decorated lintels or orthostats. Some of the stones of which these great Irish passage-graves are constructed have their surfaces carved with rows of pecked or drilled holes, a form of finishing treatment which recalls that used in the latest Maltese temples. In some cases the original designs have been superseded by those which pleased the new users of the tomb, for example the decoration on the slab by the entrance to the chamber of the New Grange tomb has been cut away by later rippling treatment of the stone.

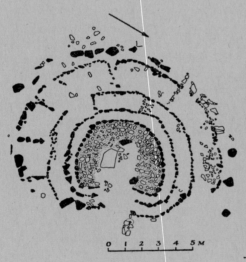

Plan of Townley Hall passage-grave, showing the rings of stones set on the ground surface below the mound, bending inwards towards the entrance. Similar rings of stones were found in the Ile Longue passage-grave (Brittany). Of the megaliths used in the tomb chamber, only three stones remain, two upright and one fallen. (10)

f 10   The ghost of one of these Boyne graves was found at Townley Hall. As the plan shows, the large stone blocks of the interior passage and chamber have nearly all been removed. Most of the cairn of small stones covering the monument had also disappeared, but enough remained to show it was circular, and surrounded by a kerb of revetting blocks. Before the cairn was built, several concentric rings of small stones were laid on the ground surface. These bend in towards the entrance to the grave, and the outer rings are broken up into segments by further radial lines of stones. These could be marking-out stones used in the preliminary survey or consecration of the ground where the tomb was to be erected. They closely resemble the stone revetments already mentioned in the interior of the cairn of the Ile Longue passage-grave in Brittany and similar features on the Los Millares monuments themselves.

The religious ritual of the Boyne tombs is related to that of Spain and the Mediterranean by such features as the anthropomorphic designs and the spiral and ocular design in their

pl 26   megalithic art and by the use of such equipment as stone basins, found in the small chambers at New Grange and elsewhere, as in

320

Spain and Malta, and single standing pillars. The single pillars instead of being in the forecourts in front of the megaliths as in Los Millares and Malta are here found, at Carrowkeel, at the chamber entrance and, at New Grange, in the centre of the burial chamber itself.

The stone basins in the latest Irish megaliths can be related to a profound change of ritual. They are thought to have contained *cremated* bone. The Mound of the Hostages, at Tara, the traditional home of the Irish kings near Dublin, was excavated recently and shown to be an untouched passage-grave, with its original contents intact, and with numerous secondary burials. This is the only untouched passage-grave or tholos which has been properly excavated either in Spain or Western Europe, and its original contents proved to be large quantities of burnt or broken bone, the remains of human cremations, which had been almost wholly incinerated and then washed completely white. Some of the cremations were placed in piles against the standing stones on the ground surface outside the chamber, under the mound itself. These must have been put there before the tomb was complete. Other piles of 'clean cremation' are on the floor in the interior, but the greater part of the grave is filled with secondary deposits, individual cremations and inhumation burials accompanied by characteristic pottery of later periods, such as food vessels and cinerary urns, inserted through the roof. The small space taken up by these cremations may explain why so many of the tombs appear to be empty, for once the tombs were opened the contents would wash away. The cremations and the Boyne tombs in general are associated with a characteristic tomb equipment which is mostly of small size, and likely to be missed, such objects as miniature hammer pendants, stone balls, bone pins with mushroom and poppy-shaped heads and a wide variety of beads. This tomb equipment is found also at Carrowkeel and Carrowmore near Sligo and, in the Boyne tombs themselves, it is accompanied by the Carrowkeel style of pottery, so that at least the latest periods at these two groups of sites must be related. However the Boyne cremation ceremony and the latest Boyne tombs, Fourknocks and the Mound of the Hostages, are dated by carbon-14 around 2000 BC. This is 500 years after the presumed date of destruction for Los Millares and a thousand years after the arrival of the first Breton, and possibly the first Irish passage-graves. The Mound of the Hostages is a small, poor relation of the great Boyne tombs, which probably contained much richer grave goods as well as the characteristic cremations.

The majestic large-scale monuments of Ireland with the enormous corbelled vaults—that of Fourknocks I would have been the largest prehistoric corbelled vault in Europe, though partly built in wood—are a late developed product in Ireland as in Brittany. This also seems to be true for some of the large colony of variant passage-graves found in the Orkneys and along the Inverness coast in Scotland. Maes Howe, the most famous tomb in the Orkneys, was broken into in the 12th century AD by the Vikings, who left runic inscriptions saying that they had removed treasure from the tomb. This presumably means gold and precious metal, and it gives some idea of the riches that may accompany some, though not all, of the last passage-graves in the British Isles.

From the Loire to Western England

Apart from the outliers of the Boyne culture, that is one or two tombs in Anglesey and near Liverpool, passage-grave influence is rare in England and Wales. It is only marked by imports such as mirror-finished jadeite axes like those in the Breton graves, and in the chalk copies of Iberian idols buried at Folkton in Yorkshire about 2200 BC. However there are other megalithic traditions, represented by the horned cairns of Ireland and south-west Scotland and the gallery-graves of the Cotswold and Severn Valley region which may be very much earlier in date than the latest passage-graves. These groups of megalith builders may well be related and it is thought that the graves around the Severn Valley represent a West French immigration, from the Loire Valley. Those on the banks of the Severn are the earliest and represent the point of landfall of the megalith builders, those inland, such as West Kennet, near Avebury, are later. Severn-Cotswold graves have a peculiar transepted plan, with two sets   f 11

pl 31

pl 11

pl 27

of lateral chambers opening off the central passage, a design which is thought to have developed in the Loire Estuary before the megalith builders left France.

The grave entrance in the earlier examples is at the wider end, and though in the latest barrows the actual entrance to the grave may be at one side, ceremonies are still conducted at the end of the barrow in front of a dummy entrance and between the horns of a curved forecourt, which relate the design to the horned cairns of Scotland and Ireland. The grave goods accompanying these tombs include plain western pottery, some of which may be related to the period of the construction, but a good deal of which is certainly of a later period.

It is difficult to find any real evidence of the character of this 'native group' of megalith building immigrants. Even the date of arrival of the culture can only be arrived at by inference. Severn-Cotswold graves, like West Kennet, in long wedge-shaped mounds seem still to be the only credible precursors in Wiltshire and Dorset for the unchambered long barrows of the Windmill-Hill culture, the earliest English farming culture. It seems that some of the original burials of the West Kennet grave may even be connected with the primary occupation at the type-site of this farming group—the camp of Windmill-Hill, about 2750 BC in date. As one early example of unchambered Windmill-Hill long barrow can be dated to 2700 BC, it is certain that the builders of the Severn-Cotswold chambered tombs came from France at least 100 years before that date, and perhaps two or three hundred years earlier. This is the earliest date at which the Windmill-Hill agriculturalists are established in Devon and on the North Wiltshire downs, and the French megalith builders may well have been partly responsible for the introduction and development of the culture, including the ditched encampments, as well as for the distinctive burial rite. The Dorset *Cursus* and that near Stonehenge, earth-banked ceremonial ways several miles long associated with the unchambered long barrows, are another English type of monument which was probably introduced from France at this time. The *Cursus* seems to be a direct translation of the Carnac stone alignments into terms suitable for the chalk downlands of Britain.

In eastern England the non-megalithic Windmill-Hill culture is succeeded by other native traditions and immigrants some of which use burial circles and religious circles of small standing stones, which derive from the Continent. In the west, on the coasts of south-west England, in Wales, coastal Scotland and throughout Ireland small megalithic cists or dolmens representing some form of burial cult are known, but these may have been for individual rather than for collective burial. The Irish examples may have been built between the arrival of the passage-graves and the horned cairns, but most of them seem to represent a native reaction to the arrival of the immigrant megalith builders.

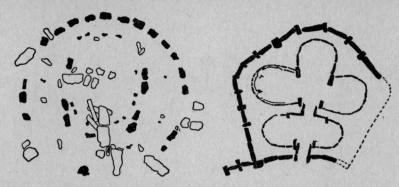

Plans of Stonehenge (left) and a Maltese megalithic temple, showing the affinity between the two in the arrangement of the interior ritual chambers in a horseshoe pattern. They are not drawn to the same scale. (12, 13)

The Temple in the North: Stonehenge

There remains one monument which deserves separate discussion. Stonehenge must be the latest megalithic monument in England. Its carbon-14 date is about 1660 BC. The fully developed design with a horseshoe plan of separate megalithic trilithons, resembling a series of gigantic doorways surrounded by a continuous trilithon circle, is quite original. Though it is placed upon the site of an earlier monument of a well-known British type, there is nothing at all like Stonehenge elsewhere in Britain or in Western Europe. The mortise and tenon-like joints holding the lintels to the orthostats suggest that the craftsmen who built the monument were used to working in wood, but the enormous carefully squared and dressed blocks make all other West European megaliths, even New Grange, look provincial.

Stonehenge has been compared with such later works as the Lion Gate Entrance to Mycenae, and to Mycenaean tombs, but it is plainly a temple and its nearest relations seem to be the contemporary Maltese temples, though we know nothing else to suggest a connection between Malta and the British Isles. If one examines the Maltese temples one is impressed by the resemblances in design between them and Stonehenge. The extreme care with which the enormous stone blocks are cut and finished is only one very general resemblance. There is also the use of separate trilithons in the internal arrangements of the temple. The horseshoe plan of the internal structure is common to Stonehenge and to the side and end chambers of all later Maltese temples, and the continuous trilithon circle at Stonehenge bears some resemblance to the outside retaining wall of a Maltese temple. Even within a common megalithic tradition such detailed resemblances are very striking, while the carbon-14 datings for these sites provide clear evidence of contemporaneity.

pl 1

pl 23
22
f 12
13

pl 24

Furthest Point: Passage-Graves in Denmark

The principal passage-graves of Scandinavia are found in Denmark, on the east coast of Jutland and in the islands of the Baltic, and on German soil, for example in the North Frisian Islands. Danish passage-grave builders succeed an earlier funnel beaker culture (TRB culture), who buried their dead in small megalithic cists. In the late Neolithic the passage-grave culture is itself succeeded by another megalithic culture who buried their dead in long gallery-graves, a group also found in south Sweden and Germany, and related to the tomb builders of the Paris basin. Graves containing the funnel beaker pottery are found all over the North German plain as far as Poland and south into Holland.

pl 20

The small cists or boxes in which the undivided burials and pottery were placed were often built in pairs or larger numbers inside rectangular enclosures outlined by stones, a form which resembles the long gallery type of megalith but is thought to have been derived from the design of long houses in which these people lived. The megalithic burial custom, which is in part earlier than the Danish passage-graves, can, in some degree, be explained by the existence of suitable raw material, as large numbers of glacial erratic boulders are found in Denmark and North Germany which were covered with an ice sheet in pleistocene times. However, as in Spain, graves built of large boulders appear to be in use before the passage-grave builders arrive.

pl 38

The Danish passage-grave culture represents a complete fusion

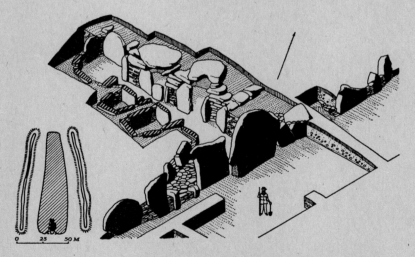

Isometric view of West Kennet long barrow, during the last stages of excavation. The plan (left) shows the very long wedge-shaped earthwork flanked by ditches on the longer sides. This plan is retained by the later unchambered long barrows in Wiltshire and Dorset. (11)

of the traditions of the native funnel beaker peoples and the immigrant megalith builders. The pottery in the passage-graves is derived entirely from the native tradition. The long houses of the funnel beaker and passage-grave settlements are similar, and the general layout of their settlements is related. The passage-grave builders appear to have been accepted and to have taken over the native tradition instead of imposing their own, as their lakeside settlements without walls are quite different from the

pl 32 hill-top defended sites of Iberia and western Europe.

The pottery at the Troldbjerg passage-grave settlement suggests that it was only occupied for 50–100 years, but the layer of cultural debris is extremely thick, showing that this settlement had a large population. There are other indications of the density of the Danish passage-grave population, especially the number and size of the passage-graves themselves. There are two types of passage-graves, those with round, polygonal or square chambers like those found in Western Europe and a developed form, the T-shaped passage-graves with a long chamber or pair of chambers at right-angles to the passage. A whole series of these T-shaped graves can be recognized where design develops one out of the other, becoming more and more eccentric. Recent excavations have shown, surprisingly enough, that this variant is not a late form as might be expected. The T-shaped graves contain the same pottery as the circular passage-graves, and are merely due to local variations in taste.

The Danish passage-grave builders are related to the Western groups both by the design of the graves and by the rituals of ancestor worship carried out in the specially lined forecourts in front of the grave. Most passage-grave forecourts contain pottery and at Grönhöj many thousand potsherds of the same age as the primary deposits in the tomb were found in the forecourt and could be joined to other pottery sherds jammed between the slabs lining the entrance to the grave. On these slabs the ceremonial vessels and ladles had been placed, with food and drink for the dead.

A special Danish extension of this ritual worship of the dead is the separate ceremonial houses related to passage-graves.

pl 39 These are small square timber and wattle-and-daub constructions
40 which appear to have no real occupation deposits, but contain banks or benches running the length of the house, littered with rows and groups of pottery, food and drink containers and pottery ladles. The vessels excavated are nearly all whole and unused. These benches must have closely resembled the altars for food offerings to be seen in present-day Hindu or Buddhist temples.

The older burial rites, as well as the passage-graves, were still used by the Danish megalithic culture. At Tustrup in Jutland a group of burials was excavated, a passage-grave, a small cist and a megalithic cist or dolmen of the kind used by the earlier funnel beaker culture. All of these contained pottery of identical type and design—in other words they were all in use at the same time. The three Tustrup graves were in adjoining fields and equidistant

pl 41 from a ceremonial house of the type described above, which also contained identical pottery. This gives us some idea of the variety of Danish funerary ritual.

The two ceremonial houses excavated at Tustrup and Ferslev were abandoned when their roof fell in after a generation or so, and contain big collections of pottery all of the same period. This is particularly interesting since there are carbon-14 dates

pl 34 for both houses. The pottery found at Ferslev is a particularly highly finished type, known as the refined style, which belongs to a late stage of the development of passage-grave pottery. The

dates for this are in the region of 2500 BC, while the Tustrup house which contained slightly earlier pottery is dated 2650 BC. It seems likely that the final passage-grave builders arrived in the Baltic about a hundred years before this date.

The earliest connection between Denmark and Iberia is of some interest as it is represented by the earliest group of metal tools in Northern Europe. This is the famous Bygholm hoard, a pl 35 group of flat copper axes, a copper dagger and spiral copper armlets. They were buried in a funnel beaker pot belonging to the first period when the earlier (funnel beaker) culture had come in contact with the passage-grave builders. The dagger has a cast rib on one side of the blade, a design which is found at Los Millares and Palmela, and must have come from Spain or Portugal about 2800 BC. Apart from this, few traces exist of the relationship between Denmark and Spain and Portugal or the other passage-grave groups in Western Europe. The enormous quantity of grave-goods such as polished flint axes and pottery found in Danish passage-graves seem in many cases to be contemporary with their erection and in all cases to belong to a native tradition of manufacture. The design of the graves is Iberian or West European, but there is no other really convincing evidence of immigration to Denmark. Unless there exist, as yet undiscovered, some traces of a primary cremation deposit with distinctive grave goods as has been found in Ireland, we will have to admit a progressive impoverishment in the cultural relationship between the different passage-grave settlers, as they move north from Iberia, and the possibility that the Danish passage-grave settlers may have been immigrants, not from Iberia itself but from Brittany or from north-east Scotland.

The Danish passage-graves culture was supported by an economy of cattle and wheat farming on the best land in Denmark and its prosperity is shown by the size of the population and its dominant relationship towards other peoples in Denmark at the same time—groups of poor shepherds and sea-fishing peoples on the coast. This culture is thought to have been in existence until perhaps 2000 BC and its tradition still played a great part in later Danish prehistoric periods.

The Ships of the Megalith Builders

The movement of the passage-grave builders presupposes long sea voyages and though little or nothing is known of their ships it is legitimate to believe that some form of sailing ship was in use. Many of the landing places could be arrived at by travelling along the coasts but this is not the case with the British Isles, and the distribution of passage-graves, particularly those in the north of Scotland and on either side of the Irish Sea, is suggestive of the use of prevailing winds. A number of carvings exist on the megaliths that are interpreted as ships, both in Malta and in Brittany, Ireland and Scotland, and it is reasonable to draw attention to the resemblances between these drawings and the drawings of ships in Cycladic pottery and on the rock carvings *f 14* in Scandinavia, though the latter may belong to the Bronze Age. It seems likely that some sort of long shallow-draught high-prowed vessel was used. This probably had a single mast and sail and also paddles, and must have resembled an angular version of the Greek and Viking longship. Small boats had been in use for thousands of years in Scandinavia and Western Europe, but the introduction of an imported design of sea-going vessel (with or without sails) from the Mediterranean must partly account for the successful penetration of the Atlantic seaboard by the megalith builders.

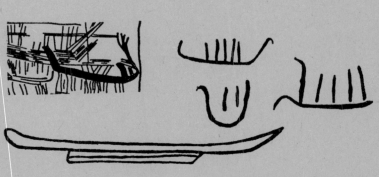

Representations of ships on early Cycladic (Aegean) pottery (left), and on megaliths at Hal Tarxien, Malta (centre top), and at Ile Longue (centre bottom), and Mané Lud, Brittany: evidence of seagoing craft of the same period as the megalithic migrations. Some indication of the possible size of the craft is given by what are most probably crew members or passengers, portrayed by vertical lines. The drawings are not to the same scale. (14)

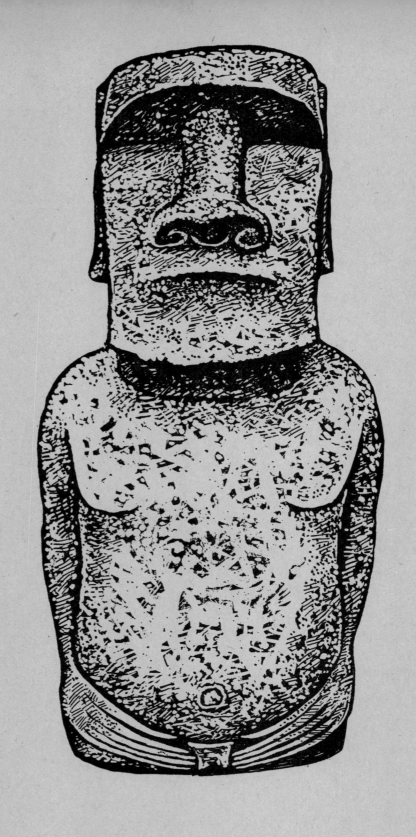

XIV NAVEL OF THE WORLD

The red-topped giants of lonely Easter Island

THOR HEYERDAHL

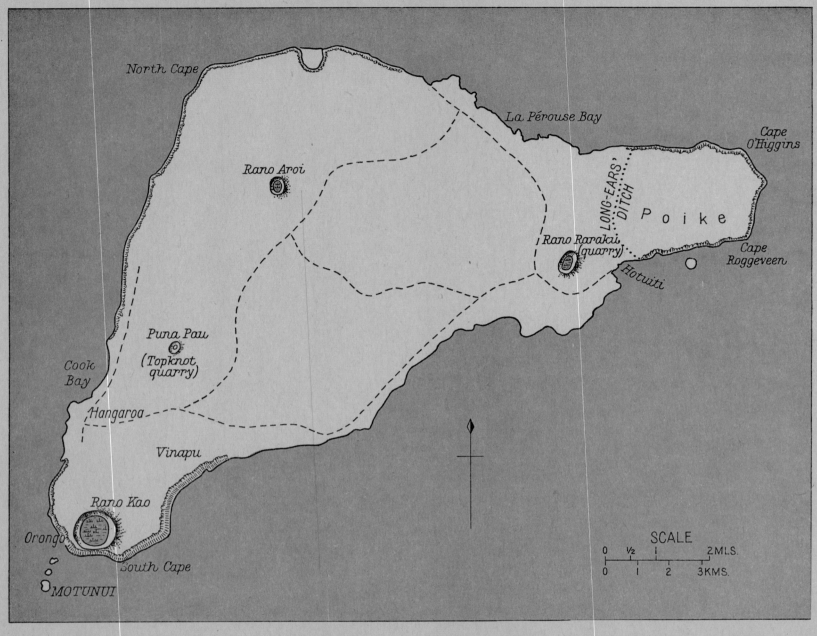

A note on chronology. No chronology of Easter Island can be anything but a patchwork of tradition, assumption and approximation, with occasional gleams of light from radio-carbon dating. With this reservation, a reasonable picture would be somewhat as follows:

Early Period before AD **300–1100?**
 Orongo cult centre and solar observatory
 Makemake sun deity
 About 15 ceremonial altars without statues, sun orientated, facing sea
 Carefully fitted masonry
 Probably lenticular stone and reed houses
 Tiahuanaco-style stone statues standing in the ground

Before **300** Arrival of first settlers from east under Hotu-matua

c. **386** Construction of defensive ditch across Poike peninsula

c. 1100 INDETERMINATE PERIOD OF ABANDONMENT AND DECAY

Middle Period AD **1100?–c. 1680**
 Bird-man cult
 Ceremonial village at Orongo, with stone houses
 Altars reconstructed, facing inland (*ahu*), supporting ancestor figures
 Giant statues from Rano Raraku quarries
 Lenticular stone and reed houses; thick-walled circular stone houses

c. **1500** Arrival of Polynesians from west under Tuu-ko-ihu ('Short-ears'). They adopt Long-ear religion and culture, and collaborate in statue-building

c. **1680** Revolt of the Short-ears. Long-ears defeated and massacred in battle of Poike ditch

Late or decadent Period c. **1680–1864**
 Semi-pyramidal *ahu* with no platform or image
 Pole-and-thatch boat-shaped houses
 Refuge caves
 Small carvings in stone and wood
 Obsidian spear points

1722 Roggeveen discovers and names Easter Island
1770 Rediscovery by Gonzalez
c. **1770** Civil war breaks out between Ko-Hotu and Ko-Tuu people
 Beginning of *huri-moai* ('statue-overthrowing time')
1774 Visit by Capt. Cook.
1786 Visit by La Pérouse. No indication of war
1804 Visit by Lishansky: more than 20 statues still standing
1805 First slave raid
1838 Visit by Adm. du Petit-Thouars: 9 standing statues seen
1840 Last standing statue overthrown
1862 Great slave raid
1864 Missionaries introduce Christianity

On the evening of Easter Day,

the 6th of April 1722, a Dutch expedition of three ships discovered and named Easter Island, a lonely speck of rock eight miles by four set in the vast expanse of the Pacific, 2,000 miles east of the coast of Peru. The following morning, says the log of Carl Friedrich Behrens, the first man to set foot ashore, they 'could see from some distance that (the natives) had prostrated themselves towards the rising sun and had kindled some hundreds of fires, which probably betokened a morning oblation to their gods.' These 'gods' were 'certain remarkably tall figures', which puzzled the Dutch sailors and have to this day remained one of archaeology's most celebrated riddles. 'These idols', Behrens wrote, 'were all hewn out of stone, and in the form of a man, with long ears, adorned on the head with a crown, yet all made with skill: whereat we wondered not a little.'

In 1774 Captain James Cook visited Easter Island on his second voyage to the South Seas. William Hodges, who accompanied him, painted this picture showing groups of these mysterious statues standing by the shore. These, the classic statues of Easter Island's Middle Period, are of a consistent pattern: long-nosed, long-eared, probably anything up to 60 tons in weight, they are cut off flat at the hips to stand on the *ahu* or ceremonial platform. The tops of their heads are also flattened to receive the *pukao*, a cylindrical topknot of red scoria. Today, except for one that was re-erected in 1956, every single statue lies tumbled off its *ahu* in a scene of wanton devastation, its red topknot rolled apart from it.

Some of the questions still remain, as they did for the old navigators. Who were the people who raised these monstrous megaliths? Where did they come from, and when, to this lonely island which they named *Te-Pito-o-te-Henua*, 'The Navel of the World'? How did they transport the statues to their sites and erect them? Today, thanks to archaeological fieldwork on Easter Island, we are nearer to an answer—at any rate a more acceptable one than that given by the islanders themselves, who, when asked how the statues were moved from quarry to site, replied, 'They walked.' (1)

When man first arrived on the island, probably some time before AD 300, he introduced a plant unknown in other Pacific islands, or anywhere else except South America. This is the freshwater reed *Scirpus riparius*, called *totora* by the natives. It soon spread to cover most of the crater lakes with a mat of vegetation (left). They used this reed in house-building—as was also done in ancient Peru—and to build boats, light, unsinkable, riding the water like a swan (opposite, right), such as still exist today on Lake Titicaca in Peru. On the ceiling of a stone house in the cult centre of Orongo, in the south-west of the island, there is a painting (opposite) of a *totora* boat with mast and sail. (4–6)

Tens of thousands of tons, hundreds of thousands of cubic feet of rock have been carved out of the yellowish-grey volcanic tuff of Rano Raraku, both on the outside of the crater (left) and within its rim. All the colossal statues of Easter Island, over 600 in all, came from this one mountain, and from here too was quarried the rock for many of the much smaller and quite different sculptures of the first period. At the foot of the crater wall great banks of scree can be seen, consisting of thousands of tons of rock chippings, the detritus of centuries of quarrying and carving. Dotted about in this are some of the enormous Middle Period statues, some broken in carving or in transit, others abandoned half-finished when, about AD 1680, the work was brought to an abrupt end by the outbreak of civil war. (2)

The first men on Easter Island were sun-worshippers, constructing huge altar-like platforms oriented with great precision in relation to the rising sun at the solstice or the equinox. On the summit of the highest volcano, Rano Kao, they built a solar observatory and temple, with a device (above) for marking the rising positions of the sun. When a pole is placed in a shallow pit bored in the rock, a shadow falls across one of three smaller holes just as the sun appears above the rim of the crater at the summer and winter solstices and at the middle position, the equinox. Sun worship and solar observatories, unknown elsewhere in Polynesia, are characteristic of ancient Peru. (3)

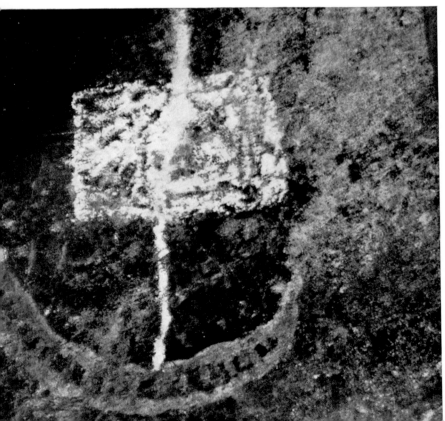

327

An unexpected find in recent years was a number of fair-sized statues in human form, antedating the huge, long-eared busts that made the island famous. The first settlers, some time before AD 300, must have brought with them an expert knowledge of stone quarrying and carving. Three of these statues are shown below. The one in the centre, which has lost its head, is a pillar-like four-sided column with stunted limbs indicated in low relief. On the left is a realistic kneeling figure, which, like the middle figure, is characteristic of the pre-Inca sun-worshipping centre at Tia-huanaco. The third figure seems, in a way, to be a prototype of the towering busts of the Middle Period. All are considerably more than lifesize. (7–9)

Another pointer to Peru as the origin of the first settlers on Easter Island is the expertly cut masonry with which they faced their altars. With crude stone picks for tools, they quarried huge blocks (below, right) and dressed them to shape with such care and skill that when correctly placed, with no mortar, not even a thin knife blade can be inserted between the blocks. Below (left) is part of a similar kind of masonry, this time from Cuzco, the Inca capital in Peru. When the Early Period, for unknown reasons, came to an end about AD 1100, the secret was lost, and the beautifully fitted masonry was largely destroyed. (10–11)

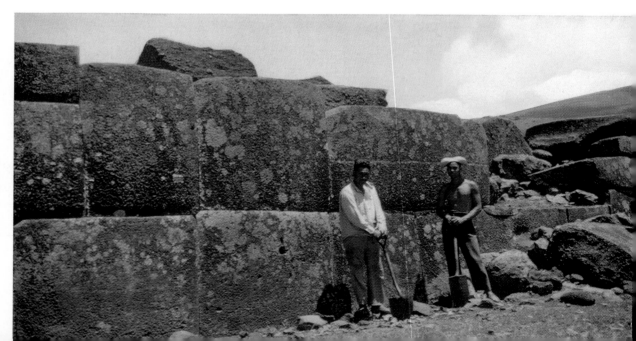

Suddenly, about AD 1100,
the original Easter Island culture came
to an end. No reason is known for the
disappearance of these Early Period
sun-worshippers; perhaps the whole
island was deserted for a time, perhaps
disease or war reduced them to a few
precariously surviving remnants. The
sun temples show evidence of a long
interval of abandonment and decay,
after which a different culture arose,
with other techniques and religious
concepts.

A strange bird-man cult replaced
the former sun religion, and an obsession with ancestor worship shows
itself. In this Middle Period the giant
statues for which Easter Island is
famous today were quarried, carved,
dragged across country and raised on
to their *ahu*, there to stand, not facing
outwards to the sun and the sea as the
temples did in the old days, but gazing
inland across the ceremonial plaza.
Finally, on the flat top of the statue's
head a massive red stone topknot was
placed. Then, and not till then, were
the eyes carved; unfinished statues still
scattered about the island have blind
eye-sockets which somehow seem to
add to their air of mystery.

For more than two hundred years
this posed a riddle without an answer.
The largest finished and erected statue
was 33 feet tall and its topknot added
another 8 feet; the combined weight
must have been over 90 tons. Towards the end of the statue-carving
period, bigger and bigger ones were
being made, one almost 70 feet long
having been found still attached to
the quarry wall. If that had been
levered up on to its platform base it
would have stood as high as a seven-
storey house. Even on an average-
sized statue, a full-grown man could
lie comfortably along the nose, his
hands behind his head, and ponder
the problem of how these colossi were
moved from quarry to platform, and
then lifted up on to a base that stood
some six feet above the ground.

Arrogant and remote, an unfinished
Middle Period statue stares sightlessly
at the sky from the slopes of the Rano
Raraku quarry. (12)

Crouching human figures with birds' heads and long, curved beaks were found incised on rocks at the summit of Rano Kao (above, right), the highest point of Easter Island, where the Early Period settlers had built their solar observatory and temple. That the bird-man cult was a later religion is shown by the fact, among others, that sometimes the bird-man image is found superimposed over the earlier big-eyed sun-symbol. Sometimes, too, the existing statues of the Early Period were overthrown and the bird-man symbols triumphantly cut on the base of the fallen figures (left, lower). Even in the last century the cult was still actively practised on Easter Island. For weeks on end the strongest of the natives would watch on the cliffs of Rano Kao until the first flocks of migrating sooty terns settled on the little island of Motunui. They would then swim out on a reed float, and the man who found the first egg became a semi-divinity for the next year, the embodiment of the bird-god. Like the earlier sun-worship, the bird-man cult is characteristic of Ancient Peru; both are unknown elsewhere in Polynesia. (13–15)

Problem: how to get this statue back on its base. Over 25 tons in weight, it lay face down, sloping downhill, its base twelve feet from the slab it once stood on. But twelve islanders showed how their long-eared forefathers used to do it. (19)

Inch by inch, first one side then the other, the dead weight of the statue is levered up with long poles, and rocks and stones are packed underneath. Level and at the correct height, the statue is painfully and slowly eased backwards to the base. (20)

How long would the sculptors have taken, with their crude hand-picks of hard andesite, to carve a statue? Pedro Atan, mayor of the island, volunteered to lead a team of six natives, lineal descendants of the Middle Period stone-workers, in an experiment to find out. From three days' progress on the head (right), rough calculations suggested a six-man team would take a year to complete a statue 15 to 20 feet long—twelve months' patient clink-clink-clink of pick against iron-hard rock until the last narrow, keel-like attachment (right, below) could be cut through. Behind the mayor (in ceremonial fern-leaf crown) are a pile of old picks collected from all over the quarry, and gourds full of water to be splashed on the rock to make the work easier. (16, 17)

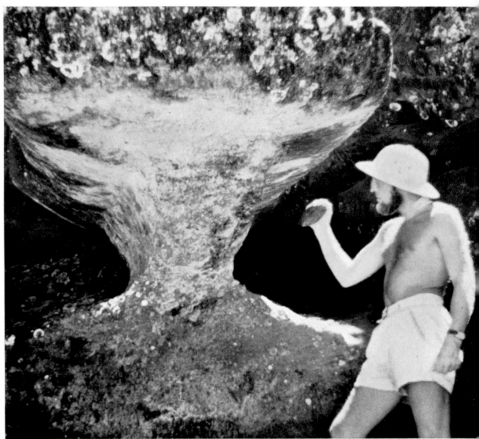

Even the transport of these giants is one of the old statue-makers' skills that has been handed down to the present-day islanders. Slowly at first, then more smoothly and easily, 180 natives showed that they could move a 12-ton statue, simply by hauling on ropes. The mayor, who organized them and cheered them on, explained that his ancestors would have had a Y-shaped wooden sledge under the statue. A larger statue could also have been jerked along by ropes passing through stout wooden shears, inching it forward in a seesawing motion on the bulge of its stomach. (18)

Correctly placed, the levering continues, day by strenuous day, under head and shoulders. Slowly the giant rises. At 45 degrees from the vertical, still safely wedged, it is secured by ropes round the neck to steady it as it is lifted higher and higher. (21)

Upright at last, the only statue on Easter Island still standing on its platform gazes out across the fields. In the old days the pile of stones would have been left for the red topknot to be levered up in the same way, and balanced on the head. (22)

Scattered about the slopes of Rano Raraku are nearly three hundred statues, abandoned at all stages. The one above, now partly excavated, was temporarily stood in a pit for its back to be finished off. Statues standing thus should not be regarded as finished and erected: they are still 'in production'. (23)

Massive topknots six feet thick or more, hewn out of the red volcanic scoria of Puna Pau, have also been found here and there about the island, abandoned where they lay when the work suddenly ceased. Three can still be seen (above) in the shallows of the south coast, suggesting that some were transported by *totora* rafts. (24)

A man feels small when excavating something this size. Left in its pit where the sculptors had propped it up for finishing, this giant stood for centuries while rain-washed debris slowly buried it up to the chest. Its total height is over 36 feet, which makes it the tallest erected statue on the island. (25)

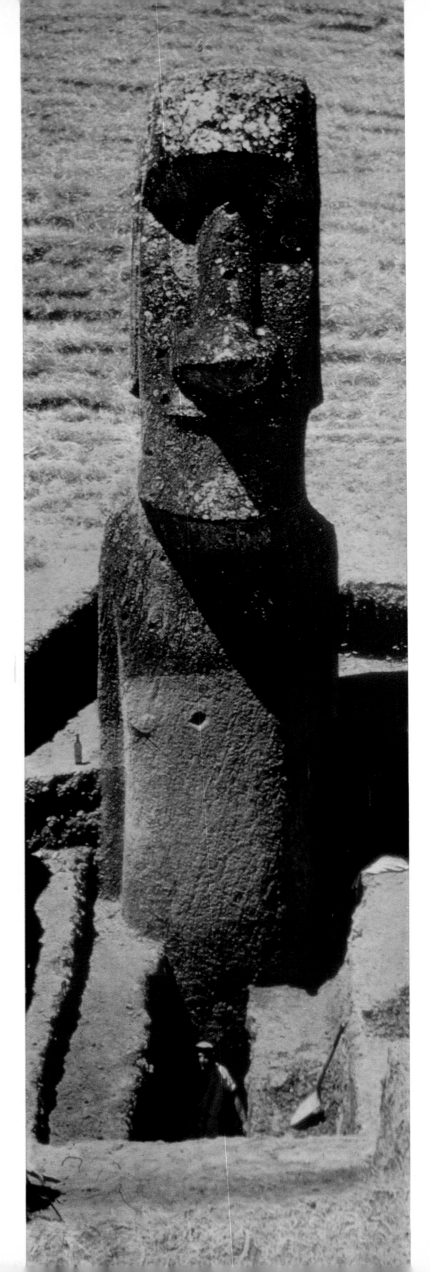

A symbol of uncertain meaning appears in relief on the back of some of the statues (below). It may represent a kind of loincloth (though the front of these statues is invariably naked), but there is a native tradition which suggests that the curving lines represent a rainbow, the circles are the sun and moon, and the M-shaped lines represent rain. (26)

One of the most perfect statues on Easter Island (right), though under twenty feet tall, is unusually broad in relation to its height, which gives an impression of strength and dignity. The sightless eyes indicate that it is unfinished: not until it finally stood on its family *ahu* were a statue's eyes 'opened'. (27)

A new element arrived

across the sea, probably about AD 1500. Polynesians from the west, perhaps from the Marquesas, came to Easter Island, not as invaders but—it almost seems—as immigrant labourers, to help with the ever-increasing work on the statues. The native Easter Islanders had the custom (reflected in their statues) of stretching their ear-lobes by inserting large disks; the newcomers, who did not do this, were called 'Short-ears' to distinguish them from the long-eared natives. Tradition has it that the Short-ears finally revolted, 'downed tools', and slaughtered all the Long-ears, men, women and children, except for one, Ororoina, who was spared to let his race continue. This revolt, marking the end of the Middle Period and the beginning of the Late Period which lasted well into historic times, has been placed by radio-carbon dating at about AD 1676.

Silent witnesses of disaster and revenge encumber the island landscape. Statues still lie where the tow-ropes were dropped (above) and, half-finished, in the quarries (below). No more statues were made, but the Short-ears appropriated the *ahu* and worshipped before the standing statues, as Roggeveen and his shipmates saw in 1722. (28, 29)

In the end, civil war broke out among the Short-ears, and lasted for many years, reducing them to a pitiful fraction of cave-dwelling cannibals. This was *huri-moai*, the 'statue-overthrowing time', when the images, pride of their short-eared inheritors, were toppled off their platforms in wanton destruction (above). In this period began the custom of hoarding property—especially small stone carvings of magical importance—in family caves under the protection of guardian spirits called *aku-aku*. Island families still have their caves, still hoard their precious objects (below). Among these secret sculptures of the Late Period (right) are the bearded head of a Long-ear, a whale with a reed hut and an oven on its back, a woman with a fish roped to her shoulders, and a skull. (30–35)

335

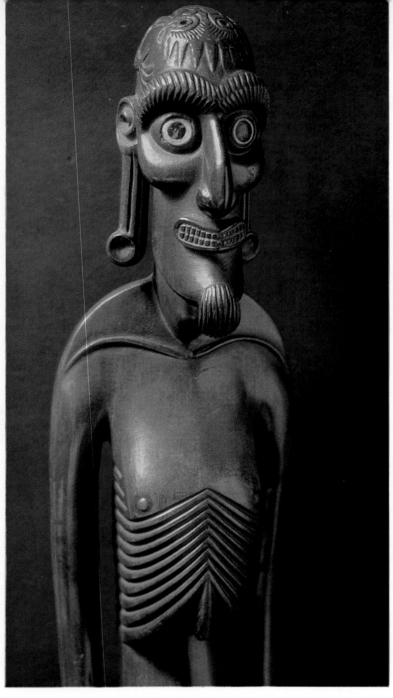

The long-eared ghost-man, *moai-kava-kava,* the most striking and characteristic product of Late Period wood-carving, is still made by Easter Islanders today. According to tradition, a king named Tuu-ko-ihu found two sleeping ghosts—or possibly two starving survivors of the massacred Long-ears—in the topknot quarry, and carved their likeness, emaciated, hook-nosed, with goatee beard and pendent ear-lobes, so that they should not be forgotten. (36).

The last of the Long-ears, the only family on the island to claim direct descent from Ororoina, sole survivor of the massacre, are the Atan family. They took the name Atan (Adam) when Christianity came to Easter Island at the end of the 19th century. On the left of the group below is Atan Atan, to his left the mayor, Pedro Atan, and on Pedro's left, leaning on a stone head, his son Juan. Juan's red hair, fair skin and European look are features that go back for generations, right back to Ororoina and the long-eared people, and to the grim, thin-lipped statues with the topknots that had to be carved from the only quarry that provided red stone. Tradition says that red hair and fair skin were seen among the very first settlers on the island; in the records of the Incas of Peru there are stories of fair-skinned, red-haired, long-eared people, builders of great stone statues, who disappeared long, long ago over the edge of the Pacific, sailing their reed boats into the eye of the setting sun. (37)

The red-topped giants
of lonely Easter Island

THOR HEYERDAHL

THE LAST major area on earth to be settled by mankind was the oceanic island-world of the Mid-Pacific. With little or no navigational accomplishment, early man from Asia had by then moved south-east by way of Indonesia into Australia and Papua-Melanesia, and north-east by way of the Bering Sea area into North, Central, and South America. Asiatic migrants had thus settled the circum-Pacific millennia before ships were designed capable of utilizing or overcoming the winds and currents that rule the vast Pacific water-wastes.

Shortly before the Christian era aboriginal craft also began to swarm into the Mid-Pacific, setting aboriginal settlers ashore on all inhabitable oceanic islands, where they remained in obscurity and isolation until Europeans found the way to America and thence debouched with the winds and currents on voyages of discovery, or rather re-discovery, in the same enormous ocean.

Loneliest of all islands found was a tiny one known by its aboriginal occupants as Te-Pito-o-te-Henua, 'The-Navel-of-the-World', but renamed by its European re-discoverer, Roggeveen, 'Easter Island', in honour of the day of his own arrival in 1722. Getting close to shore the Dutch visitors, to their surprise, saw primitive natives prostrating themselves towards the rising sun while kindling fires in front of enormous stone statues in human form. The lofty stone giants balanced huge cylinders of red rock on their heads, rising in hundreds above the barren landscape where no trees were seen that could have been used for their transport and erection. The settings for the humble worshippers and their stupendous, ever-present monuments were stony fields void of vegetation, interrupted only by small clearings of sweet potatoes and bananas, and above them the grass and fern-covered slopes of extinct volcanic cones holding the island's only supply of fresh water in their dead craters.

All around the tiny island vertical cliffs fell into the sea, consumed by hammering waves and leaving room for exceedingly few landing-places, where remnants of paved ways lead down to former slips for shallow water-craft. Born in pre-human times by a volcanic eruption on the ocean bottom, this tiny speck of solid rock had emerged utterly alone in the midst of an ocean where the current flows constantly from South America—2000 miles to the east—to the nearest inhabited island, 1600 miles to the west, and thence to Asia another 7000 miles further. Naturally, the question arose among scholars as well as among the general public: How had aboriginal civilization come to this isolated spot?

This problem was indirectly approached through a study of oral native tradition in the latter part of last century, and through a survey of surface archaeology and the living native population, their culture and language, in the first half of our own century. In the second half systematic excavations as well as pollen borings began to penetrate directly into the local past. All combine to give us certain highlights of man's remarkable history on Easter Island, and his gradual building of the unique local culture.

Pollen borings show that when aboriginal man first set foot ashore, before the Christian era, the now barren Easter Island was covered by many species of trees and shrubs. There were streams, and the fresh water of the crater lakes was open and void of vegetation, but surrounded by numerous palms and virgin forest growth. Then man arrived, and a study of the stratified pollen de-

The Pacific, showing the main oceanic currents. (1)

posits shows how the original forest came under attack while aquatic plants were introduced which covered the formerly open lakes. On man's arrival, *Polygonum acuminatum*, a strictly South American plant used by the Andean and Easter Island population for medical purposes, was planted along the edges of the lakes. It was accompanied to the island by the extremely important *totora* reed, another specifically South American fresh-water plant equally unknown in the Old World and on all other Pacific islands. Upon their introduction the local flora began to change drastically. These two useful aquatic species soon spread to cover most of the crater lakes with a partly floating bog. Simultaneously with their introduction the first fires were lit by man on the island, and after a short period the land vegetation started to disappear. Soot particles began for the first time to mix with the formerly pure soil and pollen deposits. They reflect controlled forest fires started by the first settlers to make clearings in the woods for their own dwellings and religious structures. As the indigenous forest fell, strange temples and monuments of enduring stone were raised in the open places. These constructions, which were later damaged or covered up, provide us with the best clues for a study of the cultural standing of the first immigrants and of the subsequent local evolution.

Strangers to Polynesia: the First Settlers

The people who first reached Easter Island must obviously have come from an area where stone quarrying rather than wood carving was in vogue. The trees were cut to give access to solid rock. These first settlers arrived as expert masons with a highly developed technique of shaping enormous blocks of hard basalt in such a way that their visible parts could be quadrangular, triangular, or polygonal, and yet fit together so closely that not a knife's blade could be inserted between them. This intricate form of megalithic masonry was unknown on the thousands of other islands further west in the Pacific, and is equalled in quality, style, and technique only by the specialized masonry characteristic of ancient Peru, on the continent which is Easter Island's nearest neighbour to the east. The intended effect was aesthetic or ceremonial rather than functional, and subsequent local generations were unable or unwilling to keep up the strange and exquisite masonry of the earliest island epoch.

The technique was used by the earliest island population for constructing huge altar-like platforms for worship or veneration of the sun. The conventionally fitted and smoothly dressed front

337

A type of Early Period sculpture: a flattish, quadrangular stone head with bulging eyes and no body. This represents the creator god Makemake. (2)

wall was astronomically oriented with great precision in relation to the sunrise at the summer solstice or the equinox. The interest in the movements of the sun is also revealed by the fact that on the summit of Rano Kao, the highest volcano, the early settlers constructed a solar observatory with a device for recording the annual movements of the sun. It was surrounded by a religious structure with sun symbols carved on the lava outcrops, and fires were associated with the local rites. Sun worship and solar observatories are considered not to be Polynesian features, but are again most characteristic of ancient Peru.

At the solar observatory and in the cleared and levelled plazas behind the large astronomically oriented megalithic platforms the early inhabitants of Easter Island erected a variety of fair-sized stone statues in human form. These differed remarkably from the larger busts that later made the island famous, and they were unknown to science until excavations disclosed their existence in recent years. One type was a small and flattish quadrangular head without body, with features carved in low relief, huge goggle-like eyes, pouching cheeks, and curved eyebrows running into a Y-shaped nose. A second and equally conventionalized type was a pillar-like rectanguloid column on the sides of which a full-sized human figure was outlined in relief, with stunted legs and hands placed in such a way that the fingers met below the navel. A third type was represented by a rounded and realistic kneeling statue sitting on its heels with hands on the knees and gazing upwards towards the sky, the oval face being ornamented with a small goatee. None of these types exists on any of the other islands, but all three are characteristic of the pre-Inca sun-worshipping centre at Tiahuanaco.

A fourth and final type is a small prototype of the large monuments of the later local era. The latter type represents a purely local style and evolution, and has no close counterparts on the mainland or on any other island. In fact, megalithic stone statues of any form are unknown throughout the numerous islands of Polynesia, Melanesia, and Micronesia, except for a few specimens on Raivavae, the Marquesas, and formerly Pitcairn, three island areas which, like Easter Island, form the extreme outposts towards Peru where stone statues abound. Carbon datings reveal that the few statues on these neighbouring islands were erected long after the initial period of statue making on Easter Island. Actually, radio-

carbon analysis of fires burnt below the platforms on which the oldest Marquesan statues were raised show that the local statue erection took place in the 14th, 15th, and 16th centuries AD. Man had then been active on Easter Island for at least a thousand years.

We do not yet know for certain when the forest-covered Easter Island was sighted by man for the first time. But carbon datings reveal that about AD 380 a large quantity of labour was directed by skilled military engineers in the construction of a huge defence position on the eastern headland of the island. The cliff-encircled peninsula of Poike then became cut off from the rest of the island by an artificially excavated ditch twelve feet deep, about forty feet wide, and nearly two miles long. The excavated dirt and gravel was placed as a protective rampart on the upper side, with passages left open for counter-attacks. Unless the earliest Easter Islanders were preparing for enemies expected to follow in their wake across the ocean, one may assume that the island had been occupied for quite some time prior to this enormous defensive enterprise.

We know little about these very first settlers of Easter Island, but we do know that they arrived with a high degree of culture which was necessarily developed outside the island itself, and should be traceable elsewhere in the surrounding territories. As we have seen, this imported Early Period culture was of an extraordinary type quite incompatible with other known Pacific island cultures. The religion and the monumental architecture of the island discoverers were intimately associated with the movements of the sun. The sun's positions at solstices and equinox were studied from a solar observatory, and the megalithic temples oriented accordingly. They imported a most extraordinary and specialized masonry technique employed in the facing of their large altar-like structures. On arrival they cleared the forest to open stone quarries where huge blocks were cut and dressed with great expertness. They carved both rectanguloid and realistic statues according to given conventionalized patterns, and raised them in the ground as the first anthropomorphic monuments ever to be erected in the oceanic island world. Whereas a series of fires started that would at a much later date lead to the complete destruction of the local dry-land vegetation, two identifiable aquatic plants, unknown throughout Oceania, were brought along and planted in the lakes to survive locally until the present time.

Kneeling statue from Tiahuanaco, the pre-Inca sun-worshipping centre in Peru. Compare with plate 7, carved by the sun-worshippers of Early Period Easter Island. (3)

pl 3

f 2

pl 8

pl 7

f 3

pl 9

All these introduced features clearly point to South America, where they were characteristic of pre-Inca Peru, whereas none could have been brought from other Pacific island territories, where they were non-existent. The human introduction to Easter Island of the important Peruvian *totora* reed may indicate that the transfer took place in the extremely seaworthy *totora* boats characteristic of aboriginal navigation along the Pacific coast of South America, and particularly in southern areas remote from the balsa timber of Ecuador. Winds and currents are extremely favourable for a crossing in buoyant, openwork craft from the coast below Tiahuanaco to Easter Island. Large *totora* reed boats capable of carrying a well equipped crew were navigating the Pacific coastline of Peru since early pre-Inca periods, and are depicted in the art of the early Mochica culture. Smaller *totora* boats have survived on Lake Titicaca through Inca times until the present, and were used for transporting the enormous megalithic blocks of Tiahuanaco across the stormy mountain lake. They survived in almost identical form among the native boat-builders of Easter Island. Here, too, there is reason to suspect that they were used for transporting some of the large stones around the coast.

Clay pot of the Peruvian Mochica culture, showing two paddlers in a totora reed boat. This reed, introduced by man, grows thickly on the crater lakes of Easter Island, where it was used for making similar craft. (4)

A New Religion—and New People?

Somewhere around AD 1100 the original culture on Easter Island suddenly reached its end. Some of the early temples and other structures including the solar observatory show evidence of a long period of abandonment and decay, until suddenly they were reoccupied and rebuilt to another plan and with a different masonry technique. The cause of the interruption is not yet known. Perhaps the entire island was deserted during this interregnum, perhaps local warfare had drastically reduced the Early Period population to a small group surviving in a secluded area. Certainly, at the end of the interregnum a different culture with other religious concepts reoccupied the former sites, and commenced what may be termed the Second or Middle Period in the Easter Island cultural sequence.

Except for its inferior stone masonry, the local culture as well as the actual population seem to have reached their climax in the Middle Period. At the beginning of this period the quarrying of the enormous stone statues began, which later brought the world's attention to the tiny island. The leading idea and fanatical passion of the local islanders in this epoch was to carve giant ancestor figures to be erected on top of elevated family tombs. Ancestor worship and a suddenly introduced bird-man cult replaced much of the former interest in the sun. The Early Period solar observatory was abandoned and partly overbuilt, and a new ceremonial village of semi-subterranean stone houses dedicated to the bird-man cult was erected by its side, at Orongo on top of the volcano. Crouched human figures with bird's head and long curved beak were carved in relief all over the mountain summit, frequently

covering the outlines of the older big-eyed sun symbols. The existing statues of the earlier period were overthrown and destroyed, bird-men sometimes being triumphantly incised at the upturned base of the fallen figures. The beautifully fitted megalithic masonry altars were partly or entirely torn apart, the old dressed stones, and occasionally a complete tier of masonry, being incorporated in a new architectonic manifestation known today as an *ahu*.

The function of the *ahu* was that of a raised burial platform designed with special strength to hold ponderous and unwieldy ancestor statues. In the reconstruction of the ancient altars no attention was paid to maintaining the former orientation according to the sun, the *ahu* being generally placed parallel to the adjacent coast. Nor was any care taken to maintain the former beautiful fitting of the stones; the aesthetic or ceremonial importance of the masonry style was now entirely abandoned in favour of obtaining strength and solidity for supporting heavy weights. Any stone, polygonally dressed or entirely unworked, would do, provided it served its mere practical purpose, and complete or fragmentary images of the former island culture were frequently used as fill in the masonry core or humbled by being set face inwards into the supporting wall below the large Middle Period images.

Whereas the Early Period people had put all their artistic skill and labour into the shaping of the high outer wall of their altars, facing the sun, the Middle Period people reversed the centre of ceremony towards the existing inland, or plaza, side and turned their own statues accordingly. Multiple cremation burial in stone-lined compartments in front of the high outer wall was superseded by slab-covered burial chambers built into the opposite, or plaza, side of the *ahu*. The temples did not formerly have built-in tombs. Whereas the outer wall generally retained most of its original height, the inner wall towards the plaza became stepped, and wings were added to each side of the central terrace, usually to support additional numbers of ancestor statues as time went by.

The Giants Arise

The entire focus of attention shifted to the giant statues, for which the platforms were nothing but pedestals raising them aloft to be visible far and wide across the island. They were all raised with their backs to the sea, facing the inland ceremonial plaza. Each statue had its own personal name, and represented a deceased family member of sufficiently high rank to warrant worship and deification after his death. Some few *ahu* never had more than one or two statues, but as time went on most got three to five, and some as many as thirteen, fifteen, and sixteen.

The Early Period people had opened a diversity of quarries on Easter Island, and their statues were variously carved from dark hard basalt, somewhat softer red scoria, and yellow-grey volcanic tuff. The latter material proved ideal for statuary art, and the main quarries gradually developed in the inner and outer walls of the Rano Raraku crater. These particular quarries were later taken over by the Middle Period people, who made no further experiments but carved every one of their large statues, more than six hundred in all, from the hard yellowish tuff of this particular volcano. The local quarrying was so extensive that vertical cliffs and huge gaps were gradually created in the changing volcano walls, the local forest disappeared entirely, and the palms that had covered the slopes of the Rano Raraku volcano on man's first arrival became extinct.

The statues were quarried in the crater wall by means of crude hand picks of hard andesite. Water from gourd containers was splashed at the rock to facilitate the work. Inside a soft, eroded surface the rock of the quarry was extremely hard, and about a year was needed to complete an average-size statue. In the quarry every detail of the statue's face, arms and body was finished, down to the polish of the ear ornaments or the long sophisticated nails, while the back of the statue was still unformed, like a keel attached to the bedrock. Finally the back was detached and the giant guided by ropes and ramps down the steep crater wall, frequently having to pass above precipitous terraces and niches left from earlier statues, to come to a temporary rest at a fortuitous point near the foot of the volcano. Here, before reaching level ground, a step or a hole was dug in the fallen quarry rubble, into which the statue was tilted feet foremost and guided by ropes

Reconstruction of a Middle Period 'ahu'—a raised burial platform, solidly constructed to support the ponderous statues. Each 'ahu' belonged to a separate family, and the statues, varying in number from one or two to as many as sixteen, represented ancestors of distinction. (5)

pl 23
25
into a vertical position. While the giant was thus standing temporarily erect on the hill-side, directly below the quarries, the sculptors for the first time had access to the unworked back, which was now dressed and polished with the same care as the rest of pl 27 the figure. While the front was always nude and unornamented, with breasts, navel and genitalia exposed, the back was often adorned with a relief symbol consisting of a rainbow-like arch pl 26 and one or two rings.

These classic Middle Period statues all follow one consistent pattern, and all represent busts with full bodies but with no legs. Thus, while the older statues of the Early Period had been variously carved as detached heads, as busts, or as complete figures with erect or kneeling legs, those of the Middle Period were invariably carved as busts truncated abruptly at the hip-joint to create a flat base permitting the giant figure to balance on top of a masonry *ahu*. The homogeneous statues of the Middle Period were almost without exception male representations, whereas the various types of the earlier period had been both male and female. Another characteristic of the Middle Period was that the apex of the head, which had formerly been round, was now flattened to become the base for a cylindrical *pukao*, or topknot, of red volcanic scoria which was superimposed on the finished giant. Separate red topknots were not carved for the Early Period statues.

Whereas the yellow-grey tuff quarries for the images were all located in the inner and outer slopes of the volcano Rano Raraku near the defence position of the eastern headland, the red scoria quarry for the topknots was located inside the small crater of Puna Pau, 8 miles away near the opposite end of the triangular island. From these two points of origin the images and topknots were transported to the respective *ahu* where they were to meet. Whereas the large topknots were rolled as crude cylinders and dressed to final shape only upon arrival at their final destination, the statues, as we have seen, were beautifully finished while standing free in a temporary position at the foot of the quarries. The only details left unworked on the images prior to departure from the volcano were the eye sockets. The eyes of the images were not to be opened before arrival at their own family *ahu*, and all the frequently illustrated giants standing on the slopes of the volcano awaiting transportation to their *ahu* were therefore gazing into the sky with a strange blind look.

pl 12
To avoid injury to the smoothly polished statue during transportation a padding of tough *totora* reeds was used, and the giant placed in a large sledge-like frame. A recent experiment undertaken on the island shows that 180 natives suffice to pull a twelve-pl 18 ton statue across the terrain by means of ropes and wooden skids. From 500 to 700 natives would be able to transport even the larger statues the same way, and there is reason to suspect that the transport was facilitated by piecemeal jerks on ropes passing through stout wooden shears placed across the neck of the statue. This would lever it along in a seesaw motion on the fulcrum of its bulging stomach, a method which would considerably reduce the manpower needed. Cleared roads, partly paved and levelled through cuts and fills in the rugged terrain, formerly led from the image quarries to various sections of the island. Some brief

sections led down to the sea. In some instances statues as well as topknots must also have been transported along the coast by sturdy rafts, as is revealed by the discovery of an image and two topknots in the cleared channel approach to a paved landing slip near a coastal *ahu*.

When a statue had reached its final destination, which was pl 24 invariably a family *ahu*, it was left with its feet towards the long *ahu* wall. The major engineering task still remained: to lift the giant up to the level of the elevated *ahu* platform where it would next be tilted on end to balance on its base, high above the surrounding ground. A recent test of a traditional technique revealed to the writer by the present islanders disclosed that twelve natives could lift and erect a twenty-five-ton statue in eighteen days by means of two wooden levers and a large quantity of small stones. By adding labour and levers in proportion to the weight of the statue, even the largest Middle Period giants could be erected by a small trained team in a comparatively short time.

The method used was a continuing process of levering up first one and then the other long side of the statue, inserting stones pl 19 underneath to hold the newly gained advantage of each almost invisible levering movement. In this way the statue slowly rose into the air on a steadily growing pile of crude stone masonry. When it finally lay horizontal at the level of the top of the *ahu*, simultaneous levering operations on each side of the head and pl 20 shoulder section were started, and the same process of inserting smaller and bigger stones began to raise the head above the level of the feet, until the giant reached an angle of more than 45 degrees from the horizontal. Stays were now lashed to the statue to prevent pl 21 it from toppling over, and the underbuilding continued until the final and most critical moment when the pulling of ropes caused the giant to tip into a vertical position with its flat body base resting on top of a large slab built into the surface platform of the *ahu*.

Before the numerous stones accumulated during the erection pl 22 were removed from the front of the statue, the crude pile was used as a steep ramp up which the now ready-dressed topknot was lifted by the same ingenious method of levering and under-building. In many instances the topknot was morticed to the narrow, truncated head of the supporting image. Then the stone pile was removed and generally added to the wings of the *ahu* or used in a nearby structure. Thus the image of the venerated ancestor finally balanced free with its giant red topknot high on top of the masonry tomb that concealed the bones of the human being to whose spirit it was to give perpetual life for the benefit of coming generations. Only when the statue reached its *ahu* were the eyes opened as deep concavities, and the giant could stare into the ceremonial plaza where the family or tribe was gathered in awe and veneration.

The Family Village

Near the *ahu* lay the family village. It was different from any other settlement in Polynesia. Whereas wood, commonly thatched by plaited palm leaves, was the building material for all houses throughout the other islands, the Easter Island house was built from stone and *totora* reed. Instead of using the available forest supply for building rectangular dwellings, as on the nearest islands of Polynesia, or oval ones, as on those further away, the people who reached Easter Island made clearings in the forest to build *f 6* thick-walled circular houses of stone with entrances frequently through the roof, or peculiar lenticular houses of stone covered *f 7* by large slabs in false arch, or, finally, *totora* reed houses of exactly the same lenticular or reversed boat-shaped form. None of these house types occurs on the other islands, but circular stone houses with vertical walls, slab-covered structures built in false arch, and dwellings made partly or entirely from *totora* reed are all characteristic of ancient Peru, where wood was unknown for building purposes on the Pacific side. As opposed to the Polynesian custom, the cooking oven was sometimes placed in the middle of the stone houses, while, in the case of the reed houses, an un-Polynesian pentagonal stone oven was placed in front of the hut. In the Middle Period all these three non-Polynesian house types were used side by side on Easter Island, although contiguous clusters of thick-walled circular stone houses seemed to be more common in the eastern part of the island. It is not yet certain which of the

Corbelled and lenticular slab house, partly covered with soil, at the Middle Period ceremonial village of Orongo. This type, and thick-walled circular stone houses with thatched roofs, were common on early Easter Island. They are unknown elsewhere in Polynesia, but have parallels in ancient Peru. (6)

three forms belonged to the Early Period. There are reasons to believe that the lenticular reed-house developed out of the identically shaped corbelled slab house where the pointed house-ends were dictated by practical constructional needs.

The inventory of the Easter Island house was extremely sparse. The furniture consisted of stone pillows frequently ornamented *f 8*

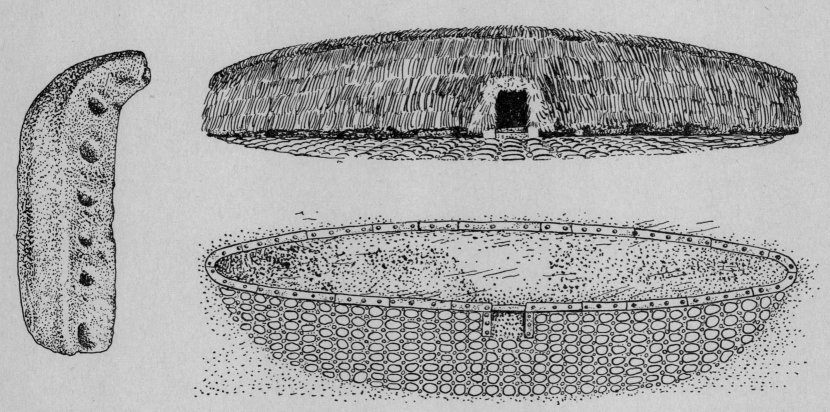

Plan (right, lower) and elevation of a house built of totora reeds. In front of the house is a cobbled area. The boat shape is laid out with 'paenga' foundation-stones in which holes were drilled (see detail, left) to take the framework holding the thatch of reeds. It seems likely that the shape derived from the identically shaped corbelled slab house, where the building method necessitated the pointed ends. (7)

Among the scanty furniture of the Easter Island houses were stone pillows, often with fertility symbols incised into them. The one above is decorated with a mask in three stages of production. (8)

Fish-hooks of polished stone or (above) of bone, simple and composite, are found in large quantities. Examples have been found of fish-hooks worked from human bone. (9)

The 'weeping eye' motif, which may represent the rain-god Hiro in a feather crown, decorates walls and ceilings of the ceremonial village at Orongo. This is a typical feature of early Peruvian cultures. (10)

with incised fertility symbols, and thick mats plaited from *totora* reeds. Beautiful polished stone bowls of hard basalt, crude picks, polished adzes and basalt saws, unique fish-hooks of polished stone *f 9* and simple and composite hooks of bone, bone needles, knitting tools for fishnets, files, grinding stones, and a variety of drills, scrapers, and cutting tools of obsidian completed their list of more imperishable utensils.

Although the religious concepts, art traditions, and architecture of the Middle Period people clearly set them apart from those of the Early Period, there is enough general correspondence between the two to indicate that they most probably came from the same general geographic area. It is interesting to note that the imported bird cult of the Middle Period is as unknown elsewhere in Polynesia as was the Early Period sun worship, whereas both are characteristic of the leading cultures in ancient Peru. Similarly, the slab-covered walls and ceilings of the Middle Period ceremonial village at Orongo were decorated with mural paintings represent-*f 11* ing hook-beaked bird deities, sickle-shaped reed boats, double-*10* bladed paddles, and the 'weeping eye' motive, non-Polynesian *pl 5* features all of which are characteristic of American cultures, and common in early Peru.

Bird-man motif incised on a rock at the ceremonial centre of Orongo. This crouching human figure with a bird's head (or bird mask) probably represents the bird-cult deity Haoa. (11)

The Coming of the Polynesians

This subdivided and disconnected, yet in many ways coherent and interrelated, double-period of apparently pure South American cult and culture on Easter Island did not extend to the end of the Middle Period. While the Middle Period cult was still at its peak with no sign of decline, a genuine Polynesian contingent arrived to collaborate in the local building of culture. The arriving Polynesians might have found the whereabouts of this tiny spot quite independently of their local predecessors by crossing for months into the contrary winds and currents of the completely empty *f 1* ocean off South America. However, archaeology indicates no conquest or other violence at the time of their arrival, and strati-

graphically there is no sudden change to a Polynesian material culture. On the contrary, the Polynesians arrived almost unnoticeably and adapted themselves quietly to locally existing non-Polynesian customs.

It is therefore an alternative possibility that they were shown this secluded spot by Middle Period Easter Islanders who had visited one of the larger and easily 'hit' down-wind groups of Polynesia and thence returned home. This impression is strengthened by the fact that the old Easter Island custom of erecting stone statues in human form spread to the Marquesas as late as during the Middle Period of Easter Island's history, indicating east-west contact between these islands just at that time. It is equally noteworthy that the Polynesians came to Easter Island in a peaceful or subdued manner, without introducing their own all-important gods, nor even such characteristic pan-Polynesian culture elements as the traditional stone pounder for beating taro into their staple *poi*, or the indispensable wooden mallet for beating the bark of the paper mulberry tree into *tapa* cloth. In spite of the fact that the Polynesian taro and paper mulberry tree were brought along to Easter Island, the arriving Polynesians abandoned entirely their *poi* pounder and the associate *poi* eating custom, and accepted the South American sweet potato as the one and only food staple of paramount importance on Easter Island. The wooden mallet was also discarded, and *tapa* was beaten into strips with a smooth pebble-stone and then sewn together with bone needle and thread, a method unlike that used on all Polynesian islands.

Even more remarkable is the fact that the arriving Polynesians abandoned their pan-Polynesian religion, including the worship of the primary gods Tu, Tane, and Tangaroa, as they were converted to the local Easter Island deities, the two gods Makemake and Haoa, unheard-of in all Polynesia. Whereas Haoa had essentially human attributes and was the centre of the important bird ceremonies that began with the Middle Period, Makemake was the real creator associated with the sun cult and depicted either as *f 12* a large-eyed mask or as a crouched feline creature with long claws, another important Peruvian trait unknown throughout Oceania.

The willingness of the Polynesian contingent to subscribe to already existing alien beliefs and customs on Easter Island, and the evidence of probable contact between Easter Island and the Marquesas group when the statuary art spread from the former to the latter area about the 14th century AD, halfway into the Middle Period, make it seem plausible that Middle Period Easter Islanders drew Polynesian labour from the Marquesas group to assist in their vast engineering tasks. There are, indeed, remarkable affinities between the Middle Period Easter Island image *ahu* and certain contemporaneous Marquesas Island statue platforms. However, apart from this and from some stone adze types that may hint at an arrival from the Marquesas, there seems to be nothing in the Middle Period material culture that might help further to pinpoint the port of embarkation of the Polynesian element that is so dominant on Easter Island today. Linguistically and physically the tie to Eastern Polynesia in general is, however, unmistakable.

Various evidence seems to reflect a period of peaceful collaboration between the arriving Polynesians and the pre-existing creators and architects of the giant image *ahu*. Archaeology clearly reveals, however, that this period of joint construction terminated in disastrous warfare with a sudden disruption of all work on the *ahu* and in the quarries. As work was abandoned statues were left in the quarry walls at all stages of progress, and the sculptors' stone tools were left scattered about in thousands all over the volcano side.

'Long-ears' and 'Short-ears': the Battle of Poike

By combining archaeologic evidence with ethnographic facts and traditional information preserved by the natives at the first advent of European settlers, we are able to reconstruct some of the main events that led to the downfall of the Middle Period culture and the initiation of the Late, or Decadent, Period that lasted well into historic times.

According to very firm beliefs on the island there were formerly two different people living together in friendship. They had come at different times and from opposite directions, and spoke two diverse languages. Traditions state that the actual island discoverer was King Hotu Matua who fled with his followers from a large country to the east when defeated in war. His home was a barren land where the sun at seasons shrivelled up all vegetation, and he discovered Easter Island by steering for two months towards the setting sun. He brought with him *kohau rongo-rongo*, or written tablets, built a village of stone houses on the east coast, and started quarrying the first statues. According to some royal genealogies this island discoverer arrived fifty-seven generations ago, according to others only thirty. At a more recent time, or twenty-two generations ago, another king named Tuu-ko-ihu arrived from an island in the opposite direction, in the far west, bringing with him the banished ancestors of most of the present Easter Islanders. Upon arrival they found the earlier people and their giant stone statues, and the Polynesian newcomers from the west 'adopted the religion which they found upon the island.' According to tradition the original Easter Island stone sculptors were termed *Hanau-eepe*, or 'Long-ears', owing to their custom of enlarging the ear lobes artificially through inserting large disks, whereas the ancestors of the present population were termed *Hanau-momoko*, or 'Short-ears', for distinction. For a period of *karau-karau*, or two hundred years, the Short-ears toiled patiently for the Long-ears by assisting them in their great works on the island. Large *ahu* were built, and ever greater statues were dragged from the Rano Raraku quarries and erected on the chiefly Long-ear tombs. Although there were instances of intermarriage between the two peoples, only six of the *ahu* images were carved with short ears; all the rest had extended lobes which clearly depicted Long-ears.

Tradition goes on to record that this two-century-long period of peaceful collaboration ended when the Long-ears had made the Short-ears clear the entire eastern peninsula of Poike of stones. The work was already done, and Poike left as a green field in contrast to the rest of the black lava-studded island, when the Short-ears were ordered to clear all the rest of the island the same way. Now their long patience was exhausted, and their kin united in revolt, chasing the Long-ears into the Poike peninsula where they fortified themselves behind the large excavated defensive ditch which they filled with brushwood to set on fire if the Short-ears attacked. By plotting with an old Short-ear woman married into the Long-ear people, some of the Short-ears got around the ditch while the others pretended a frontal attack, and when the Long-ears lit their defensive pyre they were caught by surprise and pushed into their own fire from behind. Of the adult Long-ear men only one, Ororoina, was spared to let his race continue.

According to tradition this event took place twelve generations ago, computed by genealogists to be about AD 1680, and the names of Ororoina's successors are preserved down to the still living Atan family, who are reckoned among the natives as the only direct descendants in paternal line from the formerly so important Long-ear people.

pl 37

However, the huge sand-filled Poike ditch was long thought by Europeans to be a natural formation, and little credit was given to the tradition of the pyre until the ditch was recently examined by excavation. It proved to be the elaborate work of man, and all along its length were carbon and ashes from an extensive pyre, which radio-carbon analysis dated to approximately AD 1676, which concurs perfectly with the vivid native memories.

The Downfall of the Giants

With the battle of Poike and the nearly complete extermination of the Long-ears the Middle Period ended. All megalithic work on Easter Island ceased abruptly, the quarries were left as they were, and along the roads lay blind statues deserted for ever while in the

pl 28

course of transport. The victorious Short-ears divided the land between them, and the numerous *ahu* and statues that had survived the war were considered valuable booty by the owner of the surrounding land. When work ceased nearly three hundred statues

pl 29

were abandoned lying or standing in the quarry area, some abandoned because of a flaw or accident during work, some still in the process of being sculptured. Others lay along the roads, and two hundred and thirty-one had been already erected on top of *ahu*. The largest erected on an *ahu* was 33 feet tall and weighed about 82 tons. In addition to its own height it carried a 6 by 8 feet red

The round eyes and Y-shaped nose of Makemake in the shape of a double-headed animal, carved in low relief; the two heads share a short body and each provides two legs. This is one of the many forms in which the Makemake mask appears. (12)

stone cylinder, weighing nearly 12 tons, on top of its head. The magnitude of the work was still increasing when it was interrupted. The largest blind statue raised at the foot of the quarries to have its back finished was more than 37 feet tall, and another, measuring almost 70 feet in length, was in preparation with its back still attached to the volcano wall. Topknots were abandoned under way to various parts of the island, and many were stored on the rim of the scoria crater, the largest measuring 650 cubic feet and weighing roughly 30 tons.

Weapons, which are unknown in the deposits from the Early and Middle Period on Easter Island, commence with the Poike war. Sling stones are found in the Poike ditch, and a spear-point of local obsidian, the *mataa*, was developed out of a Middle Period cutting tool and increased in importance with explosive force to become the most numerous and characteristic artifact of the Late Period, being still found today by the thousand all over the island surface. Archaeological deposits show that cutting tools for wood, too, increase remarkably with the beginning of the Late Period, indicating that wood carving rather than stone sculpturing was the handicraft of the Short-eared, or Polynesian, victors.

f 13

Heavy rain gradually washed quarry rubble and talus down the volcano slope to bury the blind, standing statues up to their chest, neck, or chin, since nobody attempted any more to move these nearly finished colossi away to their waiting *ahu*. Fire was occasionally lit in front of the blind giants at the volcano's foot, and food offerings and bundle burials at different levels were covered up by falling rubble, revealing that worship went on below the giant heads until about 1840, or well into historic times. Ceremonies also continued at the unmolested *ahu*, with white beach pebbles and seaweed being thrown onto the topknots of the open-eyed giants standing aloft gazing over the plazas, and family burials were regularly added to the *ahu* tombs.

pl 25
27

However, peace was not the result of the Poike war. A new split arose among the population. Tradition states that the inhabitants of Hotuiti near Poike and the image quarries, where Ororoina was permitted to survive, called themselves Ko-Hotu, or Hotu Matua's people, whereas the rest of the island population called themselves Ko-Tuu, or Tuu-ko-iho's people, and soon quarrels and plunderings ended in a civil war that lasted until the arrival of the missionaries about 1864. During this war nobody was spared, neither women nor children, cannibal orgies raged, houses were torn apart and burnt, and in revenge the pride of the various families, their inherited image *ahu*, were demolished and the giant statues made to fall through undermining and pulling with cords. One by one the enormous giants toppled face to the ground; some broke in the fall, with their powerful masks buried in the plaza side of the *ahu* and their huge topknots rolling away along the platform.

In this period, when even the enemy fields were scorched, the Easter Islanders abandoned their stone and reed houses and resorted to underground caves. Natural caverns formed in pre-human times by liquid under-currents of lava and by volcanic gas abound on Easter Island. Some have a quite considerable length with narrow tunnels uniting spacious chambers. Their openings were now narrowed by crude masonry to chimney-like tubes and covered by slabs to become invisible from the outside. Some twisted down underground in long right-angled steps so narrow that they could only be penetrated by wriggling with arms over-head. A few of these caves contained underground water, and here the various families lived a miserable life, in time of war ascending only at night.

This period was termed *huri-moai* by the native Easter Islanders, which means the 'Overthrow-of-statue' period. Nothing would enrage the enemy more than to see the giant statue, the pride of his land, tumble to the ground with no possibility of ever having it re-erected. Tradition recalls that the last statue to fall was the 33-foot giant Paro, with its 12-ton topknot, on the north-east coast. It was pulled down in revenge during a terrible cannibal feast about 1840. The Late Period people never attempted to re-erect a fallen statue. In periods of peace they made large *paina* figures of *tapa* stuffed with *totora* reed to erect in front of the *ahu* at mortuary ceremonies. Alternatively they often raised on their *ahu* ruins a dressed Middle Period *paenga*, or house-foundation stone, as substitute for a true statue. The failure to re-erect the overthrown giants was probably due to the lack of organized force as well as the constant threat of new enemy assaults that would triumph by toppling the giant over once more.

The Trail of Civil War

In the Late Period the fires ravaged the remaining vegetation on Easter Island. Pollen borings reveal that in the upper strata of soil deposits, representing the later levels, soot particles increased remarkably in quantity while pollen diminished, and many plant species became extinct. In the uppermost levels the pollen deposits reflect how grass and ferns conquered the former Easter Island forest and entirely dominate the now barren land, where former streams became dry ravines. Undoubtedly, these final forest fires reflect deliberate destruction during tribal wars. The fires were arrested only at the edge of the wet bogs covering the crater lakes, where the aquatic species introduced by the Early Period discoverers were left to abound until the present as the principal building material for house and water-craft.

The remains of fires, killing, and violent destruction from the *huri-moai* activities of the Late Period are ever-present on Easter Island. Everything too big to be portable was destroyed, and everything small enough to be carried away was rescued and hidden in the countless secret caves. In this period, undoubtedly, began the custom of hoarding property in secret storage caves, the entrance to which was known only to its owner or to a leading member of the family. Here portable treasures captured or in-

herited from former generations were stored and protected, and the system of guardian spirits, or *aku-aku*, became an important social factor. Whereas belief in the original gods gradually faded, and entirely disappeared with the introduction of Christianity towards the end of the 19th century, belief in a large number of *aku-aku*, or ancestral spirits, increased and still survives among a great portion of the population. The fear of punishment by an *aku-aku* was so great that a secret family storage cave would hardly be entered by an uninitiated person even if discovered by accident.

Originally, *rongo-rongo* tablets, *moai-kavakava* statuettes, and other Late Period wood carvings of ceremonial importance were hidden together with small stone sculptures from earlier periods in these caves, but as it appeared that the wooden figures decayed through time and crumbled at a touch, soft lava was resorted to as a medium of preserving and perpetuating art motifs, mythic concepts, and magic objects. The many generations of ancestor worship on Easter Island, strengthened by awe and admiration for the former creators of the giant local statues from which they could never escape on the little barren island, made former styles and concepts survive for centuries with the same rigidity as oral tradition.

A remarkable creation of Late Period origin is the *moai-kavakava*, a lean, hook-nosed, goatee-bearded, and emaciated figure with long, pendent ears. Thousand of specimens of this figure have been carved on the island, and specimens carved for tourists today are all like those obtained by Cook and other early voyagers. According to tradition the first *moai-kavakava* was carved by a Short-ear king who saw two of the last Long-ears hiding in the crater of the topknot quarries. He made the figure to ensure that the appearance of the exterminated Long-ears should be preserved for coming generations on the island.

The custom of extending the ear lobes was taken over by the victors and continued among certain Easter Islanders until recent times, possibly primarily among those who claimed to possess Long-ear blood either on the paternal or maternal side. Another characteristic expressly noted on Easter Island from the time of the first discovery until the missionary arrival, and appearing even among the Atan family of the present time, is the sporadic occurrence of very light skin and red hair, combined with Europoid features and aquiline nose. Tradition and genealogical studies show that these features run back for generations, and they seem to continue back through time as represented in the stern, tight-lipped stone giants with long ears, and topknots carved from a rock of a specially selected red colour.

Future archaeological work will probably reveal that the present population on Easter Island derives from the Marquesas Group. But the links between the founders of the earlier Easter Island cultures and ancient Peru are becoming increasingly clear and the mystery of their origin is somehow connected with that of the founders of the great South American civilizations, and more particularly the early megalithic centre of Tiahuanaco, the influence of which swept along the Andean highlands and down to the entire Pacific desert coast of early Peru. The Inca records of their fair and long-eared predecessors who were driven from their stone quarries and extensive statuary activity at Tiahuanaco to disappear westwards into the open Pacific have too much in common with the Polynesian records on Easter Island to be ignored as mere native myth, if we take the concrete archaeological and botanical evidence into account.

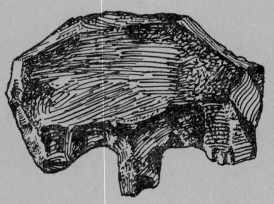  

The 'mataa', an obsidian spear-point developed from a Middle Period cutting tool. Found in thousands all over the island, it is the most characteristic Late Period artifact—a result of the Poike war and its aftermath. (13)

SELECT BIBLIOGRAPHY

LIST AND SOURCES OF ILLUSTRATIONS

INDEX

Select Bibliography

II The Fertile Sahara

BREUIL, H. 'Les Roches peintes du Tassili-n-Ajjer', extract from *Actes du IIème Congrès panafricain de Préhistoire, Alger, 1952* (1954)

CAPOT-REY, R. *Le Sahara français* (1953)

FROBENIUS, L. *Hádschra Máktuba* (1925)
Ekade Ektab (1937)

LHOTE, H. *The Search for the Tassili Frescoes* (1959)
In *Art of the World: The Stone Age* (1961)
L'Épopée du Ténéré (1961)

McBURNEY, C.B.M. *The Stone Age of Northern Africa* (1960)
Resultats scientifiques de la Mission Berliet-Ténéré-Tchad (1962)

VAUFREY, R. 'L'Art rupestre nord-africain'. *Archives de l'Institut de Paléontologie humaine*, mem. 20 (1939)

III City of Black Gold

(Abbreviation: NMSR – Occasional Papers of the National Museums of Southern Rhodesia)

BENT, T. *The Ruined Cities of Mashonaland* (1892; 3rd ed. 1895)

CATON-THOMPSON, G. *The Zimbabwe Culture* (1931)

FROBENIUS, L. *Erithräa* (1931)

HALL, R.N. *Great Zimbabwe* (1905)
Prehistoric Rhodesia (1909)

HALL, R.N. & NEAL, W.G. *The Ancient Ruins of Rhodesia* (1902)

MACIVER, D.R. *Medieval Rhodesia* (1906)

MAUCH, K. 'Reisen im Inneren von Süd-Afrika. 1865–1872' in *Petermanns Mitteilungen.* Ergänzungsheft no. 37 (1874)

MENNELL, F.R. & SUMMERS, R. 'The Ancient Workings of Southern Rhodesia' in NMSR no. 20 (1955)

POSSELT, F.W.T. *Fact and Fiction* (1935)

POSSELT, J.W. 'Early Days of Mashonaland and a Visit to the Zimbabwe Ruins' in NADA II (1924)

ROBINSON, K.R. *Khami Ruins* (1959)

SCHLICHTER, H. 'Travels and Researches in Rhodesia' in *Geographical Journ.* XIII (1899)

SCHOFIELD, J. F. 'Zimbabwe: a Critical Examination of the Building Methods Employed' in *South African Journ. of Science* XXIII (1926)

SUMMERS, R. *Inyanga* (1958)

SUMMERS, R., ROBINSON, K. R. & WHITTY, A. 'Zimbabwe Excavations 1958' in NMSR no. 23 A (1961)

WILLOUGHBY, SIR JOHN, BT *Further Excavations at Zimbabwe* (1893)

IV The X-Group Enigma

(Abbreviation: SNR – Sudan Notes and Records)

BATES, O. & DUNHAM, D. 'Excavations at Gammai' in *Harvard African Studies* VIII (1937)

BUDGE, E.W. *The Egyptian Sudan* (2 vols. 1936)

DUNHAM, D. *Royal Tombs at Meroe and Barkal* (1957)

EMERY, W. B. *Royal Tombs at Ballana and Qustul* (with chapters by L. P. KIRWAN. 2 vols. 1938)
Nubian Treasure (1948)

EMERY, W. B. & KIRWAN, L. P. *Excavations and Survey from Wadi-es-Sebua to Adindan* (2 vols. 1935)

FRAZER, P. M. 'Bibliography; Greco-Roman Egypt' in *Journ. of Egyptian Archaeology* 42 (Dec. 1961), 147. For the Greek inscription from Ikhmindi

KIRWAN, L. P. *Oxford University Excavations at Firka* (1939)
'Studies in the Later History of Nubia' in *Liverpool Annals of Archaeology and Anthropology* XXIV (1937), nos 1–2
'A Contemporary Account of the Conversion of the Sudan to Christianity' in SNR 20 (1937), 289–95
'A Survey of Nubian Origins' in SNR 20 (1937), 47–62
'The Ballana Civilization' in *Bull. de la Soc. Roy. de Géogr. d'Egypte* XXV (Mar. 1953), 103–10

KIRWAN, L. P. 'Rome Beyond the Southern Egyptian Frontier' in *Geographical Journ.* CXXII (Mar. 1957), 13–19
'Tanqasi and the Noba' in *Kush* V (1957), 37–41
'Comments on the Origin and History of the Nobatae of Procopius' in *Kush* VI (1958), 69–73
'The Decline and Fall of Meroe' in *Kush* VIII (1960), 163–73

MONNERET DE VILLARD, U. *Storia della Nubia cristaina* (1938)
'Le necropoli di Ballana e di Qostol' in *Orientalia* IX (1940), 61–75

V Who were the Ancient Ainu?

Western literature on the Ainu belongs for the most part to the end of the nineteenth century and the beginning of the present century, as do also some pioneering western books on Japanese prehistoric antiquities which are still valuable. Apart from *Japan before Buddhism* by Dr J. Edward Kidder, Jr in the *Ancient Peoples and Places* series no systematic account of the early Japanese cultures has been published in the west. There are on the other hand a number of valuable specialized works recently published by occidental scholars. No attempt is made here to indicate even the chief introductory works in Japanese, beyond listing Y. Kobayashi's *A General Introduction to Japanese Archaeology (Nihon Kōkogaku Gaisetsu)*, in which the linguistically equipped reader will find rather full reference to the Japanese literature of the subject.

ASTON, W.G. *Nihongi* (2 vols. 1896)

BATCHELOR, J. *The Ainu of Japan* (1892)

BEARDSLEY, R.K. 'Japan before History: A Survey of the Archaeological Record' in *The Far Eastern Quarterly* XIV (1955), no. 3

BUHOT, J. *Histoire des Arts du Japon* I (1949)

CHAMBERLAIN, B.H. 'An Aino Bear Hunt' in *Transactions of the Asiatic Society of Japan* XV (1884)

EJUSD *The Ainu and their Folk-Lore* (publ. by The Religious Tract Society, London, 1901)
'The Japanese Gohei and the Ainu Inao' in *Journ. Anthropological Inst. G. Britain and Ireland* XXIII (1901)
The Jōmon Pottery of Japan (1957)

GROOT, G. J. *The Prehistory of Japan* (1952)

GROOT, G. J. & SHINOTO, Y. *The Shell Mound of Ubayama* (1952)

KIDDER, J.E., Jr *Japan before Buddhism* (1959)

KOBAYASHI, Y. *Nihon Kōkogaku Gaisetsu* (1951)

MacRITCHIE, D. 'The Ainos', suppl. to *Internationales Archiv für Ethnographie* IV (1892)

MARINGER, J. 'A Core and Flake Industry of Palaeolithic Type from Central Japan' in *Artibus Asiae* XIX (1956), no. 2, 111–25

MUNRO, N.G. *Prehistoric Japan* (2nd ed. 1911)

SCHNELL, I. 'Prehistoric Finds from the Island World of the Far East' in *Bull. Mus. Far Eastern Antiquities* IV (1932), 13–104

TORII, R. *Les Ainou des Îles Kouriles* (1919)

VI The Collapse of the Khmers

BHATTACHARYA, K. *Les Religions brahmaniques dans l'ancien Cambodge* (1961)

BOISSELIER, J. *La Statuaire Khmère et son Évolution* (1955)

BRIGGS, L. P. *The Ancient Khmer Empire* (1951)

COEDÈS, G. *Pour mieux comprendre Angkor* (1947)
Les États hindouisés d'Indochine et d'Indonésie (1948)
Les Peuples de la Péninsule indochinoise (1962)

DUPONT, P. *La Statuaire préangkorienne* (1955)

GITEAU, M. *Histoire du Cambodge* (1957)

GLAIZE, M. *Les Monuments du Groupe d'Angkor* (1948)

GROSLIER, B. P. *Angkor: Art and Civilization* (1957)
'Nouvelles Recherches à Angkor', *Compte-Rendu à l'Academie des Inscriptions et Belles-Lettres, Paris* (1960)
Indochine: Carrefour des Arts (1961)

GROSLIER, G. *Recherches sur les Cambodgiens* (1921)

MARCHAL, H. *Le Décor et la Sculpture khmers* (1951)
Les Temples d'Angkor (1955)

MOUHOT, H. *Travels in the central parts of Indo-China* (1864)

PARMENTIER, H. *L'Art Khmer classique* (1939)

PELLIOT, P. *Mémoires sur les Coutumes du Cambodge par Tcheou Ta Kouan* (1951)

PYM, C. *The Ancient Civilization of Angkor* (in preparation)

RÉMUSAT, G. DE C. *L'Art Khmer: les grandes Étapes de son Évolution* (1951)

Articles in many journals especially those of G. COEDÈS, L. FINOT, V. GOLOUBEW, H. PARMENTIER and P. STERN in the *Bulletin de l'École Française d'Extrème-Orient*, the *Bulletin de la Commission Archéologique Indochinoise*, and the *Journal Asiatique*. Occasional publications of the EFEO especially *Mémoires Archéologiques* and *Inscriptions du Cambodge* (ed. G. COEDÈS). Future studies of interest are expected from K. BHATTACHARYA on Buddhism at Angkor; from P. STERN on the Bayon; and B-P. GROSLIER on excavations at Angkor.

VII The Gods that Failed

(Abbreviation: CIWP – Carnegie Institution of Washington Publications)

KELEMEN, P. *Medieval American Art* (2 vols. 1943)

KUBLER, G. *The Art and Architecture of Ancient America* (1962)

LA FARGE, O. *Santa Eulalia. The Religion of a Cuchumatan Indian Town* (1947)

LANDA, DIEGO DE 'Relación de Las Cosas de Yucatán'. English translation and notes by A. M. Tozzer. *Papers of the Peabody Museum of Archaeology and Ethnology* XVIII (1941; original c. 1566)

MARQUINA, I. 'Arquitectura prehispanica' in *Instituto Nacional de Antropología e Historia, Memorias* I (1951)

MORLEY, S.G. *The Ancient Maya* (3rd ed. revised by G.W. Brainerd, 1956)

OAKES, M. *The Two Crosses of Todos Santos. Survivals of Mayan Religious Ritual* (1951)

PROSKOURIAKOFF, T. 'An Album of Maya Architecture' in CIWP no. 558 (1946)
'A Study of Classic Maya Sculpture' in CIWP no. 593 (1950)

ROYS, R.L. 'The Indian Background of Colonial Yucatán' in CIWP no. 548 (1943)

THOMPSON, J.E.S. *The Rise and Fall of Maya Civilization* (1956)
Maya Archaeologist (1963)

VIII The Etruscan Problem

History and Antiquities

BANTI, L. *Il Mondo degli Etruschi* (1960)

BLOCH, R. *The Etruscans* (1960)

CIBA FOUNDATION *Medical Biology and Etruscan Origins* (1959)

DENNIS, G. *Cities and Cemeteries of Etruria* (3rd ed. 1883)

DUCATI, P. *Etruria Antica* (2 vols. 1927)

HEURGON, J. *La Vie quotidienne chez les Etrusques* (1961)

MACIVER, D.R. *Villanovans and Early Etruscans* (1924)

PALLOTTINO, M. *The Etruscans* (1955)
L'Origine degli Etruschi (1947)

VACANO, O.W. VON *The Etruscans in the Ancient World* (1960)

WATMOUGH, J. *The Foundations of Roman Italy* (1937)

Art

ANDRÉN, A. *Architectural Terracottas from Etrusco-Italic Temples* (1940)

BEAZLEY, J.D. *Etruscan Vase Painting* (1947)

DUCATI, P. *Storia dell'Arte Etrusca* (2 vols. 1927)

GIGLIOLI, G.A. *L'Arte Etrusca* (1935)

PALLOTTINO, M. *Art of the Etruscans* (1955)
Etruscan Painting (1952)

POULSEN, F. *Etruscan Tomb Paintings* (1922)

RIIS, P.J. *An Introduction to Etruscan Art* (1953)

SANTANGELO, M. *Musei e Monumenti Etruschi* (1960)

Religion and Language

CLEMEN, C. *Die Religion der Etrusker* (1930)

GRENIER, A. *Les Religions étrusque et romaine* (1948)

PALLOTTINO, M. *Elementi di Lingua etrusca* (1936)
Testimonia di Lingua Etrusca (1954)

IX The Sabian Mysteries

(Abbreviation AS – Anatolian Studies)

BRANDT, W. *Elchasai, ein Religionsstifter und sein Werk* (1912)

CHWOLSON, D. *Die Ssabier und der Ssabismus* (1856)

COLPE, C. 'Mandäer' in *Die Religion in Geschichte und Gegenwart* (3rd ed., ed. K. Galling, IV, 1960)

DOZY, R. & DE GOEJE, M.J. 'Nouveaux Documents pour l'Étude de la Religion des Harraniens' in *Actes du sixième Congrès international des Orientalistes tenu... à Leide* I (1884), 281–366

DROWER, E.S. *The Mandaeans of Iraq and Iran. Their Cults, Customs, Magic, Legends and Folklore* (new ed. 1962)
The Haran Gawaita (1953)

DUVAL, R. *Histoire politique, religieuse et littéraire d'Édesse jusqu'à la première Croisade* (1892; reprinted from articles in *Journ. asiatique* 8th ser. XVIII–XIX, 1891–2)

GADD, C.J. 'The Harran Inscriptions of Nabonidus' in AS VIII (1958), 35–92

KIRSTEN, E. 'Edessa' in *Reallexikon für Antike und Christentum*, ed. Th. Klauser, IV (1959)

LLOYD, S. & BRICE, W. 'Harran' in AS I (1951), 77–111

MEZ, A. *Die Stadt Harran bis zum Einfall der Araber* (1892)

PEDERSEN, J. 'The Ṣābians' in *A Volume of Oriental Studies presented to Edward G. Brown*, ed. T.W. Arnold and R.A. Nicholson (1922), 383–91

POGNON, H. *Inscriptions sémitiques de la Syrie, de la Mésopotamie et de la Région de Mossoul* (1907)

RICE, D.S. 'Medieval Harran: Studies on its Topography and Monuments, I' in AS II (1952), 38–84

SACHAU, C.E. *The Chronology of Ancient Nations... Athâr-ul-bâkiya of Albîrûnî...* (1879)

SEGAL, J.B. 'Pagan Syriac Monuments in the Vilayet of Urfa' in AS III (1953), 97–119
'Some Syriac Inscriptions of the 2nd – 3rd Century A.D.' in *Bull. of the School of Oriental and African Studies* XVI (1954), 13–36
'Mesopotamian Communities from Julian to the Rise of Islam' in *Proceedings of the British Academy* XLI (1956), 109–39
Edessa and Harran (1963)

X The Peoples of the Highland

(Abbreviations: EX – Expedition, the Bulletin of the University Museum of Pennsylvania; UMBP – University Museum Bulletin, Philadelphia)

General

CAMERON, G.G. *A History of Early Iran* (1936)

GHIRSHMAN, R. *L'Iran des Origines à l'Islam* (1951)

HERZFELD, E.E. *Iran in the Ancient East* (1941)

OLMSTEAD, A.T. *History of the Persian Empire* (1948)

VANDEN BERGHE, L. *Archéologie de l'Iran ancien* (1959)

Luristan

DUMÉZIL, G. 'Dieux cassites et dieux védiques à propos d'un bronze de Luristan' in *Revue Hittite et Asianique* X, FASC. 2 (1950), 18–37.

DUSSAUD, R. 'The Bronzes of Luristan' in A.U. Pope *A Survey of Persian Art* (1938) vol. I, 254–77 with figs. 53–68 and vol. IV, pls. 25–72
'Anciens Bronzes du Luristan et Cultes iraniens' in *Syria* XXVI (1949), 196–229

GHIRSHMAN, R. et al. *Sept Mille Ans d'Art en Iran* (catalogue of the Exhibition of Iranian Art at the Petit Palais, Paris, Oct. 1961 – Jan. 1962)

GODARD, A. *Les Bronzes du Luristan. Ars Asiatica* XVII (1931)

LEGRAIN, L. *Luristan Bronzes in the University Museum, Philadelphia* (1934)

MINORSKY, V. 'The Luristan Bronzes' in *Apollo* XIII (1931), 141–42

PRZEWORSKI, S. 'Luristan Bronzes in the Collection of Mr Frank Savery' in *Archaeologia* 88 (1940), 229–69

ROSTOVTSEV, M. 'Some Remarks on the Luristan Bronzes' in *IPEK* VII (1931), 45–56

Mannai

BARNETT, R.D. 'The Treasure of Ziwiye' in *Iraq* XVIII (1956), 111–16

DYSON, R.H. 'Iran 1956' in UMBP XXI (1957), 37–39
'Iran 1957' in UMBP XXII (1958), 25–32
'Digging in Iran. Hasanlu 1958' in EX (Spring 1959), 4–18
'Death of a City' in EX (Spring 1960), 2–11

GODARD, A. *Le Trésor de Ziwiyé.* Publications du Service Archéologique de l'Iran (1950)

PORADA, EDITH 'The Hasanlu Bowl' in EX (Spring 1959), 19–22

SULIMIRSKI, T. 'Scythian Antiquities in Western Asia' in *Artibus Asiae* XVII (1954) nos. 3–4, 282–314

Urartu

ADONTZ, N. *Histoire d'Arménie* (1946)

AKURGAL, E. 'Urartäische Kunst' in *Anatolia* IV (1959), 77–114
Die Kunst Anatoliens von Homer bis Alexander (1961)

BARNETT, R.D. & WATSON, W. 'Russian Excavations in Armenia' in *Iraq* XIV, 2 (1952), 132–47
'Further Russian Excavations in Armenia' in *Iraq* XXI, 1 (1959), 1–19

BURNEY, C.A. 'Urartian Fortresses in the Van Region' in *Anatolian Studies* VII (1957), 37–53

GROUSSET, R. *Histoire de l'Arménie* (1947)

LEHMANN-HAUPT, C. *Armenien einst und jetzt* (2 vols. 1910, 1931)

PIOTROVSKY, B.B. *Karmir-Blur* (3 vols. in Russian 1949–1955)
'L'Ourartou' in *Ourartou, Néapolis des Scythes, Kharezm* (1954)
L'Orient ancien illustré VIII (1954)
'Urartu' in *Lebende Vergangenheit* (1954)

SCHACHERMEYER, F. 'Tuschpa' in M. Ebert *Reallexikon der Vorgeschichte* XIII (1929), 487–98

XI Bridge to the Ancient East

(Abbreviations: APAMNH – Anthropological Papers of the American Museum of Natural History; MDAFA – Mémoires de la Délégation archéologique française en Afghanistan)

CASAL, J.-M. 'The Afghanistan of Five Thousand Years Ago: Excavating the Huge Bronze-Age Mound of Mundigak' in *Illus. London News* (May 7, 1959), 832–34

DUPREE, L. 'Shamshir Ghar: Historic Cave Site in Kandahar Province, Afghanistan' in APAMNH XLVI pt. 2 (1958), 141–311

FAIRSERVIS, W.A., JR 'Preliminary Report on the Prehistoric Archeology of the Afghan-Baluch Areas' in *Amer. Mus. Novitates* no. 1587 (1952)

347

FAIRSERVIS, W. A., JR 'Excavations in the Quetta Valley, West Pakistan'in APAMNH XLV pt. 2 (1956), 169–402
  'The Chronology of the Harappān Civilization and the Aryan Invasions' in *Man* LVI (1956) art. 173, 153–56
  'Archeological Surveys in the Zhob and Loralai Districts, West Pakistan' in APAMNH XLVII pt. 2 (1959), 277–447

GHIRSHMAN, R. *Fouilles de Sialk* (2 vols. 1938, 1939)
  'Fouilles de Nadi-Ali dans le Seistan afghan' in *Revue des Arts asiatiques* XIII (1939) no.1, 10–22
  L'Iran (1951)

HACKIN, J. & CARL, J. *Nouvelles Recherches archéologiques à Bamiyan* (MDAFA III, 1933)
  Recherches archéologiques à Begram (MDAFA IX, 2 vols. 1939)

HACKIN, J., CARL, J. & MEUNIE, J. *Diverses Recherches archéologiques en Afghanistan (1933–40)* (1959)

HEINE-GELDERN, R. 'The Coming of the Aryans and the End of the Harappān Civilization' in *Man* LVI (1956) art. 151, 136–40

MASSON, V. M. *Ancient Farming Cultures of Margiana* (Materialy i Issledovania po Arkheologii SSSR no. 73) (1959)

OLMSTEAD, A.T. *History of the Persian Empire* (1948)
  History of the Persian Empire (1959)

PIGGOTT, S. *Prehistoric India to 1000 BC* (1950)

SCHMIDT, E.F. 'Excavation at Tepe Hissar, Damghan' in *Publications of the Iranian Section of the University Museum, Philadelphia* (1937)

STEIN, SIR AUREL *Innermost Asia. Detailed Report of Explorations in Central Asia, Kan-Su and eastern Iran* (4 vols. 1928)
  Archaeological Reconnaissances in north-western India and south-eastern Iran (1937)

TARN, W.W. *The Greeks in Bactria and India* (2nd ed. 1951)

TATE, G. P. *Seistan. A Memoir on the History, Topography, Ruins and People* (2 vols. 1910, 1912)

VANDEN BERGHE, L. *Archéologie de l'Iran ancien* (1959)

WHEELER, SIR R. E. M. 'The Indus Civilization' in *The Cambridge History of India* (suppl. vol., 1953)

XII The Forgotten Sarmatians

BENINGER, E. 'Der westgotisch-alanische Zug nach Mitteleuropa' in *Mannus-Bibliothek* 51 (1931)

BURY, J. B. *History of the Later Roman Empire* (2 vols. 1923)
  Cambridge Ancient History, relevant chapters in vols. VIII (1930), IX (1932), XI (1936), XII (1939)

DVORNIK, F. *The Making of Central and Eastern Europe* (1949)
  The Slavs. Their Early History and Civilization (1956)

HARMATTA, J. *Studies on the History of the Sarmatians* (1950)
  Istoria Rominiei (1960), relevant chapters
  Journal of Roman Studies. Articles by I. A. Richmond and E. H. Thompson in vols. XXXIV (1944) and XLVI (1956)

LOT, F. *La Fin du Monde antique et le Début du Moyen Âge* (1927)

PAULY-WISSOWA *Real-Encyclopädie* relevant entries

PARDUCZ, M. 'Denkmäler der Sarmatenzeit Ungarns' in *Archaeologia Hungarica* XXV (1941), XXVIII (1944), XXX (1950); Acta Archaeologica Acad. Sci. Hungaricae VII (1956)

ROSTOVTSEV, M. *Iranians and Greeks in South Russia* (1922)

SCHMIDT, L. *Geschichte der deutschen Stämme* (1940)

THOMPSON, E. A. *A history of Attila and the Huns* (1948)

VERNADSKY, G. *Ancient Russia* (1944)

WERNER, J. *Beiträge zur Archäologie des Attila-Reiches* (1956)

A huge literature on the subject exists in Russian, and among the more recent studies should be mentioned those by B.N. Grakov, K.F. Smirnov, V. A. Kuznetsov, S. A. Pletnerova, A. I. Meliukova, I. V. Sinitsin, M. P. Abramova, M. I. Vyazmitina, B. A. Rybakov, etc. in the periodicals *Sovetskaya Arkheologia* vols. VI, 3, 4 (1957), XIV, 1, 2 (1959), XVII, 1 (1962); *Kratkie Soobscenia* IIMK nos. 32 (1950), 34 (1950), 37 (1951), etc.; *Materialy i Issledovania po Arkheologii* SSSR nos. 101 (1961), 106 (1962); *Arkheologia-Kiev* vols. VII, VIII (in Ukrainian). Also important is the relevant chapter in *Narysy Staradavnoi Istorii Ukrainskoi RSR* (in Ukrainian, 1957); and also the book by E. I. Solomonik on Sarmatian 'tamga' signs (1959).

XIII The Migration of the Megaliths

(Abbreviation: *Ant.* – Antiquity)

General

CHILDE, V. G. *The Dawn of European Civilization* (6th ed. 1957)
  Prehistoric Migrations in Europe (1950)

DANIEL, G. E. *The Megalith Builders of Western Europe* (1958)

PEET, T.W. *Rough Stone Monuments and their Builders* (1912)

Malta

EVANS, J. D. *Malta* (1960)
  'C 14 Date for the Maltese Early Neolithic' in *Ant.* XXXV (June 1961)

BREA, L. B. 'Malta and the Mediterranean' in *Ant.* XXXIV (June 1960)

Spain and Portugal

BLANCE, B. M. 'Early Bronze Age Colonists in Iberia' in *Ant.* XXXV (Sept. 1961)

CARTAILHAC, E. *Les Ages préhistoriques de l'Espagne et du Portugal* (1886)

JALHAY, E. & PAÇO A. DO 'A Gruta II da Necropole de Alapraia' in *Anais Academia Portuguesa da Historia* IV (1941)

LEISNER, V. & G. *Die Megalithgräber der iberischen Halbinsel. Der Suden* (1943); *Der Westen* (1956 & 1960)
  Antas do Concelho de Reguengos de Monsaraz (1951)

LEISNER, V., PAÇO, A. DO & RIBEIRA, L. 'Grutas artificias de San Pedro do Estoril' in *Memorias do Servicos Geologicos de Portugal* (1962)

MARQUEZ, C. C. & LEISNER, V. & G. *Los Sepulchros Megaliticos de Huelva* (1952)

PAÇO A. DO & SANGMEISTER, E. 'Vila Nova de San Pedro, eine befestigte Siedlung der Kupferzeit in Portugal' in *Germania* 34 (1956)

PIGGOTT, S. 'The Tholos Tomb in Iberia' in *Ant.* XXVII (Mar. 1953)

France

DANIEL, G. *The Prehistoric Chamber Tombs of France* (1960)

CAZALIS DE FONDOUCE, P. *Les Allées couvertes de la Provence* (2 vols. 1873–8)

LE ROUZIC, Z. 'Morphologie et Chronologie des Sépultures préhistoriques du Morbihan' in *L'Anthropologie* 43 (1933) 225–265
  'Le Mobilier des Sépultures préhistoriques du Morbihan' in *L'Anthropologie* 44 (1934), 485–524

PEQUART, M. & S. J., & LE ROUZIC, Z. *Corpus des Signes gravés des Monuments mégalithiques du Morbihan* (1927)

Britain and Ireland

ATKINSON, R. J. C. *Stonehenge* (1956)
  'The Dorset Cursus' in *Ant.* XXIX (Mar. 1955)

DANIEL, G. E. *The Megalith Builders of Western Europe* (1958)

PEET, T.W. *Rough Stone Monuments and their Builders* (1912)

CHILDE, V. G. *Prehistoric Communities of the British Isles* (1940)

CLIFFORD, E. M. & DANIEL, G. E. 'The Rodmarton and Avening Portholes' in *Proc. Prehistoric Society* VI (1940)

DANIEL, G. E. *The Prehistoric Chamber Tombs of England and Wales* (1950)

DE VALERA, R. 'The Court Cairns of Ireland' in *Proc. Royal Irish Academy* 61 (1961)

HARTNETT, P. J. 'Excavation of a Passage-Grave at Fourknocks, in *Proc. Royal Irish Academy* 58 (1957)

PIGGOTT, S. *The Neolithic Cultures of the British Isles* (1954)
  (Ed.) *The Prehistoric Peoples of Scotland* (1962)
  The West Kennett Long Barrow (1962)

Northern Europe

BECKER, C. T. 'Neolithic Pottery in Danish Bogs' in *Aarbøger* 1947

GLOB, P.V. *Danske Oldtidsminder* (vol. 2. 1951)

KERSTEN, K. & LA BAUME, P. *Vorgeschichte der nordfriesischen Inseln* (1958)

KJAERUM, P. 'A Neolithic Temple' in *Kuml* 1955

MARSEEN, O. 'The Ferslev House' in *Kuml* 1960

NORDMAN, C. A. 'The Megalithic Culture of Northern Europe' in *Finska Fornminnesforeningens Tidskrift* XXXIX (1935)

POWELL, T. G. E. 'Megalithic and Other Art: Centre and West' in *Ant.* XXXIV (Sept. 1960)

XIV Navel of the World

ENGLERT, P. S. *La Tierra de Hotu Matu'a. Historia, Etnologia y Lengua de Isla de Pascua* (1948)

HEYERDAHL, T. *Aku-Aku, The Secret of Easter Island* (1957)

HEYERDAHL, T. & FERDON, E. N., JR *Archaeology of Easter Island. Reports of the Norwegian Archaeological Expedition to Easter Island and the East Pacific* vol. 1. Monographs of the School of American Research and the Museum of New Mexico no. 24, pt. 1 (1961)

MÉTRAUX, A. *Ethnology of Easter Island.* B. P. Bishop Mus. Bull. no. 160 (1940)

ROUTLEDGE, K. *The Mystery of Easter Island* (1919)

THOMSON, W. J. 'Te Pito te Henua, or Easter Island' in *Rept. U. S. Nat. Mus. for the year ending June 30, 1889*

List and Sources of Illustrations

In the following list the first set of numerals indicates the page and the second plate and figure numbers. Wherever possible both the find spot and the present location of objects is stated. Owners of copyright are indicated in italic.

The following abbreviations are used for staff illustrators and photographers: DAC David A. Cox, ET Eileen Tweedy, GC Gaynor Chapman, IMK Ian Mackenzie Kerr, ISM Stephen Molnar, JEB Joan E. Bennett, JP Josephine Powell, JRF John R. Freeman, MEW Martin E. Weaver, PPP P. P. Pratt, PRW Philip R. Ward. The title page drawings are by IMK.

II The Fertile Sahara

12 Map of Sahara Region. JEB

13 1. Ténéré: tree. Photo *Henri Lhote*
2. Tassili, Wadi Tamrit: cypress. Photo *Henri Lhote*

14 3. Sefar: air view. Photo *Dominique Lajoux*
4. Aouanrhet: painted rock-shelter. Photo *Henri Lhote*
5. Tamaya: Neolithic deposit. Photo *Henri Lhote*

15 6. In Habeter: rock engravings of animals. Photo courtesy *Frobenius-Institut an der Johann Wolfgang Goethe-Universität, Frankfurt (Main)*
7. Tassili, Wadi Djerat: rock engraving of elephants. Photo *Henri Lhote*

16 8. R'chech Dirhem: rock engraving of *Bubalus antiquus* and human figure. Photo *Henri Lhote*
10. Sefar: rock painting of the 'Great God'. Copy *Henri Lhote*

17 9. Ti-n-Tazarift: rock paintings of round-headed human figures, archer and animals. Copy *Henri Lhote*
11. Aouanrhet: rock painting of 'Negro' mask and woman. Copy *Henri Lhote*

18 12. Wadi Djerat: rock engraving of hippopotamus. Photo *Henri Lhote*
13. Ain Sfafasa: rock engraving of elephants and leopard. Photo *Henri Lhote*
14. Wadi Djerat: rock engraving, *Bubalus antiquus* and spirals. Photo *Henri Lhote*

19 15. El Hamra: rock engraving of two charging *Bubalus antiquus*. Photo courtesy *Professor Raymond Vaufrey*
16. Wadi Djerat: rock engraving of animal-headed human figure. Photo *Henri Lhote*
17. Aouanrhet: rock painting of running female figure. Copy *Henri Lhote*

20 18. Jabbaren: rock painting of polychrome cattle. Copy *Henri Lhote*
19. Sefar: rock painting of sheep. Copy *Henri Lhote*

21 20. Jabbaren: rock painting of bird-headed female figures. Copy *Henri Lhote*
21. Jabbaren: rock painting of girls. Copy *Henri Lhote*

22 22. Sefar: rock painting of men, cattle and dog. Copy *Henri Lhote*

22 23. Jabbaren: rock painting of rhinoceros hunt. Copy *Henri Lhote*
24. Aouanrhet: rock painting of hippopotamus hunt. Copy *Henri Lhote*

23 25. Sefar: rock painting of man and woman. Copy *Henri Lhote*
26. Aouanrhet: rock painting, 'the Marathon Race'. Copy *Henri Lhote*
27. Jabbaren: rock painting of cattle with horn attributes. Copy *Henri Lhote*
28. Tisoukai: rock painting of sun-symbol. Copy *Henri Lhote*

24 29. Adjefou: rock painting of warriors, chariots and cattle. Copy *Henri Lhote*
30. Tin-Abou Teka: rock painting of chariot and horseman. Copy *Henri Lhote*

25 *1.* Tihemboka: pebble-tool. Musée de l'Homme, Paris. ISM

26 *2.* Admer: hand-axe and cleaver. *Henry Lhote*

27 *3.* Unprovenanced: Aterian tanged points. *Henry Lhote*
4. Ténéré: Neolithic arrowheads of green jasper. After Joubert and Vaufrey. *Henry Lhote*

28 *5.* Map: prehistoric sites of the Tassili-n-Ajjer. JEB

29 *6 left.* Azaouak: bone barbed harpoon-heads. *Henry Lhote*
6 right. In-Guezzam: bone fish hook. *Henry Lhote*
7. Jabbaren: rock painting of little devils. IMK after Breuil

30 *8.* Jabbaren: rock painting of cattle. ISM after Breuil

31 *9.* Jabbaren: rock painting of bowmen. ISM after Breuil

10. Tisoukai: rock painting of woman with pots. IMK after Breuil

32 *11.* Map: route of the chariot people. JEB after Lhote

III City of Black Gold

We are grateful to the Trustees of the National Museums of Southern Rhodesia for permission to photograph objects illustrated in plates 17–22, 24, 26 and 29, and also to the Historical Monuments Commission of Southern Rhodesia for permission to photograph the buildings illustrated in plates 3–8, 10 and 12–15.

34 Map: Southern Rhodesia and adjacent territories. JEB

35 1. Zimbabwe: air view of ruins from south. Photo *Aircraft Operating Co. (Aerial Surveys) Ltd, Johannesburg*
2. Zimbabwe, Acropolis: air view of Western Enclosure. Photo *Aircraft Operating Co. (Aerial Surveys) Ltd, Johannesburg*

36 3. Zimbabwe, Acropolis: Western Enclosure. Photo Barney Wayne
4. Zimbabwe, No. 2 Ruins: hut platforms. Photo Barney Wayne
5. Khami: terraced retaining walls. Photo Barney Wayne

37 6. Zimbabwe, Temple: Great Outer Wall from south-east. Photo Barney Wayne
7. Zimbabwe, Temple: internal view from north-west. Photo Barney Wayne
8. Nalatale: decorated wall. Photo Barney Wayne

38 9. Zimbabwe: view of Temple from Eastern Enclosure, Acropolis. Photo Ronald D. K. Hadden, courtesy *Federal Information Dept.*
12. Zimbabwe, No. 1 Ruin: example of earliest (Class *P*) walling. Photo *Barney Wayne*
13. Zimbabwe, Temple: example of later (Class *Q*) walling. Photo *Barney Wayne*

38–39 10. Zimbabwe, Acropolis: entrance to East Cave. Photo Barney Wayne

39 11. Zimbabwe, Temple: Conical Tower. Photo courtesy *Federal Information Dept.*
14. Zimbabwe, Ridge Ruins: example of final (Class *R*) walling. Photo *Barney Wayne*
15. Dhlo-Dhlo: decorated walling. Photo *Barney Wayne*

40 16. Zimbabwe, Acropolis: carved soapstone figure of bird. Groote Schuur House, Capetown (cast in National Museum of S. Rhodesia, Bulawayo). Photo Ronald D. K. Hadden, courtesy *Federal Information Dept.*
17. Zimbabwe, Philips Ruins: carved soapstone figure of bird on beam ornamented with figure of crocodile. National Museum of S. Rhodesia, Bulawayo. Photo Barney Wayne
18. Zimbabwe: carved soapstone female figurine. British Museum (cast in National Museum of S. Rhodesia, Bulawayo). Photo Barney Wayne
19. Khami: carved ivory human figurine. National Museum of S. Rhodesia, Bulawayo. Photo Barney Wayne
20. Mapungubwe: figure of rhinoceros in beaten gold sheet. Archaeological Museum, Pretoria. Photo courtesy *University of Pretoria*
21. Zimbabwe: fragment of rim of carved soapstone bowl with human and animal figures. South African Museum, Capetown (cast in National Museum of S. Rhodesia, Bulawayo). Photo Barney Wayne
22. Khami: carved ivory figurine of lion. National Museum of S. Rhodesia, Bulawayo. Photo Barney Wayne

41 23. Zimbabwe, Acropolis: preparations for rainmaking ceremony in Eastern Enclosure. Reconstruction painting GC

42 24. Zimbabwe, Acropolis: sherds of early pottery. National Museum of S. Rhodesia, Bulawayo. Photo Barney Wayne

42 25. Zimbabwe, Acropolis and Temple: later pottery. National Museum of S. Rhodesia, Bulawayo. Photo Barney Wayne
26. Khami: polychrome beaker. National Museum of S. Rhodesia, Bulawayo. Photo Barney Wayne
27. Zimbabwe: fragment of rim of carved soapstone bowl with figure of bull. Zimbabwe Site Museum. Photo Ronald D. K. Hadden, courtesy *Federal Information Dept.*
28. Zimbabwe: double iron gong and striker. Zimbabwe Site Museum. Photo Ronald D. K. Hadden, courtesy *Federal Information Dept.*
29. Khami: hoard of bronze spears. National Museum of S. Rhodesia, Bulawayo. Photo Barney Wayne

43 *1.* Plan of Zimbabwe Ruins. After Whitty, courtesy *Historical Monuments Commission of S. Rhodesia*
2. Plan of Acropolis. After Whitty, courtesy *Historical Monuments Commission of S. Rhodesia*

44 *3.* Plan of Temple. After Whitty, courtesy *Historical Monuments Commission of S. Rhodesia*
4. Map: Carl Mauch's route, 1871–2. JEB after Summers

45 *5.* Map: stone buildings of Zimbabwe period. JEB after Summers

47 *6.* Map: 'Ancient Workings' of Southern Rhodesia. JEB after Summers

48 *7.* Map: ethnic movements contributing to Zimbabwe's history. JEB after Summers

49 *8.* Zimbabwe, Acropolis: figurine of long-horned cow or bull in burnt clay from Western Enclosure. National Museum of S. Rhodesia, Bulawayo. Reconstruction DAC after Summers and Robinson
9. Zimbabwe: iron tools. National Museum of S. Rhodesia, Bulawayo. ISM

50 *10.* Zimbabwe: *P* and *Q* type walling. After Whitty

51 *11.* Map: political influence of Mambo. JEB after Summers
12. Schematic drawing showing relationship of stone walls to daga huts. DAC after Whitty

52 *13.* Map: origin of Zimbabwe imports and probable trade routes. JEB after Summers
14. Zimbabwe: copper ingot. National Museum of S. Rhodesia, Bulawayo. DAC

53 *15.* Map: Arab and Portuguese activity in SE. Africa. JEB after Summers

IV The X-Group Enigma

We are grateful to Professor W. B. Emery for his permission to prepare figures *1–5, 7, 8* and *10–16* from drawings and photographs in 'The Royal Tombs of Ballana and Qustul' and to the Ministry of Culture and National Guidance of the United Arab Republic for permission to photograph the objects in the Cairo Museum illustrated in plates 1, 6, 7, 9, 14, 15, and 17–34.

56 Map: Upper Egypt and northern Sudan. JEB

57 1. Qostol, Tomb 3: hollow-cast bronze hand lamp in form of male head. Cairo Museum. Photo Roger Wood

57 2. Ballana, Tomb 37: tumulus of earth covered with schist pebbles. Photo courtesy *Director of Antiquities Service, Cairo*

58 4. Ballana, Tomb 80: skeleton of king. Photo courtesy *Director of Antiquities Service, Cairo* and Messrs. Methuen and Co. Ltd.

58–59 3. Ballana: X-Group burial scene. Reconstruction painting GC

59 5. Ballana, Tomb 3: removal of earth tumulus. Photo courtesy *Director of Antiquities Service, Cairo* and Messrs Methuen and Co. Ltd.

60 6. Qostol, Tomb 2: bit of cast silver with rod terminals in the form of clenched hands. Cairo Museum. Photo Roger Wood
7. Qostol, Tomb 17: beaten silver plaque from casket. Cairo Museum. Photo Roger Wood
8. Qostol, Tomb 3: silver head-stall of ribbon chain with silver lion-head medallions with lapis lazuli eyes. Cairo Museum. Photo courtesy *Director of Antiquities Service, Cairo* and Messrs Methuen and Co. Ltd.
9. Qostol, Tomb 3 (tumulus): embossed leather shield. Cairo Museum. Photo Roger Wood

61 10. Qostol, Tomb 3: silver lion-head medallion from horse collar. Cairo Museum. Photo courtesy *Director of Antiquities Service, Cairo* and Messrs Methuen and Co. Ltd.
11. Qostol, Tomb 3: harness and trappings shown on model horse with reconstructed sheepskin saddlecloth and leatherwork. Cairo Museum. Photo courtesy *Director of Antiquities Service, Cairo* and Messrs Methuen and Co. Ltd.
12. Qostol, Tomb 3: iron knife with ivory handle in form of Bes. Cairo Museum. Photo courtesy *Director of Antiquities Service, Cairo* and Messrs Methuen and Co. Ltd.

13. Qostol, Tombs 36, left, and 31, right: silver-mounted pommels embossed with a figure of Isis (Tomb 36) and figures of hawk-gods (Tomb 31). Cairo Museum. Photo courtesy *Director of Antiquities Service, Cairo* and Messrs Methuen and Co. Ltd.

62 14. Ballana, Tomb 47: crown of beaten silver with rivetted fastenings, set with carnelians. Cairo Museum. Photo Roger Wood
18. Ballana, Tomb 3: necklace of gold beads and gold pendants. Cairo Museum. Photo Roger Wood
19. Ballana, Tomb 6: cast silver bracelet with lion-head terminals. Cairo Museum. Photo Roger Wood

62–63 15. Ballana, Tomb 118: crown of three strips of silver bent and rivetted, set with carnelians and green glass jewels. Cairo Museum. Photo Roger Wood

63 16. Kalabsha, Roman temple: wall engraving of Silko. Photo courtesy *Director of Antiquities Service, Cairo.*
17. Ballana, Tomb 80: silver crown set with garnets (the ram's eyes and forehead) and carnelians. Cairo Museum. Photo Roger Wood
20. Qostol, Tomb 14: earrings of beaten silver, amethyst and coral. Cairo Museum. Photo Roger Wood
21. Ballana, Tomb 47: jewelled bracelets of beaten silver with plaster fillings. Cairo Museum. Photo Roger Wood

64 22. Ballana, Tomb 95: cast and turned bronze lamp with Maltese cross. Cairo Museum. Photo Roger Wood
23. Ballana, Tomb 121: cast bronze censer in form of shrine topped by pine cone. Cairo Museum. Photo Roger Wood
24. Ballana, Tomb 121: cast and engraved bronze lamp standard with hare and hound. Cairo Museum. Photo Roger Wood
25. Ballana, Tomb 80: bronze double-burner dolphin lamp with bust of a Bacchante. Cairo Museum. Photo Roger Wood

65 26. Ballana, Tomb 114: bronze lamp standard in form of Eros (figure and base hollow-cast). Cairo Museum. Photo Roger Wood
27. Ballana, Tomb 80: bronze dolphin lamps supported by nude male figure (figure and base hollow-cast). Cairo Museum. Photo Roger Wood

66 28. Ballana, Tomb 3: cast and engraved silver plate with figure of Hermes. Cairo Museum. Photo Roger Wood
29. Qostol, Tomb 3 (tumulus): wooden dice-box *(pyrgus)* with silver fittings and ebony pieces. Cairo Museum. Photo Roger Wood
30. Qostol, Tomb 3 (tumulus): wooden gaming board with silver handle and corner pieces, inlaid with ivory; ivory dice. Cairo Museum Photo Roger Wood

67 31. Qostol, Tomb 14 (tumulus): wooden chest inlaid with ivory panels engraved with mythological figures; bronze hasps in form of couchant lions. Cairo Museum. Photo Roger Wood
32. Ballana, Tomb 80: gilded bronze miniature table. Cairo Museum. Photo Roger Wood

68 33. Ballana, Tomb 80: hollow-cast bronze censer with sliding lid with figures of lion and boar. Cairo Museum. Photo Roger Wood
34. Ballana, Tomb 80: hollow-cast bronze censer in form of lion. Cairo Museum. Photo Roger Wood
35. Persia, unprovenanced: bronze censer in form of lion; Seljuk period, 12th C. AD. Photo courtesy *Cleveland Museum of Art*, John L. Severance Fund

70 1. Qostol, Tomb 3: plan showing position of human and animal burials. ISM after *Emery*
2. Qostol, Tomb 3: section and frontal view of wooden dice-box *(pyrgus)*. Cairo Museum. IMK after *Emery*

71 3. Qostol, Tomb 3: elevation of east wall. ISM after *Emery*
4. Qostol, Tomb 3: cast and engraved silver medallion with onyx cameo (? Constantine). Cairo Museum. IMK after Emery.

72 5. Qostol, Tomb 14: bronze hanging lamp in form of dove. Cairo Museum. IMK after Emery
6. Firka, Tomb A 12: bronze hanging lamp in form of dove. Cairo Museum. IMK after Kirwan
7. Qostol, Tomb 14: Meroitic inscription on iron spear. Cairo Museum. After *Emery*

73 8. (left) Qostol, Tomb 3, and (right) Ballana, Tomb 3: inscriptions on wine jars. Cairo Museum. After *Emery*
9. Naga, temple: stone engraving of hawk-headed crocodile. IMK after Lepsius

73 10. Qostol, Tomb 17: hawk-headed crocodile embossed on silver plaque. Cairo Museum IMK after Emery

74 11. Ballana, Tomb 3: details of silver casket embossed with figures of Christ and the apostles. Cairo Museum. ISM after Emery

75 12. Ballana, Tomb 80: archer's silver bracer worn on left hand. Cairo Museum. IMK after Emery
13. Ballana, Tomb 95; arrow loose worn on right hand. Cairo Museum. IMK after Emery

76 14, 15. Ballana, Tomb 80: bronze folding table. Cairo Museum. IMK and ISM after *Emery*

77 16. Ballana, Tomb 2: Greek love-charm on gold foil. Cairo Museum. After *Emery*

V Who were the Ancient Ainu?

80 Map: Japan. JEB

81 1. Shiraoi, Hokkaido: Ainu dance. Photo courtesy *Dr J. Edward Kidder, Jr*
2. Hokkaido: commercial conference between two seated Ainu in front of witnesses. Photo *Radio Times Hulton Picture Library*

82–3 3. Jōmon village scene. Reconstruction painting GC

82 4. Unprovenanced: Jōmon stone axe and adze blades. British Museum. Photo ET
5. Yamato Province: Jōmon green stone knife blade. British Museum. Photo ET

83 6. Unprovenanced: stone and obsidian arrow-heads. *Tokyo National Museum*
7. Hiromi, Nagano: hearth of a Jōmon pit-dwelling. Photo courtesy *Kyoto University*

84 8. Unprovenanced: stone 'sceptre'. British Museum. Photo ET
9. Unprovenanced: ritual stone object in the form of a net-weight. British Museum. Photo ET
10. Misaka, Yamanashi: Middle Jōmon clay figurine. *Tokyo National Museum*
11. Kamegaoka, Aomori: Latest Jōmon clay figurine. *Kyoto University*
14. Unprovenanced: *magatama* or comma-shaped jewels of stone. Rijksmuseum voor Volkenkunde, Leiden. Photo ET

85 12. Mumuro, Saitama: Latest Jōmon clay figurine. Collection T. Nakazawa. Photo courtesy *Kyoto University*
13. Satohara, Gumma: Late Jōmon clay figurine. Collection Y. Yamasaki, Tokyo National Museum. *Photo Sakamoto Photo Research Laboratory, Tokyo*
15. Nonakado, Akita: 'sun-dial' arrangement of stones from Late Jōmon period. Photo courtesy *Dr J. Edward Kidder, Jr*
16. Tsugumo, Okayama: flexed burial of a man and burial jar of an infant from Late Jōmon period. Photo courtesy *Kyoto University*

86 17. Unprovenanced: Early Jōmon clay pot with beaded diagonal pattern. British Museum. Photo ET
18. Nikki shell-mound, Sekiyama: Early Jōmon pot with herring-bone pattern. *Tokyo National Museum*
19. Ubayama, Tokai: Middle Jōmon pot. *Östasiatiska Museet, Stockholm*

86 20. Himi, Toyama: Middle Jōmon pot with elaborate appliqué decoration. Tokyo University. Photo courtesy *S. Yamanouchi*
23. Mine-Machi, Tokyo: Late Jōmon spouted vessel. *Tokyo National Museum*
24. Hokkaido: blade and arrow-heads of obsidian. British Museum. Photo ET

87 21. Unprovenanced: heavily ornamented Middle Jōmon pot. Photo *Sakamoto Photo Research Laboratory, Tokyo*
22. Harinouchi shell-mound, Chiba: Late Jōmon pot with incised pattern. Collection T. Tani. Photo courtesy *Tokyo National Museum*
25. Aso, Akita: clay mask. Tokyo National Museum. Photo courtesy *Kyoto University*
26. Unprovenanced: carved ornamental objects of horn and ivory. *Tokyo National Museum*

88 28. Matsumaye, S. Hokkaido: part of a scroll painting by Chishima Shunri showing two Ainu exchanging salutations in front of a dead bear. Rijksmuseum voor Volkenkunde, Leiden. Photo ET
29. Matsumaye, S. Hokkaido: scroll painting by Chishima Shunri showing Ainu dancing and drinking at the bear festival. Rijksmuseum voor Volkenkunde, Leiden. Photo ET

89–90 27. Kiyosu Kōjin: screen painting by Tomioka Tessai showing scenes from an Ainu bear festival. Photo *Sakamoto Photo Research Laboratory, Tokyo*

90 30. Unprovenanced: silk scroll painting, sealed Sekkō, showing Ainu with smoking implements, *sake* container and cup on cup-stand. Rijksmuseum voor Volkenkunde, Leiden. Photo ET
31. Cape Sōya, N. Hokkaido: silk scroll painting by Toyosuke showing Ainu in bark costume. Rijksmuseum voor Volkenkunde, Leiden. Photo ET

91 32. Kunashiri, S. Kuriles: part of scroll painting by Tanabe Anzō showing Ainu dwelling, storage, bear-cage and woman weaving. Rijksmuseum voor Volkenkunde, Leiden. Photo ET
33. Kiyosu Kōjin: screen painting by Tomioka Tessai showing scenes from Ainu village life. Photo *Sakamoto Photo Research Laboratory, Tokyo*

92 34. Hokkaido: Ainu jewellery. Rijksmuseum voor Volkenkunde, Leiden. Photo ET
35. Unprovenanced: Ainu ceremonial head-dress. British Museum. Photo ET
36. Hokkaido: wooden sandals and piece of embroidered silk. Rijksmuseum voor Volkenkunde, Leiden. Photo ET
37. Unprovenanced: carved wooden dishes. British Museum. Photo ET

93 38. Horobetsu: woman's ceremonial dress. *Musée de l'Homme, Paris*
39. Hokkaido: woman's ceremonial dress. Rijksmuseum voor Volkenkunde, Leiden. Photo ET
40. Hokkaido: Japanese lacquer tea-set with Ainu mat and moustache-lifter. Rijksmuseum voor Volkenkunde, Leiden. Photo ET

94 41. Unprovenanced: *inao* with the head of a wolf. British Museum. Photo ET
42. Hokkaido: grass hunting cap. Rijksmuseum voor Volkenkunde, Leiden. Photo ET

151–2 28. Tulum: village scene. Reconstruction painting GC

151 29. Kaminaljuyu, Guatemala: polychrome two-part anthropomorphic effigy vessel. Painting Antonio Tejeda courtesy *Peabody Museum, Harvard University*
30. Punta Piedra, Quintana Roo: miniature shrine. Photo courtesy *Loring M. Hewen*

152 31. Uxmal: modern peasant's house. Photo *Victor W. von Hagen*

153 32. Unprovenanced: a page from the Dresden Codex. Saxony State Library, Dresden. Photo courtesy *Ian Graham*
Quiriguá: glyph showing a date 400,000,000 years in the past. IMK after Thompson

154 33. Bonampak: fresco showing a chief being dressed for a ceremony. Painting Antonio Tejeda courtesy *Peabody Museum, Harvard University*
34. Ratinlinxul: extended vase-painting showing the procession of an important merchant. Painting M. Louise Baker courtesy *University Museum, Philadelphia*

155 35. Bonampak: frieze showing a procession with musicians and impersonators of the gods. Painting Antonio Tejeda courtesy *Peabody Museum, Harvard University*
36. Yaxchilán: relief showing a worshipper passing a barbed cord through his tongue. *Trustees of the British Museum*
37. Yaxchilán: relief showing a blood-offering. *Trustees of the British Museum*

156 38. Yaloch, Guatemala: mythological vase showing a story from the life of the Sun-god. Formerly in Liverpool Public Museums. Painting Annie G. Hunter courtesy *University Museum, Philadelphia*
39. Teotihuacán: carved green jade pendant. British Museum. Photo ET
40. Chamá: extended vase-painting showing a chief receiving merchants. Cary collection. Painting M. Louise Baker courtesy *University Museum, Philadelphia*

157 41. Tikal: engraved flake of obsidian from a sub-stele cache. British Museum. Photo ET
42. Tikal: hollow pottery figure of a seated god. Photo W. R. Coe courtesy *University Museum, Philadelphia*
43. Tikal: pottery tripod vessel with painted stucco design. Photo W. R. Coe courtesy *University Museum, Philadelphia*
44. Tikal: plate with painting of a fish, emblem of the god Xoc. Photo W. R. Coe courtesy *University Museum, Philadelphia*

158 45. Tula: Quetzalcoatl on the Toltec Temple of the Morning-Star God. Photo courtesy *Instituto Nacional de Antropologia e Historia, Mexico*
46. Chichén Itzá: Quetzalcoatl of Toltec design. Photo courtesy *Loring M. Hewen*
47. Tula: frieze of jaguars on the Toltec Temple of the Morning-Star God. Photo courtesy *Instituto Nacional de Antropologia e Historia, Mexico*
48. Chichén Itzá: frieze of jaguars of Toltec design. Photo courtesy *Loring M. Hewen*
49. Piedras Negras: throne reconstructed from broken fragments. Photo W. R. Coe courtesy *University Museum, Philadelphia*

160 1. Copán: reconstruction of the ceremonial centre. MEW after Tatiana Proskouriakoff

161 2. Cobá: plan of the road system. ISM after Thompson

162 3. Palenque: the Temple of the Inscriptions showing the stairway and tomb. PPP after Ruz

163 4. Schematic representation of the Maya calendar. Drawing Avis Tulloch courtesy *I. Eric S. Thompson*

164 5. Examples of corbelled and true arches. MEW

165 6. (left) British Honduras, unprovenanced; (right) Quiriguá: eccentric flints. British Museum. IMK

166 7. Tula: ground plan of the Temple of the Morning-Star God. MEW after Tozzer
8. Chichén Itzá: ground plan of the Temple of the Warriors. MEW after Tozzer

167 9. Chichén Itzá: gold disc from the *cenote* showing the Toltec conquest. *Peabody Museum, Harvard University*

168 10. Mayapán: decadent pottery figure. Museo Nacional de Antropologia, Mexico. IMK
11. Chichén Itzá: reconstruction of the centre as rebuilt by the Toltecs. PPP

VIII The Etruscan Problem

170 Map: Etruscan sites in Italy (modern names in parentheses). JEB

171 1. Caere (Cerveteri): terracotta figures of man and woman on lid of sarcophagus; c. 500 BC. Museo di Villa Giulia, Rome. Photo *Georgina Masson*

172 2. Vetulonia: clay hut urn; 9th/8th C. BC. Museo Archeologico, Florence. Photo courtesy *Soprintendenza Antiquità*
3. Felsina (Bologna), Bennacci Tomb: clay *askos* with horse and rider; Villanovan. Museo Civico, Bologna. Photo *Studi Fotofast, Bologna*
4. Tarquinia, Poggio dell'Impiccato: Villanovan clay funeral urn with bronze helmet lid; 8th C. BC. Museo Archeologico, Florence. Photo courtesy *Soprintendenza Antiquità*
5. Felsina (Bologna): reconstructed Villanovan urn burial; 9th/8th C. BC. Museo Civico, Bologna

173 6. Clusium (Chiusi), Solaia: bronze 'Canopic' burial urn with clay lid; late 7th C. BC. Museo Archeologico, Florence. Photo *Martin Hürlimann*
7. Clusium (Chiusi): terracotta burial urn (the 'Gualandi ossuary') 7th C. BC. Museo Civico, Chiusi. Photo *Alinari*
8. Certosa: bronze situla (detail); late 6th/early 5th C. BC. Museo Civico, Bologna

174 9. Caere (Cerveteri): seated female terracotta figure; 7th C. BC. British Museum. Photo ET
10. Tarquinia: the 'Bocchoris vase' of faience; 734-728 BC. Museo Nazionale, Tarquinia. Photo *Anderson*
11. Praeneste (Palestrina), Bernardini Tomb: Phoenician silver cauldron; mid-7th C. BC. Museo Pigorini, Rome. Photo *Martin Hürlimann*

175 12. Caere (Cerveteri), Regolini-Galassi Tomb: gold fibula; mid-7th C. BC. Museo Gregoriano, Vatican. Photo *Scala*
13. Praeneste (Palestrina), Barberini Tomb: gold fibula; 7th C. BC. Museo di Villa Giulia, Rome. Photo *Scala*

176 14. Vulci: engraved bronze mirror; 4th C. BC. Museo Gregoriano, Vatican. Photo courtesy *Archivio Fotografico dei Gallerie e Musei Vaticani*
15. Italy, unprovenanced: bronze statuette of a *haruspex*, 4th C. BC. Museo Gregoriano, Vatican. Photo courtesy *Archivio Fotografico dei Gallerie e Musei Vaticani*
16. Tarquinia: detail of nenfro sarcophagus of Laris Pulena showing scroll; 4th C. BC. Museo Nazionale, Tarquinia. Photo *Walter Dräyer*
17. Tarquinia, Tomb of Bulls: wall painting of Achilles and Troilus; c. 530 BC. Photo *Anderson*
18. Caere (Cerveteri), Tomb of Stuccoes: interior; 3rd C. BC. Photo *Anderson*

178 19. Tarquinia, Tomb of Leopards: wall painting of banqueters; c. 470 BC. Copy Douglas Masonowicz *(St George's Gallery Prints)*

178 20. Tarquinia, Tomb of Triclinium: wall painting of dancers; c. 470 BC. Photo *Scala*

179 21. Tarquinia, Tomb of Leopards: wall painting of piper; c. 470 BC. Photo *Walter Dräyer*
22. Tarquinia, Tomb of the Lioness: wall painting of female dancer; c. 520 BC. Photo *Walter Dräyer*

180 23. Tarquinia, Tomb of Hunting and Fishing; wall painting of fishermen and bird hunter; c. 520-510 BC. Photo Aleandro Anchora
24. Tarquinia, Tomb of the Olympiad: wall painting of racing chariot; late 6th C. BC. Photo *Carlo M. Lerici*

180–1 25. Clusium (Chiusi), Tomb of the Monkey: wall painting of wrestlers; 5th C. BC. Copy Gatti, photo *Alinari*
26. Tarquinia, Tomb of Orcus: wall painting of Charun; c. 300 BC. Photo Thames and Hudson Archive
27. Tarquinia, Tomb of the Shields: wall painting of banqueting couple; c. 300 BC. Photo *Walter Dräyer*

182 28. Praeneste (Palestrina): figures on lid of bronze cista; ?4th C. BC. Museo di Villa Giulia, Rome. Photo Aleandro Anchora

182 29. Capua: figures on lid of bronze cauldron; late 6th C. BC. British Museum. Photo ET
30. Arretium (Arezzo): bronze chimaera; ? c. 300 BC. Museo Archeologico, Florence. Photo *Scala*

183 31. Praeneste (Palestrina): the Ficorini cista (bronze); c. 300 BC; Museo di Villa Giulia, Rome. Photo Aleandro Anchora
32. Praeneste (Palestrina): detail of Ficorini cista. Museo di Villa Giulia, Rome. Photo *Alinari*

184 33. Rome: Capitoline wolf; c. 500 BC. Palazzo dei Conservatori, Rome. Photo *Alinari*
34. Vulci: bronze tripod; 6th BC. Museo Etrusco Gregoriano, Vatican. Photo *Anderson*

184 35. Italy, unprovenanced: elongated bronze figurine; 3rd C. BC. Musée du Louvre. Photo *Martin Hürlimann*

185 36. Italy, unprovenanced; bronze statuette of kneeling satyr; mid 4th C. BC. Staatliche Antikensammlungen, Munich. Photo *Martin Hürlimann*
37. Italy, unprovenanced: bronze candelabra support in form of dancing female figure; Musée du Louvre. Photo Thames and Hudson Archive
38. Rome: bronze head of 'Brutus'; late 4th/early 3rd C. BC. Palazzo dei Conservatori, Rome. Photo Thames and Hudson Archive

186 39. Etruria: group of bucchero vessels; 6th/7th C. BC. British Museum. Photo ET
40. Clusium (Chiusi): bull's head jug of bucchero; late 6th C. BC. Museo Archeologico, Florence. Photo *Scala*
41. Visentium (Bizenzio): clay vase with geometric decoration; 8th/7th C. BC. Museo Archeologico, Florence. Photo *Scala*
42. Caere (Cerveteri): Caeretan hydria with blinding of Polyphemus; late 6th C. BC. Museo di Villa Giulia, Rome. Photo Aleandro Anchora

187 43. Falerii Veteres (Città Castellana): Faliscan calyx-crater with sack of Troy; 4th C. BC. Museo di Villa Giulia, Rome. Photo *Scala*
44. Vulci: 'Pontic' jug; 550-575 BC. Museo Archeologico, Florence. Photo *Scala*
45. Clusium (Chiusi): clay jug in form of duck; c. 300 BC. Musée du Louvre. Photo *Martin Hürlimann*

188 46. Certosa: funerary stele; c. 400 BC. Museo Civico, Bologna. Photo *Alinari*
47. Vulci: nenfro centaur; early 6th C. BC. Museo di Villa Giulia, Rome. Photo *Walter Dräyer*
48. Volterra: clay figures of man and woman on lid of urn (detail); mid 1st C. BC. Museo Etrusco Guarnacci, Volterra. Photo *Walter Dräyer*

189 49. Tarquinia: terracotta winged horses; c. 300 BC. Museo Nazionale, Tarquinia. Photo *Anderson*
50. Clusium (Chiusi): terracotta sarcophagus of Seianti Thanunia. *Trustees of the British Museum*

190 51. Veii: terracotta statue of Apollo; c. 500 BC. Museo di Villa Giulia, Rome. Photo *Scala*
52. Falerii Veteres (Città Castellana): terracotta bust of Apollo (detail); c. 300 BC. Museo di Villa Giulia, Rome. Photo *Alinari*
53. Etruria: terracotta head of young man; c. 100 BC. British Museum. Photo ET

191 1. Vetulonia; inscribed stone funerary stele of 'Avele Feluske'; c. 650 BC. Museo Archeologico, Florence. PRW after Soprintendenza Antichità

192 2. Tarquinia: bronze wheeled container; 7th C. BC. Museo Nazionale, Tarquinia. PRW after Banti

193 3. Kalminia, Lemnos: inscribed stone funerary stele; 6th C. BC. National Archaeological Museum, Athens. After Bloch
4. Vetulonia: iron fasces; 7th C. BC. Museo Archeologico, Florence. PRW after Soprintendenza Antichità

249 *11.* Karmir Blur: plan of the fortress. ISM after Piotrovsky

250 *12.* Toprak Kale: bronze figure of royal attendant. Staatliche Museen, Berlin. ISM after Barnett

XI Bridge to the Ancient East

252 Map: the Indo-Iranian Borderlands. JEB

253 *1.* Damb Sadaat: mother goddess figurine. American Museum of Natural History. Photo courtesy *Dr Walter A. Fairservis, Jr*
2. Bamian: the Great Buddha. Photo courtesy *Dr Walter A. Fairservis, Jr*

254 *3.* Near Mazar-i-Sherif: nomads' tents. Photo *J. J. H. Clowes*
4. Konach Mar, Hindu Kush: crops growing at 10,000 ft. Photo *Roger Forster*
5. Herat: cattle grazing by the Hari Rud. Photo *Roger Forster*
6. Seistan: a village. Photo courtesy *Dr Walter A. Fairservis, Jr*

255 *7.* Panjshir Valley, Hindu Kush: nomadic group on the move. Photo courtesy *Dr Walter A. Fairservis, Jr*
8. West Pakistan: nomadic family en route to the highlands of Afghanistan. Photo courtesy *Dr Walter A. Fairservis, Jr*

256 *9.* Namazgah Tepe, Turkestan: decorated pottery bowls. Photo courtesy *Professor V. M. Masson*
10. Seistan: prehistoric village site. Photo courtesy *Dr Walter A. Fairservis, Jr*
11. Seistan: flexed burial. Photo courtesy *Dr Walter A. Fairservis, Jr*
12. Damb Sadaat: compartmented seal. American Museum of Natural History. Photo courtesy *Dr Walter A. Fairservis, Jr*
13. Said Kala: compartmented seal. American Museum of Natural History. Photo courtesy *Dr Walter A. Fairservis, Jr*

257 *14.* (left) Sur Jangal; (centre) Damb Sadaat; (top right) Rana Ghundai; (bottom right) Damb Sadaat; decorated pottery. *American Museum of Natural History*
15. (top) Kile Ghul Mohammad: casts of matting impressions on clay vessels; (bottom left) Kile Ghul Mohammad: cast of basketry impression on clay vessel; (bottom right) Damb Sadaat: cast of basketry impression on clay vessel. *American Museum of Natural History.*
16. Quetta Valley: Faiz Mohammad ware plate with pipal leaf design. *American Museum of Natural History*

258 *17.* Periano Ghundai: clay bull's head. *American Museum of Natural History*
18. Karez Site, Damb Sadaat: clay pot with bull design. *American Museum of Natural History*
258–9 *19.* Sacrificial procession at Edith Shahr. Reconstruction painting GC

259 *20.* Edith Shahr: boulder-wall of Complex B. Photo courtesy *Dr Walter A. Fairservis, Jr*

260 *21.* Quetta: potters' marks. *American Museum of Natural History*
22. Edith Shahr: clay bull figurine and fragment of a wheeled cart. *American Museum of Natural History*
23. Baluchistan: sherds of Lando ware. Private collection. Photo courtesy *Miss B. de Cardi*

260 *24.* Seistan: spouted vessel. *American Museum of Natural History*

261 *25.* Near Balkh: a mound which may conceal the ruins of Bactra. Photo courtesy *Dr Walter A. Fairservis, Jr*
26. Balkh: the Bala Hissar. Photo courtesy *Dr Walter A. Fairservis, Jr*
27. Unprovenanced: Bactrian coins; (top left) Menander; (top centre) Eucratides; (top right) Heliocles; (bottom left) Pantaleon; (bottom right) Azes I. *American Museum of Natural History*

262 *28.* Bamian: grottoes round the remnants of a seated Buddha. Photo courtesy *Dr Walter A. Fairservis, Jr*
29. Bamian: grottoes used by the modern populace as shelters. Photo courtesy *Dr Walter A. Fairservis, Jr*
30. Bamian: the valley setting showing the giant Buddhas. Photo *J. J. H. Clowes*

263 *31.* Bamian: frescoes showing Early Christian influence. Photo courtesy *American Museum of Natural History*
32. Bamian: fresco painting of a bodhisattva. Photo courtesy *American Museum of Natural History*
33. Bamian: fresco painting showing a Corinthian column. Photo courtesy *American Museum of Natural History*

264 *34.* Begram: bronze figure of Hercules-Serapis. Kabul Museum. Photo JP
35. Begram: ivory figure of a river-goddess. Kabul Museum. Photo JP
36. Begram: plaster medallion of Pompeiian type. Kabul Museum. Photo JP
37. Begram: painted glass goblet. Kabul Museum. Photo JP
38. Begram: engraved ivory casket lid. Kabul Museum. Photo JP

267 *1.* Djeitun: partial reconstruction of a house. ISM after Masson

268 *2.* Map: prehistoric and protohistoric sites in the Seistan basin. Courtesy American Museum of Natural History

269 *3.* Damb Sadaat: 'Zhob Goddess' figurines. American Museum of Natural History. IMK after Fairservis

270 *4.* Map: main archaeological sites in the Zhob, Loralai and Quetta valleys and their relationship to the Indus Valley civilization. JEB
5. Chashmi Ali and Togau: chart showing the cultural links between northern Iran and Baluchistan. Courtesy *Dr Walter A. Fairservis, Jr*

271 *6.* Amri, Loralai and Quetta: chart showing the cultural links between the Indus valley and Baluchistan. Courtesy *Dr Walter A. Fairservis, Jr*
7. Tepe Hissar and Quetta: chart showing links between the Late Hissar and later Quetta cultures. Courtesy *Dr Walter A. Fairservis, Jr*

272 *8.* (top left) Sur Jangal; (top right and bottom left) Turkestan; (bottom right) Damb Sadaat: 'Mother Goddess' figurines. Courtesy *Dr Walter A. Fairservis, Jr*
9. Namazgah and Quetta: chart showing links between the Namazgah and Quetta cultures. Courtesy *Professor V. M. Masson*

273 *10.* Edith Shahr: reconstruction of Complex A as it probably appeared c. 2000 BC. ISM after Fairservis

275 *11.* Map: probable routes of cultural diffusion from Iran to Seistan and Baluchistan during late prehistoric times. Courtesy *Dr Walter A. Fairservis, Jr*

277 *12.* Bamian: imitation 'lantern' ceiling carved out of the rock. ISM

XII The Forgotten Sarmatians

281 *1.* Rome: cast of a relief from Trajan's column showing defeat of the Roxolani by the Romans. Photo *Alinari*
2. Chester: stone relief showing a Sarmatian warrior. Grosvenor Museum, Chester. Photo courtesy *Chester Archaeological Society*

282–3 *3.* Alan encampment on the Steppe. Reconstruction painting GC

282 *4.* Chesters, Northumberland: Sarmatian beads. Chesters Museum. Photo ET
5. Caucasus: grave hoard consisting of two rings, mirror, buckle, brooch and necklace. British Museum. Photo ET

283 *6.* Unprovenanced: sword with ivory handle. British Museum. Photo ET

284 *7.* Poiana (Prahova):? Royal Sarmatian helmet. *National Museum, Bucharest*
8. Shores of the Black Sea: silver gilt *phalera*. Cabinet des Médailles, Paris. Photo *Draeger*
9. Tanais: funerary relief of Tryphon. *State Hermitage, Leningrad*
10. Unprovenanced: coin of Marcus Aurelius. British Museum. Photo ET
11. Unprovenanced: coin of Commodus. British Museum. Photo ET
12. Unprovenanced: coin of Constantine II. British Museum. Photo ET
13. Unprovenanced: coin of Commodus. British Museum. Photo ET

285 *14.* Martinovka: silver hoard. British Museum. Photo ET
15. Maikop: bronze gilt fibula with figure brandishing the severed head of an enemy. *University Museum, Philadelphia*
16. South Caucasus: decorated sword sheath. *Institute of Archaeology, Moscow*
17. South Caucasus: decorated sword sheath. *Institute of Archaeology, Moscow*
18. Zakrzów (Sackrau): engraved bowl. Now lost. Photo courtesy *Silesian Museum*

286 *19.* Novocherkassk: electrotype copies of part of the gold hoard. Victoria and Albert Museum. (Originals in State Hermitage, Leningrad.) Photo ET
20. Caucasus: glass cup, gold and garnet ring and beads. British Museum. Photo ET

287 *21.* Herpály: electrotype copy of bronze gilt shield boss. Victoria and Albert Museum. (Original in Hungarian National Historical Museum.) Photo ET
22. Novocherkassk: electrotype copy of scent bottle from the gold hoard. Victoria and Albert Museum. (Original in State Hermitage, Leningrad.) Photo ET

288 *24.* Krivoy Rog: sacred stone inscribed with 'tamga' signs. *Museum of Archaeology, Odessa*
25. Kiev: rings of Grand Duke Vsievolod Yaroslavich. British Museum. Photo ET
26. Kerch: open-work buckle with 'Helios' monogram. British Museum. Photo ET
27. Elanskaya, Don: cauldron with 'tamga' sign. *Historical Museum, Moscow*

289 *1.* Map: the main area occupied by the Sarmatians. JEB

290 *2.* Kuban: figure of a Sarmatian warrior on a rhyton. State Hermitage, Leningrad. IMK after Rostovtsev

291 *3.* Eastern Germany: bronze fibula 'with foot turned over'. IMK

292 *4.* Map: routes of the Iazyges and Roxolani into Western Europe. ISM

294 *5.* Map: the migrations of the Western Alans. ISM

295 *6.* Salonica: Sarmatian soldiers depicted on the Arch of Galerius. ISM after Rostovtsev

296 *7.* Various sources: (top row) 'tamga' signs compared with (bottom row) Polish coats-of-arms. ISM after Sulimirski

297 *8.* Melitopol: Alan gold diadem with amber, garnet and carnelian stones. Melitopol Regional Museum. ISM
9. (right) Niederolm, Austria: artificially deformed skull; (left) normal skull for comparison. ISM

298 *10.* Map: the movements of a group of Western Alans. ISM after Sulimirski

XIII The Migration of the Megaliths

300 Map of megalithic and associated sites in Europe and the Mediterranean. JEB

301 *1.* Stonehenge: re-erected trilithon. Photo *Edwin Smith*

302 *2.* Almizeraque: phalange idol. Museo Arqueologico Nacional, Madrid. Photo courtesy *Dr Vera Leisner*
3. Comenda, Anta 2: decorated slate plaque. Photo courtesy *Dr Vera Leisner*
4. Denmark: detail of Late Passage-Grave type bowl with occulus motifs. *National Museum, Denmark*
6. Los Millares, Tomb 15: detail of interior of bowl with occulus motifs. *Museo Arqueologico Nacional, Madrid*
7. Almeria, unprovenanced: stylized alabaster figurine. *Museo Arqueologico Nacional, Madrid*

302–3 *5, 13.* Los Millares, Tomb 15: detail of exterior of bowl with occulus and stag motifs. *Ashmolean Museum, Oxford*

303 *8.* Fourknocks: decoration on capstone of west recess. Photo courtesy *Bord Fáilte Éireann*
9. Trets: decorated stele. Musée des Antiquités Nationales, St-Germain-en-Laye. Photo Jaqueline Hyde

Index

Page numbers in *italic* indicate illustrations; those in **bold** type refer to main entry.